13th European Workshop on Natural Language Generation 2011

(ENLG 11)

Nancy, France
28-30 September 2011

ISBN: 978-1-62276-440-2

Printed from e-media with permission by:

Curran Associates, Inc.
57 Morehouse Lane
Red Hook, NY 12571

Some format issues inherent in the e-media version may also appear in this print version.

Printed by Curran Associates, Inc. (2012)

Association for Computational Linguistics
209 N. Eighth Street
Stroudsburg, Pennsylvania 18360

Phone: 1-570-476-8006
Fax: 1-570-476-0860

acl@aclweb.org

Additional copies of this publication are available from:

Curran Associates, Inc.
57 Morehouse Lane
Red Hook, NY 12571 USA
Phone: 845-758-0400
Fax: 845-758-2634
Email: curran@proceedings.com
Web: www.proceedings.com

Table of Contents

Oral Presentations

Poster Presentations

Generation Challenges 2011

Introduction

It is with great pleasure that we present the current volume of papers accepted for presentation at the 13th European Workshop on Natural Language Generation (ENLG 2011), which will be held from September 28th to 30th, 2011 at Loria in Nancy, France.

The ENLG 2009 workshop continued a biennial series of workshops on natural language generation that has been running since 1987 and alternates with INLG, the International Conference on Natural Language Generation. Previous European workshops have been held at Royaumont, Edinburgh, Judenstein, Pisa, Leiden, Duisburg, Toulouse, Budapest, Aberdeen, Dagstuhl and Athens. Together with INLG, the ENLG workshop is the main regular forum for presenting and discussing research in Natural Language Generation.

ENLG 2011 invited submissions on all topics related to natural language generation. We received 41 submissions of long and short papers from all over the world. Of these 13 long papers and 12 short papers were accepted for presentation. The long papers will be presented orally, and the short papers as posters.

In addition, ENLG 2011 hosts Generation Challenges 2011. This year, three shared task evaluation competitions were organized under the umbrella of Generation Challenges 2011: the Surface Realisation Challenge (Belz, Hogan, White, and Stent), the Challenge on Generating Instructions in Virtual Environments (Striegnitz, Denis, Gargett, Garoufi, Koller, and Theune) and the Helping Our Own Challenge (Dale and Kilgariff).

The first part of this volume contains the 25 research papers that will be presented at ENLG 2011. The second part is devoted to the Generation Challenges 2011 session. It contains overview reports on the active and planned challenges and system descriptions of all participating teams.

We are indebted to the authors and to the members of our program committee whose hard work contributed to making this a collection of high quality research papers. We are also delighted that Oliver Lemon, Johanna Moore and Jeff Orkin agreed to give invited talks at ENLG 2011. And last but not least, many thanks go to the local organisation team, Nicolas Alcaraz, Anne Lise Charbonnier, Alexandre Denis, Alejandra Lorenzo, Shashi Narayan and Laura Perez-Beltrachini for handling the preparation of the meeting.

Claire Gardent and Kristina Striegnitz
Program co-Chairs for ENLG 2011

Program Co-Chairs:

Claire Gardent, CNRS/Loria, Nancy, France
Kristina Striegnitz, Union College, USA

Local Organizers:

Nicolas Alcaraz, INRIA Nancy, France
Anne-Lise Charbonnier, INRIA Nancy, France
Alexandre Denis, CNRS/LORIA, Nancy, France
Alejandra Lorenzo, INRIA/LORIA, Nancy, France
Shashi Narayan, U. Nancy/LORIA, Nancy, France
Laura Perez-Beltrachini, U. Nancy/LORIA, Nancy, France

Program Committee:

John Bateman, University Bremen, Germany
Anja Belz, University of Brighton, UK
Bernd Bohnet, University Stuttgart, Germany
Stephan Busemann, DFKI, Germany
Christian Chiarcos, University of Potsdam, Germany
Norman Creaney, University of Ulster, Ireland
Robert Dale, Macquarie University, Australia
Kees van Deemter, University of Aberdeen, Scotland
Seniz Demir, Tubitak-Bilgem, Turkey
Alexandre Denis, CNRS/LORIA Nancy, France
David DeVault, USC Institute for Creative Technologies, USA
Barbara Di Eugenio, University of Illinois, USA
Roger Evans, University of Brighton, UK
Leo Ferres, University of Concepcion, Chile
Jennifer Foster, Dublin University, Ireland
Albert Gatt, University of Malta, Malta
Josef van Genabith, Dublin City University, Ireland
Pablo Gervas, Universidad Complutense de Madrid, Spain
Markus Guhe, University of Edinburgh, UK
John Kelleher, Dublin Institute of Technology, Ireland
Alistair Knott, University of Otago, New Zealand
Alexander Koller, University of Saarbrcken, Germany
Stefan Kopp, University of Bielefeld, Germany
Eric Kow, University of Brighton, UK
Emiel Krahmer, Tilburg University, The Netherlands
Geert-Jan Kruijff, DFKI, Germany
Ivana Kruijff-Korbayova, DFKI, Germany
Oliver Lemon, Heriot Watt University, Edinburgh, Scotland

James Lester, North Carolina State University, USA
Keith van der Linden, Calvin College, USA
François Mairesse, University of Cambridge, UK
Kathleen McCoy, University of Delaware, USA
David McDonald, SIFT, Inc., USA
Chris Mellish, University of Aberdeen, Scotland
Jon Oberlander, University of Edinburgh, Scotland
Cécile Paris, CSIRO ICT Centre, Australia
Paul Piwek, The Open University, UK
Richard Power, The Open University, UK
Ehud Reiter, University of Aberdeen and Data2Text Ltd, Scotland
Donia Scott, University of Sussex, UK
Advaith Siddharthan, University of Aberdeen, Scotland
Ielka van der Sluis, Trinity College Dublin, Ireland
Yaji Sripada, University of Aberdeen, Scotland
Manfred Stede, University of Potsdam, Germany
Amanda Stent, AT&T Labs Research, USA
Matthew Stone, Rutgers, USA
Michael Strube, EML Research, Germany
Mariët Theune, University of Twente, The Netherlands
Takenobu Tokugana, Tokyo Institute of Technology, Japan
Jette Viethen, Macquarie University, Australia
Carl Vogel, Trinity College Dublin, Ireland
Michael White, Ohio State University, USA
Sandra Williams, the Open University, UK
Tie-Jun Zhao, Harbin Institute of Technology, China
Michael Zock, CNRS/LIF Université de la Méditerrannée Aix-Marseille II, France

Invited Speakers:

Oliver Lemon, Heriot Watt University, Scotland
Johanna Moore, University of Edinburgh, Scotland
Jeff Orkin, MIT Media Lab, USA

ENLG 2011 is sponsored by

informatics mathematics
Inria

Loria
Laboratoire lorrain de recherche
en informatique et ses applications

cnrs
dépasser les frontières

Nancy-Université

lorraine
conseil régional

Conference Program

Wednesday, September 28, 2011

8:30–9:15 Registration

9:15–9:30 Opening Remarks

9:30–10:30 Invited Talk

Talkin' bout a revolution (statistically speaking)
Oliver Lemon

10:30–11:00 Coffee Break

ENLG Talks: Tailoring text to users

11:00–11:30 *Text Simplification using Typed Dependencies: A Comparision of the Robustness of Different Generation Strategies*
Advaith Siddharthan

11:30–12:00 *Generating Affective Natural Language for Parents of Neonatal Infants*
Saad Mahamood and Ehud Reiter

12:00–12:30 *What is in a text and what does it do: Qualitative Evaluations of an NLG system – the BT-Nurse – using content analysis and discourse analysis*
Rahul Sambaraju, Ehud Reiter, Robert Logie, Andy Mckinlay, Chris McVittie, Albert Gatt and Cindy Sykes

12:30–1:30 Lunch

ENLG Talks: Referring expression generation

1:30–2:00 *Evaluating Salience Metrics for the Context-Adequate Realization of Discourse Referents*
Christian Chiarcos

2:00–2:30 *The Impact of Visual Context on the Content of Referring Expressions*
Henriette Viethen, Robert Dale and Markus Guhe

2:30–3:00 Coffee Break

Wednesday, September 28, 2011 (continued)

ENLG Talks: Referring expression generation

3:00–3:30 *A Cross-Linguistic Study on the Production of Multimodal Referring Expressions in Dialogue*
Ielka Van Der Sluis and Saturnino Luz

3:30–4:00 *Two Approaches for Generating Size Modifiers*
Margaret Mitchell, Kees Van Deemter and Ehud Reiter

1:30-2:30 Birds-of-a-Feather sessions / SimpleNLG User Group Meeting

6:30-8:00 Bowling and Drinks

Thursday, September 29, 2011

9:30–10:30 Invited Talk

Using Online Games to Capture, Generate, and Understand Natural Language
Jeff Orkin

10:30–11:00 Coffee Break

ENLG Talks: Knowledge representation and NLG — expressing semantic, rhetorical and temporal relations

11:00–11:30 *Content selection from an ontology-based knowledge base for the generation of football summaries*
Nadjet Bouayad-Agha, Gerard Casamayor and Leo Wanner

11:30–12:00 *Deriving rhetorical relationships from semantic content*
Richard Power

12:00–12:30 *If it may have happened before, it happened, but not necessarily before*
Albert Gatt and François Portet

12:30–1:30 Lunch

Thursday, September 29, 2011 (continued)

Generation Challenges Talks and Posters

1:30–1:40 Generation Challenges Introductory Remarks

1:40–2:55 Result Presentation: Surface Realization (SR), Helping Our Own (HOO), Generating Instructions in Virtual Environments (GIVE)

2:55–3:40 Presentation of Planned Tasks: SR Spanish, Question Generation 2nd Edition, Generating Route Instructions under Uncertainty in Virtual Environments (GRUVE)

3:40–5:00 Generation Challenges Poster Session (with coffee)

6:00–7:00 Guided Tour in the Old Town

7:30 Banquet

Friday, September 30, 2011

ENLG Talks: Optimizing task success in interactive systems

9:30–10:00 *Adaptive Information Presentation for Spoken Dialogue Systems: Evaluation with real users*
Verena Rieser, Simon Keizer, Oliver Lemon and Xingkun Liu

10:00–10:30 *Combining Hierarchical Reinforcement Learning and Bayesian Networks for Natural Language Generation in Situated Dialogue*
Nina Dethlefs and Heriberto Cuayáhuitl

10:30–11:00 *Combining symbolic and corpus-based approaches for the generation of successful referring expressions*
Konstantina Garoufi and Alexander Koller

11:00–12:30 ENLG Posters (see below for a detailed list)

12:30–1:30 Lunch

Friday, September 30, 2011 (continued)

1:30–2:30 Invited Talk

Language Generation for Spoken Dialogue Systems
Johanna D. Moore

2:30–3:00 Coffee Break

3:00–5:00 Generation Challenges Working Groups

5:00–5:30 Reports from the Working Groups and Closing Remarks

ENLG Poster Presentations

Adapting SimpleNLG to German
Marcel Bollmann

EasyText: an Operational NLG System
Laurence Danlos, Frédéric Meunier and Vanessa Combet

Towards Generating Text from Discourse Representation Structures
Valerio Basile and Johan Bos

A Policy-Based Approach to Context Dependent Natural Language Generation
Thomas Bouttaz, Edoardo Pignotti, Chris Mellish and Peter Edwards

Levels of organisation in ontology verbalisation
Sandra Williams, Allan Third and Richard Power

Using semantic roles to improve summaries
Diana Trandabâţ

Building a Generator for Italian Sign Language
Alessandro Mazzei

Investigation into Human Preference between Common and Unambiguous Lexical Substitutions
Andrew Walker, Advaith Siddharthan and Andrew Starkey

Talkin' bout a revolution (statistically speaking)

Oliver Lemon
Heriot-Watt University
Edinburgh, United Kingdom
o.lemon@hw.ac.uk

This talk will describe new methods for generating Natural Language in interactive systems – methods which are similar to planning approaches, but which use statistical machine learning to develop adaptive NLG components. Employing statistical models of users, generation contexts, and of Natural Languages themselves, has several potentially beneficial features: the ability to train models on real data, the availability of precise mathematical methods for optimisation, and the capacity to adapt robustly to previously unseen situations. Rather than emulating human behaviour in generation (which can be sub-optimal) these methods can even find strategies for NLG which improve upon human performance.

Recently, some encouraging results have been obtained with real users of 3 different systems developed using these methods, for the tasks of Information Presentation in an automated tourist guide, Referring Expression Generation in a technical support system, and generation of Temporal Referring Expressions in an appointment scheduling system. The results show that optimised NLG significantly outperforms related prior approaches, and can also improve the global performance of dialogue systems.

As well as explaining the core Reinforcement Learning and user modelling methods and concepts behind this work, I will also cover some recent work from other researchers which fits with this general perspective on NLG. Finally, I discuss some future directions for this research area, for example the issues of incremental generation and generation under uncertainty.

References

Srini Janarthanam and Oliver Lemon. 2010a. Learning to adapt to unknown users: Referring expression generation in spoken dialogue systems. In *Proceedings of ACL*.

Srinivasan Janarthanam and Oliver Lemon. 2010b. Adaptive referring expression generation in spoken dialogue systems: evaluation with real users. In *Proceedings of SIGDIAL*.

Srinivasan Janarthanam, Helen Hastie, Oliver Lemon, and Xingkun Liu. 2011. 'the day after the day after tomorrow?' a machine learning approach to adaptive temporal expression generation: training and evaluation with real users. In *Proceedings of SIGDIAL*.

Oliver Lemon, Srini Janarthanam, and Verena Rieser. 2010. Generation under uncertainty. In *Proceedings of the Generation Challenges Session at INLG*.

Oliver Lemon. 2011. Learning what to say and how to say it: joint optimization of spoken dialogue management and natural language generation. *Computer Speech and Language*, 25(2).

Verena Rieser and Oliver Lemon. 2009. Natural language generation as planning under uncertainty for spoken dialogue systems. In *Proceedings of EACL*.

Verena Rieser, Oliver Lemon, and Xingkun Liu. 2010. Optimising information presentation for spoken dialogue systems. In *Proceedings of ACL*.

Proceedings of the 13th European Workshop on Natural Language Generation (ENLG), page 1,
Nancy, France, September 2011.

Text Simplification using Typed Dependencies: A Comparison of the Robustness of Different Generation Strategies

Advaith Siddharthan
University of Aberdeen
Department of Computing Science
advaith@abdn.ac.uk

Abstract

We present a framework for text simplification based on applying transformation rules to a typed dependency representation produced by the Stanford parser. We test two approaches to regeneration from typed dependencies: (a) **gen-light**, where the transformed dependency graphs are linearised using the word order and morphology of the original sentence, with any changes coded into the transformation rules, and (b) **gen-heavy**, where the Stanford dependencies are reduced to a DSyntS representation and sentences are generating formally using the RealPro surface realiser. The main contribution of this paper is to compare the robustness of these approaches in the presence of parsing errors, using both a single parse and an n-best parse setting in an overgenerate and rank approach. We find that the gen-light approach is robust to parser error, particularly in the n-best parse setting. On the other hand, parsing errors cause the realiser in the gen-heavy approach to order words and phrases in ways that are disliked by our evaluators.

1 Introduction

In this paper, we present a system, REGENT, for text regeneration tasks such as text simplification, style modification or paraphrase. Our system applies transformation rules specified in XML files, to a typed dependency representation obtained from the Stanford Parser (De Marneffe et al., 2006). There are currently rule files for simplifying coordination (of verb phrases and full clauses), subordination, apposition and relative clauses, as well as conversion of passive to active voice; for instance, simplifying:

> The original police inquiry, which led to Mulcaire being jailed in 2007, also discovered evidence that he has successfully intercepted voicemail messages belonging to Rebekah Brooks, who was editor of the Sun when Mulcaire was working exclusively for its Sunday stablemate.

to:

> The original police inquiry led to Mulcaire being jailed in 2007. The police inquiry also discovered evidence that he has successfully intercepted voicemail messages belonging to Rebekah Brooks. Rebekah Brooks was editor of the Sun. This was when Mulcaire was working exclusively for its Sunday stablemate.

The main aim of this paper is to describe and compare two methods for generating sentences from the transformed dependency graphs:

1. **gen-heavy:** We use RealPro (Lavoie and Rambow, 1997), a statistical realiser to generate, making all decisions related to morphology and word ordering.
2. **gen-light:** We reuse word order and morphology from the original sentence, and specify any changes to these as part of each transformation rule.

Both options have pros and cons. In the gen-light approach described in detail in Siddharthan (2010) and summarised in §3.1, we can reuse information from the input sentence as much as possible, leading to very efficient generation. The downside is

Proceedings of the 13th European Workshop on Natural Language Generation (ENLG), pages 2–11,
Nancy, France, September 2011.

that we need to encode some generation decisions within transfer rules, making them cumbersome to write and difficult to learn automatically. A case can be made, particularly for the issue of subject-verb agreement, for such issues to be handled by a generator. This would make the transfer rules simpler to write, and indeed easier to learn automatically in a supervised setting. While many syntactic simplification rules are quite easy to formulate by hand, this might be an important consideration if we were trying to learn stylistic improvements or other general paraphrase rules from corpora. To explore the feasibility of using a full surface realiser for text simplification, we implemented a module that converts the Stanford dependencies to a DSyntS representation, and used RealPro (Lavoie and Rambow, 1997) to generate sentences. This module is briefly described in §3.2, before we evaluate both approaches in §4.

Summary: To summarise our findings, we find that that the gen-light approach is fairly robust to parsing errors, particularly when the n-best parses are used in an overgenerate-and-rank approach. However, the gen-heavy approach fares less well, since the process of applying transformation rules to an incorrect analysis and then generating with a statistical realiser often leads to garbled output. The gen-heavy approach can be made slightly more robust by using the n-best parses, but the judges in our evaluation still find its word and phrase ordering decisions much less acceptable. Based on our evaluation, we conclude that the preferred solution to regeneration tasks would use a gen-heavy approach for verb features (tense, mood, voice, agreement etc.) and argument ordering, while otherwise reusing word and phrase order from the input.

2 Related work

Text simplification is the process of reducing the grammatical and lexical complexity of a text, while retaining its information content and meaning. The main goal of simplification is to make information more accessible to the large numbers of people with reduced literacy. The National Literacy Trust (http://www.literacytrust.org.uk) estimates that one in six adults in the UK have poor literacy skills; other potential beneficiaries include non-native speakers and children. While there is a large body of evidence that manual text simplification is an effective intervention, there has been relatively little work on automatic simplification.

2.1 Vocabulary, Syntax and Comprehension

There is a large body of research that suggests that there are differences in the way highly skilled and poor readers read. The most striking difference is perhaps at the word level, and people for whom mapping words to meanings requires effort tend to be bad readers (Anderson and Freebody, 1981). However, various studies also highlight the role of syntax in comprehension; for instance, splitting complex sentences into several shorter ones results in better comprehension for less skilled readers (Mason and Kendall, 1979). Similarly, students' reading comprehension has shows to improve when texts have been manually rewritten to make the language more accessible (L'Allier, 1980), or to make the content more transparent (Beck et al., 1991). L'Allier (1980) found that text revision brought low ability readers above the performance level of middle ability readers on the original text and Linderholm et al. (2000) also found that reformulating causal relations for relatively difficult texts had a significant facilitatory effect for readers with low reading skills. However, manually revising texts to fit readers' level of expertise is expensive in terms of both time and money, and there is a need for automatic text simplification systems.

2.2 Automatic Text Simplification

Previous work on automatic syntactic simplification has applied transformation rules to phrasal parse trees. In early work, Chandrasekar and Srinivas (1997) induced simplification rules from a comparison of the structures of the chunked parses of the original and hand-simplified text. The learning algorithm worked by flattening subtrees that were the same on both sides of the rule, replacing identical strings of words with variables and then computing tree→trees transformations to obtain rules in terms of these variables. This work simplified relative clauses, apposition and subordination. The PSET project (Devlin and Tait, 1998; Carroll et al., 1998), which aimed at simplifying news reports for aphasics, followed the approach of Chandrasekar and Srinivas (1997) for syntactic simplification and focused mainly on lexical simplification (replacing difficult words with easier ones). The PSET project used *WordNet* (Miller et al., 1993) to identify synonyms and the Oxford Psycholinguistic Database (Quinlan, 1992) to determine the relative difficulty of words (Devlin and Tait, 1998).

In more recent work, we have examined syntactic simplification and, in particular, the way syntactic rewrites interact with discourse structure and text cohesion (Siddharthan, 2003; Siddharthan, 2006). This work has spurred subsequent research in using text simplification for second language acquisition (Petersen, 2007) and for increasing access to the web for people with low literacy (Gasperin et al., 2010). However, all these approaches are limited in the kinds of simplification they can perform. For instance, Petersen (2007) found through comparison with manually simplified text that while 87% of split points identified by the Siddharthan (2006) system were correct, these accounted for only 37% of the simplification operations identified in the manually simplified text. Siddharthan (2010) developed a framework that can potentially handle a much wider range of lexico-syntactic simplification operations using transformation rules over type dependency structures, demonstrating their approach using rules to reformulate sentences expressing causality (e.g., " The cause of the explosion was an incendiary device" to " The explosion occurred because of an incendiary device"). In this paper, we build on that work and focus on the issue of robustness in the face of incorrect parser analyses.

2.3 Other text regeneration tasks

Sentence compression is a related research area that aims to shorten sentences for the purpose of summarising the main content. There are similarities between our interest in reformulation and existing work in sentence compression. Sentence compression has usually been addressed in a generative framework, where transformation rules are learnt from parsed corpora of sentences aligned with manually compressed versions. The compression rules learnt are therefore tree-tree transformations (Knight and Marcu, 2000; Galley and McKeown, 2007; Riezler et al., 2003) of some variety. These approaches focus on *deletion* operations, mostly performed low down in the parse tree to remove modifiers. Further they make assumptions about isomorphism between the aligned tree, which means they cannot be readily applied to more complex reformulation operations such as *insertion* and *reordering*. Cohn and Lapata (2009) provide an approach based on Synchronous Tree Substitution Grammar (STSG) that in principle can handle the range of reformulation operations. However, given their focus on sentence compression, they restricted themselves to local transformations near the bottom of the parse tree. Siddharthan (2010) compared different representations and concluded that phrasal parse trees were inadequate for learning complex lexico-syntactic transformation rules and that dependency structures were more suited. Indeed dependency structures are now increasingly popular for other text regeneration tasks, such as sentence fusion (Krahmer et al., 2008; Marsi and Krahmer, 2005; Barzilay and McKeown, 2005).

3 Simplification using typed dependencies

We now summarise REGENT, our system for regenerating text, including two approached to generation: **gen-light** (§3.1) and **gen-heavy** (§3.2).

As mentioned before, we use the Stanford parser (De Marneffe et al., 2006) to obtain a typed dependency representation of the input sentence. These are triplets consisting of a relation-type and two arguments. We will use the following sentence to illustrate the process (note that the parser provides word position and part-of-speech tags in addition to dependency relations):

```
The/DT cat/NN was/VBD chased/VBN
by/IN the/DT dog/NN ./.

det(cat-2, The-1)
nsubjpass(chased-4, cat-2)
auxpass(chased-4, was-3)
det(dog-7, the-6)
agent(chased-4, dog-7)
punct(chased-4, .-8)
```

To generate, we note that these dependencies represent a tree[1] (we have not shown the punctuation

[1] In fact, the typed dependencies are only 'almost' acyclic. There are a small number of (predictable) relations that introduce cycles .

arc for simplicity):

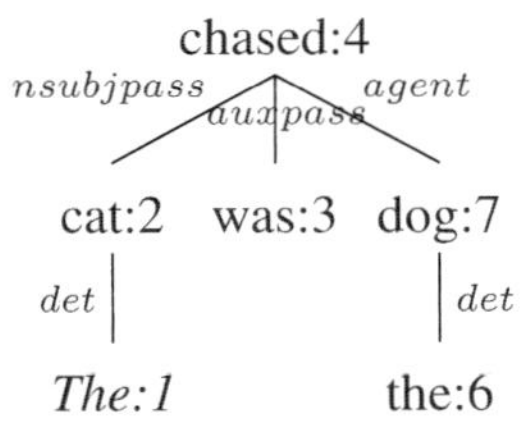

To generate from a dependency tree, we need to know the order in which to process nodes - in general tree traversal will be "inorder"; i.e, left subtrees will be processed before the root and right subtrees after. These are generation decisions that would usually be guided by the type of dependency and statistical preferences for word and phrase order. However, using a gen-light approach, we could simply use the word positions (1–7) from the original sentence, noting that the *agent* relation introduces the word "by".

As typed dependencies can be represented as a flat list, we can write transformation rules quite easily. For instance, a transformation rule to convert the above to active voice would require three deletions and two insertions:

1. Match and Delete:
   (a) nsubjpass(??X0, ??X1)
   (b) auxpass(??X0, ??X2)
   (c) agent(??X0, ??X3)
2. Insert:
   (a) nsubj(??X0, ??X3)
   (b) dobj(??X0, ??X1)

Applying this transformation to the dependency list above creates a new dependency tree:

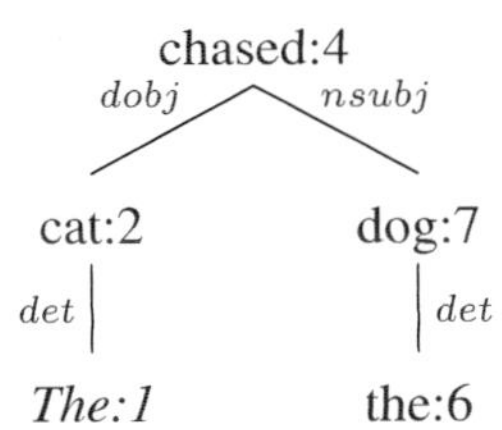

We can no longer rely on the original word order to determine the order in which to traverse the tree for generation. Now, to generate from this structure, we have two options: gen-light and gen-heavy, summarised below.

3.1 The gen-light approach

If we choose the gen-light approach, our transformation rules, in addition to Deletion and Insertion operations, also need to provide rules for tree traversal order. These only need to be provided for nodes where the transform has reordered subtrees ("??X0", which instantiates to "chased:4" in the trees above). Our rule would thus include:

3. Traversal Order Specifications:
   (a) Node ??X0: [??X3, ??X0, ??X1]

This states that for node ??X0, the traversal order should be subtree ??X3 followed by current node ??X0 followed by subtree ??X1. Using this specification would allow us to traverse the tree using the original word order for nodes with no order specification, and the specified order where a specification exist. In the above instance, this would lead us to generate:

The dog chased the cat.

Our transfer rule is still incomplete and there is one further issue that needs to be addressed – operations to be performed on nodes rather than relations. There are two node-level operation that might be required for sentence reformulation:

Lexical substitution: We still need to ensure number agreement for the verb "chase" (??X0). By changing voice, the verb now has to agree with ??X3 (the dog) rather than ??X1 (the cat). Further the tense of ??X0 was encoded in the auxiliary verb ??X2 (was) that has been deleted from the dependency list. Neither of these matter in the above example, but consider instead a rule for simplifying "The cat is chased by the dogs" to "the dogs chase the cat". We need the transfer rule to encode the lexical substitution required for node ??X0:

4. Lexical substitution:
   (a) Node ??X0: Get tense from ??X2 and number agreement from X3.

Other lexical substitution are easier to specify; for instance to reformulate "*John jumped because David shouted.*" as "*David's shouting caused John to jump*", the following lexical substitution rule is required for node ??Xn representing "shout" that replaces its suffix "ed" with "ing":

Lexical substitution: Node ??Xn: Suffix="ing"

Node deletion: This is an operation that removes a node from the tree. Any subtrees are moved to the parent node. If a root node is deleted, one of the children adopts the rest. By default, the right-most child takes the rest as dependents, but we allow the rule to specify the new parent. In the above example, we want to remove the node ??X2 ("was") (note that deleting a relation does not necessarily remove a node – there might be other nodes connected to ??X2 in the graph). We would like to move these to the node ??X0 ("cause"):

5. Node Deletion:
   (a) Node ??X2: Target=??X0

Node deletion is easily implemented using search and replace on sets of GRs. It is central to any reformulations that alter syntactic categories; for instance, to reformulate "*The cause of X is Y*" as "*Y causes X*", we need to delete the verb "is" and move its dependents to the new verb "causes".

To summarise, the gen-light approach requires transfer rules to specify five lists:

1. CONTEXT: Transform only proceeds if this list of GRs can be unified with the input GRs.
2. DELETE: List of GRs to delete from input.
3. INSERT: List of GRs to insert into input.
4. ORDERING: List of nodes with subtree order specified
5. NODE-OPERATIONS: List of lexical substitutions and deletion operations on nodes.

For most reformulations, the CONTEXT and DELETE lists are one and the same, but one can imagine reformulation tasks where extra context needs to be specified to determine whether reformulation is appropriate.

3.2 The gen-heavy approach

The alternative to specifying lists for changes in word/phrase ordering and morphology is to use a formal generator to make these decisions. We use an existing widely used generator RealPro (Lavoie and Rambow, 1997) that uses a typed dependency formalism. For this purpose we have written a convertor that translates the Stanford dependency types into the DSyntS notation required by RealPro. The DSyntS notation differs in two basic ways:

1. In DSyntS, words are presented as lemmas, with tense, voice, aspect, mood, taxis, number, person, gender, etc. represented as features. This means we need to analyse part-of-speech tags, auxilliary verbs and pronouns to provide RealPro with the correct input.
2. Unlike the Stanford Dependencies that contains 52 fine-grained types, DSyntS uses only the following seven types: 'I', 'II', 'III', 'IV', 'ATTR', 'DESC-ATTR' and 'APPEND'. Thus, we need to map each of the Stanford dependencies to one of these types. There are some subtleties regarding coordination and relative clauses, but the mapping is for the most part straightforward.

The DSyntS representation created by tranforming the Stanford Dependencies for "the dog chased the cat" is:

```
DSYNTS:
 "chase" [class:"verb" voice:"act"
          tense:"past" aspect:"simple"
          taxis:"nil" polarity:"nil"]
   (
    I  "dog" [class:"common_noun"
            number:"sg" article:"def"]
    II "cat" [class:"common_noun"
            number:"sg" article:"def"]
   )
END:
```

The advantage of the gen-heavy approach is that generation decisions such as ordering and agreement no longer need to be encoded in the transformation rules, making them easier to learn automatically.

3.3 Applying multiple transformation rules

One advantage of using typed dependencies as a representation for applying transformation rules is that we can iteratively apply multiple transformations on the same set of dependency relations. As an illustration, consider:

The cat was chased by a dog that was barking

det(cat-2, The-1)
nsubjpass(chased-4, cat-2)
auxpass(chased-4, was-3)
det(dog-7, a-6)
agent(chased-4, dog-7)
nsubj(barking-10, dog-7)
aux(barking-10, was-9)
rcmod(dog-7, barking-10)

We apply two rules; the first simplifies relative clauses:

1. Match and Delete:
   (a) rcmod(??X0, ??X1)
   (b) nsubj(??X1, ??X0)

2. Insert:
   (a) nsubj(??X1, ??X0)

This rule removes the embedding "rcmod" relation, when there is a subject available for the verb in the relative clause. Then we apply the rule to convert passive to active voice, as described in §3. Following these two rule applications, we are left with the following list of dependencies:

det(cat-2, The-1)
dobj(chased-4, cat-2)
det(dog-7, a-6)
nsubj(chased-4, dog-7)
aux(barking-10, was-9)
nsubj(barking-10, dog-7)

This list now represents two trees with *chased* and *barking* as root nodes:

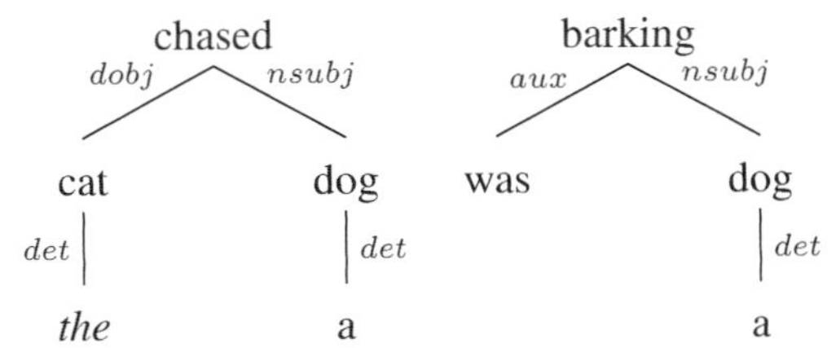

This generates (using either gen-light or gen-heavy):

> A dog chased the cat. The dog was barking.

Note that we employ a postprocessor for generating referring expressions when a noun phrase is repeated. This includes the head noun and either a definite article or a title (e.g., *Mr* or *President*).

3.4 The n-best parse setting

During the development of the system, we found that most of the errors in the output could be traced back to inaccurate parsing. For instance, the top parse for the sentence:

> Cars and pick-up trucks with badly twisted and still smouldering frames littered the three compounds, which housed villas and four-storey blocks.

identified *which housed* as a relative clause, and *villas* and *blocks* as verbs. This incorrect analysis got simplified (using gen-light) as:

> The three compounds housed. Cars and pick-up trucks with badly twisted and still smouldering frames littered the compounds, villas and four-storey. And Cars blocks.

We ask the question, can we use the n-best parses and try to rank the simplified texts in some way? And to what extent can this increase the robustness of the system?

The question arises, how can we evaluate the quality of the generated sentences? Our first attempt calculated n-gram overlap with the original sentence, but this was not found to be useful. Essentially, every transformation of the input sentence reduces ngram overlap between the input and the output, so this method penalises the application of any transforms. This proved to be a problem even for simple transforms such as coordination and subordination that introduce sentence breaks. It proved a bigger problem for embedded constructs such as relative clauses and apposition, and of course the metric is almost meaningless for voice change and other transformations that reorder constituents or change words. Indeed a metric based on comparison with the original would make little sense for text modification applications.

Our final approach was to manually go through the simplifications of the 50 best parses of 100 sentences and identify patterns of infelicities in them. We identified patterns such as:

1. Sentences ending in subject pronouns, prepositions or conjunctions

2. Word repetition (e.g., "is is" or "to to")
3. Prepositions followed by subject pronouns (e.g., "of he")
4. Bad sequences of conjunctions and prepositions (e.g., "because but" or "until for")

Our metric deducted a point for each identified infelicity. In addition we penalised very short sentences (4 words or less) and simplifications that resulted in many fewer words than the original.

In addition to the above penalties, we used the following positive scores:

1. Bigram and trigram overlap with original sentence (as a fraction)
2. The number of sentences in the output (this is to encourage the application of simplification rules)
3. A bonus if the simplification was performed on the top-ranked parse (as this is the most likely to be correct)

In the next section on testing, we report results for system settings using a single parse, and the n-best parses, where we produce n outputs and select the best one according to the criterion described in this section.

4 Evaluation of generation strategies

In this paper we have proposed a framework for complex lexico-syntactic text regeneration. Our system, REGENT, comes with 63 rules for simplifying coordination, subordination, relative clauses, apposition and passive voice. In addition, our system offers two generation options (**gen-light** and **gen-heavy**) in two settings (single and n-best parse).

We emphasise that our purpose in this paper is not to evaluate the simplification rules for their effect on comprehension for different categories of users, but only to test the framework for robustness in the face of parsing errors. We will focus on comparing the four different system settings with respect to how many simplifications have been performed and whether these have been done correctly. Specifically, we will not evaluate whether simplification is found to be useful to different categories of users. With these narrow goals, we report results using:

- **Extent:** The level of simplification achieved, based on the number of transforms performed and the average sentence length in the simplified text.

- **Precision:** The proportion of transformed sentences for which the rules have been applied accurately, so that the output is grammatical with (a) correct verb agreement and inflexion and (b) modifiers/complements appearing in acceptable orders.

Measuring precision as defined above is tricky. As a developer trying to evaluate the framework, the pertinent question is whether the transformation rules have been applied correctly. This however requires knowledge of the transformation rules, which only the developer has. However, we also need external unbiased judgements by testers not involved with the development of the system. These would necessarily conflate issues arising from the quality of the transformation rules with issues arising from the parsing and generation aspects of the system. We present developer test results in §4.1, and an additional evaluation with external testers in §4.2.

4.1 Developer Testing

Our data is six news articles totalling 175 sentences selected as follows: We picked the first two news reports each from the main webpage of three online British news sources (news.bbc.co.uk, guardian.co.uk and thesun.co.uk) at a single time.

We summarise our testing results (with accuracy judged by the developer) in Table 2. In addition, Table 1 provides examples of accurate and inaccurate transformations, as judged by the developer (our judges in §4.2 did not always agree). As Table 2 shows, using the n-best parse setting increases the average number of simplification operations performed by 9 % points and the number of sentences modified by 5 % points. This reduces the average sentence length of the output by around one word. We attribute this improvement to the greater likelihood of a transformation rule matching a dependency parse when multiple parses are considered. More importantly, we also observe an improvement in accuracy from using multiple parses, suggesting that our approach to ranking (§3.4) is valid.

Accurate and Inaccurate Transformations
1 I am very relieved to have won my appeal and for recognition I was treated unfairly and unlawfully.
√I am very relieved to have won my appeal. And for recognition I was unfairly and unlawfully treated.
× I am very relieved to have won my appeal. And I was unfairly and unlawfully treated for recognition.
2 One user of the social network, christonabike, tweeted...
× One user of the social network tweeted. The network is christonabike...
3 It is believed to include recordings Mulcaire made of messages left on Rice's mobile phone, including several from friends and families.
√It is believed to include recordings Mulcaire made of messages left on Rice's mobile phone. This includes several from friends and families.
× It is believed to include recordings Mulcaire, made of messages, left on Rice's mobile phone. This includes several from friends and families.
4 Lo and behold the taxpayers subsidised a $30,000 kitchen and he's refusing to give all the details.
√The taxpayers lo and behold subsidised a $30,000 kitchen. And he is refusing to give all the details.
5 On Thursday, Serbian TV showed footage of the former general wearing a baseball cap and walking slowly as he appeared in court in Belgrade for the first time.
√Serbian TV showed footage of the former general wearing a baseball cap and slowly walking on Thursday. This is as he appeared in court in Belgrade for the first time.

Table 1: Examples of automatic reformulations.

System Setting	Av S Len	#Trans/S	%S Trans	%Acc
Original	20.9			
gen-l/1 parse	15.3	0.65	50.2	83.9
gen-l/50 parses	14.3	0.74	55.4	87.9
gen-h/1 parse	14.8	0.65	50.2	70.8
gen-h/50 parses	14.0	0.74	55.4	77.7

Table 2: Test results for four configurations of the system: **gen-l**ight and **gen-h**eavy in single parse and 50-best parses modes. The columns report average sentence length in words, average number of transformations performed on each input sentence, percentage of input sentences with at least one transformation, the correctness of the transformations.

Manual inspection of the mistakes reveals that for the gen-light approach with n-best parses, these are mostly due to relative clause attachment errors by the parser – these result in incorrect simplification, but no disfluency in the output (cf. Ex 2 in Table 1).

The gen-heavy approach makes many more errors; these are usually due to mis-parses (cf. Ex 1 and 3 in Table 1; in 3, while the word order is fine, the parser has incorrectly detected a reduced relative clause, and RealPro has placed this within commas). In addition, the gen-heavy approach often results in different phrase orders that might be harder to read, for instance in Ex 4 and 5. These have been treated as accurate in this evaluation.

4.2 Acceptability measurements

In the previous section, the developer was testing whether the rules have been applied accurately. This is different from evaluating the acceptability of the output. We selected 50 sentences from our test set at random and asked two native speakers to label each of the four reformulations (gen-light and gen-heavy in single and 50-best parse settings) as either acceptable or unacceptable. The judges were shown both the original sentence and reformulations, without being provided information about system settings. We found quite a low pair-wise agreement ($kappa < 0.55$) between the two judges and also with the developer's judgements for these sentences (Table 3). Table 4 shows the acceptability results are lower than the developer's assessments in the previous section, particularly for the gen-heavy approach. The two judges deemed sentences unacceptable for a variety of reasons that were not penalised by the developer in his testing (e.g., disfluencies that were carried over from the input, incorrect capitalisation, lack of punctuation, bad sentence order, etc.).

In addition, the judges also deemed examples such as 5 in Table 1 unacceptable because of the copula being in present tense. The "this is" construct is introduced by the transformation rules for subordination; however, this fact is only known to the developer (who thus deemed the transformation accu-

Judge 1	Judge 2	κ	% Agreement
A	B	.55	78%
A	Developer	.52	79%
B	Developer	.32	68%

Table 3: Pairwise agreement on acceptability

System	% Acceptable			
	J1	J2	Developer	Majority
gen-l/1 parse	.59	.66	.79	.69
gen-l/50 parses	.62	.69	.86	.78
gen-h/1 parse	.19	.40	.62	.40
gen-h/50 parses	.20	.45	.71	.43

Table 4: The percentage of transformed sentences acceptable to the three raters (the developer and two judges) for 4 reformulations each of 50 sentences. The final column treats a transformation as acceptable if at least 2 raters find it acceptable.

rate) and not to the two judges (who thus deemed the output unacceptable).

We believe that these two evaluation provide a good indication of the performance of our system and its different settings, as well as the quality of the transformation rules. The main conclusion that we draw from these tests is that users can be quite intolerant towards suboptimal word ordering, and that using an off-the shelf sentence realiser is not a good option for text regeneration tasks, unless it can reuse ordering information from the input in some way.

5 Conclusions and future work

We have presented a system for text simplification based on applying transformation rules to typed dependencies. The main contribution of this paper is to demonstrate that the robustness of the system to parsing errors can be improved by using the n-best dependency parses in a overgenerate-and-rank approach. In addition, we explore the question of whether an existing surface realiser can be used for text regeneration tasks. We find that this approach is brittle, and misanalyses by the parser can result in unacceptable word and constituent orders in the generated texts. This problem would, we believe, be overcome if the generator could make use of word and phrase order in the input sentence, using deep generation only for verb features (mood, tense, voice, etc.), number agreement and argument order.

Acknowledgements

This work was supported by the Economic and Social Research Council (Grant Number RES-000-22-3272).

References

Richard Anderson and Peter Freebody. 1981. Vocabulary knowledge. In John Guthrie, editor, *Comprehension and Teaching: Research Reviews*, pages 77–117. International Reading Association, Newark, DE.

Richard Anderson. 1981. A proposal to continue a center for the study of reading. Technical Report 487, University of Illinois, Center for the Study of Reading, Urbana-Champaign.

Regina Barzilay and Lillian Lee. 2003. Learning to paraphrase: An unsupervised approach using multiple-sequence alignment. In *HLT-NAACL 2003: Main Proceedings*, pages 16–23.

Regina Barzilay and Kathleen McKeown. 2005. Sentence fusion for multidocument news summarization. *Computational Linguistics*, 31(3):297–328.

Isabel L. Beck, Margaret G. McKeown, Gale M. Sinatra, and Jane A. Loxterman. 1991. Revising social studies text from a text-processing perspective: Evidence of improved comprehensibility. *Reading Research Quarterly*, pages 251–276.

John Carroll, Guido Minnen, Yvonne Canning, Siobhan Devlin, and John Tait. 1998. Practical simplification of English newspaper text to assist aphasic readers. In *Proceedings of AAAI98 Workshop on Integrating Artificial Intelligence and Assistive Technology*, pages 7–10, Madison, Wisconsin.

Raman Chandrasekar and Bangalore Srinivas. 1997. Automatic induction of rules for text simplification. *Knowledge-Based Systems*, 10:183–190.

Raman Chandrasekar, Christine Doran, and Bangalore Srinivas. 1996. Motivations and methods for text simplification. In *Proceedings of the 16th International Conference on Computational Linguistics (COLING '96)*, pages 1041–1044, Copenhagen, Denmark.

Trevor Cohn and Mirella Lapata. 2009. Sentence compression as tree transduction. *Journal of Artificial Intelligence Research*, 34(1):637–674.

Trevor Cohn, Chris Callison-Burch, and Mirella Lapata. 2008. Constructing corpora for the development and evaluation of paraphrase systems. *Computational Linguistics*, 34(4):597–614.

Meredyth Daneman and Patricia Carpenter. 1980. Individual differences in working memory and reading. *Journal of Verbal Learning and Verbal Behavior*, 19:450–466.

Marie-Catherine De Marneffe, Bill MacCartney, and Christopher D. Manning. 2006. Generating typed dependency parses from phrase structure parses. In *Proceedings of LREC*, volume 6, pages 449–454. Citeseer.

Siobhan Devlin and John Tait. 1998. The use of a psycholinguistic database in the simplification of text for aphasic readers. In J. Nerbonne, editor, *Linguistic Databases*, pages 161–173. CSLI Publications, Stanford, California.

Michel Galley and Kathleen McKeown. 2007. Lexicalized Markov grammars for sentence compression. In *Human Language Technologies 2007: The Conference of the North American Chapter of the Association for Computational Linguistics; Proceedings of the Main Conference*, pages 180–187, Rochester, New York, April. Association for Computational Linguistics.

Caroline Gasperin, Erick Maziero, and Sandra Aluísio. 2010. Challenging choices for text simplification. *Computational Processing of the Portuguese Language*, pages 40–50.

Ali Ibrahim, Boris Katz, and Jimmy Lin. 2003. Extracting paraphrases from aligned corpora. In *Proceedings of The Second International Workshop on Paraphrasing*.

Nobuhiro Kaji, Daisuke Kawahara, Sadao Kurohash, and Satoshi Sato. 2002. Verb paraphrase based on case frame alignment. In *Proceedings of the 40th Annual Meeting of the Association for Computational Linguistics (ACL'02)*, pages 215–222, Philadelphia, USA.

Kevin Knight and Daniel Marcu. 2000. Statistics-based summarization — step one: Sentence compression. In *Proceeding of The American Association for Artificial Intelligence Conference (AAAI-2000)*, pages 703–710.

Emiel Krahmer, Erwin Marsi, and Paul van Pelt. 2008. Query-based sentence fusion is better defined and leads to more preferred results than generic sentence fusion. In *Proceedings of the 46th Annual Meeting of the Association for Computational Linguistics on Human Language Technologies: Short Papers*, pages 193–196. Association for Computational Linguistics.

James J. L'Allier. 1980. *An evaluation study of a computer-based lesson that adjusts reading level by monitoring on task reader characteristics*. Ph.D. thesis, University of Minnesota, Minneapolis, MN.

Benoit Lavoie and Owen Rambow. 1997. A fast and portable realizer for text generation systems. In *Proceedings of the fifth conference on Applied natural language processing*, pages 265–268. Association for Computational Linguistics.

Tracy Linderholm, Michelle G. Everson, Paul van den Broek, Maureen Mischinski, Alex Crittenden, and J. Samuels. 2000. Effects of Causal Text Revisions on More-and Less-Skilled Readers' Comprehension of Easy and Difficult Texts. *Cognition and Instruction*, 18(4):525–556.

Erwin Marsi and Emiel Krahmer. 2005. Explorations in sentence fusion. In *Proceedings of the European Workshop on Natural Language Generation*, pages 109–117.

Jana Mason and Janet Kendall. 1979. Facilitating reading comprehension through text structure manipulation. *Alberta Journal of Medical Psychology*, 24:68–76.

George A. Miller, Richard Beckwith, Christiane D. Fellbaum, Derek Gross, and Katherine Miller. 1993. Five Papers on WordNet. Technical report, Princeton University, Princeton, N.J.

Sarah E. Petersen. 2007. *Natural language processing tools for reading level assessment and text simplification for bilingual education*. Ph.D. thesis, University of Washington, Seattle, WA.

Stephen P. Quigley and Peter V. Paul. 1984. *Language and Deafness*. College-Hill Press, San Diego, California.

Philip Quinlan. 1992. *The Oxford Psycholinguistic Database*. Oxford University Press, U.K.

Stefan Riezler, Tracy H. King, Richard Crouch, and Annie Zaenen. 2003. Statistical sentence condensation using ambiguity packing and stochastic disambiguation methods for lexical-functional grammar. In *Proceedings of the Human Language Technology Conference and the 3rd Meeting of the North American Chapter of the Association for Computational Linguistics (HLT-NAACL'03)*, Edmonton, Canada.

Advaith Siddharthan and Napoleon Katsos. 2010. Reformulating discourse connectives for non-expert readers. In *Proceedings of the 11th Annual Conference of the North American Chapter of the Association for Computational Linguistics (NAACL-HLT 2010)*, Los Angeles, CA.

Advaith Siddharthan. 2003. Preserving discourse structure when simplifying text. In *Proceedings of the European Natural Language Generation Workshop (ENLG), 11th Conference of the European Chapter of the Association for Computational Linguistics (EACL'03)*, pages 103–110, Budapest, Hungary.

Advaith Siddharthan. 2006. Syntactic simplification and text cohesion. *Research on Language and Computation*, 4(1):77–109.

Advaith Siddharthan. 2010. Complex lexico-syntactic reformulation of sentences using typed dependency representations. In *Proceedings of the 6th International Natural Language Generation Conference (INLG 2010)*, pages 125–133. Dublin, Ireland.

Generating Affective Natural Language for Parents of Neonatal Infants

Saad Mahamood and Ehud Reiter
Department of Computing Science
University of Aberdeen
Scotland, United Kingdom
{s.mahamood, e.reiter}@abdn.ac.uk

Abstract

This paper presents several affective NLG strategies for generating medical texts for parents of pre-term neonates. Initially, these were meant to be personalised according to a model of the recipient's level of stress. However, our evaluation showed that all recipients preferred texts generated with the affective strategies, regardless of predicted stress level.

1 Introduction

In recent years there has been a great interest in building NLG systems that do not only inform but also take into consideration the recipients emotional state. The need to take such additional factors into account arises from the fact that end users in various contextual circumstances can have more than informational needs to meet. This is particularly apparent for parents of babies that are being looked after in a Neonatal Intensive Care Unit (NICU). This is an environment that has many challenges in receiving and understanding information. It is also an environment in which parents have to come to terms with information that they are not familiar with and have to deal with the emotional impact of the information presented to them. However, whereas medical staff can express affect through voice-tone and body language, the affect-limited nature of text means that information given to recipients by computers must carry the appropriate affective tone in the way that words are expressed to the recipient. The use of empathy to recognise and express emotions to efficiently convey the affective tone of information could allow computers to influence the mood of their users (Picard, 1997). NLG technology has made it possible to produce data-to-text information summaries for human recipients. However, very few NLG systems have any form of strategies that take into consideration the recipients emotional state when communicating information.

In this paper, we discuss our effort to do this in the context of the BabyTalk (Gatt et al., 2009) project. In particular, this paper will focus on the affective approaches used by the BabyTalk-Family system, which was designed to communicate medical information summaries for parents of pre-term neonatal infants. We describe the design, construction, and evaluation of this system in the hope to stimulate discussion on how best to incorporate human emotions as a component of communication between computers and humans.

2 Background

In the United Kingdom 12% of newly born babies need specialist medical care in a NICU or in a Special Care Baby Unit (SCBU). The length of stay for such infants can range from a few days to several months. Inside these units, critical life support, physiological monitoring, and medical attention are provided twenty-four hours a day. The babies that are cared for may have complex and serious medical problems. The environment of neonatal care is one of "high technology" in which babies are looked after in incubators surrounded by monitors, wires, and tubes.

For parents of children in NICU, the need for information that is tailored to emotional and informational needs is very much evident. The birth

Proceedings of the 13th European Workshop on Natural Language Generation (ENLG), pages 12–21,
Nancy, France, September 2011.

of a child that requires neonatal care is a particular circumstance that has the potential to cause a considerable amount of stress and anxiety for the parents. The sequence of events in NICU can be akin to a roller coaster ride, with many unexpected ups, downs, and turns of events. Parents rarely feel safe from the fear and uncertainty of the problems that can occur whilst the child is in care (McGrath, 2001). In addition, the stress and shock of having a sick child in neonatal intensive care might also mean that parents will not be able to process large amounts of information (Brazy et al., 2001). However, the provision of information is important in giving parents a sense of hope and a feeling of involvement in their child's care (Charchuk and Simpson, 2005).

2.1 NLG and e-Health systems

NLG systems have been increasingly used for the creation of e-Health systems (Hüske-Kraus, 2003), such as generating information for smoking cessation patients (Reiter et al., 2000), breast surgery patients (DiMarco et al., 2007), and so forth. Within healthcare, increasing amounts of patient data are being stored within computerised health databases. This information is being stored in patient records and is combined with drug databases and knowledge bases of medical terminology. Besides helping to provide information support to clinicians, NLG is playing a greater role in providing patients with access to information in a personal form. One prime example is the HealthDoc project that aimed to customise patient information at an individual level based upon their medical condition, demographic, personality profile, and other relevant factors (DiMarco et al., 2007). Such personalisation compares favourably when compared to traditional patient literature which is often limited in its effectiveness by having to address a wide audience (DiMarco et al., 1995).

2.2 Affective NLG

Recently, the NLG community has explored the use of emotion as a way of adapting information to the recipient. This development has led to the rise of 'Affective' NLG (ANLG), which has been defined as "NLG that relates to, arises from, or deliberately influences emotions or other non-strictly rational aspects of the hearer" (de Rosis and Grasso, 2000). In other words, it is a form of NLG that outputs text from a non-linguistic source, but unlike most NLG systems it also takes into account the emotional aspects of the recipient and modifies its textual output for the intended recipient. ANLG attempts to redefine NLG methods and knowledge sources to produce more affective texts (de Rosis and Grasso, 2000). One approach proposed by de Rosis and Grasso (2000) was to introduce models at the sentence planning stage that adapts the message for the intended recipient's communicative goal and also employs rule-based heuristics for the usage of empathy in the resultant text. Other ANLG systems have used emotional or physiological models to define the type of affective text generation. For example, the PERSONAGE system, whilst strictly not dealing with emotion, has shown that by using the 'Big Five' personality traits model it is possible to generate tailored output for particular personality traits (Mairesse and Walker, 2007).

A review of past work in ANLG by Belz (2003) concluded that the research in ANLG has not yet been successful in making the connection between emotion and NLG. Empirical testing of ANLG systems can also pose many challenges as well, with very few past systems being tested. Work by van der Sluis and Mellish (2009) on measuring the emotions of recipients when given positively slanted texts has recently shown it is possible to measure the emotional effect. However, the overall lack of empirical testing from past ANLG systems makes it hard to determine the effectiveness of previous ANLG implementations and the relative importance of their individual techniques.

2.3 The BabyTalk Project

The goal of the BabyTalk project (Gatt et al., 2009) is to develop software that generates English summaries of medical data about babies in a NICU. The babies that are cared for may have complex and serious medical problems, and could require critical life support, physiological monitoring, and medical attention twenty-four hours a day. Large quantities of data (a megabyte per day or more) are generated from the real-time monitoring of the baby's physiological condition (e.g., heart rate, blood pressure) and discrete medical events (e.g., equipment settings, drug administration, parent interactions) are also logged. This large, diverse array of information is stored by modern NICUs in an Electronic Medical Record (EMR). Typically, these EMRs are accessed by medical practitioners through a computer beside the baby's cot.

The main aim for all of the BabyTalk systems is to generate English summaries of EMR data for a variety of readers and purposes. They use signal analysis and medical data interpretation techniques to identify key events and inter-relationships, and NLG to express these events and relationships as a textual narrative. The overriding philosophy of BabyTalk is to use information only within the medical record and not to rely on any additional data input from its recipients. So as not to inconvenience clinicians, nurses, and parents with additional demands. Three BabyTalk (BT) systems have been built. BT-45 (Portet et al., 2007) generates summaries for medical professionals, to assist in real-time decision making; BT-Nurse (Hunter et al., 2011) generates summaries for nurses, to assist in shift handover; and BT-Family generates summaries for parents, to keep them informed about the condition of their child.

Our focus in this paper is on the BT-Family system. This is a system where it is essential that the texts generated be comprehensible to people who are not medical professionals, that the texts do not cause unnecessary stress and anxiety, and most importantly, the texts communicate the information that parents want to know.

3 Stress Modelling in BabyTalk-Family

To develop a more effective approach to communicating information to parents, BT-Family must take into account the possible state of mind of the intended recipient and the context or climate that the message would be received in (Berry, 2004). In neonatal care, one of the most predominate emotions that parents face is one of stress. The level of distress experienced by parents can be significant especially if their child is critically ill (Shields-Poë and Pinelli, 1997). Parents can also become distressed by noticing colour changes such as Jaundice, or witnessing episodes of Apnea or respiratory distress (Miles and Holditch-Davis, 1997; Bass, 1991). The small, fragile and undeveloped appearance of an infant in NICU whilst being surrounded by medical apparatus such as respirators, intravenous fluid lines, and monitoring equipment can be very stressful for parents (Miles et al., 1991; Holditch-Davis and Miles, 2000). Parents can find the experience of having their child looked after in a technological environment considerably distressing and oppressive (Jämsä and Jämsä, 1998). The baby's appearance can have such an impact that even at one month of age, mothers of very low birthweight infants show a higher degree of stress compared to mothers of full-term infants (Jackson et al., 2003).

Since neonatal care is a dynamic environment, the sources and levels of stress for parents can change over time and therefore it is important to obtain repeated stress measurements to obtain an accurate assessment of parental stress (Reid et al., 2007). In BT-Family this was done through a stress prediction model called PNSS (Predictive Neonatal Stress Score). Unlike traditional stress self-questionnaire instruments for parents of pre-term neonatal infants, the focus of this model was to have a repeatable non-invasive way of calculating the recipient's level of stress. A detailed explanation of this model's implementation is beyond the scope of this paper, but in essence the model focused on utilising the baby's EMR data to generate a stress score on a three point Likert scale. The higher the score, the more likely the parent could potentially be stressed. The PNSS model composed of thirteen elements. These elements were derived from a partial subset of the Parental Stress Scale (PSS): NICU (Miles et al., 1991) and the Neonatal Unit Parental Stress (Reid et al., 2007) questionnaire instruments. As one of the main factors of parental stress is the physiological health of the child (Shields-Poë and Pinelli, 1997; Seideman et al., 1997), most of the elements in the PNSS model focus on this particular aspect. Another reason to focus on the physiological aspect was due to the fact that most data contained with the baby's EMR focused on the physiological state or medical treatments of the patient. Information about the parents is sparsely recorded or not recorded at all. Therefore, any attempt to simply use all the elements within existing stress questionnaire instruments is not possible.

To evaluate the accuracy of the PNSS model, it was validated against a set of PSS: NICU scores that were obtained from eight mothers who had a child actively receiving care in a neonatal unit. Statistical analysis of the results obtained showed that the PNSS score had no statistically significant non-parametric correlation with the PSS: NICU score ($p=0.204$, $r_s=-0.504$). These forms of discrepancy could possibly be attributed to the lack of elements that describe the parental role in the PNSS model. This is primarily because this information is not available in the EMR. Whilst the philosophy of BabyTalk is to avoid asking external information from users (such as clinicians, nurses, and parents), in the case of stress scores such input would be required from parents. Further work is required in this area to produce a more accurate predictive stress score.

4 Implementing ANLG in BT-Family

The ANLG architecture (illustrated in Figure 1) used in BT-Family is an extension of the NLG data-to-text architecture that was proposed by Reiter (2007), in which natural language text is generated from a non-linguistic data source. Most of the core parts of this system are based upon the BT-Nurse system, in which there are six core components: *Badger EMR Database*, *BabyTalk Ontology*, *Signal Analysis*, *Data Interpretation*, *Document Planner*, and *Microplanner & Realisation*. A detailed explanation of how these core modules function can be found in Gatt et al., (2009) and Mahamood (2010).

The system presented in this section is built upon the BT-Nurse system, but there are crucial differences between these two systems that make both unique from each other. BT-Family contains additional affective extensions to produce textual output that takes into consideration the emotional status of the recipient. The modifications and innovations in the BT-Family system rest in three key areas:

1. Implementation of a stress model within a traditional NLG architecture.
2. The development of a selective document planner that reacts to parental level of distress.
3. The application of multiple affective strategies that attempt to mitigate emotional affect.

Figures 2 & 3 shows the difference between the 12-hour BT-Nurse and 24-hour BT-Family reports produced from the same EMR record.

The PNSS model implemented in BT-Family is based on the work described in the previous section. The implementation uses the BabyTalk ontology to query for the existence of particular factual details about the baby's records to help determine the score for each of the thirteen separate stress factors. This score is stored and made accessible to all other components of the BT-Family system. However, the PNSS score could be calculated by other means or even directly entered by a parent or medical staff; this would not affect the rest of the system.

BT-Nurse – Patient: 100299, Shift Ending: 2004-02-16 20:00
Background
The baby was born at 24 weeks weighing 755 g. He is 7 weeks old, with corrected gestational age of 30 weeks and 4 days, and weighs 1113 g. He is in an intensive care nursery.

Current problems

- Oxygen or ventilator requirement at 28 days of age (since 31/01/2004).
- Hyponatraemia (since 02/02/2004).
- PDA (since 07/02/2004).
- Thrombocytopaenia (since 09/02/2004).
- Confirmed bacterial sepsis (since 10/02/2004).

Respiratory Support
Currently, the baby is on CPAP in 27 % O2. CPAP pressure is 4.4 cms H2O.
SaO2 is variable within the acceptable range and there have been some desaturations.
The most recent blood gas was taken at around 11:45. There is fully compensated respiratory acidosis or secondary compensation of metabolic acidosis. pH is 7.32. CO2 is 9.52 kPa. BE is 9.7 mmol/L. The last oral suction was done at about 16:30.

Events During the Shift
Between 09:00 and 11:30, RR decreased from 81 to 38.
At around 10:00, the baby was given caffeine.

Current Status
Currently, HR is stable within the acceptable range although there have been some bradycardias. At about 19:45, it decreased from 157 bpm to 141 bpm. T1 is variable within the acceptable range.

Figure 2: A partial BT-Nurse report example.

The BT-Family system has a document planner that generates a text structure in a more accessible narrative format for parents rather than producing technical diagnostic texts for nurses. Research findings from past knowledge acquisition phases with parents of neonatal infants were used to create additional subject matter in the generated reports that were of particular interest to parents, but not considered to be clinically relevant (Mahamood et al.,

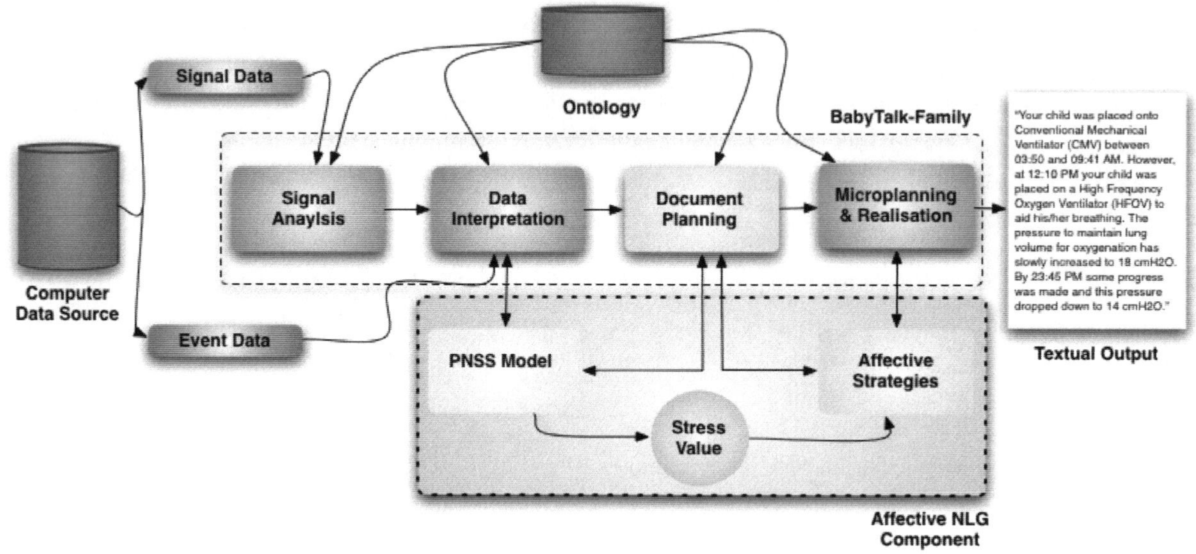

Figure 1: Diagram illustrating the overall ANLG architecture

BT-Family – Baby 100299, 16/02/2004 08:00 to 17/02/2004 08:00

John was in intensive care. Your child was stable during the day and night. Since last week, his weight increased from 860 grams (1 lb 14 oz) to 1113 grams (2 lb 7 oz). He was nursed in an incubator.

Yesterday, John was on a ventilator. The mode of ventilation is Bilevel Positive Airway Pressure (BiPAP) Ventilation. This machine helps to provide the support that enables him to breathe more comfortably. Since last week, his inspired Oxygen (FiO2) was lowered from 56% to 21% (which is the same as normal air). This is a positive development for your child.

During the day, Nurse Johnson looked after your baby. Nurse Stevens cared for your baby during the night.

Since last week Milk feeds have increased from 3.0 mls per every hour to 7.0 mls per every hour. This is a reassuring development for your baby.

Baby John had Mummy & Daddy provide some care to him yesterday. John had a gastric milk feed. Also, baby John had some visitors who came to visit him yesterday.

Figure 3: An equivalent BT-Family report.

2008; Moncur et al., 2009). This included matters such as addressing the nursing staff details, listing the parental based care given to child, a reminder of information leaflets given to the parents, and even details on whether the baby had slept well during the night. Some of the content topics are only addressed if the relevant medical details are present within the baby's medical record. Likewise, BT-Nurse also contains detailed clinical information that is not present in BT-Family, such as blood gas test results (pH, CO2, and Base Excess (BE) levels).

The initial core of the BT-Family document planner, however, relies on addressing four main physiological topics in its textual reports:

1. Details of the baby's weight.
2. Ventilation and inspired oxygen details.
3. Baby's feeding details.
4. Arterial and IV tube insertion/removal details.

What makes these four subject matters different from BT-Nurse is how they are handled in the BT-Family document planner. Instead of just simply reporting the factual details, additional information is also generated to accompany these subject matters. Each of the four main subject matters uses one or more of these additional affective information types, which can consist of:

1. Explanatory Justifications / Details
2. Positive Trend Descriptions
3. Reassurance statements

The main fundamental difference between BT-Family and BT-Nurse resides within the document planner module of the two systems. In BT-Nurse, the document planner utilises several algorithms that specify the maximum length of the document and the minimum importance an event must have to be mentioned. Key events are specifically identified by the BT-Nurse document planner whose importance exceeds a preset threshold and these events are placed at the head of a paragraph, with each paragraph being ordered by the time of occurrence of the key events (Gatt et al., 2009). This implementation differs substantially from BT-Family, where the document planner is based upon fixed categorical topics and clinical events are described in more general terms rather than having the specificity found in BT-Nurse.

4.1 Explanatory justification

Explanatory justification is an affective technique that aims to provide additional explanatory textual information to parents for why particular medical actions have occurred by stressing the positive effects for the baby. For example, if a child is moved from one ventilation equipment type to another, that could be viewed by the parents as a negative reflection on the child's well being. But with an explanatory justification statement, the positive benefits are stated for the parents to offset any possible negative perceptions. These statements were implemented as fixed statements that are inserted into the document plan automatically for the last three main topics, besides the baby's weight. This strategy is similar to one employed by Haimowitz (1991) and de Rosis et al. (1999) in which empathy is used by "stressing favourable information while downplaying or offsetting unfavourable information" (Haimowitz, 1991).

> *"This machine helps to provide the support that enables him to breathe more comfortably."*

Figure 4: Explanatory justification example.

4.2 Positive Trend Descriptions

Trend descriptions, on the other hand, present trend information over the previous twenty-four hours or week weight, inspired oxygen, and feeding quantities. This is BT-Family's second affective technique. Unlike other strategies BT-Family has discretion when reporting trends. Only those trends that could be considered positive or stable by the parents are reported as such. If no positive or stable trends could be identified, then BT-Family will always present the current value by itself without any trend description. The trend analysis module tries to determine a positive or stable trend by analysing previous medical data to see if a relative decline or increase has occurred in the given timeframe. Twenty-four hour trends are only computed by the system when the infant has been hospitalised for less than seven days. For inspired oxygen, IV feeds, and nitric oxide, a positive trend was one that has declined over time, whereas for milk feeds and weight, a positive trend was defined as a trend that increased over a specific time period. Table 1 details the trend expectations of parents for each of the different data sources. If no positive or stable trend could be identified, then no additional trend statement was created at all and the factual statement, such as the babys weight, would be presented on it's own.

It was hoped that the use of trend statements would give parents a better understanding of the medical situation that their child faces. The provision of such extra information could prevent parents from feeling that they are not being told every detail and thus would lose hope or assume the worst (Charchuk and Simpson, 2005).

> *"Since last week, his inspired Oxygen (FiO2) was lowered from 56% to 21% (which is the same as normal air)."*

Figure 5: Trend description example.

4.3 Reassurance Statements

Finally, within BT-Family there are two forms of reassurance statements: Positive Assurance and Supportive Reassurance statements. If no positive or stable trend from the parents perspective was identified by the system, then a supportive reassurance sentence would be used instead. This would help to reassure the parent that whilst no additional progress has been made, the medical staff nevertheless will continue to support the baby. Such a strategy is also used to help parents cope with the distress of seeing their child having a temporary downturn by helping to reassure parents that the baby has made significant progress over the long term: *"We'll continue to monitor your baby's condition and provide all the support he needs."*

For Positive Assurance, statements like *"Your baby has made good progress today"* are used by the

Data Source	Trend Expectation	Trend Explanation
Babys Weight	Positive	*Increases in the Babys weight in grams over a 24-hour / 7-day period.*
IV Feed Fluid	Negative	*Decreases in the amount of Dextrose (mls) over a 24-hour / 7-day period.*
Milk Feed	Positive	*Increases in the amount of Milk (mls) over a 24-hour / 7-day period.*
Inspired Oxygen	Negative	*Decreases in the amount of Inspired Oxygen (%) over a 24-hour / 7-day period.*
Nitric Oxide	Negative	*Decreases in the amount of Nitric Oxide (%) over a 24-hour / 7-day period.*

Table 1: Trend expectations listing for each data source

system to assure parents that positive physiological progress is being made by the child.

4.4 Affective and non-Affective Texts

The PNSS model was simply used as a means of switching the affective strategies on or off. In practice this resulted in two forms of text: Affective and non-Affective texts for a given situation. Statements such as trend descriptions and reassurance statements were used as part of an Affective text if the strategies were turned on, but otherwise remained absent from their equivalent non-affective text.The affective strategies would be activated at key junctures of the document planner that dealt with any of the four core physiological topics listed above. Other information types such as explanatory justifications can differ between affective and non-affective texts as shown in Figure 6. Both explanatory statements try to communicate the same concept to the parent. However the affective version is far more concise than the non-affective version so that parents would be prevented from being overwhelmed with information.

Affective Version
The mode of ventilation is Conventional Mechanical Ventilation (CMV). This machine helps to provide the support that enables him to breathe more comfortably.

Non-Affective Version
The mode of ventilation is Conventional Mechanical Ventilation (CMV). This kind of ventilation helps your babys breathing by inflating his lungs, oxygenating the blood, and removing carbon dioxide so that he breathe a lot more easily.

Figure 6: A comparison of explanatory justification statements

Figure 7 shows the difference between the non-affective and affective texts when describing inspired oxygen information for a neonate. From the version it is apparent that the affective version attempts to reassure the parent far more than the non-affective version. On the other hand, the non-affective version attempts to only communicate the factual status of the baby. The affective version not only addresses the parents information need like the non-affective version but also goes beyond and attempts to reassure as well.

Non-Affective Text Version:
"Since yesterday, he was in air (which is the same as 21% oxygen)."

"In the evening, John was fed on specialised milk at 56 mls. John was able to take his milk feeds well yesterday. ."

Affective Text Version:
"Since last week, his inspired Oxygen (FiO2) was lowered from 56% to 21% (which is the same as normal air). This is a positive development for your child."

"Milk feeds have increased since last week from 53.0 mls per every three hours to 56.0 mls per every three hours. This is a reassuring development for your baby. John was able to take his milk feeds well yesterday."

Figure 7: A comparison between non-affective and affective versions of inspired oxygen information and milk feeds.

5 Evaluation

BT-Family was evaluated with parents that previously had a child in neonatal care (intensive care, high dependency care, or special care) to see the effectiveness of several aspects of the generated texts. A total of thirteen parents were recruited for this study. Recruited participants were mostly socio-economically affluent and well-educated. Parents with babies currently in NICU were not used for this study due to ethical constraints.

Methodology:

The thirteen participants were asked to evaluate two different types of text that communicated the same information over ten different medical scenarios, making a total of twenty texts in total. These two types of texts were the computer generated BT-Family reports that were presented as "affective" and "non-affective" variants to the participants. These texts were presented to parents randomly labelled as either text 'A' or 'B', with no indication given of which text was which. In order to reduce the time required for the study, parents were shown only half of a BT-Family report instead of a complete report.

One of the main objectives of this evaluation was to understand the parent's preference for either an "affective" or "non-affective" text for a given medical scenario. In particular, did the participating parents share the same preferences for affective texts in complex medical scenarios and for non-affective texts in simpler medical situations? As subjects could not be made stressed for ethical reasons, they were instead given medical details for each scenario and were asked to imagine that they were the parent of the baby. The PNSS score was used as a way of indirectly identifying between complex and simple medical scenarios as the majority of the score's indicators dealt with the baby's physiological health. Ten different medical scenarios were chosen with five medical scenarios having a high PNSS score and the other five scenarios having a low PNSS score.

To present the two texts for each scenario, the researcher gave a verbal description describing the medical condition and circumstances of the baby in the scenario. This description helped the participant to mentally familiarise themselves with the situation of the baby in the given scenario without prejudicing their preferences. After presenting the participants with a verbal description of the medical circumstance of the baby, they were asked to examine the two texts generated by BT-Family for the given scenario. The participants were informed that the system can produce two types of texts that can express the same information but were not informed about the explicit reason why the texts differ, so as not to prejudice their choice. Following which the researcher asked the participants the following sets of questions:

1. Text style preference: Whether the participants preferred either text A or B for the given scenario.
2. The level of understandability for text A and B (Likert scale of 1 to 5) .
3. The helpfulness for both text A and B (Likert scale of 1 to 5).
4. The level of which both text A and B appropriately considers the parents' emotional state in the given scenario (Likert scale of 1 to 5).
5. Participant's comments about the two texts.

Results: An overwhelming number of parents (80%) preferred the affective text version than compared to the non-affective text version (20%) in the first five high PNSS score scenarios. Contrary to expectations, in the low PNSS score scenarios, the non-affective text version was disapprovingly looked upon by the parents (13%) compared to the affective text version (87%). It seems that for both cases, parents overwhelmingly prefer the affective text version compared to the non-affective version representing the same information regardless of the baby's scenario. On average, all of the understandability, helpfulness, and emotional appropriateness ratings were weighted in favour of the affective texts across all scenarios.

Several reasons were given by participants for their overwhelming preference for affective texts across all scenarios. For the high PNSS scenarios, the affective texts were favoured due to the fact that the non-affective texts were viewed as "too technical" for some of the parents or that they contain "too much information". Secondly, for low PNSS scenarios, the opposite reaction occurred. Parents stated that the non-affective texts contained less information compared to the affective version, as they contained additional trend and reassurance statements that were not present in the non-affective text. The use of positive reassurance statements in the affective texts were well received by the parents and also were perceived as producing "more friendly text". However, one parent in particular did find the language used by some of the affective texts "a bit patronising". Additionally, the presence of trend statements for the baby's weight, inspired oxygen, and feeds were positively welcomed by the parents. The combination of these factors led most parents to prefer the affective text version in all scenarios regardless of the emotional and situational circumstances of the scenario.

From the ratings results gathered, a two-tailed Pearson cross-correlation statistical test was calculated. The null hypothesis was that there should be no correlations between any of the affective and non-affective ratings in all of the three categories. This proved to be incorrect, as three significant results were identified. The first result shows a statistically significant positive correlation between the emotional appropriateness rating and the helpfulness rating for affective texts ($p=0.049$, $r=0.633$). Additionally, the emotional appropriateness rating had a second statistically significant correlation with understanding ratings for affective texts ($p=0.001$, $r=0.885$). What these two results seem to indicate is that there is a relationship between the emotional appropriateness rating for affective texts and the rating scores given by parents for the levels of helpfulness and understandability for the affective texts. The non-affective texts showed only one significant result, a positive correlation between the level of emotional appropriateness and the level of helpfulness ($p=0.006$, $r=0.793$).

6 Current Work

BT-Family is still work in progress. Work on BT-Family is preparing for on-ward evaluations with parents, scheduled for late 2011. Using the feedback from parents in the previous section and comments from clinicians, refinements have been made in the textual output of the system and additional topics have been added that were not covered previously, such as drug medication, blood sugar levels, stool and urine output, details of the baby's cot location, and more. Ideas such as the PNSS model and non-affective text output have been removed as ultimately they have proved to be unsuccessful when evaluated.

Ethical permission was sought and granted for two on-ward evaluations with parents of neonatal infants. The first evaluation will focus on refining the quality of the texts from a content and readability perspective with parents providing direct feedback on texts generated for their own baby. The second evaluation will focus on evaluating the usefulness of the texts by seeing how frequently parents access the texts through a web based portal. We will also conduct post-discharge interviews with participating parents to see if they thought BT-Family texts were communicating appropriate and understandable information. These two evaluations will ultimately help to assess the usefulness of generating such reports for parents.

7 Conclusion

We have presented in this paper several affective strategies for communicating medical information for parents of neonatal infants. Initially, we tried to personalise this for the recipient's level of stress. We found that all recipients preferred texts generated with our affective strategies. The key finding is that the use of such affective strategies may be appropriate whenever an NLG system is communicating emotional sensitive information to an non-expert recipient.

Acknowledgements

This work is funded by the UK Engineering and Physical Sciences Council (EPSRC) under a Doctoral Training Award and Digital Economy grant EP/H042938/1. Many thanks to Chris Mellish and the other members of the Babytalk team for their help.

References

Linda S. Bass. 1991. What do parents need when their infant is a patient in the NICU? *Neonatal Network*, 10(4):25–33, December.

Anja Belz. 2003. And now with feeling: Developments in emotional language generation. Report itri-03-21, Information Technology Research Institute, University of Brighton.

Dianne C. Berry. 2004. *Risk, Communication and Health Psychology*. Open University Press.

Jane E. Brazy, Barbara M. H. Anderson, Patricia T. Becker, and Marion Becker. 2001. How parents of premature infants gather information and obtain support. *Neonatal Network*, 20(2):41–48, March.

Margo Charchuk and Christy Simpson. 2005. Hope, Disclosure, and Control in the Neonatal Intensive Care Unit. *Health Communication*, 17(2):191–203.

Fiorella de Rosis and Floriana Grasso. 2000. Affective natural language generation. *Affective Interactions, Springer Lecture Notes in AI*, pages 204 – 218.

Fiorella de Rosis, Floriana Grasso, and Dianne C. Berry. 1999. Refining instructional text generation after evaluation. *Artificial Intelligence in Medicine*, 17(1):1–36.

Chrysanne DiMarco, Graeme Hirst, Leo Wanner, and John Wilkson. 1995. Healthdoc: Customizing patient information and health eduction by medical condition and personal characteristics. In *Workshop on Artificial Intelligence in Patient Education,*, Glassgow, Scotland, UK.

Chrysanne DiMarco, H. Dominic Covvey, P. Bray, D. Cowan, V. DiCiccio, E. Hovy, and D. Mulholland J. Lipa. 2007. The Development of a Natural Language Generation System For Personalized e-Health Information. In *12th International Health (Medical) Informatics Congress*, Brisbane, Australia. Medinfo 2007.

Albert Gatt, François Portet, Ehud Reiter, Jim Hunter, Saad Mahamood, Wendy Moncur, and Somayajulu Sripada. 2009. From Data to Text in the Neonatal Intensive Care Unit: Using NLG Technology for Decision Support and Information Management. *AI Communications*.

Ira J. Haimowitz. 1991. Modelling all dialouge system participants to generate empathetic responces. *Computer Methods and Programs in Biomedicine*, 35(4):321–330, August.

D. Holditch-Davis and M.S. Miles. 2000. Mothers' Stories about Their Experiences in the Neonatal Intensive Care Unit. *Neonatal Network*, 19(3):13–21.

James Hunter, Yvonne Freer, Albert Gatt, Ehud Reiter, Somayajulu Sripada, Cindy Sykes, and Dave Westwater. 2011. BT-Nurse: Computer Generation of Natural Language Shift Summaries from Complex Heterogeneous Medical Data. *Journal of the American Medical Informatics Association*, 18:621–624.

D. Hüske-Kraus. 2003. Text Generation in Clinical Medicine — a review. *Methods of Information in Medicine*, 1:51–60.

Karin Jackson, Britt-Marie Ternestedt, and Jens Schollin. 2003. From alienation to familarity: experiences of mothers and fathers of preterm infants. *Journal of Advanced Nursing*, 43(2):120–129.

Kaisa Jämsä and Timo Jämsä. 1998. Technology in neonatal intensive care — a study on parents' experiences. *Technology and Health Care*, 6(4):225–230, March.

Saad Mahamood, Ehud Reiter, and Chris Mellish. 2008. Neonatal Intesive Care Information for Parents – An Affective Approach. In *Proceedings of 21st IEEE International Symposium on Computer-Based Medical Systems*, Jyväskylä, Finland.

Saad Mahamood. 2010. *Generating Affective Natural Language for Parents of Neonatal Infants*. Ph.D. thesis, University of Aberdeen, Department of Computing Science, Aberdeen, Scotland, United Kingdom.

François Mairesse and Marilyn Walker. 2007. PERSONAGE: Personality generation for dialogue. In *Annual Meeting-Association For Computational Linguistics*, volume 45, pages 496–503.

Jacqueline M. McGrath. 2001. Building Relationships with Families in the NICU: Exploring the Guarded Alliance. *Journal of Perinatal & Neonatal Nursing*, 15(3):74–83.

Margaret Shandor Miles and Diane Holditch-Davis. 1997. Parenting the Prematurely Born Child: Pathways of Influence. *Seminars in Perinatology*, 21(3):254–266, June.

Margaret Shandor Miles, Sandra G. Funk, and Mary Ann Kasper. 1991. The Neonatal Intensive Care Unit Enviroment: Sources of Stress for Parents. *AACN Clinical Issues in Critical Care Nursing*, 2(2):346–354.

Wendy Moncur, Saad Mahamood, Ehud Reiter, and Yvonne Freer. 2009. Involving Healthcare Consumers in Knowledge Acquisition for Virtual Healthcare. Technical Report FS-09-07, AAAI Press, Menlo Park, California, USA, November.

Rosalind W. Picard. 1997. *Affective Computing*. MIT Press, Cambridge (Mass.).

François Portet, Ehud Reiter, Jim Hunter, and Somayajulu Sripada. 2007. Automatic generation of textual summaries from neonatal intensive care data. In *Proceedings of the 11th Conference on Artificial Intelligence in Medicine (AIME '07)*. LNCS, July.

Tilly Reid, Ros Bramwell, Nicola Booth, and A. M. Weindling. 2007. A new stressor scale for parents experiencing neonatal intensive care: the NUPS (Neonatal Unit Parental Stress) scale. *Journal of Reproductive and Infant Psychology*, 25(1):66–82, February.

Ehud Reiter, Roma Robertson, and Liesel Osman. 2000. Knowledge acquisition for natural language generation. In *First International Conference on Natural Language Generation (INLG-2000)*, pages 217–224.

Ehud Reiter. 2007. An architecture for data-to-text systems. In *Proceedings of the 11th European Workshop on Natural Language Generation (ENLG'07)*, June.

Ruth Young Seideman, Margaret A. Watson, Karen E. Corff, Phillip Odle, Joan Haase, and Jane L. Bowerman. 1997. Parent Stress and Coping in NICU and PICU. *Journal of Pediatric Nursing*, 12(3):169–177, June.

Donna Shields-Poë and Janet Pinelli. 1997. Variables Associated with Parental Stress in Neonatal Intensive Care Units. *Neonatal Network*, 16(1):29–37, February.

Ielka van der Sluis and Chris Mellish. 2009. Towards Empirical Evaluation of Affective Tactical NLG. In *Proceedings of the Twelfth European Natural Language Generation Conference (ENLG 2009)*.

What is in a text and what does it do: Qualitative Evaluations of an NLG system – the BT-Nurse – using content analysis and discourse analysis.

Rahul Sambaraju
Queen Margaret Univ, UK
rsambaraju@qmu.ac.uk

Ehud Reiter
Univ of Aberdeen, UK
e.reiter@abdn.ac.uk

Robert Logie
Univ of Edinburgh, UK
rlogie@staffmail.ed.ac.uk

Andy McKinlay
Univ of Edinburgh, UK
hos.ppls@ed.ac.uk

Chris McVittie
Queen Margaret Univ, UK
cmcvittie@qmu.ac.uk

Albert Gatt
Univ of Malta, Malta
albert.gatt@um.edu.mt

Cindy Sykes
Edinburgh Royal Infirmary, U.K
Cindy.Sykes@luht.scot.nhs.uk

Abstract

Evaluations of NLG systems generally are quantiative, that is, based on corpus comparison statistics and/or results of experiments with people. Outcomes of such evaluations are important in demonstrating whether or not an NLG system is successful, but leave gaps in understanding why this is the case. Alternatively, qualitative evaluations carried out by experts provide knowledge on where a system needs to be improved. In this paper we describe two such evaluations carried out for the BT-Nurse system, using two different methodologies (content analysis and discourse analysis). The outcomes of such evaluations are discussed in comparison to what was learnt from a quantitiave evaluation of BT-Nurse. Implications for the role of similar evaluations in NLG are also discussed.

1 Introduction

Natural-Language Generation (NLG) systems are usually evaluated quantitatively, by measuring impact on task performance, human opinions on Likert-like scales, and/or similarity to a gold-standard corpus. While such evaluations are essential, we believe there is also a role for qualitative evaluations, especially when the goal of the evaluation is formative that is, assessing weaknesses and identifying how the NLG system could be improved.

In this paper we describe how we used two qualitative methodologies, content analysis and discourse analysis, to evaluate texts produced by the BT-Nurse system (Hunter et al., 2011). These methodologies require a human analyst to read and analyse the generated texts; and indeed for both types of analysis it is helpful to conduct a similar analysis of human-written corpus texts, so that generated texts can be compared to manually-authored texts. From a practical perspective this means that only a relatively limited number of texts can be analysed using these methodologies; but nevertheless we believe they can substantially help in formative evaluation of NLG systems.

2 Background

2.1 *Evaluation in NLG*

The great majority of published evaluations of NLG systems are quantitative: as described by Reiter and Belz (2009), they either measure the impact of a generated text on task performance, ask human subjects to rate generated texts on a Likert-like scale, or compare the similarity of generated texts to corpus texts using automatic metrics such as BLEU (Papineni et al., 2002). Reiter and Belz point out that many human-based quantitative NLG evaluations also solicit free-text comments from their subjects, and these are very helpful in diagnosing and fixing problems in generated texts. Soliciting such comments, however is usually a secondary goal of evaluations of NLG systems, the primary goal being quantitative.

One instance of the use of qualitative methodologies in evaluating NLG systems was that by McKinlay et al (2010) who used discourse analysis to analyse texts generated by the BT45 NLG system (Portet et al., 2009). The evaluation revealed certain problems with generated texts, such as a

Proceedings of the 13th European Workshop on Natural Language Generation (ENLG), pages 22–31,
Nancy, France, September 2011.

poor narrative structure (Reiter et al., 2008). The discourse analysis work presented here uses a similar approach to McKinlay et al (2010).

2.2 *BT-Nurse*

The BT-Nurse system (Hunter et al., 2011) generates nursing shift handover reports for babies in a Neonatal Intensive Care Unit (NICU), from data stored in the baby's electronic medical record. The input data include numeric time-series data (e.g., heart rate), ad-hoc structured data (e.g., lab results), and descriptions of actions and observations of medical and nursing staff (such as administering drugs and performing surgical procedures). The handover report is produced at the end of a 12-hour nursing shift, and is given to the incoming nurse on the next shift as part of the handover process. Its purpose is to help the incoming nurse plan her care activities, and also ensure that she is aware of the baby's circumstances.

BT-Nurse is part of the BabyTalk family of systems (Gatt et al., 2009), and like other BabyTalk systems it combines signal analysis and pattern matching, data interpretation based on expert medical knowledge, and NLG techniques. It was developed in close consultation with NICU nurses, and used no input data other than what was stored in the electronic medical record.

As part of the development process, an expert NICU nurse wrote a corpus of 32 example nursing summaries based on data in the medical record related to 10 babies collated over a period of 3 months. The babies concerned here were diagnosed to have a range of medical conditions affecting various body systems at differing levels of pathology. These texts differed from real-world existing handover reports in two ways: (1) they were much longer and more detailed (on-duty nurses do not have the time to write detailed shift-handover reports), and (2) they were purely based on the electronic patient record (and not, for example, on visual observation of the baby).

BT-Nurse was designed so that the output texts resemble corpus texts with the aim of complementing nurses engaged in their duties. In the remainder of this paper, *corpus text* refers to one of the specially written summaries above for the purposes of designing the system, and *actual handover text* refers to a real-world handover report written by an on-duty nurse for a baby she was looking after. At the time of analysis the BT-Nurse was focusing on producing texts that described only the baby's clinical history and respiratory system, so qualitative analyses were limited to these parts of the corpus texts, actual handover texts and BT-Nurse generated texts.

An extract from an actual handover text is shown in Figure 1, an extract from nurse-written corpus text is shown in Figure 2, and an extract from the corresponding BT-Nurse text is shown in Figure 3 (the complete texts are several pages long).

Nurse Shift Summary	
dbpatid	103362
working weight	840.0
nursedin	Incubator
Problems during shift	
resp distress	Oxygen requirement
stools	Changed
Respiratory	
resp support	SIMV
resp notes	rate 25 pressure 20/4
Fluids / Feeds	
prescribed daily feeds	175.0
type milk	Breast
vol mil per feed	6.0
feed given by	OGT
frequency of feeds	hly
adequate urine vol	Yes
stools	Changed
Medication	
drugs	
Social	
social visited	Mother|Father
length parent visit	1-3 hours
Developmental support	
developmental support	Incubator cover used|Positioning aids used|Containment given
Notes	
other notes	settled night, no change in ventilation. Obs stable in 438-44% O2. Suction x2 yeilding 2-3 M ET and Oral. Pud BO. Drugs given as prescribed.
signature designation	Staff nurse

Figure 1: Actual handover text

2.3 *Quantitative Evaluation:*

BT-Nurse was evaluated by deploying the system on-ward in the NICU, asking nurses to use it as part of the shift handover process, and soliciting ratings and free-text comments from nurses as to the understandability, accuracy, and helpfulness of BT-Nurse texts (Hunter et al., 2011). Overall, 90% of nurses thought BT-Nurse texts were understandable, 70% thought they were completely accurate, and 60% thought they were helpful. Free-text comments focused on specific content issues (requests for additional information, complaints about incorrect content, suggestions to remove content). There were fewer comments about language issues. These tended to be fairly specific when addressing microplanning issues (for example "*would prefer not to see the word 'since' with the date*"), but vaguer when addressing document-planning and narrative issues (for example, "*this summary does not convey the feeling that the baby has made progress*" and "*The above comments are accurate statements, however they do not present a 'picture' of current condition*").

This evaluation worked well from the perspective of getting some numbers on the system's perceived utility, which was its primary goal. However, from the perspective of diagnosing problems and suggesting enhancements, it worked much better for content and low-level phrasing issues than for document structure and narrative issues. This suggests that other methodologies, probably involving analysts with specialist expertise in narrative and structural issues, might be needed to diagnose and address these issues. In the remainder of this paper we describe how we used two such methodologies, content analysis and discourse analysis, to gain a better understanding of BT-Nurse's deficiencies from this perspective.

3 Evaluation using content analysis

3.1 Content Analysis

Content analysis is widely used as a data exploratory tool by qualitative researchers in psychology, linguistics and other social sciences. In content analysis, qualitative data, mainly texts, are coded according to some coding scheme which is usually predetermined, either from previous research or researcher expectations. Following this, frequencies can be calculated to enable a numerical comparison. A unit of analysis (sentence, paragraph or a page) is identified and classified according to specific codes. These codes could either be descriptive or analytic (Richards, 2009). The level of coding and what is done on these codes depends to a good extent on the research question (Saldaña, 2009). Here we were interested in what sorts of data representation was contained within BT-Nurse generated texts as compared to that in corpus texts. Therefore, the analysis had as its focus identifying content in these texts which was reflective of representations of data in textual form.

3.2 Method

The corpus of 32 nurse written texts was first analyzed to come up with a coding scheme; this was then applied to corpus texts, BT-Nurse texts, and actual handover texts. The extent of corpus texts subjected to analysis was defined in two ways: (1) focus here was on identifying lexical items that communicated 'complex' information; for example temporal relations and causality (but not simple statements of parameter values such as heart rate) and (2) as mentioned above those parts of the texts relating to babies' clinical history and respiratory system only. Analysis led to the identification of various items that were abstracted into higher order 'codes' forming the coding scheme A sample of nurse written corpus text was made available to a doctorate student with brief notes on what was being looked for in those texts and to form some sort of codes relating to data representation. Codes identified were checked against the first authors' for agreement (Cohen's κ = .74), in line with common practices of doing such analyses with codes (Saldaña, 2009). The coding scheme presented here was used to calculate frequency of occurrence of each item in nurse written corpus texts, BT-Nurse summaries and actual handover texts.

3.3 Coding Scheme

Items on the coding scheme can be usefully differentiated into descriptive items that describe various particulars of information and inferential elements, which provide for inferences amongst data items.

1) Descriptive items in the coding scheme:

a) <u>Temporal information</u>: Data items, have time stamps, that is, they are presented as having occurred at *some* time:

i. <u>Specific clock times</u>: Temporal information is provided in terms of normative clock times – 11:00 or 13:30. E.g.: "The last blood gas was at *18:30* and no changes were made".

ii. <u>Vague temporal markers</u>: Temporal information provided in terms that do not readily specify the exact point in clock times, such as: 'morning', 'a few minutes ago' and others. E.g.: "but this *afternoon* he also looks pale".

iii. Shift time: shift start and end times are made use of as temporal markers. E.g.: "Insulin *just* commenced".

iv. References to other events: Clock time is provided for one event 'A' and another event 'B' is temporally located via references to 'A'. E.g.: "He *received morphine prior to intubation at 00:30*; no spontaneous respiratory effort *noted since being re-ventilated*".

b) *Time intervals*: Provision of temporal *information* for events that do not have a single temporal marker but two that refer to the start and end times, is made as unitary condensed entities. E.g.: "However, *over the day* his oxygen requirements generally have come down from 30% to 25%".

c) *Trends in parameter values*: Recordings of parameter values are made to capture changes in *the* parameter over a period of time providing the initial and final values along with the direction of such change. E.g.: "Baseline SpO2 *drifted down* from *95% to 88%* accompanied by *increasing* SpO2 variability associated with handling". [SpO2 – Oxygen saturation in blood]

d) *Evaluations of parameter values*: Parameter *values* are also evaluated either in terms of what is physiologically normal or in terms of what is locally taken to be normal for that particular shift and that particular baby. E.g.: "ABG at 23:10 showed CO2 *increased* from 7.7 to 9.27 in three hours". [ABG – Arterial Blood Gas; CO2 – Carbon Di-oxide]

e) *Events in temporal relation with other events*: *Information* about certain events and data items is presented as preceding or succeeding other events. E.g.: "Received one dose of surfactant *after* admission to NNU". [NNU – Neonatal Unit]

2) Inferential items in the coding scheme:

a) *Event characterizations*: Events are those data items that indicate a recording of a parameter value, a change in a parameter value, interventions and such.

i. Events 'marked up': Events are presented as important within the local context via providing clock times and describing other events in relation to this particular event. The use of one event 'A' as a temporal anchor for another 'B' presents it as consequential to 'A'. E.g.: "*Electively re-intubated at 00:30* to CMV rate 50, pressures 18/4 in 30% oxygen. *On ventilation*, oxygen requirement reduced to 30% and *ABG initially improved*". [CMV – Continuous Mandatory Ventilation]

ii. Event presented as forming a context for other events: Events are presented as occurring over a period of time and then other events are presented as having occurred in the contextual background of the former event. E.g.: "*While on BiPAP*, oxygen requirement increased to 50% by 23:00." [BiPAP – Bi-level Positive Airway Pressure]

b) *Evaluation*: The presentation of parameter values or medical interventions forms an evaluation of a prior event or parameter value. E.g.: "ABG taken 2 hours post-extubation was *reasonably good*: pH 7.33 and pCO2 7.08". [pCO2 – Partial pressure of Carbon Di-oxide]. Evaluative information together with the temporal marker anchored in 'extubation' serves to present changes in ABG as an evaluation of the outcomes of 'extubation'.

c) *Parameters grouped together*: Two or more dissimilar parameter descriptions are made together with a conjunctive indicating some sort of an association between the two parameters. E.g.: "*Desaturation* to 15% *with bradycardia* to 50-60s".

d) *Grouping similar events*: descriptions of two or more event descriptions are juxtaposed to each other. As above these descriptions are of their temporal status, outcomes and such. E.g.: "*Tried off CPAP once* but *put back on after 30 minutes* due to increased work of breathing; otherwise has not been off CPAP". [CPAP – Continuous Positive Airway Pressure]. Here, descriptions attend to two events: being on CPAP and being off CPAP. Including descriptions on these two events provides for inferences as to the reasons, outcomes and other such features of those events.

e) *Causation*: Events are presented to be causally related to each other either via an explicit discourse marker or presenting the parameter recordings or events in temporal relation to each other that makes relevant causal links between them. E.g.: "several episodes (about 3 per hour) of bradycardia with desaturation that *only resolved after* stimulation or increase in FiO_2".

3.4 Results and Discussion

Results shown in Table 1 include frequencies of coding items in corpus texts, BT-Nurse texts, and in actual handover texts. BT-Nurse texts score

	Coding item	Human Corpus	BT-Nurse	Actual Handover
1)	**Descriptive Items**			
a)	Temporal information			
i)		4	29	19
ii)	Vague	3	27	19
iii)	Shift times	8	2	4
b)	Time Periods	27	0	17
c)	Trends	19	99	31
d)	Evaluations	13	38	28
e)	Temporal relations	23	15	13
2)	**Inferential Items**			
a)	Event presentations			
i)	'Marked up'	8	2	10
ii)	Context forming	5	0	16
b)	Evaluations	8	0	16
c)	Grouping Parameters	14	10	12
d)	Grouping events	8	7	8
e)	Causation	8	0	17

Table 1: Frequencies of coding items.

more on descriptive items: they contain quantitatively more temporal information, higher reporting of trends in parameters, and more items of evaluation on parameter values. However, they do not contain representations of 'time intervals' (1 (b)). Representing time intervals can be thought of as using at least two time stamps on a temporal axis: the 'start' and 'end' (Adlassnig et al., 2006). BT-Nurse software apparently does not enable such representation, the outcome of which is reflected in item 2 (a) ii. The lack of representing an event 'B' as occurring over a period of time in BT-Nurse texts does not make for characterizing an event 'A' as occurring in the background context of the ongoing event 'B' (the event 'B' having 'start' time and an 'end' time). Although BT-Nurse texts do contain inferential items, overall these items are less frequent compared to nurse written corpus texts. Moreover, inferential items presented do not readily make it clear as to the nature of the relationship (see 4.3 below). These findings then reveal how representing temporal information has outcomes on other forms of data representation in BT-Nurse texts, and thus contribute to the design of the system.

Analysis of actual handover texts served to attend to issues of external validity of the evaluation. Results indicate that actual handover texts are more similar to nurse written corpus texts in containing more inference enabling items and more instances of explicit inferences. These results at one level are not very surprising as nurses engaged in doing their duties would arguably require information of this sort. In that sense, this evaluation has pointed to features of data-to-text systems that are indicative of the sorts of requirements users of these systems have. Thus, by providing more information on relevant parameters, a better trend detection ability and producing an easily usable textual document, BT-Nurse has significant potential to enhance nurse care planning in the NICU.

4 Evaluation using discourse analysis

4.1 Discourse analysis:

The other qualitative evaluation employed discourse analysis, which has as its focus pragmatic outcomes of texts. Discourse analysis specializes in the analysis of spoken or written discourse, as a topic of study in its own right (McKinlay et al., 2008). In contrast to content analysis, discourse analysis takes as its focus the action-orientation of discourse. The analyst focuses on identifying properties within the text, such as the design of individual discourse elements and how sets of such elements are sequentially organized in order to accomplish particular pragmatic outcomes in that, discourse is considered for the sorts of actions that ensue from specific forms of usage. Discourse analysis differs from other forms of linguistic analyses (such as those based on Rhetorical Structural Theory (Thompson et al., 1987) or Discourse Structural Relations (Hovy, 1993)) in focusing on the ways in which language gets used for specific outcomes, that is, the focus is on an analysis of discourse rather than on linguistic features of any fixed 'unit' of text. The analysis seeks to draw out those aspects of discourse production and reception which are treated by participants in a particular discursive interaction as 'everyday' or 'commonsense' but which are, at the same time, central to a full understanding of what is written. Outcomes of discourse analysis then are of a psychological nature than merely linguistic.

A prior use of such methodology in conducting an evaluation of another data-to-text system – BT-45 – showed that corpus texts written by domain experts had better narrative structures than system generated texts (McKinlay et al., 2010). These are considered to be desirable aspects in texts generated by NLG systems (Reiter et al., 2008), therefore we conducted an evaluation using this methodology.

This evaluation was in fact conducted on a preliminary version of BT-Nurse, and some changes were made to the final version of BT-Nurse based on this evaluation; for example the way 'causality' was expressed was changed in some cases to enhance clarity. The content analysis and quantitative evaluations, in contrast, were carried out on the final version of BT-Nurse.

4.2 Method

For reasons of illustration and space we provide here a comparative analysis of one nurse written corpus text and the corresponding BT-Nurse generated text for one 12 hour shift. This particular shift summary pair was randomly selected amongst the 32 pairs available. Analysis provided here aims to demonstrate the utility of discourse analysis in formative evaluations of NLG systems. The analysis was conducted by three of the authors on an extract taken from each of these texts that detailed occurrences within the shift related to baby's respiratory system. Analysis involved identification of lexical items (words, sentences and such) that were selected for inclusion and how they were sequentially combined within the summary. The identification of such was considered for the sorts of outcomes made available. Here, this led to the identification of three pragmatic discursive features present in nurse written corpus texts. These analytic findings were subsequently made use of in evaluating BT-Nurse output texts.

4.3 Analyses:

Figure 2 is an example nurse written corpus text that includes descriptions of baby's respiratory status. Figure 3 is the corresponding BT-Nurse generated text produced for the same baby for the same shift. It can readily be seen that they are similar in terms of producing a list of events that occurred during the said shift. The following comparative analysis aims to show the pragmatic outcomes of these two summaries. For the purposes of this paper, the analysis is presented along three main pragmatic features:

a) *Foregrounding the actor*:

The summary in Figure 2 begins with the admission of the baby and the status of his respiration. Through the use of 'he' at line 2, the author explicitly introduces the baby as a character. This first item also specifies a particular, desirable health status for the baby at that time: 'in air'. This provides a context for the rest of the description organized around the baby as a central character in a sequence of events. The final item selected for inclusion at lines 21-22 also makes explicit reference to the baby, thereby presenting a conclusion that is designed to highlight health of the central character at the end of the sequence.

Figure 3, however, begins at line 2 by describing an event, namely a decrease in oxygen saturation, occurring over an extended period of time which commences towards the beginning of shift. Thus, this account treats as the first reportable item a description of an event and not of the baby. It is not until line 7 of the summary that we see any mention of the baby himself. This relatively late introduction of the baby into the summary fails to foreground the baby himself as a central character in relation to the events that are being described. Additionally, the final item on the list makes no reference to the initial topic or a change in baby's respiratory status.

b) *Temporal organization of events*:

The description in Figure 2 begins at the start of the shift and concludes at the end, and the intervening events are temporally marked in a sequential order. The list begins at line 2 with a description located at the start of the period of observation. Subsequent items are designed in terms of their temporal connections to this starting point. The temporal marker 'Within an hour' at line 3 describes the next item on the list in relation to the commencement of observation. The next item at lines 8-14 is temporally indexed to be subsequent in the overall listing of events. Similarly, at lines 15-17, descriptions of the baby's respiratory status are temporally marked in relation to the time of occurrence and the age of the baby. Finally, at lines 21-22, concluding descriptions temporally mark events as occurring at the end of the shift by the use of 'now' (line 20).

Shift 23 written by Human Nurse

EVENTS THIS SHIFT
On admission he was in air.
Within an hour his respiratory rate was 63 with moderate recession, nasal flaring, occasional grunting and SpO2 falling to the low 80s. He was placed prone and put into 24% incubator oxygen.
At 5 hours of age he was in 45% incubator oxygen, and was electively intubated (morphine and sux were given) and put onto CMV ventilation: rate 50, pressures 19 / 5, iTime 0.3 in 30% oxygen, tidal volumes were 5ml. ETT is size 3, and 8cm at the lips.
At 16:20 (6 hours of age) surfactant was given, 240 mg, first dose, and he was in air within an hour after that.
Ventilation has been weaned with CBGs to the present settings.
Recession is now just mild. Breathing has settled and he is taking spontaneous breaths.

Figure 2: Nurse written corpus text.

Shift 23 generated by BT-Nurse

Events During the Shift
Between 11:30 and 14:30, SaO2 decreased from 93 % to 84 %.
A CBG was taken at 12:15. Parameters were acceptable. pH was 7.37. CO2 was 7.02 kPa. Be was -1.9 mmol/L.
The baby was intubated at around 15:15 and was moved from Inc O2 to CMV. Vent RR was 50 breaths per minute. Pressures were 19/5 cms H2O. He was in air. Tidal volume was 8.9.
At around 15:15, he was given morphine.
At about 15:15, he was given suxamethonium.
At around 18:30, he was given a first dose of 240 mg of surfactant.

Figure 3: BT-Nurse generated text.

Such temporal organization in Figure 3 however is limited. The initial description does make explicit reference to specific times and so marks the starting point for a temporally organised summary. As the listing of events continues, at a number of points specific events are also temporally marked in order to indicate their relationship to the chronological starting point of the description, ending at lines 15-16 with a description of drug administration presented as occurring towards the end of the period of observation. This sequence, however, is not organised entirely chronologically, in that the temporal reference at line 4 to '12.15' precedes the second such reference at line 2 which is to '14.30'. To the extent that the description provided is framed by reference to times near the start and end of the observational period it is presented in the form of a temporal sequence.

c) *Causal connectivity*:

Descriptions of events in Figure 2 highlight causal connectedness of preceding and subsequent events and actions. For instance, the description at lines 8-14 takes up as relevant the topic introduced at the conclusion of the preceding item, that of 'incubator oxygen'. This topic flow causally connects events described to that topic by detailing steps taken to support the breathing of the baby at that time. In addition, events found within this description are explicitly linked through the use of grammatical markers and the conjunctive 'and'. The parenthetical 'morphine and sux' at line 10 can be read as relevant to the immediately preceding description of intubation, making explicit for the reader the connection between these events. Following this, at lines 15-17 the description makes an explicit connection between two events, namely the medication given and the subsequent status of the baby. Further, the description of the baby as being 'in air' can be heard as a desirable state of affairs, in contrast to previous descriptions. This positive description provides a context for description of ventilation being 'weaned', which also suggests an improvement as a result of the actions taken. Finally, at lines 21-20, the summary concludes with a description that takes as its explicit topic 'breathing' and describes actions of the baby at this time. The reference here to 'taking spontaneous breaths' can be heard as desirable, and in so doing to be a continuation of the baby's breathing status set out previously. As such, the description draws together disparate elements – the baby as the actor in the events being described, his respiratory status, and the temporal context – in offering a hearably positive upshot to the sequence of events that occurred during the shift. Together, the continuation of topic and linking of events presents the events being described as connected and as located within an ongoing narrative relating to the breathing of the baby over the course of the shift.

With respect to causal connectivity, in Figure 3 there is seen to be variation in how events are causally linked. First, some events are explicitly linked: at lines 7-8, the process of intubation is clearly marked as linked to the baby being moved from incubator oxygen to 'CMV' (CMV is a form of mechanical ventilation that follows from being intubated). Second, some are not marked in this way but can be read as being connected through the consecutive descriptions of particular actions and states: at lines 4-6, we see a description of a blood gas measurement being taken, an evaluation of parameters, and descriptions of particular measurements that allow them to be treated as consequentially relevant and the later descriptions to be treated as presenting the outcomes of the procedure. Third, the form of description works to suggest that there is no immediate connection between different events being described: at lines, 7-14, we are given a description of a process of intubation, of the baby being given morphine, and of the baby being given suxamethonium. Explicitly describing these events as occurring at a similar approximate time suggests that these are not related events occurring in a connected manner but rather are discrete events that simply happen to have occurred at the same time in the shift. This combination of descriptions that are explicitly linked, those that can be read as linked and those that are presented in an unconnected manner fails to provide a coherent ongoing causal narrative for the period of observation.

4.4 Discussion

Taken together, these pragmatic features function to present descriptions in Figure 2 in a recognisably narrative form. Figure 3, however differs from Figure 2 in the following ways. The selection of reportable events, particularly the first and last items in the summary, differs markedly from those in Figure 2. The first reported item provides little, if any, context for the descriptions to follow and makes no reference to the baby as the focus of the summary. Further, the causal organization of the events being described is variable, making some connections explicit, other connections inferable, and failing to make relevant causality in instances where it might be appropriate. In these respects, the text produced by the NLG system does not have the narrative form seen in the nurse-written corpus text in Figure 2. However, temporal organization of events and inclusion of some causal elements provide a more coherent organization of descriptions and thus make available at least some causal connections between events. To this extent, the NLG system appears to have produced text that more closely resembles that produced in nurse written corpus text. These findings show that discourse analysis represents a useful tool for evaluation of NLG systems. The analyses identified a range of pragmatic features which are desirable features in a text which seeks to describe in an efficient and useable manner the sequence of events and occurrences which can arise in nursing shifts in an NICU.

These findings have implications for the design of NLG systems. First, in terms of content selection, corpus texts show that the nurse does not merely select items as being topically relevant, but *treats* these items as topically relevant in terms of how descriptions of actions and events are designed and of how these descriptions are sequentially organized. In this respect, topical relevance must be viewed not as an objective feature of the situations being described, but rather as a pragmatic outcome of texts themselves. Second, it is apparently important to carefully select those items that are reported at the very start and the very end of the text. The first and last entries function to introduce the topic of the summary and offer an upshot of the matters at the end, that is these items take up *functional* 'slots'. Third, the human nurse expert attends to the topic flow: the sequential organization of a text to provide for readily recognizable shifts from one topic to another; this is absent from the text produced by the BT-Nurse system.

These issues come together in the issue of narrative structure. Narrative can be viewed as a form of talk or text in which descriptions of events are sequentially ordered so as to tell a story about those events. The human nurse's text contains pragmatic features such as identifying the baby as an actor in events, and indicating causal relationships among the actions and events being described, which features make it likely for it being treated as having a narrative form (Daiute et al., 2003).

5 General Discussion

5.1 Findings on BT-Nurse:

In terms of types of content, BT-Nurse texts have more instances of trend detection and recordings of parameter values, and fewer instances of inference enabling data representations than the corpus texts. This is perhaps a natural consequence of the differences in capabilities between a computer (good at crunching numbers) and a person (good at making domain inferences). It probably makes sense to accept this distinction and try to determine how a computer-generated text can most usefully support a nurse: an improved analysis of numeric data.

The evaluation using discourse analysis showed that BT-Nurse texts are deficient from a narrative perspective. They show a minimal foregrounding of the baby as a central character, inconsistent temporal organization of events and variable causal connectivity. Narrative form is a desirable feature of texts from an understandability and utility perspective (Reiter et al., 2008) more so because narratives are a pervasive feature of human interaction (Jefferson, 1978; Sacks, 1992).

5.2 Implications for NLG systems:

A content analysis of corpus texts reveals various ways in which domain experts represent various domain relevant types of information. For instance, here we see various ways in which both temporal markers and events are presented in corpus texts which can inform ways in which inferential items can potentially be included in NLG system generated texts. Knowledge of this sort then is certainly useful in designing NLG systems to produce texts which present information in appropriate ways for the domain.

Discourse analysis differs from content analysis in providing an understanding of ways in which users engaged in their daily duties present summaries or similar texts as part of their duties and helps in producing texts that take up such concerns. Here, aspects of presenting the baby as a central character was one feature of producing corpus texts. This is readily seen to be relevant for activities performed by nurses in that their duties are about caring and/or providing nursing care for one particular party, namely 'the baby'. To see that human users take up aspects such as these to be relevant features is knowledge useful in the design of NLG systems that are to be deployed in specific domains. Another finding of relevance is the role of items that occupy the start and final positions in a text. The inclusion of specific items at certain points in a text by human users allows them to do specific functions: doing an introduction, offering an upshot and others. Of note is that such features *serve* to make the text more of a narrative.

The interesting thing about the above findings is that they did *not* arise from the quantitative evaluation of BT-Nurse. To us, this suggests that such findings are more likely to arise from a qualitative evaluation conducted by analysts with expertise in discourse analysis or content analysis; they are not likely to be spontaneously suggested by subjects who have domain expertise but no expertise in analysis of texts.

5.3 Limitations:

Although, the extent of texts covered in these analyses is limited, outcomes of such evaluations are useful and a complete analysis is likely to throw up further useful knowledge. For instance, across the corpus texts foregrounding the baby as a central character and how descriptions offered are made in ways to make overall evaluations of the baby's status, such as being 'okay' or 'deteriorating' are seen to be consistent features.

Additionally matters that appear to be of a quantitative nature were revealed as relevant aspects of these texts only posterior to qualitative analyses. For example, the content analysis showed a difference in the frequency of trend descriptions of parameter values between corpus texts and BT-Nurse texts. This could probably be tested using quantitative techniques; this would require annotating the texts, and the annotation scheme could be based on the scheme used in content analysis. In theory a task evaluation study could even be performed to evaluate the impact of having more trend descriptions, although this would be an expensive undertaking.

6 Conclusion

The qualitative evaluations presented above make use of two different but complementary methodologies. Content analysis provides us with knowledge on the sorts of items present in a text. Discourse analysis on the other hand moves a step further and makes clear aspects of ways in which these items are presented in the service of certain actions (making the baby a central character, for instance). In particular, content analysis is appropriate in showing what goes into a text and discourse analysis reveals what the texts are designed to do.

Qualitative analyses described above identified many differences between generated texts and corpus texts. Some of the differences identified may be desirable, such as the fact that BT-Nurse texts contain more trend descriptions than corpus texts. Other differences are probably not desirable, such as narrative deficiencies in the generated texts. However, the key point is that qualitative analyses have identified these differences, so that developers are aware of them and can decide what action to take.

Acknowledgements

This research was funded by the UK Engineering and Physical Sciences Research Council under grants EP/D049520/1, EP/D05057X/1, and EP/E011764/1. The authors would like to thank other members of the BABYTALK project including François Portet, Jim Hunter, Somayajulu Sripada, and Neil McIntosh for their help.

References

K Adlassnig, C Combi, A Das, E Keravnou, and G Pozzi. 2006. Temporal representation and reasoning in medicine: Research directions and challenges. *Artificial Intelligence in Medicine, 38(2):* 101 - 113.

C Daiute and C Lightfoot. 2003. *Narrative analysis: Studying the development of individuals in society.* London: Sage.

A Gatt, F Portet, E Reiter, J Hunter, S Mahamood, W Moncur, and S Sripada. 2009. From data to text in Neonatal Intensive Care Unit: Using NLG technology for decision support and information management. *AI Communications, 22:* 153 - 186.

E Hovy 1993. Automated Discourse Generation Using Discourse Structure Relations. *Artificial Intelligence, 63(1-2):* 341 - 386.

J Hunter, Y Freer, A Gatt, E Reiter, S Sripada, C Sykes, and D Westwater. 2011. BT-Nurse: Computer generation of natural language shift summaries from complex heterogenous medical data., *Journal of American Medical Informatics Association* **18**:621-624.

G Jefferson 1978. Sequential aspects of storytelling in conversation. In, J. Schenkein (Ed), *Studies in the organization of conversational interaction.* London: Academic Press.

A McKinlay, C McVittie, E Reiter, Y Freer, C Sykes, and R Logie. 2010. Design issues for socially intelligent user-interfaces: A Discourse analysis of a data-to-text system for summarizing clinical data. *Methods of Information in Medicine, 49(4):* 379 - 387.

A McKinlay and C McVittie. 2008. *Social Psychology & Discourse.* Sussex: Wiley-Blackwell.

K Papineni, S Roukos, T Ward, and W Zhu. 2002. BLEU: A method for automatic evaluation of machine translation. *Proceedings of ACL-2002,* pages 311-318.

F Portet, E Reiter, A Gatt, S Sripada, Y Freer, and C Sykes. 2009. Automatic generation of textual summaries from neonatal intensive care data. *Artificial Intelligence, 173(7,8):* 789 - 816.

E Reiter and A Belz. 2009. An investigation into the validity of some metrics for automatically evaluating Natural Language Generating systems. *Computational Linguistics, 35:* 529 - 558.

E Reiter, A Gatt, F Portet, and M van der Meulen. 2008. The importance of narrative and other lessons from an evaluation of an NLG system that summarizes clinical data. *Proceedings of INLG-08,* pages 147-155

L Richards. 2009. *Handling Qualitative Data: A Practical Guide.* London: SAGE.

H Sacks. 1992. *Lectures on Conversation.* Oxford: Blackwell's.

J Saldaña. 2009. *The Coding Manual for Qualitative Researchers.* London: SAGE.

S Thompson and W Mann. 1987. Rhetorical Structure Theory: A framework for the Analysis of Texts. *IPRA Papers in Pragmatics, 1:* 79 - 105.

Evaluating Salience Metrics for the Context-Adequate Realization of Discourse Referents

Christian Chiarcos
chiarcos@uni-potsdam.de
Universität Potsdam

Abstract

We describe the application of a framework for salience metrics and linguistic variability with respect to the contextually adequate choice of referring expressions and grammatical roles: Where multiple meaning-equivalent candidate realizations are available that differ in one of these aspects, NLG systems can apply salience metrics to predict contextually adequate realization preferences. We evaluate this claim and a number of parameters of salience metrics found in the theoretical literature on two German newspaper corpora.
Key features of the approach described here include the application of a two-dimensional model of salience, how its theoretical predictions can be exploited to develop salience metrics for a particular phenomenon, and that these salience metrics can be subsequently applied to other phenomena. This approach can be applied to develop classifiers to predict packaging preferences for phenomena where little training data is available.

1 Motivation and Background

For an example sentence from the RST Discourse Treebank (Carlson et al., 2003, file 3), example (1) illustrates how the same 'thought' can be realized, or 'packaged' (Chafe, 1976) in many different ways: Three referents, the insurance agent *Toni*, her sister *Cynthia* and their *apartment* suffer from an earthquake, the central protagonist of the paragraph is *Toni*, and the text goes on elaborating her situation.

(1) *The apartment she shares with her sister was rattled ...*

(a) *The apartment* **the agent** *shares with her sister ...*

(b) **The earthquake rattled** *the apartment she shares ...*

We consider two packaging phenomena: **Referring expressions** (1a: definite NP vs. pronoun), and **grammatical roles** (1b: active vs. passive).[1]

These variants are meaning-equivalent in the sense of Dorr et al. (2004), but according to theories of referential coherence (Sgall et al., 1986; Grosz et al., 1995; Givón, 2001), they express different discourse functions, often described with reference to the notion of 'discourse salience'.[2] Accordingly, the local discourse context – or, better, a salience score calculated on this basis – can help to predict contextually adequate packaging preferences.

In NLG, discourse salience has been employed to generate referring expressions (McCoy and Strube, 1999), to assign grammatical roles (Stede, 1998), and word order preferences (Kruijff et al., 2001). More recently, however, salience-based approaches have been increasingly superseded by statistical approaches, that nevertheless build on earlier theories of salience, e.g., Shiramatsu et al. (2007) for referring expressions, Zarrieß et al. (2011) for voice alternation, and Cahill and Riester (2009) for word order. One of the reasons for this methodological shift may be the observation (noted, for example, by

[1] Along with referring expressions and grammatical roles, word order alternation has been described in a similar way, and it is of particular importance for the motivation of two-dimensional models of salience (Chiarcos, 2011b). For reasons of space, however, this paper concentrates on referring expressions and grammatical roles.

[2] Discourse salience is to be distinguished from other types of salience, that are either not specific to discourse referents (e.g., salience of semantic features, Ortony et al. 1985), or defined with respect to other modalities (e.g., visual salience, Itti 2003, Kelleher 2011).

Proceedings of the 13th European Workshop on Natural Language Generation (ENLG), pages 32–43,
Nancy, France, September 2011.

Navaretta, 2002) that the existing approaches developed until the late 1990s were only partially compatible with each other, as they employed different theories of referential coherence.

Major theories of referential coherence, e.g., Centering (Grosz et al., 1995), its instantiations (Poesio et al., 2004), Topicality (Givón, 2001) and Functional Generative Description (Sgall et al., 1986, FGD) share a set of common insights, in particular, the close association between referential coherence and attentional states (as manifested in the salience of discourse referents), but they focus on different aspects of referential coherence and formalize them in different ways.[3]

Even worse, the field is notoriously plagued by a multitude of incompatible terminologies: 'Salience', for example, is used as a near-synonym of 'givenness' (Sgall et al., 1986, p.54f.), but also as a near-synonym of 'newness (for the hearer)' (Davis and Hirschberg, 1988), or 'degree of interest (of the speaker)' (Langacker, 1997, p.22). Therefore, the operationalization of discourse salience in NLG requires a theoretical foundation and a formalization of salience and its effects on information packaging.

This paper takes its point of departure from a theoretical framework of discourse salience that has been developed as a generalization over Centering, Topicality and FGD. This framework, as sketched in Sect. 2, resolves the terminological difficulties associated with the notion of salience by distinguishing two dimensions of salience, with independent effects on referring expressions, grammatical roles and word order. One advantage of this theory-based approach as compared to a plain statistical classifier is that it incorporates a set of theoretical assumptions that guide the development of salience metrics, and that predict an impact of a salience metric even on phenomena not considered during the development of this particular metric.

Section 3 identifies a number of parameters that allow to reconstruct different instantiations of Centering, Topicality and FGD salience within this model. Section 4 deals with the empirical evaluation of these parameters on two German newspaper corpora, in Sections 4.1 and 4.2 elementary metrics for both dimensions of salience are developed, and Sect. 4.3 confirms theoretical predictions on the impact of both dimensions of salience on noun phrase complexity and grammatical roles.

2 A Framework of Salience in Discourse

Inspired by Givón's topicality measurements and hierarchies of grammatical devices associated with them, Chiarcos (2010; 2011a) developed an operationalizable formalization of functional-cognitive theories of information packaging within the Mental Salience Framework (MSF), a framework for the development and interpretation of salience metrics in discourse. Below, we sketch the reconstruction of Centering, Topicality and FGD salience within this approach. We provide a brief, technical description only, as the focus of this paper is to evaluate the resulting salience metrics.

The framework, schematically illustrated in Fig. 1, consists of the following components:

- a theoretical model of salience, grounded in cognitive linguistics and functional grammar (Chiarcos, 2011a),
- the specification of two dimensions of salience, backward-looking hearer salience, and forward-looking speaker salience (Sect. 2.1), and the corresponding metrics (Sect. 2.2),
- packaging hierarchies, i.e., rankings of grammatical devices for different packaging phenomena (Sect. 2.3), that are aligned with cumulated salience scores calculated from hearer salience and speaker salience (Sect. 2.4), and
- principles for the mapping between packaging hierarchies and salience scores (Sect. 2.5).

As opposed to related models in functional-cognitive linguistics, e.g., Mulkern (2007), our formalization is operationalizable for NLG applications: It allows to predict packaging preferences for discourse referents from numerical salience scores (Sect. 2.5).

Metrics of salience applied in Natural Language Processing are dominated by research on anaphora

[3]For example, Grosz et al.'s Centering posits an adjacency constraint, whereas FGD and Topicality employ distance measurements. FGD predicts constraints on word order and referring expressions, but it differs from Centering and Topicality in that in formalizes only the backward-looking aspect of salience in discourse.

resolution in the tradition of Lappin and Leass (1994). Such salience metrics do, however, focus on the backward-looking, hearer-oriented aspect of salience, whereas the speaker-oriented, forward-looking aspect of salience is neglected. This tradition also had a strong impact on NLG, in particular in the field of generating referring expressions (GRE). Current metrics of discourse salience in GRE are thus essentially concerned with hearer salience,[4] although the relevance of speaker-oriented factors has been recognized for other aspects of NLG, e.g., for German word order as being sensitive to a domain-specific 'aboutness' criterion (Filippova and Strube, 2007).

Within the MSF, Centering, Topicality and FGD salience can be reconstructed as configurations of hearer and speaker salience. As opposed to earlier generalizations over some of these theories, e.g., Krahmer and Theune (2002), this paper adopts a two-dimensional model of salience for NLG. This bidimensionality not only helps to resolve conflicts between different terminological traditions, it also accounts for newer evidence that many packaging phenomena require the differentiation of (at least) two dimensions of discourse salience (Kaiser and Trueswell, 2010; Chiarcos, 2011b).

The most important parameters are summarized in Sect. 3.

2.1 Salience

In neurobiology and psychology, salience is defined as a gradual assessment of attentional states (Itti et al., 2005), and it is used in this sense also in functional grammar (Sgall et al., 1986), cognitive linguistics (Talmy, 2000) and computational linguistics (Grosz et al., 1995). In order to resolve the terminological difficulties mentioned above, we distinguish two dimensions of salience in discourse associated with different roles regarding the flow of attention in discourse.

From the perspective of an NLG system, 'attentional states' are primarily those **of the speaker**: Information that is relevant to the speaker is more salient than information not considered relevant (Pattabhiraman, 1992; Reed, 2002). Beyond this, a cooperative speaker takes the perspective of the addressee into consideration, i.e., she acts according to her assumptions about the attentional states **of the hearer** (Prince, 1981). Generating text that is both coherent (for the hearer) and goal-directed (for the speaker) requires both perspectives.

The resulting multidimensionality of salience is not specific to dialog, but has also been confirmed for written, monologuous discourse, e.g., by Kaiser and Trueswell (2010) and Chiarcos (2011b). The latter also provides evidence for a differentiation between a backward-looking and a forward-looking dimension of salience. Taking up Centering terminology, assumed attentional states of the hearer can indeed be characterized as being primarily *backward-looking* (the preceding discourse allows to approximate the attentional states of the hearer), whereas attentional states of the speaker involve a *forward-looking* aspect (subsequent discourse can unveil the speaker's earlier intentions to elaborate on a particular issue).

This difference is modelled here by distinguishing two independent dimensions of discourse salience: (i) **speaker salience** represents the attentional states of the speaker (that express her intentions to guide the hearer's focus of attention), and (ii) **hearer salience** represents the speaker's approximation of the attentional states of the hearer.

Cross-linguistic research indicates that both aspects of attention control in discourse are necessary to chose of referring expressions, and to assign grammatical roles appropriately.[5]

2.2 Salience metrics

Salience is represented by means of numerical scores, so that a principally unlimited number of attentional states can be distinguished, cf. Sgall et al. (1986), Ariel (1990), and Lappin and Leass

[4]This is true even for multidimensional models of salience in GRE such as van der Sluis and Krahmer (2001): Their 'focus-space salience' is concerned with the visual environment, 'inherent salience' is a semantic criterion (uniqueness within a domain), 'linguistic salience' is the hearer-oriented, backward-looking aspect of discourse salience.

[5]Referring expressions are associated with hearer salience (Ariel, 1990; Gundel et al., 1993; for German see Heusinger; 1997), demonstratives also with speaker salience (attention guidance, contrast) (Ehlich, 1982; Diessel, 2006; for German see Bosch et al., 2007). The assignment of grammatical roles is sensitive to hearer salience (Fillmore, 1977; Sgall et al., 1986) as well as speaker salience (foregrounding) (Pustet, 1995; Tomlin, 1995).

Figure 1: The Mental Salience Framework, schematically

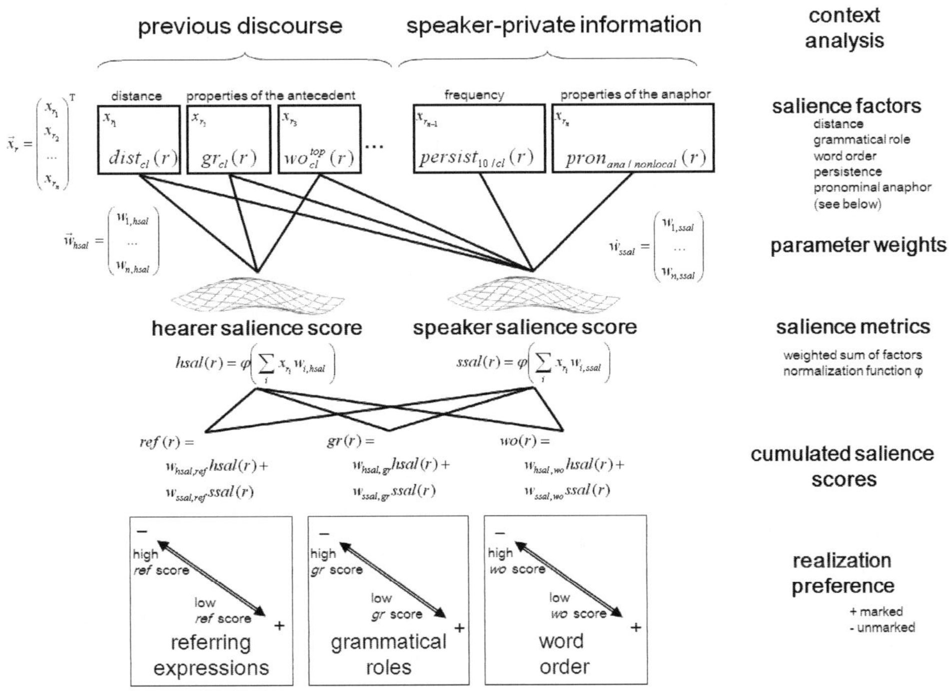

(1994). The salience of a referent r is assessed by means of one metric of hearer salience, $\text{hsal}(r)$, and one metric of speaker salience, $\text{ssal}(r)$. Backward-looking salience factors that pertain to the preceding discourse are available to both speaker and hearer; they represent primarily **factors of hearer salience**. Forward-looking factors that take the subsequent discourse into consideration are **factors of speaker salience**: If the speaker intended to guide the hearer's attention in a planful way – to prepare him for the following development of discourse – the subsequent discourse provides a rough approximation of the speaker's intentions at the moment the current utterance was produced.

For a referent r, the salience factor i is represented as a numerical value x_{r_i} with $0 \leq x_{r_i} < 2$. Hearer salience and speaker salience are calculated from the weighted sum of these factors. The weights $w_{i,hsal} \in \mathcal{R}$ and $w_{i,ssal} \in \mathcal{R}$ correspond to the relative impact that a particular salience factor x_{r_i} has on the salience scores $\text{hsal}(r)$ and $\text{ssal}(r)$. If x_{r_i} is speaker-private, then $w_{j,hsal} = 0$.

Salience scores are normalized to the range $0 \leq \text{sal}(r) < 2$: Scores greater than 1 indicate a high degree of salience, 0 the absence of salience. For distance-sensitive factors of hearer salience, we employ the normalization function $n(x,k) = \frac{x}{k\,x+1}$ where k represents the distance from the last mention of the referent (e.g., the number of intermediate clauses), and x the salience score that the referent would have if the last mention was in the preceding utterance. All theories mentioned above assume that a referent r mentioned in the last utterance is more hearer salient than any referent in the utterance before, i.e., $x > n(2,1) = \frac{2}{3}$. We thus adopt 0.8 as minimum value for x. For presentational reasons, we further assume that 1.0 is the average hearer salience score for a referent mentioned in the preceding utterance, possible values of x are thus normalized to the range $0.8 \leq x \leq 1.2$.[6]

2.3 Packaging hierarchies

Figures 2 and 3 illustrate the predicted impact of salience on referring expressions and grammatical roles. These hierarchies generalize over several

[6]Hearer salience scores greater than 1.2 are obtained if a referent's hearer salience is calculated not only from its mention, but if salience scores from the entire referential chain are added up (as in Lappin and Leass' original proposal). This paper, however, follows Centering, Topicality and FGD and only considers the last mention of the referent.

rankings and scales of grammatical devices developed in cognitive and functional linguistics (footnote 5): They are assumed to be applicable cross-linguistically, and also to English (Chafe, 1994; Cornish, 2007; Fillmore, 1977; Tomlin, 1995), and thus illustrated for ex. 1:

(1a): In accordance with Fig. 2, the use of *the agent* in place of the pronoun is possible as a means to express a high degree of speaker salience, e.g., in order to put *Toni* in the foreground. However, as *Toni* already is the maximally hearer salient referent in the preceding discourse, this is not necessary and thus avoided.

(1b): In the original, *Toni* is the subject of a relative clause attached to the subject *apartment*. In (1b), the relative clause is attached to the direct object, and in accordance with Fig. 3, this indicates a lower degree of hearer salience and speaker salience as compared to the original realization. This is justified only if the *earthquake* was speaker salient, e.g., because it would be the intended main protagonist of the following sentences (what it isn't), (1b) is thus dispreferred as it would distract the hearer's focus of attention from *Toni*.

2.4 Cumulated salience scores

We employ cumulated salience scores for the mapping between salience scores and packaging hierarchies: For every packaging phenomenon, the cumulated salience score is the weighted sum of hearer salience score $\mathrm{hsal}(r)$ and speaker salience score $\mathrm{ssal}(r)$, i.e., $\mathrm{ref}(r)$ for referring expressions and $\mathrm{gr}(r)$ for grammatical roles.

$$\begin{aligned} \mathrm{ref}(r) &:= w_{\mathrm{hsal,ref}}\,\mathrm{hsal}(r) + w_{\mathrm{ssal,ref}}\,\mathrm{ssal}(r) \\ \mathrm{gr}(r) &:= w_{\mathrm{hsal,gr}}\,\mathrm{hsal}(r) + w_{\mathrm{ssal,gr}}\,\mathrm{ssal}(r) \end{aligned}$$

As a convention, the realization favored by a high degree of hearer salience is associated with high, positive cumulated salience scores. If a high degree of speaker salience favors the same realization, ssal is assigned a positive weight (as for $\mathrm{gr}(r)$), if ssal favors a deviation from hsal preferences, it is assigned a negative weight (as for $\mathrm{ref}(r)$).

In practical application, the relative weights of hsal and ssal for a particular phenomenon, say, sentence-initial word order, can be trained with a simple Multi-Layer Perceptron (MLP) with one hidden node: hsal and ssal scores serve as input nodes and two nodes representing $\pm$initial as output nodes. After training the MLP, the weights of hearer salience and speaker salience can be extrapolated from the activation function of the hidden node.

2.5 Predicting packaging preferences

Cumulated salience scores are interpreted against a packaging hierarchy by means of hierarchy alignment: The referent with the highest cumulated salience score is assigned the highest-ranking grammatical device available, etc. For grammatical roles, for example, the candidate realization would be preferred that minimizes the deviations between the salience ranking of discourse referents and their relative syntactic prominence (e.g., when a highly referent is assigned object role while a non-salient referent is assigned subject role).

This hierarchy alignment, as well as additional realization thresholds that express, for example, that pronouns require a certain minimum of salience, can be implemented as constraints in an optimality-theoretic setting. Alternatively, alignment between salience scores and their most likely realization can also be formulated as a minimization problem, so that standard approaches to optimization problems can be applied (Pattabhiraman, 1992). A similar ranking-based approach has been applied, for example, by Zarrieß et al. (2011) for voice alternation in German. Another possibility to derive packaging preferences from salience metrics is to train a classifier that makes use of cumulated salience scores as one (or even the only) factor.

3 Parameters of salience metrics

The framework sketched above specifies a number of parameters of salience metrics, i.e.,

- salience factors that involve (a) different aspects of the **linguistic realization** of previous/subsequent mentions of the referent, (b) different **distance** measurements from the last mention of the referent, or (c) different **frequency** measurements,
- weights of salience factors for the calculation of $\mathrm{hsal}(r)$ and $\mathrm{ssal}(r)$,
- weights of $\mathrm{hsal}(r)$ and $\mathrm{ssal}(r)$ for the calculation of cumulated salience scores, and

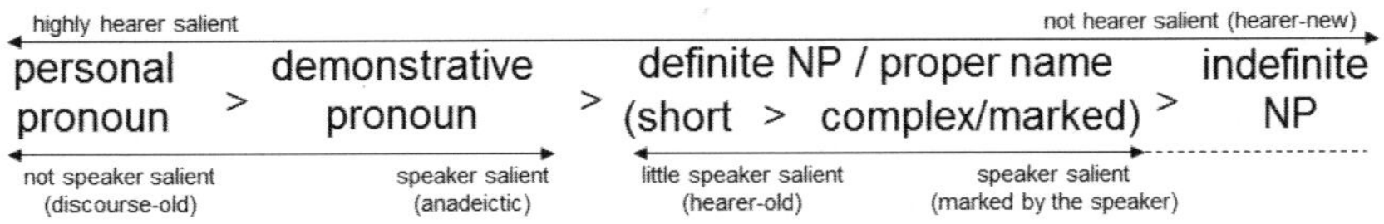

Figure 2: Salience and referring expressions

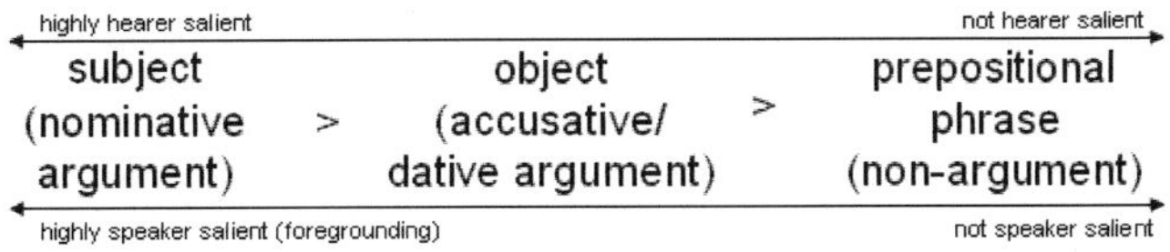

Figure 3: Salience and grammatical roles

- optional realization thresholds

Different theories of referential coherence entail different parameter configurations, as observed by Hajičová and Kruijff-Korbayová (1997), Krahmer and Theune (2002) and others for differences between Centering and FGD, and by Poesio et al. (2004) for different instantiations of Centering. The parameter configurations for these theories, as well as for Givón's Topicality – whose operationalization as part of an NLG system has not been considered so far – are shortly introduced below.

3.1 Topicality parameters

Givón (1983, 2001) established two dimensions of 'topicality' – abbreviated TOP –, anaphoric topicality and cataphoric topicality, and described correlations between both dimensions of topicality and the choice of grammatical devices.

The anaphoric topicality of a referent r is measured by the distance from its last mention, cataphoric topicality by its persistence (frequency) within the subsequent n utterances:

$$\text{dist}_{cl}(r) = \begin{cases} \frac{1}{k+1} & \text{with } k \geq 0 \text{ intermediate clauses} \\ & \text{since last mention of } r \\ 0 & \text{if no previous mention of } r \end{cases}$$

$$\text{persist}_{n/cl}(r) = \frac{\boxed{\text{mentions of } r \text{ within the next } n \text{ clauses}}}{n}$$

Here and below, the subscript cl indicates that a factor is defined with reference to clauses. Alternatively, sentences could be considered (subscript s).

Hearer salience corresponds to anaphoric topicality, and speaker salience to cataphoric topicality, i.e., $\text{hsal}_{TOP}(r) = \text{dist}_{cl}(r)$ and $\text{ssal}_{TOP}(r) = \text{persist}_{10/cl}(r)$. As for cumulated salience scores, Givón (2001) predicts that (i) high values of $\text{hsal}(r)$ result in high $\text{ref}(r)$ scores (anaphoric topicality favors pronominal realization), and that (ii) high $\text{ssal}(r)$ scores result in high scores for $\text{gr}(r)$ (subject assignment indicates foregrounding):

$$\begin{aligned} \text{ref}_{TOP}(r) &= \text{hsal}_{TOP}(r) \\ \text{gr}_{TOP}(r) &= \text{ssal}_{TOP}(r) \end{aligned}$$

3.2 Centering parameters

For Centering (Grosz et al., 1995) – abbreviated CT –, hearer salience corresponds to the ranking of referents in the preceding utterance, with the ranking subject > object > other, implemented here as an extension of the dist(r) function above:

$$\text{gr}_{cl}(r) = \begin{cases} \frac{\text{gr}_{ante}(r)}{k\ \text{gr}_{ante}(r)+1} & \text{with } k \geq 0 \text{ intermediate clauses} \\ & \text{since last mention of } r \\ 0 & \text{if no previous mention of } r \end{cases}$$

$$\text{with } gr_{ante}(r) = \begin{cases} 1.2 & \text{if antecedent is subject} \\ 1.0 & \text{if antecedent is object} \\ 0.8 & \text{otherwise} \end{cases}$$

The numerical scores of $\text{gr}_{ante}(r)$ reflect the relative ranking proposed by the theory, and that they are equally distributed between 0.8 and 1.2.[7]

In accordance with the concept of "backward-looking center" (C_B), speaker salience can be defined with respect to the following utterance: A referent is speaker salient if it represents the C_B of the following utterance. To prevent cyclic definitions, the C_B of the following utterance (clause) can

[7] While later studies may involve empirically justified numbers for $\text{gr}_{ante}(r)$, this paper only considers theory-internal evidence to motivate numerical salience factors. The numerical values are thus chosen such that they reflect the original ranking, but the exact numerical values of salience factors are arbitrary. Important for their appropriate interpretation and for the training of decision trees on individual factors is only that relative differences are preserved.

be heuristically identified by pronominal realization (Centering Rule 1):

$$\text{pron}_{ana/cl}(r) = \begin{cases} 1.0 & \text{iff } r \text{ realized as pronoun in the following clause} \\ 0 & \text{otherwise} \end{cases}$$

Pronominalization is associated with the C_B (Centering Rule 1), i.e., the most (hearer-) salient referent in the current utterance, high $\text{hsal}(r)$ scores thus entail high $\text{ref}(r)$ scores:

$$\text{ref}_{CT}(r) = \text{hsal}_{CT}(r)$$

Grammatical roles determine the C_B of the following utterance, so that high $\text{ssal}(r)$ scores entail high $\text{gr}(r)$ scores. Further, Centering Rule 2 predicts a preference for C_B continuity, so that $\text{hsal}(r)$ has a positive influence on $\text{gr}(r)$:

$$\text{gr}_{CT}(r) = 0.5\ \text{hsal}_{CT}(r) + 0.5\ \text{ssal}_{CT}(r)$$

3.3 Functional parameters

Functional Centering (Strube and Hahn, 1999) and Functional Generative Description (Sgall et al., 1986) introduce $\text{hsal}(r)$ factors that evaluate the type of referring expression of the antecedent and its word order: Following Strube and Hahn (1999) the functions $\text{ref}_{cl}^{top}(r)$ and $\text{wo}_{cl}^{top}(r)$ can be defined in analogy with $\text{gr}_{cl}(r)$ above with the following subfunctions:

$$\text{ref}_{ante}^{top}(r) = \begin{cases} 1.2 & \text{iff } r \text{ realized as pronoun, proper name, or simple definite NP} \\ 1.0 & \text{iff } r \text{ realized as possessive NP or complex definite NP} \\ 0.8 & \text{iff } r \text{ realized as indefinite NP} \end{cases}$$

$$\text{wo}_{ante}^{top}(r) = \left(0.8 + 0.4\frac{m-n}{m}\right)$$

with m number of words in antecedent sentence, and $n < m$ number of words preceding the antecedent

The functions $\text{ref}_{ante}^{top}(r)$ and $\text{wo}_{ante}^{top}(r)$ formalize the claim that referents with topical (given) antecedents are more hearer salient than referents with focal (new) antecedents. The opposite claim, formulated by Sgall et al. (1986), requires alternative formulations of these salience factors $\text{ref}_{ante}^{foc}(r) := 2 - \text{ref}_{ante}^{top}(r)$ and $\text{wo}_{ante}^{foc}(r) := 2 - \text{wo}_{ante}^{top}(r)$.

4 Evaluation

The parameters identified above are evaluated against referring expressions and grammatical roles in two German newspaper corpora that combine syntactic and anaphoric annotations, i.e., a coreference-annotated subcorpus of the NEGRA corpus (Skut et al., 1997; Schiehlen, 2004), and the Potsdam Commentary Corpus (Stede, 2004; Krasavina and Chiarcos, 2007, PCC).

4.1 Pronominalization and hsal metrics

Hearer salience is evaluated with respect to pronominalization. As shown in Fig. 2, personal pronouns are characterized by a high degree of hearer salience (otherwise, a definite description would have been used) and a low degree of speaker salience (otherwise, a demonstrative pronoun would have been used). As speaker salience is neutralized, pronominalization provides a test case for metrics of hearer salience.

For the study of hearer salience, we applied CART and C4.5 decision trees and classified hearer salience scores against the pronominal and nominal realization of third-person referents. Both learning algorithms produced almost identical results (Tab. 1). All hsal factors outperformed the baseline (predict nominal), and with the exception of $\text{dist}_{cl}(r)$ on NEGRA, this improvement was statistically significant as confirmed by a χ^2 test. For all factors, high salience scores were identified with a preference to pronominal realization, thereby confirming the predicted influence of hearer salience on the choice of referring expressions (Fig. 2).

With respect to plain distance measurements, sentence-level segmentation outperformed clause-level segmentation. This configuration was thus adopted for hearer salience factors that take the form of the antecedent into consideration. The overall best results were achieved with $\text{ref}_s^{top}(r)$ and $\text{ref}_s^{foc}(r)$.

Closer inspection of the classifier revealed that prominent realization compensates distance, i.e., a referent that is realized in a prominent way in U_{k-2} (e.g., as subject) is more likely to occur as a pronoun than a referent that is realized in a non-prominent way in U_{k-1} (e.g., as non-argument). The classification results did thus not provide a concrete pronom-

Table 1: Correctness of hsal factors for the prediction of nominal and pronominal realization (C4.5), χ^2 significance of correctness improvements over baseline

salience factor	correctness (significance) NEGRA	PCC
baseline	.799	.726
$\text{dist}_{cl}(r)$	.819 (not sig.)	.836 ($p < .001$)
$\text{dist}_s(r)$	.845 ($p < .001$)	.853 ($p < .001$)
$\text{gr}_s(r)$	.845 ($p < .001$)	.861 ($p < .001$)
$\text{ref}_s^{top}(r)$	.969 ($p < .001$)	.942 ($p < .001$)
$\text{ref}_s^{foc}(r)$	.969 ($p < .001$)	.942 ($p < .001$)
$\text{wo}_s^{top}(r)$	.863 ($p < .001$)	.887 ($p < .001$)
$\text{wo}_s^{foc}(r)$	.861 ($p < .001$)	.886 ($p < .001$)
total (# ref.exp)	976	2355

Table 2: Pronominalization thresholds for $\text{ref}^{top}(r)$, $\text{ref}^{foc}(r)$, and $\text{gr}(r)$ as identified with a single conjunctive rule learner

salience factor	corpus	threshold	predicted pronouns prec.	recall	f
$\text{gr}_s(r)$	PCC	.472	.695	.84	.761
	NEGRA	.472	.569	.837	.678
$\text{ref}_s^{top}(r)$	PCC	.523	.830	.899	.863
	NEGRA	.523	.782	.913	.842
$\text{ref}_s^{foc}(r)$	PCC	.389	.631	.899	.741
	NEGRA	(conjunctive rule learner failed)			

inalization threshold, but rather, multiple classes scattered along the range of possible hsal scores.

In experiments with a single conjunctive rule learner (that forces a binary partition of salience scores) $\text{ref}_s^{top}(r)$ outperformed the other factors in precision and recall of pronoun prediction (Tab. 2). For subsequent experiments, we adopt $\text{ref}_s^{top}(r)$ as the primary metric of hearer salience.

4.2 Subject role assignment and ssal metrics

Speaker salience is evaluated here against the assignment of grammatical roles. The subject represents either a high degree of hearer salience or a high degree of speaker salience (Fig. 3). For the study of speaker salience, we eliminated the influence of hearer salience by considering only sentences where one non-subject referent was at least as hearer salient ($\text{ref}_s^{top}(r)$) as the subject. The relatively low number of sentences that match this pattern (approx. 10%) indicates that subjects tend to be hearer salient. To

Table 3: Correctness of ssal factors for the prediction of subject/non-subject status (CART, subsection of NEGRA+PCC)

factor	correctness	(significance)
baseline (non-subject)	.521	
$\text{persist}_{10/s}(r)$	.595	($p < .05$)
$\text{persist}_{3/s}(r)$	.576	(not sig.)
$\text{persist}_{1/s}(r)$	.613	($p < .01$)
$\text{persist}_{10/cl}(r)$	.585	($p < .1$)
$\text{persist}_{3/cl}(r)$	.571	(not sig.)
$\text{persist}_{1/cl}(r)$	.562	(not sig.)
$\text{pron}_{ana/cl}(r)$	.571	(not sig.)
$\text{pron}_{ana/s}(r)$	.627	($p < .01$)
$\text{pron}_{ana}(r)$	.636	($p < .001$)
total (# ref.exp)	216	

compensate for data sparsity, data from NEGRA and PCC was combined.

We trained decision trees to predict subject or non-subject realization (Tab. 3). Both C4.5 and CART classifiers confirmed that high speaker salience entails a subject preference.

All persistence measurements outperform the baseline (non-subject), and we find that sentence-level segmentation performs better than clause-level segmentation. As for Centering-inspired speaker salience factors that address the pronominalization of the anaphor, three different variants were tested: pronominalization in the immediately following clause $\text{pron}_{ana/cl}(r)$, in the immediately following sentence $\text{pron}_{ana/s}(r)$ and pronominalization of the anaphor without contextual restriction $\text{pron}_{ana}(r)$. Factor $\text{pron}_{ana}(r)$ achieved highest correctness, closely followed by $\text{pron}_{ana/s}(r)$, and $\text{persist}_{1/s}(r)$ and then by $\text{persist}_{10/s}(r)$. For other salience factors, the correctness improvement over the baseline was marginally significant or insignificant.

4.3 Beyond pronouns and subjects

Having identified $\text{ref}_s^{top}(r)$ and $\text{pron}_{ana}(r)$ as suitable measurements of hearer salience and speaker salience, Fig. 4 illustrates their application to NP complexity and grammatical roles. Different grammatical devices are ordered according to their average salience scores. Edges between two scores indicate highly significant differences between the

Figure 4: Average salience scores for selected grammatical devices (NEGRA+PCC)

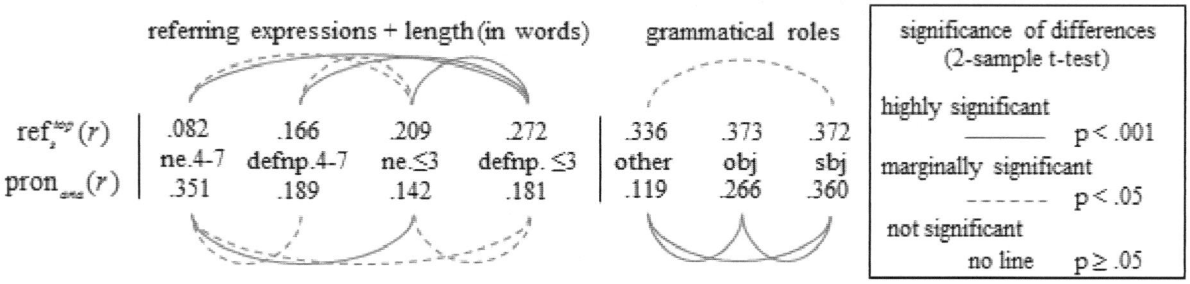

salience scores for two grammatical devices (two-sample t-test, $p < .001$), dotted edges indicate marginally significant differences ($p < .05$), no edge indicates an insignificant difference ($p \geq .05$).

The results obtained mirror the theory-based predictions on salience metrics summarized in Figs. 2 and 3. Remarkable here is that these phenomena were not taken in consideration when the salience metric was developed (resp., a salience factor selected for its approximation). For pron$_{ana}(r)$ and ref$_s^{top}(r)$, these effects were not even anticipated by the researchers who proposed the salience factors in the first place: Neither Centering nor Functional Centering predict a difference between complex and non-complex proper names. Such differences are, however, fully in line with assumptions of the theoretical literature, Ariel (1990), for example, postulated a gradual decrease of complexity with increasing salience.

Figure 4 shows two types of extensions in the application of salience metrics as compared to the data sets they were developed on: (1) change of domain (pron$_{ana}(r)$ applied to referring expressions), and (2) change of granularity (pron$_{ana}(r)$ applied to differentiate non-subject referents, ref$_s^{top}(r)$ applied to differentiate nominal expressions). For both types of extension, the theory-based predictions of the MSF could be confirmed, and on this basis, a classifier for packaging preferences can be developed (Sect. 2.5). For the development of such a classifier from an establishes salience metric, it is sufficient to consider only the salience scores and the respective target realizations. With so few parameters, a small amount of data is sufficient to train a classifier for this task.

This is of practical relevance to NLG because it allows us to develop a salience metric for an easily observable phenomenon with loads of training data, and then apply it to another domain, where little training data is available, just sufficient to perform the necessary adjustments (e.g., to calculate the relative weight of hearer salience and speaker salience for the phenomon under discussion). An interesting prediction is, for example, that speaker salience (and absence of hearer salience) entails differences in accentuation (following Ariel, 1990, and Levelt, 1989, prosodically prominent expressions are more 'complex' than prosodically non-prominent expressions, and thus subject to the complexity predictions of Fig. 2). Corpora with prosodic and coreference annotation are available, but expensive to create, and thus relatively small (e.g., the German radio news corpus DIRNDL, with 3221 sentences annotated for prosody and information structure, Eckert et al., 2011). But with salience metrics developed for text corpora, this limited amount of data is sufficient to evaluate whether the salience metrics yield the predicted effects, and to develop a classifier for the salience-based prediction of prosody from previously established metrics.

5 Results and Discussion

This paper described the application of a framework of salience in discourse that introduces a formal distinction between metrics of (backward-looking) hearer salience and (forward-looking) speaker salience, and a definition of information packaging as an alignment between the salience ranking of discourse referents and hierarchies of grammatical devices.

Our model extends Centering in that it assigns every referent a numerical score rather than concentrating on the top-level element in a ranking of referents from the preceding utterance. By doing so, it is possible to study the effect of distance measurements and to predict packaging preferences for all referents in an utterance, whereas Centering is restricted to adjacent utterances and constraints on possible realizations of the backward-looking center and the preferred center only. Further, our framework is not restricted to pronominalization, but capable to cover elaborate hierarchies of referring expressions.

Evaluation results on the choice of referring expressions and grammatical roles in German confirmed the theoretical predictions on how hearer salience and speaker salience affects both packaging phenomena (cf. Figs. 2 and 3). Essential assumptions about packaging hierarchies and associated aspects of salience could thus be confirmed.

(Subhierarchies of) the rankings in Figs. 2 and 3 have previously been applied in NLG: Fig. 2 covers standard assumptions about pronominal, definite and indefinite descriptions that can be found in similar form in the GRE algorithms of Dale and Reiter (1995) and McCoy and Strube (1999), and in the generation direction of optimality-theoretic models of anaphor interpretation and generation (Beaver, 2004; Byron and Gegg-Harrison, 2004). Thes salience ranking of grammatical roles has been employed for lexicalization of verbs, e.g., by Stede (1998). Zarrieß et al. (2011) describe an experiment to generate voice alternation on the basis of an implicit notion of hearer salience ('information status', approximated from surface features such as pronominalization and definiteness, cf. (Cahill and Riester, 2009) for a similar approach on word order).

The two-dimensional model of salience generalizes over Centering, Topicality and FGD, but it also allows us to formulate novel predictions, e.g., that subsequent pronominalization has an effect on NP complexity, or that the same notion of speaker salience is affecting both grammatical roles and the choice of referring expressions. Both claims have not been stated as such within the original theories.

Furthermore, the evaluation showed that the theory-guided adaption of salience metrics from one packaging phenomenon to another is possible. The theoretical background model adopted here may thus provide us with an opportunity to develop salience-based predictors for domains with relative little training data available.

By combining information drawn from different packaging phenomena, new metrics of salience may be developed and integrated into existing NLG algorithms to predict referring expressions and grammatical roles (as well as word order) in a contextually adequate way.

Acknowledgements

The research described in this paper was partially conducted within the Collaborative Research Center (SFB) 632 'Information Structure', Universität Potsdam, and financially supported by the Linguistics Department, Universität Potsdam. I would also like to thank Manfred Stede and three anonymozs reviewers.

References

Mira Ariel. 1990. *Accessing Noun-Phrase Antecedents*. Routledge, London, New York.

David I. Beaver. 2004. The optimization of discourse. *Linguistics and Philosophy*, 27(1).

Peter Bosch, Graham Katz, and Carla Umbach. 2007. The non-subject bias of German demonstrative pronouns. In Monika Schwarz-Friesel, Manfred Consten, and Mareile Knees, editors, *Anaphors in Texts. Cognitive, Formal and Applied Approaches to Anaphoric Reference*, pages 145–164. John Benjamins, Amsterdam.

António Branco, Tony McEnery, Ruslan Mitkov, and Fátima Silva, editors. 2007. *Proceedings of the 6th Discourse Anaphor and Anaphor Resolution Colloquium (DAARC 2007), Lagos (Algarve), Portugal, 2007, March 29-30.* Centro de Linguistica da Universidade do Porto, Porto.

Donna K. Byron and Whitney Gegg-Harrison. 2004. Evaluating optimality theory for pronoun resolution algorithm specification. In *Proceedings of the Discourse Anaphora and Reference Resolution Colloquium (DAARC 2004)*, pages 27–32, September.

Aoife Cahill and Arndt Riester. 2009. Incorporating information status into generation ranking. In *Proceedings of the Joint Conference of the 47th Annual Meeting of the ACL and the 4th International Joint Conference on Natural Language Processing of the AFNLP*, pages 817–825, Suntec, Singapore, August.

Lynn Carlson, Daniel Marcu, and Mary Ellen Okurowski. 2003. Building a discourse-tagged corpus in the framework of Rhetorical Structure Theory. In Jan van

Kuppevelt and Ronnie Smith, editors, *Current Directions in Discourse and Dialogue*, pages 85–112. Kluwer, Dordrecht.

Wallace Chafe. 1976. Giveness, contrastiveness, definiteness, subjects, topics, and point of view. In Charles N. Li, editor, *Subject and Topic*, pages 25–55. Academic Press, New York.

Wallace Chafe. 1994. *Discourse, Consiousness, and Time. The Flow and Displacement of Conscious Experience in Speaking and Writing*. University of Chicago Press, Chicago and London.

Christian Chiarcos. 2010. *Mental Salience and Grammatical Form*. Ph.D. thesis, Universität Potsdam, Jun.

Christian Chiarcos. 2011a. The mental salience framework. In Christian Chiarcos, Berry Claus, and Michael Grabski, editors, *Salience. Multidisciplinary Perspectives on Its Function in Discourse*. Mouton de Gruyer, Berlin.

Christian Chiarcos. 2011b. On the dimensons of discourse salience. *Bochumer Linguistische Arbeitsberichte*, 3:31–44, February.

Francis Cornish. 2007. Deictic, discourse-deictic and anaphoric uses of demonstrative expressions in English. In *Workshop on Anaphoric Uses of demonstrative Expressions at the 29th Annual Meeting of the DGfS*, Siegen.

Robert Dale and Ehud Reiter. 1995. Computational interpretation of the Gricean maxims in the generation of referring expressions. *Cognitive Science*, 2(19):233–263.

James Raymond Davis and Julia Hirschberg. 1988. Assigning intonational features in synthesized spoken directions. In *Proceedings of the 26th Annual Meeting of the Association for Computational Linguistics (ACL 1988)*, pages 187–193, Buffalo, June.

Holger Diessel. 2006. Demonstratives, joint attention, and the emergence of grammar. *Cognitive Linguistics*, 17:463–489.

Bonnie J. Dorr, Rebecca Green, Lori Levin, Owen Rambow, David Farwell, Nizar Habash, Stephen Helmreich, Eduard Hovy, Keith J. Miller, Teruko Mitamura, Florence Reeder, and Advaith Siddharthan. 2004. Semantic annotation and lexico-syntactic paraphrase. In *Proceedings of the Workshop on Building Lexical Resources from Semantically Annotated Corpora, LREC 2004*, Portugal.

Kerstin Eckert, Arndt Riester, and Katrin Schweitzer. 2011. A discourse information radio news database for linguistic analysis. unpublished ms. Institut für Maschinelle Sprachverarbeitung, Universität Stuttgart.

Konrad Ehlich. 1982. Anaphora and deixis: Same, similar, or different? In Robert J. Jarvella and Wolfgang Klein, editors, *Speech, Place and Action. Studies in Deixis and Related Topics*, pages 315–338. John Wiley, Chichester.

Katja Filippova and Michael Strube. 2007. The German vorfeld and local coherence. *Journal of Logic, Language and Information*, 16(4):465–485.

Charles J. Fillmore. 1977. Topics in lexical semantics. In Roger W. Cole, editor, *Current Issues in Linguistic Theory*, pages 76–138. Indiana University Press, Bloomington.

Talmy Givón, editor. 1983. *Topic Continuity in Discourse: A Quantitative Cross-Language Study*. John Benjamins, Amsterdam and Philadelphia.

Talmy Givón. 2001. *Syntax*. John Benjamins, Amsterdam and Philadelphia. 2nd, revised ed.

Barbara J. Grosz, Aravind K. Joshi, and Scott Weinstein. 1995. Centering: A framework for modelling the local coherence of discourse. *Computational Linguistics*, 21(2):203–225.

Jeanette K. Gundel, Nancy A. Hedberg, and Ron Zacharski. 1993. Cognitive status and the form of referring expressions in discourse. *Language*, 69(2):247–307.

Eva Hajičová and Ivana Kruijff-Korbayová. 1997. Topics and centers: A comparison of the salience-based approach and the Centering theory. *Prague Bulletin of Mathematical Linguistics*, 67:25–50.

Klaus von Heusinger. 1997. *Salienz und Referenz. Der Epsilonoperator in der Semantik der Nominalphrase und anaphorischer Pronomen*. Akademie Verlag, Berlin.

Laurent Itti, Geraint Rees, and John K. Tsotsos, editors. 2005. *Neurobiology of Attention*. Elsevier.

Laurent. Itti. 2003. Visual attention. In *Handbook of Brain Theory and Neural Networks*. 2nd edition.

Elsi Kaiser and John Trueswell. 2010. Investigating the interpretation of pronouns and demonstratives in Finnish: Going beyond salience. In Edward Gibson and Neal J. Pearlmutter, editors, *The Processing and Acquisition of Reference*. MIT Press, Cambridge, Mass.

John D. Kelleher. 2011. Visual salience and the other one. In Christian Chiarcos, Berry Claus, and Michael Grabski, editors, *Salience. Multidisciplinary Perspectives on Its Function in Discourse*. Mouton de Gruyer, Berlin.

Emiel Krahmer and Mariët Theune. 2002. Efficient contextsensitive generation of referring expressions. In Kees van Deemter and Rodger Kibble, editors, *Information Sharing: Reference and Presupposition in Language Generation and Interpretation*, pages 223–264. CSLI, Stanford.

Olga Krasavina and Christian Chiarcos. 2007. PoCoS - Potsdam Coreference Scheme. In *Proceedings of the*

Linguistic Annotation Workshop. Held in Conjunction with the ACL-2007, pages 156–163, Prague, Czech Republic, June.

Geert-Jan M. Kruijff, Ivana Kruijff-Korbayová, John Bateman, and Elke Teich. 2001. Linear order as higher-level decision: Information structure in strategic and tactical generation. In Helmut Horacek, editor, *Proceedings of the 8th European Workshop on Natural Language Generation*, pages 74–83, Toulouse, France, July 5-6.

Ronald W. Langacker. 1997. Constituency, dependency, and conceptual grouping. *Cognitive Linguistics*, 8:1–32.

Shalom Lappin and Herbert J. Leass. 1994. An algorithm for pronominal anaphora resolution: A critical evaluation. *Computational Linguistics*, 20(4):535–561.

Willem J.M. Levelt. 1989. *Speaking: From Intention to Articulation*. MIT Press.

Kathleen F. McCoy and Michael Strube. 1999. Generating anaphoric expressions: Pronoun or definite description? In *Proceedings of the ACL-1999 Workshop on the Relation of Discourse/Dialogue Structure and Reference*, pages 63–71, Maryland, June.

Ann E. Mulkern. 2007. Knowing who's important: Relative discourse salience and Irish pronominal forms. In Nancy A. Hedberg and Ron Zacharski, editors, *The Grammar-Pragmatics Interface: Essays in honor of Jeanette K. Gundel*, pages 113–142. John Benjamins, Amsterdam and Philadelphia.

Costanza Navaretta. 2002. Combining information structure and centering-based models of salience for resolving intersentential pronominal anaphora. In Antonio Branco, Tony McEnery, and Ruslan Mitkov, editors, *Proceedings of the 4th Discourse Anaphora and Anaphora Resolution Colloquium (DAARC 2002)* , pages 135–140, Lisbon, September 18-29.

Andrew Ortony, R.J. Vondruska, M.A. Foss, and J.E. Jones. 1985. Salience, similes and the asymmetry of similarity. *Journal of Memory and Language*, 24:569–594.

Thiyagarajasarma Pattabhiraman. 1992. *Aspects of Salience in Natural Language Generation*. Ph.D. thesis, Simon Fraser University, August.

Massimo Poesio, Barbara Di Eugenio, Rosemary Stevenson, and Janet Hitzeman. 2004. Centering: A parametric theory and its instantiations. *Computational linguistics*, 30(3):309–363.

Ellen F. Prince. 1981. Toward a taxonomy of given-new information. In P. Cole, editor, *Radical Pragmatics*, pages 223–256. Academic Press, New York.

Regina Pustet. 1995. Obviation and subjectivization: The same basic phenomenon? A study of participant marking in Blackfoot. *Studies in Language*, 19:37–72.

Chris Reed. 2002. Saliency and the attentional state in natural language generation. In *Proceedings of the 15th European Conference on Artificial Intelligence (ECAI 2002)*, pages 440–444, Lyon, France.

Michael Schiehlen. 2004. Optimizing algorithms for pronoun resolution. In *Proceedings of the 20th International Conference on Computational Linguistics (COLING)*, pages 515–521, Geneva, August.

Petr Sgall, Eva Hajićová, and Jarmila Panevova. 1986. *The Meaning of the Sentence in its Semantic and Pragmatic Aspects*. Reidel, Dordrecht.

Shun Shiramatsu, Kazunori Komatani, Kôiti Hasida, Tetsuya Ogata, and Hiroshi G. Okuno. 2007. Meaning-game-based Centering model with statistical definition of utility of referential expression and its verification using Japanese and English corpora. In *(Branco et al., 2007)*, pages 121–126.

Wojciech Skut, Brigitte Krenn, Thorsten Brants, and Hans Uszkoreit. 1997. An annotation scheme for free word order languages. In *Proceedings of the 5th Conference on Applied Natural Language Processing (ANLP)*, Washington, D.C.

Manfred Stede. 1998. A generative perspective on verb alternations. *Computational Linguistics*, 24(3):401–429.

Manfred Stede. 2004. The Potsdam Commentary Corpus. In Bonnie Webber and Donna K. Byron, editors, *Proceedings of the ACL-2004 Workshop on Discourse Annotation*, pages 96–102, Barcelona, July.

Michael Strube and Udo Hahn. 1999. Functional Centering - Grounding referential coherence in information structure. *Computational Linguistics*, 25(3):309–344.

Leonard Talmy. 2000. *Toward a Cognitive Semantics*, volume I. Concept Structuring Systems. MIT Press, Cambridge and London.

Russel S. Tomlin. 1995. Focal attention, voice, and word order. An experimental, cross-linguistic study. In Mickey Noonan and Pamela Downing, editors, *Word Order in Discourse*, pages 517–554. John Benjamins, Amsterdam and Philadelphia.

Ielka van der Sluis and Emiel Krahmer. 2001. Generating referring expressions in a multimodal context: An empirically oriented approach. In Walter Daelemans et al., editor, *Selected Papers from the 11th CLIN Meeting*. Rodopi, Amsterdam and Atlanta.

Sina Zarrieß, Aoife Cahill, and Jonas Kuhn. 2011. Underspecifying and predicting voice for surface realisation ranking. In *Proceedings of the 49th Annual Meeting of the Association for Computational Linguistics: Human Language Technologies*, pages 1007–1017, Portland, Oregon, USA, June. Association for Computational Linguistics.

The Impact of Visual Context on the Content of Referring Expressions

Jette Viethen[1,2]
h.a.e.viethen@uvt.nl
[1]TiCC
University of Tilburg
Tilburg, The Netherlands

Robert Dale[2]
robert.dale@mq.edu.au
[2]Centre for Language Technology
Macquarie University
Sydney, Australia

Markus Guhe[3]
m.guhe@ed.ac.uk
[3]School of Informatics
University of Edinburgh
Edinburgh, UK

Abstract

Traditional approaches to referring expression generation (REG) have taken as a fundamental requirement the need to distinguish the intended referent from other entities in the context. It seems obvious that this should be a necessary condition for successful reference; but we suggest that a number of recent investigations cast doubt on the significance of this aspect of reference. In the present paper, we look at the role of visual context in determining the content of a referring expression, and come to the conclusion that, at least in the referential scenarios underlying our data, visual context appears *not* to be a major factor in content determination for reference. We discuss the implications of this surprising finding.

1 Introduction

Traditional approaches to referring expression generation are based on the idea of distinguishing the intended referent from the other entities in the context (Dale and Reiter, 1995; Gardent, 2002; Krahmer and Theune, 2002; Krahmer et al., 2003; Gatt and van Deemter, 2006). The task is generally characterised as involving the construction of a *distinguishing description* consisting of those attributes of the intended referent that distinguish it from the other entities with which it might be confused; building a referring expression thus requires us to have an appropriate formalisation of the notion of *context*. Earlier work (for example, (Dale, 1989)) took its cue from work on discourse structure (in particular, (Grosz and Sidner, 1986)), and defined the context in terms of the set of discourse-accessible referents; more recent work has tended to focus on visual scenes (for example, (Viethen and Dale, 2006; Gatt et al., 2008; Gatt et al., 2009)), with the context being defined as the set of all the objects in the scene.

Most of the early approaches to REG (Dale, 1989; Dale and Haddock, 1991; Dale and Reiter, 1995; Krahmer et al., 2003) were proposed without the support of rigorous empirical testing. Probably the most fundamental shift in the field in the last five years has been the move towards the development of algorithms that attempt to replicate corpora of human-produced referring expressions. This work has only really become possible with the advent of a number of publicly-available corpora of human-produced referring expressions collected under controlled circumstances: these include the TUNA Corpus (van der Sluis et al., 2006), the Drawer Corpus (Viethen and Dale, 2006), and the GRE3D3 and GRE3D7 Corpora (Viethen and Dale, 2008; Viethen and Dale, 2011). All of these corpora contain descriptions of target referents using a small number of attributes in simple visual scenes containing only a very small number of distractor objects. The descriptions in all these cases were elicited in isolation, with no preceding discourse: the reference task they represent has sometimes been called 'one-shot reference'. So there is no *discourse* context that provides a set of potential distractors, but there is a *visual* context of potential distractors.

The idea that the process of constructing a reference to an object in a visual scene needs to take account of the other entities in that scene in order to ensure that the reference is successful seems so obvious that it might be thought ridiculous to doubt it. However, our exploration of a dataset that contains referring expressions for objects in visual scenes of somewhat greater complexity and involving dialogic discourse calls this fundamental assumption into question.

In (Viethen et al., 2011), we presented a machine-learning approach to REG, and distinguished two main kinds of features that might play a role in subsequent reference: 'traditional' REG features, which are concerned with distinguishing the intended referent from visual and discourse distractors; and 'alignment' features, representing aspects of the discourse history (Clark and Wilkes-Gibbs, 1986; Pickering and Garrod, 2004). We used feature ablation in a decision tree approach to investigate the role of the traditional features, and found that the impact of these features was negligible compared to that of the alignment features. The bad performance of these features caused us to ask whether the method of determining

Proceedings of the 13th European Workshop on Natural Language Generation (ENLG), pages 44–52,
Nancy, France, September 2011.

the visual distractors that were taken into account was to be blamed. In the present paper, we explore this question by trying out two different ways of determining the set of visual distractors and by varying the size of this set.

In Section 2 we provide some background by situating the investigation presented here with respect to the literature. In Section 3, we describe the corpus we work with, and in Section 4, we describe our machine-learning framework for exploring the data this corpus provides. In Section 5, we present the results of some experiments that attempt to determine the role of visual context in REG, and in Section 6 we draw some conclusions.

2 Background

Some of the earliest work in REG (for example, (Dale, 1989)) adopted what we might think of as an 'extreme rationalist' characterisation of the task: build a description that has no more and no less information than is required to distinguish the intended referent (a *minimal distinguishing description*).

It was soon recognised that this was not a good characterisation of what people did, in particular because human-produced descriptions are often over-specified, rather than being minimal in the sense just described. The incremental algorithm (IA; (Dale and Reiter, 1995)) diluted the extreme position with the acknowledgement that something akin to habit also played a role in REG: the basic idea here was that, on the basis of experience, people learn 'preference orders' for properties that tend to work well, and when faced with the need to create a new description, they use these preference orders to guide the search for an appropriate description. The IA still hung on to the need to build a distinguishing description, but the preference order mechanism meant that some descriptions might be longer than necessary, containing redundant information.

In (Dale and Viethen, 2010), we proposed a further weakening of the traditional model, suggesting that attributes in a referring expression might be chosen independently, rather in a fashion whereby each depends on the attributes previously chosen (a characteristic of earlier algorithms that we refer to as *serial dependency*). But even this attribute-centric model takes the view that the discriminatory power of the individual attributes plays a role in decision-making. The requirement that we should take account of the context in determining how to refer to something has thus been kept more or less centre-stage in computational work through the last 20 years or so.

Meanwhile, work in psycholinguistics has explored the idea that quite orthogonal factors are at play in choosing the content of descriptions. Starting with the early work of Carroll (1980), a distinct strand of research has explored how a speaker's form of reference to an entity is impacted by the way that entity has been previously referred to in the discourse or dialogue. The general idea behind what we will call the *alignment approach* is that a conversational participant will often adopt the same semantic, syntactic and lexical alternatives as the other party in a dialogue. This perspective is most strongly associated with the work of Pickering and Garrod (2004). With respect to reference in particular, speakers are said to form *conceptual pacts* in their use of language (Clark and Wilkes-Gibbs, 1986; Brennan and Clark, 1996). The implication of much of this work is that one speaker introduces an entity by means of some description, and then (perhaps after some negotiation) both conversational participants share this form of reference, or a form of reference derived from it, when they subsequently refer to that entity. Recent work by Goudbeek and Krahmer (2010) supports the view that subconscious alignment does indeed take place at the level of content selection for referring expressions: the participants in their study were more likely to use a dispreferred attribute to describe a target referent if this attribute had recently been used in a description by a confederate.

One way of characterising these developments is that, on the one hand, the original very precise and somewhat rigid computational approaches to REG have been progressively weakened in the face of real human data; and on the other hand, work in a distinct discipline has offered a quite separate view of how reference works. Of course, these two broad approaches may not be incompatible. The truth may lie 'in-between', involving insights and ideas from both ways of thinking about the problem. In the present paper we aim to put one of the remaining fundamental tenets of the computational approaches to the test: does visual context really matter when we construct a referring expression?

3 Referring Expressions in the iMAP Corpus

The iMAP Corpus (Louwerse et al., 2007) is a collection of 256 dialogues between 32 participant-pairs who contributed 8 dialogues each. Both participants had a map of the same environment, but one participant's map showed a route winding its way between the landmarks on the map (see Figure 1 for examples). The task was for this participant, the instruction giver (IG), to describe the route in such a way that their partner, the instruction follower (IF), could draw it onto their map; this was complicated by some discrepancies between the two maps, such as missing landmarks, the unavailability of colour in some regions due to ink stains, and small differences between some landmarks. Note that the maps contain a relatively large number of objects compared to the visual stimuli used in other REG corpora.

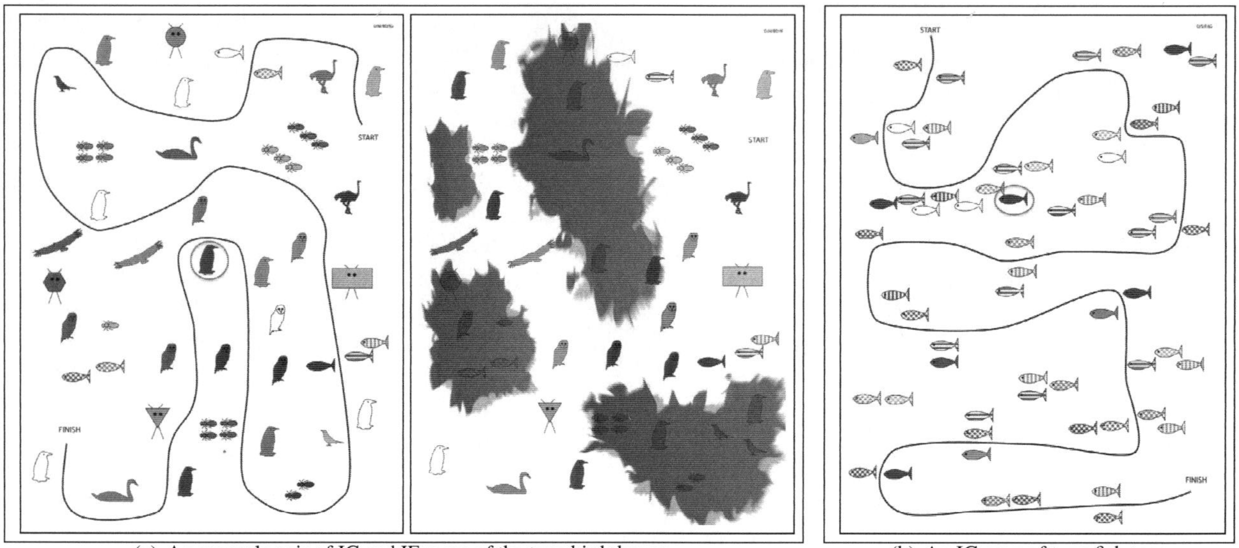

(a) An example pair of IG and IF maps of the type bird+house.

(b) An IG map of type fish+car.

Figure 1: Three example maps.

There are eight types of landmarks, grouped into pairs of one animate and one inanimate type each: alien+trafficsign, bird+house, fish+car, and bugs+trees. Each of these pairs defines a map type, which contains landmarks which are mostly of one of the two types of the pair. Half of the maps contain a few landmarks of types other than the main type; for example, a bird+house map contains mostly birds or houses, but might also contain a small number of other landmarks. The maps in Figure 1(a) are bird+house maps containing mainly birds with a few landmarks of other types mixed in, and the map in Figure 1(b) is an unmixed fish–car map for the IG, containing only fish landmarks. Note the high density of landmarks on the map in Figure 1(b) compared to those in Figure 1(a) (each cluster of same-coloured bugs on the bird maps counts as a single landmark). Overall there are 32 maps, which differ by the map type (four levels), the animatedness of the landmark types (two levels, e.g. fish vs. cars), the mixedness of the landmark types (two levels: only the main landmark type or also a few landmarks of different types), and the shape of the ink blots on the IF's map (two levels: one large blot or several smaller ones).

Apart from their type, the landmarks differ in colour, and one other attribute, which is different for each type of landmark. For example, there are different *kinds* of birds and houses (eagle, ostrich, penguin, ...; church, castle, ...); fish and cars differ by their *patterns* (dotted, checkered, plain, ...), aliens and traffic signs have different *shapes* (circular, hexagonal, ...), and bugs and trees appear in small clusters of differing *numbers*. In addition to these three inherent attributes of the landmarks, participants used spatial relations to other items on the map. Each of the 34,403 referring expression in the corpus is annotated with the semantic values of the attributes that it contains. This collection of annotations forms the basic data we use in our experiments.

We removed from the data all referring expressions that made reference to more than one landmark and those—in particular, pronouns—that did not contain any of the four main landmark attributes, type, colour, relation, or the landmark's other distinguishing attribute. However, all filtered expressions are taken into account in the computation of the features for the machine learner. The final data set contains 22,727 referring expressions, of which 6,369 are initial references and 16,358 are subsequent references.

We can think of each referring expression as being realised from a *content pattern*: this is the collection of attributes that are used in that description. The attributes can be derived from the property-level annotation given in the corpus. So, for example, if a particular reference appears as the noun phrase *the blue penguin*, annotated semantically as ⟨blue, penguin⟩, then the corresponding content pattern is ⟨colour, kind⟩. Our aim is to replicate the content pattern of each referring expression in the corpus. Table 1 lists the 15 content patterns that occur in our data set in order of frequency.

The high frequency of the ⟨other⟩ pattern is in part due to the annotation of the kind of birds and houses as other, which could also be argued to be a more fine-grained type attribute. We accepted this annotation as it was provided in the corpus, but we may alter it in future studies.

Content Pattern	Count	Proportion
⟨other⟩	7561	33.27%
⟨other, type⟩	5975	26.29%
⟨other, colour⟩	2364	10.40%
⟨other, colour, type⟩	1954	8.60%
⟨colour⟩	1029	4.53%
⟨relation⟩	796	3.50%
⟨other, relation⟩	738	3.25%
⟨type⟩	662	2.91%
⟨colour, type⟩	596	2.62%
⟨other, relation, type⟩	463	2.04%
⟨relation, type⟩	262	1.15%
⟨other, colour, relation⟩	124	0.55%
⟨colour, relation⟩	101	0.44%
⟨other, colour, relation, type⟩	82	0.36%
⟨colour, relation, type⟩	20	0.09%
total	22,727	

Table 1: The 15 different content patterns that occur in our data and their frequencies.

Map Features	
Main_Map_type	most frequent type of LM on this map
Main_Map_other	other attribute if the most frequent type of LM
Mixedness	are other LM types present on this map?
Ink_Orderliness	shape of the ink blot(s) on the IF's map
LMprop Features	
other_Att	type of the other attribute of the target
*[att]*_Value	value for each *att* of target
*[att]*_Difference	was *att* of target different between the two maps?
Missing	was target missing one of the maps?
Inked_Out	was target inked]_out on the IG's map?
Speaker Features	
Dyad_ID	ID of the pair of participant-pair
Speaker_ID	ID of the person who uttered this RE
Speaker_Role	was the speaker the IG or the IF?

Table 2: The Map, LMProp and Speaker feature sets.

Visual TradREG Features	
Count_Vis_Distractors	number of visual distractors
Prop_Vis_Same_*[att]*	proportion of visual distractors with same *att*
Dist_Closest	distance to the closest visual distractor
Closest_Same_*[att]*	has the closest distractor the same *att*?
Dist_Closest_Same_*[att]*	distance to the closest distractor of same *att* as target
Cl_Same_type_Same_*[att]*	has the closest distractor of the same type also the same *att*?
Discourse TradREG Features	
Count_Intervening_LMs	number of other LMs mentioned since the last mention of the target
Prop_Intervening_*[att]*	proportion of intervening LMs for which *att* was used AND which have the same *att* as target

Table 3: The TradREG feature set.

4 A Machine Learning Approach to Content Determination

The number of factors that can be hypothesised as having an impact on the form of a referring expression in a dialogic setting associated with a visual domain is very large. Attempting to incorporate all of these factors into parameters for a rule-based system, and then experimenting with different settings for these parameters, is prohibitively complex. Instead, we here capture a wide range of factors as features that can be used by a machine learning algorithm to automatically induce from the data a classifier that predicts for a given set of feature values the attributes that should be used in a referring expression.

The features we extracted from the data set are outlined in Tables 2–4.[1] They fall into a number of subsets. **Map** features capture design characteristics of the map-pair the current dialogue is about; **Speaker** features capture the identity and role of the participants; and **LMprop** features capture the inherent visual properties of the target referent. The **TradREG** features allow the machine learner to capture factors that the traditional computational approaches to referring expression generation take account of. Of particular interest for our present considerations are the **Visual TradREG** features, which represent knowledge about the visual context. **Alignment** features capture factors that we would expect to play a role in the psycholinguistic models of alignment and conceptual pacts. When we refer to the complete feature set, we use the abbreviation **allF**.

For our experiments, we use the Weka Toolkit (Witten and Frank, 2005) to learn one decision tree for each of the four attributes which decides whether or not to include that attribute. We then combine the attributes for which a positive decision was made into a content pattern that can be compared to the content pattern found in the corpus for the same instance.[2]

In (Viethen et al., 2011) we showed that dropping the complete TradREG feature set from allF does not decrease the performance of this model on subsequent reference. The relevant numbers from that experiment are shown in italics in the first two lines of Table 5.

One question this kind of work raises is: just what gets included in the visual context? Considering that most of the TradREG features depend on the visual context, it might be possible that the lack of impact of this feature set was due to the size of the visual context having been chosen incorrectly. A second consideration is that the TradREG features might have more of an impact on

[1] In these tables, *att* is an abbreviatory variable that is instantiated once for each of the four attributes type, colour, relation, and the other distinguishing attribute of the landmark. The abbreviation LM stands for landmark.

[2] We also tried an alternative approach of learning the whole content pattern at once with very similar results, which we do not report here due to space limitations.

Alignment Features – Recency	
Last_Men_Speaker_Same	who made the last mention of target?
Last_Mention_*[att]*	was *att* used in the last mention of target?
Dist_Last_Mention_Utts	distance to the last mention of target in utterances
Dist_Last_Mention_REs	distance to the last mention of target in REs
Dist_Last_*[att]*_LM_Utts	distance in utterances to last use of *att* for target
Dist_Last_*[att]*_LM_REs	distance in REs to last use of *att* for target
Dist_Last_*[att]*_Dial_Utts	distance in utterances to last use of *att*
Dist_Last_*[att]*_Dial_REs	distance in REs to last use of *att*
Dist_Last_RE_Utts	distance to last RE in utterances
Last_RE_*[att]*	was *att* mentioned in the last RE?
Alignment Features – Frequency	
Count_*[att]*_Dial	how often has *att* been used in the dialogue?
Count_*[att]*_LM	how often has *att* been used for target?
Quartile	quartile of the dialogue the RE was uttered in
Dial_No	number of dialogues already completed +1
Mention_No	number of previous mentions of target +1

Table 4: The Alignment feature set.

initial reference than on the subsequent referring expressions that were at focus in our previous work. We explore these possibilities next.

5 The Effects of Variation in Visual Context

In (Viethen et al., 2011), the size of the visual context was set for each map type in such a way that each landmark on any map of that type would have six distractors on average. We will refer to this way of setting the visual context size as *average–6*.

Because we are here particularly interested in the performance of the features that depend on the visual context (i.e., the Visual TradREG features), we performed two more ablation steps, in which we separately excluded only the Visual TradREG features and the Discourse TradREG features for both subsequent and initial references. Table 5 confirms that, using the *average–6* method to determine the visual context, the Visual TradREG features have no significant effect for either subsequent or initial referring expressions on the Accuracy with which the model replicates the referring expressions in our corpus. Perhaps surprisingly, this is true not only for subsequent reference, but also for initial reference, where one might expect that distinguishing from the visual context would be of more importance.

Considering the difference in density and uniformity of landmarks on the different types of maps (compare Figure 1(a) with 42 diversely shaped landmarks in the IG map to Figure 1(b) with 59 uniformly shaped landmarks), we wondered whether the *average–6* method of setting the visual context might be too inflexible. For example, one might hypothesise that fewer surrounding objects might get taken into account in describing the blue penguin marked by a circle in the left map in Figure 1(a) than in describing the purple fish marked by a circle in Figure 1(b).

	all	initial	subseq.
allF	61.5%	68.6%	*58.8%*
allF – TradREG	61.3%	69.4%	*58.2%*
allF – Discourse TradREG	61.3%	68.6%	58.4%
allF – Visual TradREG	61.6%	69.4%	58.5%
no of REs	22727	6369	16358

Table 5: Ablation of Discourse and Visual TradREG features using *average–6* to determine the visual context. Performance is measured in percentage of perfect matches. Numbers in italics were prevously reported in (Viethen et al., 2011).

We therefore split our data into four sets according to the four different map types and tried out a range of different visual context sizes for each type separately. Two different ways of determining the visual context might be at play. One possibility is that people might indeed be taking into account (roughly) the same number of surrounding objects for each landmark, while this number might be different for different map types due to their different landmark densities. We call this the *count* method of determining the visual context. Alternatively, one might draw an imaginary circle around each landmark, and consider all objects whose centres fall within the radius of this circle to be distractors. We call this the *distance* method of determining the visual context.

In order to explore whether there is one 'correct' size of visual context for each map type, we tried all distances from 0 to 675 pixels in 15 pixel steps (each map is 488× 675 pixels) and all possible distractor counts from 0 to 61 (the maximum number of landmarks on the most dense map pair is 61). If the bad performance of the Visual TradREG features so far was indeed due to the visual context being too inflexible or set incorrectly, we would expect to find at least one visual context size for each map type that outperforms all others. There should also be a peak of performance around that size, with the performance falling if the size grows or shrinks from the ideal size (if the visual context is set too small, we might expect to see references containing too many attributes; if the visual context is set too large, we might expect to see references with too few attributes).

We trained the decision trees on 80% of the data for each map type and tested on the remaining 20%. The training–test splits were stratified for the content patterns of the referring expressions, the Speaker_IDs of the participants who produced the expressions, and the Quartiles of the dialogue in which the references occurred. Table 6

map type	train	test	total
alien+sign	4,425	967	5,392
fish+car	4,021	813	4,834
bird+house	5,492	1,264	6,756
tree+bug	4,703	1,042	5,745
total	18,641	4,086	22,727

Table 6: Sizes of the training and test sets for the different map types.

maptype	best sizes	all REs	best sizes	initial REs	best sizes	subseq. REs
alien+sign	43	63.5%	5	68.3%	43	62.5%
fish+car	44, 46	59.2%	43	60.6%	13	59.0%
house+ bird	3, 22	72.6%	22	75.6%	13, 19, 28	71.8%
trees+ bugs	3	70.5%	0, 1, 3, 11, 12	74.8%	33	68.4%
weighted average		67.1%		71.1%		65.9%
all maps *average-6*		61.5%		68.6%		58.8%

Table 7: Maximum possible Accuracy using all features achieved by choosing the best performing visual context by the *count* method for each map type, compared to the performance of the *average-6* visual contexts.

maptype	best sizes	all REs	best sizes	initial REs	best sizes	subsequ. REs
alien+sign	90, 105	59.5%	90	65.1%	240, 285	57.9%
fish+car	75	57.3%	75, 180	62.4%	75	55.9%
house+ bird	150	73.3%	300, 540-675	74.8%	480	73.4%
trees+ bugs	210	70.4%	585, 660, 675	76.6%	210, 420, 525	67.2%
weighted average		65.9%		70.9%		64.3%
all maps *average-6*		61.5%		68.6%		58.8%

Table 8: Maximum possible Accuracy using all features achieved by choosing the best performing visual context by the *distance* method for each map type, compared to the performance of the *average-6* visual contexts.

shows the sizes of the four different training–test splits.

Table 7 shows that if we choose the best performing count of distractors for each map type, the overall performance (weighted average over all map types) does indeed improve over the old *average-6* method of choosing the visual context. Table 8 shows the same results for the distance method of determining the visual context. (For both methods $p \ll 0.01$, using the χ^2 statistic with $df = 1$ for all, initial, and subsequent references.)

However, Figures 2 to 5 demonstrate that there is no consistent effect of the size of the visual context on the performance of our model using the *number* method of setting visual context sizes. None of the graphs show a clear performance peak around one particular visual context; instead, performance oscillates in a fairly narrow percentage band both when using all features and when using only the Visual TradREG features that are directly impacted by the visual context. For most map types it becomes clear that even a model using only the features that are not affected by the visual context (the flat lines labelled *noVisualTrad*) outperforms allF with many of the settings for visual context size. This means that, unless we are certain that we are using the best performing setting for visual context, using the Visual TradREG features is risky, as choosing the wrong visual context can easily lead to a worse match with human behaviour.

For space reasons we do not show all four graphs for the *distance* method. However, Figure 6 shows the performance for all map types when using all feature sets. Again, the performance oscillates as the size of the visual context varies, rather than showing a real peak around an ideal context size.

Although the performance of the overall system can be increased over the old *average-6* method by setting the visual context to a map type-specific optimum, these results show that this increase is somewhat a matter of luck. Short of trying out (almost) all possible sizes of the visual context, as we did here, there is no systematic way in which to determine the size of the visual context that gives the best performance; and by using features dependent on the visual context one might just as likely hit on a visual context that decreases performance. The oscillations in the graphs in Figures 2 to 6 indicate that it is unlikely that people are taking the visual content into account in the way that our model suggests.

6 Discussion

In this paper we have put forward what might be considered a rather heretical position: that during the construction of a referring expression, contrary to what is assumed by much work in the field, a speaker does not seem to take account of the visual context of reference. Using a collection of human-produced referring expressions of landmarks on moderately complex maps, we have shown that there is no principled way in which to determine a visual context that might make a significant difference to the ability of a machine-learned algorithm to replicate the human data. The implication of this would seem to be that humans generate referring expressions with little regard for the visual context, or at least that the role of visual context is masked by other factors (such as alignment) that play a bigger role. So, we might conclude that

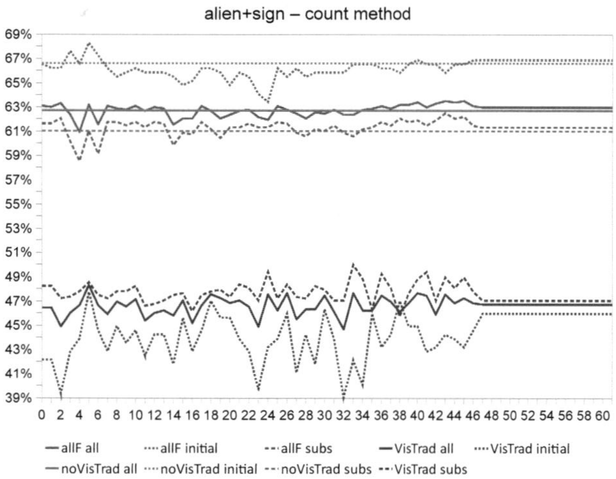

Figure 2: Accuracy for different visual contexts (determined by the *count* method) for the alien+sign maps.

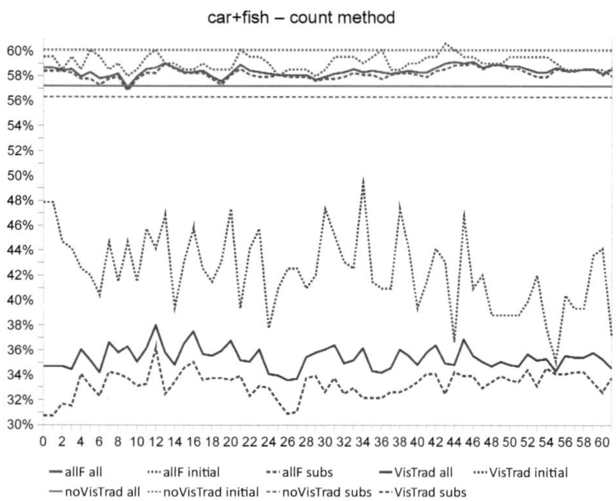

Figure 3: Accuracy for different visual contexts (determined by the *count* method) for the fish+car maps .

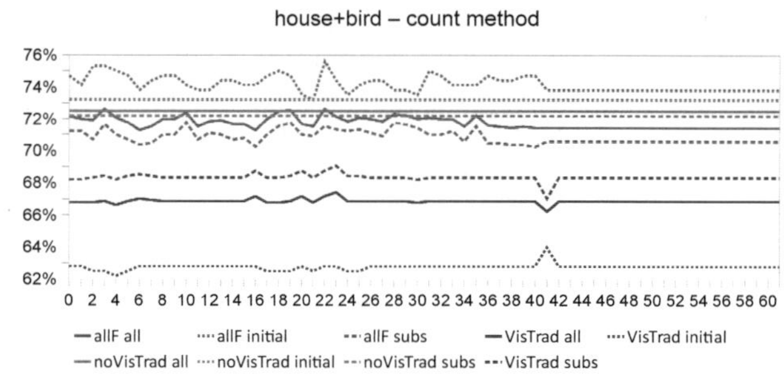

Figure 4: Accuracy for different visual contexts (determined by the *count* method) for the bird+house maps.

Figure 5: Accuracy for different visual contexts (determined by the *count* method) for the bugs+trees maps.

the view that reference is about deliberately constructing distinguishing descriptions should be considered suspect.

It could be argued that this is a somewhat plausible position if we look only at *subsequent* reference as we did in (Viethen et al., 2011): once an entity has been introduced into the discourse, perhaps how it is referred to subsequently depends more on the preceding discourse than it does on the visual context at the time of reference. Indeed, once an entity has been referred to, the description that has been constructed 'factors in' the visual context, and so any subsequent reference to that entity does not require re-computation of the description; referring to the entity in the way that it was referred to before should still do the job (unless, of course, the context has changed in some relevant way). Such a model has the twin appeals of being both more computationally efficient, and consistent with explanations based on the alignment approach.

But surely, we would want to say, context must still be taken account of when constructing an initial reference; and if the context is a visual one, then that first reference constructed needs to distinguish the intended referent from the other entities in the scene. Surprisingly, even here, our experimental results support the view that visual context doesn't matter.

So what's going on? Intuition suggests that, in real world scenes, we *do* take account of the distinguishing ability of our referring expressions; when we describe an intended referent, we do not do so blindly without considering whether the referring expression might be confusing or ambiguous. But our data suggests, at least in the scenarios we have looked at, that this is not the case.

One possible explanation is that neither of the two ways of determining the visual context that we tried out in our experiments accurately models the visual context that the speakers in our corpus take into account. Firstly, while acknowledging that there are differences between the different types of maps that might influence the number of distractors to be taken into account, we still kept

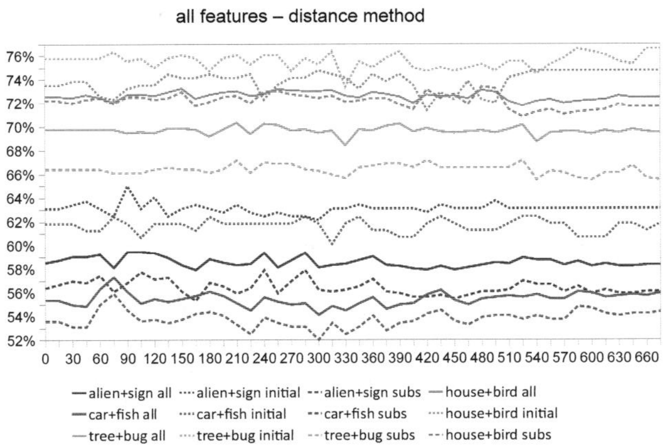

Figure 6: Accuracy for different visual contexts determined by the *distance* method for all map types.

the size of the visual context constant for all landmarks on a given map. It is conceivable that this is still too simplistic an assumption and that distractor numbers have to be determined on a landmark-by-landmark basis instead. For instance, it is likely that, at least for the IG, the course of the path influences the shape of the visual context, with objects along the path being more likely to be taken into account than those further away. This is a consideration that was taken into account to some extent by Guhe (2007; 2009). Similarly, what counts as the visual context is probably influenced by the linguistic context as well. For example, in uttering as well as resolving an instruction such as *go left until you get to the red alien*, the red alien has to be distinguished mostly from objects to its right and not so much from anything that lies beyond it to its left.

To explore these kinds of hypotheses, a lot more preparatory work would be necessary. The dialogues would need to be annotated with information about the point on the path that the IG and IF have reached, and with possibly relevant information in the dialogue context. However, to obtain a more definite answer to the question of which landmarks are taken into account when people refer in dialogue, we will ultimately have to look beyond the text of the dialogue transcriptions. With technologies such as eye-tracking it might be possible to reveal which other landmarks speakers look at while or before they construct a referring expression.

Another possible explanation for the surprising outcome of our experiment is that our scenarios are too simple: they do not reflect the complexity of real-world visual scenes, and so the complex mechanisms we think are required for REG more generally are simply not required in these simple scenes. Rather than compute a reference that takes account of the context, the subjects in the iMAP Task perhaps recognise that the scenes are simple enough to use referring expressions that are not carefully computed on the basis of context.

But this then raises a methodological issue. An assumption implicit in much recent work on evaluation in REG is that, by initially using simplistic domains and tasks, the in-principle capabilities of algorithms can be tested before scaling up to more complex real-world settings. The visual scenarios that are represented by the TUNA Corpus, the Drawer Corpus, and the GRE3D3 and GRE3D7 Corpora are very abstract and arguably quite unlike any real-world scenes where a speaker needs to construct a reference. For the work presented here, we attempted to consider more 'realistic' scenes involving speakers discussing larger numbers of objects in a distinct task; but even here, the scenario is still very simple with much fewer attributes to choose from than speaker are usually presented with when referring 'in the wild'. But if this is the case, then what do we learn by developing algorithms that work in these simple scenarios?

We do not believe that the idea that human speakers deliberately build distinguishing descriptions in order to uniquely identify their intended referents should be abandoned: this seems to us a fundamentally important aspect of successful referential behaviour. But if we want to understand how it is that people do this, we should be wary of thinking we can learn about these processes by looking at how people refer in vastly simplified models of the real world. To move forward, we need to focus on the complexity of real-world reference scenarios.

7 Conclusions

Traditional REG algorithms are based on the aim of distinguishing the target referent from the other objects in its context. However, using a corpus of maptask dialogues, we found in earlier work that using features based on the same considerations as those underlying the traditional REG algorithms does not help in machine learning which attributes people use in a given situation. In this paper, we used two different methods of varying the size of the visual context that gets taken into account in computing the values for these features. We found that it is not possible to systematically determine an ideal context size using these methods, which seems to point to the conclusion that, for the speakers in our corpus, visual context was not an important consideration. Alternatively, even more fine-grained methods of determining the visual context than those we tried might be necessary, or the scenarios on the maps underlying our corpus are too simplistic to elicit real-world behaviour from the speakers. This points to the conclusion that it might be time for the field to move on to more complex visual scenes when researching content selection mechanisms for referring expression generation.

References

Susan E. Brennan and Herbert H. Clark. 1996. Conceptual pacts and lexical choice in conversation. *Journal of Experimental Psychology: Learning, Memory, and Cognition*, 22:1482–1493.

John M. Carroll. 1980. Naming and describing in social communication. *Language and Speech*, 23:309–322.

Herbert H. Clark and Deanna Wilkes-Gibbs. 1986. Referring as a collaborative process. *Cognition*, 22(1):1–39.

Robert Dale and Nicholas Haddock. 1991. Generating referring expressions involving relations. In *Proceedings of the 5th Conference of the European Chapter of the Association for Computational Linguistics*, pages 161–166, Berlin, Germany.

Robert Dale and Ehud Reiter. 1995. Computational interpretations of the Gricean maxims in the generation of referring expressions. *Cognitive Science*, 19(2):233–263.

Robert Dale and Jette Viethen. 2010. Attribute-centric referring expression generation. In Emiel Krahmer and Marit Theune, editors, *Empirical Methods in Natural Language Generation*, volume 5980 of *Lecture Notes in Computer Science*, pages 163–179. Springer.

Robert Dale. 1989. Cooking up referring expressions. In *Proceedings of the 27th Annual Meeting of the Association for Computational Linguistics*, Vancouver BC, Canada.

Claire Gardent. 2002. Generating minimal definite descriptions. In *Proceedings of the 40th Annual Meeting of the Association for Computational Linguistics*, pages 96–103, Philadelphia PA, USA.

Albert Gatt and Kees van Deemter. 2006. Conceptual coherence in the generation of referring expressions. In *Proceedings of the 21st International Conference on Computational Linguistics and the 44th Annual Meeting of the Association for Computational Linguistics*, pages 255–262, Sydney, Australia.

Albert Gatt, Anja Belz, and Eric Kow. 2008. The TUNA Challenge 2008: Overview and evaluation results. In *Proceedings of the 5th International Conference on Natural Language Generation*, pages 198–206, Salt Fork OH, USA.

Albert Gatt, Anja Belz, and Eric Kow. 2009. The TUNA-REG Challenge 2009: Overview and evaluation results. In *Proceedings of the 12th European Workshop on Natural Language Generation*, pages 174–182, Athens, Greece.

Martijn Goudbeek and Emiel Krahmer. 2010. Preferences versus adaptation during referring expression generation. In *Proceedings of the 48th Annual Meeting of the Association for Computational Linguistics*, pages 55–59, Uppsala, Sweden.

Barbara J. Grosz and Candance L. Sidner. 1986. Attention, intentions, and the structure of discourse. *Computational Linguistics*, 12(3):175–204.

Markus Guhe. 2007. Marking theme and rheme in preverbal messages. In *Proceedings of the Seventh International Workshop on Computational Semantics*, pages 330–333, Tilburg, The Netherlands.

Markus Guhe. 2009. Generating referring expressions with a cognitive model. In *Proceedings of the Workshop Production of Referring Expressions: Bridging the Gap between Computational and Empirical Approaches to Reference*, Amsterdam, The Netherlands.

Emiel Krahmer and Mariët Theune. 2002. Efficient context-sensitive generation of referring expressions. In Kees van Deemter and Rodger Kibble, editors, *Information Sharing: Reference and Presupposition in Language Generation and Interpretation*, pages 223–264. CSLI Publications, Stanford CA, USA.

Emiel Krahmer, Sebastiaan van Erk, and André Verleg. 2003. Graph-based generation of referring expressions. *Computational Lingustics*, 29(1):53–72.

Max M. Louwerse, Nick Benesh, Mohammed E. Hoque, Patrick Jeuniaux, Gwyneth Lewis, Jie Wu, and Megan Zirnstein. 2007. Multimodal communication in face-to-face computer-mediated conversations. In *Proceedings of the 28th Annual Conference of the Cognitive Science Society*, pages 1235–1240.

Martin J. Pickering and Simon Garrod. 2004. Toward a mechanistic psychology of dialogue. *Behavioral and Brain Sciences*, 27(2):169–226.

Ielka van der Sluis, Albert Gatt, and Kees van Deemter. 2006. Manual for the TUNA corpus: Referring expressions in two domains. Technical Report AUCS/TR0705, Computing Department, University of Aberdeen, UK.

Jette Viethen and Robert Dale. 2006. Algorithms for generating referring expressions: Do they do what people do? In *Proceedings of the 4th International Conference on Natural Language Generation*, pages 63–70, Sydney, Australia.

Jette Viethen and Robert Dale. 2008. The use of spatial relations in referring expression generation. In *Proceedings of the 5th International Conference on Natural Language Generation*, pages 59–67, Salt Fork OH, USA.

Jette Viethen and Robert Dale. 2011. GRE3D7: A corpus of distinguishing descriptions for objects in visual scenes. In *Proceedings of the Workshop on Using Corpora in Natural Language Generation and Evaluation*, Edinburgh, UK.

Jette Viethen, Robert Dale, and Markus Guhe. 2011. Generating subsequent reference in shared visual scenes: Computation vs. re-use. In *Proceeding the 2011 Conference on Empirical Methods in Natural Language Processing*, Edinburgh, UK.

Ian H. Witten and Eibe Frank. 2005. *Data Mining: Practical Machine Learning Tools and Techniques*. Morgan Kaufmann, San Francisco CA, USA.

A Cross-Linguistic Study on the Production of Multimodal Referring Expressions in Dialogue

Ielka van der Sluis
Communication and Information Studies
University of Groningen, the Netherlands
i.f.van.der.sluis@rug.nl

Saturnino Luz
Department of Computer Science
Trinity College Dublin, Ireland
luzs@scss.tcd.ie

Abstract

This paper presents a cross-linguistic data elicitation study on fully realised referring expressions (REs) in a dialogue context. A web-based experiment was set up in which participants were asked to choose REs to be uttered by one of two agents for identifying five targets in a scripted dialogue. Participants were told that the agent would point at the referents while uttering their chosen linguistic descriptions. The study was conducted in English, Japanese, Portuguese and Dutch and yielded a total of 1190 referring expressions. Our hypotheses concern sets of objects that need to be considered for identification depending on the effect of the pointing gesture. Results show interesting and significant differences between the language groups.

1 Introduction

Generation of referring expressions (GRE) has been a central task in Natural Language Generation for many years, and numerous algorithms which automatically produce referring expressions (REs) have been developed (Gardent, 2002; Krahmer et al., 2003; Jordan and Walker, 2005; Van Deemter, 2006). Existing GRE algorithms generally assume that both speaker and addressee have access to the same information. In most cases this information is represented by a knowledge base that contains the objects and their properties present in the domain of conversation in terms of attribute-value pairs. A typical algorithm (Dale and Reiter, 1995) takes as input an object or a set of objects (Van Deemter, 2002), the target referent of the description, and a set of distractors from which the target needs to be distinguished. The task of a GRE algorithm is to determine which set of properties is required to single out the target from the distractors.

Much of the work on GRE focusses on the use of REs in the English language. However, in recent years, other languages have attracted increased interest (Funakoshi et al., 2006; Pareira and Paraboni, 2008; Spanger et al., 2009; Theune et al., 2010). In this paper we present a cross-linguistic study on human production of REs in English, Japanese, Dutch and Brazilian Portuguese. The study originated from a project in which the perception of multimodal REs was studied in a virtual world in a Japanese and an English-speaking setting (Van der Sluis and Luz, 2011; Van der Sluis et al., to appear). In the present paper, the materials from a production study initially conducted for Japanese to validate our Japanese translation of a dialogue written in English, have been translated and further adapted to Dutch and Portuguese. We draw on the results of this study to analyse how well different languages match a typical GRE algorithm that uses a list of preferred properties, such as the algorithm proposed by Dale and Reiter (1995).

The REs considered in this study are part of a scripted dialogue between two agents in a furniture sales setting. The study focusses on 'first-mention' REs that identify objects that have not been talked about earlier in the discourse. In the dialogue the furniture seller agent refers to objects in the domain by uttering each scripted RE combined with a pointing gesture directed to the target. Since human com-

Proceedings of the 13th European Workshop on Natural Language Generation (ENLG), pages 53–62,
Nancy, France, September 2011.

munication includes gestures as well as language various algorithms for the generation of such multimodal REs have been proposed (André and Rist, 1996; Kranstedt et al., 2006; Van der Sluis and Krahmer, 2007). Interestingly, we know from other studies (Piwek, 2009; Van der Sluis and Krahmer, 2007) that the use of pointing gestures can have a particular influence on the REs in that they reduce the distractor set such that often less properties are needed to uniquely distinguish the target. In this paper we test two hypotheses about the composition of the distractor set.

The paper is structured as follows: Section 2 describes the materials and setting of the study, Section 3 presents our hypotheses and our evaluation method, Section 4 details the results, Section 5 discusses the findings and Section 6 concludes the paper.

2 Production Study

2.1 Setting: Dialogue and REs

A dialogue script was written by hand for two agents in a furniture store. Figure 1 presents a schematic layout of the furniture shop marking the positions of the agents and the furniture items. The shop contains 26 objects of which 14 were used as target referents, the others were used as distractors. The dialogue consists of 19 utterances and features a conversation between a female agent purchasing furniture for her office, and a male shop owner describing some furniture items that she could consider for her purposes. Results from a pilot study used for validation of the dialogue and the setting showed that the dialogue was acceptable to an English speaking audience (Breitfuss et al., 2009).

The dialogue was used as a template in which five first-mention REs could be varied. The REs used to fill out these slots were chosen carefully to cover various aspects of REs currently studied in the GRE literature. These aspects include: (1) cardinality, the REs targeted three singular objects and two larger sets of items; (2) locative expressions, the REs included three absolute locative expressions and two relative locative expressions; and (3) the position of the referent. The targets were distributed in the domain of conversation such that one referent was located near to the stationary agents, two referents were located far away from the agents, and two sets of referents were located somewhere in between those two extremes.

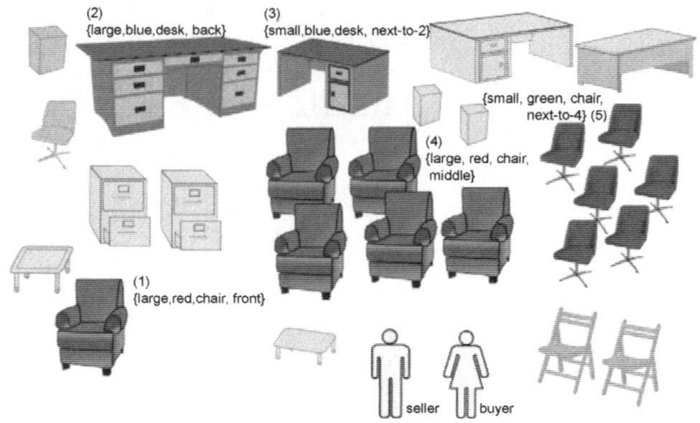

Figure 1: Bird's-eye sketch of the virtual furniture shop.

Figure 1 shows 14 furniture items that are used for assessing multimodal GRE output: (1) a large red chair (bottom left); (2) a large blue desk (top left), (3) a small blue desk (next to the large one); (4) a set of five large red chairs (in the middle), and (5) a set of six small green chairs (next to the set of reds), as well as a number of distractors (greyed-out items). We stipulated that the agents would stay stationary at the position indicated in Figure 1 and point in the direction where the targets can be found. The targets can be described with the attributes usually considered in GRE research (i.e. *type*, *colour*, *size*, *location*) and were realised as follows:

- RE1: large red chair in the front of the shop
- RE2: large blue desk in the back of the shop
- RE3: small blue desk next to it (where 'it' refers to the target of RE2)
- RE4: large red chairs in the middle of the shop
- RE5: small green chairs next to the red ones

The dialogue was translated to Japanese, Brazilian Portuguese and Dutch such that the dialogue was adapted to the normative, communicative and inferential rules of the respective cultures but the REs were as close to the English originals as possible. The translations and localisations for Portuguese and Dutch followed a similar pattern as the process for Japanese described in (Van der Sluis and Luz, 2011). Validation of the translated dialogues was conducted by three native speakers in the respective languages and revisions were made accordingly.

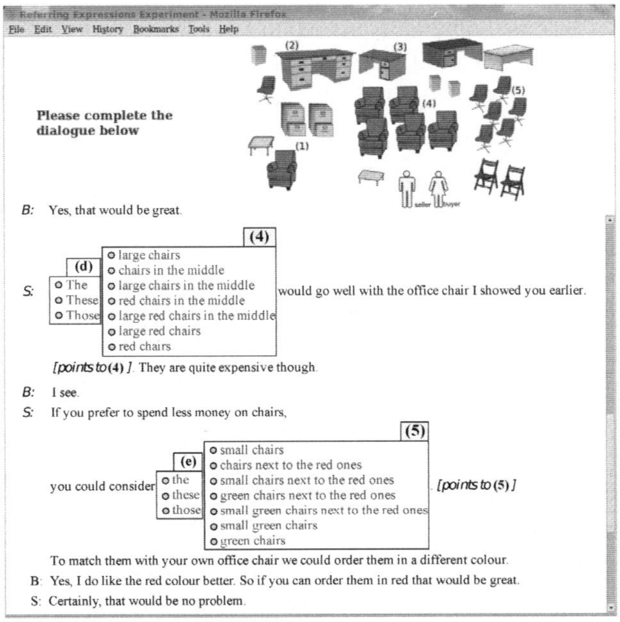

Figure 2: Screenshot of the application in which participants were asked to choose their preferred REs. Utterances by the Seller and Buyer are marked with "S:" and "B:", respectively. Options were presented as shown in the DE-boxes marked *(d)* and *(e)*, and RE-boxes marked *(4)* and *(5)*.

2.2 Materials

The study was conducted over the Web and consisted of three pages. The first page presented a tutorial in which the participants were told about the goals of the study, what they were going to see on the next page, and what they would be asked to do. The second page is shown in Figure 2. At the top of the screen a picture of the domain was presented. The bottom part of the screen contained the dialogue through which the participants could scroll and select the REs they preferred from a set of options, all of which were simultaneously available to the participant while reading the sentence. The picture of the domain was always visible on the top part of the screen. The five REs of interest were each presented with two boxes as illustrated by, for instance, the items marked (e) and (5) in Figure 2: the DE-box, in which participants could select a determiner or demonstrative and the RE-box, in which combinations of properties could be chosen.

The RE-box contained seven possible REs in which the inclusion of *colour*, *size* and *location* were varied; all REs contained the relevant value for *type* as a noun. For instance, in the case of RE2 the options would be 'large desk', 'blue desk', 'desk in the back', 'large blue desk', 'large desk in the back', 'blue desk in the back' and 'large blue desk in the back'. After each RE-box, it was indicated that the agent's utterance of the RE would be combined with a pointing gesture in the direction of the target. The DE-box offered a number of options to compose deictic expressions in line with the determiners available in the respective languages. We refer to (Luz and van der Sluis, 2011) for our analysis of the determiners that were collected with this study. The third page of our study consisted of a "thank you" note and information about a prize draw, as a reward for participating in the study. All materials used in this study were fully translated into the languages considered.

3 Hypotheses

Because we study the perception of REs by presenting them to potential users in their own language and localised contexts (i.e. a context adapted to the normative, communicative and inferential rules of their cultural background) we used null hypothesis significance testing. In other words, our null hypotheses are that participants do not differ in their preferences dependent on their cultural background. If significant differences are observed, we can regard these differences as evidence towards alternative hypotheses.

The hypotheses for the REs to be selected by the participants are based on findings from cognitive linguistics (Pechmann, 1989; Arts et al., 2010) that show that absolute properties (e.g. *colour*) are preferred over relative properties (e.g. *size*). Following Krahmer and Theune (2002) we expect locative expressions to be even less preferred than relative properties. In our set up we presented the discourse domain including the agents that featured in the dialogue in a two-dimensional fashion. However, we asked the participants to imagine that the furniture seller agent included a pointing gesture to accompany the linguistic descriptions to refer to the targets. Hence we asked participants to imagine the distinguishing effect that this pointing gesture would have in a three-dimensional environment. As we cannot be sure about the scope of these pointing gestures in the minds of the participants and their effect on the distractor set on which the participants based their choice of RE, we decided to test two hypotheses, which are summarised in Table 1.

Table 1: Expected REs for referents *RE1* to *RE5* for two hypotheses *H1* and *H2* on the content of the REs.

Target	H1: Whole domain	H2: Gesture scope
RE1	colour, location	colour
RE2	colour, size	colour, size
RE3	colour, size	colour, size
RE4	colour, location	colour
RE5	colour, location	colour

Our first hypothesis, H1, is that participants in our study will consider all distractors in the domain as depicted in Figure 2 for each RE (i.e., the pointing gesture has no effect, it does not rule out any distractors). Accordingly, for RE1 we expect that participants will first include *colour* to rule out all objects in the domain that are not red. For RE1, *size* will not remove any distractors, but we expect that *location* will be included to rule out the group of red chairs in the middle of the shop. For RE2, we expect that *colour* will be selected to rule out all objects that are not blue. Secondly, *size* will be added to remove the remaining smaller blue desk and thereby empty the set of distractors. For RE3, we expect participants to include *colour* to rule out all distractors that are not blue and add *size* to rule out the large blue desk and thereby uniquely distinguish the target of RE3. RE4 will be distinguishing by first adding *colour* to rule out all objects that are not red. Then *location* will be added to remove the only remaining distractor, that is the singular red chair in the front of the shop. RE5 is expected to include *colour*, which leaves only green distractors, and *location* to remove the singular green chair on the left-hand side of the domain.

Our second hypothesis, H2, is that participants only consider the set of distractors located in the scope of the pointing gesture performed by the agent to distinguish the target. For all five targets we tentatively defined the scope of the pointing gestures as depicted in Figure 3, where the areas covered by the pointing gestures are of the same size, but differ in terms of the covered areas that include the target in the centre of the gesture's scope. Note, however, that the participants in our study were not provided with these gesture scopes, they had to imagine the effect of the gesture themselves. Accordingly, their representation might have been different from the scopes presented in Figure 3. For the sake of illustration, we define the set of distractors as including all objects that are located fully or partly within the projected lines that indicate the scope of the gesture. For all five REs we assume that the algorithm first adds a pointing gesture to the RE which results in a decrease of the number of distractors. For all five REs, however, inclusion of the pointing gestures does not result in distinguishing REs and participants are still expected to add linguistic properties to identify the targets uniquely. For RE1, *colour* should be added to empty the distractor set (i.e. the pointing gesture had already ruled out the group of red chairs in the middle of the shop). For RE2, *colour* and *size* are expected to be included; the pointing gesture's scope has decreased the target set but still includes some objects with a different colour as well as the smaller blue desk. RE3 also requires *colour* and *size* to respectively rule out the objects in the gesture's scope that are not blue as well as the large blue desk. Both RE4 and RE5 require *colour* to remove the remaining distractors located in the scope of the respective pointing gestures.

Figure 3: Furniture shop divided into five areas that cover the scope of the pointing gestures produced by the Seller agent to accompany the REs *R1* to *R5*.

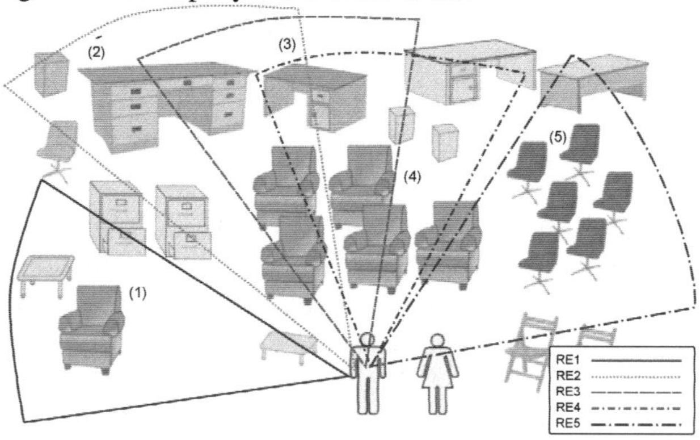

3.1 Evaluation Metric

To test our hypotheses, H1 to H2, we compared the participants' choices with the realised output of a typical GRE algorithm that uses a preferred attribute list alike the algorithm proposed by (Dale and Reiter, 1995) that mimics human preferences (i.e. [*colour*, *size*, *location*]). We chose the Dice coefficient as our evaluation metric, which accounts for a degree of overlap between two descriptions. Dice computes the degree of similarity between two sets by scaling the number of attributes that the two descriptions have in common, by the overall size of the two sets:

$$dice(H_a, R) = \frac{2 \times |H_a \cap R|}{|H_a| + |R|} \quad (1)$$

where H_a is the set of attributes in the description produced by a human author, and R the set of attributes in the reference description generated by the algorithm. Dice yields a value between 0 (no agreement) and 1 (perfect agreement). The attributes are chosen from a set $A = \{c, s, l\}$, denoting colour, size and location, respectively, so that possible H_a will be elements of $\mathcal{A} = 2^A \setminus \emptyset$. We summarise the Dice scores by their expected values for a particular object. That is, we report the mean scores weighted according to the probability p_a that a combination of attributes $a \in \mathcal{A}$ is chosen, as set out in equation (2).

$$E[dice(H, R)] = \sum_{a \in \mathcal{A}} p_a \times dice(H_a, R) \quad (2)$$

For comparison, we computed a baseline score (B) where p_a is a uniform distribution (i.e. all feature combination choices are equally likely) as a special case of (2) that is: $B = 1/7 \sum_{a \in \mathcal{A}} dice(H_a, R)$

The 'perfect recall percentage', (PRP), that is the proportion of times the hypotheses match the participants' choices exactly, is also reported.

4 Results

4.1 Participants

The address (URL) for the study was distributed through sending invitations for participation by email. Participants included 54 native speakers of Japanese (female: 26%(14), male: 74%(40)), 91 native speakers of English (female: 60%(55), male: 40%(36)), 42 native speakers of Brazilian Portuguese (female: 60%(25), male: 40% (17)) and 51 native speakers of Dutch (female: 55%(28), male: 45%(23)). Table 2 summarises the characteristics of the participants that took part in our study.

4.2 Referring Expressions

Table 3 presents the REs that were selected by the participants in our study per language group. As regards which RE was chosen by the majority of each language group we find that for RE1, 'large red chair in the front', speakers of Portuguese and Dutch agree in their selection of *colour* and *location*. In contrast, Japanese participants largely preferred the RE including only *colour* and English participants preferred to include all available properties in the description. For RE2, 'large blue desk in the back', a majority in all four language groups chooses to include all available properties. For RE3, 'small blue desk next to it', the majorities of the four language groups also agree and select a description that includes *size* and *location* (note that this is not a possible algorithmic output when we assume the proposed preference order in the current domain). However, for RE3, the Japanese data presents a tie, indicating that an equally large group of participants selected all available properties to distinguish the target. For RE4, 'large red chairs in the middle', Japanese and Portuguese speaking participants team up with a majority vote for inclusion of only *colour*, while both English and Dutch participants prefer *colour* and *location*. Finally, for RE5, 'small green chairs next to the red ones', the Japanese and Portuguese speakers again agree with a majority vote for *colour*, while Dutch participants select *colour* and *size* and English speakers prefer to include all available properties to refer to the target.

Per language group we find that the majority of the Japanese participants chose an RE that only include *colour* for RE1, RE4 and RE5 (all between 40 and 50%). For RE2 and RE3 the Japanese majority chose to include all available properties. The English participants show different preferences, namely including all available properties in RE1, RE2 and RE5, *size* and *location* for RE3, and for RE4 *colour* and *location*. Speakers of Portuguese and Dutch present more variability. Portuguese speakers select only *colour* for RE4 and RE5, while the majority prefers different descriptions for RE1, RE2 and RE3. The majority of Dutch speakers chooses *colour* and *location* for RE1 and RE4 and prefers various descriptions for RE2, RE3 and RE4.

Table 2: Participants in our study per *L*anguage (*E*nglish, *J*apanese, *P*ortuguese and *D*utch) in terms of *N*umber of subjects, number of subjects per *Age* band, where *1* = 20-30, *2* = 31-40, *3* = 41-50, *4* = 61-70 and *5* = over 70 years old, and per *Occupation* as *S*tudent, *A*cademic or *O*ther.

L	N	Age	Occupation
J	54	1=57%(31); 2=28%(15); 3=15%(8)	S=52%(28); A=13%(7); O=35%(19)
E	91	1=52%(47); 2=23%(21); 3=22%(20); 4=2%(2); 5=1%(1)	S=44%(40); A=26%(23); O=31%(28)
P	42	1=71%(30); 2=26%(11); 3=2 %(1)	S=29%(12); A=57%(24); O=%(6)
D	51	1=22%(11); 2=33%(17); 3=26%(13); 4=14%(7); 5=6%(3)	S=4%(2); A=14%(7); O=80%(42)

Table 3: Means and standard deviations of REs collected per *L*anguage (*E*nglish, *J*apanese, *P*ortuguese and *D*utch) for *RE1* to *RE5* for which the values of the available attributes *colour*, *size* and *location* are indicated, as well as the actual choices made by the participants in the study as combinations of *c*olour, *s*ize and *l*ocation. The PRP scores for H1 and H2 are presented in boldface.

L		RE1	RE2	RE3	RE4	RE5
	colour, size, location	*red, large, front*	*blue, large, back*	*blue, small, next*	*red, large, middle*	*green small, next*
J	c	**42.6%** (23)	7.4% (4)	3.7% (2)	**46.3%** (25)	**48.1%** (26)
E		**7.7%** (7)	0% (0)	0% (0)	**11.1%** (10)	**14.3%** (13)
P		**26.2%** (11)	2.4% (1)	2.4% (1)	**33.3%** (14)	**38.1%** (16)
D		**15.7%** (8)	2% (1)	0% (0)	**11.8%** (6)	**17.6%** (9)
J	s	7.4% (4)	14.8% (8)	9.3% (5)	3.7% (2)	9.3% (5)
E		1.1% (1)	1.1% (1)	4.4% (4)	1.1% (1)	4.4% (4)
P		4.8% (2)	0% (0)	0% (0)	2.4% (1)	4.8% (2)
D		3.9% (2)	2% (1)	9.8% (5)	2.0% (1)	0% (0)
J	l	1.9% (1)	3.7% (2)	5.6% (3)	1.9% (1)	0.0% (0)
E		3.3% (3)	3.3% (3)	4.4% (4)	0% (0)	2.2% (2)
P		0% (0)	0% (0)	14.3% (6)	4.8% (2)	7.1% (3)
D		5.9% (3)	3.9% (2)	9.8% (5)	9.8% (5)	3.9% (2)
J	cs	29.6% (16)	20.4% (11)	7.4% (4)	13% (7)	27.8% (15)
E		12.1% (11)	17.6% (16)	1.1% (1)	7.7% (7)	25.3% (23)
P		19% (8)	11.9% (5)	11.9% (5)	7.1% (3)	4.8% (2)
D		0% (0)	17.6% (9)	2% (1)	0% (0)	39.2% (20)
J	cl	**5.6%** (3)	**5.6%** (3)	**14.8%** (8)	**24.1%** (13)	**7.4%** (4)
E		**31.9%** (29)	**5.5%** (5)	**4.4%** (4)	**35.2%** (32)	**16.5%** (15)
P		**28.6%** (12)	**19%** (8)	**9.5%** (4)	**28.6%** (12)	**26.2%** (11)
D		**43.1%** (22)	**9.8%** (5)	**2%** (1)	**43.1%** (22)	**11.8%** (6)
J	sl	3.7% (2)	9.3% (5)	29.6% (16)	3.7% (2)	0.0% (0)
E		6.6% (6)	9.9% (9)	48.4% (44)	8.8% (8)	9.9% (9)
P		2.4% (1)	21.4% (9)	35.7% (15)	9.5% (4)	4.8% (2)
D		3.9% (2)	11.8% (6)	41.2% (21)	13.7% (7)	5.9% (3)
J	csl	9.3% (5)	38.9% (21)	29.6% (16)	7.4% (4)	7.4% (4)
E		37.4% (34)	62.6% (57)	37.4% (34)	25.3% (23)	27.5% (25)
P		11.9% (5)	45.2% (19)	26.2% (11)	14.3% (6)	14.3% (6)
D		27.5% (14)	52.9% (27)	35.3% (18)	19.6% (10)	21.6% (11)

4.3 Distractor Sets

Table 4 displays the Dice scores for the collected data and our baseline per hypotheses per language group computed for the REs for which the hypotheses rendered different output (i.e. RE1, RE4 and RE5). Recall that H1 predicts that participants would take all objects in the domain into account as distractors when selecting their preferred description, while H2 predicts that participants would only consider the objects located in the scope of the pointing gesture that would accompany the linguistic description. Except for the Japanese data for RE1 and RE5 on H1, all Dice scores seem well above the baseline. This reinforces that for all three REs the figures show that the choice of the speakers of Japanese matches H2 best, while the other three languages match better with H1. T-tests at the $p < .05$ level comparing the Dice scores per RE per language show significant differences for the collected English REs for the targets of all three REs (RE1 t=8.786, RE4 t=8.805 and RE5 t=3.574). For Japanese REs significant differences were found for the targets of RE1 and RE5 (RE1 t=3.046 and RE5 t=5.177). The Dutch data displayed significant differences for RE1 and RE4 (RE1 t=6.137 and RE4 t=8.058). Differences between the Dice scores for the Portuguese data are not significant.

Table 4: Dice scores for the RE1, RE4 and RE5 computed per *L*anguage (*E*nglish, *J*apanese, *P*ortuguese and *D*utch) and the *B*aseline, where significant differences between the Dice scores of H1 and H2 are denoted with '*' at the $p < .05$ level and '**' at the $p < .01$ level.

L		*H1-Dice*	*H2-Dice*	*H1 vs H2*
J	**RE1**	.59	.71	**
E		.78	.56	**
P		.71	.64	
D		.81	.58	**
B		.59	.40	
J	**RE4**	.70	.75	
E		.78	.52	**
P		.74	.64	
D		.80	.50	**
B		.59	.40	
J	**RE5**	.59	.75	**
E		.67	.56	**
P		.73	.66	
D		.66	.62	
B		.59	.40	

4.4 Cross-linguistic Findings

Table 5 displays the significant differences between the languages per hypotheses (H1: distractors = all objects in the domain safe the target, and H2: distractors = objects in the scope of the pointing gesture), per RE (RE1, RE4 and RE5) that were found through a multivariate ANOVA with posthoc Tukey's HSD tests. For RE1, 'large red chair in the front' the REs from the Japanese speakers significantly differed from all three other languages, indicating that the collected Brazilian Portuguese, English and Dutch REs better match H1 than the Japanese REs. For RE5 we also found a significant difference between the Japanese and the Portuguese group for H1. Results further show that for all REs the choices of the Japanese group differed significantly from the choices of the English group when comparing the Dice scores for hypothesis H2, indicating that H2 was a significantly better match for the REs selected by the participants in the Japanese group than the REs selected by the English group. For RE4, the Japanese REs also differed from the Dutch ones for H2.

Table 5: Multivariate ANOVA per referring expression (*RE1*, *RE4* and *RE5*), per hypothesis (*H1* and *H2*) reporting *Mean* differences and standard errors (*StdE*) for significant differences between language pairs (*E*nglish, *J*apanese, *P*ortuguese and *D*utch), where differences are denoted with '*' at the $p < .05$ level and '**' at the $p < .01$ level.

RE	*H*	*L-pair*	*Mean(StdE)*	*P*
RE1	H1	J - D	.22(.042)	**
		J - E	.19(.037)	**
		J - P	.12(.044)	*
	H2	J - E	.15(.048)	*
RE4	H2	J - D	.24(.062)	**
		J - E	.23(.045)	**
RE5	H1	J - P	.13(.045)	*
	H2	J - E	.20(.052)	**

Overall, we found significant effects between languages. RE1, large red chair in the front, showed such an effect for H1 (*F*(3,234)=11.903, *MSE*=.554 $p < .001$) and H2 (*F*(3,234)=3.482, *MSE*=.280 $p < .05$). RE4, 'large red chairs in the middle', only for H2 (*F*(3,234)=7.563, *MSE*=.280 $p < .05$), and RE5,'small green chairs next to the red ones', for H1 (*F*(3,234)=2.954, *MSE*=.143 $p < .001$) and H2 (*F*(3,234)=4.867, *MSE*=.438 $p < .01$).

5 Summary and Discussion

The REs collected with our web experiment display many differences between the four language groups included in our study. Most notably is the fact that the majority of Japanese participants preferred shorter descriptions than the majorities of the participants in the other language groups. Especially, the Japanese majority chose only to include the property *colour* in the object descriptions RE1, RE4 and RE5, while the majorities of the English and Dutch participants also chose *location* and sometimes *size*. Interestingly, the Portuguese speakers, like the Japanese, chose only *colour* for RE4 and RE5.

For RE2, 'large blue desk in the back', the majorities of all four language groups agreed in selecting all available properties for the RE. This might be explained by the fact that the focus in the dialogue shifted from a furniture item in the front of the shop (i.e. the large red chair in the front located near to the agents) to the back of the shop (i.e. far away from the agents). Note that the target of RE3, 'small blue desk next to it' was equally far away from the agents as the target of RE2. However, when the target of RE3 is discussed in the script, the focus of attention was already in the back area of the shop.

As regards our hypotheses, we found that the REs selected by the Japanese participants best matched H2, indicating that they considered a reduced distractor set in composing their REs due to the scope of the accompanying pointing gesture. In contrast, the REs selected by the participants in the other language groups better matched H1, stating that people would consider all objects in the conversation domain as distractors when identifying targets.

We also found various significant differences between the Dice means of the four language groups per RE, indicating that Japanese speakers employ different strategies in composing REs than participants in the English, Dutch and Portuguese groups.

The fact that the Japanese participants in our study are predominantly male (74%) may have been a potential confounding factor in our results. As men are known to be less verbal than women, the reported effect could be a gender rather than a language effect. We ran a separate statistical analysis on gender effects on our Japanese data. It turned out that gender affected the use of the *location* attribute with t=3.05 at the $p < .05$ level indicating that Japanese females used *location* more often than Japanese males (in 57% and 36% of REs, respectively). Comparing the hypotheses H1 and H2 per object with respect to gender, Japanese males had a significant preference for H2 over H1 for RE1 (mean Dice scores 75% vs. 60%, t=2.38, $p < .05$) while Japanese females exhibited no clear preference (57% vs 58%, non-signif). Both genders preferred H2 for RE5 (56% vs 73% for males and 68% vs 82% for females, $p < .05$. There was no gender effect with respect to RE4. Further studies are required to investigate gender across different languages.

Another reason for the effects we observed in our study may be related to differences in the use of pointing gestures in the languages we considered. For instance, (Kita and Özürek, 2003) showed differences in gesturing between English and Japanese speakers (not about pointing though), and it is conceivable that the observed language differences are caused by gesture differences. In future work it would be interesting to add a condition to the experiment in which pointing gestures are not included.

6 Conclusion and Future Work

This paper has presented a cross-linguistic study of the production of REs by native speakers of English, Japanese, Dutch and Brazilian Portuguese, which displayed many significant differences between the language groups. These differences were related to the set of distractors that was taken into account, which was hypothesised to be influenced by the effect of pointing gestures that accompanied the REs. One limitation of this study is clearly that the pointing gestures to accompany the linguistic descriptions were scripted and the effect of those gestures in the minds of the participants could only be assumed. Instead of linguistically described pointing gestures, animations of pointing gestures may be more effective for deriving the effect of pointing on a linguistic description. We refer to (Van der Sluis et al., to appear) for an attempt in this direction.

Another limitation is that only five predefined realisations of REs were used to elicit object descriptions from the participants. The REs, however, were carefully chosen as to reflect on issues currently being studied in GRE. The situated and life-like dialogue that was used in the study, specially in terms of focus shifts, might also have influenced the participants' choice of REs. In addition, perhaps overhearer effects to do with attention and engagement may have played a role. However, with our with 'static' study we have not attempted to mimic an interactive, real-time situation.

Upon completing their choices participants were offered the opportunity to enter free-form comments in a text box. From the participants' comments we know that people were positively engaged in the study. Some participants, however, indeed criticised the limited choice of descriptive attributes and their suitability for the sales domain. While the criticism is valid, our choice of REs was based on previous work on RE generation where the furniture domain is used very often (i.e., through the COCONUT corpus (Di Eugenio et al., 2000) and the TUNA corpus (Van Deemter et al., To Appear)).

In summary, although limited in terms of expressiveness, the range of attributes available allowed us to identify general differences in RE production styles between the languages. With inspecting almost 1200 REs, we can conclude that a typical GRE algorithm that uses a well established preference order does not match the human production of multimodal REs for all languages and further studies are necessary to inform the design of GRE algorithms that can be employed in multilingual, multimodal and interactive environments.

7 Acknowledgements

This research is supported by the Science Foundation Ireland (Grant 07/CE/I1142) as part of the Centre for Next Generation Localisation (www.cngl.ie) at Trinity College Dublin.

References

E. André and T. Rist. 1996. Coping with temporal constraints in multimedia presentation planning. In *Proc. of the AAAI'96.*

A. Arts, A. Maes, L. Noordman, and C. Jansen. 2010. Overspecification facilitates object identification. *Journal of Pragmatics*, 43(1):361–374.

W. Breitfuss, I. Van der Sluis, S. Luz, H. Prendinger, and M. Ishizuka. 2009. Evaluating an algorithm for the generation of multimodal referring expressions in a virtual world: A pilot study. In *Proc. of IVA-09*, Amsterdam. 2009.

R. Dale and E. Reiter. 1995. Computational interpretations of the Gricean maxims in the generation of referring expressions. *Cognitive Science*, 18:233–263.

K. Van Deemter, A. Gatt, I. Van der Sluis, and R. Power. To Appear. Generation of referring expressions: Assessing the incremental algorithm. *Cognitive Science.*

K. Van Deemter. 2002. Generating referring expressions: Boolean extensions of the incremental algorithm. *Computational Linguistics*, 28(1):37–52.

K. Van Deemter. 2006. Generating referring expressions that involve gradable properties. *Computational Linguistics*, 32(2):195–222.

B. Di Eugenio, P. Jordan, R. Thomason, and J. Moore. 2000. The agreement process: An empirical investigation of human-human computer-mediated collaborative dialogues. *Intl. Journ. Human-Comp. Studies*, 6:1017–1076.

K. Funakoshi, S. Watanabe, and T. Tokunaga. 2006. Group-based generation of referring expressions. In *Proc. of the INLG-06*, pages 73–80.

C. Gardent. 2002. Generating minimal definite descriptions. In *Proc. of the ACL-02.*

P. Jordan and M. Walker. 2005. Learning content selection rules for generating object descriptions in dialogue. *Journal of Artificial Intelligence Research*, 24:157–194.

S. Kita and A. Özürek. 2003. What does cross-linguistic variation in semantic coordination of speech and gesture reveal?: Evidence for an interface representation of spatial thinking and speaking. *Journal of Memory and Language*, 48(1):16–32.

E. Krahmer and M. Theune. 2002. Efficient context-sensitive generation of referring expressions. In K. van Deemter and R. Kibble, editors, *Information Sharing: Reference and Presupposition in Language Generation and Interpretation.* CSLI Publications.

E. Krahmer, S van Erk, and A. Verleg. 2003. Graph-based generation of referring expressions. *Computational Linguistics*, 29(1):53–72.

A. Kranstedt, A. Lücking, T. Pfeiffer, H. Rieser, and I. Wachsmuth. 2006. Deictic object reference in task-oriented dialogue. In G. Rickheit and I. Wachsmuth, editors, *Situated Communication.* Mouton de Gruyter.

S. Luz and I. van der Sluis. 2011. Production of demonstratives in Dutch, English and Portuguese dialogues. In *Proceedings of the 13th European Workshop on Natural Language Generation (ENLG'11).*

D. Pareira and I. Paraboni. 2008. From TUNA attribute sets to Portuguese text: a first report. In *Procs. of INLG'08.*

T. Pechmann. 1989. Incremental speech production and referential overspecification. *Linguistics*, 27:89–110.

P. Piwek. 2009. Salience and pointing in multimodal reference. In *Proc. of preCogsci 2009: Production of Referring Expressions: Bridging the gap between computational and empirical approaches to reference. At CogSci'09*, Amsterdam, The Netherlands.

I. Van der Sluis and E. Krahmer. 2007. Generating multimodal referring expressions. *Discourse Processes*, 44(3):145–174.

I. Van der Sluis and S. Luz. 2011. Issues in translating and producing Japanese referring expressions for dialogues. *Linguistic Issues in Language Technology*, 5(1):1–46.

I. Van der Sluis, S. Luz W. Breitfuß, M. Ishizuka, and H. Prendinger. to appear. Cross-cultural assessment of automatically generated multimodal referring expressions in a virtual world. *International Journal of Human-Computer Studies*.

P. Spanger, Y. Masaaki, I. Ryu, and T. Takenobu. 2009. A Japanese corpus of referring expressions used in a situated collaboration task. In *Proc. of the ENLG-09*.

M. Theune, R. Koolen, and E. Krahmer. 2010. Cross-linguistic attribute selection for REG: Comparing Dutch and English. In *Procs. INLG'10*.

Two Approaches for Generating Size Modifiers

Margaret Mitchell
University of Aberdeen
Aberdeen, Scotland, U.K.
m.mitchell@abdn.ac.uk

Kees van Deemter
University of Aberdeen
Aberdeen, Scotland, U.K.
k.vdeemter@abdn.ac.uk

Ehud Reiter
University of Aberdeen
Aberdeen, Scotland, U.K.
e.reiter@abdn.ac.uk

Abstract

This paper offers a solution to a small problem within a much larger problem. We focus on modelling how people use size in reference, words like "big" and "tall", which is one piece within the much larger problem of how people refer to visible objects. Examining size in isolation allows us to begin untangling a few of the complex and interacting features that affect reference, and we isolate a set of features that may be used in a hand-coded algorithm or a machine learning approach to generate one of six basic size types. The hand-coded algorithm generates a modifier type with a high correspondence to those observed in human data, and achieves 81.3% accuracy in an entirely new domain. This trails oracle accuracy for this task by just 8%. Features used by the hand-coded algorithm are added to a larger set of features in the machine learning approach, and we do not find a statistically significant difference between the precision and recall of the two systems. The input and output of these systems are a novel characterization of the factors that affect referring expression generation, and the methods described here may serve as one building block in future work connecting vision to language.

1 Introduction

The task of referring expression generation (REG) has often been contextualized as a problem of generating uniquely identifying reference to visible items. Properties such as COLOR, SIZE, LOCATION, and ORIENTATION have been treated as exemplars of attributes used to distinguish a referent (Dale and Reiter, 1995; Krahmer et al., 2003; van Deemter, 2006; Gatt and Belz, 2008). This paper is no exception. However, we approach the task of REG by examining in depth what it means to uniquely identify something that is visible. We specifically address the attribute of *size* and explore ways to connect the dimensional properties of real-world objects to surface forms used by people to pick out a referent. This work contributes to recent research examining naturalistic reference in visual domains explicitly (Kelleher et al., 2005; Viethen and Dale, 2010; Koolen et al., 2011).

Traditionally, to create an algorithm for the generation of reference, one considers a set of different properties and develops ways to decide which properties to include in a final surface string. This may be considered a *breadth-based* methodology, where many properties are considered, but the details of how those properties are input to the algorithm is left unspecified. Here, we begin creating an algorithm for the generation of naturalistic reference by considering a single property – size – and tracing how it is realized based on a variety of different inputs and outputs. This we will call a *depth-based* methodology. This is a departure from previous approaches to the construction of an REG algorithm. Instead of a more general-purpose algorithm, a small set of abstract semantic types are mapped to a variety of surface forms. This allows us to understand the task of referring expression generation at a fine-grained level, analyzing the specific visual characteristics that need to be considered in order to generate reference similar to that produced by people.

The algorithm is developed for the microplanning stage of a natural language generation system (Reiter and Dale, 2000), generating a size type that directly informs lexical choice and surface realization

Proceedings of the 13th European Workshop on Natural Language Generation (ENLG), pages 63–70,
Nancy, France, September 2011.

of a final string. Comparisons made by the algorithm may also be represented as features within classifiers that predict size type, and so we compare the size algorithm with such a method, using decision trees to model human participants' selection of size modifiers.

We introduce two broad size classes, *individuating* size modifiers and *overall* size modifiers. *Individuating* size modifiers pick out specific configurations of object axes. *Overall* size modifiers identify the overall size of an object. This follows distinctions made in psycholinguistic work on size (Hermann and Deutsch, 1976; Landau and Jackendoff, 1993) that until now have not been formalized. Each class contains several modifier types, and these map to sets of modifier surface forms.

	Type	Axis	Polarity
Individuating	(<ind,y>, 1)	y	+
	(<ind,y>, 0)	y	-
	(<ind,x>, 1)	x	+
	(<ind,x>, 0)	x	-
Overall	(<over>, 1)	x,y	+
	(<over>, 0)	x,y	-

Table 1: Size types.

Type	Examples		
(<ind,y>, 1)	taller	thicker	longer
(<ind,y>, 0)	shorter	thinner	short
(<ind,x>, 1)	longer	thicker	wider
(<ind,x>, 0)	thinner	shorter	narrower
(<over>, 1)	larger	bigger	big
(<over>, 0)	smaller	small	smallest

Table 2: Top three surface forms for each size category in the size corpus.

2 Background

One of the most common algorithms for the generation of referring expressions is Dale and Reiter's 1995 Incremental Algorithm. This algorithm analyzes a *context set*, which is represented as a series of <attribute:value> pairs that apply to each item in a scene. The context set is made up of the referent and the *contrast set*, the group of other items in the scene, or the *distractors*. The algorithm reasons over an ordered list of attributes (the preference order) to determine which attributes rule out at least one distractor. Chosen <attribute:value> pairs are added to a *distinguishing description*, and the algorithm stops once all members of the contrast set have been ruled out. The distinguishing description can then be realized as a referring expression, for example, (<COLOR:red>, <SIZE:big>, <TYPE:lamp>) may be realized as "big red lamp". Krahmer et al. (2003) follow a comparable procedure, utilizing a graph-based algorithm that relies on edge costs rather than a preference order, which can generate different kinds of expressions depending on how the costs are assigned. Both of these approaches treat size as a simple attribute, with its basic form defined as input. As such, whether to generate an expression like "the big tortoise", "the fat tortoise" or "the tall tortoise" is left to other stages of the generation process.

Such approaches may be further refined by reasoning about the semantic content of each property relevant to the scene. For example, with an attribute like SIZE, we know that the dimensional properties of the referent itself must be analyzed in order to determine what kind of modifier to produce. Hermann and Deutsch (1976) show that when people are presented with an object with two axes of different sizes than a distractor's, they are more likely to refer to the axis with the larger difference. Landau and Jackendoff (1993) discuss how a modifier like "big" selects different dimensions depending on the nature of the object, and tends to be used in cases where an object is large in either two or all three of its dimensions, while modifiers like "thick" and "thin" may be applied when an object extends in a single dimension. Brown-Schmidt and Tanenhaus (2006) and Sedivy et al. (1999) document that dimensional modifiers are likely to be used in visual scenes when there is another object of the same type as the target referent.

3 Predicting Size Types

Within each broad size class, we define several size types. Individuating size modifiers refer to at least one axis, and here we focus on the x-axis, running horizontally across an object (width), and the y-axis, running vertically across an object (height). There are also different polarities for each type, with words like "tall" and "big" denoting a positive polarity (1), and words like "small" and "thin" denoting a negative polarity (0). The six abstract size types based on these distinctions are listed in Table 1, and a few

Figure 1: Example stimuli in the size corpus (Mitchell et al., 2011a).

examples of corresponding surface forms are listed in Table 2. These types may be used to generate different surface realizations from the same underlying semantic form, for example, (<ind,y>, 0) may be used to produce adjectives ("the short box"), relative clauses ("that is shorter"), and prepositional phrases ("with less height"). We refer to these different kinds of constituents using the broad term *modifier*.

We predict modifiers according to the proposed classes in two domains: A study that specifically elicits size modification (Mitchell et al., 2011b) (the size corpus), and a corpus of instructive reference available from Mitchell et al. (2010) (the craft corpus). The size corpus informs the design of the size algorithm and serves as training data for the decision tree models. Example stimuli are given in Figure 1. The algorithm and the decision trees are then tested on a new domain, the craft corpus.

The size algorithm reasons about the difference in the height and width axes between a referent and a distractor to generate a single size modifier type. It is constructed based on the findings listed in Figure 2, and we discuss the algorithm in further detail in the next section. The classifiers use a set of size features that characterize each image, as well as a set of features reflecting the comparisons made in the hand-coded algorithm. This is discussed in further detail in Section 5.

1. When two dimensions differ in the same direction between a referent object and another object of the same type, an overall size modifier will be produced more often than an individuating size modifier.
2. When two dimensions differ in opposite directions between a referent object and another object of the same type, an individuating size modifier will be produced more often than an overall size modifier.
3. The closer the aspect ratio of an object, the more likely participants are to use an overall size modifier.

Figure 2: Size findings reported in Mitchell et al. (2011b).

4 The Size Algorithm

The size corpus provides information about size when there is a single distractor of the same type, however, in practice, a referent may be competing against several distractors. To address this, the algorithm must compare the referent's height and width against a larger set of heights and widths. A straightforward way to apply such a comparison is to take the *average* height and width of the items in the contrast set. Since size is more common when an item of the same type is in the scene (Brown-Schmidt and Tanenhaus, 2006), it may be suitable for the algorithm to compare size using the height and width average of other items of the same type. This also provides a simple way to model the size expectations of the referent relative to similar items. Such an approach is tested in Section 7.

We introduce the size algorithm in Figure 3 below. It is based on the findings listed in Figure 2, and is used when the following preconditions are met:

1. There is a target referent and one or more distractors
2. Each distractor has two dimensions that can be compared with the target referent's dimensions

As input, the algorithm takes the width and height of the referent (rx, ry) and the width and height of the distractor of the same type or average of the distractors of the same type as the referent (dx, dy). The algorithm outputs one of the size types listed in Table 1.

Lines 3 and 6 of SIZEMOD model the first finding in Figure 2, creating a structure to generate an overall size modifier ('over') with the appropriate polarity (0 for a negative difference, 1 for a positive).

Input: Referent height, width (ry, rx),
Average height, width for distractors of referent's type (dy, dx).
Output: Size modifier type (See Table 1).

```
SIZEMOD(rx, ry, dx, dy):
 1.  axes = <rx, ry, dx, ry>
 2.  case (mod, pol) of:
 3.    ry > dy and rx > dx:   (<'over'>, 1)
 4.    ry > dy and rx < dx:   LargestDimDiff(axes)
 5.    ry > dy and rx == dx:  (CalcRatio(axes, 'y'), 1)
 6.    ry < dy and rx < dx:   (<'over'>, 0)
 7.    ry < dy and rx > dx:   LargestDimDiff(axes)
 8.    ry < dy and rx == dx:  (CalcRatio(axes, 'y'), 0)
 9.    ry == dy and rx > dx:  (CalcRatio(axes, 'x'), 1)
10.    ry == dy and rx < dx:  (CalcRatio(axes, 'x'), 0)
11.    ry == dy and rx == dx: (None, None)
12.  return (mod, pol)

LARGESTDIMDIFF(<rx, ry, dx, dy>):
  axis = axis with largest difference between r and d (x or y)
  pol = direction of difference (0 or 1)
  return (<'ind', axis>, pol)

CALCRATIO(<rx, ry, dx, dy>, axis):
  if ry > rx: greater = ry, smaller = rx
  else: smaller = ry, greater = rx
  p = (greater/smaller) - 1
  if p > 1: p = 1
  v = round(100 * p)
  i = random integer between 1 and 100
  if i > v: mod = <'over'>
  else: mod = <'ind', axis>
  return mod
```

Figure 3: Size algorithm.

Lines 4 and 7 create a structure to generate an individuating size modifier ('ind') referring to the axis with the largest difference, with the appropriate polarity. Here, the modifier type selection reflects the second finding in Figure 2, while the selected axis is chosen based on the conclusions of Hermann and Deutsch (1976).

Lines 5, 8, 9, and 10 are all cases where one axis is different from the distractor and one axis is not. In these cases, following the third finding in Figure 2, we calculate the ratio of difference between the axes (CALCRATIO). This is a stochastic process that models speaker preference for a modifier type as a function of the object's aspect ratio. The closer the ratio of the x / y axes is to 1, the more likely the algorithm is to generate an overall size modifier.

Line 11 handles the case where both the referent and distractor have the same height and width. In this case, no size modifier is generated.

#	ID	Description
REFERENT FEATURES		
1	ry	target height
2	rx	target width
3	rrat	target height:width
4	ryrxdf	target height - target width
5	rsurfar	surface area of target
DISTRACTOR FEATURES		
6	dy	distractor height
7	dx	distractor width
8	drat	distractor height:width
9	dydxdf	distractor height - distractor width
10	dsurfar	surface area of distractor
COMPARISON FEATURES		
11	ydf	target height - distractor height
12	yratio	target height / distractor height
13	xdf	target width - distractor width
14	xratio	target width / distractor width
15	ratdf	target ratio - distractor ratio
16	discx	1 if rx > dx; 2 if rx == dx; 3 if rx < dx
17	discy	1 if ry > dy; 2 if ry == dy; 3 if ry < dy

Table 3: Visual features for each expression. Features 16 and 17 mirror the size algorithm's comparisons.

5 Machine Learning

One of the strengths of applying machine learning to this task is that it may be constructed as a series of binary classification problems, where a model is built for each size type. This allows more than one modifier to be generated for each referent, while avoiding issues of data sparsity inherent in training every combination of size as a separate class. The machine learning approach therefore has functionality that the hand-coded size algorithm does not have; it is able to predict sets of modifiers for a referent instead of being limited to a single modifier. This flexibility is a benefit to the machine learning approach over the hand-coded algorithm, and we return to this issue in Section 8.

To build robust models for this task, we use the data from the experiment in Mitchell et al. (2011a), which includes 414 native or fluent speakers of English. Each expression is annotated to mark the size modifiers and their types (Table 1).

A random selection of 10% of the dataset was checked for inter-annotator agreement. We found that many of the annotated brownie references picked out the z-axis, the third dimensional axis pointing inwards in the picture; although the im-

Type	<ind, y>		<ind, x>		<over>	
	1	0	1	0	1	0
Observed	22	10	3	0	51	43

Table 4: Frequency of observed size modifier types in the craft corpus.

ages are two-dimensional, both annotators reasoned about the three-dimensional shape to resolve references to all three axes. This is probably especially true for the brownies stimuli due to the angle of the camera, where differences in height may appear to be along the z-axis. In future work, it would be better to control this aspect, perhaps making only two dimensions visible. For this data, we group those modifiers for z- and y-axes together. Inter-annotator agreement was quite high at $\kappa = 0.94$.[1]

The models are constructed using C4.5 decision tree classifiers as implemented within Weka (Hall et al., 2009), with default parameter settings. We did not find a significant improvement in accuracy on our development set with different pruning methods or normalization. Each feature vector used by the models lists visual size features that characterize each image, such as the size of the referent and distractor's axes, and differences between the two. We also provide a set of features reflecting the comparisons made in the hand-coded algorithm. The feature set is listed in Table 3.

6 Testing Corpus

To evaluate how well the models perform in a new domain, we use the craft corpus from the experiment reported in Mitchell et al. (2010). The 2010 experiment is a different task, and differs in several critical ways from the 2011 experiment: (1) It was conducted in-person, using three-dimensional objects; (2) the referring expressions were produced orally; (3) there were many different objects in the scene, and (4) the objects had a variety of different features: texture, material, color, sheen, etc., as well as size along all three dimensions. A picture of the objects in the experiment is shown in Figure 4. Subjects referred to objects as, for example, "the longer silver ribbon", and "small green heart". Table 4 lists the frequency of each observed size type in this corpus.

[1] 729 size modifiers were compared for the agreement score; 5 modifiers only labeled by one annotator are excluded.

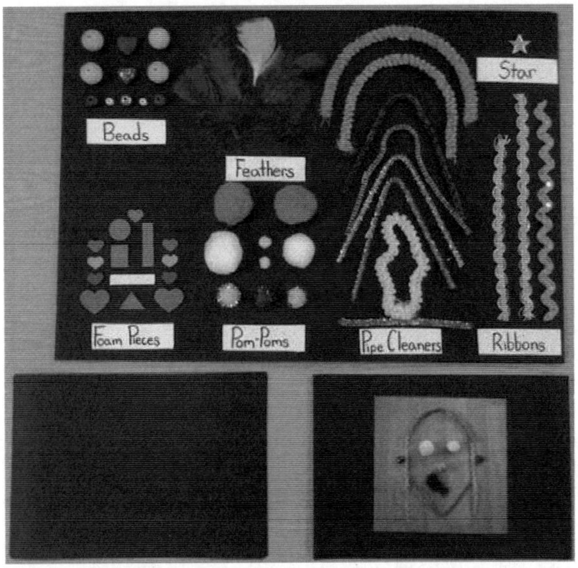

Figure 4: Object board for craft corpus.

As discussed above, we adapt the size algorithm to the new domain by taking the average height and width of all distractors of the same type, and comparing the referent against this average. The implications of this are three-fold: (1) Comparisons are limited to those items of the same type; (2) comparisons are limited to those items in an immediately surrounding group; and (3) comparisons are against a general 'gist' of the surrounding scene, instead of individual measurements.

To adapt the classifiers to the new domain, we remove all direct measurement features from training and testing; work on our development set suggests that including all listed features achieves the best precision and recall when training and testing in the same domain, however, when expanding to a new domain, certain features should be removed for optimal performance. This includes features 1 (ry, target height), 2 (rx, target width), 4 (ryrxdf, target height - width), 6 (dy, distractor height), 7 (dx, distractor width), 9 (dydxdf, distractor height - width), 11 (ydf, target height - distractor height), 13 (xdf, target width - distractor width). Removing these features allows the classifiers to build models from relative measurement features alone, and helps minimize overfitting to any one domain.

7 Evaluation

Before testing on the new domain, we test how well the two approaches do on the size corpus. The con-

```
discy <= 1: no
discy > 1
|   discx <= 1: no
|   discx > 1
|   |   drat <= 1
|   |   |   xratio <= 0.909: yes
|   |   |   xratio > 0.909
|   |   |   |   discy <= 2: no
|   |   |   |   discy > 2
|   |   |   |   |   rrat <= 0.455
|   |   |   |   |   |   xratio <= 0.910: yes
|   |   |   |   |   |   xratio > 0.910
|   |   |   |   |   |   |   rrat <= 0.413: yes
|   |   |   |   |   |   |   rrat > 0.413: no
|   |   |   |   |   rrat > 0.455: yes
|   |   drat > 1: no
```

Figure 5: Example decision tree: Training on Mechanical Turk data, direct measurement features removed, model for inclusion of (<over>, 0). Values in cm.

struction of the size algorithm was informed by this corpus, and so this provides a measure of how well the algorithm does in the domain for which it was designed. The decision trees are evaluated in this domain using leave-one-out validation, where the set of expressions for a referent containing at least one size modifier is tested against the models trained on the size expressions for all other referents. An example tree is shown in Figure 5. Features developed from the hand-coded algorithm (features 16 and 17 in Table 3) appear to have high discriminative utility in the trained models.

Unlike the machine learning approach, the size algorithm generates no more than one size type for each referent, although participants may produce several. To understand the upper bound of both approaches, we therefore implement an oracle method for the size algorithm (ORACLE$_{alg}$) that always guesses the most common size type for each referent, and an oracle method for the classifiers (ORACLE$_{tree}$) that always guesses the most common set of size types for each referent.

To understand the lower bound, we implement a baseline method that guesses the most common size type and most common set of size types in the training data for each testing fold. We find that the most common set of size types across folds contains a single modifier, making the baseline of the two approaches equivalent.

We evaluate the systems using precision and recall. Since we are comparing the set of predicted modifiers with the set of modifiers that a description contains, it would have been possible to use the

Model	Mturk precision/recall	Crafts precision/recall
BASELINE	25.7% / 24.5%	16.4% / 16.4%
ORACLE$_{alg}$	80.5% / 72.7%	89.1% / 89.1%
ORACLE$_{tree}$	79.5% / 76.0%	89.1% / 89.1%
SIZE ALGORITHM	69.7% / 63.4%	81.3% / 81.3%
DECISION TREE	65.4% / 65.7%	80.5% / 81.3%

Table 5: Precision and recall for models, testing on expressions that contain size. The size algorithm is averaged over 5 iterations.

DICE metric (Dice, 1945), as has often been done in evaluations of REG algorithms (Gatt and Belz, 2008). But DICE does not distinguish between recall (i.e., modifiers that are not predicted but should have been) and precision (i.e., modifiers that are predicted but should not have been), collapsing both of these into one single metric. For our purposes, it will be more informative to separate precision and recall. Given:

$\mathbb{O}_e$ = The set of size modifier types observed in an expression e

$\mathbb{P}_r$ = The set of size modifier types predicted for a referent r

$\mathbb{E}$ = The multiset of expressions in the corpus

$\mathbb{E}_r$ = The multiset of expressions for a referent r

$$\textbf{Precision} = \frac{\sum_{e \in \mathbb{E}_r \in \mathbb{E}} \frac{|\mathbb{P}_r \cap \mathbb{O}_e|}{|\mathbb{P}_r|}}{|\mathbb{E}|}$$

$$\textbf{Recall} = \frac{\sum_{e \in \mathbb{E}_r \in \mathbb{E}} \frac{|\mathbb{P}_r \cap \mathbb{O}_e|}{|\mathbb{O}_e|}}{|\mathbb{E}|}$$

Table 5 shows how well the different systems perform. Testing instances are limited to those that contain a size modifier. The second column lists precision and recall on the size corpus. The difference in results between the two systems is not statistically significant.

The third column of Table 5 lists how well the systems do when tested on the new domain, the craft corpus. The precision and recall values here are identical for the systems that generate one modifier because almost all size expressions in the craft corpus contain just one modifier. This also allows a more direct comparison between the two systems, as both the lower bounds (BASELINE) and upper bounds (ORACLE) of the two systems are equal.

As discussed in Section 6, both systems are adapted slightly for the new domain. The size algorithm uses the height and width *average* of items that are the same type as the referent. The decision trees are trained on the full size corpus, and when the models are built from all of the features listed in Table 3, precision / recall on this task is 44.1% / 48.1%. However, once we adapt the classifiers to the subset of relative measurement features, there is a large jump for both measures.

The two systems perform similarly. The size algorithm achieves just over 81.3% precision and recall, while the machine learning approach reaches 80.5% precision and 81.3% recall, and the differences between the two methods are not statistically significant. Oracle accuracy is higher by around 8%, suggesting that both systems are reasonable, and further work may want to finesse the kinds of size information that each uses.

8 Discussion

It is interesting that both systems perform better in the new domain. Both were built based on typed reference to one of two rectilinear solids in a two-dimensional photograph, and still produce reasonable output to spoken reference to one of several three-dimensional objects with different shapes in a much more descriptive task. The two systems likely perform better on the craft corpus than the one they were developed on because in the craft corpus, almost all expressions contain just one size modifier (only one expression had more).[2]

The machine learning approach does poorly when it uses the same set of features in both domains, however, by removing those features that may lead to overfitting – the direct measurements of individual objects – it dramatically improves in the new domain. The difference in precision and recall between the two systems is not statistically significant, with values above 80%.

A notable difference between the two systems is that the machine learning approach can predict any number of size modifiers, while the size algorithm is limited to predicting one modifier (or none). The upper and lower bounds are the same for both in the craft corpus discussed here, however, the classifiers' ability to predict when several size modifiers will be included may help extend this method in other domains.

One immediate question that arises from this work is how to move from abstract size type to surface form. For some modifiers, this will be relatively straightforward, but for others, e.g., using (<over>, 1) to generate the phrase "the second largest one", further functionality must be in place to reason about individual sizes of objects in the contrast set.

Both systems may be developed further by modelling speaker variation. Adding speaker label as a feature within the decision tree models guides the construction of distinct speaker clusters (Mitchell et al., 2011b) that generate different kinds of output. Such a technique can be applied here to generate language for a particular speaker cluster. In this case, the ability of the machine learning approach to generate any number of modifiers may aid in tuning it to specific speaker preferences.

In the size algorithm, speaker variation may be applied several ways. Currently, the algorithm's CALCRATIO function decides which of the two broad size modifier classes to generate by using a random number generator. This was implemented based on speaker variation in cases where the aspect ratio of an object approaches 1 (Figure 2). A similar technique may be applied throughout the algorithm, where a prior is assigned to various decisions based on an analysis of how speakers behave. Another method could apply slightly different versions of the algorithm to different speaker models, where some more detailed aspects of the algorithm are varied for different speaker profiles – for example, placing a preference on height over width within a threshold of axis size similarity.

9 Conclusions

We have presented two methods for generating size modifiers. Both utilize the dimensional aspects of objects in a scene to decide among six broad size categories, which may be used to inform the selection

[2]This was "the smallest long ribbon", which both models fail to predict.

of size modifier in a realized surface string. Both work relatively well and are extensible to a new domain.

One of the next clear steps in developing the hand-coded size algorithm is to add functionality for generating sets of modifiers. We would also like to explore different features and the effect they have on the overall accuracy of the different approaches. We hope to address modifiers that pick out specific configurations of multiple axes, e.g., "stout" may be realized from $\{(<\mathrm{ind}, \mathrm{x}>, 1), (<\mathrm{ind}, \mathrm{y}>, 0)\}$. Methods for reasoning about the distance and relative orientation between the target object and its distractors may guide which axis is referred to, and the systems should be further expanded to real-world objects by adding mechanisms to handle a third z-axis. A better understanding of when a difference along an axis is small enough not to be salient would help connect these approaches more closely to a visual input, placing constraints on when the outlined cases apply.

We hope to address other kinds of properties of real-world referents using a similar methodology, for example, reasoning about the inclusion of spatial prepositions between objects. By further defining when different properties are used, how distinct properties interact, and the features affecting their realization, we hope to continue to expand the methods to generate naturalistic reference.

10 Acknowledgments

This research was funded by the Scottish Informatics and Computer Science Alliance (SICSA) and the Overseas Research Students Awards Scheme (ORSAS). Thanks to help from Ellen Bard, Brian Roark, and the anonymous reviewers.

References

Sarah Brown-Schmidt and Michael K. Tanenhaus. 2006. Watching the eyes when talking about size: An investigation of message formulation and utterance planning. *Journal of Memory and Language*, 54:592–609.

Robert Dale and Ehud Reiter. 1995. Computational interpretations of the gricean maxims in the generation of referring expressions. *Cognitive Science*, 19:233–263.

Lee R. Dice. 1945. Measures of the amount of ecologic association between species. *Ecology*, 26(3):297–302, July.

Albert Gatt and Anja Belz. 2008. Attribute selection for referring expression generation: New algorithms and evaluation methods. *Proceedings of Fifth International Natural Language Generation Conference*, pages 50–58.

Mark Hall, Eibe Frank, Geoffrey Holmes, Bernhard Pfahringer, Peter Reutemann, and Ian H. Witten. 2009. The weka data mining software: An update. *SIGKDD Explorations*, 11(1).

Theo Hermann and Werner Deutsch. 1976. *Psychologie Der Objektbenennung*. Huber Verlag, Bern.

John Kelleher, Fintan Costello, and Josef van Genabith. 2005. Dynamically structuring, updating and interrelating representations of visual and linguistic discourse context. *Artificial Intelligence*, 167:62–102.

Ruud Koolen, Martijn Goudbeek, and Emiel Krahmer. 2011. Effects of scene variation on referential overspecification. *Proceedings of the 33rd annual meeting of the Cognitive Science Society (CogSci 2011)*.

Emiel Krahmer, Sebastiaan van Erk, and André Verleg. 2003. Graph-based generation of referring expressions. *Computational Linguistics*, 29(1):53–72.

Barbara Landau and Ray Jackendoff. 1993. "What" and "where" in spatial language and spatial cognition. *Behavioral and Brain Sciences*, 16:217–265.

Margaret Mitchell, Kees van Deemter, and Ehud Reiter. 2010. Natural reference to objects in a visual domain. *Proceedings of the Sixth International Natural Language Generation Conference (INLG-10)*.

Margaret Mitchell, Kees van Deemter, and Ehud Reiter. 2011a. Applying machine learning to the choice of size modifiers. *Proceedings of the 2nd PRE-CogSci Workshop*.

Margaret Mitchell, Kees van Deemter, and Ehud Reiter. 2011b. On the use of size modifiers when referring to visible objects. *Proceedings of the 33rd Annual Conference of the Cognitive Science Society*.

Ehud Reiter and Robert Dale. 2000. *Building Natural Language Generation Systems*. Cambridge University Press.

Julie C. Sedivy, Michael K. Tanenhaus, Craig G. Chambers, and Gregory N. Carlson. 1999. Achieving incremental semantic interpretation through contextual representation. *Cognition*, 71:109–147.

Kees van Deemter. 2006. Generating referring expressions that involve gradable properties. *Computational Linguistics*, 32(2):195–222.

Jette Viethen and Robert Dale. 2010. Speaker-dependent variation in content selection for referring expression generation. *Proceedings of the 8th Australasian Language Technology Workshop*, pages 81–89.

Using Online Games to Capture, Generate, and Understand Natural Language

Jeff Orkin
MIT Media Laboratory
Cambridge, MA, USA
jorkin@media.mit.edu

While the game industry has excelled at simulating combat, dynamically generating social interaction and natural language dialogue has proven intractable. The gaming landscape today, with millions of people playing games together online, provides opportunities to radically rethink our approach to developing conversational, socially intelligent characters. This talk will present a data-driven, human-machine collaborative approach to automating characters using data recorded from online human-human interactions, including a crowd-sourced annotation framework, and a new real-time planning system driven by thousands of annotated human gameplay traces. The approach will be demonstrated with examples from three novel games: The Restaurant Game has recorded over 16,000 people playing as customers and waitress, Improviso is currently recording players on the set of a low-budget science fiction movie, and Mars Escape has recorded hundreds of online human-robot interactions for eventual transfer to a real robot.

Proceedings of the 13th European Workshop on Natural Language Generation (ENLG), page 71,
Nancy, France, September 2011.

Content selection from an ontology-based knowledge base for the generation of football summaries

Nadjet Bouayad-Agha
Gerard Casamayor
DTIC, University Pompeu Fabra
Barcelona, Spain
`firstname@lastname.upf.edu`

Leo Wanner
ICREA and
DTIC, University Pompeu Fabra
Barcelona, Spain
`leo.wanner@icrea.es`

Abstract

We present an approach to content selection that works on an ontology-based knowledge base developed independently from the task at hand, i.e., Natural Language Generation. Prior to content selection, a stage akin to *signal analysis* and *data assessment* used in the generation from numerical data is performed for identifying and abstracting patterns and trends, and identifying relations between individuals. This new information is modeled as an extended ontology on top of the domain ontology which is populated via inference rules. Content selection leverages the ontology-based description of the domain and is performed throughout the text planning at increasing levels of granularity. It includes a main topic selection phase that takes into account a simple user model, a set of heuristics, and semantic relations that link individuals of the KB. The heuristics are based on weights determined empirically by supervised learning on a corpus of summaries aligned with data. The generated texts are short football match summaries that take into account the user perspective.

1 Introduction

Content selection (or determination) forms one of the major tasks in Natural Language Generation (NLG). Traditionally, it has been done from purpose-built KBs intertwined with discourse structuring; see, e.g., (Hovy, 1993; Moore and Paris, 1993). In an attempt to systematize the structure of the used KBs and to build an intermediate knowledge-oriented layer between them and linguistic structures, language-oriented ontologies such as the Upper Models (Bateman et al., 1990; Henschel, 1992, 1993; Bateman et al, 1995) have been developed. However, in view of the rise of the semantic web and the rapidly increasing volumes of KBs codified in OWL/RDF, the question on content selection from large scale purpose-neutral ontologies becomes very essential—at least for practical applications of NLG— and has scarcely been addressed.

In what follows, we present a framework for content selection from large scale OWL/RDF ontology-based domain KBs that were developed independently from the task of NLG. The framework is novel in that it (i) foresees a separation of the *domain communication* ontology from the general purpose domain ontology, and (ii) implements mechanisms for selecting content from large scale (at least for NLG standards) ontology-based knowledge bases.

To identify and abstract regular patterns and trends and introduce semantic relations between the individuals of a generic domain ontology, which are critical for high quality generation, but absent from any general purpose ontology, prior to content selection a stage akin to *signal analysis* and *data assessment* used for the generation from numerical data (Reiter, 2007; Wanner et al., 2010) is performed. This new information is modeled as an additional layer on top of the domain ontology, which is populated via rule-based inferences. Content selection proper then takes place at a number of levels of increasing granularity. First, a content bounding task is in charge of selecting, based on the user query, a subset of the KB that includes the maximal set of information that might be communicated to the user. Next the main topics to be included in the content plan are selected, taking into account: 1) a user model, 2) a set of heuristics, and 3) the seman-

Proceedings of the 13th European Workshop on Natural Language Generation (ENLG), pages 72–81,
Nancy, France, September 2011.

tic relations that link individuals of the KB. Finally, discourse unit determination in the discourse structuring submodule is in charge of deciding which details to include (or not) in each message. The whole text planning procedure that includes both content selection and discourse structuring is presented in (Bouayad-Agha et al., 2011).

The framework has been implemented with a KB that models the First Spanish Football League competitions for the generation (in Spanish) of short user perspective-tailored summaries of the individual matches. The user model is a simple model that contains the preference of the user for one of the teams. The content bounding parameters include the time, location and protagonists of the match of interest. The heuristics are based on weights determined empirically by supervised learning on a corpus of summaries aligned with data, as in (Duboue and McKeown, 2003). The following is an example generated summary:[1]

> "Victoria del F.C. Barcelona. *El Barcelona ganó contra el Almería por 2-1 gracias a un gol de Ronaldinho en el minuto 34 y otro de Eto'o en el minuto 56. El Barcelona ganó aunque acabó el partido con 10 jugadores a causa de la expulsión de Eto'o. Gracias a esta victoria, permanece en la zona de champions.* En la vigésimo quinta jornada, se enfrentará al Villarreal."

The first and the last sentences of the text are template-based. The content selection strategy is responsible for dynamically selecting the contents used to generate the text in between. For this example the system selected 30 RDF triples involving 17 individuals and 8 datatype values. For example, the fragment "a goal by Ronaldinho in minute 34 and another goal by Eto'o in minute 56" is generated from the following 6 triples: `minute(goal-1, 34), player(goal-1, player-1), name(player-1, Ronaldinho), minute(goal-2, 56), player(goal-2, player-2),name(player-2, Eto'o)`.

[1]Translation: 'Victory of F.C. Barcelona. Barcelona won against Almería by 2-1 thanks to a goal by Ronaldinho in minute 34 and another goal by Eto'o in minute 56. Barcelona won despite ending the match with 10 players because of the sent off of Eto'o. Thanks to this victory, Barcelona remains in the Champions zone (of the classification). Gameweek 25 Barcelona will meet Villareal.'

In the next section, we outline the base and extended ontologies and their corresponding knowledge bases. In Section 3, we discuss the ontology-based content selection procedure. In Section 4, we present a corpus-based evaluation of the content selection procedure, before reviewing some related work in Section 5 and providing some conclusions and discussing future work in Section 6.

2 Creation of an ontology-based KB

In an ontology-based KB, the KB is an instantiation (or population) of the corresponding ontologies. In what follows, we thus first outline the (manual) design of the ontology underlying our framework and describe then their (automatic) instantiation (or population).

2.1 Design of the ontology

As mentioned in Section 1, our framework foresees a two-layer ontology, the base ontology and the extended ontology. The **base ontology** models the domain in question, namely a football league competition. It is composed of two different ontologies: an object ontology which deals with structural information of the domain and an event ontology. The object ontology contains the specification of the teams, competition phases, matches, players, etc. The event ontology covers the events that may happen in a match (penalties, goals, cards, etc.). The object base ontology consists of 24 classes and 42 properties, with 4041 instances in the corresponding KB; the top level classes of the object ontology are: Competition, Match, Period, Person, Result, Season, Team, TeamCompositionRelation and Title. The event ontology consists of 23 classes and 8 properties, with 63623 instances in the corresponding KB; the top level classes of the event ontology are: ActionFault, Card, Corner, Fault, FaultKick, Goal, GoalKick, Interception, OffSide, Pass, Stop, Throw-in, Shot and Substitution.

The **extended ontology** models types of knowledge that can be considered as inferred from the concepts of the base ontology. This knowledge and consequently the rules to infer it were obtained by manual analysis of a subset of the corpus of football match summaries described in Subsection 3.2 below. It includes (i) the most frequently verbalized concepts that could be deduced from the events and states of a match specified in the base ontology,[2], and (ii) the semantic relations that implicitly hold between the individuals of the base and extended ontology concepts.[3]

The knowledge deduced from the events and states of a match is divided into five categories, each of them captured by several classes in the extended ontology: 1. result, 2. classification, 3. set, 4. match time, and 5. send-offs. *Result*-related knowledge (nominal result and the points scored in the competition) is inferred from the numerical result of the match available in the base ontology (with winner/loser/drawing opponents specified). *Classification*-related knowledge models information related to the position of each team in the competition, its accumulated points and relative zone. For the zone, in addition to the four official zones Champions, UEFA, neutral or relegation, we introduce two internal zones—Lead and BottomOfLeague. Furthermore, it is of relevance to obtain after each gameweek a team's tendency (ascending, descending, stable) and distance with respect to its previous classification. In addition to the real tendency, teams are assigned a virtual tendency which represents the team's change of zone taking a (virtual) result that may be different from the actual match result (for instance, if the team would have drawn instead of winning, what would be the tendency of its classification in the league table). *Set*-related knowledge models sets of events or processes for a given team in a match or for a given match. It is needed to be able to talk about events or processes together in accordance with their chronological occurrence (first goal, team was winning then it drew, etc.). *Match time*-related knowledge models the state of the match along its duration, creating intermediate results after each goal. Thus, a team could be winning after a goal, even though the final result is a draw. It is also possible to refer to specific reference time points such as 'beginning of the match', and 'conclusion of the first period'. *Send-offs* related knowledge includes the expulsion of a player after a red card and the number of players left after an expulsion.

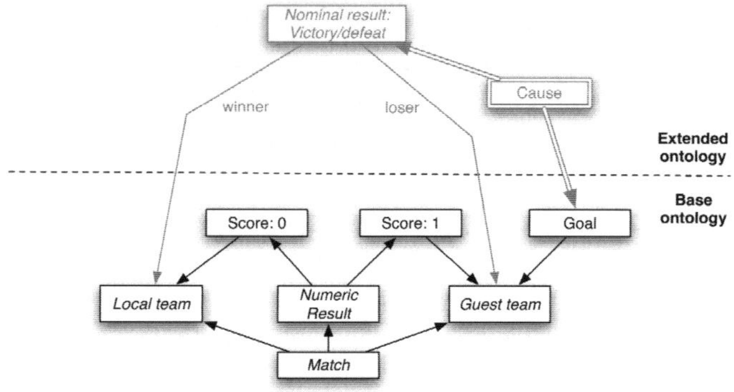

Figure 1: Fragment of the base and extended ontologies

In total, the five categories are modeled by 18 classes, among them: NominalResult, CompetitionResult, Tendency (a team's change of zone in the competition), Distance (to a higher/lower zone), Set, ConstituentSet,[4] Expulsion, PlayersInField, and IntermediateResult.

Consider Figure 1 for illustration.

Each class of deduced knowledge triggers the inference of a number of semantic relations; for instance:

- a cause relation is instantiated between the set of goals of a team and the final nominal result;
- a violation-of-expectation relation is instantiated between an instance of PlayersInField and a final winning/drawing result (e.g., *despite playing with 10, the team won*);
- a relation of precedence is instantiated between pairs of constituents in a set to show their immediate temporal precedence relation;
- a contrast relation is instantiated between the contrasting classification distances or tendencies of both teams of the match (e.g., *team A*

[2]Statistical information about matches within a season and across seasons (best scorer, consecutive wins, first victory in a given stadium, etc.), although mentioned in human produced summaries, has been excluded for now since it requires the assessment of a sequence of matches.

[3]More marginally, the extended ontology contains some information added to make the navigation easier for the mapping to linguistic realization and for the inference of new knowledge—for instance, 'for' and 'against' properties are added to the Goal class in order to know which team scored the goal and which team received it as this information was only available indirectly in the base ontology via the player who scored the goal.

[4]Set and ConstituentSet also allow us to simply refer to the number of constituents within it (cf. *the team had two red cards*).

goes up in the classification whilst team B goes down).

The semantic relations are modeled in terms of the class LogicoSemanticRelation and subclasses such as Cause, Implication, ViolationOfExpectation, Meronymy, Precedence, and Contrast.

2.2 Creation of the KB

The base KB has been automatically populated with data scraped from web pages about the Spanish League seasons to include general information about competitions, players, stadiums, etc, and specific information about matches. Currently, it contains three seasons: 2007/2008, 2008/2009 and 2009/2010. The scrapping was done by *ad hoc* programs that extract all the information required by the classes defined in the base ontologies.[5] The extended ontology population was carried out using the inference engine provided by Jena.[6] The engine works with a set of user-defined rules consisting of two parts: head (the set of clauses that must be accomplished to fire the rule) and body (the set of clauses that is added to the ontology when the rule is fired). We defined 93 rules, with an estimated average of 9,62 clauses per rule in the head part. Consider the following example of a rule for classifying the difference between the scores of the two teams as "important" if it is greater than or equal to three:

```
[rule2: (?rn rdf:type base:NumResult)
(?rn base:localScore ?localScore)
(?rn base:visitorScore ?visitorScore)
(?localScore base:result ?local)
(?visitorScore base:result ?visitor)
differenceAbs(?local, ?visitor, ?r)
ge(?r, 3) ->
(?rn inference:resultDiff "important")]
```

For the 38 gameweeks of the regular football season, the inference engine generates, using the 93 rules from the data in the base ontologies, a total of 55894 new instances. The inference rules are organized into five groups corresponding to the five categories of inferred knowledge described in Subsection 2.1.

[5]Object and event information were extracted from the Sportec (`http://futbol.sportec.es`) and AS (`http://www.as.com/futbol`) portals respectively.

[6]`http://jena.sourceforge.net/`

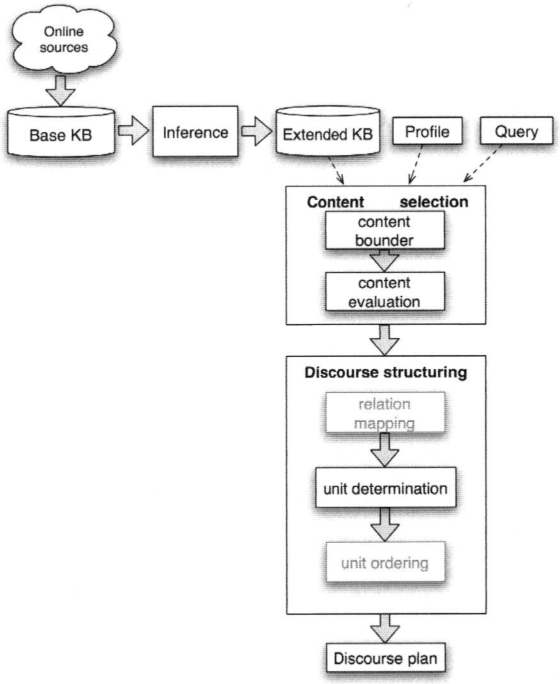

Figure 2: The view on text planning involving content selection *(the sub-modules that do not perform any content selection are grayed out)*

3 Ontology-based content selection

3.1 Approach to content selection

As mentioned in Section 1, content selection is performed at different stages of text planning, in increasing granularity. It includes content bounding and main topic selection performed within the content selection module proper, and fine-grained content selection performed during the discourse unit determination task of the discourse structuring module; see Figure 2 for the overall picture of text planning in which content selection is involved.

The content bounding sub-module selects from the ontology-based KB individuals that are relevant to the match for which a text is to be generated and the semantic relations that link these individuals. The selection works with a set of hand-written rules that draw upon relevance criteria concerning the direct involvement of the individuals (e.g., the players of the teams in question, goals during the match, etc.) and the general context of the competition (e.g., the league's classification).

Given the large size (by NLG standards) of the

KB, the motivation for the content bounder is to filter out irrelevant information and to make thus the subsequent content selection task more manageable. The output of the content bounder is a fragment of the KB which constitutes the maximal set of data available for generating any sort of summary for a given match.

The content evaluation submodule is in charge of evaluating the relevance of the content according to 1) a simple user model, 2) a set of heuristics, and 3) the semantic relations that link individuals in the KB. Both the user model and the heuristics are numeric functions that map instances of concepts in the KB to a numeric measure of their relevance. The user model consists of the specification of the user's team of interest for the requested match or of a "neutral" profile—if the user has no favorite team. The heuristics measure relevance according to empirical knowledge extracted from a corpus of texts.[7] The content evaluation currently gives a weight of '1' if the node is related to the user's team of interest or if the user profile is "neutral" and '0' otherwise. This weight is multiplied by the node's relevance measure, which is set to '1' if the heuristic weight for selecting the instance outweighs the heuristic weight for not selecting it. Otherwise it is set to '0'. Finally, the nodes that represent the semantic relations are marked as relevant if they link two nodes with a positive relevance weight. This ensures the coherence of the content being selected. In Subsection 3.2 below, we describe how the relevance measures were empirically obtained.

The discourse unit determination is template-based. That is, we use our expertise of what can be said together in the same proposition in a football match summary. Currently, we have defined eleven discourse unit templates that cover the types of propositions that can be found in football summaries. Each core node, i.e., node that can be the argument of a discourse relation, can form a discourse unit. So, for each core node, a list of (possibly recursive) paths in the form *edge>Vertex* (where the edge is the object property and the vertex is the class range) is given to find in the graph the list of nodes that can be included in the discourse unit of that core node, starting from the core node. The individuals that are not included in those discourse units are excluded from the final text. For example, the following is an excerpt of the template for expressing the result of a match:

```
partido>Partido,
periodo>PeriodoPartido,
resultNom>ResultNom,
resultNom>ResultNom>ganador>Equipo,
resultNom>ResultNom>perdedor>Equipo,
resultNom>ResultNom>protagonist>Equipo
```

3.2 Empirical Determination of Relevance Measures

The weights of the instances that are to be selected are obtained by supervised training on a corpus of aligned data and online articles. The corpus consists of eight seasons of the Spanish League, from 2002/2003 to 2009/2010 with a total of 3040 matches, downloaded from different web sources. The articles typically consist of explicitly marked up title, summary and body. The data for each match consist of the teams, stadium, referee, players, major actions like goals, substitutions, red and yellow cards, and some statistical information such as number of penalties. Table 1 shows the verbalization of some categories in each of the three article sections considered for a single season in any of the sources. These categories were automatically marked up using the alignment of text with data described below. As can be seen, the result of the match (whether nominal or numerical) is almost always included in all the sections, whilst the verbalization of other categories is more extensive in the article body than in the summary, and in the summary more extensive than in the title. In our work on the generation of summaries, we focused on learning weights for league classifications, goals and red cards.

The data-text alignment procedure implies as a first step a preprocessing phase that includes tokenization and number-to-digit conversion. Then, instances of the relevant categories (i.e., specific goals, specific red cards, etc.) are detected using data anchors in the text (such as player names and team names) and regular expressions patterns compiled from the most frequent N word sequences of the corpus (where $1<N<5$). Data anchors are given priority over the use of regular expressions.

[7]Relevance could also be measured according to other sources (e.g., past interaction with the user).

	title	summary	body
result	92.4%	90.8%	97.6%
classification	16.3%	22%	51.3%
goal	19.6%	43.6%	95.2%
red card	9.3%	32.2%	77.1%
stadium	19.2%	38.2%	82.4%
referee	2.9%	3.7%	80%
substitution	0%	0.17%	18.1%

Table 1: Verbalization of some categories in title, summary and body of Spanish Football League articles (2007/2008 season) in all sources

For the description of a goal or a red card, we used the same set of over 100 feature types since we considered them both as match events. The features include information about the current event (minute, event number in the match), the player involved (name,position, proportion of goals/cards in the match and in the season up to the match, proportion of games played in season up to the match, etc), the current game, gameweek, season and team (including classification and statistical information), and comparison of the current event with previous and next event of the same class (e.g., deltas of minute, player and team).

For modeling the classification, we used a more systematic approach to feature extraction by regarding a team's classification as the event of a specific gameweek, comparing it to the events of the previous gameweek—that is, to the 20 classifications[8] of the previous gameweek and to the events of the same gameweek (also 20 classifications), such as the delta of category, points and team between classifications. In this way, we obtained a total of 760 feature types.

In order to classify the data, we used Boostexter (Schapire and Singer, 2000), a boosting algorithm that uses decision stumps over several iterations and that has already been used in previous works on training content selection classifiers (Barzilay and Lapata, 2005; Kelly et al., 2009).[9] For each of the three categories (goal, red card, classification), we experimented with 15 different classifiers by considering a section dimension (title, summary and title+summary) and a source dimension (espn, marca, terra, any one of them (any) and at least two of them). We divided the corpus each time into 90-10% of the matches for training and testing.

4 Content selection evaluation

Our evaluation of the content selection consisted of three stages: (1) evaluation of the automatic data-article alignment procedure, (2) evaluation of the performance of the classifiers for the empirical relevance determination, and (3) evaluation of the content selection as a whole.

The evaluation of the automatic alignment against 158 manually aligned summaries resulted in an F-score of 100% for red cards, 87% for goals and 51% for classification. The low performance of classification alignment is due to the low efficiency of its anchors: positions, zones and points are seldom mentioned explicitly and both team names often appear in the summary, leading to ambiguity. For this reason, classification alignment was edited manually.

Table 2 shows the performance of the classifiers for the determination of the relevance of the three categories (goal, red card and classification) with respect to their inclusion into the summary section, comparing it to the baseline, which is the majority class. For red cards, the results correspond to considering title and summary from a source together, given that the results are not significant when considering summary section only (accuracy is 78.1%, baseline accuracy is 65.4% and $t = 4.4869$ with $p<0.0001$). In all cases, the best performance is obtained by considering the content from any of the online sources.

The evaluation of the content selection as a whole is done by comparing the content of generated summaries with that of existing summaries (the gold standard). We say "as a whole" since this evaluation also considers the template-based content selection performed during discourse unit determination.[10]

Our test corpus consists of 36 randomly selected matches from the set of matches of the 2007–2008 season, each with three associated summaries from

[8]The Spanish League competition involves 20 teams.

[9]After a number of experiments, the number of iterations was set to 300.

[10]However, we do not evaluate discourse unit determination itself.

category	source	sample size	classifier	baseline	paired t-test
goal	any	1123	64%	51%	t = 6.3360 (p<0.0001)
	terra	1121	65%	59%	t = 3.4769 (p=0.0005)
card	any	62	85%	53%	t = 4.4869 (p<0.0001)
classif	any	295	75%	61%	t = 4.4846 (p<0.0001)

Table 2: Performance of the best classifiers (vs majority baseline) on a test set for the summary section (+title in case of red cards)

three different web sources (namely espn, marca, terra). We compiled a list of all individuals considered for inclusion in the content selection and discourse unit determination modules and for which explicitly references could be found in target texts, including instances of the semantic relations, which were modelled as classes in the KB. For each of the 108 (36×3) summaries, we manually annotated whether an individual was verbalized or not. We also annotated for each text the team of interest by checking whether the majority of content units was from one team or another; in case of equality, the user profile was considered neutral. This allowed us to compare the generated text of a given match for a given profile with the text(s) for the same profile.[11] As baseline, we always select both teams and the final result regardless of profile since the result (and most likely the associated teams—as shown in Table 1) is almost always included in the summaries. This baseline is likely to have high precision and lower recall.

We performed three runs of generation: (1) a full run with relevance weights determined by the trained models ("estimated"), (2) a run in which the relevance of the instances is determined from the aligned texts, taking the profile into account ("real w., prof."), and (3) a run like (2), but without taking into account the user profile when determining relevance ("real w., no prof."). Table 3 shows the results of the evaluation for each of the three sources. In the context of sports commentaries, readers usually tolerate better a certain excess of information than lack of (relevant) information. Therefore, recall can be considered of higher prominence than precision.

Precision and recall are obtained by measuring the individuals included in the content plan by the estimated or baseline model against the individuals mentioned in the gold standard. The recall is predictably lower in the baseline than in the other runs. The F-measure in the source Marca is considerably lower for the three runs than the baseline. This is because the summaries in this source are very much like short titles (for marca, we had an average of 2 individuals mentioned per summary vs. 4 for espn and 6 for terra). The runs without profile have understandably a higher recall since content selection is less discriminative without a user profile (or rather with a *neutral* user profile). Nonetheless, they show a somewhat lower F-measure than those with a profile, especially for the two sources with the longest summaries. Finally, the performance of content selection with empirically estimated relevance is comparable to the performance of content selection with relevance taken from the target texts—which indicates that there are benefits in using supervised learning for estimating relevance.

Although a more formal error analysis would be needed, here are a few issues that we encountered during the (manual) counting of the individuals for the evaluation:

1. errors in the automatic alignment for goals and red cards;
2. errors in the KB (we found at least a missing instance, and an error in the final score which meant that it was a draw instead of a victory);
3. some inferred content is missing, among them sets of goals for a given player or a given period of the match (e.g., first half) as well as some relations (e.g., violation of expectation between the fact that team A did not win and team B played with less than 11 players during a determined period of the game);

[11] Our observation is that sports commentaries (at least in web-based news media) are by far not always neutral and address thus readers with a specific (biased) profile.

source	#individuals	baseline			estimated			real w., prof.			real w., no prof.		
		prec.	rec.	F1	prec.	rec.	F1	prec.	rec.	F1	prec.	rec.	F1
espn	157	83.3	57.3	67.9	43.2	77.1	55.4	42.5	79.6	55.4	35.1	85.4	49.7
marca	74	49.0	63.5	55.3	21.8	79.7	34.2	20.2	79.7	32.2	17.7	90.5	29.6
terra	223	98.1	47.5	64.0	54.2	64.1	58.7	56.1	65.9	60.6	44.8	75.8	56.3

Table 3: Content selection evaluation results

4. some of the considered individuals are never included in the final content plan; for instance, the sets of goals without the listing of the individual goals (to say that a team marked 3 goals).

With respect to the second issue, although we did not evaluate the correctness of the KB, we are aware that it is not error-free and that more testing and mending is needed. With respect to the third and fourth issues, the question comes up how to systematize the discovery of new inferred knowledge (including relations) and how to get relevance heuristics for content selection. Supervised learning can be unreliable and/or painstaking, especially if the data is scarce and/or requires manual annotation. Another promising avenue of research is to obtain those heuristics from the user using reinforcement learning.

5 Related Work

The task of content selection in NLG can be characterized along three dimensions: 1) *what* is the source of the content, 2) *where* in the generation pipeline it is selected, and 3) *how* it is selected. The first dimension specifies, for instance, whether the content is structured or unstructured data in a relational database or hierarchical knowledge in a knowledge base, and whether the data / knowledge representation is built for the purposes of NLG or whether it is task-independent. The second dimension specifies whether content selection occurs before the actual generation (as an expert system task) or during it, and whether it is performed in a separate module or is integrated to a lesser or greater degree with other tasks. The third dimension reflects the strategy used: statistical or symbolic, top-down or bottom-up. Traditionally, content selection in NLG involves structured, purpose-built KBs processed using symbolic top-down approaches such as schemas or plan-based operators that perform content selection together with discourse structuring; see, e.g., (Hovy, 1993; Moore and Paris, 1993).

In a step towards more flexible content selection, (O'Donnell et al., 2001) put forward a proposal to select content by navigating a text potential. Also, in the recent past, determination of the relevant episodes in large time-series gained prominence (Yu et al., 2007; Portet et al., 2009). Although some of the data of a football league competition can also be expressed in terms of a time-series, in general, it goes beyond a numeric attribute-value pair sequence.

Statistical techniques on numerical data have also been investigated—among them (Duboue and McKeown, 2003; Barzilay and Lapata, 2005; Demir et al., 2010). Some of these techniques use classifiers trained with supervised learning methods to decide on the selection of individual units of data (e.g., a row of a table in a relational database, or entities in an RDF graph). Others construct a graph-based representation of the content and apply an optimisation algorithm for network analysis (i.e. a flow or a centrality algorithm) to find out the most relevant subset of content.

Ontologies have a long standing tradition in NLG, the most notable of which is the Upper Model (Bateman et al., 1990; Henschel, 1992, 1993; Bateman et al, 1995) which is a a linguistically motivated ontology. More directly related to our approach are ontology-oriented proposals in NLG whether to leverage linguistic generation (Bontcheva and Wilks, 2004), to verbalize ontologies (Wilcock, 2003; Power and Third, 2010) or to select content for the purpose of ontology verbalization (Mellish and Pan, 2008).

6 Conclusions and future work

We have presented an NLG content selection approach performed on a task-independent ontology-based knowledge base. The lack of domain communication knowledge (Kittredge et al., 1991) in the ontology was remedied by adding to the basic ontology a second layer populated using inference rules that includes the modelling of semantic relations between individuals. Ontological information, that is knowledge of classes and properties, was exploited at all stages of content selection, whether using schemas or empirically determined relevance measures for the main classes to include in the target text.[12] This latter task of selecting the main topics that are to be included in the final text takes into account coherence by exploiting the semantic relations between individuals, and the wanted perspective on the generated text by incorporating a simple user model and relevance measures empirically determined on a corpus of aligned text and data pairs. In the future, instead of using a heuristic-based content extraction approach for the main topic selection task, we plan to apply a set of general purpose content extraction algorithms such as PageRank (Demir et al., 2010).

In the medium-term, we also plan to make the tasks of our content selection and discourse structuring modules domain-independent, that is, parametrizable to a given domain, but with clearly domain-independent mechanisms. This goal is currently being addressed by applying the approach to ontology-based content selection to a completely different domain, namely environmental information. The environmental domain has been modeled in an ontology-based knowledge base which has been extended with domain communication knowledge. We want to be able to bound the content using a general algorithm that exploits domain-specific criteria.

We are also planning additional work on discourse unit determination, as it is still template-based and thus of restricted flexibility.

[12] As pointed out by Referring Expression Generation researchers (Jordan and Walker, 2005), content selection occurs also further down the chain; for example, during the selection amongst the property for name, dorsal number, and role (e.g., attacker) to refer to a given player. In our generator, these properties are passed down to the linguistic generator for selection, although ad-hoc rules are used rather than strict ontological knowledge.

References

Regina Barzilay and Mirella Lapata. 2005. Collective Content Selection for Concept-to-Text Generation. *Proceedings of the Joint Human Language Technology and Empirical Methods in Natural Language Processing Conferences (HLT/EMNLP-2005)* Vancouver, Canada.

John A. Bateman, Robert T. Kasper, Johanna D. Moore, and Richard A. Whitney 1990 A General Organization of Knowledge for Natural Language Processing: the Penman Upper Model *Technical Report.* USC/Information Sciences Institute, Marina del Rey, California.

John A. Bateman, Renate Henschel, and Fabio Rinaldi 1995 Generalized Upper Model 2.0: documentation. *Technical Report.* GMD/Institut für Integrierte Publikations- und Informationssysteme, Darmstadt, Germany.

Kalina Bontcheva and Yorick Wilks. 2004. Automatic Report Generation from Ontologies: the MIAKT approach. *Proceedings of the Nineth International Conference on Applications of Natural Language to Information Systems (NLDB'2004).* Manchester, UK.

Nadjet Bouayad-Agha, Gerard Casamayor, Leo Wanner, Fernando Díez, and Sergio López Hernández. 2011. FootbOWL: Using a generic ontology of football competition for planning match summaries. *Proceedings of the 8th Extended Semantic Web Conference (ESWC2011).* Heraklion, Greece.

Seniz Demir, Sandra Carberry and Kathleen F. McCoy. 2010. A Discourse-Aware Graph-Based Content-Selection Framework. Proceedings of the International Language Generation Conference. Sweden.

Pablo A. Duboue and Kathleen R. McKeown. 2003. Statistical Acquisition of Content Selection Rules for Natural Language Generation. Proceedings of the 2003 conference on Empirical Methods in Natural Language Processing (EMNLP). Sapporo, Japan.

Renate Henschel 1992, 1993. Merging the English and German Upper Models. *Technical Report.* GMD/Institut für Integrierte Publikations- und Informationssysteme, Darmstadt, Germany.

Eduard Hovy. 1993 *Automated discourse generation using discourse relations.* Artificial Intelligence. 63 , 341 – 385.

Pamela W. Jordan and Marilyn A. Walker 2005 *Learning content selection rules for generating object descriptions in dialogue* Journal of Artificial Intelligence Research 24, 157–194.

Colin Kelly, Ann Copestake, and Nikiforos Karamanis. 2009 Investigating content selection for language generation using machine learning. *Proceedings of the 12th European Workshop on Natural Language Generation.*. 130–137.

Richard Kittredge, Tanya Korelsky, and Owen Rambow. 1991. On the need for domain communication knowledge. *Computational Intelligence* 7(4):305–314.

Chris Mellish and Jeff Z. Pan. 2008 Language Directed Inference from Ontologies. *Artifi cial Intelligence.* 172(10):1285-1315.

Johanna D. Moore and Cécile L. Paris. 1993 Planning texts for advisory dialogs: capturing intentional and rhetorical information. *Computational Linguistics.* 19(4), 651-694.

Mick ODonnell, Chris Mellish, Jon Oberlander, and Alistair Knott. 2001. ILEX: an architecture for a dynamic hypertext generation system. *Natural Language Engineering.* 7(3):225–250.

François Portet, Ehud Reiter, Albert Gatt, Jim Hunter, Somayajulu Sripada, Yvonne Freer and Cindy Sykes. 2009. Automatic generation of textual summaries from neonatal intensive care data. *Artifi cial Intelligence* 173(7-8): 789-816.

Richard Power and Allan Third. 2010. Expressing OWL axioms by English sentences: dubious in theory, feasible in practice. *Proceedings of the 23rd International Conference on Computational Linguistics (COLING 2010).* Beijing, China.

Ehud Reiter 2007. An Architecture for Data-to-Text Systems. *Proceedings of the 11th European Natural Language Generation* Schloss Dagstuhl, Germany. page 97-104.

Robert E. Schapire and Yoram Singer 2000 BoosTexter: A boosting-based system for text categorization. *Machine Learning* 39(2/3):135–168.

Leo Wanner, Bernd Bohnet, Nadjet Bouayad-Agha, Francois Lareau, and Daniel Nicklaß. 2010 MARQUIS: Generation of User-Tailored Multilingual Air Quality Bulletins. *Applied Artifi cial Intelligence.* 24(10):914–952.

Graham Wilcock 2003 Talking owls: Towards an ontology verbalizer. *Proceedings of the Human Language Technology for the Semantic Web and Web Services, ISWC-2003.* 109–112. Sanibel Island, Florida.

Jin Yu, Ehud Reiter and Jim Hunter. 2007 Choosing the content of textual summaries of large time-series data sets. *Natural Language Engineering.* 13:25-49.

Deriving rhetorical relationships from semantic content

Richard Power
Department of Computing
Open University, UK
r.power@open.ac.uk

Abstract

This paper investigates to what extent rhetorical relations can be assigned purely on the basis of propositional content, without any reference to speaker goals or other pragmatic information. This task confronts any NLG system designed to generate coherent text from a set of formally represented statements; we consider it here in the context of an ontology verbaliser, for which the input is a set of axioms encoded in the web ontology language OWL. A simple set-theoretical model of the possible semantic relationships between two statements is proposed; this model allows 46 logically consistent relationships, of which we hypothesise that 11 are rhetorically coherent. This hypothesis is tested through an empirical survey which also provides evidence on how the coherent patterns are expressed linguistically.

1 Introduction

Perhaps the murkiest area in the language sciences is the issue of how statements are combined in a discourse. Much research has been based (more or less strictly) on Rhetorical Structure Theory (RST), (Mann and Thompson, 1987), a theory grounded in intuitions about naturally occurring texts and more concerned with comprehensive coverage than formal adequacy. Categories like 'concession' and 'elaboration' have to be assigned through human judgement, and remain somewhat subjective despite efforts to refine them and clarify their definitions (Carlson and Marcu, 2001). Other researchers have looked more deeply into the meaning of the relations, analysing them through rhetorical features (Hobbs, 1985; Sanders et al., 1992; Knott, 1996) with more emphasis on theory than on the requirements of practical annotation.

In this paper we attack the problem from a new direction. Instead of starting from naturally occurring texts, and human judgements thereupon, we consider the far more restricted issue of how a rhetorical relationship could be assigned to two axioms drawn from an ontology, and hence to the sentences generated from these axioms by an ontology verbaliser,[1] using only information that is internal to the ontology. This means that we accept the strict limitations of the ontology formalism, assumed to be OWL-DL (Horrocks et al., 2003); statements that cannot be represented in this formalism are excluded. It also means that the ontology is the *only* source of knowledge about the domain, and that no pragmatic information is available at all, beyond the implicit fact that each axiom has been asserted. This is precisely the situation that confronts an NLG (Natural Language Generation) system that aims to generate a coherent text from an OWL ontology, using only generic methods (i.e., methods that require no additional domain knowledge). How can such a system decide whether two statements from the ontology are related, and if so, classify the relationship in a way that guides their linguistic realisation?

An example will clarify both the exact task, and how it might be approached. Suppose that an on-

[1] Examples of ontology verbalisers are SWAT Tools (SWAT Project, 2011), described by Williams et al. (2011), ACE (Attempto Project, 2011), and OntoVerbal (Liang et al., 2011).

Proceedings of the 13th European Workshop on Natural Language Generation (ENLG), pages 82–90,
Nancy, France, September 2011.

	OWL statement	Example of verbalisation
1	*ClassAssertion(C,I)*	Butch is a dog
2	*ObjectPropertyAssertion(P,I,J)*	Mary owns Butch
3	*ClassAssertion(ObjectSomeValuesFrom(P,C),I)*	Butch lives in a kennel
4	*SubClassOf(C,D)*	Every dog is a canine
5	*SubClassOf(C,ObjectHasValue(P,I))*	Every dog likes Mary
6	*SubClassOf(C,ObjectSomeValuesFrom(P,D))*	Every dog lives in a kennel
7	*DisjointClasses(C,D)*	No dog is a cat
8	*EquivalentClasses(C,D)*	A dog is defined as a domestic canine

Table 1: Common axiom patterns in OWL. A study of over 200 ontologies indicated that these patterns comprise over 95% of all axioms (Power and Third, 2010). Variables C, D denote classes, I, J denote individuals, and P denotes a property.

tology contains the axioms in table 1, and that we are interested in the relationship between the axioms numbered 6 and 3:

> Every dog lives in a kennel.
> Butch lives in a kennel.

Even within our restricted formulation of the task, there are two sources of evidence that can be exploited here. First, confining our attention to these two statements alone, we may note that they share the same predicate term 'lives in a kennel' (corresponding to a constructed class in OWL). On this basis we might presume that the statements are related, and propose a neutral method of linking them such as 'Every dog lives in a kennel; so does Butch'. However, we can go further if we exploit the second source of evidence, *the other statements in the ontology* — and in particular statement 1 which connects the terms 'Butch' and 'dog'. Taking this into account, we could interpret the second statement in our pair (3) as an implication of the first statement (6), or perhaps as an example of it:

Every dog lives in a kennel; therefore so does Butch.
Every dog, including Butch for example, lives in a kennel.

The purpose of this paper is to model systematically the patterns of relationship among the terms in two statements, and to show through an empirical study which pairs are judged to be rhetorically related, and which are not. For pairs judged to be related, we also present evidence on how the statements could be combined linguistically (e.g., using aggregation and/or discourse connectives).

2 Coherence model

We begin by constructing a simple model which covers OWL statements based on three axiom functors: *ClassAssertion*, *ObjectPropertyAssertion*, and *SubClassOf*.[2] The commonest patterns are shown in axioms 1-6 of table 1, along with sample English realisations conforming to most verbalisers (Kaljurand and Fuchs., 2007; Hart et al., 2008; Schwitter and Meyer, 2007).

For the axioms considered, we can give a simple uniform semantics in which each statement links two sets, one denoted by the subject, the other by the predicate; the meaning of the statement is that the predicate set contains the subject set. To accommodate individuals within this scheme we can replace them by enumerated classes with only one member (in OWL these can be constructed using the functor *OneOf*). Thus 'Butch is a dog' means that the set containing only Butch is a subset of the set of dogs; 'Butch lives in a kennel' means that the set containing only Butch is a subset of the set of things that live in kennels, and so forth. Both statements in a pair can then be reduced to a pair of sets SP, where S is the subject set and P is the predicate set, the structure of the pair being $S_1P_1 + S_2P_2$.[3] With four sets we now have six potential relationships to consider: S_1P_1, S_1S_2, S_1P_2, P_1S_2, P_1P_2, and S_2P_2. Two of these (S_1P_1, S_2P_2) correspond to the original statements; the other four may be addressed elsewhere in

[2]Elsewhere (Power and Third, 2010) we have shown that these functors cover around 80% of all axioms.

[3]Note that this semantics is derived from the underlying OWL formulas, and would not be applicable to some sentences in English (e.g., ones expressing existential statements such as 'At least one dog likes Mary').

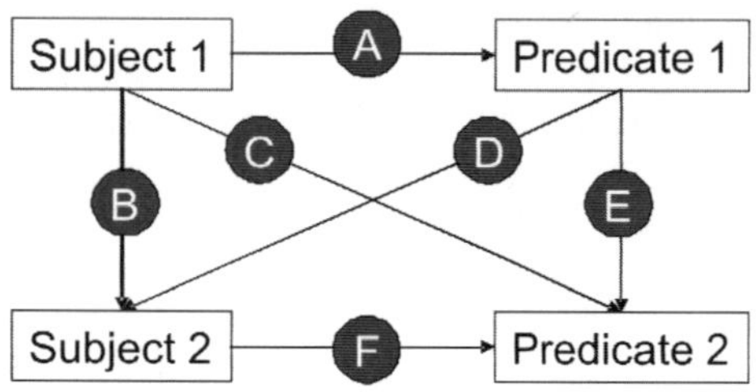

Figure 1: Subject-Predicate relations for two statements

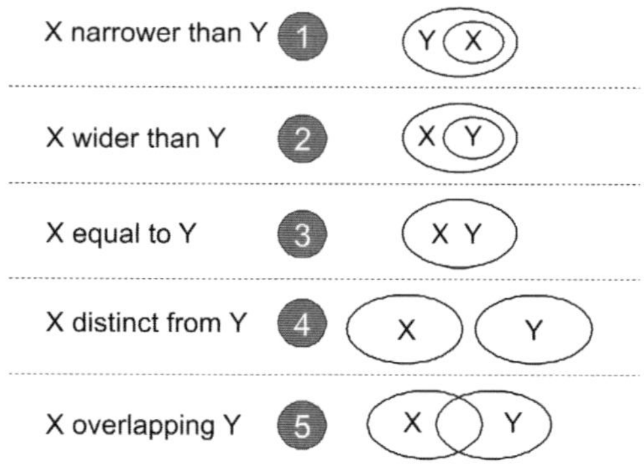

Figure 2: Relations among two sets

the ontology, thus providing additional information on whether and how the statements are rhetorically related. The six relationships are shown diagrammatically in figure 1 by the arrows labelled A–F.

The next question is how these relationships among sets should be classified. Among various possibilities, a plausible method is shown in figure 2: given two sets X and Y, either X will be narrower than Y, or wider, or equal, or distinct, or overlapping. These relations are represented in OWL as follows: (1) narrower by *SubClassOf(X,Y)*; (2) wider by *SubClassOf(Y,X)*; (3) equal by *EquivalentClasses(X,Y)*; (4) distinct by *disjointClasses(X,Y)*; and (5) overlapping, implicitly, by absence of the above. A similar set of relations has been proposed by MacCartney and Manning (2009) for the textual entailment task.[4]

With this model, the rhetorical relationship between two statements can be profiled by assigning an integer from 1–5 (figure 2) to each of the relationships A–F (figure 1); to represent such assignments succinctly we will use a six-number code such as 131231 meaning A=1, B=3, C=1, D=2, E=3, F=1. If we assume that subjects are always narrower than predicates, two of these relations (A and F in figure 1) will always be 1. This leaves a potential 5^4 or 625 combinations for the other four relations (B to E in figure 1). However, most of these combinations are contradictory; by writing a Prolog program[5] which applies consistency constraints, we have shown that the consistent combinations number only 46 (Power, 2011a). These are presented with handcrafted examples suggesting that some of the patterns are rhetorically coherent, while others, although logically consistent, are not. On the basis of these examples, the author judged that 11 pairs out of 46 were rhetorically related and 35/46 were not. The list was then given to two colleagues who picked out exactly the same eleven patterns, illustrated in table 2. In this table the patterns are also grouped, and given names which we hope are intuitively easier to grasp than their codes. On inspection, it turns out that a simple rule explains our selections: we judged a pattern coherent either if the two statements had a set in common (i.e., if the cross-statement relations B-E contained relation 3), or if all cross-statement relations were disjoint (i.e., 144441).

3 Empirical validation

The empirical study described in this section has two aims. First, we seek firmer evidence regarding the division of the 46 logically consistent patterns into coherent and incoherent (i.e., rhetorically related and unrelated). However intuitive this division, it is interesting not only to confirm it, but to see whether there are degrees of coherence both within the sheep (so to speak) and the goats. Secondly, where people judge that two statements have sufficient affinity to be presented together, we are interested in how they combine them linguistically, and whether each pattern is associated with characteristic discourse connectives or syntactic configurations.

To generate examples for testing, it is convenient to construct an ontology that contains just enough material to produce at least one example for each

[4]MacCartney and Manning actually use seven relations, because they distinguish as a separate case disjoint and overlap relations in which the classes X and Y cover all entities in the domain (i.e., every entity must belong either to X or to Y or both). This refinement is not relevant for our purposes.

[5]The program can be downloaded from the website at Power (2011b).

N	Code	Name	Example
1	131211	Widening Elaboration	Dogs are canines; dogs are vertebrates
2	131221	Narrowing Elaboration	Dogs are vertebrates; dogs are canines
3	131251	Additive Elaboration	Dogs are canines; dogs are domestic mammals
4	111231	Widening Comparison	Dogs are vertebrates; canines are vertebrates
5	121231	Narrowing Comparison	Canines are vertebrates; dogs are vertebrates
6	141231	Disjoint Comparison	Dogs are vertebrates; cats are vertebrates
7	151231	Additive Comparison	Canines are vertebrates; domestic mammals are vertebrates
8	111311	Forward Reasoning	Dogs are canines; canines are vertebrates
9	123221	Backward Reasoning	Canines are vertebrates; dogs are canines
10	144441	Contrast	Dogs are canines; cats are felines
11	131231	Restatement	Dogs are canines; dogs are canines

Table 2: Classification of the coherent patterns

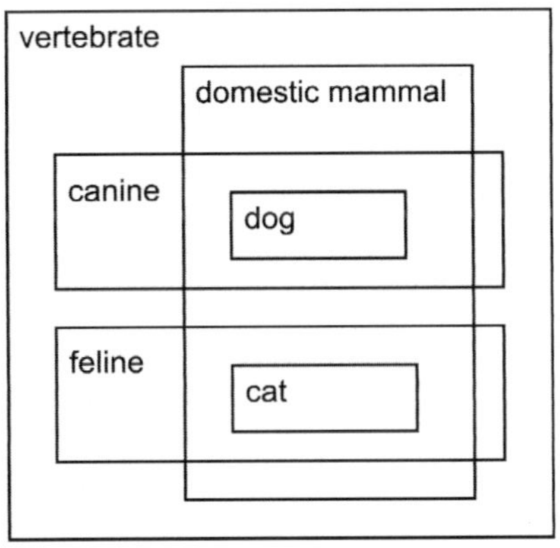

Figure 3: Minimal ontology for coherent patterns

pattern. For the eleven patterns hypothesised to be coherent, the *minimal* such ontology is shown diagrammatically in figure 3. The important feature of this diagram is not the names of the classes, but their relationships; by varying the names it would be possible to generate test examples in different domains. Note that to generate examples for all 46 consistent patterns, we would have to add more classes, the main reason being that incoherent patterns like 155551 require several classes that partially overlap one another (corresponding to weakly related concepts). However, using only the minimal ontology it is possible to generate 10 examples that were *not* selected as coherent. It is therefore convenient to test the proposed coherence partition using only material generated from the minimal ontology: this ensures that the concepts used in all patterns are as similar as possible, and also yields two groups of roughly equal size. In fact, by eliminating the arguably trivial restatement pattern, in which the two statements in the pair are exactly the same, we obtain exactly ten patterns in the group presumed coherent, and ten in the group presumed incoherent; all of these patterns are shown in table 3. To save space this table uses an abbreviated wording in the 'Example' column; the wording actually used is illustrated in figure 4, with 'Dogs' replaced by 'A dog', a formulation preferred by subjects in an evaluation of the SWAT verbaliser (Stevens et al., 2011).[6]

To present each participant with a conveniently brief task (in our experience, anything over five minutes yields a high drop-out rate), two surveys were compiled from the patterns in table 3, each composed of five patterns from the coherent group and five from the incoherent group, arbitrarily selected and then arranged in a random order (the same for all subjects doing a given survey). Survey I was sent to the SIGDIAL mailing list, Survey II to the SIGGEN list. When uptake proved much greater for Survey II, we also sent Survey I to a local departmental list, and invited people on the SIGGEN list to do Survey I as well as (or instead of) II; since the questions were all different, no duplication resulted if a participant did both surveys. Overall 45 participants completed Survey I and 52 completed Survey II.[7]

A snapshot from Survey I is shown in figure 4.

[6]The issue of how best to word a universal statement requires further research. 'Every X is a Y' is perhaps most precise, but sometimes sounds unnatural; 'Xs are Ys' and 'an X is a Y' are more natural but more open to other interpretations. For the statements in the survey we assume it was obvious that a generic interpretation was intended, and no subjects commented that the sentences were ambiguous or in any way unclear.

[7]It can therefore be inferred from table 3 which questions belonged to which survey.

N	Code		Freq	%	Example
1	WiEl	131211	25/45	56%	Dogs are canines; dogs have backbones
2	NaEl	131221	37/52	71%	Dogs have backbones; dogs are canines
3	AdEl	131251	30/45	67%	Dogs are canines; dogs are domestic mammals
4	WiCp	111231	37/45	82%	Dogs have backbones; canines have backbones
5	NaCp	121231	34/45	76%	Canines have backbones; dogs have backbones
6	DiCp	141231	50/52	96%	Canines have backbones; felines have backbones
7	AdCp	151231	24/52	46%	Canines have backbones; domestic mammals have backbones
8	FwRe	111311	51/52	98%	Dogs are canines; canines have backbones
9	BwRe	123221	42/52	81%	Canines have backbones; dogs are canines
10	CoRe	144441	43/45	96%	Dogs are canines; cats are felines
Total			373/485	77%	
11	Incoh	111511	0/45	0%	Dogs are canines; domestic mammals have backbones
12	Incoh	125221	9/52	17%	Canines have backbones; dogs are domestic mammals
13	Incoh	141211	2/45	4%	Dogs are domestic mammals; cats have backbones
14	Incoh	141221	4/52	8%	Dogs have backbones; cats are domestic mammals
15	Incoh	141411	2/45	4%	Dogs are canines; felines have backbones
16	Incoh	141451	12/52	23%	Dogs are canines; cats are domestic mammals
17	Incoh	141511	0/45	0%	Dogs are domestic mammals; felines have backbones
18	Incoh	144221	2/52	4%	Dogs have backbones; cats are felines
19	Incoh	144251	2/45	4%	Dogs are domestic mammals; cats are felines
20	Incoh	145221	3/52	6%	Canines have backbones; cats are domestic mammals
Total			36/485	7%	

Table 3: Coherence judgements for each pattern. Subjects were asked to judge whether the statements in each pair could be appropriately presented together. The data are the number of 'Yes' responses to this question. Patterns 1–10 were hypothesised coherent, patterns 11–20 incoherent.

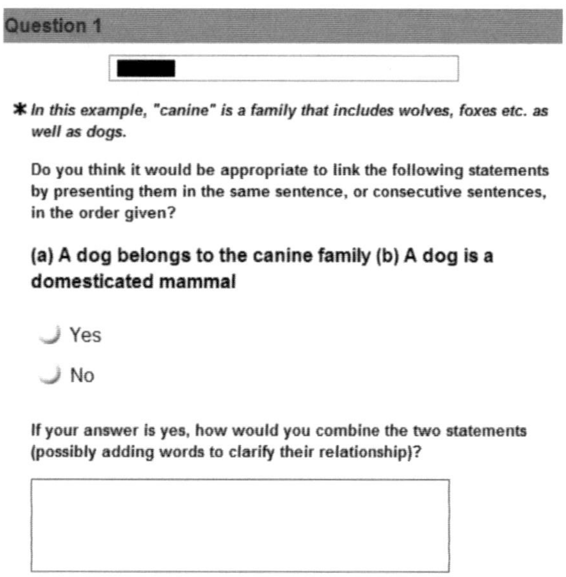

Figure 4: First question in Survey I

Participants were asked to judge whether it would be appropriate to link the two statements in a text (in the given order), by presenting them either in the same sentence or in consecutive sentences; if they answered this question in the affirmative, there was an optional follow-up question asking them to indicate, by typing freely into a text box, how they might combine them. To score these responses, we counted four features:

And: The statements were combined neutrally using 'and', or a full stop or a semicolon, without any discourse connective.
Con: A discourse connective was employed (possibly in addition to 'and').
Agg: Either the subject or predicate terms of the statements were aggregated.
Rel: One statement was expressed as a relative clause inside the other.

The resulting counts for the coherent patterns are shown in table 4. Frequencies for specific discourse connectives (excluding 'and') are shown in table 5.

Pattern	Connectives
Widening Elaboration	therefore (4), hence (1), so (1), which means that (1)
Narrowing Elaboration	also (2), because (2), in addition (2), more specifically (2), furthermore (1), moreover (1)
Additive Elaboration	however (1), therefore (1)
Widening Comparison	because (6), in fact (5), like (5), as (4), as do (2), since (2), so (2), as does (1), for example (1), in general (1), as well as (1), more generally (1), therefore (1)
Narrowing Comparison	therefore (8), so (5), hence (4), for example (3), as (2), like (2), as does (1), as well (1), in particular (1), including (1), ipso facto (1), such as (1)
Disjoint Comparison	also (6), too (6), as well as (2), so does (2), just like (1), similarly (1)
Additive Comparison	as do (2), actually (1), also (1), for (1), in general (1), like (1), so do (1), too (1)
Forward Reasoning	also (1), therefore (1)
Backward Reasoning	for example (5), e.g. (2), example is (2), as (1), by the way (1), therefore (1)
Contrast	whereas (11), while (10), but (3), however (1), as (1)

Table 5: Connectives suggested for each pattern, with their frequencies

Pattern	And	Con	Agg	Rel
Widening Elaboration	14	7	8	3
Narrowing Elaboration	27	10	9	0
Additive Elaboration	19	2	6	11
Widening Comparison	2	32	12	2
Narrowing Comparison	2	30	9	1
Disjoint Comparison	30	18	22	0
Additive Comparison	12	9	10	0
Forward Reasoning	36	2	2	1
Backward Reasoning	23	12	0	2
Contrast	16	26	0	0

Table 4: Frequencies of various devices for combining the statements in the ten coherent patterns presented. 'And' = Linked only by 'and' or punctuation; 'Con' = Connective; 'Agg' = Aggregation; 'Rel' = Relative clause.

4 Analysis of results

4.1 Coherent and incoherent

The first question is whether the results confirm our intuitive classification of the patterns into coherent and incoherent. Table 3 demonstrates clearly that they do. Summing across all subjects, we obtained 373/485 (77%) positive responses for patterns that satisfied our coherence criterion (upper half of table 3), compared with 36/485 (7%) positive responses for patterns that did not satisfy this criterion (lower half) – obviously a highly significant association[8]. Overall, judgements were fairly evenly divided between positive and negative, with 409 'Yes' answers against 561 'No' answers.

Looking in more detail at the coherent group, we found clear differences in degree, with several patterns obtaining positive responses of 95% and over, with others not far above the 50% level (and one just below). On a two-tailed binomial test assuming equal *a priori* probabilities for 'Yes' and 'No', frequencies over 70% are significant at the $p < 0.01$ level and frequencies over 75% at the $p < 0.001$ level; thus we have three patterns (widening elaboration, additive elaboration, additive comparison) for which there is not a clear consensus that the statements are related closely enough to be combined in a discourse.

4.2 Distinctive realisation

The second question is whether we find evidence that the coherent patterns are *distinctive*, as shown by the linguistic devices by which they are combined. Here table 4 shows that the realisation profiles for the ten patterns differ sharply. With relatively few responses these results should be seen only as suggestive, but several trends are already apparent:

- For widening and narrowing comparison, a discourse connective is almost always used; for the other patterns, combinations using only 'and' or a full stop are common.

- Conversely, for additive elaboration and forward reasoning a discourse connective is almost never

[8] On a 2x2 χ^2 test for association between pattern (coherent vs incoherent) and judgement (positive vs negative) we obtain χ^2=480 with *df*=1, two-tailed $p < 0.00001$.

used; for the other patterns connectives other than 'and' are common.

- Aggregation is commonly used for comparisons, and especially for disjoint comparison (e.g., 'Canines and felines have backbones').

- Relative clause combinations are commonly used only for one pattern, additive elaboration (e.g., 'Dogs, which are domesticated mammals, belong to the canine family').

4.3 Discourse connectives

The final question is whether the discourse connectives proposed for the coherent patterns are distinctive, and linked to familiar rhetorical relations such as EVIDENCE and EXAMPLE. Here again the results are only suggestive, but consistent themes do emerge from the subjects' choices. For widening and narrowing elaboration these choices signal the EVIDENCE relation ('therefore', 'because') as well as ELABORATION ('also', 'moreover'). For widening and narrowing comparison EVIDENCE is also common, with more signs of sensitivity to generalising or specifying ('more generally', 'in particular'), a rhetorical move somewhat neglected in RST and other theories. For all comparisons, but especially disjoint comparison, the connectives often signal SIMILARITY. Backward reasoning is the only pattern for which choices often signalled EXAMPLE. Finally, choices for our contrast pattern were dominated by 'whereas' and 'while', marking as one would expect the CONTRAST relation.

5 Discussion

5.1 Comparison with other approaches

The most similar work, both in spirit and substance, is the taxonomy of coherence relations proposed by Sanders et al. (1992), who also aim to cover a restricted set of relations using relatively precise theoretical concepts. Their fundamental distinction is between *causal* and *additive* relations, where 'cause' is defined (oddly) as an *implication* between two discourse segments: thus if one statement implies the other we have a causal relation; if not we have an additive one. Causal relationships are further distinguished by order of presentation: if antecedent precedes consequent the order is *basic*, otherwise *non-basic*. The theory also distinguishes whether the relation is semantic or pragmatic, and whether statements are presented in positive or negative polarity; these features are not distinguished in our model which is restricted to semantic relations and positive polarity. Combining the values of their four features, Sanders et al. list 12 patterns of which three are comparable with ours: (1) Causal-Semantic-Basic-Positive, (2) Causal-Semantic-Nonbasic-Positive, and (3) Additive-Semantic-Positive; the first two are labelled 'Cause-consequence' and the third 'List'.

In our model, the causal-additive distinction is easily made for the elaboration patterns (i.e., those with equivalent subject terms): if the predicate terms are widening or narrowing the relation is 'causal', if they overlap it is 'additive' (hence our choice of that word). The basic order for elaboration is widening elaboration (e.g., 'dogs are canines' implies 'dogs are vertebrates'); narrowing elaboration is non-basic. For comparison patterns (those with equivalent predicate terms) the same distinctions hold, except that this time the basic order is narrowing comparison, and widening comparison is non-basic. Note however that we find no evidence that the basic order is preferred: on the contrary, positive coherence judgements were more common for the non-basic orders both for the elaboration and comparison patterns (although the differences are not large). We also find quite different realisation profiles for widening elaboration and narrowing comparison (both Causal-Basic in Sanders et al.'s taxonomy), and for narrowing elaboration and widening comparison (both Causal-Nonbasic). In line with Sanders et al. we obtain discourse connectives signalling implication ('therefore', 'since' etc.) for all these 'causal' patterns, but we also obtain connectives signalling generalisation or specification ('more generally', 'in particular') and exemplication ('for example') that depend on our more detailed classification.

Comparing our classification with RST is harder since the approaches are so different. Unlike Sanders et al., RST is not concerned with order of presentation, and has instead an asymmetry in the *importance* of the two statements, most relations having a 'nucleus' and a 'satellite'. At present we have no way of assigning importance levels from the information encoded in an OWL ontology. Regarding coverage, we can informally link our patterns to the following RST relations (Carlson and Marcu, 2001): comparison, contrast, elaboration-additional, elaboration-general-specific, example, and restatement.[9] On the other hand we cover some relations apparently missing from RST, which lacks any notion of co-premise (found in our forward and backward reasoning patterns), or of moving from specific to general or vice-versa (our distinction between widening and narrowing).

5.2 Limitations

As already mentioned, the methods proposed here are bounded by characteristics of the ontology verbalisation task: since the OWL standard (Horrocks et al., 2003) lacks any representation of pragmatics, or time, or causal relations between events, or modality, or probability, many relations dependent on these concepts lie outside our compass. However, even within this restriction of coverage, the theory and evaluation described here are far from complete.

Recall first of all that we have covered only those patterns in which the subject of each statement denotes a *subclass* of the predicate (relation number 1 in our code). Thus we cover 'every dog is a canine' (dogs are a subclass of canines), but not the following sentence patterns:

> (2) Only canines are dogs (subject is superclass of predicate)
> (3) A dog is defined as a domestic canine (subject and predicate are equivalent)
> (4) No dog is a cat (subject and predicate are disjoint)
> (5) Some pets are canines[10] (subject and predicate overlap)

In verbalising ontologies it would be unnecessary to cover pattern (2), which is merely an awkward inversion of *SubClassOf*, or (5), which is represented in OWL only indirectly. However, patterns (3) and (4) should be covered, since they correspond to the OWL functors *DisjointClasses* and *EquivalentClasses*, and their inclusion would raise the total number of patterns from 46 to 297, and the subset conforming to our coherence rule from 11 to 62.[11]

A second limitation concerns the empirical validation, which addresses only a single very small content domain. Looking at a wider set of examples, it might emerge that the fivefold classification of semantic relations used here is oversimple, and that the taxonomic information in ontologies can be put to better use. To take just one example, the coherence of the disjoint comparison pattern might plausibly depend on the subject terms being not only disjoint, but also *siblings* in the taxonomy (Milosavljevic, 1997) – i.e., concepts at the same level of generality: subjects might be less inclined to judge the example coherent if canines were compared with kittens rather than felines, even though canines and kittens are also disjoint.

Next, we could probably produce a more flexible and generally applicable model if the semantic relations among sets were relaxed so that they allowed exceptions. In particular, by enforcing strict consistency we lose the pattern 131241, disjoint elaboration, in which a subject term is assigned to two incompatible predicates (e.g., 'Butch is a wolf; Butch is a pet'). If we defined relations 1-4 in a way that allowed a little leeway (e.g., X is nearly a subclass of Y; X and Y are nearly disjoint; etc.), the repertoire of 'consistent' patterns could be expanded, and we would obtain a plausible context for the relations typically signalled by 'but' and 'however' (e.g., CONCESSION). Such a model would be useful for a system generating from data, which might find a few instances of wolf pets in a dataset where nearly all wolves are non-pets and nearly all pets are non-wolves, and thus generate 'Butch is a pet even though he is a wolf'.

Finally, we have considered only how a rhetorical relationship could be assigned to a *pair* of statements, ignoring the issue of how a globally coherent text could be planned from pairwise assignments. However, this topic is already addressed in the literature, for instance by Marcu's (1997) bottom-up planning algorithms.

[9] The restatement pattern 131231 was deemed too trivial for inclusion in the survey, but might plausibly occur either for emphasis or to explain technical terms – for instance 'Corgis are domestic canines, that is, they are dogs'.

[10] Actually this sentence is an oversimplified rendition of overlap, which would also require that some pets are not canines and some canines are not pets.

[11] For details on how these numbers are computed see Power (2011b).

6 Conclusion

We have sketched a model through which an NLG system could decide whether two formally encoded statements are rhetorically related, and if so how, by examining cross-statement semantic relations evidenced by other statements in the knowledge base. Although in its early stages, the work suggests that a formal basis for assigning rhetorical relations is possible, at least for some relations. As well as guiding NLG systems that generate from ontologies and/or data, our method might prove useful in automatically detecting rhetorical relations in naturally-occurring text; in fact it has already been applied successfully to the task of textual entailment (MacCartney and Manning, 2009), which could be regarded as a special case in which the only rhetorical relation of interest is CONSEQUENCE.

Acknowledgments

The SWAT project (Semantic Web Authoring Tool) is supported by the UK Engineering and Physical Sciences Research Council (EPSRC) grants G033579/1 (Open University) and G032459/1 (University of Manchester). Thanks are also due to colleagues and reviewers for their comments and suggestions.

References

Attempto Project. 2011. ACE OWL Verbalizer. Website. http://attempto.ifi.uzh.ch/site/tools/.

Lynn Carlson and Daniel Marcu. 2001. Discourse tagging manual. Technical report, ISI Tech Report ISI-TR-545.

Glen Hart, Martina Johnson, and Catherine Dolbear. 2008. Rabbit: Developing a control natural language for authoring ontologies. In Manfred Hauswirth, Manolis Koubarakis, and Sean Bechhofer, editors, *Proceedings of the 5th European Semantic Web Conference*, pages 348–360.

Jerry Hobbs. 1985. On the coherence and structure of discourse. Technical report, Stanford University.

Ian Horrocks, Peter F. Patel-Schneider, and Frank Van Harmelen. 2003. From shiq and rdf to owl: The making of a web ontology language. *Journal of Web Semantics*, 1:2003.

Kaarel Kaljurand and Norbert Fuchs. 2007. Verbalizing OWL in Attempto Controlled English. In *OWLED: OWL Experiences and Directions*.

A. Knott. 1996. A data-driven methodology for motivating a set of coherence relations. Technical report, University of Edinburgh. Ph.D. thesis.

Shao Fen Liang, Donia Scott, Robert Stevens, and Alan Rector. 2011. Unlocking Medical Ontologies for Non-Ontology Experts. In *Proceedings of the 49th Annual Meeting of the Association for Computational Linguistics: Human Language Technologies*.

Bill MacCartney and Christopher D. Manning. 2009. An extended model of natural logic. In *Proceedings of the Eighth International Conference on Computational Semantics*, IWCS-8 '09, pages 140–156, Stroudsburg, PA, USA. Association for Computational Linguistics.

W. Mann and S. Thompson. 1987. Rhetorical structure theory: a theory of text organization. In L. Polyani, editor, *The structure of discourse*, Norwood, NJ. Ablex.

Daniel Marcu. 1997. From Local to Global Coherence: A Bottom-Up Approach to Text Planning. In *AAAI/IAAI*, pages 629–635.

Maria Milosavljevic. 1997. Augmenting the user's knowledge via comparison. In *In Proceedings of the 6th International Conference on User Modelling*, pages 119–130.

Richard Power and Allan Third. 2010. Expressing OWL axioms by English sentences: dubious in theory, feasible in practice. In *Proceedings of the 23rd International Conference on Computational Linguistics*.

Richard Power. 2011a. Coherence relations in ontologies. Technical Report Technical Report TR2011-01, ISSN 1744-1986, Department of Computing, Open University.

Richard Power. 2011b. Rhetorical Coherence Patterns. Website. http://mcs.open.ac.uk/rp3242/rhetoric.html.

T. Sanders, W. Spooren, and L. Noordman. 1992. Toward a taxonomy of coherence relations. *Discourse Processes*, (15):1–35.

Rolf Schwitter and Thomas Meyer. 2007. Sydney OWL Syntax - towards a Controlled Natural Language Syntax for OWL 1.1. In *OWLED: OWL Experiences and Directions*.

Robert Stevens, James Malone, Sandra Williams, Richard Power, and Allan Third. 2011. Automating generation of textual class definitions from owl to english. *Journal of Biomedical Semantics*, 2(S 2:S5), May.

SWAT Project. 2011. SWAT Natural Language Tools. Website. http://swat.open.ac.uk/tools/.

Sandra Williams, Allan Third, and Richard Power. 2011. Levels of organisation in ontology verbalisation. In *Proceedings of the 13th European Workshop on Natural Language Generation*, Nancy, France.

If it may have happened before, it happened, but not necessarily before

Albert Gatt
Institute of Linguistics
University of Malta
Tal-Qroqq, Msida MSD2080
Malta
albert.gatt@um.edu.mt

François Portet
LIG UMR 5217, UJF-Grenoble 1
Grenoble INP / UPMF-Grenoble 2 / CNRS,
Laboratoire d'Informatique de Grenoble
Grenoble, F-38041, FRANCE
francois.portet@imag.fr

Abstract

Temporal uncertainty in raw data can impede the inference of temporal and causal relationships between events and compromise the output of data-to-text NLG systems. In this paper, we introduce a framework to reason with and represent temporal uncertainty from the raw data to the generated text, in order to provide a faithful picture to the user of a particular situation. The model is grounded in experimental data from multiple languages, shedding light on the generality of the approach.

1 Introduction

Natural Language Generation (NLG) systems which take raw data as input often need to transform it by performing operations such as inference, abstraction or approximation. However, in many domains, input data is riddled with uncertainty or inaccuracy. For example, a patient database may contain records of interventions which were entered well after they actually occurred (Gatt et al., 2009). This problem is particularly acute in systems where the temporal dimension of the data is important; it is exacerbated by the lack of a principled way of handling temporal information in existing database management systems (Terenziani et al., 2005).

Temporal uncertainty – that is, uncertainty about the precise time at which an event occurred – can affect NLG systems at the data processing and document planning stages, since it affects temporal and/or causal relationships between events. It also impacts microplanning and realisation, since decisions must be made as to whether a proposition is to be simply asserted or modalised to express some degree of epistemic (un)certainty. Simply asserting a proposition will normally give rise to the presupposition that the state of affairs described is known for certain (Karttunen, 1972); conversely, modalising the proposition impacts its truth conditions (Papafragou, 2006).

In this paper, we argue that temporal uncertainty should be explicitly communicated, and we focus on the use of modalised propositions to acheive this[1], taking a multilingual perspective. Our aim is to address two empirical questions. The first concerns the (non-linguistic) representation and quantification of uncertainty: given the raw data about an event, as well as general knowledge that enables a limited amount of reasoning about a situation, we are interested in quantifying the degree of 'subjective' uncertainty about the time of an event and the resulting degree of uncertainty about the temporal relations between it and other events (e.g *x happened before y*). We propose a formalism to handle this, showing that its predictions have a good correspondence to human intuitions. Our second question concerns the way in which modal expressions can be *grounded* in subjective uncertainty arising from raw data. We describe an experimental design that enables us both to quantify subjective uncertainty in a given situation, and to map from subjective uncertainty to modal expressions. Our experiments are conducted in three different languages which, though culturally fairly

[1]In what follows, our use of the term 'modality' refers to the semantic or 'notional' category (Kratzer, 1981). As Kratzer argues, this can be expressed in a variety of ways, ranging from modal auxiliaries to adverbs of possibility, among others.

Proceedings of the 13th European Workshop on Natural Language Generation (ENLG), pages 91–101,
Nancy, France, September 2011.

close (insofar as they are European), are typologically diverse. In this way, we seek both to validate our methodology using data from multiple languages, and to investigate the implications that differences between languages can have for a proper account of modality in NLG.

We begin with an overview of related work (Section 2), followed by a description of the reasoning formalism (Section 3), and the experiment and results (Section 4). We conclude in Section 5 with some pointers to future work.

2 Epistemic uncertainty in language

The expression of uncertainty is usually achieved through modal expressions, which are concerned with the degree of possibility or necessity associated with a particular proposition. Modality, which is often associated (and in some languages, conflated) with the category of Irrealis, can be characterised in terms of assertion (Palmer, 2001): an unmodalised proposition is simply asserted (thereby presupposing certainty about the matter); its modalised counterpart is not, or only with some qualification as to the degree of evidence that the speaker has for it.

We are primarily interested in how the resources that a language makes available to express epistemic modality can be harnessed to express temporal uncertainty in data-to-text systems, thus avoiding misleading the reader. While the importance of this problem has been pointed out in recent work (Portet et al., 2009; Gatt et al., 2009), modality lacks a principled treatment in NLG (but see Klabunde (2007)). As Klabunde notes, NLG systems which use modals in their output (Elhadad, 1995; Reiter et al., 2003) do not seem to select these expressions in a principled way. The following example illustrates some of the difficulties in dealing with epistemic modality, especially from a cross-linguistic perspective:

(1) A bank robbery occurred yesterday afternoon. An investigator is trying to reconstruct the scene from eye-witness reports. He knows for certain that the robbers were inside the bank for no more than 45 minutes. He also knows for certain that the police took 30 minutes to arrive on the scene after being alerted. He has also interviewed some eye-witnesses. Here is what they said: **The robbers entered the bank at 16:00. The police were alerted some time between 16:15 and 16:45.**

Consider now the proposition *The police were on the scene before the robbers left the bank.* In this scenario, the certainty of this proposition is affected by the fact that the event of the police being alerted occurs within an uncertain interval. From an NLG perspective, we would like to be able to (a) quantify the degree of certainty associated with the occurrence time of the two events, as well as their temporal relation; and (b) choose the right expression to express this. A prerequisite for both these tasks is a computationally tractable account of how modal expressions are grounded in temporal data, which also supports fine-grained choices, such as that between *may* and *possibly*.

However, it is unlikely that a model of such choices can be built completely language-independently, since modality exhibits considerable cross-linguistic variation (Palmer, 2001). Languages like English and French would commonly modalise a proposition using modal auxiliaries (2a) or adverbials (2b). Whether the two systems (auxiliaries and adverbials) are equivalent with respect to the degree of uncertainty they express is an empirical question, one that has a direct impact on the lexicalisation strategies used by an NLG system.

(2) (a) *La* *police* **pourrait/doit** *avoir* *été*
the.fsg police may.3pl/must.3pl have be.3sg.ps
sur *les* *lieux* *avant que* *les* *voleurs*
on def.pl scene.pl before the.pl robber.pl
quittent *la* *banque.*
leave.3pl.ps the.fsg bank
'The police **may/must** have been on the scene before the robbers left the bank.'

(b) *La* *police* *était* **surement/peut-être** *sur*
the.fsg police be.3sg.ps definitely/possibly on
les *lieux* *avant que* *les* *voleurs*
def.pl scene before the.pl robber.pl
quittent *la* *banque.*
leave.3pl.pl the.fsg bank
'(**Possibly**) the police were (**definitely**) on the scene before the robbers left the bank.'

The above example suggests certain similarities between English and French, despite their different genetic classification (Anglo-Saxon vs. Romance). The difficulties increase when other language families are considered. We will also consider a European language which comes from a third language family, namely Maltese (Semitic), where the modal auxilaries that have been identified (Vanhove et al., 2009) tend to be more restricted in their use. For example, the auxiliary *seta'* (can.3sgm.pfv; 'could have') can be used to express epistemic possibility or likelihood, but this is only possible with the imperfective form and is more frequently rendered in a construction involving clausal subordination using *li* ('that'), a form that is also commonly used with adverbs like *bilfors* (e.g. *bilfors li*; lit. 'by force that', i.e. 'definitely') and *żgur* ('certainly') (3a). One adverbial that normally occurs without explicit subordination of the matrix VP is the Romance-derived *forsi* ('maybe/perhaps') (3b). However, current descriptive work on these modals does not give a clear picture of the difference in the distribution of these expressions and suggests that some of them may be highly restricted in their use.

(3) (a) *Il-pulizija* **jista' jkun/bilfors/żgur** *li* *kienu*
the-police could be/definitely/certainly that be.pl.ps
fuq *ix-xena* *qabel ma* *l-ħallelin* *telqu*
on the-scene before the-robber.pl leave.pl.ps
mill-bank.
from.the-bank

'The police **may have/definitely/certainly** left the scene before the robbers left the bank.'

(b) *Il-pulizija* **forsi** *kienu* *fuq* *ix-xena*
the-police possibly be.3pl.ps on the-scene
qabel ma *l-ħallelin* *telqu* *mill-bank.*
before the-robber.pl leave.3pl.ps from.the-bank

'**Possibly** the police were on the scene before the robbers left the bank.'

The examples from the three languages under consideration serve to illustrate a subset of the grammatically diverse expressions that different languages make available to express epistemic uncertainty, as well some possible differences that may arise among them despite their cultural proximity (insofar as all three are European languages). A consideration of languages which are even more diverse – historically, culturally and typologically – would presumably shed light on even greater differences in modal systems and their interaction with the expression of time, in line with recent work that questions the existence of absolute 'universals' across languages (Evans and Levinson, 2009). An investigation of such cross-linguistic differences is beyond the scope of the present paper, though the methodology illustrated in the following sections is not restricted to particular languages.

Neither of the two questions we have raised – that of representing and quantifying uncertainty, and that of mapping from this to the right modal expression in a particular language – has been treated exhaustively in the NLG literature. To our knowledge, the only recent approach to handling modals in NLG is Klabunde (2007), who focuses on the generation of deontic modals (those related to obligation, rather than epistemic certainty) in the CAN system, which advises students about university courses (Klabunde, 2005; Klabunde, 2007). Klabunde's approach is based on the influential possible worlds framework proposed by Kratzer (Kratzer, 1977; Kratzer, 1981; Portner, 2009), in which the truth of a modalised proposition is evaluated against a (contextually determined) set of relevant possible worlds or situations, ordered by their accessibility from the current world or situation. In an epistemic context, this set contains the worlds which are compatible to some degree with the propositions which constitute the underlying 'evidence' for the statement.

Most semantic work on modality has been based on this framework (but see Papafragou (1998) for a relevance-theoretic account, and Sweetser (1990) for a cognitive-functionalist account). Neither of these theories is straightforwardly applicable to the type of problem illustrated in (1). Intuitively, the temporal uncertainty of the proposition in the example, which arises due to an event having a fuzzy temporal interval, would be evaluated on a continuous scale: given the knowledge that something occurred between times t_1 and t_2, a person may feel more certain of the occurrence towards the middle of the interval, less so as one approaches its start or end. If a continuous certainty scale is what is required, it is difficult to see how approaches based on a treatment of propositions as (crisp) sets of possible worlds can be applied. Nor is it immediately obvious, were the problem amenable to such a treatment, that this is the most cognitively plausible or computationally tractable way of representing uncertainty, relying as it does on an exhaustive consideration of alternative situations (Johnson-Laird, 1978). In the following section, we consider an alternative proposal.

3 Temporal representation and reasoning

The formalism used to represent and reason with events and relations between events is based on the Metric Temporal Constraint Network (TCN) (Dechter et al., 1991) approach.

This approach differs from purely qualitative approaches — such as the one based on Allen's thirteen mutually exclusive binary relations (Allen, 1983)— as it considers only metric-based temporal relations (e.g., 'Mary left 10 minutes before James arrived' as opposed to 'Mary left before James arrived') and represents events as time-points rather than intervals The time-point metric approach is capable of representing intervals through start and end points and can translate most qualitative intervals or point relations into metric relations (e.g., a before b can be reformulated as $b-a \in [1, \infty)$) though recuding the expressiveness of the interval relations (see Vilain et al. (1987)). Moreover, there are numerous algorithms to compute the consistency of a TCN network efficiently, depending on the allowed experessivity, though expressive power and computational tractability tend to be inversely related. Other interesting properties of TCNs are that they can be used to represent numerical temporal information that can then be queried or used to model expert knowledge (Palma et al., 2006; Gao et al., 2009). For more information about temporal reasoning and the aforementioned formalisms the reader is refereed to (Zhou and Hripcsaka, 2007; Artikis et al., 2010).

In the TCN formalism, temporal representation relies on time points and time is considered as a linearly ordered discrete set of instants ($t_0 < t_1 < \cdots < t_i < \dots$) where $\forall i \in \mathbf{N}, t_{i+1} - t_i = \Delta_t$. Δ_t is a constant that represents the sampling period (e.g. 1 microsecond, 1 month, 1 century). We assume that temporal information is composed of instantaneous events and finite durative events. An instantaneous event or **event** a is a tuple $\langle t, o \rangle$, where $t \in \mathbf{N}$ and $o \in \mathcal{O}$. t is the known date of occurrence of the event and o represents some structured data corresponding to this event (e.g. database record, inference, user input). Among other things, o can correspond to a type (concept) in a knowledge repository such as an ontology $\mathcal{O}$. A durative event or **interval** A is a tuple $\langle as, ae, c, o \rangle$, where as (resp. ae) is an instantaneous event representing the start (resp. end) of the durative event, c is a numerical constraint such that $ae - as \in (0, c]$ and o is the description of the durative event.

Briefly, a TCN $\mathcal{N}$ consists of a set of instantaneous events (a, b, c) with constraints between them. Each constraint T between a and b is represented by a set of binary constraints ($\{I_1, \dots, I_n\} = \{[t_{s1}, t_{e1}], \dots, [t_{sn}, t_{en}]\}$) that represent the temporal knowledge about a situation. For instance, the set of facts in example (1), can be represented by the TCN depicted in Figure 1 where all durative events are translated into pairs of events (e.g. 'were inside the bank' $\rightarrow$ 'robbers enter' and 'robbers leave') and all temporal relations are translated into binary temporal constraints (e.g., 'for no more than 45 minutes' $\rightarrow [1, 45]$). This also applies to absolute times, which are represented with respect to the origin of the day.

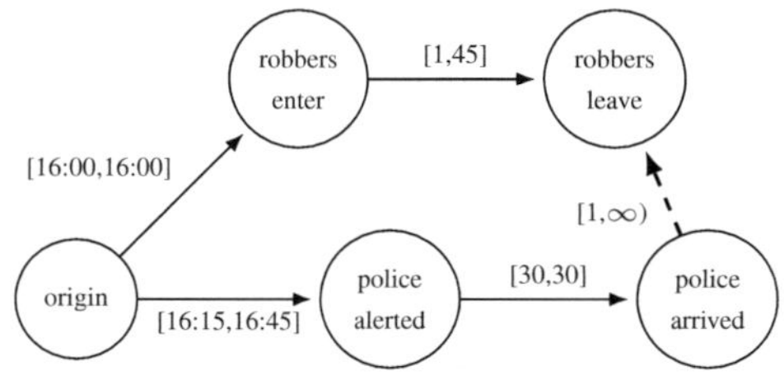

Figure 1: Robbers example represented as a TCN.

In the TCN approach, reasoning is seen as a temporal constraint satisfaction problem (TCSP), which consists in finding a solution that satisfies a set of inequalities (e.g., $t_{s1} \leq b - a \leq t_{e1} \vee \cdots \vee t_{sn} \leq b - a \leq t_{en}$). Briefly, this consists in applying algorithms that solve the shortest path problem to generate the minimal network (i.e., the network with the tightest constraints). If one constraint is not satisfied then no solution exists and the network is inconsistent. For instance, if one wants to test the assertion *The police were on the scene before the robbers left the bank*, this constraint can be integrated into the network (before $\rightarrow [1, \infty)$; see the dashed edge in Figure 1) and the consistency checking algorithm will find no solution, because the latest possible departure time of the robbers is 16:45 and the earliest police presence is 16:45, which is not strictly before the robbers' departure. While such reasoning is perfectly correct, it might not correspond to the intuitive answer a human would give. A human reader is likely to take much more liberty with the interpretation of the reported temporal facts, particularly if it is a report made by another person. For instance, the statement that the police took 30 minutes to arrive might result in some allowance being made for their arriving after 29 minutes, or after 31. A slight change in the interpretation of the constraints would lead to very different results. To better capture these intuitions, it is possible to represent each temporal constraint as a fuzzy set (Zadeh, 1965).

There are several implementations of Fuzzy Temporal Constraint Networks (FTCNs) (Barro et al., 1994; Vila and Godo, 1994; Campos et al., 2002). We will focus on the one implemented in the FuzzyTIME engine (Barro et al., 1994; Campos et al., 2002). FuzzyTIME is a general purpose engine that can represent intervals as well as instants and all common qualitative and quantitative temporal relations between them. All definitions are translated into metric relations between time points on which the reasoning is performed. In this approach, a binary constraint between two events is defined by a normalised, unimodal possibility distribution π which restricts the temporal distance between two events. Recall that in possibility theory (Dubois et al., 2003), the uncertainty about a temporal relation r between two events a and b can be evaluated by the two dual measures of possibility Π and necessity (also called certainty) N, as follows:

$$\Pi(r_{a,b}) = \pi_r(b - a) \quad (4)$$

$$N(r_{a,b}) = 1 - \Pi(\bar{r}_{a,b}) \quad (5)$$

Where $\pi_r(b - a) \in [0, 1]$ is the possibility distribution of the temporal distance between the events a and b, representing the degree to which these two events are possibly linked via relation r, and $\bar{r}_{a,b}$ is the complement of $r_{a,b}$. The necessity of the relation r between a and b can be summarised as follows: $r_{a,b}$ is certain only if no relation contradicting $r_{a,b}$ (i.e., $\bar{r}_{a,b}$) is possible.

An example FTCN is represented in Figure 2 where the arrival time of the police is translated into a possibility distribution expressing the following interpretation : *it is completely possible that the police took 30 minutes to arrive, less possible that they took 28-30 minutes or 30-32 minutes, and impossible otherwise.* All other constraints are represented as a uniform possibility distribution (e.g., the constraint $[1, 45]$ is translated into a possibility distribution for which any value in its range is completely possible).

In FTCN, the solutions to the network can satisfy the constraints only to a certain degree σ, given

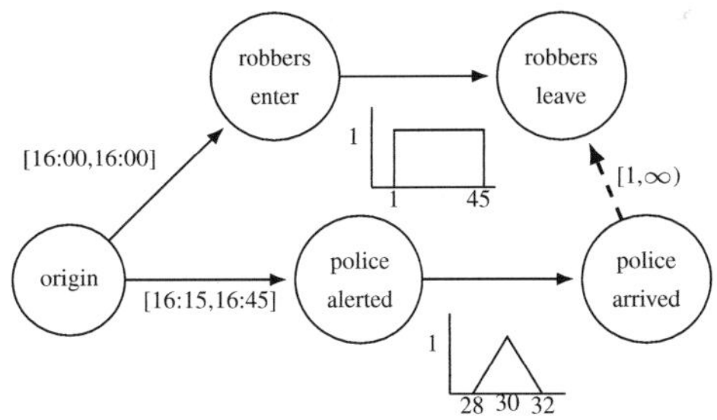

Figure 2: Robbers example represented as a FTCN.

that temporal constraints may be fuzzy. In FuzzyTIME, an algorithm that combines exhaustively all constraints is applied to obtain the minimal network (i.e., in which the constraints have the smallest possible degree of imprecision) (Barro et al., 1994). For instance, incorporating the assertion *The police were on the scene before the robbers left the bank.* with $\Delta_t = 1$ minute leads to a network consistent with only .5 possibility and 0 necessity (because the 'after' relation is completely possible).

This model therefore offers us the possibility of quantifying the possibility and necessity of an event, given a formalisation of the background knowledge. Thus, this formalism can handle the first of the two problems pointed out in the previous section, namely, to quantify temporal uncertainty of events in a fine-grained manner. Our next question is how these values can be mapped to linguistic expressions by an NLG system.

4 Experiment

In this section, we describe an experiment whose aims were (1) to validate the possibility-theoretic formalism against human data, by comparing uncertainty computations to human subjective evaluations based on the same scenarios; (2) to map subjective certainty judgements to the classes of modal expressions in French, Maltese and English introduced in Section 2, thereby also testing whether the formalism itself can adequately capture subjective uncertainty judgements by speakers of different languages. The experiment replicated the one reported by Portet and Gatt (2010), with some differences in the choice of materials, and with the crucial difference that it was carried out on three groups of native speakers of the three languages under consideration. Furthermore, we go beyond their analysis in comparing the possibility-theoretic formalism to human judgements.

English	French	Maltese
must	doit	bilfors
may	pourrait	jista' jkun
possbily	peut-être	forsi
definitely	sûrement	żgur

Table 1: Modal expressions used in the experiment.

Design and procedure The experiment exposed participants to scenarios such as those in example (1) through a web interface; this is partially displayed in Figure 3. Each scenario presented some background information, and then presented two propositions about two different *key events* (shown in boldface in (1). Key events always contained either an exact or fuzzy temporal expression, which could refer to the clock time of an event (e.g. *at 16:00*, *between 16:00 and 16:45*) or to its date (e.g. *in 1890*, *between 1890 and 1895*), depending on the scenario. The scenarios were designed to make it explicit that the events themselves actually happened for certain and that uncertainty was only related to their timing. After reading a scenario, participants performed two tasks:

1. *Judgement*: Participants were given a proposition involving a simple event or a temporal relation between two events, and were asked to judge their subjective certainty about the proposition on a scale (Figure 3, top). To elicit these subjective certainty judgements, we used a slider representing the Ψ-scale developed by Raufaste et al. (2003). This combines both possibility and necessity into a single scale, which ranges from 'impossible' ($\Psi = 0$) to 'completely certain' ($\Psi = 1$). From this Ψ measure, the corresponding possibility (Π) and necessity (N) values can easily be reconstructed using (6) and (7) below.

$$\Pi(P) = \begin{cases} 2 \times \Psi & \text{if } \Psi \leq 0.5 \\ 1 & \text{if } \Psi > 0.5 \end{cases} \tag{6}$$

$$N(P) = \begin{cases} 0 & \text{if } \Psi \leq 0.5 \\ 2 \times \Psi - 1 & \text{if } \Psi > 0.5 \end{cases} \tag{7}$$

2. *Expression choice*: For each scenario, participants were also presented with a list of 6 different versions of the proposition they had judged in random order and asked to choose the one that they felt best reflected their degree of certainty (Figure 3, bottom). The list invariably included the original unmodalised proposition (hereafter referred to as the *default* case), as well as a negated version. These were intended to cover the cases of complete certainty about the truth of a proposition (by hypothesis, in the conditions with no uncertainty), or about its falsity (hence, certainty that the proposition is false). Apart from these, there were 4 versions containing the expressions exemplified for the three languages in examples (2) and (3) and summarised in Table 1. Note that the expressions are grouped together in this Table based on the authors' intuitions for convenience of presentation; whether or not the expressions in the three languages correspond precisely is one of the empirical questions we seek to address.

The experimental scenarios represented combinations of two within-participants factors. *Uncertainty* (3 levels) manipulated the amount of temporal uncertainty in scenario, where either both key events were given an exact time (e.g. *at 16:00*), or one had a fuzzy temporal interval (e.g. *between 16:00 and 16:45*) or both did. *Proposition Type* (4 levels) manipulated the type of proposition whose subjective certainty participants were asked to judge, namely: a simple proposition describing either of the two key events alone (e.g. *the robbers left the bank at 16:45*); or a compound proposition describing a temporal relation between them using one of the temporal connectives *before, after*, or *during*. This design yields $3 \times 4 = 12$ conditions. We added a thirteenth condition, in order to balance the design by ensuring that, for every level of uncertainty, there was a simple proposition describing either the first key event or the second. There was also a third, between-groups factor, namely Language (Maltese/English/French). Thus, our experiment had a mixed 3 (Uncertainty) $\times 4$ (Proposition Type) $\times 3$ (Language) design.

Materials and participants Thirteen scenarios were constructed; each one had a version in English, Maltese and French. Within each language, each one had 13 different versions corresponding to

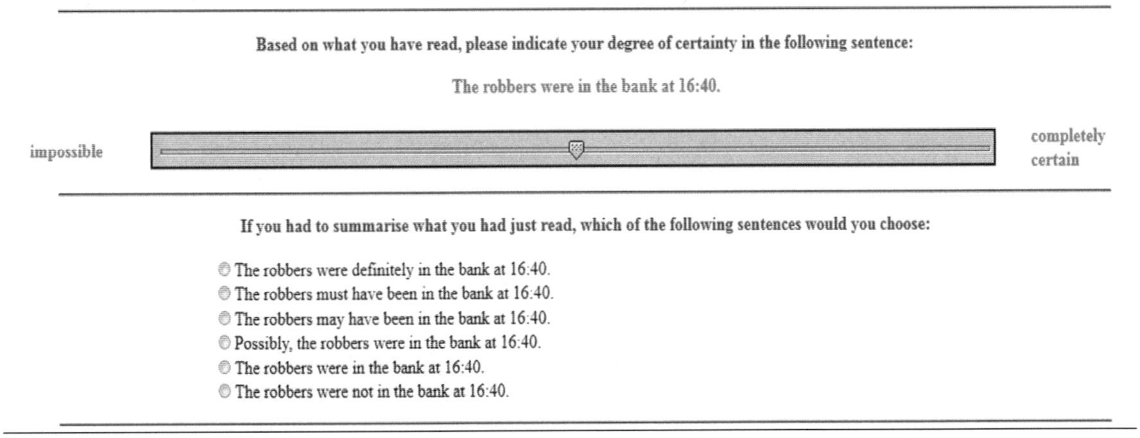

Figure 3: Partial screenshot of the experiment interface

each of the 13 conditions. The scenarios were rotated through a latin square to create 13 versions of the experiment in each language, where each scenario appeared in each condition exactly once across the 13 versions. The present analysis is based on data from 3 different groups of 13 native speakers of each language. Within each group, each participant did one of the versions of the experiment.

4.1 Results

We first test the effects of Uncertainty and Proposition Type on subjective uncertainty judgements using the Ψ scale and compare the subjective judgements made by experimental participants to the output of the reasoning engine on the same scenarios. We then attempt to model statistically the mapping from subjective uncertainty to choice of linguistic expressions.

4.1.1 Subjective uncertainty

Table 2 summarises the mean Ψ ratings overall and within each language, as a function of the different levels of Proposition Type. At a glance, there is a clear tendency for subjective certainty to decrease as scenarios introduce more temporal uncertainty, as expected. However Proposition Type seems to affect ratings less drastically. To test these intuitions, we used a linear mixed effects analysis, with our three factors (Uncertainty, Proposition Type and Language) as fixed effects, and participants and items as random effects, with mean Ψ value as dependent variable. Our strategy was to fit a simple model first, and compare it to increasingly complex models, using a log likelihood test for goodness of fit. Table 3 summarises models and indicates whether they are different from the simplest one (Model 0).[2]

Model	Fixed effects	Random effects	Fit	p
0	Uncertainty	item	NA	NA
1	Uncert.	participant	0	1
2	Uncert.	participant + item	0.916	$> .3$
3	Uncert. + Lang.	item	3.31	$> .06$
4	Uncert. + Prop. + Lang.	item	3.98	$> .3$
5	Uncert. $\times$ Prop. + Lang.	item	4.32	$> .2$
6	Uncert. $\times$ Prop. $\times$ Lang.	item	5.45	$> .4$

Table 3: Linear mixed effects models. Goodness of fit tests compare models to Model 0 using -2 log likelihood

Model 0 is a simple model incorporating only Uncertainty as fixed effect, with item as random effect. This was found to have a high goodness of fit relative to a model with only the intercept and no effects (log $\lambda = 152.4$). The linear mixed effects analysis for this model showed a strong main effect of Uncertainty on Ψ values ($t = 4.887, p < .001$). No subsequent model provided a better fit: Model 1, which incorporates participant as the only random effect, and Model 2, which incorporates both item and participant, are no better, suggesting that the variance among participants was marginal, unlike that of items (scenarios). The impact of different scenarios is likely due to the difference between those where event times were dates and those using clock times – the former are inherently 'fuzzier' since they involve a larger temporal interval.

Once item was established as the only significant random effect, we tested several other models in-

[2]The χ^2 values in the table are the $-2LL$ values.

	No uncertainty				**1 uncertain proposition**				**2 uncertain propositions**		
	after	before	during	simple	after	before	during	simple	after	before	during
en	0.543 (0.48)	0.672 (0.44)	0.505 (0.50)	0.706 (0.43)	0.217 (0.34)	0.340 (0.43)	0.594 (0.41)	0.159 (0.34)	0.183 (0.36)	0.106 (0.28)	0.604 (0.47)
fr	0.554 (0.48)	0.672 (0.44)	0.411 (0.49)	0.728 (0.41)	0.375 (0.39)	0.311 (0.45)	0.562 (0.44)	0.051 (0.17)	0.185 (0.38)	0.315 (0.44)	0.502 (0.47)
mt	0.736 (0.36)	0.743 (0.38)	0.492 (0.47)	0.656 (0.42)	0.308 (0.38)	0.346 (0.46)	0.434 (0.46)	0.186 (0.33)	0.360 (0.48)	0.255 (0.42)	0.454 (0.47)
overall	0.614 (0.43)	0.696 (0.41)	0.471 (0.48)	0.697 (0.42)	0.298 (0.37)	0.332 (0.43)	0.530 (0.43)	0.1325 (0.30)	0.241 (0.41)	0.2225 (0.39)	0.522 (0.46)

Table 2: Mean Ψ values across languages and conditions (standard deviation in parentheses)

corporating more fixed effect combinations. The main effect of Uncertainty persisted, but Model 3 found only a marginal main effect of language ($t = 1.818, p = .06$) and Model 4 showed no main effect of Proposition Type ($t = 0.811, p > .4$). None of the interactions (Models 5 and 6) yielded a better fit. This replicates the finding of Portet and Gatt (2010), who also found no effect of Proposition Type and no interactions. Perhaps more strikingly, there was no significant difference among participants across the three different languages, suggesting that suggesting that, in our data, the language used to describe scenarios didn't affect uncertainty judgements much. Note that this does not imply that linguistic expressions across languages do not differ, only that for a given set of facts associated with a scenario, the level of subjective uncertainty was independent of the language in which that scenario was described.

	r	p
fr	.45	$< .001$
en	.55	$< .001$
mt	.42	$< .001$
overall	.62	$< .001$

Table 4: Correlations between computed and elicited Ψ judgements.

This finding is encouraging, as it suggests that, to the extent that the reasoning formalism described in Section 3 adequately matches human judgements, it can be used to compute possibility and necessity values (though not their mapping to expressions) independently of the target language in which a given scenario is described. To test this, we computed the Π and N values for each scenario using the reasoning engine described in Section 3, making two assumptions: (i) if a scenario stated that an event occurred at a specific time (or within a fuzzy interval), the event was represented with that time or interval as its start time; (ii) we assumed that, over a given fuzzy interval, the possibility distribution for an event was uniform, that is, if an event was stipulated as having started between t_0 and t_1, it was equally possible/necessary during any subinterval of $[t_0, t_1]$. From the computed values for Π and N the value of Ψ was derived and correlated to the mean Ψ value obtained from participants. Table 4 summarises the correlations for each language, and overall. All correlations were positive and highly significant, and higher when averaged over all languages. The value of $r = .62$ for the 'overall' correlation suggests that we can account for approximately ($.62^2 =$) roughly 40% of the variance in the data. While this is not perfect, it does suggest that the model is on the right track.

4.1.2 Choice of linguistic expression

To address our second question, we attempted to predict the choice of expression made by participants from their subjective uncertainty ratings. This was done for each language separately. Means and frequencies are displayed in Table 5.

In all three languages, the table suggests a clustering of expressions, with higher Π and N for the default, *must* and *definitely* cases, and lower values for *may* and *possibly*. However, there are also divergences: in French, the counterpart for *definitely* has a much lower N than in English or Maltese. French *may* and *possibly* also have lower Π values. Maltese Π values for *may* and *possibly* are also closer to those for other expressions than they are in French or English, although the corresponding N values are similar.

Since our aim is ultimately to develop a function that can map from a particular level of subjective uncertainty to a modal expression in a given language, we modelled these results using a multinomial logistic regression (essentially, a Maximum Entropy model). This amounts to treating our problem as a classification problem: given a scenario and a temporal relation, with associated Π and N values, what linguistic expression do these values map to? Our model used the *default* as the reference category, to which others are compared. We simplified the

English			French			Maltese		
	Π	N		Π	N		Π	N
default (27)	0.96	0.82	default (50)	0.97	0.92	default (39)	1	0.76
must (20)	1	0.92	doit (10)	1	0.81	bilfors li (18)	0.94	0.82
definitely (27)	1	0.94	sûrement (19)	0.96	0.49	żgur (26)	0.98	0.78
may (54)	0.86	0.09	pourrait (38)	0.71	0.09	jista' jkun li (55)	0.95	0.14
possibly (28)	0.90	0.11	peut-être (35)	0.73	0.04	forsi (20)	0.90	0.16
negation (23)	0.58	0.04	negation (17)	0.24	0	negation (12)	0.29	0

Table 5: Mean Π and N values by phrase choice. Frequency of each choice is in parentheses.

modelling process by dividing the subjective Π and N ratings into four intervals at increments of 0.25 (i.e. the new coding grouped together $\Pi < .025$, $0.25 \geq \Pi < 0.5$ etc), effectively recoding the predictor variables into categorical ones.

For both English and French, the model incorporating both Π and N yielded an excellent goodness of fit (English: model $\chi^2 = 265.03, p < .001$; French: $\chi^2 = 205.46, p < .001$). However, this was not the case for Maltese, where the combined model was not significantly better than a model containing only the intercept. For this language, a model with only N as predictor turned out to be better ($\chi^2 = 134.87, p < .001$). This is relatively unsurprising, considering that the possibility values for the Maltese data are quite consistently high, with the exception of the negated expressions. This may reflect a genuine difference between Maltese and the other two languages under consideration; however, given that the samples used in the present study were relatively small, further testing will be required to establish the reliability of this finding.

4.1.3 Lexical choice of modals in NLG

A regression model such as the one developed above can be used to classify particular instances (combinations of Π and N values), to identify the best modal expression to use to express the temporal uncertainty. To take an example suppose the reasoning engine predicts $\Pi = 1$ and $N = 0$ for the proposition *the police were on the scene before the robbers left the bank*. The model for English predicts no change in the likelihood of choosing the default expression (i.e. the unmodalised proposition) where possibility values are high, all other things being equal. However, in the present case, the low necessity value substantially decreases the odds associated with the default. In this case, therefore, the model would swing the choice in favour of that expression whose probability increases, relative to the default, as necessity decreases. In this case, the most likely such expression is *possibly*. The model would work in the same way for the other two languages under consideration. Furthermore, given that our results suggest that the actual uncertainty ratings for scenarios are independent of language (Section 4.1.1), we hypothesise that extending the model to other languages would not require substantial alterations to the reasoning formalism described in Section 3, but only to the specific classification model.

5 Conclusions

This paper presented a formalism to reason with temporal uncertainty and a model to map from uncertainty to modal expressions in different languages. Our data shows that subjective uncertainty varies as a function of the temporal uncertainty associated with events in a scenario; moreover, subjective uncertainty correlates well with the values computed by our model. Although we find no evidence of a strong effect of participant variation in our data, in future work we plan to investigate to what extent subjective uncertainty differs between participants using larger samples, as previous work has shown that individual reasoning strategies may differ (Benferhat et al., 2005).

We also described a logistic regression model to predict the best expression in a particular language given a specific degree of subjective uncertainty. The experimental data suggests that there are substantial differences between the sets of expressions tested for the three languages. More data from more participants will be required to validate it and this is our aim in the medium term, in addition to extending our model to cover more linguistic expressions.

Acknowledgments

François Portet is supported by the French national project Sweet-Home (ANR-09-VERS-011). Thanks to Manuel Campos Martnez for letting us use the FuzzyTIME engine.

References

J. F. Allen. 1983. Maintaining knowledge about temporal intervals. *Communications of the ACM*, 26(11):832–843.

Alexander Artikis, Georgios Paliouras, Franois Portet, and Anastasios Skarlatidis. 2010. Logic-based representation, reasoning and machine learning for event recognition. In *DEBS 2010*, pages 282–293.

S. Barro, R. Marín, J. Mira, and A. Paton. 1994. A model and a language for the fuzzy representation and handling of time. *Fuzzy Sets and Systems*, 61:153–175.

S. Benferhat, J.F. Bonnefon, and R. da Silva Neves. 2005. An overview of possibilistic handling of default reasoning, with experimental studies. *Synthese*, 146:53–70.

M. Campos, A. Cárceles, J. Palma, and R. Marín. 2002. A general purporse fuzzy temporal information management engine. In *EurAsia-ICT 2002*, pages 93–97.

R. Dechter, I. Meiri, and J. Pearl. 1991. Temporal constraint networks. *Artificial Intelligence*, 49:61–95.

D. Dubois, H.A. Allel, and H. Prade. 2003. Fuzziness and uncertainty in temporal reasoning. *Journal of Universal Computer Science*, 9(9):1168–1194.

M. Elhadad. 1995. Using argumentation in text generation. *Journal of Pragmatics*, 24:189–220.

N. Evans and S.C. Levinson. 2009. The myth of language universals: Language diversity and its importance for cognitive science. *Behavioral and Brain Sciences*, 32:429–492.

F. Gao, S. Sripada, J. Hunter, and F. Portet. 2009. Using temporal constraints to integrate signal analysis and domain knowledge in medical event detection. In *12th Conference on Artificial Intelligence in Medicine (AIME 09)*, volume 5651 of *LNAI*, pages 46–55.

A. Gatt, F. Portet, E. Reiter, J. Hunter, S. Mahamood, W. Moncur, and S. Sripada. 2009. From data to text in the neonatal intensive care unit: Using NLG technology for decision support and information management. *AI Communications*, 22:153–186.

P. Johnson-Laird. 1978. The meaning of modality. *Cognitive Science*, 2:17–26.

L. Karttunen. 1972. Possible and must. In J. Kimball, editor, *Syntax and Semantics*, volume 1. Academic, New Yowk.

R. Klabunde. 2005. When must should be chosen. In *Proceedings of the 10th European Workshop on Natural Language Generation (ENLG-05)*.

R. Klabunde. 2007. Lexical choice for modal expressions. In *Proceedings of the 11th European Workshop on Natural Language Generation (ENLG-07)*.

A. Kratzer. 1977. What *must* and *can* must and can mean. *Linguistics and Philosophy*, 1:337–355.

A. Kratzer. 1981. The notional category of modality. In H-J Eikmeyer and H. Rieser, editors, *Words, Worlds and Contexts: New Approaches to Word Semantics*. Walter de Gruyter and Co., Berlin.

J. Palma, J.M. Juareza, M. Camposa, and R. Marina. 2006. Fuzzy theory approach for temporal model-based diagnosis: An application to medical domains. *Artificial Intelligence in Medicine*, 38(2):197–218.

F.R. Palmer. 2001. *Mood and modality*. Cambridge University Press, Cambridge, 2 edition.

A. Papafragou. 1998. Inference and word meaning: The case of modal auxiliaries. *Lingua*, 105:1–47.

A. Papafragou. 2006. Epistemic modality and truth conditions. *Lingua*, 116:1688–1702.

F. Portet and A. Gatt. 2010. Towards a possibility-theoretic approach to uncertainty in medical data interpretation for text generation. In D. Riano, A. ten Teije, S. Miksch, and M. Peleg, editors, *Knowledge Representation for Health-Care: Data, Processes and Guidelines*, LNAI 5943. Springer, Berlin and Heidelberg.

F. Portet, E. Reiter, A Gatt, J. Hunter, S. Sripada, Y. Freer, and C. Sykes. 2009. Automatic generation of textual summaries from neonatal intensive care data. *Artificial Intelligence*.

P. Portner. 2009. *Modality*. Oxford University Press, Oxford.

E. Raufaste, R. Da Silva Neves, and C. Mariné. 2003. Testing the descriptive validity of possibility theory in human judgments of uncertainty. *Artificial Intelligence*, 148(1-2):197–218.

E. Reiter, R. Robertson, and L. Osman. 2003. Lessons from a failure: Generating tailored smoking cessation letters. *Artificial Intelligence*, 144:41–58.

E. E. Sweetser. 1990. *From etymology to pragmatics*. Cambridge University Press, Cambridge.

P. Terenziani, R.T. Snodgrass, A. Bottrighi, M. Torchio, and G. Molino. 2005. Extending temporal databases to deal with telic/atelic medical data. In *Proceedings of the 10th Conference on Artificial Intelligence in Medicine (AIME 05)*.

M. Vanhove, C. Miller, and D. Caubet. 2009. The grammaticalisation of modal auxiliaries in maltese and arabic vernaculars of the mediterranean area. In B. Hansen and F. de Haan, editors, *Modals in the languages of Europe*. Mouton, Berlin.

L. Vila and L. Godo. 1994. On fuzzy temporal constraint networks. *Mathware and soft computing*, 3:315–334.

M. Vilain, H. Kautz, and P. van Beek. 1987. Constraint propagation algorithms for temporal reasoning: A revised report.

L.A. Zadeh. 1965. Fuzzy sets. *Information and Control*, 8(3):338–353.

L. Zhou and G. Hripcsaka. 2007. Temporal reasoning with medical data — a review with emphasis on medical natural language processing. *Journal of Biomedical Informatics*, 40(2):183–202, April.

Adaptive Information Presentation for Spoken Dialogue Systems: Evaluation with human subjects

Verena Rieser[1], **Simon Keizer**[1,2], **Xingkun Liu**[1], **Oliver Lemon**[1]

[1] Heriot-Watt University
Edinburgh, United Kingdom

[2] University of Cambridge
Cambridge, United Kingdom

{v.rieser,s.keizer,x.liu,o.lemon}@hw.ac.uk

Abstract

We present evaluation results with human subjects for a novel data-driven approach to Natural Language Generation in spoken dialogue systems. We evaluate a trained Information Presentation (IP) strategy in a deployed tourist-information spoken dialogue system. The IP problem is formulated as statistical decision making under uncertainty using Reinforcement Learning, where both content planning and attribute selection are jointly optimised based on data collected in a Wizard-of-Oz study. After earlier work testing and training this model in simulation, we now present results from an extensive online user study, involving 131 users and more than 800 test dialogues, which explores its contribution to overall 'global' task success. We find that the trained Information Presentation strategy significantly improves dialogue task completion, with up to a 9.7% increase (30% relative) compared to the deployed dialogue system which uses conventional, hand-coded presentation prompts. We also present subjective evaluation results and discuss the implications of these results for future work in dialogue management and NLG.

1 Introduction

Natural Language Generation (NLG) for Spoken Dialogue Systems serves two goals. On the one hand the "local" NLG task is to present "enough" information to the user (for example helping them to feel confident that they have a good overview of the search results) while keeping the utterances short and understandable. On the other hand, better Information Presentation should also contribute to the "global/ overall" dialogue task, so as to maximise task completion.

We have developed a novel framework for adaptive Natural Language Generation (NLG) where the problem is formulated as incremental decision making under uncertainty, which can be approached using Reinforcement Learning (Lemon, 2008; Rieser and Lemon, 2009; Rieser et al., 2010).This model is also being explored by other researchers (Dethlefs et al., 2011; Dethlefs and Cuayáhuitl, 2011) and (Janarthanam and Lemon, 2010; Janarthanam et al., 2011). We have applied the theory to a variety of NLG problems, such as referring expression generation, and here we focus on adaptive Information Presentation (IP) in spoken dialogue. The IP model is adaptive to noisy feedback from the current generation context (e.g. a user, a surface realiser, and a TTS engine), and it incrementally adapts the IP policy at the turn level. Reinforcement Learning is used to automatically optimise the IP policy with respect to a data-driven objective function.

In previous simulation-based work, we demonstrated that this IP model "locally" outperforms other IP strategies as used by conventional dialogue systems (Rieser and Lemon, 2009), as well as a more elaborate IP baseline strategy mimicking human "wizard" IP behaviour (Rieser et al., 2010). We have now integrated this policy into a full online dialogue system using Voice Over IP (VoIP), and evaluated its performance with real users. In particular, we test its ability to contribute to overall dialogue task success.

In Section 2 we briefly review the NLG framework as planning under uncertainty and how it was tested and trained in simulation. Section 3 explains

Proceedings of the 13th European Workshop on Natural Language Generation (ENLG), pages 102–109,
Nancy, France, September 2011.

how this trained policy was integrated into a fully working spoken dialogue system. Section 4 describes the experimental setup. In Section 5 we present the results, and in Section 6 we conclude with a discussion.

2 NLG as planning under uncertainty

We follow the overall framework of NLG as planning under uncertainty (Lemon, 2008; Rieser and Lemon, 2009; Rieser et al., 2010), where each NLG action is a sequential decision point, based on the current dialogue context and the expected long-term utility or "reward" of the chosen NLG action. Other recent approaches describe this task as planning, e.g. (Koller and Petrick, 2008), or as utility-based decision making (Deemter, 2009), but not as a statistical planning problem, where uncertainty in the stochastic environment is explicitly modelled. Below, we apply this framework to Information Presentation strategies in SDS using Reinforcement Learning (RL) (Sutton and Barto, 1998), where the example task is to present a set of search results (e.g. restaurants) to users. In particular, we consider 7 possible policies for structuring the content (see Figure 1): Recommending one single item, comparing two items, summarising all items, or ordered combinations of those actions, e.g. first summarise all the retrieved items and then recommend one of them. The IP module has to decide which action to take next, how many attributes to mention, and when to stop generating. We use a sentence generator based on the stochastic sentence planner SPaRKy (Stent et al., 2004) for surface generation.

Prior work has presented a variety of IP strategies for structuring information (see examples in Table 1). For example, the SUMMARY strategy is used to guide the user's "focus of attention". It draws the user's attention to relevant attributes by grouping the current results from the database into clusters, e.g. (Polifroni and Walker, 2008; Demberg and Moore, 2006). Other studies investigate a COMPARE strategy, where the attributes of individual items from the database result are compared, e.g. (Walker et al., 2007; Nakatsu, 2008). Most work in SDS however uses a RECOMMEND strategy, where only the top ranking item from the database result is presented, e.g. (Young et al., 2007).

We jointly optimise these 7 content structuring strategies together with attribute selection, i.e. how many attributes to mention in each strategy (e.g. SUMMARY(3)+RECOMMEND(2) with number of attributes in brackets). Attribute types are ranked according to a pre-defined user model (i.e. cuisine, price range, location, food quality, and service quality). We formulate the problem as a Markov Decision Process (MDP), where states are dialogue system contexts and actions are NLG decisions. Each state-action pair is associated with a transition probability, which is the probability of moving from state s at time t to state s' at time $t+1$ after having performed action a when in state s. This transition probability is computed by the environment model (i.e. the user simulation and realiser), and explicitly captures the uncertainty in the generation environment. This is a major difference to other non-statistical planning approaches. Each transition is also associated with a reinforcement signal (or "reward") r_{t+1} describing how good the result of action a was when performed in state s. The aim of the MDP is to maximise the long-term expected reward of its decisions, resulting in a *policy* which maps each possible state to an 'optimal' action in that state (i.e. the action with the highest expected long-term reward) (Rieser and Lemon, 2011).

$$\begin{bmatrix} \text{ACTION:} & \begin{bmatrix} \textit{IP:}\begin{Bmatrix}\text{SUMMARY}\\ \text{COMPARE}\\ \text{RECOMMEND}\end{Bmatrix}\begin{Bmatrix}\text{attr: } \texttt{1-5}\end{Bmatrix}\end{bmatrix} \\ \text{STATE:} & \begin{bmatrix} \texttt{attributes:}\{\texttt{1-15}\} \\ \texttt{sentence:}\{\texttt{2-18}\} \\ \texttt{dbHitsFocus:}\{\texttt{1-100}\} \\ \texttt{userSelect:}\{\texttt{0,1}\} \\ \texttt{userAddInfo:}\{\texttt{0,1}\} \\ \texttt{userElse:}\{\texttt{0,1}\} \end{bmatrix} \end{bmatrix}$$

Figure 2: State-Action space for the IP problem

We treat IP as a hierarchical joint optimisation problem, where first one of the IP structures (1-3) is chosen and then the number of attributes is decided, as shown in Figure 2. At each generation step, the MDP can choose 1-5 attributes. This results in 215 possible strategies, given the ordering constraints displayed in Figure 1. Generation stops as soon as the user is predicted to select a presented item, i.e. the "local" IP task is successful.

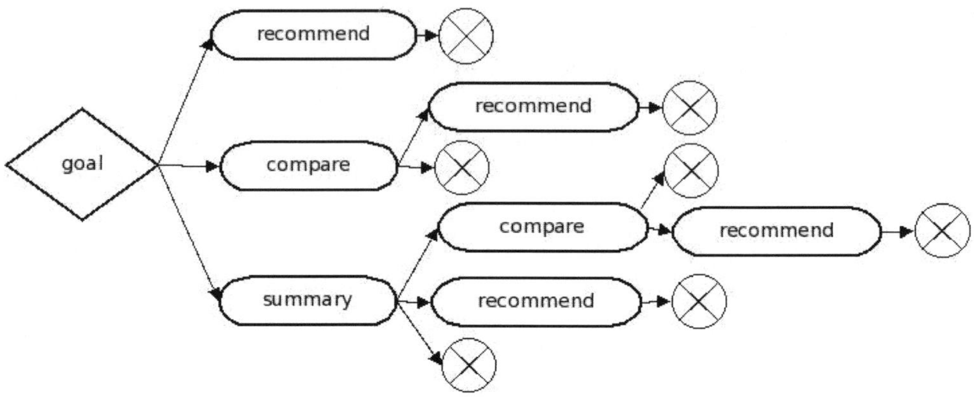

Figure 1: Possible Information Presentation structures (X=stop generation)

Strategy	Example utterance
SUMMARY	26 restaurants meet your query. There are 10 restaurants which serve Indian food and are in the cheap price range. There are also 16 others which are more expensive.
COMPARE	The restaurant called Maharajah and the restaurant called The Gandhi are both Indian restaurants. However, The Gandhi is in the cheap price range while Maharajah is moderately priced.
RECOMMEND	The restaurant called The Gandhi has the best overall quality amongst the matching restaurants. It is an Indian restaurant, and it is in the cheap price range.

Table 1: Example realisations, generated when the user provided `cuisine=Indian`, and where the NLG component has also selected the additional attribute `price` for presentation to the user.

States are represented as sets of dialogue system context features. The state space comprises "lower-level" features about the realiser behaviour (two discrete features representing the number of attributes and sentences generated so far) and three binary features representing the user's predicted next action, as well as "high-level" features provided by the Dialogue Manager (DM) (e.g. current database hits in the user's focus (`dbHitsFocus`)).

We train the policy in a simulated environment which is constructed from Wizard-of-Oz data (Liu et al., 2009). Simulated users for testing and training, as well as a data-driven reward function have been trained and evaluated using this data (Rieser et al., 2010). The data-driven reward function is formulated as a linear regression in equation (1) ($R^2 =$ .26), which indicates that users like to be focused on a small set of database hits, which will enable them to choose an item ($valueUserReaction$), while keeping the IP utterances short (where $\#sentence$ is in the range [2-18]):

$$\begin{aligned} Reward \ = \ & 0.121 \times valueUserReaction \\ & -1.2 \times \#DBhits \\ & -1.43 \times \#sentence \end{aligned} \quad (1)$$

The policy was trained using the SHARSHA algorithm (a hierarchical version of SARSA) (Shapiro and Langley, 2002) with linear function approximation (Sutton and Barto, 1998).

3 System Integration

In order to evaluate our NLG strategy with real users, it was integrated into the 'CamInfo' system (Young et al., 2010), a spoken dialogue system providing tourist information for real locations in Cambridge. This baseline system has been made accessible by phone using VoIP technology, enabling out-of-lab evaluation with large numbers of users. Apart from practical advantages in managing evaluation campaigns, this development effort was also intended as a step towards evaluating spoken dialogue systems under more realistic conditions. Please note, however, that the users in this evaluation were still recruited and asked to complete predefined tasks (see Section 4), and therefore the evaluation might not be as realistic as an evaluation of a final deployed application with real users having real goals (Black et al., 2011).

The speech recogniser (ASR), semantic parser (SLU) and dialogue manager (DM) have all been developed at Cambridge University. For speech synthesis (TTS), the Baratinoo synthesiser, developed at France Telecom, was used.

The DM uses a POMDP (Partially Observable Markov Decision Process) framework, allowing it to process N-Best lists of ASR hypotheses and keep track of multiple dialogue state hypotheses. The DM policy is trained to select system dialogue acts given a probability distribution over possible dialogue states. It has been shown that such dialogue managers can exploit the information in the N-Best lists (as opposed to only using the top ASR hypothesis) and are therefore particularly effective in noisy conditions (Young et al., 2010).

The natural language generation component of this baseline system is a standard rule-based surface realiser covering the full range of system dialogue acts that the dialogue manager can produce. It has only one IP strategy, i.e., the system only provides information about database entries in the form of single venue recommendations (the RECOMMEND strategy, see Table 1). The attributes of the venue to be presented are selected heuristically. In the extended version of the system, the IP strategy is replaced by our trained NLG component, which is optimised to decide between different IP strategies.

We follow a hybrid between statistical and rule-based approaches in order to integrate the trained policy: higher-level hand-coded rules impose a set of constraints on the statistical policy. Note that the possibility of constraining statistical policies with hard-coded rules is increasingly required for developing commercial dialogue systems (Williams, 2008). We follow a modular approach for integration, where the NLG and Dialogue Management strategies were trained separately (we discuss this issue further below).

We impose the following rule-based constraints on our policy in order to make it compatible with the (separately trained) DM policy:

- The chosen IP strategy must end with in a RECOMMEND action, since the DM expects (exactly one) named entity to be mentioned.

- COMPARE actions are excluded in order to not introduce new named entities that the user may refer to later (since the DM was not optimised under this condition).

- The attribute selection is forced to present at least the attributes chosen by the DM.

The remaining decision points are: choosing between RECOMMEND and SUMMARY+RECOMMEND, as well as selecting additional attributes to present to the user. Although this is a somewhat limited version of the fully optimised IP strategy, it is still interesting to discover whether even a limited amount of NLG optimisation (in terms of more elaborate IP strategies and attribute selection) has an effect on overall global system performance.

Hence, in this real user evaluation, we compared the baseline system, incorporating a single recommendation IP strategy only, with the extended system, incorporating our trained NLG IP policy. In a previous proof-of-concept study (Rieser and Lemon, 2009) a similar rule-based baseline NLG strategy (RECOMMEND only) was shown to be outperformed in simulation. We now test whether these results transfer to real user settings. In the remainder of this paper we will refer to the baseline system as *BASE* system and to the system with the integrated trained IP strategy as *TIP*.

4 Experimental Setup

For the evaluation of the two systems, two approaches to managing subjects were taken. In the first approach, subjects were recruited using mailshots and web-based advertising amongst people from Cambridge and Edinburgh, mostly students. From the resulting pool of subjects, people were gradually invited to start the tasks, in their own time, and within a given trial period of around two weeks. After the trial period, they were paid (using PayPal) per completed task, with a required minimum of 15 tasks, and a maximum of 40 tasks. For the two systems, this resulted in a corpus of 304 dialogues. In the second approach, an alternative method of managing subjects was used, using Amazon Mechanical Turk (Jurcicek et al., 2011). In this setup, tasks are published as so-called HITs (Human Intelligence Tasks) on a web-server and registered workers can complete them. This setup resulted in 532 collected dialogues for the two systems compared[1]. In the remainder of this paper, we will refer to the corpus

[1]This evaluation was part of a bigger evaluation campaign, in which 2046 dialogues were collected in total.

obtained with 'locally' managed subjects as *Feb11-LOC* and to the corpus obtained using Amazon Mechanical Turk as *Feb11-AMT*.

In both of the above-mentioned approaches, the subjects were directed to a webpage with detailed instructions and for each task, a phone number to call and the scenario to follow. The subjects were randomly assigned to interact with one of the systems (BASE or TIP). A scenario describes a place to eat in town, with some constraints, for example: *"You want to find a moderately priced restaurant and it should be in the Riverside area. You want to know the address, phone number, and type of food."*. After the dialogue, the subjects were asked to fill in a short questionnaire, assessing the impact of IP strategies on the users' perception of various system components:

Q1. Did you find all the information you were looking for? [Yes / No]

Please state your attitude towards the following statements:

Q2. The system understood me well. [1 – 6]

Q3. The phrasing of the system's responses was good. [1 – 6]

Q4. The system's voice was of good quality. [1 – 6]

1: strongly disagree	4: slightly agree
2: disagree	5: agree
3: slightly disagree	6: strongly agree

Table 2 summarises the two corpora of collected data. For the Feb11-AMT corpus, considerably more subjects were used, although many of them did only a small number of tasks. For the Feb11-LOC corpus, it was more difficult to recruit many subjects, but in this setup, the subjects could be asked to complete a minimum number of tasks, hence the higher average number of dialogues per user.

Also note, that the Word Error Rate (WER) is relatively high in both corpora. This is partly due to the fact that the ASR module had not been trained properly for this particular domain due to lack of training data. Furthermore, some of the subjects were non-native speakers and some subjects used Skype to call the systems, which causes distortion of the audio signal. These conditions are the same for both BASE and TIP systems. Despite the high ASR error rates, overall task completion rates were high, due to the robustness of the POMDP dialogue manager.

Corpus	nDials	AvgTurns	nUsers	nDsUsr	WER
Feb11-LOC	304	11.48	19	16.00	56.5
Feb11-AMT	532	10.09	113	4.71	53.6

Table 2: Overview of collected data, with for each corpus the number of dialogues (nDials), the average number of user turns per dialogue (AvgTurns), the number of unique users (nUsers), the average number of dialogues per user (nDsUsr), and the word error rate (WER).

The overall most frequently employed IP strategy is SUMMARY(2)+RECOMMEND(2), see Table 3. Also, note that the trained policy never employed more than 3 attributes, and always chose to use the same number of attributes for its combined IP strategies.

Frequ.	Strategy(Attributes)
1	RECOMMEND(1)
123	RECOMMEND(2)
163	RECOMMEND(3)
254	SUMMARY(1)+RECOMMEND(1)
778	SUMMARY(2)+RECOMMEND(2)
270	SUMMARY(3)+RECOMMEND(3)

Table 3: Frequency of occurrences of each IP strategy observed in the evaluation with number of attributes in brackets.

5 Results

After processing the log files and completed user questionnaires, both objective and subjective performance measures were computed in order to compare the systems.

5.1 Objective evaluation

For the objective evaluation of the two dialogue systems we focused on measuring goal completion rates, which can be done in different ways. First, we can take the goal specification assigned to the user for each dialogue and then analyse the system dialogue acts. *Partial completion* (ObjSucc-PC) is achieved when the system has offered a venue that matches the constraints as specified in the assigned goal, for example it has provided the name of a cheap chinese restaurant in the riverside area. *Full completion* (ObSucc-FC) is achieved when the system has also provided the required additional information about that venue, for example the phone number and address.

In Table 4, all success rates obtained from the February 2011 evaluation are given, for the corpus

Corpus	System	nDials	nTurns	SubjSucc	ObjSucc-PC	ObjSucc-FC
Feb11-LOC	BASE	199	11.69	65.33 (6.61)	73.37 (6.14)	46.73 (6.93)
	TIP	105	11.02	60.00 (9.37)	77.23 (8.02)	49.50 (9.56)
Feb11-AMT	BASE	402	9.86	64.18 (4.69)	51.00 (4.89)	28.86 (4.43)
	TIP	130	10.83	56.15 (8.53)	60.77 (8.39)	37.69 (8.33)
Feb11-TOT	BASE	601	10.46	64.56 (3.82)	58.40 (3.94)	34.78 (3.81)
	TIP	235	10.91	57.87 (6.31)	**68.09 (5.96)**∗	**42.98 (6.33)**∗

Table 4: Overview of all success rates (%) obtained for the two corpora, including subjective success obtained from Q1 of the user questionnaire(SubjSucc), objective success based on assigned goals (ObjSucc-PC for partial completion and ObjSucc-FC for full completion). 95% confidence intervals for all success rates are indicated in brackets; statistically significant improvements ($p < 0.05$ using a z-test) are indicated with an asterisk (*). Also given are the number of dialogues (nDials) and dialogue length in terms of the average number of user turns per dialogue(nTurns).

with data from locally recruited subjects (Feb11-LOC), and the corpus with data from Amazon Mechanical Turk workers, as well as both corpora pooled together (Feb11-TOT). The results show that the system with our NLG component (TIP) outperforms the baseline system (BASE) on all objective success rates in both corpora. Relative improvements of up to 30% for full completion on the Feb11-AMT corpus were obtained. After pooling the two corpora together, we have a sufficient number of dialogues to show that the improvement from our NLG strategy is statistically significant on both partial and full completion (using a 2-tailed z-test for two proportions).

It is also interesting to note that the average number of user turns per dialogue is not significantly different between systems in both corpora, suggesting that the contribution of the trained IP policy to system performance manifests itself primarily in terms of effectiveness rather than efficiency. By providing more useful information to the user, the system might help them to find an appropriate venue in fewer turns, but due to the lengthy system prompts, more turns might be needed to recover from speech recognition errors (see WER in Table 2).

5.2 Subjective evaluation

Table 5 summarises the subjective user scores from the questionnaire (see Section 4). In terms of subjective success rates (Q1), the baseline system (BASE) obtains slightly higher scores on both corpora, although no statistically significant differences were found. We will further discuss these results in section 6.

When comparing the other subjective scores (Q2–Q4) on a scale of [1–6], using a Mann-Whitney

Corpus	System	Q1	Q2	Q3	Q4
Feb11-LOC	BASE	65.33	3.69	3.94	**4.23**∗
	TIP	60.00	3.44	3.70	3.91
Feb11-AMT	BASE	64.18	3.92	4.16	3.81
	TIP	56.15	3.87	4.30	3.85
Feb11-TOT	BASE	64.56	3.85	4.10	3.95
	TIP	57.87	3.68	4.03	3.88

Table 5: Subjective evaluation results, based on the questionnaire [Q1-Q4], where an asterisk (*) denotes a significant difference at $p < 0.05$ (using a z-test for Q1 and a Mann-Whitney test for Q2–Q4).

test, the only case where a statistically significant difference is found between the two systems is the score for *Q4:VoiceQuality* in the Feb11-LOC corpus, where the baseline system is significantly better. Since the the TTS voice is exactly the same for both systems, the difference in perceived voice quality might be influenced by the longer system prompts for the TIP system. However, we don't see this pattern in the Feb11-AMT corpus.

We also compared the Mechanical Turk setup to the setup where subjects where recruited locally (Feb11-AMT vs. Feb11-LOC for both systems). For the TIP system, *Q2:Understanding* and *Q3:Phrasing* are significantly higher in the Feb11-AMT corpus compared to the FEB11-LOC corpus. Similarly, the BASE system performs significantly better for *Q3:Phrasing* under the Mechanical Turk setting. However, when combining the results for all the subjective scores (similar to the objective scores), none of the differences are significant.

In sum, there is no difference in user ratings between the original BASE system and the TIP system with the integrated trained NLG strategy, except for *Q4:VoiceQuality*, which is better rated for the BASE system in the Feb11-LOC corpus, even though the systems had identical TTS. The difference in ratings between the Feb11-LOC and Feb11-AMT corpora suggests that the way in which subjects are recruited, instructed and payed, as well as the user population targeted, has an impact on subjective ratings obtained.

6 Discussion

Following previous work on a novel NLG model in which content planning and attribute selection are formulated as statistical planning under uncertainty, this paper has presented results of the evaluation of this NLG model with real users, focussing on contribution to overall task success in spoken dialogue systems. The NLG model that was trained in a simulated environment was integrated in a deployed spoken dialogue system for tourist information and evaluated in an online experiment with 131 real users and over 800 dialogues. The results showed that the trained Information Presentation model significantly improves objective dialogue task completion, with up to a 30% relative increase (+9.7% raw improvement) compared to a state-of-the-art deployed dialogue system that generates conventional, hand-coded presentation prompts. This outcome confirms earlier results from a previous proof-of-concept study (Rieser and Lemon, 2009), where a similar baseline was shown to be outperformed in simulation.

The subjective scores however were quite similar between the two systems, and in terms of perceived success rate, the baseline system scored better, though not statistically significantly. One possible explanation is that the more elaborate TIP strategy might have somehow obscured the users' perceptions of task completion (even though the objective task completion was significantly higher).

An important factor that may have influenced the results, was that the word error rate was relatively high throughout the data. The more elaborate information presentation prompts from the integrated system (TIP) might have exacerbated the many speech recognition problems, where the DM might have falsely initiated a lengthy Information Presentation prompt after a mis-recognition error. This is also suggested by the analysis of dialogue length, which turned out to be very similar between the two systems. By providing more useful information to the user, the TIP system might help them to find an appropriate venue in fewer turns, but due to the lengthy system prompts, more turns might be needed to recover from speech recognition errors.

Although these evaluation results are very positive, a system setup which combines separately trained dialogue manager and NLG components is not ideal. In this case the dialogue manager was trained in a setup where only the single item recommendation strategy for IP is used. Therefore, for the dialogue manager state update, only dialogue acts for such IP prompts are expected. If the trained NLG model decides to use an alternative IP strategy, a mismatch is then potentially caused between what the dialogue manager planned and what is actually presented to the real user. Therefore, the NLG module might result in user behaviour that the dialogue manager is not optimised for. As a practical compromise it was therefore decided (as explained above) to require all IP prompts to end with a single item recommendation, and the COMPARE strategy was blocked during the evaluation. Therefore, neither DM nor NLG were trained for the final operating conditions that they would experience in this application, though the constraints on NLG mentioned above meant that the DM's chosen actions were maintained. In future work we therefore strive to jointly optimise the DM and NLG strategies (see also (Lemon, 2011)), and it is likely that full use of an optimised IP strategy would lead to an even greater performance boost in the overall system. We would expect that a joint optimisation of DM and NLG policies would prevent the DM from initiating long IP prompts after likely mis-recognitions. We predict that the results obtained in this study would be even stronger for a jointly-optimised DM+NLG strategy, and we pursue this in current work.

Finally, we note that the overall framework has also been used for optimising generation of referring expressions, including adaptive generation of temporal referring expressions, where similar results have been found in boosting overall task success of spoken dialogue systems (Janarthanam et al., 2011). This set of results shows that there are significant 'global' benefits to be gained by viewing NLG as statistical planning under uncertainty.

Acknowledgments

The research leading to these results has received funding from the EC's 7th Framework Programme (FP7/2007-2013) under grant agreement no. 216594 (CLASSiC project `www.classic-project.org`), and (FP7/2011-2014) under grant agreement no. 270019 (SpaceBook project).

References

Alan W Black, Susanne Burger, Alistair Conkie, Helen Hastie, Simon Keizer, Oliver Lemon, Nicolas Merigaud, Gabriel Parent, Gabriel Schubiner, Blaise Thomson, Jason D. Williams, Kai Yu, Steve Young, and Maxine Eskenazi. 2011. Spoken Dialog Challenge 2010: Comparison of Live and Control Test Results. In *Proceedings of SIGDIAL*.

Kees van Deemter. 2009. What game theory can do for NLG: the case of vague language. In *12th European Workshop on Natural Language Generation (ENLG)*.

Vera Demberg and Johanna Moore. 2006. Information presentation in spoken dialogue systems. In *Proc. of the Conference of the European Chapter of the ACL (EACL)*.

Nina Dethlefs and Heriberto Cuayáhuitl. 2011. Hierarchical Reinforcement Learning and Hidden Markov Models for Task-Oriented Natural Language Generation. In *Proc. of ACL*.

Nina Dethlefs, Heriberto Cuayáhuitl, and Jette Viethen. 2011. Optimising Natural Language Generation Decision Making For Situated Dialogue. In *Proc. of SIGDIAL*.

Srinivasan Janarthanam and Oliver Lemon. 2010. Adaptive Referring Expression Generation in Spoken Dialogue Systems: Evaluation with Real Users. In *Proceedings of SIGDIAL*.

Srinivasan Janarthanam, Helen Hastie, Oliver Lemon, and Xingkun Liu. 2011. "The day after the day after tomorrow?" a machine learning approach to adaptive temporal expression generation: training and evaluation with real users. In *Proc. of SIGDIAL*.

F. Jurcicek, S. Keizer, M. Gasic, F. Mairesse, B. Thomson, K. Yu, and S. Young. 2011. Real user evaluation of spoken dialogue systems using amazon mechanical turk. In *Proc. Interspeech*, Florence, Italy, August.

Alexander Koller and Ronald Petrick. 2008. Experiences with Planning for Natural Language Generation. In *ICAPS*.

Oliver Lemon. 2008. Adaptive natural language generation in dialogue using Reinforcement Learning. In *Proc. of the 12th SEMdial Workshop on on the Semantics and Pragmatics of Dialogues*, London, UK, June.

Oliver Lemon. 2011. Learning what to say and how to say it: joint optimization of spoken dialogue management and Natural Language Generation. *Computer Speech and Language*, 25(2):210–221.

Xingkun Liu, Verena Rieser, and Oliver Lemon. 2009. A Wizard-of-Oz interface to study information presentation strategies for spoken dialogue systems. In *Proc. of the 1st International Workshop on Spoken Dialogue Systems*.

Crystal Nakatsu. 2008. Learning contrastive connectives in sentence realization ranking. In *Proc. of SIGdial Workshop on Discourse and Dialogue*.

Joseph Polifroni and Marilyn Walker. 2008. Intensional Summaries as Cooperative Responses in Dialogue Automation and Evaluation. In *Proceedings of ACL*.

Verena Rieser and Oliver Lemon. 2009. Natural Language Generation as Planning Under Uncertainty for Spoken Dialogue Systems. In *Proc. of EACL*.

Verena Rieser and Oliver Lemon. 2011. Learning and Evaluation of Dialogue Strategies for new Applications: Empirical Methods for Optimization from Small Data Sets. *Computational Linguistics*, 37(1).

Verena Rieser, Oliver Lemon, and Xingkun Liu. 2010. Optimising Information Presentation for Spoken Dialogue Systems. In *Proceedings of ACL*, pages 1009–1018, Uppsala, Sweden, July.

Dan Shapiro and P. Langley. 2002. Separating skills from preference: Using learning to program by reward. In *Proc. of the 19th International Conference on Machine Learning (ICML)*, pages 570–577, Sydney, Australia, July.

Amanda Stent, Rashmi Prasad, and Marilyn Walker. 2004. Trainable sentence planning for complex information presentation in spoken dialog systems. In *Proc. ACL*.

R. Sutton and A. Barto. 1998. *Reinforcement Learning*. MIT Press.

Marilyn Walker, Amanda Stent, François Mairesse, and Rashmi Prasad. 2007. Individual and domain adaptation in sentence planning for dialogue. *Journal of Artificial Intelligence Research (JAIR)*, 30:413–456.

Jason D. Williams. 2008. The best of both worlds: Unifying conventional dialog systems and POMDP. In *Proceedings of Interspeech*.

SJ Young, J Schatzmann, K Weilhammer, and H Ye. 2007. The Hidden Information State Approach to Dialog Management. In *ICASSP 2007*.

S. Young, M. Gašić, S. Keizer, F. Mairesse, B. Thomson, and K. Yu. 2010. The Hidden Information State model: a practical framework for POMDP based spoken dialogue management. *Computer Speech and Language*, 24(2):150–174.

Combining Hierarchical Reinforcement Learning and Bayesian Networks for Natural Language Generation in Situated Dialogue

Nina Dethlefs
Department of Linguistics,
University of Bremen
dethlefs@uni-bremen.de

Heriberto Cuayáhuitl
German Research Centre for Artificial Intelligence
(DFKI), Saarbrücken
heriberto.cuayahuitl@dfki.de

Abstract

Language generators in situated domains face a number of content selection, utterance planning and surface realisation decisions, which can be strictly interdependent. We therefore propose to optimise these processes in a joint fashion using Hierarchical Reinforcement Learning. To this end, we induce a reward function for content selection and utterance planning from data using the PARADISE framework, and suggest a novel method for inducing a reward function for surface realisation from corpora. It is based on generation spaces represented as Bayesian Networks. Results in terms of task success and human-likeness suggest that our unified approach performs better than a baseline optimised in isolation or a greedy or random baseline. It receives human ratings close to human authors.

1 Introduction

Natural Language Generation (NLG) systems that work in situated domains and need to generate utterances during an interaction are faced with a number of challenges. They need to adapt their decisions to a continuously changing interaction history and spatial context as well as to the user's properties, such as their individual information needs and verbal or nonverbal responses to each generated utterance. Decisions involve the tasks of content selection, utterance planning and surface realisation, which can be in many ways related and interdependent. For the former two tasks, e.g., there is a trade-off between how much information to include in an utterance (to increase task success), and how much a user can actually comprehend online. With regard to surface realisation, decisions are often made according to a language model of the domain (Langkilde and Knight, 1998; Bangalore and Rambow, 2000; Oh and Rudnicky, 2000; White, 2004; Belz, 2008). However, there are other linguistic phenomena, such as alignment (Pickering and Garrod, 2004), consistency (Halliday and Hasan, 1976), and variation, which influence people's assessment of discourse (Levelt and Kelter, 1982) and generated output (Belz and Reiter, 2006; Foster and Oberlander, 2006). We therefore argue that it is important to optimise content selection, utterance planning and surface realisation in a unified fashion, and we suggest to use Hierarchical Reinforcement Learning (HRL) with Bayesian networks to achieve this. Reinforcement learning (RL) is an attractive framework for optimising NLG systems, where situations are mapped to actions by maximising a long term reward signal (Rieser et al., 2010; Janarthanam and Lemon, 2010). HRL has the additional advantage of scaling to large search spaces (Dethlefs and Cuayáhuitl, 2010). Since an HRL agent will ultimately learn the behaviour it is rewarded for, the reward function is arguably the agent's most crucial component. Previous work has therefore suggested to learn a reward function from human data as in the PARADISE framework (Walker et al., 1997). We will use this framework to induce a reward function for content selection and utterance planning. However, since PARADISE relies heavily on task success metrics, it is not ideally suited for surface realisation, which depends more on linguistic phenomena like frequency, consistency and variation. Linguistic and psycho-

Proceedings of the 13th European Workshop on Natural Language Generation (ENLG), pages 110–120,
Nancy, France, September 2011.

logical studies (cited above) show that such phenomena are worth modelling in an NLG system. The contribution of this paper is therefore to induce a reward function from human data, specifically suited for surface generation. We obtain Bayesian Networks (BNs) (Jensen, 1996) from a human corpus and use them to inform the agent's learning process. We compare their performance against a greedy and a random baseline. In addition, we suggest to optimise content selection, utterance planning and surface realisation decisions in a joint, rather than isolated, fashion in order to correspond to their interrelated nature. Results in terms of task success and human-likeness show that our combined approach performs better than baselines that were optimised in isolation or act on behalf of the language model alone. Since generation spaces in our approach can be obtained for any domain for which corpus data is available, it generalises to different domains with limited effort and reduced development time.

2 Related Work

Related approaches using graphical models for NLG include Barzilay and Lee (2002) and Mairesse et al. (2010). Barzilay and Lee use multiple sequence alignment to obtain lattices of surface form variants for a semantic concept. Mairesse et al. use Dynamic Bayesian networks and learn surface form variants from semantically aligned data. Both approaches demonstrated that graphical models can yield good results for surface realisation.

Related work has also shown the benefits of treating interrelated decisions jointly. Lemon (2010) suggests to use RL to jointly optimise dialogue management and language generation for information presentation, where the system needs to learn when presentation is most advantageous. Cuayáhuitl and Dethlefs (2011b) use HRL for the joint optimisation of spatial behaviours and dialogue behaviours in an agent that learns to give route instructions by taking the user's individual prior knowledge into account. Angeli et al. (2010) treat content selection and surface realisation in a joint fashion using a log-linear classifier, which allows each decision to depend on all decisions made previously. These recent investigations show that jointly optimised policies outperform policies optimised in isolation.

3 The Generation Domain

We address the generation of navigation instructions in a virtual 3D world in the GIVE scenario (Koller et al., 2010). In this task, two people engage in a 'treasure hunt', where one participant instructs the other in navigating through the world, pressing a sequence of buttons and completing the task by obtaining a trophy. The GIVE-2 corpus (Gargett et al., 2010) provides 63 English and 45 German transcripts of such dialogues. We complemented the English dialogues with a set of semantic annotations, please see Sec. 5.1 for the knowledge base of the learning agent, which corresponds to the annotation scheme.

A key feature of the situated approach to generation we are addressing is a tight coupling of system and user behaviour as is also standard in dialogue management.[1] It allows the system to constantly monitor the user's behaviour and change its strategy as soon as the user shows signs of confusion. Since the user needs to process system utterances online, we face a tradeoff between generating few utterances (preferred by users) and generating utterances which are easy to comprehend online (increasing task success). Figure 1 contrasts the dynamics of two possible NLG system architectures, a traditional pipeline and the joint architecture suggested here. In the traditional model, an interaction always starts with information about the user, the dialogue history and the spatial setting being sent to the **content selection** (CS) component. Here, the system chooses whether to use a high-level (e.g, 'go to the next room') or a low-level navigation strategy (e.g., 'go straight, turn left'). High-level instructions are forms of contracted low-level instructions. CS also determines a level of detail for an instruction based on the number of present objects, lengths of instructions and confusion of the user. A first semantic form[2] is constructed here and passed on to **utterance planning** (UP). Here, the system decides whether to use temporal markers, conjunctions, a marked or unmarked theme as well as a mode of presentation (all together or one by one). It then

[1] In fact, some content selection decisions we treat as part of NLG here concerning the user or next system utterance may be shared with a dialogue manager in a complete dialogue system.

[2] Semantic forms contain an instruction type ('destination', 'direction', 'orientation', 'path' or 'straight'), a direction of navigation, and salient landmarks along the path of navigation.

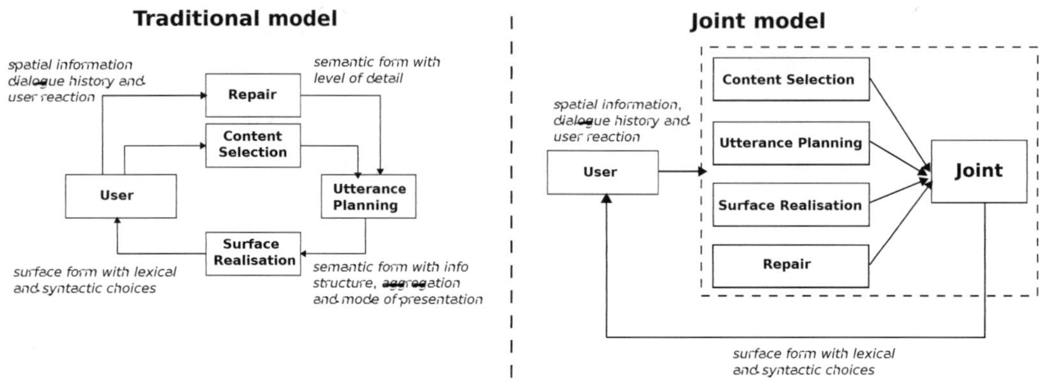

Figure 1: Left: traditional pipeline architecture of an NLG system for CS, UP and SR. Right: an architecture for joint decision making among these tasks. Information passed between components is given in cursive fonts.

consults **surface realisation** (SR) for a final realisation. The SR component addresses the one-to-many relationship between a semantic form and its possible realisations. It optimises the tradeoff between alignment and consistency (Pickering and Garrod, 2004; Halliday and Hasan, 1976) on the one hand, and variation (to improve text quality and readability) on the other (Belz and Reiter, 2006; Foster and Oberlander, 2006). The SR component produces a string of words and presents it to the user whose reaction is observed. The utterance is then either repaired (if the user hesitates or performs an undesired action) or the next one is generated. Note that CS, UP and SR are closely related in this setting. For successful CS, we may wish to be as detailed as possible in an utterance. On the other hand, redundant detail may confuse the user and make it difficult to process utterances online. In UP, we may want to generate as few utterances as possible and thus aggregate them. However, if instructions are too many, a one by one presentation may ease comprehension. In SR, a short utterance is often most likely according to a language model, but it may not be ideal when the user needs more detail. In the joint architecture, there is thus no sequential order on decision making. Instead, one best utterance is generated by considering all variables jointly across subtasks.

4 HRL with Bayesian Networks for NLG

4.1 Hierarchical Reinforcement Learning

The concept of *language generation as an optimisation problem* is as follows: given a set of generation states, a set of actions, and an objective reward function, an optimal generation strategy maximises the objective function by choosing the actions leading to the highest reward for every reached state. Such states describe the system's knowledge about the generation task (e.g. CS, UP, SR). The action set describes the system's capabilities (e.g. *'use high level navigation strategy'*, *'use imperative mood'*, etc.). The reward function assigns a numeric value for each action taken. In this way, language generation can be seen as a finite sequence of states, actions and rewards $\{s_0, a_0, r_1, s_1, a_1, ..., r_{t-1}, s_t\}$, where the goal is to induce an optimal strategy. To do that we use HRL in order to optimise a hierarchy of generation policies rather than a single policy. We denote the hierarchy of RL agents as M^i_j, where the indexes i and j only identify a model in a unique way, they do not specify the execution sequence of subtasks because that is learnt. Each agent of the hierarchy is defined as a Semi-Markov Decision Process (SMDP) consisting of a 4-tuple $< S^i_j, A^i_j, T^i_j, R^i_j >$. S^i_j is a set of states, A^i_j is a set of actions, and T^i_j is a probabilistic state transition function that determines the next state s' from the current state s and the performed action a. $R^i_j(s', \tau|s, a)$ is a reward function that specifies the reward that an agent receives for taking an action a in state s lasting τ time steps (Dietterich, 1999). Since actions in SMDPs may take a variable number of time steps to complete, the random variable τ represents this number of time steps. Actions can be either primitive or composite. The former yield single rewards, the latter correspond to SMDPs and yield cumulative rewards. The goal of

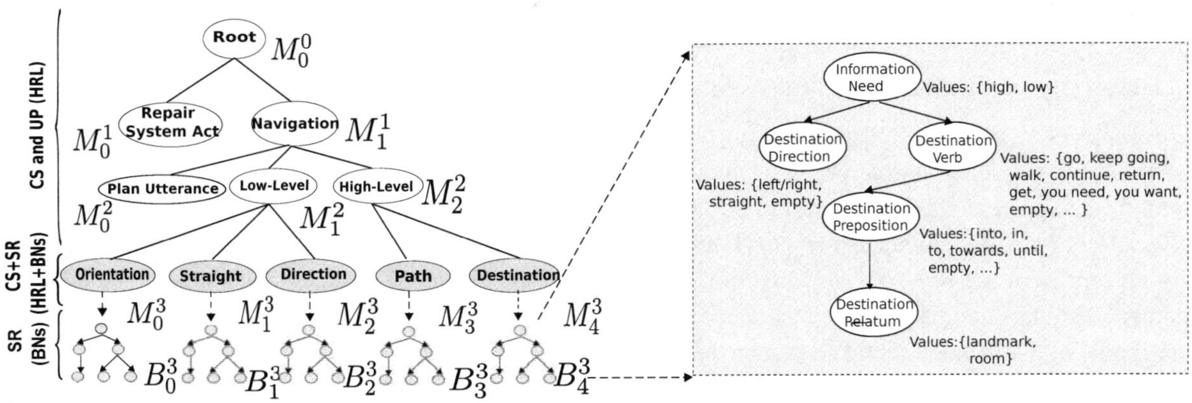

Figure 2: Hierarchy of learning agents (left). The top three layers are responsible for decisions of content selection (CS) and utterance planning (UP), and use HRL. The shaded agents in the bottom use HRL with a Bayesian Network-based reward function and joint optimisation of CS and surface realisation (SR). The BNs represent generation spaces for SR. An example BN, representing the generation space of 'destination' instructions, is shown on the right.

each SMDP is to find an optimal policy π^* that maximises the reward for each visited state, according to $\pi^{*i}_j(s) = \arg\max_{a \in A} Q^{*i}_j(s, a)$, where $Q^i_j(s, a)$ specifies the expected cumulative reward for executing action a in state s and then following π^*. For learning NLG policies, we use HSMQ-Learning, see (Cuayáhuitl, 2009), p. 92.

4.2 Bayesian Networks for Surface Realisation

We can represent a surface realiser as a BN which models the dynamics between a set of semantic concepts and their surface realisations. A BN models a joint probability distribution over a set of random variables and their dependencies based on a directed acyclic graph, where each node represents a variable Y_j with parents $pa(Y_j)$ (Jensen, 1996). Due to the Markov condition, each variable depends only on its parents, resulting in a unique joint probability distribution $p(Y) = \Pi p(Y_j|pa(Y_j))$, where every variable is associated with a conditional probability distribution $p(Y_j|pa(Y_j))$. We use random variables to represent semantic concepts and their values as corresponding surface forms. A random variable with the semantics 'destination process' e.g. can have different values 'go', 'walk', 'elided surface form' (empty) etc. The BNs were constructed manually so as to capture two main dependencies. First, the random variable 'information need' should influence the inclusion of all optional semantic constituents (on the right of Figure 2, e.g., 'destination direction') and the process of the utterance ('destination verb'). Second, a sequence of dependencies spans from the verb to the end of the utterance. In Figure 2, this is from the verb over the preposition to the relatum. The first dependency is based on the intuition that whenever the user's information need is high, optional semantic information is more likely to be included than when the information need is low.[3] Also, we assume that high frequency verb forms are preferable in cases of a high information need. The second dependency is based on the hypothesis that the value of one constituent can be estimated based on the previous constituent. In the future, we may compare different configurations and designs as well as effects of word order. Since BNs allow for probabilistic reasoning, that is the calculation of posterior probabilities given a set of query variable-value pairs, we can perform reasoning over surface forms. Given the word sequence represented by linguistic variables $Y_0...Y_n$ (lexical and syntactic information), and context and situation-based variables $Y_0...Y_m$, we can compute the posterior probability of a random variable Y_j. We use efficient implementations of the variable elimination and junction tree algorithms (Cozman, 2000) for probabilistic reasoning. Initial prior and conditional probability tables were estimated from the GIVE corpus using Maximum Likelihood Estimation.

[3]This is key to the joint treatment of CS and SR: if an utterance is not ideally informative in terms of content, it will receive bad rewards, even if good SR choices have been made (and vice versa).

5 Experimental Setting

5.1 Hierarchy of Agents: State and Action Sets

Figure 2 shows a (hand-crafted) hierarchy of learning agents for navigating and acting in a situated environment. Each agent represents an individual generation task. The models shown in the bottom of the figure represent the BNs $B_0^3 ... B_4^3$ that inform SR decisions. The state representation contains all situational and linguistic knowledge the agent requires for optimal decision making. The following are the state and action sets of the agents in Figure 2 (see the corresponding feature structures). Model M_0^0 is the root agent, it decides whether to generate the next instruction, repair a previous utterance (M_0^1), or confirm the user's behaviour. Model M_1^1 is responsible for navigation instruction generation.[4] It has information about the situational context (e.g., visible objects, route length), the status of the utterance, and the user. It chooses a navigation level, and an utterance plan.[5] State variable names can be reused in later agents. The value 'filled' means that a decision has been made, 'unfilled' means it is still open. Model M_0^2 performs UP. It makes decisions concerning aggregation, info structure, temporal markers and utterance presentation. Decisions are based on the user's information need, and the number of instructions, and do not exclude each other. Model M_1^2 generates low level instructions (direction, orientation, 'straight') based on the user's information need and waiting behaviour. Model M_2^2 generates high-level instructions (destination, path). Model M_0^3 is responsible for orientation instructions. It chooses surface forms for semantic constituents based on the user's information need and behaviour. State variables correspond to semantic concepts, their values to realisation variants. Similarly, model M_1^3 generates 'straight', and model M_2^3 direction instructions. They represent low-level navigation. Model M_3^3 generates path, and model M_4^3 destination instructions. They realise high-level navigation. The hierarchical agent has $|S \times A| = \sum_{i,j} |S_j^i| \times |A_j^i| = 2.5$ million state-action pairs.

[4] Models M_0^0 and M_0^1 are omitted, since we focus on the right branch of the hierarchy in this paper, i.e. from M_1^1 down.

[5] Bold-face (composite) actions pass control between agents. Each time an agent is called, it takes between 7 and 10 (composite or primitive) actions, the exact number varies per agent.

S_1^1:
- v1:GoalVisible ← 0=true,1=false
- v2:InformationNeed ← 0=low,1=high
- v3:NavigationLevel ← 0=unfilled,1=filled
- v4:PreviousUserReaction ← 0=none,1=perform action, 2=perform undesired action,3=wait, 4=request help
- v5:RepairStatus ← 0=unfilled,1=filled
- v6:RouteLength ← 0=short,1=long
- v7:RouteStatus ← 0=unfilled,1=filled
- v8:UserPosition ← 0=on track,1=off track
- v9:UserWaits ← 0=true,1=false
- v10:UtterancePlan ← 0=short,1=long

A_1^1: fetchRoute(), dontRepair(), useHighLevelPlan(), useLowLevelPlan(), **repairUtterance(), generateHighLevel(), planUtterance(), generateLowLevel(),**

S_0^2:
- v11:Aggregation ← 0=unfilled,1=filled
- v12:InfoStructure ← 0=unfilled,1=filled
- v13:NumInstructions ← 1=1,2=2,3=3 or more
- v14:Presentation ← 0=unfilled,1=filled
- v15:TemporalMarker ← 0=unfilled,1=filled, v4, v8

A_0^2: aggregate(), dontAggregate(), temporalMarkers(), noTemporalMarkers(), markedTheme(), unmarked-, Theme(), jointPresentation(), incrementalPresent.

S_1^2:
- v16:LowLevelContent ← 0=direction,1=orientation, 2=straight; v2, v4, v8, v9
- v17:NavigationAbstractness ← 0=unfilled,1=filled

A_1^2: explicitUtterance(), implicitUtterance(), **generateDirection(), generateOrientation() generateStraight()**

S_2^2:
- v18:HighLevelContent ← 0=destination,1=path v2, v4, v8, v9, v17

A_2^2: explicitUtterance(), implicitUtterance(), **generateDestination(), generatePath()**

S_0^3:
- v19:Degrees ← 0=empty,1=filled
- v20:Destination ← 0=empty,1=filled
- v21:Direction ← 0=empty,1=filled
- v22:AddInfo ← 0=path,1=destination,2=empty 3=direction,4=orientation,5=location
- v23:Verb ← 0=turn,1=keep going,2=look..., v8

A_0^3: insert turn, insert direction, insert path, etc. (all 14 surface form variants and combinations)

S_1^3:
- v24:Direction ← 0=straight,1=forward,2=ahead, ...
- v25:Verb ← 0=walk,1=go,2=continue..., v8, v22

A_1^3: insert go, insert straight, insert orientation, etc. (all 11 surface form variants and combinations)

S_2^3:
- v26:Preposition ← 0=to(your),1=to(the),2=empty...
- v27:Verb ← 0=turn,1=go,2=bear..., v8, v21, v22

A_2^3: insert go, insert to(your), insert direction, etc. (all 12 surface form variants and combinations)

S_3^3:
- v28:Preposition ← 0=down,1=along,2=through,...
- v29:Verb ← 0=walk,1=go,2=follow...
- v30:Relatum ← 0=tunnel,1=space,2=point..., v8, v22

A_3^3: insert go, insert through, insert tunnel, etc. (all 13 surface form variants and combinations)

S_4^3:
- v31:Preposition ← 0=into,1=towards,2=until,...
- v32:Verb ← 0=walk,1=go,2=return..., v8, v21, v22
- v33:Relatum ← 0=room,1=point,2=empty,

A_4^3: insert go, insert to, insert point, etc. (all 12 surface form variants and combinations)

5.2 A Reward Function for CS and UP

According to the PARADISE framework (Walker et al., 2000), the performance of a system can be modelled as a weighted function of task success and dialogue cost measures (e.g., number of turns, interaction time). We argue that PARADISE is also useful to assess the performance of an NLG system. To identify the strongest predictors of user satisfaction (US) in situated dialogue/NLG systems, we performed an analysis of subjective and objective dialogue metrics based on PARADISE. In a human evaluation study in a real setting (Dethlefs et al., 2010), 26 participants were asked to interact with a route-giving dialogue system and follow the system's instructions. Subsequently, participants provided subjective ratings of the system's performance to indicate their US. The study revealed that users prefer short interactions at maximal task success. We also found that task success metrics that penalise the degree of task difficulty correlate higher with US than binary (success/failure) metrics.[6] We therefore define graded task success (GTS) by assigning a value of 1 for finding the target location (FTL) without problems, $2/3$ for FTL with small problems and 0 for FTL with severe problems. The value with small problems was assigned for short confusions of the user, the value for severe problems was assigned if the user got lost at least once. More specifically, in order to identify the relative contribution that different factors have on the variance found in US scores, we performed a standard multiple regression analysis on the data. First results showed that 'user turns' (UT) and 'graded task success' (GTS) (which are negatively correlated) were the only predictors. In a second multiple regression analysis involving only these metrics we obtained the performance function $Performance = 0.38\mathcal{N}(GTS) - 0.87\mathcal{N}(UT)$, where 0.38 is a weight on the normalised value of GTS and 0.87 is a weight on the normalised value of UT. This result is significant at $p < 0.01$ and accounts for 62% of the variation found in US. Using this reward function (and -1 for each other action), the agent is rewarded for short interactions (few user turns) at maximal (graded) task success. User turns correspond to the behaviour with which a user reacts to an utterance. If the user reacts positively (carries out the instructions), task success is rated with 1; if they hesitate, it is $2/3$ and if they get lost (carry out a wrong instruction), it is 0. In this way the agent receives the highest rewards for the shortest possible utterance followed by a positive user reaction. This reward function is used by all CS and UP agents $M_0^0 \dots M_2^2$. Rewards are assigned after each system instruction presented to the user and the user's reaction. This reward is propagated back to all agents that contributed to the sequence of decisions leading to the instruction.

[6]Graded metrics show a high correlation with user satisfaction, binary metrics only show a moderate correlation.

5.3 A Reward Function for Surface Realisation

Due to its unique function in an RL framework, we suggest to induce a reward function for SR from human data. To this end, we use BNs to provide feedback to an agent learning to optimise SR decisions. Whenever the agent has generated a word sequence (and reaches a goal state), it receives $P(w_0...w_n)$ as a reward. This corresponds to $\sum P(Y_j = v_x | pa(Y_j) = v_y)$, the sum of posterior probabilities given the chosen values v_x and v_y of random variables and their dependencies. It receives a reward of $+1$ for maintaining an equal distribution of alignment and variation. In this way, the agent learns to balance the most likely surface forms against the benefits of variation and nonlinguistic context. [7] The agent receives a reward of -1 for any other action (to encourage efficiency). Agents $M^3_{0...4}$ use this reward function.

6 Experiments and Results

6.1 The Simulated Environment

The simulated environment has two parts: simulating the spatial context of an utterance and simulating the user's reaction to it. The first part was designed using unigrams modeling features of the context [8] and the user. [9] This lead to 23 thousand dif-

[7]The distribution of alignment and variation is measured by dividing the number of surface variants used before by the total number of variants used. The agent is then rewarded for keeping the resulting number around 0.5, i.e. for a middle way between alignment and variation (Dethlefs and Cuayáhuitl, 2010).

[8]previous system act, route length, route status (known/unknown), objects within vision, objects within dialogue history, number of instructions, alignment(proportion)

[9]previous user reaction, user position, user waiting(true/false), user type(explorative/hesitant/medium)

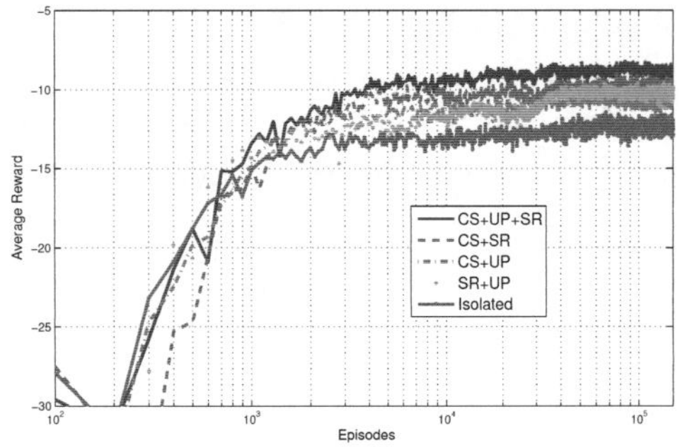

Figure 3: Performance of navigation instruction generation policies, jointly optimised and in isolation. See explanation in Section 6.2 and sample dialogue in Table 2.

Compared Instructions	F-Measure	KL-Divergence
Real1 - Real2	0.58	1.77
Real - 'HRL with BNs'	0.38	2.83
Real - 'HRL with *greedy*'	0.49	4.34
Real - 'HRL with *random*'	0.0	10.06

Table 1: Evaluation of generation behaviours with Precision-Recall and KL-divergence.

ferent configurations which we estimated from the GIVE corpus to ensure the system is trained under multiple circumstances. Since the corpus contains three different worlds, we estimated the training environment from worlds 1 and 2, and the test environment from world 3. We addressed the simulation of user reactions with a Naive Bayes Classifier. It is passed a set of features describing the current context and user and a set of semantic features describing the generated utterance.[10] Based on this, the classifier returns the most likely user reaction of *perform_desired_action, perform_undesired_action, wait* and *request_help*. It reached 82% of accuracy in a 10-fold cross validation. Simulating user reactions helps to assess the quality of instructions and provides feedback to the agent's learning process.

6.2 Comparison of Learnt Policies

We have made two main claims in this paper: (1) that CS, UP and SR decisions should all be learnt in a joint fashion to achieve optimal performance, and (2) that BNs can prove beneficial for learning SR variants. To address the first claim, Figure 3 shows the performance (in terms of average rewards)[11] of our agent with (a) isolated optimisation of CS, UP and SR, (b) joint optimisation of CS and SR, (c) joint optimisation of CS and UP, (d) joint optimisation of SR and UP and (e) joint optimisation of all subtasks. All policies were trained[12] for 150 thousand episodes, where one episode corresponds to one generated utterance. We can see that learning a joint policy for all three subtasks achieves the best performance. In terms of **content selection**, the agent learns to prefer high level navigation strategies, which allow more efficient instruction giving, and switch to low level whenever the user gets confused. Regarding **utterance planning**, the agent prefers incremental displays for three or more instructions, and joint presentations otherwise. For **surface realisation**, the agent learns to choose a (short) most likely surface form when the user has a low information need, but include more information otherwise. It learns to balance variation and alignment in an about equal proportion. Trained in isolation, a non-optimal behaviour is learnt. The reason is that all three components have a repertoire of actions, which are different in nature, but can have similar effects. For example, assume that for a user with medium information need the CS component makes a decision favouring an efficient instruction giving. It chooses a high-level navigation strategy, which contracts several low-level instructions. The next component, UP, should now take an action to balance the earlier efficiency decision and correspond to the user's increased cognitive load. However, without access to the earlier decision, it may itself make an efficiency choice, and thus increase the likelihood of the user hesitating or requesting help.

The second claim concerning the advantage of BNs for SR is addressed by Table 1. Here, we tested the human-likeness of SR decisions by com-

[10]navigation level(high / low), repair(yes / no), instruction type(destination / direction / orientation / path / straight), aggregation(yes / no), info structure(marked / unmarked), presentation(joint / incremental), temporal markers(yes / no)

[11]Since the reward function assigns a reward of -1 for each action taken, rewards stay in negative values.

[12]For training, the step-size parameter α (learning rate) was initiated with 1 and then reduced over time by $\alpha = \frac{1}{1+t}$, where t is the time step. The discount rate γ, which indicates the relevance of future rewards in relation to immediate rewards, was set to 0.99, and the probability of a random action ϵ was 0.01. See (Sutton and Barto, 1998) for details on these parameters.

Conv.	Policy	Action (composite in italics)	Utterance
USR		*request_route (low info need, on track)*	*'How do I get to the trophy?'*
	π_0^0	**CS:** *navigation*, dontConfirm	
	π_1^1	*generateHighLevel, planUtterance*, dontRepair	
	π_2^2	*generateDestination, generateDirection*	
	π_0^2	**UP:** jointPresentation, noTempMarkers	
	π_2^3	**SR:** turnVP, emptyPP, insertLocation	
	π_4^3	emptyVP, emptyPP, pointRelatum	Turn left at the end of the hall.
USR			*[waits]*
SYS	π_0^0	**CS:** *navigation*,	
	π_1^1	*generateLowLevel, planUtterance, repairUtterance*	
	π_0^1	switchNavigationStrategy	
	π_1^2	*generateDirection, generatePath*	
	π_0^2	**UP:** aggregateClauses, incrementalPresentation	
	π_2^3	**SR:** turnVP, emptyPP, noLocation	Turn right,
	π_3^3	goVP, downPrep, pathRelatum	and go down the hallway.
USR			*[executes navigation instructions]*
SYS	π_0^0	**CS:** *navigation, dontConfirm*	
	π_1^1	*generateLowLevel, planUtterance, dontRepair*	
	π_1^2	*generateDirection*	
	π_0^2	**UP:** incrementalPresentation, tempMarkers	
	π_2^3	**SR:** bearVP, emptyPP	Now bear left.
USR			*[executes navigation instructions]*
SYS	π_0^0	confirmation	Well done.

Table 2: Sample dialogue for the jointly learnt policy. See Section 5.1 for corresponding policies and actions. The agent starts using a high level navigation strategy. When the user gets confused, it temporarily switches back to low level; nonverbal behaviour is given in square brackets.

paring them with the human-authored instructions from the GIVE corpus. We compare our jointly learnt policy ('HRL with BNs') with a greedy baseline ('HRL with *greedy*', where SR decisions are made purely based on frequency) and a random baseline ('HRL with *random*' where SR decisions only aim to produce a grammatical form). For the comparison we use Precision-Recall based on the F-Measure score, and dialogue similarity based on the Kullback-Leibler (KL) divergence (Cuayáhuitl et al., 2005), which computes the difference between two probability distributions. In all cases, we compared word strings of human-authored instructions against word strings of instructions generated by each of our policies. Table 1 shows results of the comparison of two human data sets 'Real1' vs 'Real2' and both of them together, as the gold standard, against our policies. While 'HRL with *greedy*' receives higher F-Measure scores, the learnt policy is more similar to the human data. This is due to variation: in contrast to the greedy baseline, which always exploits the most likely variant, the 'HRL with BNs' policy learns to vary surface forms. This leads to lower F-Measure scores, but achieves higher similarity with human authors. This ultimately is a desirable property, since it enhances the quality and naturalness of our instructions. The 'HRL with *random*' baseline, which generates random variation, performs worst according to both metrics.

Table 2 shows an example dialogue using the jointly learnt policy. Here, the user has prior knowledge of the environment and a low information need. The system decides to give instructions efficiently and chooses a high-level navigation strategy ('Turn left at the end of the hall'). When the user hesitates (waits), it repairs its previous utterance, switches the navigation strategy to low-level and rephrases the utterance ('Turn right, and go to the end of the hall.

Conv.	Utterance
USR	*'How do I get to the trophy?'*
SYS	Go to the end of the hall and then turn left.
USR	*[waits]*
SYS	Turn right, go straight and follow the corridor. Then turn left.
USR	*[turns right, requests help]*
SYS	Go to the end of the hall and turn left.
USR	*[undesired action: turns left]*
SYS	Wait! Go back, then straight and then follow the corridor.
USR	*[executes instructions]*
SYS	Very good. Turn left.
USR	*[executes instructions]*
SYS	Very good.

Table 3: Sample dialogue using policy optimised in isolation. In terms of CS and UP, the agent prefers efficient instruction giving. There is no variation in surface forms.

Now bear left'). It also chose to aggregate the messages using the conjunction 'and' (to minimise the number of instructions), and present them in a one-by-one fashion (to ease comprehensibility). This interrelated decision making is possible due to their joint optimisation. In contrast, Table 3 shows a dialogue for the same situation using the policy optimised in isolation, where the user gets confused several times. Since decision making is not interrelated, all components prefer efficiency decisions (a high-level navigation strategy, aggregation and joint presentation whenever possible). There is no variation in surface forms, and repair strategies affect only the immediately preceding utterance.

6.3 Human Evaluation Study

To get a more reliable idea of the quality and human acceptance of our instructions, we asked 12 participants[13] to rate 96 sets of instructions. Each set contained a spatial graphical scene with a person, mapped with one human, one jointly learnt, and one instruction learnt in isolation. Participants were asked to rate navigation instructions to an object, e.g. 'go left and press the yellow button', on a 1-5 Likert scale (where 5 is the best) for their helpfulness on guiding the displayed person to the referent. Scenes were presented in a random order. We then asked the participants to circle the object they thought was the intended referent. Human instructions were rated with a mean of 3.86 (with a standard deviation (SD) of 0.89). The jointly learnt instructions were rated with a mean of 3.57 (SD=1.07) and instructions learnt in isolation with a mean of 2.35 (SD=0.85). The difference between human and jointly learnt is not significant ($p < 0.29$) according to a t-test. The effect size r is 0.14. The difference between human and learnt in isolation is significant at $p < 0.001$ with an effect size r of 0.65 and the difference between jointly learnt and learnt in isolation is significant at $p < 0.003$ and has an effect size r of 0.53. Users were able to identify the intended referent in 96% of all cases.

[13] 7 female, 5 male with an age average of 25.6.

7 Conclusion

We have presented a novel approach to optimising NLG for situated interactions using HRL with BNs. We also suggested to jointly optimise the tasks of CS, UP and SR using reward functions induced from human data. For the former two, we used the PARADISE framework to obtain a reward function that favours short interactions at maximal task success. We then proposed a method for inducing a reward function for SR from human data: it uses BNs to represent the surface realiser and inform the HRL agent's learning process. In this way, we are able to address a number of challenges arising with situated NLG and correspond to the interrelated nature of different NLG tasks. Results showed that our jointly learnt policies outperform policies learnt in isolation and received human ratings similar to human instructions. We also found that our hybrid approach to SR using HRL with BNs generates language more similar to human data than a greedy or random baseline enhancing language quality and naturalness. Future work can transfer our approach to different domains, or address the effects of SR variants on human ratings in a more detailed study. Other graphical models, e.g. Dynamic Bayesian Networks, can be explored for SR. In addition, adaptive NLG during an interaction can be explored assuming a continuously changing learning environment, as shown for situated dialogue management by Cuayáhuitl and Dethlefs (2011a).

Acknowledgements Thanks to the German Research Foundation DFG, the SFB/TR8 'Spatial Cognition' and the EU-FP7 project ALIZ-E (ICT-248116) for partial support of this work.

References

Gabor Angeli, Percy Liang, and Dan Klein. 2010. A simple domain-independent probabilistic approach to generation. In *Proceedings of the Conference on Empirical Methods in Natural Language Processing (EMNLP)*.

Srinivas Bangalore and Owen Rambow. 2000. Exploiting a probabilistic hierarchical model for generation. In *Proceedings of the 18th Conference on Computational Linguistics (ACL) - Volume 1*, pages 42–48.

Regina Barzilay and Lillian Lee. 2002. Bootstrapping lexical choice via multiple-sequence alignment. In *Proceedings of the 2002 Conference on Empirical Methods in Natural Language Processing (EMNLP)*, pages 164–171.

Anja Belz and Ehud Reiter. 2006. Comparing Automatic and Human Evaluation of NLG Systems. In *Proceedings of the European Chapter of the Association for Computational Linguistics (EACL)*, pages 313–320.

Anja Belz. 2008. Automatic generation of weather forecast texts using comprehensive probabilistic generation-space models. *Natural Language Engineering*, 1.

Fabio G. Cozman. 2000. Generalizing variable elimination in Bayesian networks. In *IBERAMIA/SBIA, Workshop on Probabilistic Reasoning in Artificial Intelligence*, pages 27–32, Sao Paulo, Brazil.

Heriberto Cuayáhuitl and Nina Dethlefs. 2011a. Optimizing Situated Dialogue Management in Unknown Environments. In *Proceedings of INTERSPEECH*, Florence, Italy.

Heriberto Cuayáhuitl and Nina Dethlefs. 2011b. Spatially-aware dialogue control using hierarchical reinforcement learning. *ACM Transactions on Speech and Language Processing (Special Issue on Machine Learning for Robust and Adaptive Spoken Dialogue Systems*, 7(3).

Heriberto Cuayáhuitl, Steve Renals, Oliver Lemon, and Hiroshi Shimodaira. 2005. Human-Computer Dialogue Simulation Using Hidden Markov Models. In *Proceedings of the Automatic Speech Recognition and Understanding Workshop ASRU*, pages 290–295.

Heriberto Cuayáhuitl. 2009. *Hierarchical Reinforcement Learning for Spoken Dialogue Systems*. Ph.D. thesis, School of Informatics, University of Edinburgh.

Nina Dethlefs and Heriberto Cuayáhuitl. 2010. Hierarchical Reinforcement Learning for Adaptive Text Generation. *Proceeding of the 6th International Conference on Natural Language Generation (INLG)*.

Nina Dethlefs, Heriberto Cuayáhuitl, Kai-Florian Richter, Elena Andonova, and John Bateman. 2010. Evaluating task success in a dialogue system for indoor navigation. In *Proceedings of the Workshop on the Semantics and Pragmatics of Dialogue (SemDial), Poznan, Poland.*

Thomas G. Dietterich. 1999. Hierarchical Reinforcement Learning with the MAXQ Value Function Decomposition. *Journal of Artificial Intelligence Research*, 13:227–303.

Mary Ellen Foster and Jon Oberlander. 2006. Data-driven generation of emphatic facial displays. In *Proceedings of the European Chapter of the Association for Computational Linguistic (EACL)*, pages 353–360.

Andrew Gargett, Konstantina Garoufi, Alexander Koller, and Kristina Striegnitz. 2010. The GIVE-2 corpus of giving instructions in virtual environments. In *Proceedings of the 7th International Conference on Language Resources and Evaluation (LREC)*.

Michael A. K. Halliday and Ruqaiya Hasan. 1976. *Cohesion in English*. Longman, London.

Srinivasan Janarthanam and Oliver Lemon. 2010. Learning to adapt to unknown users: referring expression generation in spoken dialogue systems. In *Proceedings of the Annual Meeting of the Association for Computational Linguistics (ACL)*, pages 69–78.

Finn V. Jensen. 1996. *An Introduction to Bayesian Networks*. Springer Verlag, New York.

Alexander Koller, Kristina Striegnitz, Donna Byron, Justine Cassell, Robert Dale, Johanna Moore, and Jon Oberlander. 2010. The first challenge on generating instructions in virtual environments. In M. Theune and E. Krahmer, editors, *Empirical Methods on Natural Language Generation*, pages 337–361, Berlin/Heidelberg, Germany. Springer.

Irene Langkilde and Kevin Knight. 1998. Generation that exploits corpus-based statistical knowledge. In *Proceedings of the 36th Annual Meeting of the Association for Computational Linguistics (ACL)*, pages 704–710.

Oliver Lemon. 2010. Learning what to say and how to say it: joint optimization of spoken dialogue management and natural language generation. *Computer Speech and Language*, 25(2).

Willem J. M. Levelt and S Kelter. 1982. Surface form and memory in question answering. *Cognitive Psychology*, 14.

François Mairesse, Milica Gašić, Filip Jurčíček, Simon Keizer, Blaise Thomson, Kai Yu, and Steve Young.

2010. Phrase-based statistical language generation using graphical models and active learning. In *Proceedings of the Annual Meeting of the Association for Computational Linguistics (ACL)*, pages 1552–1561.

Alice H. Oh and Alexander I. Rudnicky. 2000. Stochastic language generation for spoken dialogue systems. In *Proceedings of the 2000 ANLP/NAACL Workshop on Conversational systems - Volume 3*, pages 27–32.

Martin J. Pickering and Simon Garrod. 2004. Toward a mechanistc psychology of dialog. *Behavioral and Brain Sciences*, 27.

Verena Rieser, Oliver Lemon, and Xingkun Liu. 2010. Optimising information presentation for spoken dialogue systems. In *Proceedings of the Annual Meeting of the Association for Computational Lingustics (ACL)*, pages 1009–1018.

Richard S. Sutton and Andrew G. Barto. 1998. *Reinforcement Learning: An Introduction*. MIT Press, Cambridge, MA, USA.

Marilyn A. Walker, Diane J. Litman, Candace A. Kamm, and Alicia Abella. 1997. PARADISE: A framework for evaluating spoken dialogue agents. In *Proceedings of the Annual Meeting of the Association for Computational Linguistics (ACL)*, pages 271–280.

Marilyn Walker, Candice Kamm, and Diane Litman. 2000. Towards developing general models of usability with PARADISE. *Natural Language Engineering*, 6(3):363–377.

Michael White. 2004. Reining in CCG chart realization. In *Proceedings of the International Conference on Natural Language Generation (INLG)*, pages 182–191.

Combining symbolic and corpus-based approaches for the generation of successful referring expressions

Konstantina Garoufi and **Alexander Koller**
Area of Excellence "Cognitive Sciences"
University of Potsdam, Germany
{garoufi, akoller}@uni-potsdam.de

Abstract

We present an approach to the generation of referring expressions (REs) which computes the unique RE that it predicts to be fastest for the hearer to resolve. The system operates by learning a maximum entropy model for referential success from a corpus and using the model's weights as costs in a metric planning problem. Our system outperforms the baselines both on predicted RE success and on similarity to human-produced successful REs. A task-based evaluation in the context of the GIVE-2.5 Challenge on Generating Instructions in Virtual Environments verifies the higher RE success scores of the system.

1 Introduction

The generation of referring expressions (REs) is one of the best-studied problems in natural language generation (NLG). Traditional approaches (Dale and Reiter, 1995) have focused on defining the range of possible valid REs (e.g., as those REs that describe the target object uniquely) and on simple heuristics for choosing one valid RE (e.g., minimal REs). Recently, the question of how to choose the best RE out of the possible ones has gained increasing attention (Krahmer et al., 2003; Viethen et al., 2008). This process has been accelerated by the systematic evaluation of RE generation systems in the context of RE generation challenges (Belz and Gatt, 2007; Gatt and Belz, 2010).

Almost all of these approaches optimize the *humanlikeness* of the NLG system, i.e. the similarity between system-generated REs and human-generated REs from some corpus. However, in order to be most helpful to the user, an NLG system should arguably produce REs that are *easy to understand*. As Belz and Gatt (2008) show, these are not the same: In particular, the scores for humanlikeness and usefulness in task-based evaluations of systems participating in the TUNA RE generation challenge are not correlated. It would therefore be desirable to optimize a system directly for usefulness.

A second characteristic of most existing RE generation systems is that they are limited to generating single noun phrases in isolation. By contrast, planning-based approaches (Appelt, 1985; Stone et al., 2003; Koller and Stone, 2007) generate REs in the context of an entire sentence or even discourse (Garoufi and Koller, 2010), and can therefore exploit and manipulate the linguistic and non-linguistic context in order to produce succinct REs (Stone and Webber, 1998). However, these approaches have not been combined with corpus-based measures of humanlikeness or understandability of REs.

In this paper, we present the mSCRISP system, which extends the planning-based approach to NLG with a statistical model of RE understandability. mSCRISP uses a metric planner (Hoffmann, 2002) to compute the best REs that refer uniquely to the target referent, and thus combines statistical and symbolic reasoning. We obtain the cost model by training a maximum entropy (maxent) classifier on a corpus of human-generated instruction giving sessions (Gargett et al., 2010) in which every RE can be automatically annotated with a measure of how easy it was for the hearer to resolve. Although mSCRISP is in principle capable of generating complete in-

Proceedings of the 13th European Workshop on Natural Language Generation (ENLG), pages 121–131,
Nancy, France, September 2011.

struction discourses, we only evaluate its RE generation component here. It turns out that mSCRISP generates more understandable REs than a purely symbolic baseline, according to our model's estimation of understandability. Furthermore, mSCRISP generates REs that are more similar to high-quality human-generated REs than either the symbolic or a purely statistical baseline. Finally, a full task-based evaluation in the context of the GIVE-2.5 Challenge on Generating Instructions in Virtual Environments[1] (Koller et al., 2010; Striegnitz et al., 2011) verifies the higher referential success of the system.

Plan of the paper. We first compare our model to earlier work in Section 2. We then introduce the planning-based approach to NLG on which mSCRISP is based in Section 3. Section 4 lays out how we obtain a maximum entropy model of RE attribute preferences from our corpus, and Section 5 shows how we bring the two approaches together using metric planning. We present the evaluation in Section 6 and conclude in Section 7.

2 Related work

Our work stands in a recent tradition of approaches that attempt to learn optimal RE generation strategies from corpora. For instance, Viethen et al. (2008) tune the parameters of the graph-based algorithm of Krahmer et al. (2003) by learning attribute costs from the TUNA corpus (Gatt et al., 2007). Stoia et al. (2006) share with us a focus on situated generation in a virtual environment. They train a decision tree learner using a wide range of context features, including dialog history, spatio-visual information and features capturing relations between objects in the scene. The context features we use in this paper are partially inspired by theirs. However, our work differs from this line of research in that we do not primarily attempt to replicate the REs produced by humans, but to train a system to produce REs that are easy to understand by humans.

There are a number of related systems which optimize for understandability. Paraboni et al. (2007) present two rule-based RE generation systems which can deliberately produce redundant REs, and evaluate these systems to show that they outperform earlier systems in terms of understandability. On the other hand, their approach is not corpus-based and is therefore harder to fine-tune to the communicative needs of hearers using empirically determined parameters. Golland et al. (2010) present a maximum entropy model which acts optimally with respect to a hearer model; but their system is focussed on spatial descriptions of objects in non-dynamic scenes. Furthermore, dialogue and NLG systems based on reinforcement learning optimize their expected utility for human or simulated users. However, because of the complexity of reinforcement learning, this has for the greatest part been applied to RE generation only in the most rudimentary way, e.g. to distinguish whether or not to use jargon in a technical dialogue (Janarthanam and Lemon, 2010). Decision-making problems of a broader scope have started getting addressed by such techniques only very recently (Dethlefs et al., 2011).

Finally, NLG systems based on planning, such as Koller and Stone (2007), typically optimize for RE size instead of either humanlikeness or understandability. One exception is Bauer and Koller (2010), where sentence generation with a probabilistic grammar formalism is performed using a metric planner. That work generates REs which are probable and therefore in a certain sense humanlike; yet it focuses on syntactic choice and does not take understandability into account, neither has it been evaluated on RE generation tasks.

3 Planning utterances in situated context

We build upon CRISP (Koller and Stone, 2007), a planning-based NLG model which encodes sentence generation with tree-adjoining grammars (TAG; (Joshi and Schabes, 1997)) as an automated planning problem. The CRISP model solves the problem of translating a given communicative goal into a complete natural language sentence in a single step. Although we only use CRISP to generate REs that are individual noun phrases here, these are in fact part of a comprehensive integrated sentence planning and realization process, which has also been extended to the generation of entire discourses of navigation instructions (Garoufi and Koller, 2010).

CRISP assumes a TAG lexicon in which each elementary tree has been enriched with semantic and

[1] `http://www.give-challenge.org/research/page.php?id=give-2.5-index`

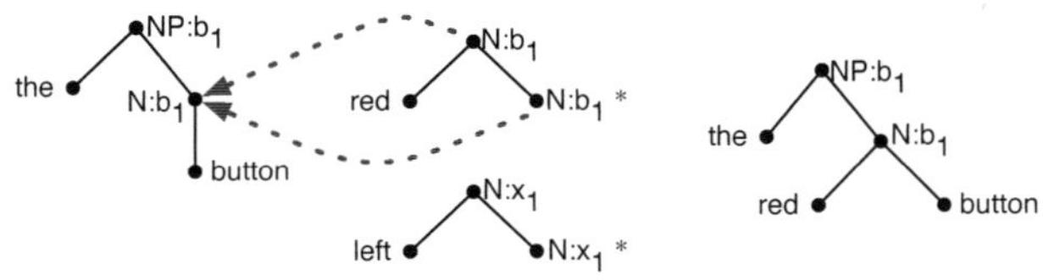

Figure 1: A simplified example of a CRISP lexicon and the derivation of the RE "the red button" describing b_1.

red(u, x):
Precond: $\mathsf{canadjoin}(\mathrm{N}, u), \mathsf{ref}(u, x), \mathsf{red}(x), \ldots$
Effect: $\forall y. \neg\mathsf{red}(y) \rightarrow \neg\mathsf{distractor}(u, y), \ldots$

left(u, x):
Precond: $\forall y. \neg(\mathsf{distractor}(u, y) \wedge \mathsf{left\text{–}of}(y, x)),$
$\mathsf{canadjoin}(\mathsf{N}, u), \mathsf{ref}(u, x), \ldots$
Effect: $\forall y. (\mathsf{left\text{–}of}(x, y) \rightarrow \neg\mathsf{distractor}(u, y)), \ldots$

the–button(u, x):
Precond: $\mathsf{subst}(\mathsf{NP}, u), \mathsf{ref}(u, x), \mathsf{button}(x), \ldots$
Effect: $\forall y. (\neg\mathsf{button}(y) \rightarrow \neg\mathsf{distractor}(u, y)),$
$\neg\mathsf{subst}(\mathsf{NP}, u), \ldots$

Figure 2: Simplified CRISP planning operators for the lexicon of Figure 1.

pragmatic information in addition to the syntactic information it encodes. The generator obtains awareness of the domain entities a hearer knows about, their semantic content and the relations holding between them by tapping into a knowledge base that models the scene. It then generates REs for these entities by reasoning about how its lexicon entries can be combined into well-formed derivation trees that amount to correct and distinguishing descriptions of the referents. Given an example knowledge base $\{\mathsf{button}(b_1), \mathsf{red}(b_1), \mathsf{button}(b_2), \mathsf{blue}(b_2), \mathsf{left\text{–}of}(b_2, b_1))\}$, and a communicative goal that involves describing b_1, Figure 1 shows with a simplified version of CRISP's lexicon how the derivation of "the red button" referring to b_1 is performed.

In order to generate this RE, CRISP converts the lexicon of Figure 1 and the given communicative goal into a planning problem, whose operators are shown in simplified form in Figure 2. Preconditions of an operator determine which logical propositions must be true in a given state so that the operator can be executed, while its effects specify how the truth conditions of these propositions change after the execution. It is important to notice that both syntactic preconditions and effects (e.g., subst specifies open substitution nodes, ref connects syntax nodes to the semantic individuals to which they refer, and canadjoin indicates the possibility of an auxiliary tree adjoining the node) and semantic ones are integrated into these operators. In particular, **red** includes a precondition $\mathsf{red}(x)$, whereas **left** includes a more complex precondition estimating the eligibility of an entity to be described as "left" at a given state of the derivation. This way CRISP ensures that the attributes selected are applicable to the entities described and that the resulting REs are correct.

The planning problem adopts the facts of the knowledge base in its initial state and sets as its goal the fulfillment of the communicative goal along with the satisfaction of a set of syntactic and semantic constraints. The former encode syntactic completeness of the derivation while the latter are specified as $\forall u \forall x. \neg\mathsf{distractor}(u, x)$, conveying that a complete derivation tree must eliminate all possible distractors from any entities it refers to, thus making sure that all generated REs are distinguishing. With these constraints, it is easy to examine what reasoning CRISP follows for the generation of an RE describing b_1. Having executed the action **the–button**(n_1, b_1), it can eliminate all entities of the domain that are not buttons from the set of distractors for b_1. However, the button b_2 in the domain remains as a distractor. To change this, CRISP goes on to check the preconditions of other available operators. It finds that even though **left**(n_1, b_1) is not applicable, as b_2 and not b_1 is the leftmost button in the scene, **red**(n_1, b_1) is. Since this operator now eliminates b_2 (which is blue) as a distractor, the goals have been achieved and the planner terminates.

4 A maxent model for successfulness

We now present how to obtain a corpus which allows to determine how fast a hearer understood an RE, and discuss how to train a maxent model that predicts this.

4.1 RE attributes in the GIVE-2 corpus

We use the GIVE-2 corpus of Giving Instructions in Virtual Environments[2] (Gargett et al., 2010), which

[2] http://www.give-challenge.org/research/page.php?id=give-2-corpus

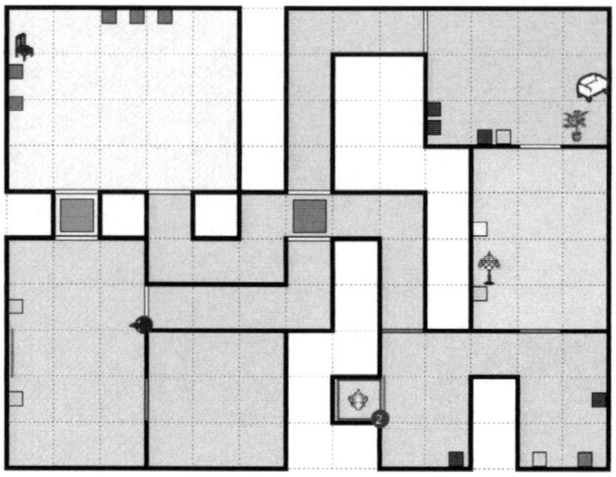

Figure 3: Map of a virtual world from the GIVE-2 corpus.

RE attribute type	%
Absolute property (color; e.g. "red")	79.83
Taxonomic property (type; e.g. "button")	59.80
Viewer-centered (e.g. "on the right", "the left one")	19.33
Micro-level landmark intrinsic (e.g. "by the chair")	17.37
Macro-level landmark intrinsic (e.g. "next to the doorway")	8.54
Distractor intrinsic (e.g. "next to the yellow button")	7.00

Table 1: The six most frequent attribute types in the English edition of the GIVE-2 corpus.

consists of instruction giving sessions in 3D virtual worlds. In these sessions a human instruction giver (IG) guides a human instruction follower (IF) through the world with the goal of completing a treasure hunting task. Although the worlds feature varied types of objects (e.g. movable objects such as chairs and immovable features of rooms such as doorways), instruction followers can directly manipulate only one type of targets before picking up the treasure, which is buttons. Figure 3 presents a bottom-up view of one of the three corpus worlds.

Gargett et al. have annotated the expressions referring to button targets of manipulation in the corpus with the types of attributes of which they are made up. In this work we focus on the six most frequent attribute types, shown in Table 1. Notice that each attribute type is a semantic concept which may be realized in different ways, according to the properties of the referent. We refer to the resulting realizations as attributes (e.g. "red" and "blue" are attributes of the type "absolute"). Of the 714 annotated REs in the English edition of the GIVE-2 corpus, 598 only use attributes of the above six types.

4.2 Successfulness of REs

Annotated REs in the GIVE-2 corpus are issued by the human IGs in order to help their partners identify targets of manipulation in the world. In this task-based setting, we can assess whether an RE has served its purpose with success or not by determining whether it leads the IF to manipulating the intended referent. A manual annotation of RE success reveals that 92% of all human-produced REs in the corpus allow the IF to correctly identify the referent.

This task-based success measure could be a good candidate for determining the understandability of a RE, except that data in which one class accounts for 92% of all instances is too skewed to be useful for machine learning. We can achieve a more even split of the data by assuming that an IF who understands the RE easily will walk towards the correct referent quickly and directly; in other words, the average speed at which they approach the referent is a measure of understandability. We define the *successfulness* $succ(r)$ of an RE r as follows:

$$succ(r) = \begin{cases} 0 & \text{if } r \text{ was not correctly resolved} \\ \frac{\Delta S}{\Delta T} & \text{otherwise,} \end{cases}$$

where ΔS is the distance in the GIVE world (including turning distance) between the target referent and the hearer's location at the time when they are presented with the RE, and ΔT is the time elapsed between the presentation of the RE and the manipulation of the referent. We can now split the REs in the corpus into a class of high successfulness and one of low successfulness as follows:

$$succ^*(r) = \begin{cases} 0 & \text{if } succ(r) \leq \tilde{S} \\ 1 & \text{otherwise} \end{cases} \quad (1)$$

where $\tilde{S}$ is the median of all values that $succ(r)$ takes for all REs r in the data. This *binarized successfulness* abstracts away from the exact numeric value of an RE's successfulness, which is not important for our purpose, and allows us to create a balanced dataset with two classes of equal size.

4.3 Context features

We assume that in any given context, all attributes of the same type are equally easy to understand for a hearer. However, we do not assume that the same attribute types are easy to understand (i.e., have high successfulness) in all possible contexts. A color attribute may be easier to understand in a scene where there are no distractors of the same color as the referent—not just because it is conspicuous, but also because the hearer will not be visually distracted by similar distractors. Conversely, if a visually salient landmark is available for describing the target referent, it might be harder to process the referent's color than its location relative to the landmark (Viethen and Dale, 2008).

We model this connection of the RE resolution process with the currently visible scene through a collection of ten *context features*, which we list in Table 2. For our experiments, we extract most of these features from the corpus automatically, except for the *Round* and *ReferenceAttempt* features, which we annotated manually. For each object relations and referent's distinctiveness feature, we consider as scope of comparison (near the referent, in the referent's room or in the whole virtual world) the one that yields best results in Subsection 6.1. Note that some context features (such as *MicroLandmarkInRoom*) take binary values, whereas others (e.g. *Angle*) take a range of numeric values.

4.4 The maximum entropy model

Now we combine the information we have about human RE choices, the context in which they were issued and their relative successfulness in order to train a maximum entropy model that can estimate the successfulness of any RE in any context. We model an RE r as a set of attributes and let $a_j(r) = 1$ (where $j = 1, \ldots, 6$) iff r contains an attribute of type a_j. We further assume that $c_i(s)$ (where $i = 1, \ldots, 10$) takes the value of the feature c_i on the scene s, and combine attributes and context features into derived features of the form

$$\phi_{ij}(r, s) = c_i(s) \cdot a_j(r).$$

The derived features allow us to cast the problem as a simple binary classification task, in which our goal is to estimate the conditional probability of an RE r issued in a scene s being successful, given a joint representation of attributes and context:

$$P\left(succ^*\left(r\right) = 1 \mid \{\phi_{ij}\left(r, s\right)\}_{i,j}\right)$$

We train a maximum entropy model to learn this distribution. This choice of model has several advantages; among others, that we can later convert the model parameters into parameters for a planning model quite easily (see Section 5). For training we use the logistic regression implementation of the Weka data mining workbench (Hall et al., 2009). The model estimates the above probability as:

$$\hat{P}(succ^*(r) = 0 \mid \{\phi_{ij}(r, s)\}_{i,j}) = \frac{1}{1 + e^{-z(r,s)}}, \quad (2)$$

where $z(r, s) = \sum_{i,j}(w_{ij} \cdot \phi_{ij}(r, s)) + w_0$ for model coefficients w_{ij} and intercept w_0. By letting $v_j(s) = \sum_i (w_{ij} \cdot c_i(s))$, we can rewrite this equation as $z(r, s) = \sum_j (v_j(s) \cdot a_j(r)) + w_0$. In this way, we can obtain *attribute weights* $v_j(s)$ for each attribute type a_j. Notice that the weight of an attribute type depends on the current scene s (as seen through the context features). In our data, we observe that every context feature in Table 2 affects the weight of at least one attribute type.

5 Optimizing successfulness using metric planning

We can now describe the mSCRISP system, which combines the planning-based NLG algorithm from Section 3 with the maxent model for assigning successfulness estimates to REs from Section 4. We employ for this the formalism of *metric planning* (Fox and Long, 2003), which we use to assign to each planning operator a *cost*. The cost of a plan is the sum of the costs of the actions that were used in it, and a metric planner will try to find a plan of minimal total cost. Because the original planning problem already enforces that an RE must refer uniquely, this amounts to finding the RE of lowest cost among the distinguishing ones.

Notice that most off-the-shelf planners (such as the MetricFF planner (Hoffmann, 2002), which we used in our experiments) do not guarantee that they actually find an optimal plan for efficiency reasons, but in practice the plans that our planner finds are close to optimal (see Section 6).

Object relations	
RoomSameTypeDisNum	the number of distractors of the same type as the referent in the room
MicroLandmarkInRoom	whether there are any micro-level (i.e. movable) landmarks in the room
MacroLandmarkNearby	whether there are any macro-level (i.e. immovable) landmarks near the referent
Spatio-visual	
Distance	the Euclidean distance (in GIVE space units) between the IF and the referent
Angle	the angle (in radians) between the center of the IF's field of view and the referent
Referent's distinctiveness	
ColorUnique	whether the referent's color is unique (i.e. not shared by other objects) in the world
LandmarkTypeUnique	whether a landmark with unique type in the world exists in the referent's room
Interaction history	
Round	the number of times the referent has been target of manipulation in a whole session
ReferenceAttempt	the number of times the referent has been referred to in the same round
SeenDeltaTime	the time elapsed (in seconds) since the referent was last seen by the IF

Table 2: Features putting the REs of the corpus into context.

5.1 Computing the costs of RE attributes

Each attribute that we might want to use as part of an RE is represented as a single planning operator in the planning problem of Section 3. The key problem we must solve is to determine the cost we want to assign to each of these operators.

We can approach this problem by inspecting how the individual attribute weights $v_j(s)$ contribute to the successfulness probability in (2). If for a given j, $v_j(s)$ is a negative value, then an RE r for which $a_j(r) = 1$ will have a higher $P(succ(r) = 1 \mid r, s)$ than an RE r' that is like r except that $a_j(r') = 0$. If $v_j(s)$ is positive, then the effect is reversed: choosing a_j will lower the probability of high successfulness. The effect that choosing a_j has on the probability grows with the absolute value of $v_j(s)$.

It therefore seems natural to use $v_j(s)$ as the cost of all planning operators for attributes of type a_j. Indeed, it can be shown that under this assumption, if a plan expresses the RE r, then the plan has minimal cost among all correct plans just in case r has maximal successfulness probability among all uniquely referring REs. Therefore we can reduce the problem of computing a successful RE to that of solving a metric planning problem.

5.2 Working around planner limitations

There is one final technical complication which we must address: Most off-the-shelf metric planners do not accept negative operator costs (because otherwise the action could be executed again and again in order to lower the total plan cost), but $v_j(s)$ may be a negative value. Such negative weight attributes improve the successfulness estimate of an RE even if they are not necessary to distinguish the referent, and we would like the NLG system to include them in the (redundant) RE it generates.

We work around this problem by introducing, for each attribute type a_j, a special action **non-**a_j. Executing this action in a plan corresponds to the choice to *not* include any attribute of type a_j in the RE; because it does not encode a lexicon entry from the TAG grammar, the action has no preconditions or effects pertaining to syntax or semantics. We can enforce that every RE must contain for every j either an attribute of type a_j or the action **non-**a_j by inserting atoms $\mathsf{needtodecide}(a_j, u)$ whenever some planning action introduces the RE u, and requiring that the final state of the planning problem may not include any needtodecide atoms. These atoms can be removed only by executing actions for attributes of type a_j or the action **non-**a_j. Now we assign the cost $\mathsf{cost}(a_j) = \max\{0, v_j(s)\}$ to each attribute action and the cost $\mathsf{cost}(\neg a_j) = \max\{0, -v_j(s)\}$ to **non-**a_j. Notice that $\mathsf{cost}(a_j) - \mathsf{cost}(\neg a_j) = v_j(s)$ regardless of whether $v_j(s)$ is positive or negative. Thus we obtain a metric planning problem in which all action costs are zero or positive, and whose minimal-cost plans correspond to maximal-probability REs.

5.3 An example

As an example, consider the planning operators for the attribute "red" and for **non-absolute**, shown in

red(u, x):
Precond: $\mathsf{referent}(x), \mathsf{canadjoin}(\mathrm{N}, u), \ldots$
Effect: $\neg\mathsf{needtodecide}(\mathsf{absolute}, u), \ldots$
Cost: $\mathsf{cost}(\mathsf{absolute})$

non-absolute(u):
Precond: $\mathsf{needtodecide}(\mathsf{absolute}, u)$
Effect: $\neg\mathsf{needtodecide}(\mathsf{absolute}, u)$
Cost: $\mathsf{cost}(\neg\mathsf{absolute})$

Figure 4: Simplified mSCRISP planning operators for an absolute attribute.

Figure 4. These replace the operator for **red** shown in Figure 2; the other operators from Figure 2 are changed analogously.

The initial state of the planner might contain the atoms $\mathsf{subst}(\mathsf{NP}, n_1)$ and $\mathsf{ref}(n_1, b)$ indicating that we want to generate an NP (with node name n_1 in the derivation tree) referring to b. Let's say it also contains the atoms $\mathsf{button}(b)$ and $\mathsf{red}(b)$, indicating that b is a red button. Lastly, there will be an atom $\mathsf{needtodecide}(\mathsf{absolute}, n_1)$. The planner can start by selecting the action **the-button**(n_1, b), incurring the cost for a taxonomic attribute. The planner must then apply either the action **red**(n_1, b), incurring the cost for an absolute attribute, or the action **non-absolute**(n_1), with the cost of not choosing an absolute attribute; one of the two must be applied because we cannot be in a final state before all needtodecide atoms have been removed. If b is the only button in the domain, the choice between the two actions depends on which of $\mathsf{cost}(\mathsf{absolute})$ and $\mathsf{cost}(\neg\mathsf{absolute})$ is greater. If another button exists, it may be that the planner is forced to apply **red** in order to distinguish b, regardless of the relative costs. In this way, the metric planner will not compute the cheapest combination of arbitrary attributes, but the cheapest RE among all uniquely referring ones.

6 Evaluation

We evaluate our model against two baselines. The MaxEnt baseline builds an RE by selecting all attributes a_j for which $v_j(s) \leq 0$ for a given scene s. This is a purely statistical model, which does not verify the applicability or discriminatory power of the attributes it selects, and thus makes no correctness or uniqueness guarantees. The EqualCosts baseline is a version of our mSCRISP model in which all attribute costs are equal. This is a purely symbolic model which always computes a correct and unique RE, but does this without any empirical guidance about expected successfulness.

Human	*the green button on the left*
MaxEnt	*the button to the left of the picture*
EqualCosts	*the left button,* *to the left of the right button*
mSCRISP	*the button to the left of the picture*

Table 3: REs produced by a human IG, our model and the two baselines in the bottom-left room of Figure 3.

Table 3 presents example REs that a human IG, our model and the two baselines issue for one of the buttons in the bottom-left room of Figure 3. As the IF is entering the room, they see from left to right a green button, a picture, and another green button. All REs in this example are distinguishing. However, the human-produced RE, which favors the use of an absolute ("green") and a viewer-centered ("on the left") attribute over one pointing to the micro-level landmark ("to the left of the picture"), was not particularly successful in the scene: After hearing it, the IF spent time scanning the room further to the left before finally approaching the referent. MaxEnt and mSCRISP generate a different RE, using a landmark, which they judge to be more successful. By contrast, EqualCosts generates a correct but more complex RE.

6.1 Accuracy of successfulness estimations

We train the maxent model on a dataset consisting of REs in the virtual worlds 1 and 2 of the GIVE-2 corpus. All evaluations are performed on a test set consisting of REs in world 3 (Figure 3). Both corpora contain all REs (a) in which the IF is already in the same room as the referent (so as to prevent interference between navigation instructions and REs) and (b) which only contain the attribute types shown in Table 1. This amounts to 358 REs in the training set and 174 REs in the test set.

The *accuracy* of the maxent model, i.e. the proportion of REs whose binarized successfulness it estimates correctly, differs between the training and test set. On the training data, the accuracy is 75.1%; on the test data, it is 62.1%. This compares favorably to a majority classifier, which would achieve

	succ. prob.
Human	0.467***
MaxEnt	**0.984****
EqualCosts	0.649***
mSCRISP	0.957

Table 4: Average probabilities of high successfulness. Differences to mSCRISP are significant at $^{**}p < 0.01$, $^{***}p < 0.001$ (paired t-tests).

	DICE		
	low succ.	high succ.	all
MaxEnt	0.320***	0.449*	0.371***
EqualCosts	**0.512**	0.475	**0.497**
mSCRISP	0.457	**0.519**	0.482
#REs	78	51	129

Table 5: Average DICE coefficients across datasets. Differences to mSCRISP are significant at $^{*}p < 0.05$, $^{***}p < 0.001$ (paired t-tests).

50% accuracy on the training dataset (since it is balanced); that is, the maxent model actually does learn to predict successfulness. The difference in accuracy shows that the training and test data are varied enough for a fair evaluation. In addition, the drop suggests that more training data might further improve the system's overall performance.

6.2 Successfulness probability

We now use our system and the two baselines to generate REs for the referents in the test corpus, and use the maxent model to estimate the probability (2) that the generated RE is in the high successfulness class. We define the domain entity set of the planning-based models to be the objects that are visible within the target referent's room, and we restrict ourselves to those scenes in which the target is among these objects. The results are shown in Table 4.

We find that the MaxEnt baseline significantly outperforms all other models. This is not surprising, as the metric of evaluation here is exactly what this baseline directly optimizes for. However, MaxEnt picks the different attributes independently, ignoring whether the resulting RE is semantically informative; correctness and uniqueness of an RE are not captured by the maxent model. Of the models which guarantee that the generated RE refers uniquely, mSCRISP performs the best.

6.3 Humanlikeness

Although this was not the main focus of this work, we also looked at the similarity of the system-generated REs with the original REs produced by the IGs. We model the degree of humanlikeness by the Dice coefficients of the two REs (Dice, 1945; Gatt et al., 2007). The results are shown in Table 5, both for all REs in the test set and for the REs of high and low human-achieved successfulness separately.

This test reveals that the REs computed by MaxEnt are less humanlike than those computed by either of the planning-based systems. This can be explained by the fact that, in contrast to MaxEnt, the planning-based models generate their REs on the basis of a set of correctness and uniqueness principles, which are, at least to some extent, shared by humans. Even though the difference is not statistically significant, mSCRISP reaches a higher degree of humanlikeness than EqualCosts on REs of *high* successfulness. Importantly, this is reversed in the low successfulness dataset. The distinction is relevant because mSCRISP does not attempt to mimic human IG choices under all circumstances; it only does so when it believes that the human IG choices are highly successful. If this is not the case, it makes different choices—those that a more successful IG might make in the situation.

6.4 Task-based evaluation

To verify the model's performance in the context of real interactions with human IFs, we entered mSCRISP and the correct RE generating baseline EqualCosts as participating NLG systems for the 2011 edition of the GIVE Challenge (Garoufi and Koller, 2011; Striegnitz et al., 2011). Both systems operate by first generating an RE (the *first-attempt* RE) for a given button target as soon as the IF is in the target's room and can see the target. Subsequently, the systems issue follow-up REs at regular intervals until the IF responds with a manipulation act or navigates away from the target.

Follow-up REs may differ from first-attempt REs, especially for the mSCRISP system, which relies for its attribute selection on several dynamically changing context features of the scene (see Table 2). Indeed, mSCRISP issues follow-up REs that are dif-

	resol. success		successfulness	
	all	non-rephr.	all	non-rephr.
EqualCosts	86%***	86%	0.32	0.38***
mSCRISP	**95%**	**89%**	**0.33**	**0.52**

Table 6: Task-based evaluation results. Differences to mSCRISP are significant at $***p < 0.001$ (Pearson's χ^2 test for resolution success rates; unpaired two-sample t-tests for the rest).

ferent from the original more often than the purely symbolic system (in 85% of the cases, as compared to only 59% for EqualCosts). Follow-up REs are important for the GIVE task, yet the fact that they are issued regardless of whether the IF is on the right track or not poses a problem on automatic methods of assessing success. We therefore base our analysis only on first-attempt REs. To control for the effect of rephrasing, we separately examine the subset of REs for which all follow-up REs were *non-rephrasing*, i.e. exactly the same as the original. We conduct the analysis on the latest currently available snapshot of the challenge results, which contains 74 valid games for each of our two systems. We first look into two metrics for referential success, as shown in Table 6.

In terms of resolution success, which represents the rate of REs whose intended referents have been correctly identified by the hearer (regardless of how fast), we find that mSCRISP significantly outperforms the baseline with a high success rate of 95%. Though the results are measured on different datasets and are thus not directly comparable, it is interesting to note that this surpasses the 92% success rate of human IGs in the GIVE-2 corpus. The system's performance remains better than the baseline's, though not significantly so, in the non-rephrased RE dataset. Turning to the metric of successfulness as defined in Subsection 4.2, we see that the two systems do not differ significantly when all first-attempt REs are considered. However it is clear that rephrasing affects the hearer's response, since processing new REs takes additional time. Examining the portion of non-rephrased first-attempt REs, we find that our model does generate REs that humans resolve significantly faster.

Finally, from the questionnaire data collected in the challenge, we consider a subjective metric of RE success as reported by the IFs in response to the post-task question "I could easily identify the buttons the system described to me". Although a Tukey's test does not find the difference to be statistically significant, it is worth mentioning that our model receives higher rates than the baseline with respect to this subjective metric, too. The average scores for mSCRISP and EqualCosts are 38.59 and 16.42, respectively (on a scale of -100 to 100).

7 Conclusion

In this paper, we have shown how to extend a symbolic system for generating REs with a statistical model of successful REs. Our system operates by training a maximum entropy model on a corpus in which the successfulness of REs is marked up, and mapping the maxent weights to action costs in a metric planning problem. Our evaluation, which also draws from real interactions with human hearers in the task-based setting of the GIVE-2.5 Challenge, shows that our model learns to distinguish highly successful attribute choices from less successful ones, and outperforms both a purely symbolic and a purely statistical baseline.

Although the system as we have presented it here builds on a planning-based model, nothing particular hinges on this choice: As far as generation of noun phrase REs is concerned, the planner makes similar choices to e.g. the system of Krahmer et al. (2003), and our cost function could be used in other systems as well. However, one strength of planning-based systems is that they are not limited to generating isolated noun phrases. In a situated setting like GIVE, it has been shown that they can be made to generate navigation instructions which (if successful) modify the non-linguistic context in a way that makes simpler REs possible later (Garoufi and Koller, 2010). It is an interesting issue for future work to extend our successfulness model to navigation instructions, and obtain a system that deliberately interleaves navigation and RE generation in order to maximize overall communicative success.

Acknowledgments

We are thankful to Ivan Titov and Verena Rieser for fruitful discussions about the maxent model, and to our reviewers for their many thoughtful comments.

References

Douglas E. Appelt. 1985. *Planning English sentences*. Cambridge University Press, Cambridge, England.

Daniel Bauer and Alexander Koller. 2010. Sentence generation as planning with probabilistic LTAG. In *Proceedings of the 10th International Workshop on Tree Adjoining Grammar and Related Formalisms*, New Haven, CT.

Anja Belz and Albert Gatt. 2007. The attribute selection for GRE challenge: Overview and evaluation results. In *Proceedings of UCNLG+MT*, Copenhagen, Denmark.

Anja Belz and Albert Gatt. 2008. Intrinsic vs. extrinsic evaluation measures for referring expression generation. In *Proceedings of the 46th Annual Meeting of the Association of Computational Linguistics: Human Language Technologies*, Columbus, OH.

Robert Dale and Ehud Reiter. 1995. Computational interpretations of the Gricean maxims in the generation of referring expressions. *Cognitive Science*, 19.

Nina Dethlefs, Heriberto Cuayáhuitl, and Jette Viethen. 2011. Optimising natural language generation decision making for situated dialogue. In *Proceedings of the 12th annual SIGdial Meeting on Discourse and Dialogue*, Portland, OR.

Lee Raymond Dice. 1945. Measures of the amount of ecologic association between species. *Ecology*, 26(3):297–302.

Maria Fox and Derek Long. 2003. PDDL2.1: an extension to PDDL for expressing temporal planning domains. *J. Artif. Int. Res.*, 20:61–124.

Andrew Gargett, Konstantina Garoufi, Alexander Koller, and Kristina Striegnitz. 2010. The GIVE-2 Corpus of Giving Instructions in Virtual Environments. In *Proceedings of the 7th Conference on International Language Resources and Evaluation*, Valletta, Malta.

Konstantina Garoufi and Alexander Koller. 2010. Automated planning for situated natural language generation. In *Proceedings of the 48th Annual Meeting of the Association for Computational Linguistics*, Uppsala, Sweden.

Konstantina Garoufi and Alexander Koller. 2011. The Potsdam NLG systems at the GIVE-2.5 Challenge. In *Proceedings of the Generation Challenges Session at the 13th European Workshop on Natural Language Generation*, Nancy, France.

Albert Gatt and Anja Belz. 2010. Introducing shared task evaluation to NLG: The TUNA shared task evaluation challenges. In E. Krahmer and M. Theune, editors, *Empirical methods in natural language generation*, volume 5790 of *LNCS*. Springer.

Albert Gatt, Ielka van der Sluis, and Kees van Deemter. 2007. Evaluating algorithms for the generation of referring expressions using a balanced corpus. In *Proceedings of the 11th European Workshop on Natural Language Generation*, Schloss Dagstuhl, Germany.

Dave Golland, Percy Liang, and Dan Klein. 2010. A game-theoretic approach to generating spatial descriptions. In *Proceedings of the 2010 Conference on Empirical Methods in Natural Language Processing*, Cambridge, MA.

Mark Hall, Eibe Frank, Geoffrey Holmes, Bernhard Pfahringer, Peter Reutemann, and Ian H. Witten. 2009. The WEKA data mining software: an update. *SIGKDD Explorations*, 11(1).

Jörg Hoffmann. 2002. Extending FF to numerical state variables. In *Proceedings of the 15th European Conference on Artificial Intelligence*, Lyon, France.

Srinivasan Janarthanam and Oliver Lemon. 2010. Learning to adapt to unknown users: Referring expression generation in spoken dialogue systems. In *Proceedings of the 48th Annual Meeting of the Association for Computational Linguistics*, Uppsala, Sweden.

Aravind K. Joshi and Yves Schabes. 1997. Tree-Adjoining Grammars. In G. Rozenberg and A. Salomaa, editors, *Handbook of Formal Languages*, volume 3, pages 69–123.

Alexander Koller and Matthew Stone. 2007. Sentence generation as planning. In *Proceedings of the 45th Annual Meeting of the Association of Computational Linguistics*, Prague, Czech Republic.

Alexander Koller, Kristina Striegnitz, Donna Byron, Justine Cassell, Robert Dale, Johanna Moore, and Jon Oberlander. 2010. The First Challenge on Generating Instructions in Virtual Environments. In M. Theune and E. Krahmer, editors, *Empirical Methods in Natural Language Generation*, volume 5790 of *LNCS*, pages 337–361.

Emiel Krahmer, Sebastiaan van Erk, and André Verleg. 2003. Graph-based generation of referring expressions. *Computational Linguistics*, 29(1):53–72.

Ivandre Paraboni, Kees van Deemter, and Judith Masthoff. 2007. Generating referring expressions: Making referents easy to identify. *Computational Linguistics*, 33(2):229–254.

Laura Stoia, Darla M. Shockley, Donna K. Byron, and Eric Fosler-Lussier. 2006. Noun phrase generation for situated dialogs. In *Proceedings of the 4th International Natural Language Generation Conference*, Sydney, Australia.

Matthew Stone and Bonnie Webber. 1998. Textual economy through close coupling of syntax and semantics. In *Proceedings of the 9th International Workshop on Natural Language Generation*, Niagara-on-the-Lake, Canada.

Matthew Stone, Christine Doran, Bonnie Webber, Tonia Bleam, and Martha Palmer. 2003. Microplanning with communicative intentions: The SPUD system. *Computational Intelligence*, 19(4):311–381.

Kristina Striegnitz, Alexandre Denis, Andrew Gargett, Konstantina Garoufi, Alexander Koller, and Mariet Theune. 2011. Report on the Second Second NLG Challenge on Generating Instructions in Virtual Environments (GIVE-2.5). In *Proceedings of the 13th European Workshop on Natural Language Generation*, Nancy, France.

Jette Viethen and Robert Dale. 2008. The use of spatial relations in referring expression generation. In *Proceedings of the 5th International Natural Language Generation Conference*, Salt Fork, OH.

Jette Viethen, Robert Dale, Emiel Krahmer, Mariet Theune, and Pascal Touset. 2008. Controlling redundancy in referring expressions. In *Proceedings of the 6th International Language Resources and Evaluation Conference*, Marrakech, Morocco.

Language Generation for Spoken Dialogue Systems

Johanna D. Moore
School of Informatics, University of Edinburgh
Edinburgh, United Kingdom
j.moore@ed.ac.uk

The goal of spoken dialogue systems (SDS) is to offer efficient and natural access to applications and services. A common task for SDS is to help users select a suitable option (e.g., flight, hotel, restaurant) from the set of options available. When the number of options is small, they can simply be presented sequentially. However, as the number of options increases, the system must have strategies for summarizing the options to enable the user to browse the option space. In this talk, we evaluate two recent approaches to information presentation in SDS: (1) the Refiner approach (Polifroni et al., 2003) which generates summaries by clustering the options to maximize coverage of the domain, and (2) the user-model based summarize and refine (UMSR) approach (Demberg and Moore, 2006) which clusters options to maximize utility with respect to a user model, and uses linguistic devices (e.g., discourse cues, adverbials) to highlight the trade-offs among the presented items.

To evaluate these strategies, we go beyond the typical "overhearer" evaluation methodology, in which participants read or listen to pre-prepared dialogues, which limits the evaluation criteria to users' perceptions (e.g., informativeness, ease of comprehension). Using a Wizard-of-Oz methodology to evaluate the approaches in an interactive setting, we show that in addition to being preferred by users, the UMSR approach is superior to the Refiner approach in terms of both task success and dialogue efficiency, even when the user is performing a demanding secondary task. Finally, we hypothesize that UMSR is more effective because it uses linguistic devices to highlight relations (e.g., trade-offs) between options and attributes. We report the results of two studies which show that the discourse cues in UMSR summaries help users compare different options and choose between options, even though they do not improve verbatim recall.

References

V. Demberg and J.D. Moore. 2006. Information Presentation in Spoken Dialogue Systems. In *Proceedings of the 11th Conference of the European Chapter of the Association for Computational Linguistics (EACL)*.

J. Polifroni, G. Chung, and S. Seneff. 2003. Towards the Automatic Generation of Mixed-Initiative Dialogue Systems from Web Content. In *Proceedings of Eurospeech*, pages 2721–2724.

Proceedings of the 13th European Workshop on Natural Language Generation (ENLG), page 132,
Nancy, France, September 2011.

Adapting SimpleNLG to German

Marcel Bollmann
Department of Linguistics
Ruhr-University Bochum
44780 Bochum, Germany
bollmann@linguistics.rub.de

Abstract

This paper describes SimpleNLG for German, a surface realisation engine for German based on SimpleNLG (Gatt and Reiter, 2009). Several features of the syntax of German and their implementation within the current framework are discussed, with a special focus on word order phenomena. Grammatical coverage of the system is demonstrated by means of selected examples.

1 Introduction

Surface realisation is the task of generating natural language sentences from semantic input representations. The final step in any realisation process is the mapping of representations of syntactic structures to well-formed output strings, while considering the grammar rules of the target language. This includes, but is not limited to, correctly inflecting words and applying punctuation and sentence orthography. As these tasks are rather mechanical and a necessary part of every NLG application, developers can greatly benefit from a realisation engine which specialises on this process and implements it in an easy and intuitive way. SimpleNLG, as described in Gatt and Reiter (2009), is a realisation engine for English that fulfills this description. This paper results from an effort to adapt the SimpleNLG engine to German.

In SimpleNLG, sentences are constructed by combining `LexicalItem` objects and `PhraseSpecs`, which represent various phrasal subtypes, in a modular way. Canned text can always be used interchangeably with non-canned representations, while specifics of the final realisation are controlled via features.

German, when compared to English, displays features that make an adaption of the framework a non-trivial task. First, the German inflectional system is much richer, calling for a more systematic way of describing inflection classes and generating inflected word forms. On a related note, there are many more agreement phenomena to be taken care of. As word order in German is much freer than in English, the need for reordering of constituents arises; e.g., the subject can no longer unconditionally be realised at the beginning of a sentence. This area was a special focus for this implementation.

SimpleNLG for German is a Java framework derived from version 3.8 of SimpleNLG[1]; as of June 2011, version 4.3 has been released. While there are plans to port this package to the new 4.x architecture, all claims about SimpleNLG in this paper refer to the older version.

2 Characteristics of German

This section discusses some of the changes made to the SimpleNLG system to account for German grammar rules. Section 2.1 describes the implementation of inflection, while section 2.2 discusses topics related to agreement. Section 2.3 deals with the issue of word order, which prompted fundamental changes to the system, and section 2.4 explains changes regarding modal verbs.

[1]The original SimpleNLG is available from: http://code.google.com/p/simplenlg/

Proceedings of the 13th European Workshop on Natural Language Generation (ENLG), pages 133–138,
Nancy, France, September 2011.

2.1 Inflection

As inflection in English is very limited, SimpleNLG properly inflects most English words using a set of regular expressions; the use of a lexicon is possible, but not required. German, on the other hand, has a rich inflectional system that requires knowledge of the inflection class for each word, thus increasing the importance of a lexicon.

In SimpleNLG for German, inflection is encapsulated in separate classes called *inflection patterns*, which largely resemble inflection classes from traditional grammars, e.g. Eisenberg (2004). Technically, an inflection pattern stores an array of suffixes and provides methods to append them to a stem; the types and number of suffixes depends on the respective part of speech. Additionally, a pattern can have a number of features which influence the inflection process. Plural umlaut for nouns is a prominent example for this, as is *'e'* elision in certain stems ending in *–el/er*:

- *sammeln* 'to collect' ⟶ *ich sammle* 'I collect'

Special consideration is required for verbs with separable prefixes, as stem and prefix can appear both joined and separated:

- *ankommen* 'to arrive' ⟶ *ich komme an* 'I arrive'

Therefore, a verb prefix is always stored separately from the base verb. The inflection class of separable verbs can always be derived from the base verb alone, without considering the prefix. This is of particular relevance for the lexicon, which only needs an entry for the base verb in order to be able to generate all combinations of separable prefixes with that verb. Separable verbs can be instantiated by placing a vertical bar between the base verb and the prefix (e.g. `an|kommen`). The boundary has to be specified manually by the user, as there are several verbs which are ambiguous in this regard: e.g., *umfahren* is separable in the meaning of 'to knock (something) over', but inseparable in the meaning of 'to drive around (something)'.

Compound nouns are a similar case: the inflection class of a compound is equal to that of its final stem. Also, as compounding is a highly productive morphological process in German, it is not feasible to list every single compound in the lexicon. Therefore, compounding has been implemented in the same way: e.g., specifying `Heimat|stadt` 'hometown' creates a compound derived from *Stadt* 'town'.

Lexicon files are currently stored in XML format; for testing and evaluation purposes, lexicon entries were imported from IMSLex (Fitschen, 2004).

2.2 Agreement

Agreement in English is mostly confined to the 3. SG. PRES. IND. suffix *–(e)s* for verbs. In German, there is a more distinct subject–verb agreement, but also other types of agreement, e.g. determiner–noun or adjective–noun. This section discusses two topics related to agreement: the problems arising with use of canned text, and the agreement of relative pronouns.

2.2.1 Canned text

In SimpleNLG, canned text can be used interchangeably with lexical items and phrase specifications. This functionality is retained in SimpleNLG for German, as it is fundamental to the "simple" aspect of the framework. Proper nouns are typical candidates to be represented by canned text, as they show no or minimal inflection and can not generally be expected to be found in a lexicon. However, in German, this approach is problematic, as the following examples show:

(1) *beim FC Liverpool*
at.the FC Liverpool

(2) *bei der Eintracht Frankfurt*
at the Eintracht Frankfurt

Here, the names of football clubs are used together with a definite article, which agrees with the following noun in gender. Note that the article in (1) is contracted with the preposition. The examples show that even proper nouns referring to abstract concepts, such as football clubs, can be assigned different genders in German. Gender information, however, is not available when working with canned text. Consequently, whenever gender information is required—for example, when combining a proper noun with a specifier, or replacing it with a pronoun—simple canned text can not be used. Instead, a new lexical item has to be manually constructed from the canned text, and assigned the appropriate gender value. This undermines the simplicity of the system to some extent, but also highlights an intrinsic difficulty in adapting the SimpleNLG approach to languages with richer agreement morphology.

2.2.2 Relative clauses

Relative pronouns in German agree with the antecedent in gender and number, while also inflecting for case based on their function within the relative clause. To make their creation as simple as possible, explicit support for relative clauses has been added.

The `NPPhraseSpec` class now provides a method which requires a sentence (to be embedded as the relative clause) and the function of its head noun in the relative clause. The process of constructing the relative clause then consists of two steps. First, a relative pronoun is generated, referring to the head noun; this includes setting the appropriate agreement features (gender and number). Second, the relative pronoun is inserted into the sentence with the specified grammatical function; this ensures the correct case value.

(3) *die Frau, [auf die] ich stolz bin*
the woman of whom I proud am
'the woman of whom I am proud'

(4) *die Frau, [deren Kind] schön ist*
the woman whose child beautiful is
'the woman whose child is beautiful'

More complex embeddings can also be realised this way: if a preposition is given instead of a grammatical function, a new prepositional phrase is constructed, with the relative pronoun as its head. This is shown in (3). To generate (4), a noun phrase is required to which the relative pronoun is added as a specifier. All of these functions have in common that they facilitate the creation of relative clauses for the user, as they take care of mechanical steps (e.g., selecting the correct pronoun to ensure agreement), highlighting the "simple" aspect of the framework.

Relative clauses can still be constructed manually, without the use of these helper methods. This requires more code, but is actually useful, as the resulting relative clause can be embedded in phrases other than the NP containing the antecedent, thereby enabling relative clause extraposition.

2.3 Word order

German, in contrast to Modern English, has verb-second word order, i.e. the verb always has to be the second constituent in main clauses. Verb-initial and verb-final sentences are also possible, which had to be accounted for in SimpleNLG for German. More interesting, however, is the order of non-verb constituents, which is relatively free when compared to English. The examples below show that it is possible for every non-verb constituent to appear at the front of a sentence, though the order of constituents after the verb is variable, too. The preferred word order depends on many factors, which can be syntactic, semantic, or pragmatic in nature, and is therefore hard to determine automatically. Also, different word orders can, for example, be used to emphasise certain constituents. It is therefore desirable for a generation system to be able to realise these variants, which was a main focus for this implementation.

(5) *Die Frau gab dem Mann gestern*
the woman gave the man yesterday
ein Buch.
a book
'Yesterday, the woman gave a book to the man.'

(6) *Dem Mann gab die Frau gestern ein Buch.*

(7) *Ein Buch gab gestern die Frau dem Mann.*

(8) *Gestern gab die Frau dem Mann ein Buch.*

An important model in German syntax is the topological model as described in, e.g., Askedal (1986). It defines various topological fields: e.g., the first constituent of a declarative main clause is placed in the vorfeld, while the elements between the finite verb and the verb cluster constitute the mittelfeld. As we will see in the following sections, many internal representations in SimpleNLG for German correspond to topological fields in this model.

2.3.1 Subject realisation

Significant changes had to be made to the original SimpleNLG architecture to enable free constituent ordering. The most important change regards the realisation of subjects, which was moved from the sentence to the verb phrase.

front	*pre*-S	**S**	*post*-S	*pre*-I	**I**	*post*-I	*pre*-O	**O**	*post*-O	default

Figure 1: Position values for SIO word order

In SimpleNLG, subjects are always realised at sentence level, while other complements of the verb are realised in the (embedded) verb phrase. This already poses a few technical challenges for passive sentences, as a complement from the verb phrase has to be raised to subject position, while a passive complement has to be built from the subject and inserted into the verb phrase. Following a similar approach for subject movement would introduce even further complexity, but more importantly, it would imply treating subject placement differently from the placement of other constituents. Placing the subject between two VP elements after the realisation process is practically impossible, too, as the verb phrase (like all phrases) is realised as a unit and returns a single text string. For these reasons, the realisation of subjects has been moved to the verb phrase.

Although SimpleNLG for German is not built after any syntactic theory in particular, it should be noted that there are theories supporting this change: e.g., Haider (1993, p. 142 ff.) provides arguments for a VP-internal subject position, while Oppenrieder (1991) argues that a VP constituent which separates the subject from other arguments of the verb can not be justified for German.

2.3.2 Ordering the constituents

As one of the goals was to preserve the simplicity of use of SimpleNLG, the free ordering of constituents had to be implemented in an intuitive, user-friendly way. To achieve this, a two-layered system has been devised: the order of verb complements is defined through a property of the verb phrase, while the placement of other constituents is specified either relative to a complement or with an absolute value.

In SimpleNLG for German, every verb phrase has a *word order* property, which determines the order of its complements. Word order can be any permutation of subject (S), direct object (O), and indirect object (I). This is unambiguous because multiple complements of the same function are always aggregated into one coordinate phrase. Genitive objects are relatively rare and are treated like direct objects for this purpose. The default word order for new verb phrases is SIO, which is the syntactically unmarked word order in German (Eisenberg, 2004, p. 406 ff.).

Modifiers, e.g. adverbs or prepositional phrases, are realised after any complements by default. To control their placement, they can be given a *position* value. Position can be given either as an absolute value, which allows modifiers to be placed at the beginning or the end of the verb phrase, or relative to a complement, e.g. before or after the direct object. This placement specification will be obeyed even if the complement word order is later changed.

For example, assume that the variable `s` contains sentence (5) with all constituents except for the adverb *gestern* 'yesterday'. To generate (7), the adverb could be specified to be placed before the subject, and the word order must be changed to OSI:

(9)
```
s.setWordOrder(OSI);
s.addModifier(PRE_SUBJECT,
    "gestern")
```

If the word order is later changed to SIO again, the result is (8): the adverb is now realised in the vorfeld, so it still appears before the subject.

Placement specification is not restricted to modifiers, but can also be used for subordinate clauses and automatically generated passive complements.

Internally, each position can be thought of as a slot into which constituents can be placed. Complements (S, I, O) always have a fixed position slot assigned to them, while modifiers can be freely placed in any of the non-complement slots. The ordering of these slots is determined by the (complement) word order; figure 1 shows the position values for the default SIO word order. During realisation, the positions are traversed from left to right; if there is more than one constituent at any given position, they are realised in the order in which they were added. The constituent which is the first one to be realised this way is then moved to the vorfeld.

2.4 Modal verbs

In German, it is possible for a sentence to contain more than one modal verb. This necessitates the change to have a list of modal verbs for each verb phrase rather than just a single slot. Apart from that, sentences with modals have the property that the modal verb can be realised in perfect tense separately from the main verb:

(10) *Sie hat es tun können.*
she have it do can
'She was able to do it.'

(11) *Sie kann es getan haben.*
she can it done have
'She might have done it.'

In SimpleNLG for German, when a sentence is set to perfect tense, it is always the finite verb which is realised as perfect, as in (10). To be able to realise (11), a feature was added that explicitly sets the main verb to perfect tense. If no modal verb is included in the sentence, there is no difference between setting this feature and setting perfect tense in the traditional way. A combination of both settings to realise both the finite and the main verb in perfect tense is also possible.

3 Grammatical coverage

A proper evaluation of grammatical coverage is a difficult task due to the sheer number of possible constructions. In a short, non-representative survey examining five randomly selected Wikipedia articles[2], 115 of 152 sentences (75.66%) were covered by the system's grammar. Sentences were classified based on whether they could be realised within the framework using canned text only for uninflectable elements. To this end, each type of grammatical construction was recreated once within the system. The results suggest that the framework is already suitable for real-world applications.

Features and grammatical constructions supported so far include:

- morphological operations, including handling of inflection classes, separable verb prefixes, compounding, and preposition-article-contraction;
- modal verb clusters and perfect formation;
- relative clauses and relative clause extraposition; and
- constituent reordering.

However, a number of aspects remain which are not yet (fully) implemented. Verb phrase coordination is probably the most important one, as it is responsible for most of the unrealisable sentences in the above-mentioned survey. Negation is implemented only rudimentarily and is confined to the insertion of the negation particle *nicht* at a fixed position. Semi-modal verbs ('Halbmodalverben') take an infinitive with *zu*, which is not yet explicitly supported. Also, verb cluster fronting is currently not realisable:

(12) *Gesehen hatte er mich nicht.*
seen had he me not
'He had not seen me.'

In the current implementation, the position of the verb cluster is fixed, and its elements are kept separately from other sentence constituents. Therefore, sentences like (12) require further modifications to the internal representation. However, sentences of this type are pragmatically marked, so their realisation might be a peripheral problem.

In conclusion, the grammatical coverage of SimpleNLG for German is already considerable, but far from being complete. It is worth noting that some of the features mentioned above, e.g. relative clause extraposition, constitute non-trivial problems for syntactical theories of German, but are realisable in this framework in a surprisingly simple manner. The paper also highlighted several technical and conceptual problems that a realisation engine for German has to face, and offered potential solutions for some of them.

The full Java package of SimpleNLG for German will be made available online after it has been prepared for release.

Acknowledgments

I would like to thank my supervisor, Prof. Ralf Klabunde, for his guidance and support during this project.

[2] 'Josef Bartoň-Dobenín der Jüngere', 'Michael Joseph Savage', 'Saljut 7 EO-1', 'Zubringerstraße', 'Hapag-Lloyd-Flug 3378'; all retrieved on 18.05.2011.

References

John Ole Askedal. 1986. Über 'Stellungsfelder' und 'Satztypen' im Deutschen. *Deutsche Sprache*, 14:193–223.

Peter Eisenberg. 2004. *Grundriß der deutschen Grammatik. Bd. 2: Der Satz*. Metzler, Stuttgart, 2nd edition.

Arne Fitschen. 2004. *Ein Computerlinguistisches Lexikon als komplexes System*. Doctoral dissertation, University of Stuttgart.

Albert Gatt and Ehud Reiter. 2009. SimpleNLG: A realisation engine for practical applications. In *Proceedings of the 12th European Workshop on Natural Language Generation (ENLG 2009)*, pages 90–93.

Hubert Haider. 1993. *Deutsche Syntax – generativ: Vorstudien zur Theorie einer projektiven Grammatik*. Narr, Tübingen.

Wilhelm Oppenrieder. 1991. *Von Subjekten, Sätzen und Subjektsätzen: Untersuchungen zur Syntax des Deutschen*. Niemeyer, Tübingen.

EasyText: an Operational NLG System

Laurence Danlos
Univ Paris Diderot,
Sorbonne Paris Cité,
ALPAGE, UMR-I 001 INRIA
Danlos@linguist.jussieu.fr

Frédéric Meunier
WatchSystem Assistance
Meunier@watchsystance.com

Vanessa Combet
WatchSystem Assistance
Combet@watchsystance.com

Abstract

This paper introduces EasyText, a fully operational NLG system. This application processes numerical data (in tables) in order to generate specific analytical commentaries of these tables. We start by describing the context of this particular NLG application (communicative goal, user profiles, etc.). We then shortly present the theoretical background which underlies EasyText, before describing its implementation, realization and evaluation.

1 Introduction

EasyText is a NLG system which is operational at Kantar Media, a French subsidiary company of TNS-Sofres[1]. The company compiles numerical data for its customers on their advertising investments and sends to each customer seven tables every month, see Figure 1 for an example of a table. Before the existence of EasyText, these tables were presented with a general commentary written by a media analyst. Kantar decided to accompany these tables with specific charts and commentaries in order to make their reading comfortable and easy. They survey 600 segments and there are 7 tables per segment: Manually writing these analytical commentaries was inconceivable. The idea of having an automatic system producing them naturally arose, but Kantar encountered major difficulties with the text generation task. Therefore, they subcontracted this project to Watch System Assistance. Figure 1 shows an example of an analytical commentary generated by EasyText.

Section 2 describes the architecture of EasyText. Section 3 presents its implementation: EasyText is an instantiation of Kantar Media's needs in a ready-to-use NLG framework, TextElaborator. Section 4 gives some details on the realization and evaluation of EasyText.

2 Architecture of EasyText

EasyText follows a standard architecture as described in (Reiter and Dale, 2000). It includes a document planner for the content determination and document structuring tasks, and a tactical component.

The **content determination** task for a given table amounts to detecting the relevant cells of the table. This task was guided by business rules indicated by Kantar Media's analysts. These rules were hard-coded, i.e. without any reasoning module.

The content of a cell is transformed into the conceptual representation of an eventuality whose predicate is given by the column heading. This predicate subcategorizes two arguments, the first one corresponding to the line heading, the second one to the value of the cell. Therefore, the output of the content determination module can be seen as a conjunction of conceptual representations of eventualities.

The **document structuring** task consists in introducing rhetorical relations between the semantic content of the highlighted cells. For instance, if two opposite evolutions over a given period are observed (one decreasing, the other one increasing), the relation $Contrast$ is introduced. On the contrary, would

[1]Kantar Media is one of the leaders in advertising expenditure monitoring, exploring all existing media (radio, internet, mobile telephony, etc.).

Proceedings of the 13th European Workshop on Natural Language Generation (ENLG), pages 139–144,
Nancy, France, September 2011.

Évolution des investissements par Secteur / Variété

Investissements publicitaires plurimedia - Tri décroissant sur le cumul de l'année en cours - En k€

	Mai 2008	Mai 2009	Evol%	Cumul janvier à mai 2008	Cumul janvier à mai 2009	Evol%
ORGANISMES FINANCIERS	16 587	26 312	59 %	216 948	177 353	-18 %
CREDIT PERSONNEL O.F	5 868	11 227	91 %	50 610	53 772	6 %
-MULTIPROD.ORG.FINANCIERS	3 243	7 463	130 %	53 191	51 718	-3 %
CREDIT RENOUVELABLE O.F	3 930	1 994	-49 %	60 094	34 987	-42 %
INTERNET TELEMATIQUE 583	2 648	4 687	77 %	16 460	27 613	68 %
RACHAT DE CREDITS O.F	777	732	-6 %	15 817	5 637	-64 %
CREDIT AUTO MOTO O.F	79	110	39 %	5 638	993	-82 %
CREDIT TRAVAUX O.F		86		535	797	49 %
PARRAINAGE MECENAT O.F				80	0	-100 %

Dans votre univers, les investissements marquent une très forte progression (+59%) dans le secteur ORGANISMES FINANCIERS en mai 2008 par rapport à mai 2007. Toutefois, pour le cumul à date de l'étude, ils connaissent une baisse de 18%.

Dans ce secteur, les investissements ont doublé (+130%) pour la variété MULTIPROD.ORG.FINANCIERS en mai 2008 par rapport à mai 2007. Par ailleurs, les investissements pour la variété CREDIT PERSONNEL O.F marquent une progression de 6% pour le cumul à date étudié. Au contraire, pour la variété MULTIPROD.ORG.FINANCIERS, ils voient leur volume diminuer (-3%) sur la même période.

(Within your business area, ad spending ramps up (+59%) for sector ORGANISMES FINANCIERS in May 2008 compared with May 2007. However, year to date, it falls 18%. Within this sector, ad spending doubles (+130%) for segment MULTI-PROD.ORG.FINANCIERS in May 2008 compared to May 2007. Furthermore, ad spending for segment CREDIT PERSONNEL OF increases of 6% year to date. On the contrary, for segment MULTIPROD.ORG.FINANCIERS, it decreases (-3%) over the same period.)

Figure 1: Example of a table and its automatically generated comment

they have been going in the same direction, the relation $Parallel$ would have been introduced, along with some hints to prepare an aggregation operation in the tactical component.

The discourse theory on which the document structuring module relies is SDRT (Segmented Discourse Representation Theory) (Asher, 1993; Asher and Lascarides, 2001), following (Danlos et al., 2001). The output of the document structuring component is therefore consistent with a SDRS (SDRT structure), considered as a "conceptual" representation in which concepts (discourse relations, eventualities, entities) are embedded in a dependency structure (which is mathematically a Directed Acyclic Graph).

The **tactical component** (macro/micro-planner and surface realizer) is based on G-TAG formalism (Danlos, 2001), the latter being itself founded on lexicalized Tree Adjoining Grammars (TAG), (Joshi, 1985).[2] G-TAG deals with the *How to say it?* issue, understood as covering all (and only) linguistic decisions: segmentation of the text into sentences and linear ordering of these sentences[3], choice of discourse connectives and other lexical items, syntactic constructions within sentences, aggregation operations, referring expressions, semantic and syntactic parallelism, etc.

The surface realizer is designed to use the syntactic and lexical information of a TAG grammar. This TAG grammar is extended to handle multi-sentential texts and not only isolated sentences[4]. Therefore, the macro/mico planner is designed as a TAG extension. More precisely, the architecture of G-TAG is outlined in Figure 2:

- The output of the macro/mico planner is a "g-derivation tree". In TAG, a derivation tree is

[2]Since it was put forward by A. Joshi that TAG is an especially well suited grammatical theory for text generation, adapting TAG for generation has been widely explored, among many others, let us cite (Stone and Doran, 1997) and (Gardent and Kow, 2007). However, it is not in the scope of this paper to compare G-TAG with these other approaches.

[3]These tasks are not considered as part of the document structuring component. This is why the term macro/mico-planner is used in Figure 2.

[4]The idea of extending TAG to handle multi-sentential texts is also used in text interpretation, e.g. D-LTAG (Webber, 2004) and D-STAG (Danlos, 2009).

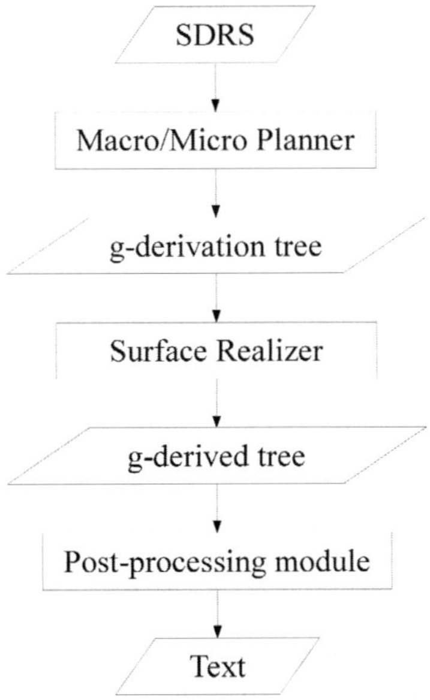

Figure 2: G-TAG tactical component

not only seen as the history of the derivation but also as a linguistic representation, close to semantics, which can serve as a basis for a deeper semantic analysis (Kallmeyer, 2002). A g-derivation tree in G-TAG is closer to semantics than a derivation tree in TAG: it is a semantic dependency tree annotated with syntactic information. Moreover, a g-derivation tree represents a text while a derivation tree represents a unique sentence.

The macro/micro planner relies on lexical databases associated with the various concepts (discourse relations, eventualities, entities) that are relevant for the NLG application. A lexical database for a given element records the lexemes lexicalizing it with their argument structure, and the mappings between the conceptual and semantic arguments. With such a lexicalized planner, the process for computing a g-derivation tree relies upon a single type of operation: lexicalization, i.e. choice of a lexeme and its syntactic realization to convey an instance of a concept. Since all the main decisions are made during this process, G-TAG can be considered as a fully lexicalized formalism for text generation.

- Thanks to a TAG grammar (which specifies the mapping between the semantic and syntactic arguments), a g-derivation tree specifies a unique "g-derived tree", in the same way as a derivation tree specifies a unique derived tree. A g-derived tree is a syntactic tree annotated with morphological information.

- From a g-derived tree, a post-processing module computes a text by performing morphological computations[5] and formatting operations.

Lexical databases for EasyText have been developed by a linguist, V. Combet, who was working in close collaboration with Kantar Media's analysts. Particular attention was paid to linguistic variation in order to avoid producing tiresome texts for Kantar Media's customers. This variation mainly concerns:

- the lexical choices: the databases associated to a given concept are as exhaustive as possible. For example, the concept INCREASE with a MAGNITUDE argument is lexicalized either with the verb *augmenter*, *doubler* or *tripler* or with the light verb construction *être en hausse/augmentation* or *enregistrer une hausse/augmentation*[6]. Moreover, a verb can be modified with an adverb, e.g. *faiblement, fortement, modéremment* for *augmenter* and *presque/pratiquement/plus que* for *doubler* or *tripler*[7], while the noun in a light verb construction can be modified with a preposed adjective, e.g. *faible/forte*, or a postposed one, e.g. *modérée*[8].

- the order of the phrases: some phrases can appear more or less freely in different places in a sentence. This is the case for duration adverbials such as *pendant le mois de mai* (*during May*) and also for different prepositional phrases such as *les investissements [pour la variété X] augmentent [pour la variété X]* (*ad*

[5]Morphological operations include elisions (*la augmentation* → *l'augmentation*) and contractions (*de le mois* → *du mois*).

[6]In English, verbs *increase*, *double* or *triple* and light verb constructions *be on the increase* or *record an increase*.

[7]In English, adverbs *slightly, seriously, moderately* for *increase* and *almost, nearly, more than* for *double* or *triple*.

[8]In English, an adjective is always preposed.

spendings [for sector X] increase [for sector X]).

3 Implementation

A prototype of G-TAG was first implemented in Ada (Meunier, 1997). G-TAG has been re-implemented as a ready-to-use framework, TextElaborator. TextElaborator is based on the Microsoft .Net framework. Particular attention was paid on functional and business issues while taking advantage of .Net for technical and non functional issues (persistence, reliability, scalability, etc.). We chose to rely on classical design patterns[9], which garantee an effortless reusability of the different components.

Our main implementation effort for TextElaborator was to build an IDE (Integrated Development Environment) incorporating tools which facilitate the linguistic work, i.e. feeding, editing, debugging and testing the various lexical databases — tasks which are crucial in G-TAG, not only in the development but also the maintenance phases.

A screenshot of this IDE is shown in Figure 3. The left column gives the domain ontology hierarchized as Abstract Objects (discourse relations and eventualities) and Entities. When clicking on a concept of the domain ontology (e.g. `Hausse` in Figure 3), the tab `LexicalPredicates` indicates the G-TAG lexical database associated with this concept. When choosing an element of this database, the corresponding g-derivation tree is displayed, along with some essential corollary information.

EasyText is an instantiation of TextElaborator for Kantar Media's needs, constiting in an ontology and its corresponding lexical databases. TextElaborator is written in C# language and is built and run upon the Microsoft .Net framework. Thanks to .Net, its integration into Kantar Media's information system was easy. Generating a comment as the one shown in Figure 1 requires an average of 400ms.

[9]DAO (Data Access Object, `http://en.wikipedia.org/wiki/Data_access_object`) and DTO (Data Transfer Object, `http://en.wikipedia.org/wiki/Data_transfer_object`).

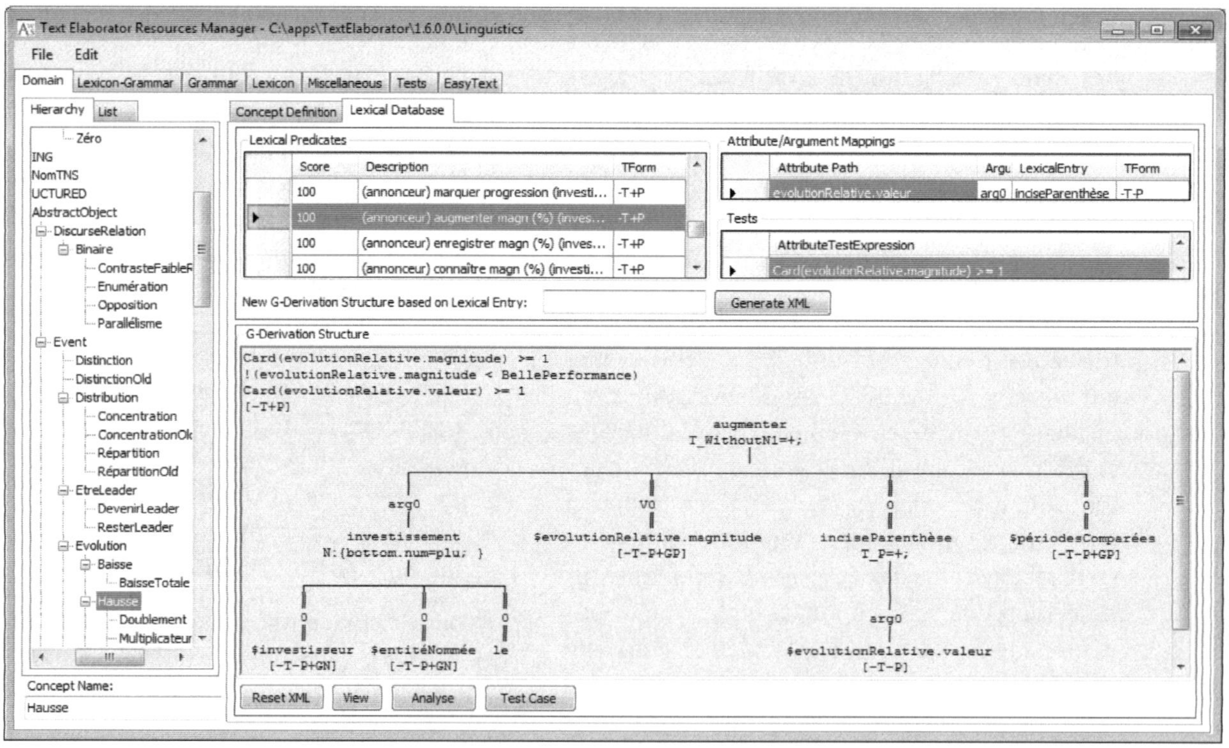

Figure 3: Sceenshot of TextElaborator's integrated development environment

4 Realization and Evaluation

The development of EasyText took 7 mm (men month) altogether:

- 1 mm was dedicated to the linguist's training to TAG and G-TAG;
- 1 mm to interviews with Kantar's media analysts;
- 3 mm to design TextElaborator and its IDE;
- 2 mm to fill the lexical databases.

During these 7 months, we were never in contact with Kantar's customers directly, but worked in close interaction with the two departments involved in the project. On the one hand, we obviously interacted with Kantar's media analysts. They shared with us all their know-how on writing commentaries on Kantar's tables, enabling us to create lexical databases corresponding to their editorial habits.

On the other hand, EasyText was developed in close collaboration with Kantar's Information system department, so as to meet their technical requirements: performance and compatibility with the existing infrastructure.

When we released the first version of EasyText, Kantar decided to send the automatically generated commentaries to a couple of customers, without saying anything about the way they had been written.

These customers made some critics[10] but gave Kantar Media the feedback that they were satisfied with this new offer. Therefore, Kantar Media decided in April 2010 to commercialize this new product and acknowledged that the commentaries were automatically generated. They keep on commercializing it, which seems to mean that their customers are satisfied.

EasyText evaluation was made by Kantar's media analysts during several months. This evaluation was qualitative and concerned the relevance of the commentaries (the choice of the cells to comment) and their accordance to the editorial habits. We remind the reader (Section 1) that EasyText commentaries had never been handwritten. Therefore, we cannot make any comparison between the generated texts and handwritten ones. This situation seems to be common in NLG, since applications are likely to be commercialized when automatic writing doesn't replace hand writing[11]. Indeed, the few commercial NLG systems we are aware of are in the same situation.[12]

[10] The main critic concerned the laying-out of these commentaries.

5 Conclusion

We have presented an operational system and, while many NLG prototypes exist, not many are commercialized, eventhough NLG technology is mature.

EasyText is an instantiation of a ready-to-use framework, TextElaborator, which is based on solid scientific basis concerning not only its architecture — the standard one (Reiter and Dale, 2000) — but also the particular instantiation of this architecture with well-established analysis formalisms (SDRT and TAG) which have been adapted to text generation.

It is foreseen that TextElaborator will be used for other applications and will produce texts in other languages than French, since it was developed as a ready-to-use framework. For a new application, the domain ontology has to be adapted and the G-TAG lexical databases associated with the concepts have to be filled. When moving to another language, only the lexical databases will have to be changed, hopefully.

A demonstration of EasyText will be presented during the conference.

References

Nicholas Asher and Alex Lascarides. 2001. Indirect speech acts. *Synthese*, 128(1–2):183–228.

Nicholas Asher. 1993. *Reference to Abstract Objects in Discourse*. Kluwer, Dordrecht.

Laurence Danlos, Bertrand Gaiffe, and Laurent Roussarie. 2001. Document structuring à la SDRT. In *International workshop on text generation - ACL*, pages 94–102, Toulouse.

Laurence Danlos. 2001. G-TAG: A lexicalized formalism for text generation inspired from TAG. In

[11] Guy Lapalme's personal communication in the late 90's.

[12] See the NLG applications developed in the American business world by Cogintex (`http://www.cogentex.com`) and in the French business world by Yseop (`http://www.yseop.com`).

A. Abeillé and O. Rambow, editors, *TAG Grammar*. CSLI.

Laurence Danlos. 2009. D-STAG: a formalism for discourse analysis based on SDRT and using synchronous TAG. In *Proceedings of the 14th Conference on Formal Grammar (FG'09)*, pages 1–20, Bordeaux, France.

Claire Gardent and Eric Kow. 2007. A symbolic approach to near-deterministic surface realisation using tree adjoining grammar. In *Proceedings of the 45th Annual Meeting of the Association of Computational Linguistics*, pages 328–335, Prague, Czech Republic, June. Association for Computational Linguistics.

Aravind Joshi. 1985. Tree-adjoining grammars. In D. Dowty, L. Karttunen, and A. Zwicky, editors, *Natural language parsing*, pages 206–250. Cambridge University Press.

Laura Kallmeyer. 2002. Using an enriched tag derivation structure as basis for semantics. In *Proceedings of the TAG+6 Workshop*, pages 101–110, Venice.

Frédéric Meunier. 1997. *Implémentation du formalisme G-TAG*. Thèse de doctorat en informatique, Université Denis Diderot, Paris 7.

Ehud Reiter and Robert Dale. 2000. *Building Natural Language Generation Systems*. Cambridge University Press, Cambridge.

Matthew Stone and Christine Doran. 1997. Sentence planning as description using tree adjoining grammar. In *Proceedings of the 35th Annual Meeting of the Association for Computational Linguistics*, pages 198–205, Madrid, Spain, July. Association for Computational Linguistics.

Bonnie Webber. 2004. D-LTAG: extending lexicalized TAG to discourse. *Cognitive Science*, 28(5):751–779.

Towards Generating Text from Discourse Representation Structures

Valerio Basile
Humanities Computing
University of Groningen
v.basile@rug.nl

Johan Bos
Humanities Computing
University of Groningen
johan.bos@rug.nl

Abstract

We argue that Discourse Representation Structures form a suitable level of language-neutral meaning representation for micro planning and surface realisation. DRSs can be viewed as the output of macro planning, and form the rough plan and structure for generating a text. We present the first ideas of building a large DRS corpus that enables the development of broad-coverage, robust text generators. A DRS-based generator imposes various challenges on micro-planning and surface realisation, including generating referring expressions, lexicalisation and aggregation.

1 Introduction

Natural Language Generation, NLG, is often viewed as a complex process comprising four main tasks (Bateman and Zock, 2003): i) **macro planning**, building an overall text plan; ii) **micro planning**, selecting referring expressions and appropriate content words; iii) **surface realisation**, selection of grammatical constructions and linear order; and iv) **physical presentation**, producing final articulation and layout operations. Arguably, the output of the macro planning component in an NLG system is some sort of abstract, language-neutral representation that encodes the information and messages that need to be conveyed, structured by rhetorical relations, and supported by information that is presupposed to be common ground.

We argue that the Discourse Representation Structures (DRSs) from Discourse Representation Theory (Kamp, 1984) form an appropriate representation for this task. This choice is driven by both theoretical and practical considerations:

- DRT, being a theory of analysing meaning, is by principle language-neutral;
- Many linguistic phenomena are studied in the framework provided by DRT;
- DRT has a model-theoretical backbone, allowing applications to perform logical inferences with the aid of theorem provers.

As a matter of fact, DRT has means to encode presupposed information in a principled way (Van der Sandt, 1992), and connections with rhetorical relations are spelled out in detail (Asher, 1993). Moreover, the formal integration of DRS with named entities, thematic roles and word senses is natural.

These are, mostly, purely theoretical considerations. But in order to make DRSs a practical platform for developing NLG systems a large corpus of text annotated with DRSs is required. Doing this manually is way too costly. But given the developments in (mostly statistical) parsing of the last two decades we are now in a position to use state-of-the-art tools to semi-automatically produce gold (or nearly gold) standard DRS-annotated corpora.

Such a resource could form a good basis to develop (statistical) NLG systems, and this thought is supported by current trends in broad-coverage NLG components (Elhadad and Robin, 1996; White et al., 2007), that take deep semantic representations as starting points for surface realisation. The importance of a multi-level resource for generation is underlined by Bohnet et al. (2010), who feel the lack of such a resource is hampering progress in the field.

In this paper we show how we are building such a corpus (SemBank, Section 2), what the exact nature of the DRSs in this corpus is, and what phenomena are covered (Section 3). We also illustrate what challenges it poses upon micro planning and surface realisation (Section 4). Finally, in Section 5, we discuss how generating from DRSs relates to the traditional NLG pipeline.

2 The Groningen SemBank

Various semantically annotated corpora of reasonable size exist nowadays: PropBank (Palmer et al.,

Proceedings of the 13th European Workshop on Natural Language Generation (ENLG), pages 145–150,
Nancy, France, September 2011.

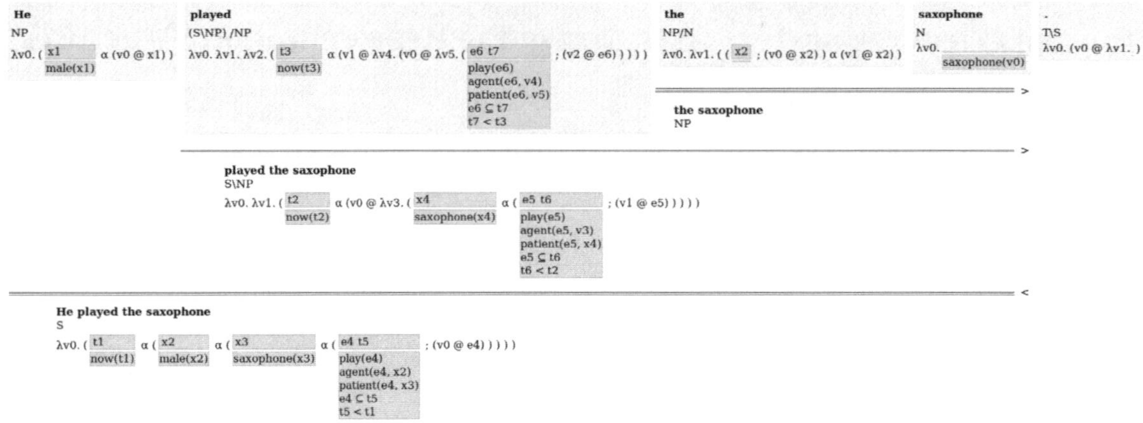

Figure 1: Screenshot of SemBank's visualisation tool for the syntax-semantics interface combining CCG and DRT.

2005), FrameNet (Baker et al., 1998), the Penn Discourse TreeBank (Prasad et al., 2005), and several resources developed for shared tasks such as CoNNL and SemEval. Annotated corpora that combine various levels of annotation into one formalism hardly exist. A notable exception is OntoNotes (Hovy et al., 2006), combining syntax (Penn Treebank style), predicate argument structure (based on PropBank), word senses, and coreference. Yet all of these resources lack a level comprising a formally grounded "deep" semantic representation that combines various layers of linguistic annotation.

Filling this gap is exactly the purpose of SemBank. It provides a collection of semantically annotated texts with **deep rather than shallow semantics**. Its goal is to **integrate phenomena instead of covering single phenomena** into one formalism, and representing **texts, not sentences**. SemBank is driven by linguistic theory, using CCG, Combinatory Categorial Grammar (Steedman, 2001), for providing syntactic structure, employing (Segmented) Discourse Representation Theory (Kamp, 1984; Asher and Lascarides, 2003) as semantic framework, and first-order logic as a language for automated inference tasks.

In our view, a corpus developed primarily for research purposes must be widely available to researchers in the field. Therefore, SemBank will only consists of texts which distribution isn't subject to copyright restrictions. Currently, we focus on English newswire text from an American newspaper whose articles are in the public domain. In the future we aim to cover other text genres, possibly integrating resources from the Open American National Corpus (Ide et al., 2010). The plan is to release a stable version of SemBank in regular intervals, and to provide open access to the development version.

The linguistic levels of SemBank are, in order of analysis depth: part of speech tags (Penn tagset); named entities (roughly based on the ACE ontology); word senses (WordNet); thematic roles (VerbNet); syntactic structure (CCG); semantic representations, including events and tense (DRT); rhetorical relations (SDRT). Even though we talk about different levels here, they are all connected to each other. We will show how in the following section.

Size and quality are factors that influence the usefulness of annotated resources. As one of the things we have in mind is the use of statistical techniques in NLG, the corpus should be sufficiently large. However, annotating a reasonably large corpus with gold-standard semantic representations is obviously a hard and time-consuming task. We aim to provide a trade-off between quality and quantity, with a process that improves the annotation accuracy in each periodical stable release of SemBank.

This brings us to the method we employ to construct SemBank. We are using state-of-the-art tools for syntactic and semantic processing to provide a rough, first proposal of semantic representation for a text. Among other tools, the most important are the C&C parser (Clark and Curran, 2004) for syntactic analysis, and Boxer (Bos, 2008) for semantic analysis. This software, trained and developed on the Penn Treebank, shows high coverage for texts in the newswire domain (up to 98%), is robust and fast, and therefore suitable for this task.

The output of these tools are corrected by crowd-

Table 1: Illustration of linguistic information integration in SemBank

Level	Theory/Source	Internal DRS Encoding
semantics	DRT (Kamp and Reyle, 1993)	`drs(...,...)`
named entity	ACE	`named(X,'Clinton',per)`
thematic roles	VerbNet (Kipper et al., 2008)	`rel(E,X,'Agent')`
word senses	WordNet (Fellbaum, 1998)	`pred(X,loon,n,2)`
rhetorical relations	SDRT (Asher and Lascarides, 2003)	`rel(K1,K2,elaboration)`

sourcing methods, comprising (i) a group of experts that are able to propose corrections at various levels of annotation in a wiki-based fashion; and (ii) a group of non-experts that provide information for the lower levels of annotation decisions by way of a *Game with a Purpose*, similar to the successful Phrase Detectives (Chamberlain et al., 2008) and Jeux de Mots (Artignan et al., 2009).

3 Discourse Representation Structures

A DRS comprises two parts: a set of discourse referents (the entities introduced in the text), and a set of conditions, describing the properties of the referents and the relations between them. We adopt well-known extensions to the standard theory to include rhetorical relations (Asher, 1993) and presuppositions (Van der Sandt, 1992). DRSs are traditionally visualised as boxes, with the referents placed in the top part, and the DRS conditions in the bottom part. The convention in SemBank is to sort the discourse referents into entities (variables starting with an x), events (e), propositions (p), temporalities (t), and discourse segments (k), as Figure 2 shows.

The DRS conditions can be divided into basic and complex conditions. The basic conditions are used to describe names of discourse referents (`named`), concepts of entities (`pred`), relations between discourse referents (`rel`), cardinality of discourse referents denoting sets of objects (`card`), or to express identity between discourse referents (=). The complex conditions introduce embedded DRSs: implication ($\Rightarrow$), negation ($\neg$), disjunction ($\vee$), and modalities ($\Box$, $\Diamond$). DRSs are thus of recursive nature, and the embedding of DRSs restrict the resolution of pronouns (and other anaphoric expressions), which is one of the trade mark properties of DRT.

The aim of SemBank is to provide fully resolved semantic representations. Obviously, natural language expressions can be ambiguous and picking the most likely interpretation isn't always straightforward: Some pronouns have no clear antecedents, word senses are often hard to distinguish, and scope orderings are sometimes vague. In future work this might give rise to adding some underspecification mechanisms into the formalism.

DRSs are formal structures and come with a model-theoretic interpretation. This interpretation can be given directly (Kamp and Reyle, 1993) or via a translation into first-order logic (Muskens, 1996). This is interesting from a practical perspective, because it permits the use of efficient existing inference engines developed by the automated deduction community. Applying logical inference can play a role in tasks surrounding NLG (e.g., summarisation, question answering, or textual entailment), but also dedicated components of NLG systems, such as generating definite descriptions, which requires checking contextual restrictions (Gardent et al., 2004).

Figure 1 illustrates how SemBank provides the compositional semantics of each sentence in the text in the form of a CCG derivation. Here each token is associated with a supertag (a lexical CCG category) and its corresponding lexical semantics, a partial DRS. The CCG derivation, a tree structure, shows the compositional semantics in each step of the derivation, with the aid of the λ-calculus (the @ operator denotes function application).

Table 1 shows how the various levels of annotation are integrated in DRSs. Thematic roles (VerbNet) are implied by the neo-Davidsonian event semantics employed in SemBank, and are represented as two-place relations. The named entity types form part of the basic DRS condition for names, and Word senses (WordNet) are represented as a feature on the one-place conditions for nouns, verbs and modifiers. Rhetorical relations are already part and parcel of SDRT. Hence, SemBank provides all these different layers of information within a DRS. Figure 2 shows an SDRS for a small text of SemBank.

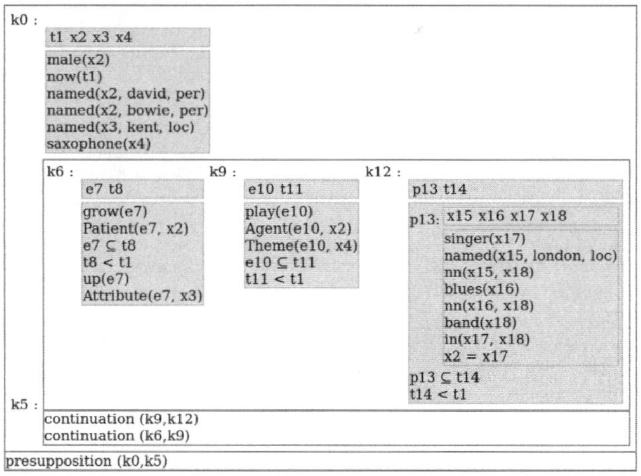

Figure 2: SDRS for the text "David Bowie grew up in Kent. He played the saxophone. He was a singer in London blues bands", as shown in SemBank.

4 Challenges for Text Generation

We believe that taking DRS as the basis for NLG will introduce not only variants of known problems, but will impose many new challenges. Here we focus on just three of them: generating referring expressions, lexicalisation, and aggregation.

4.1 Generating referring expressions

Viewed from a formal perspective, DRT is said to be a *dynamic* theory of semantics: the interpretation of an embedded DRS depends on the interpretation of the DRSs that subordinate it — either be sentence-internal structure, or by the structure governed by rhetorical relations. A case in point is the treatment of anaphoric expressions including pronouns, proper names, possessive constructions and definite descriptions.

In DRT, anaphoric expressions are resolved to a suitable antecedent discourse referent. Proper names and definite descriptions are too, but if finding a suitable antecedent fails then a process usually referred to as *presuppositional accommodation* introduces the semantic material of the anaphoric expression on an accessible level of DRS (Van der Sandt, 1992). The result of this process yields a DRS in which all presupposed information is explicitly distinguished from asserted information. This gives rise to an interesting challenge for NLG.

A DRS corresponding to a discourse unit will contain free variables for semantic material that is presupposed or has been linked to the preceeding context. On encountering such a free variable denoting an entity, the generator has a couple of choices in the way it can lexicalise it: as a quantifier, pronoun, proper name, or definite description. Even though the DRS context may provide information on names and properties assigned to this free variable, we expect it will be non-trivial to decide what properties to include in the corresponding expression. Text coherence probably plays an important role here, but whether thematic roles and rhetorical relations will be sufficient to predict an appropriate surface form remains a subject for future research. It is also interesting to explore the insights from approaches dedicated to generating referring expressions using logical methods (van Deemter, 2006; Gardent et al., 2004) with robust surface realisation systems.

4.2 Aggregation

Coordinated noun phrases are known to be potentially ambiguous between distributive and collective interpretations. A simple DRT analysis for the distributive interpretation yields two possible ways to generate strings: one where the noun phrases are coordinated within one sentence, and one where the noun phrases involved are generated in separate sentences. For instance, the DRSs corresponding to "Deep Purple and Pink Floyd played at a charity show" (with a distributive interpretation) and "Deep Purple played at a charity show, and Pink Floyd played at a charity show", would be equivalent. This is due to copying semantic material in the compositional process of computing the meaning of the coordinated noun phrase "Deep Purple and Pink Floyd". (Note that the *collective* reading, as in "Deep Purple and Pink Floyd played together at a charity show" would not involve copying semantic material, and would result in a different DRS, with a different interpretation.) It is the task of the aggregation process to pick one of these realisations, as discussed by White (2006). Doing this from the level of DRS poses an interesting challenge, because one would need to recognise that such an aggregation choice is possible in the first place. Alternatively, instead of copying, one could use an explicit operator that signals a distributive reading of a plural noun phrase, for instance as suggested by Kamp and Reyle (1993). Arguably, this is required anyway to adequately represent sentences such as "Both Deep Purple and Pink Floyd played at a charity show".

4.3 Lexicalisation

The predicates (the one-place relations) found in a DRS correspond to concepts of an hierarchical ontology. Time expressions and numerals have canonical representations in SemBank. The representation for noun and verb concepts are based on the synonym sets provided by WordNet (Fellbaum, 1998). A WordNet synset can be referred to by its internal identifier, or by any of its member word-sense pairs. For instance, synset `102999757` is composed of the noun–sense pairs `strand-3`, `string-10`, and `chain-10`. The lexicalisation challenge is to select the most suitable word out of these possibilities. Local context might help to choose: a "string of beads" is perhaps better than a "chain of beads" or "strand of beads". As another example, consider the synset {`loon-2`,`diver-3`} representing the concept for a kind of bird. American birdwatchers would use the noun "loon", whereas in Britain "diver" would be preferred to name this bird.

5 Discussion

In the DRT-based framework that we propose for generating text, the issue arises *where* in the traditional NLG pipeline DRSs play a role. In the introduction of this paper we suggested that DRSs would be output by the macro planner, and hence fed as input to the micro planner. On the one hand this makes sense, as in a segmented DRS all content to be generated is present and the rhetorical structure is given explicitly. But then the question remains whether the theoretical distinction between micro planning and surface realisation really works in practice or would just be counter-productive. Perhaps a revised architecture tailored to DRS generation should be tried instead. This issue is closely connected to the level of semantic granularity that one would like to see in a DRS. We illustrate this by four examples:

- **pronouns** — we have made a particular proposal using free variables, but we could also have followed Kamp and Reyle (1993), introducing explicit referents for pronouns;

- **distributive noun phrases** — as the discussion in Section 4.2 shows, it is unclear which represention for distributive noun phrases would be most suitable for the purpose of sentence planning;

- **sentential and verbal complements** — should there be a difference in meaning representation between "Tim expects to win" and "Tim expects that he will win"?

- **active vs. passive voice** — should a meaning representation reflect the difference between active and passive sentences?

At this moment, it is not clear whether one wants a more abstract DRS and give more freedom to sentence planning, or a more specific DRS restricting the number of sentential paraphrases of its content. Perhaps even an architecture permitting both extremes would be feasible, where the task of micro planning would be to add more constraints to the DRS until it is specific enough for the surface realisation component to generate text from it. It is even thinkable that such a planning component would take over some tasks of the macro planner, making the distinction between the two fuzzier.

A final point that we want to raise is a possible role that inference can play in our framework. DRSs can be structurally different, yet logically equivalent. This could influence the design of a generation system and have a positive impact on its output. For instance, it would be thinkable to equip the NLG system with a set of meaning-preserving tranformation rules that change the structure of a DRS, consequently producing different surface forms.

6 Conclusion

SemBank provides an annotated corpus combining shallow with formal semantic representations for texts. The development version is currently available online with more than 60,000 automatically annotated texts; the release of a first stable version comprising ca. 1,000 texts is planned later this year. We expect SemBank to be a useful resource to make progress in robust NLG. Using DRSs as a basis for generation poses new challenges, but also could offer fresh perspectives on existing problems in NLG.

Acknowledgments

We are grateful to Michael White, who provided us with useful feedback to the idea of using a DRS corpus for developing and training text generation systems. We also would like to thank the three anonymous reviewers of this article. They gave extremely valuable comments that considerably improved our paper.

References

Guillaume Artignan, Mountaz Hascoët, and Mathieu Lafourcade. 2009. Multiscale visual analysis of lexical networks. *Information Visualisation, International Conference on*, 0:685–690.

N. Asher and A. Lascarides. 2003. *Logics of conversation*. Studies in natural language processing. Cambridge University Press.

Nicholas Asher. 1993. *Reference to Abstract Objects in Discourse*. Kluwer Academic Publishers.

Collin F. Baker, Charles J. Fillmore, and John B. Lowe. 1998. The Berkeley FrameNet project. In *36th Annual Meeting of the Association for Computational Linguistics and 17th International Conference on Computational Linguistics. Proceedings of the Conference*, pages 86–90, Université de Montréal, Montreal, Quebec, Canada.

John Bateman and Michael Zock. 2003. Natural Language Generation. In R. Mitkov, editor, *Oxford Handbook of Computational Linguistics*, chapter 15, pages 284–304. Oxford University Press, Oxford.

Bernd Bohnet, Leo Wanner, Simon Mille, and Alicia Burga. 2010. Broad coverage multilingual deep sentence generation with a stochastic multi-level realizer. In *Proceedings of the 23rd International Conference on Computational Linguistics*, pages 98–106.

Johan Bos. 2008. Wide-Coverage Semantic Analysis with Boxer. In J. Bos and R. Delmonte, editors, *Semantics in Text Processing. STEP 2008 Conference Proceedings*, volume 1 of *Research in Computational Semantics*, pages 277–286. College Publications.

John Chamberlain, Massimo Poesio, and Udo Kruschwitz. 2008. Addressing the Resource Bottleneck to Create Large-Scale Annotated Texts. In Johan Bos and Rodolfo Delmonte, editors, *Semantics in Text Processing. STEP 2008 Conference Proceedings*, volume 1 of *Research in Computational Semantics*, pages 375–380. College Publications.

Stephen Clark and James R. Curran. 2004. Parsing the WSJ using CCG and Log-Linear Models. In *Proceedings of the 42nd Annual Meeting of the Association for Computational Linguistics (ACL '04)*, pages 104–111, Barcelona, Spain.

Michael Elhadad and Jacques Robin. 1996. An overview of SURGE: a reusable comprehensive syntactic realization component. Technical report.

Christiane Fellbaum, editor. 1998. *WordNet. An Electronic Lexical Database*. The MIT Press.

Claire Gardent, Hélène Manuélian, Kristina Striegnitz, and Marilisa Amoia. 2004. Generating definite descriptions: Non-incrementality, inference and data. In Thomas Pechmann and Christopher Habel, editors, *Multidisciplinary approaches to language production*, pages 53–85. Walter de Gruyter, Berlin.

Eduard Hovy, Mitchell Marcus, Martha Palmer, Lance Ramshaw, and Ralph Weischedel. 2006. Ontonotes: the 90% solution. In *Proceedings of the Human Language Technology Conference of the NAACL, Companion Volume: Short Papers*, pages 57–60, Stroudsburg, PA, USA.

Nancy Ide, Christiane Fellbaum, Collin Baker, and Rebecca Passonneau. 2010. The manually annotated sub-corpus: a community resource for and by the people. In *Proceedings of the ACL 2010 Conference Short Papers*, pages 68–73, Stroudsburg, PA, USA.

Hans Kamp and Uwe Reyle. 1993. *From Discourse to Logic; An Introduction to Modeltheoretic Semantics of Natural Language, Formal Logic and DRT*. Kluwer, Dordrecht.

Hans Kamp. 1984. A Theory of Truth and Semantic Representation. In Jeroen Groenendijk, Theo M.V. Janssen, and Martin Stokhof, editors, *Truth, Interpretation and Information*, pages 1–41. FORIS, Dordrecht – Holland/Cinnaminson – U.S.A.

Karin Kipper, Anna Korhonen, Neville Ryant, and Martha Palmer. 2008. A large-scale classification of English verbs. *Language Resources and Evaluation*, 42(1):21–40.

Reinhard Muskens. 1996. Combining Montague Semantics and Discourse Representation. *Linguistics and Philosophy*, 19:143–186.

Martha Palmer, Paul Kingsbury, and Daniel Gildea. 2005. The proposition bank: An annotated corpus of semantic roles. *Computational Linguistics*, 31(1):71–106.

Rashmi Prasad, Aravind Joshi, Nikhil Dinesh, Alan Lee, Eleni Miltsakaki, and Bonnie Webber. 2005. The Penn Discourse TreeBank as a resource for natural language generation. In *Proc. of the Corpus Linguistics Workshop on Using Corpora for Natural Language Generation*, pages 25–32.

Mark Steedman. 2001. *The Syntactic Process*. The MIT Press.

Kees van Deemter. 2006. Generating referring expressions that involve gradable properties. *Computational Linguistics*, 32(2):195–222.

Rob A. Van der Sandt. 1992. Presupposition Projection as Anaphora Resolution. *Journal of Semantics*, 9:333–377.

Michael White, Rajakrishnan Rajkumar, and Scott Martin. 2007. Towards broad coverage surface realization with CCG. In *Proceedings of the Workshop on Using Corpora for NLG: Language Generation and Machine Translation (UCNLG+MT)*.

Michael White. 2006. Efficient realization of coordinate structures in combinatory categorial grammar. *Research on Language & Computation*, 4:39–75.

A Policy-Based Approach to Context Dependent Natural Language Generation

Thomas Bouttaz, Edoardo Pignotti, Chris Mellish, and Peter Edwards
Computing Science, University of Aberdeen,
Aberdeen AB24 5UA, UK
{t.bouttaz, e.pignotti, c.mellish, p.edwards}@abdn.ac.uk

Abstract

This paper presents a method for tailoring Natural Language Generation according to context in a web-based Virtual Research Environment. We discuss a policy-driven framework for capturing user, project and organisation preferences and describe how it can be used to control the generation of textual descriptions of RDF resources.

1 Introduction

Adaptive interfaces change the style and content of interaction according to the context of use. In particular, adaptive hypertext (O'Donnell et al., 2001) adapts the content and form of natural language text. Systems like this introduce the need for a good model of the context and how it influences language. This context can, in general, include aspects of the user themselves, general aspects of the situation and also the task the user is currently performing. Many interactive systems use sets of attribute-value pairs to implement the user and general context models. They then encode the method of decision making in each task context, taking into account the information in the two models (e.g. Savidis et al., 2005). We are investigating a different approach where the representation of user (coming possibly from several sources), general context and task context are combined in a declarative way through the construction of *policies*. In this approach, preferences are expressed in terms of obligations, prohibitions and permissions, possibly arising from different sources, using semantic web ontologies. Combining information from multiple sources has been used in user modelling (Kobsa, 1993) and there has also been some use of ontologies in user modelling (Hatala and Wakkary, 2005), but ours is the first system that uses ontologies for the encoding of all user actions, task contexts, permissions and user preferences.

Although policies can be used to control a number of aspects of adaptation, here we concentrate on their use within Natural Language Generation (NLG), mainly for content determination. In general NLG is often conceived as being responsive to multiple *goals* or *constraints* (e.g. Hovy, 1990). In addition, the content and form of a generated text often needs to be tailored to at least certain aspects of the user (Paris, 1988; Bateman and Paris, 1989). However, not many general mechanisms have been presented for dynamically combining different aspects of the context for guiding NLG. Plan-based tailoring (Paris, 1988; Paris et al., 2004) might provide part of such a mechanism, but it assumes a top-down approach to text planning, which is not natural for applications that just have to express some of what happens to be there in the input data (Marcu, 1997). Requirements on style, syntax, content, etc. can all be expressed and combined in constraint-based NLG (Piwek and van Deemter, 2007), but existing implementations only use general constraint-satisfaction mechanisms for particular parts of the generation problem. Generation based on Systemic Grammar (Bateman, 1997) provides a clear mechanism for decision-making and tailoring (Bateman and Paris, 1989) but is less clear on the representation of context. In generation by classification (Reiter and Mellish, 1992), contexts are complex objects classified into an ontology. Aspects relevant

Proceedings of the 13th European Workshop on Natural Language Generation (ENLG), pages 151–157,
Nancy, France, September 2011.

to particular generation decisions are then inherited according to where the context has been classified. Although this is elegant in theory, in practice, such ideas are now used more as part of object-oriented programming approaches to NLG (White and Caldwell, 1998). It thus remains to be seen both to what extent declarative representation of contexts and NLG decision making is possible, and also to what extent control of NLG can use similar mechanisms to other types of adaptation. The current work can be seen as further exploration of this territory.

In this paper, we report on policy-driven control of NLG as we have integrated it in a Virtual Research Environment (VRE) called ourSpaces[1]. This system has been developed to facilitate collaboration and interaction between researchers by enabling users to track the provenance of their digital artifacts and processes, and to capture the provenance around a user's social network, e.g. activities within the environment, relationships between members, and membership of projects and groups. Provenance (also referred to as lineage or heritage) aims to provide additional documentation about the processes that led to the creation of an artifact. Within this environment, a short textual description of an artifact, person or project can be valuable to a user. We have developed an NLG service to generate text descriptions of those resources based on the RDF metadata held by the system. This service has to perform "ontology verbalisation" (i.e. translate ontology fragments into natural language), a topic on which there has been much previous research (e.g. Sun and Mellish, 2007; Power and Third, 2010). Our own approach builds on the system of Hielkema (2010). However, work on ontology verbalisation has not yet presented general mechanisms for content determination from semantic web data. This paper discusses how policies can be used to tailor the content selected for an NLG service like ours, so that it adapts according to the context of use.

2 Capturing Context

Underpinning the VRE is a rich and pervasive RDF (Klyne and Carroll, 2004) metadata infrastructure built upon a series of OWL ontologies (McGuinness and van Harmelen, 2004) describing aspects of the provenance of digital artifacts, projects, organisations, people and social networking activities. Through our experience with a number of case-study groups we have identified three dimensions that together characterise the context used to generate text descriptions:

The provenance of the resource being described. At the core of the VRE is a representation based on the Open Provenance Model (OPM) (Moreau et al., 2011). OPM provides a specification to express data provenance, process documentation and data derivation. It is based on three primary entities namely *Artifact*, *Process* and *Agent* and associated causal relationships namely *used*, *wasGeneratedBy*, *wasTriggeredBy*, *wasDerivedFrom* and *wasControlledBy*. The context behind the description of a digital resource is provided by a provenance ontology developed in OWL, which defines the primary entities of OPM and additional provenance ontologies which extend the concepts defined in the OPM ontology with domain-specific classes (see Figure 1 top).

The user's social context. In the VRE, the link between the social network and digital artifacts is established formally, by the integration of the FOAF social networking vocabulary (Brickley and Miller, 2010) with our provenance ontologies. FOAF characterises an individual and their social network by defining a vocabulary describing people, the links between them and the things they create and do. Moreover, we have extended our framework to allow links between people and projects, groups and organisations (see Figure 1 bottom-right).

Specific user, project, organisation and system policies. Within our system, users and their behaviours are managed by enforcing certain policies. Policies can be created by the user, by an administrator of a project, group or organisation, or by a system developer. For example, a user may impose certain access constraints on digital artifacts that they own, e.g. certain information about the artifact may only be accessible to users who are members of a particular project and who contributed towards the artifact itself. A project might also be required to archive artifacts to the UK Social Science Data Archive (UKDA) [2] and follow certain docu-

[1] http://www.ourspaces.net

[2] http://www.data-archive.ac.uk/

mentation requirements. More specifically, a policy may be created by the Principal Investigator of a project, specifying that certain information about an artifact has to be provided during the upload.

In the VRE we define such policies as a combination of *Obligation*, *Prohibition* or *Permission* instances described by the properties *hasObligation**, *hasProhibition** and *hasPermission** in the ontology illustrated in Figure 1 bottom-left. Each *Obligation*, *Prohibition* or *Permission* has an associated set of *Condition* instances. A condition in our ontology is a combination of a subject (an *opm:Artifact* or an *opm:Process*) and a rule describing the condition (see Figure 3 and 4).

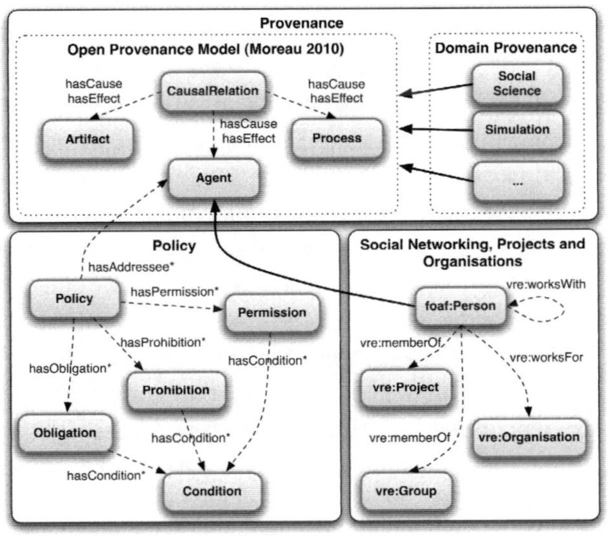

Figure 1: Capturing context in the ourSpaces VRE.

3 Generating Context-Dependent Text Descriptions

In order to enable collaboration between researchers, the VRE makes use of a number of repositories and services to store research resources, and offers a number of tools to manage and visualise such resources (see Figure 2). One of the most important components of the VRE is a *Text Generator* service which is able to generate short textual descriptions from the RDF metadata associated with resources stored in the *Metadata Repository* (e.g. title, author, date of publication). In order to generate the text, we have implemented a RESTful service that invokes a *Text Generator* service based on the RDF ID of the resource being described, passed as a parameter by the Web interface. This service generates text containing a description of the resource using a deep model of the syntactic structure of sentences and their combinations, inspired by the work of Hielkema (2010).

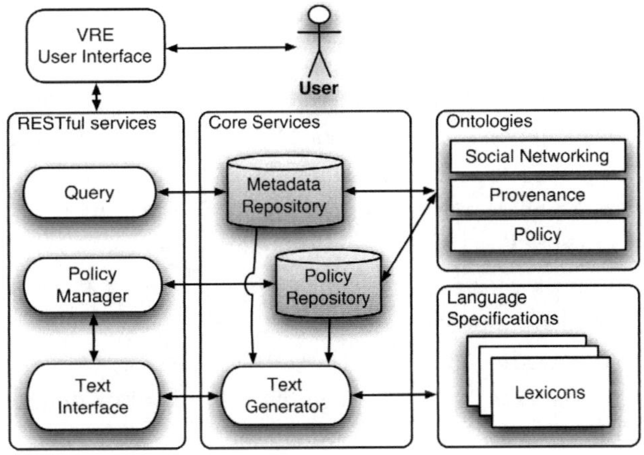

Figure 2: Architecture enabling context-dependent NLG.

The *Text Generator* builds an internal RDF model of the resource being described by querying the *Metadata Repository*. The text is then produced by converting axioms inside the model to plain text using the appropriate language specifications. A language specification is composed of a set of lexicons encoded in XML which describe how to render the text corresponding to a RDF property (e.g. syntactic category, source node, target node, verb tense). For example, if the property *transcribedBy* of a resource of type *Transcript* has a value of *"Thomas Bouttaz"*, the XML file corresponding to that property will specify that this information must be rendered as: "It was transcribed by Thomas Bouttaz" (see Figure 5 left). By following the hyperlinks available in the resource description, the user is then able to expand the text to access more information about related resources. For instance, in this example the user can click on the hyperlink *Thomas Bouttaz* to get more information about that person. This is done by invoking the *Text Generator* service with the ID of the RDF representation of that person. The description returned by the service is then appended to the original text by the *Text Interface*.

Due to the complexity of metadata associated

with a resource, context plays a vital role in supporting the selection of information to be displayed to the user. Using policies, it is possible to enforce context-dependent preferences while the text is being generated by the *Text Generator*. This is achieved in our framework by invoking the *Policy Manager* which implements a policy reasoning service based on the ontology described in Figure 1 bottom-left. Our framework is composed of a repository storing RDF triples representing policies, and a provenance policy reasoner based on the TopBraid SPIN API (Knublauch et al., 2011). In our framework, before realising the descriptive text of a resource, policies are checked against the model containing the RDF graph. The *Policy Manager* checks if any of the policies stored in the *Policy Repository* can be activated by the current RDF model by running the SPIN reasoner against the rules associated with the policies.

To illustrate the use of policies within the VRE, consider an example where the Principal Investigator of a project needs to make sure that confidential information about the project is protected. This can be achieved by constructing a policy with a rule similar to the one shown in Figure 3.

```
CONSTRUCT {
  _:b0 a spin:ConstraintViolation .
  _:b0 spin:violationRoot ?process .
  _:b0 spin:violationPath pggen:location .
  _:b0 spin:violationPath pggen:hasStartDate .
  _:b0 spin:violationPath pggen:hasEndDate .
}
WHERE {
  ?artifact pggen:wasGeneratedByInfer ?process .
  NOT EXISTS {
    ?artifact pggen:producedInProject ?project .
    ?project project:hasMemberRole ?role .
    ?role project:roleOf [USER_ID] .
  }.
}
```

Figure 3: Rule protecting confidential information of "process" artifacts.

The rule presented in Figure 3 specifies that it is not possible to view location, start date and end date of the process that generated a resource, unless the user is a member of the project which produced that artifact. Similarly, another rule could protect the identity of the person that transcribed an artifact. On the other hand, an individual user might want to express his preferences regarding what information is rendered in the textual description of a resource. For instance a user could declare that he is not interested in knowing who deposited a resource if that person is already part of his social network.

When the user requests a textual description of a resource, the VRE detects if certain policies are activated depending on the context surrounding the user and the resource being described. If policies are active, the *Text Generator* service takes into account the constraints associated with such policies. If a violation is detected, the service will remove the information described by the *spin:violationPath* property from the internal RDF model describing the resource. Therefore when the realiser generates the text from the model, those details will be omitted.

While this example demonstrates how the system can remove axioms associated with confidential information, policies can also be used to expand the description of a resource. For instance, the Principal Investigator might want to express that if a user non-member of the project tries to generate a description of a protected resource, the description should include information about who to contact to obtain access to that resource (e.g. the email address of the PI of that project). This preference can be represented by a policy which includes a rule indicating where to retrieve contact information, and how to expand the internal model, as illustrated by the rule in Figure 4.

```
CONSTRUCT {
  ?artifact nlg:forObtainingAccess ?mbox .
}
WHERE {
  ?artifact pggen:producedInProject ?project .
  ?project project:hasMemberRole ?role .
  NOT EXISTS {
    ?role project:roleOf [USER_ID] .
  } .
  ?role a project:PrincipalInvestigator .
  ?role project:roleOf ?pi .
  ?pi foaf:mbox ?mbox .
}
```

Figure 4: Rule adding contact information to obtain access to an artifact, for project non-members.

The rule shown in Figure 4 defines a new *nlg:forObtainingAccess* property about the artifact being described in the local model, if the user requesting the description is not a member of the project which produced that artifact. This property is defined in a utility ontology only used by the NLG service.

The example in Figure 5 shows two text descriptions of the same interview transcript. On the left-hand side, the description is generated for a user member of the project in which the transcript was produced. On the right-hand side, the description is generated for a non-member who has indicated that he is not interested in information about users in his social network.

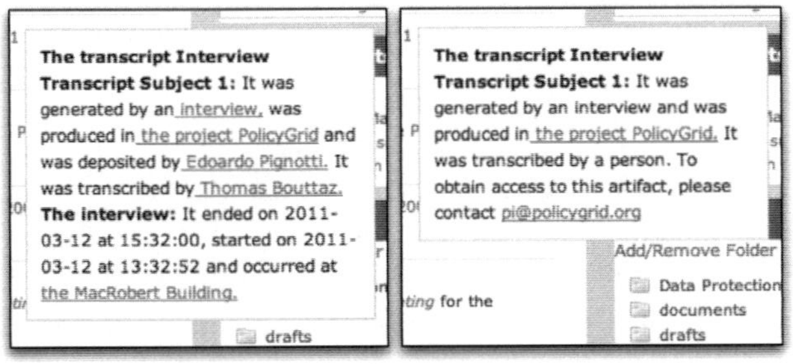

Figure 5: Two examples of text descriptions about the same transcript artifact.

Using this framework it is possible to declare policies that apply to different contexts involving users, projects and organisations. Context may also include which VRE page the user is currently browsing. By taking into account all of these factors, this architecture allows tailored content determination for the generation of resource descriptions.

4 Conclusions & Future Work

In this paper we have presented a software architecture able to deliver context-dependent textual descriptions of resources described by RDF metadata. This architecture has been developed to work in a VRE to provide a tool for researchers to explore the provenance of research artifacts. Due to the volume of metadata associated with a resource in the VRE, we argued that context plays a vital role in supporting the selection of the information to be displayed to the user. We have identified three factors to determine context: a) the provenance of the resource being described; b) the user's social context; c) specific user, project, organisation and system policies.

We discussed how policy reasoning could be used to provide a flexible mechanism to define and enforce context-dependent preferences. We presented an example where the textual description of an interview transcript was tailored to the user context to assure that confidential information about the interview was only disclosed to members of a specific project. In our future work we plan to investigate other ways in which context could be used to influence the generation of text. For example, how descriptions of resources could be generated depending on different user's domain vocabularies. Moreover, we plan to investigate other ways in which the context representation described here can influence the system in general.

Usability and conflicts between policies are two important issues that have not been explored in our work to date. We are currently investigating the use of conflict resolution strategies, such as setting ranks reflecting the degree of importance of a policy. Using such a strategy, the *Policy Manager* would be able to determine how to prioritise conflicting policies applying to a particular resource. To determine if two policies may conflict, we plan to use a conflict detection mechanism similar to the one proposed by Şensoy et al. (2010). Moreover regarding usability, we need to implement a system that would allow users to easily create SPIN rules representing their policies, possibly using a NLG interface.

Finally, we need to evaluate the extent to which the techniques presented in this paper actually enhance the user's ability to perform tasks using the VRE. We plan to do this by comparing the use of the main system with the use of versions that have specific features (NLG service, policy-driven NLG service) disabled, following a similar methodology to that used by Hielkema (2010).

Acknowledgments

This work is supported by the UK Economic & Social Research Council (ESRC) under the Digital Social Research programme; award RES-149-25-1075.

References

John A. Bateman. Enabling technology for multilingual natural language generation: the KPML development environment. *Nat. Lang. Eng.*, 3:15–55, March 1997.

John A. Bateman and Cecile Paris. Phrasing a text in terms the user can understand. In *Proceedings of the 11th international joint conference on Arti-*

ficial intelligence - Volume 2, pages 1511–1517, San Francisco, CA, USA, 1989. Morgan Kaufmann Publishers Inc.

Dan Brickley and Libby Miller. FOAF vocabulary specification. Technical report, W3C, 2010.

Murat Şensoy, Timothy J. Norman, Wamberto W. Vasconcelos, and Katia Sycara. OWL-POLAR: semantic policies for agent reasoning. In *Proceedings of the 9th international semantic web conference on The semantic web - Volume Part I*, ISWC'10, pages 679–695, Berlin, Heidelberg, 2010. Springer-Verlag.

Marek Hatala and Ron Wakkary. Ontology-based user modeling in an augmented audio reality system for museums. *User Modeling and User-Adapted Interaction*, 15:339–380, August 2005.

Feikje Hielkema. *Using Natural Language Generation to Provide Access to Semantic Metadata*. PhD thesis, University of Aberdeen, 2010.

Eduard H. Hovy. Pragmatics and natural language generation. *Artif. Intell.*, 43:153–197, May 1990.

Graham Klyne and Jeremy J. Carroll. Resource description framework (RDF): Concepts and abstract syntax. World Wide Web Consortium, Recommendation REC-rdf-concepts-20040210, February 2004.

Holger Knublauch, James A. Hendler, and Kingsley Idehen. SPIN - Overview and Motivation. Technical report, W3C, 2011.

Alfred Kobsa. User modeling: Recent work, prospects and hazards. In M. Schneider-Hufschmidt, T. Kühme, and U. Malinowski, editors, *Adaptive User Interfaces: Principles and Practice*, pages 111–128. North-Holland, Amsterdam, 1993.

Daniel Marcu. From local to global coherence: A bottom-up approach to text planning. In *Proceedings of the 14th National Conference on Artificial Intelligence*, pages 629–635, 1997.

Deborah L. McGuinness and Frank van Harmelen. OWL web ontology language overview. Technical Report REC-OWL-features-20040210, W3C, 2004.

Luc Moreau, Ben Clifford, Juliana Freire, Joe Futrelle, Yolanda Gil, Paul Groth, Natalia Kwasnikowska, Simon Miles, Paolo Missier, Jim Myers, Beth Plale, Yogesh Simmhan, Eric Stephan, and Jan Van den Bussche. The open provenance model core specification (v1.1). *Future Gener. Comput. Syst.*, 27:743–756, June 2011.

M. O'Donnell, C. Mellish, J. Oberlander, and A. Knott. ILEX: an architecture for a dynamic hypertext generation system. *Nat. Lang. Eng.*, 7: 225–250, September 2001.

Cécile Paris. Tailoring object descriptions to a user's level of expertise. *Comput. Linguist.*, 14:64–78, September 1988.

Cécile Paris, Mingfang Wu, Keith Vander Linden, Matthew Post, and Shijian Lu. Myriad: An architecture for contextualized information retrieval and delivery. In *AH2004: International Conference on Adaptive Hypermedia and Adaptive Web-based Systems*, pages 205–214, 2004.

Paul Piwek and Kees van Deemter. Generating under global constraints: the case of scripted dialogue. *Research On Language and Computation (ROLC)*, page to appear, 2007.

Richard Power and Allan Third. Expressing OWL axioms by english sentences: dubious in theory, feasible in practice. In *Proceedings of the 23rd International Conference on Computational Linguistics: Posters*, COLING '10, pages 1006–1013, Stroudsburg, PA, USA, 2010. Association for Computational Linguistics.

Ehud Reiter and Chris Mellish. Using classification to generate text. In *Proceedings of the 30th annual meeting on Association for Computational Linguistics*, ACL '92, pages 265–272, Stroudsburg, PA, USA, 1992. Association for Computational Linguistics.

Anthony Savidis, Margherita Antona, and Constantine Stephanidis. A decision-making specification language for verifiable user-interface adaptation logic. *International Journal of Software Engineering and Knowledge Engineering*, 15:1063–1094, 2005.

Xiantang Sun and Chris Mellish. An experiment on "free generation" from single RDF triples. In *Proceedings of the Eleventh European Workshop on Natural Language Generation*, ENLG '07, pages

105–108, Stroudsburg, PA, USA, 2007. Association for Computational Linguistics.

Michael White and Ted Caldwell. Exemplars: A practical, extensible framework for dynamic text generation. In *Proceedings of the Ninth International Workshop on Natural Language Generation*, pages 266–275, 1998.

Levels of organisation in ontology verbalisation

Sandra Williams, Allan Third and Richard Power
Computing Department, The Open University
Walton Hall, Milton Keynes, MK7 6AA, U.K.
s.h.williams@open.ac.uk a.third@open.ac.uk r.power@open.ac.uk

Abstract

The SWAT TOOLS ontology verbaliser generates a hierarchically organised hypertext designed for easy comprehension and navigation. The document structure, inspired by encyclopedias and glossaries, is organised at a number of levels. At the top level, a heading is generated for every concept in the ontology; at the next level, each entry is subdivided into logically-based headings like 'Definition' and 'Examples'; at the next, sentences are aggregated when they have parts in common; at the lowest level, phrases are hyperlinked to concept headings. One consequence of this organisation is that some statements are *repeated* because they are relevant to more than one entry; this means that the text is longer than one in which statements are simply listed. This trade-off between organisation and brevity is investigated in a user study.

1 Introduction

Since OWL (Web Ontology Language) became the standard language for the semantic web in 2004,[1] several research groups have developed systems, known as 'verbalisers', for generating Controlled English from OWL ontologies (Kaljurand and Fuchs, 2007; Dolbear et al., 2007; Schwitter and Tilbrook, 2004; Funk et al., 2007). The resulting texts may contain linguistic errors, especially when the lexicon is inferred from identifier names (as in SWAT TOOLS) rather than handcrafted, but they are still easier to understand than formal languages (Kuhn, 2010). We describe here a generic verbaliser[2] (applicable to any OWL-DL ontology with English identifiers/labels) which delivers its output (e.g., figure 1) in the form of an organised hypertext,[3] akin to an online encyclopedia or glossary, and investigate whether this extra organisation makes the text easier to understand and navigate.

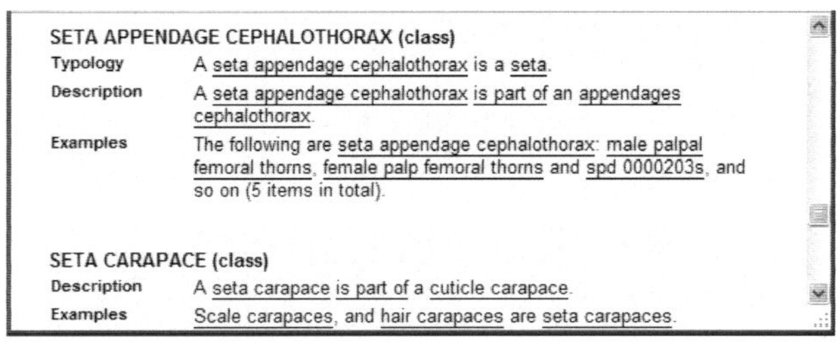

Figure 1: A section of SWAT TOOLS encyclopedia-style output, length 7746 words or 25 A4 pages, generated from an ontology about spider anatomy.

Elsewhere (Stevens et al., 2010; Stevens et al., 2011) we reported two evaluations with bioinformatics staff in which the glossary-style verbalisation was judged effective, for instance in detecting errors in the knowledge; however, these studies were not designed to test the value of organisation, through comparison with an unorganised list of statements. It might seem obvious that organisation will help: indeed, teachers of reading comprehension are required to ensure that

[1] http://www.w3.org/2004/01/sws-pressrelease

[2] SWAT TOOLS available at http://swat.open.ac.uk/tools/

[3] The hypertext in figure 1 was generated from spider.owl from owl.cs.manchester.ac.uk/repository/

Proceedings of the 13th European Workshop on Natural Language Generation (ENLG), pages 158–163,
Nancy, France, September 2011.

their students are aware of the use of textual features such as headings and subheadings in locating information (Steeds, 2001); and it comes as no surprise that reading strategies differ between a text structured as an encyclopedia and one organised as, say, a poem (Hanauer, 1998). However, organisation actually has one potential disadvantage, in that statements may be relevant in more than one context, and must thus be repeated. We describe here a study which checks this point by pitting organisation against brevity for a task requiring accurate retrieval of information from a text.

2 Verbalising statements

The input to a verbaliser is a set of OWL statements describing individuals, classes or properties; the simplest output therefore consists of a set of sentences, one per statement, as illustrated in figure 2, where the sentence 'A cribellar spigot is part of a cribellum' has been generated from the following statement:[4]

```
subClassOf(class(#SPD_0000276),
  objectSomeValuesFrom(
    objectProperty(#part_of),
    class(#SPD_0000115)))
```

The basic verbalisation method in SWAT TOOLS has been described in detail elsewhere (Stevens et al., 2011). Briefly, the OWL/XML input is transcoded to Prolog,[5] using the format illustrated in the example just given; then a lexicon for realising atomic terms (individuals, classes or properties) is inferred from their identifier names or labels; finally, a sentence is generated from each statement using a Definite Clause Grammar (Clocksin and Mellish, 1987) covering almost all of OWL-DL, using wording influenced by earlier work on controlled languages (Schwitter et al., 2008; Kaljurand and Fuchs, 2007; Dolbear et al., 2007).

Sentences are ordered according to the alphabetical order of their underlying OWL statements: i.e., sentences generated from `ClassAssertion` statements will come before those generated from `SubClassOf` statements.

[4]The 'non-semantic' identifiers #SPD_0000276 and #SPD_0000276 are annotated with English labels elsewhere in the ontology.

[5]The verbaliser is implemented in SWI Prolog

3 Document structuring

The highest levels of organisation, illustrated in figure 1, are headings and subheadings. Subheadings are inspired mainly by Berzlanovich et al.'s (2008) 'information oriented' discourse labels (name, definition, description, etc.) from their analysis of the discourse structure of encyclopedia articles; and also by Aristotle's genus-differentia descriptions.[6]

Lower levels of organisation were also influenced by Berzlanovich et al. (2008), whose investigation of lower-level lexical cohesion in encylopedia entries highlighted the high incidence of hypernymic lexical cohesion.

3.1 Headings

The top level of organisation is an alphabetical series of headings corresponding to atomic terms in the ontology (i.e., individuals, classes, or object/data properties), taken directly from the lexicon that the system infers from the ontology's identifier names or labels. Where singular and plural forms have been inferred, the singular is used, as illustrated by 'SETA CEPHALOTHORAX (class)' in figure 1.

An OWL statement is selected for inclusion under a heading if the class, property or individual that the heading refers to occurs as a top-level argument in the statement.[7] Inevitably, sentences that apply to more than one group are duplicated, e.g., 'a seta appendage cephalothorax is a seta' is added to entries for both SETA APPENDAGE CEPHALOTHORAX and SETA.

3.2 Subheadings

The second level of organisation is a set of subheadings. Within each entry, statements are organised into sub-groups according to their logical type. Subheadings are always generated in a fixed order (Definition, Taxonomy, Description, Distinctions, Examples) similar to that found in encyclopedia entries (Berzlanovich et al., 2008). For classes, `EquivalentClasses` statements in which the atomic class is the first

[6]en.wikipedia.org/wiki/Genusdifferentia_definition

[7]Theoretically, this could mean that some statements are omitted altogether because their top-level arguments are non-atomic, but in practice such statements are almost never found (Power and Third, 2010).

argument occur under the definition subheading, the taxonomy is the superclass (from an OWL `SubClassOf` statement), descriptive statements correspond to the OWL functor `SubClassOf`, distinctions to `DisjointClasses`, and examples to the individuals belonging to the class. For individuals the class is given first (from an OWL `ClassAssertion` statement), followed by descriptions typically corresponding to `ObjectPropertyAssertion`. For properties, the descriptive statements specify the domain and range, and features such as functionality and transitivity, and examples are provided by statements about individuals or classes in which the property is used.

3.3 Aggregating and truncating

A third level of organisation occurs when statements with identical structures and one identical argument are aggregated; see Williams and Power (2010) for more details. For some ontologies, this process can lead to very long lists of subclasses or individuals, so under the 'Examples' subheading where these occur we truncate them to a predefined maximum length and add the phrase 'and so on (N items in total)'. Figure 1 shows an example of aggregation and truncation in the sentence 'The following are seta appendage cephalothorax: male palpal femoral thorns, female palp femoral thorns and spd 0000203s, and so on (5 items in total)'. An obvious refinement would be to add a facility to view the entire list, if desired.

3.4 Hypertext links

The final and lowest level of organisation occurs when hyperlinks are introduced for each phrase corresponding to a class, individual or property; these link to the headings of their entries.

3.5 Related systems

To our knowledge, SWAT TOOLS takes document structuring further than other domain-*independent* ontology verbalisers. We are aware of only one other domain-independent system that attempts document structuring, ACE (Kaljurand and Fuchs, 2007). ACE lists statements under class, individual and property headings; and it inserts hyperlinks; but it has no intermediate levels of organisation.

Regarding domain-*dependent* systems, most of them aggregate statements and generate referring expressions (Bontcheva and Wilks, 2004; Dongilli, 2008; Galanis and Androutsopoulos, 2007; Hielkema, 2009; Liang et al., 2011). Only one attempts further discourse structuring: Laing et al.'s system for verbalising medical ontologies organises text according to rhetorical structure.

4 Evaluation

The evaluation study reported here focusses on the following question: Does the organisation just described help people to understand and navigate a text in spite of its longer length? This is addressed through a navigation task in which people were asked to locate information in either an organised text or an unorganised one and then give a judgement on how difficult the information was to find. The study design is between-subjects in two independent groups. Participants were 57 members of the ACL special interest groups SIGGEN[8] and SIGdial[9].

4.1 Materials and method

The texts were generated from an ontology about spider anatomy.[3] One group saw the encyclopedia-styled version illustrated in figure 1, henceforth the 'organised text'; the other saw the same information as a list of sentences[10] as shown in figure 2 ('*un*organised text'). At 7746 words (25 A4-sized pages), the organised text is much longer than the unorganised one (4803 words, 9-pages) mainly because of duplicated information and headings (as explained in section 3). To render the unorganised text's appearance as similar as possible to the organised one, spaces were introduced every fourth line with blocks of text placed on a taupe-coloured background identical to that of the entries in the organised text.

The same five navigation and information location tasks (table 1) were used for both groups. The survey was administered via SurveyMonkey[11] in which each navigation question was followed

[8] www.siggen.org

[9] www.sigdial.org

[10] Sentences were ordered alphabetically by their underlying OWL statements as described in section 2.

[11] www.surveymonkey.com

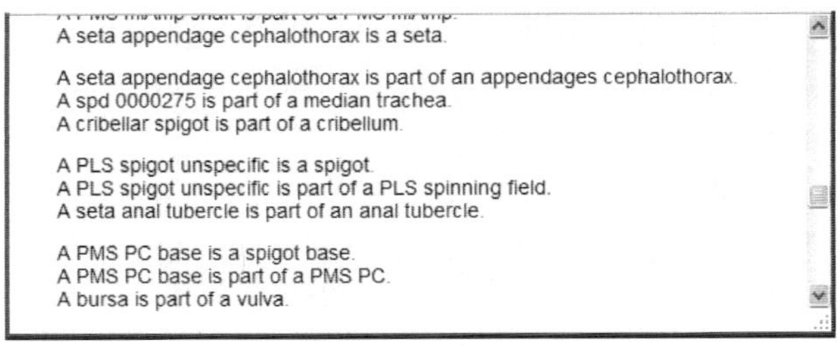

Figure 2: A section of SWAT TOOLS sentence-list-style output, 4,803 words or 9 A4 pages, the 'unorganised text' of our study generated from the spider anatomy ontology.

by a judgement 'How difficult was it to find the information?' on a 5-point scale ('Very Easy' to 'Very Hard').

Regarding search for information to answer the questions, both texts were viewed on-line and of course could be navigated with the usual 'Find' menu items, `CTRL-F` key sequence, and so on. To determine whether textual features such as headings, subheadings and hyperlinks had been used, subjects with the organised text were asked whether the following features had helped them to search for information: (i) heading, (ii) typology subheading, (iii) description subheading, (iv) examples subheading, (v) alphabetical ordering of entries,(vi) hyperlinks within entries, and (vii) totals for number of items in lists (section 3.3). Subjects given the unorganised text answered instead seven questions about techniques used for navigation, e.g., 'Did you use scrolling?'.

No.	Questions
Q1	What is a tarsus?
Q2	Name 3 kinds of spigot shaft.
Q3	What is a palp?
Q4	Name 2 kinds of silk cable.
Q5	How many kinds of seta appendage cephalothorax are there in total?

Table 1: Questions for the navigation tasks

Lastly, we had chosen the spider anatomy ontology because we hoped that the subject would be unfamiliar to participants causing them to consult the text (as we instructed) rather than using their own general knowledge to answer the questions. The final question in the survey asked about familiarity with spider anatomy.

4.2 Results

Table 2 shows that despite the drop in performance on question 5 (and question 1 for the unorganised text group), both groups were relatively successful in locating information. However, difficulty judgements differed significantly between groups (see table 3), with the group using the organised text judging the tasks much easier. This preference was confirmed by a non-parametric independent samples Mann-Whitney U test over all judgements ($p < 0.0001$). Results for questions about usage of specific organisational features (answered only by the group that viewed the organised text) are given in table 4. None of the participants claimed to be expert in spider anatomy.

n	Text	Q1	Q2	Q3	Q4	Q5
28	Unorganised	20	27	26	27	19
29	Organised	28	27	26	27	25

Table 2: Results for numbers of correct answers (n = number of participants per group)

Q	n	Text	VE	Easy	Neith	Hard	VH
Q1	28	Unorg	2	6	7	11	2
	29	Org	10	12	3	4	0
Q2	28	Unorg	3	13	4	6	2
	29	Org	11	10	6	2	0
Q3	28	Unorg	1	11	6	5	5
	29	Org	11	13	4	1	0
Q4	28	Unorg	6	17	2	2	1
	29	Org	12	13	3	1	0
Q5	28	Unorg	0	1	12	10	4
	29	Org	10	11	4	3	1

Table 3: Results for difficulty judgements (Q = question number, n = number of participants per group, Unorg = unorganised text, Org = organised text, VE = Very easy, Neith = neither hard or easy, VH = Very hard).

5 Discussion

In our earlier user studies (Stevens et al., 2010; Stevens et al., 2011), experts in bioinformatics assessed technical descriptions corresponding to glossary entries, with statements linked by aggregation but not grouped by logical subheadings. The consensus was that these were understandable, and useful to developers as a means of checking accuracy. However, various criticisms were made,

Organisational Feature	Used by
Headings	17
Typology subheadings	17
Description subheadings	20
Examples subheadings	22
Alphabetical ordering	20
Hyperlinks	19
Totals for items in truncated lists	21

Table 4: Results for usage of organisational features (number of people who used them out of 29 participants who viewed the organised text).

the main theme being that natural English should be priveleged over fidelity to OWL semantics.

The SWAT TOOLS system evaluated here incorporates some stylistic changes proposed in the earlier study, and retains the aggregation feature which combines several statements into a single sentence (thus potentially reducing fidelity to the underlying OWL); it also adds grouping by subheadings. None of this organisation is directly encoded in an OWL ontology: it represents rather a further move towards making the verbalisation more natural and humanlike.

From our study comparing organised and unorganised texts, two main points emerge: first, we find no evidence that people viewing the organised text perform a navigation task more accurately; second, people viewing the organised texts found the task easier. One explanation for these findings would be that people do whatever is necessary to achieve a desired level of performance, so that when provided with superior tools they achieve roughly the same result but with less effort.[12]

The drop in performance by the unorganised text group on question 1 might have been due to unfamiliarity with a sentence-list type of text (all participants answered question 1 first since questions were always presented in the same order). Improvements on later questions could have been the result of a learning effect with this group. The near-perfect performance of the organised text group on the first questions demonstrates the benefit of viewing a familiar genre. A drop in performance by the unorganised text group on question 5, 'How many kinds of seta appendage cephalothorax are there in total?' was expected since it is a harder question that requires a search of the entire unorganised text whilst simultaneously counting instances. It is not clear why four people in the organised text group failed to get the correct answer to question 5 since it merely requred them to understand the text '5 items in total' under 'Examples' (see figure 1).

Regarding the analysis of different organisational features, the overall response was that all these features were considered useful by a majority of users, although none of them stood out as particularly important.

6 Conclusion

We assume that most users prefer an ontology verbalisation that is worded and organised like a naturally occurring text of the appropriate genre — i.e., an encyclopedia or technical glossary. One possible objection is that such a text provides a loose rendering of OWL semantics, introducing organisational principles that are not present in the original code; however, as evidenced by the earlier studies we have cited, this attitude is not taken even by OWL specialists. A second possible objection is that the organised text is necessarily longer than a bare list of sentences; this point is tested in the study reported here, which suggests that organisation makes the texts easier to use, with no loss of performance. In future work we intend to look more closely at how the texts are used in retrieval tasks, and to obtain accurate measures of time differences.

Acknowledgments

The SWAT project (Semantic Web Authoring Tool) is supported by the UK Engineering and Physical Sciences Research Council (EPSRC) grants G033579/1 (Open University) and G032459/1 (University of Manchester). We would also like to thank colleagues and reviewers for their comments and suggestions.

References

I. Berzlanovich, M. Egg, and G. Redeker. 2008. Coherence structure and lexical cohesion in expository

[12]In this case responses for organised texts should be faster, a point we intend to check in future work.

and persuasive texts. In *A. Benz, P. Kuhnlein and M. Stede (Eds.), Proceedings of the Workshop Constraints in Discourse III, Potsdam, Germany*, pages 19–26.

K. Bontcheva and Y. Wilks. 2004. Automatic report generation from ontologies: the MIAKT approach. In *Nineth International Conference on Applications of Natural Language to Information Systems (NLDB'2004)*, pages 214–225, Manchester, UK.

F. Clocksin and Chris Mellish. 1987. *Programming in Prolog*. Springer-Verlag, 3 edition.

Cathy Dolbear, Glen Hart, Katalin Kovacs, John Goodwin, and Sheng Zhou. 2007. The RABBIT Language: Description, Syntax and Conversion to OWL. Technical Report Technical Report, Ordnance Survey Research.

Paolo Dongilli. 2008. Natural language rendering of a conjunctive query. Technical Report Knowledge Representation Meets Databases (KRDB) Research Centre Technical Report: KRDB08-3, Free University of Bozen-Bolzano.

Adam Funk, Valentin Tablan, Kalina Bontcheva, Hamish Cunningham, Brian Davis, and Siegfried Handschuh. 2007. Clone: Controlled language for ontology editing. In *K. Aberer et al. (Eds.) Proceedings of ISWC/ASWC 2007*, pages 142–155. Springer-Verlag Berlin Heidelberg 2007.

Dimitrios Galanis and Ion Androutsopoulos. 2007. Generating multilingual descriptions from linguistically annotated owl ontologies: the naturalowl system. In *Proceedings of the Eleventh European Workshop on Natural Language Generation*, pages 143–146, Saarbrücken, Germany, June. DFKI GmbH. Document D-07-01.

David Hanauer. 1998. The genre-specific hypothesis of reading: Reading poetry and encyclopedic items. *Poetics*, 26:63–80.

Feikje Hielkema. 2009. *Using Natural Language Generation to Provide Access to Semantic Metadata*. Ph.D. thesis, University of Aberdeen.

Kaarel Kaljurand and Norbert E. Fuchs. 2007. Verbalizing owl in attempto controlled english. In *Proceedings of Third International Workshop on OWL: Experiences and Directions, Innsbruck, Austria (6th–7th June 2007)*, volume 258.

Tobias Kuhn. 2010. An evaluation framework for controlled natural languages. In Norbert E. Fuchs, editor, *Proceedings of the Workshop on Controlled Natural Language (CNL 2009)*, volume 5972 of *Lecture Notes in Computer Science*, pages 1–20, Berlin / Heidelberg, Germany. Springer.

Shao Fen Liang, Donia Scott, Robert Stevens, and Alan Rector. 2011. Unlocking medical ontologies for non-ontology experts. In *Proceedings of BioNLP 2011 Workshop*, pages 174–181, Portland, Oregon, USA, June. Association for Computational Linguistics.

Richard Power and Allan Third. 2010. Expressing OWL axioms by English sentences: dubious in theory, feasible in practice. In *Proceedings of the 23rd International Conference on Computational Linguistics*.

R. Schwitter and M. Tilbrook. 2004. Controlled natural language meets the semantic web. In *Proceedings of the Australasian Language Technology Workshop*, pages 55–62, Macquarie University.

Rolf Schwitter, Kaarel Kaljurand, Anne Cregan, Catherine Dolbear, and Glen Hart. 2008. A comparison of three controlled natural languages for owl 1.1. In *OWL: Experiences and Directions (OWLED)*, page online.

Andrew Steeds. 2001. Adult literacy core curriculum including spoken communication. Technical report, Cambridge Training and Development Ltd. on behalf of The Basic Skills Agency. ISBN 1-85990-127-1.

Robert Stevens, James Malone, Sandra Williams, and Richard Power. 2010. Automating class definitions from owl to english. In *Proceedings of Bio-Ontologies 2010: Semantic Applications in Life Sciences, SIG at 18th Annual International conference on Intelligent Systems for Molecular Biology (ISMB 2010)*.

R. Stevens, J. Malone, S. Williams, R. Power, and A. Third. 2011. Automating generation of textual class definitions from owl to english. *Journal of Biomedical Semantics*, 2(Suppl 2):S5.

Sandra Williams and Richard Power. 2010. Grouping axioms for more coherent ontology descriptions. In *6th International Natural Language Generation Conference (INLG 2010)*.

Using semantic roles to improve summaries

Diana Trandabăț
Faculty of Computer Science
University "Alexandru Ioan Cuza" Iasi
Iasi, Romania
dtrandabat@info.uaic.ro

Abstract

This paper describes preliminary analysis on the influence of the semantic roles in summary generation. The proposed method involves three steps: first, the named entities in the original text are identified using a named entity recognizer; secondly, the sentences are parsed and semantic roles are extracted; thirdly, selection of the sentences containing specific semantic roles for the most relevant entities in text. Although the method is language independent, in order to check its viability, we tested the proposed approach for Romanian summaries.

1 Introduction

Text summarization refers to the task of shortening a long text. There are two major directions in text summarisation: the *extractive* and the *abstractive* paradigm (Mani, 2001). The first approach in creating summaries (most common) is based on identifying important words in texts by using their frequencies, and determining those sentences that contain a bigger number of important words. These sentences are extracted from the original text, and taken to constitute the summary. In this paradigm, the summarization is performed through sentence extraction: the summary is a subset of the sentences in the original text.

An alternative approach is to build a summary consisting of sentences that don't necessarily have to show up in that specific form in the source text. This requires a certain amount of deeper understanding of the text. This method can also be applied in the case of very large texts, such as a whole novel, where neither the determination of most significant sentences based on occurrences of frequent words, nor building discourse structures could be of help. In these cases, other methods, mainly expanding a collection of predefined flexible summary patterns (based for instance on the genre of the novel, or on some data on the main characters of the novel, a time and place positioning, and a rather shallow sketch of the initiation of the action) could be applied.

Our approach to summary building uses the first method, sentence extraction. However, the novelty of our approach consists in basing the extraction of different sentences from the original text on semantic role analysis, an association which is not yet explored at its full potential. The method is language independent, provided that named entity and semantic roles extraction modules are available.

The next Section introduces the sentence extraction phase of the summary generation using semantic roles. Section 3 presents the named entity recognition system use to identify entities in the initial text, while Section 4 presents the semantic role labeling procedure. The last section presents preliminary results obtained on 20 summaries, and discusses further development of the system.

2 Generating Summaries based on Semantic Roles

The natural language processing community has recently experienced a growth of interest in semantic roles, since they describe WHO did WHAT to WHOM, WHEN, WHERE, WHY, HOW etc. for a given situation, and contribute to the construction of meaning. If for text analysis, semantic roles have gained their way into natural language analysis systems (see for instance Lluis et al., 2008; Surdeanu et al., 2003), they are rarely used at their full potential for text generation.

Christopherson (1981) was among the first to investigate the usefulness of semantic roles in summaries. More recently, Suanmali et al. (2010) used semantic roles and WordNet (Fellbaum, 1998) to compute the semantic similarity of two sentences in order to decide if the sentences are to be kept or not in the summary. The proposed method is a further step in this direction, combining semantic roles and named entity for sentence extraction.

The overall pipeline architecture of the proposed method is presented in Figure 1.

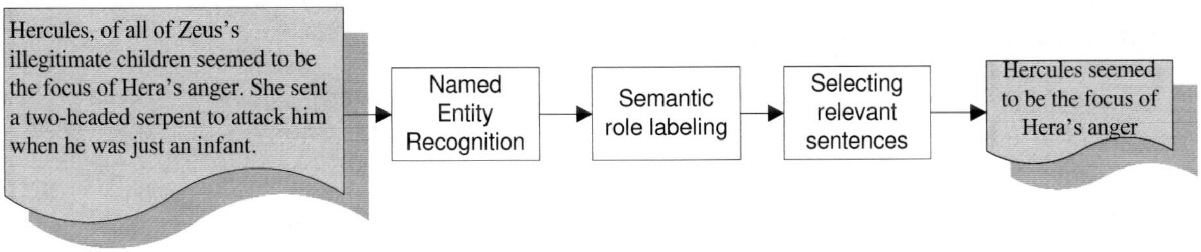

Figure 1. Overall architecture of the proposed summary generation method based on semantic roles

The method presented in this paper works in three steps: first, the original text is parsed for named entities; secondly, semantic roles are extracted from the sentences containing named entities; thirdly, sentences are selected to be kept in the summary, based on the semantic role the named entity has. Each module is detailed in the Sections below.

2.1 Identifying entities

In order to identify the semantic role a specific entity express, the entity must be first identified in the text. This is the task of named entity recognition (NER). NER systems typically use linguistic grammar-based techniques or statistical models (an overview is presented in (Nadeau and Satoshi Sekine. 2007)). Hand-crafted grammar-based systems typically obtain better precision, but at the cost of lower recall and months of work by experienced computational linguists. Besides, they are hard to adapt to new domains. Statistical NER systems typically require a large amount of manually annotated training data. Machine learning techniques, such as the ones discussed in (Scurtu et al., 2009) or (Nadeanu, 2007), allow systems to be adapted to new domains and perform very well for coarse-grained classification, but require large training data.

Thus, as a preprocessing module for our summary generation system, we used a Named Entity Recognition component for Romanian, based on linguistic grammar-based techniques and a set of resources. The NER system is based on two modules, the named entity identification module and the named entity classification module. After the named entity (NE) candidates are marked for each input text, each candidate is classified into one of the considered categories, such as Person, Organization, Place, Country, etc.

The major drawback of the sentence extraction approach for summaries generation is that it ignores the referential expressions that could occur in the initial text and should have been kept in the summary. Thus, due to the elimination of previous sentences, their antecedents may not be present anymore, resulting in incomprehensive readings. For example, consider the following text to be summarized:

Hercules, of all of Zeus's illegitimate children seemed to be the focus of Hera's anger. She sent a two-headed serpent to attack him when he was just an infant.

The summary of this very short fragment, using the sentence elimination method, could (hypothetically) be:

She sent a two-headed serpent to attack him.

which is really incomprehensible if no explanation is provided of who is "*she*" or "him".

One way to increase the coherence of such summaries is to derive first the discourse structure of the text and to guide the selection of the sentences to be included into the summary by a score that considers both the relevance of the sentence in a discourse tree and the coherence of the text[1], as given by solving anaphoric references. For the summary example above, solving anaphoric references means identifying "`she`" as `Hera` and "`him`" as `Hercules`. Thus, the provided summary becomes readable:

`Hera sent a two-headed serpent to attack Hercules.`

Therefore, after identifying named entities and their types (person, organization, place, etc.), a simple anaphora resolution method, based on a set of reference rules, is applied to our input text, in order to link all entities to their referees.

The anaphoric system we used is a basic rule-based one, focusing on named entity anaphoric relations. Thus, we developed a rule-based system that performs the following actions:

- identifies a subset of a named entity with the full named entity, if it appears as such in the same text. For instance, *Caesar* is identified with *Julius Caesar* if both entities appear in the same text. Similarly, the *President of Romania* and the *President* are considered anaphoric relations of the same entity, if they appear in a narrow word window in the text.
- solves acronyms using a gazetteer we have initially built over the Internet, and which is continuously growing in size. For instance, *United States of America* and *USA* are co-references.
- searches for different addressing modalities and matches the ones that are similar. For instance, *John Smith* is co-referenced with *Mr. Smith*, and *Mary and John Smith* is co-referenced with *The Smiths*, or *The Smith Family*.
- solve pronominal anaphora in a simplistic way. Thus, if a pronoun (i.e. *she, he, him, his* etc.) is found in the text, and in the preceding sentence a named entity with the entity type person is found, then we create an anaphoric link between the pronoun and its antecedent. A similar rule exists for companies, where the pronoun *it* may be linked to *the Insurance Company*, for instance. Lists stating these correspondences are presently used and, although the rules are limited so far, our tests show that the overall accuracy of the summarization system benefits from this simple anaphoric resolution system for named entities.

The next step is the identification of the semantic roles that each named entity plays.

[1] A detailed analysis of the coherence of different texts is presented in (Cristea and Iftene, 2011).

2.2 Identifying semantic roles

Fillmore in (Fillmore, 1968) defined six semantic roles: *Agent*, *Instrument*, *Dative*, *Factive*, *Object* and *Location*, also called *deep cases*. His later work on lexical semantics led to the conviction that a small fixed set of deep case roles was not sufficient to characterize the combinatorial properties of lexical items, therefore he added *Experiencer*, *Comitative*, *Location*, *Path*, *Source*, *Goal* and *Temporal*, and then other cases. This ultimately led to the theory of Frame Semantics (Fillmore, 1982), which later evolved into the FrameNet project[2].

In the last decades, hand-tagged corpora that encode such information for the English language were developed (VerbNet[3](Levin and Rappaport, 2005), FrameNet (Baker et al., 1998) and PropBank [4] (Palmer et al., 2005)). For other languages, such as German, Spanish, and Japanese, semantic roles resources are being developed. For Romanian, Trandabăț and Husarciuc (2008) have started to automatically build such a resource.

For role semantics to become relevant for language technology, robust and accurate methods for automatic semantic role assignment are needed. With the SensEval-3 competition[5] and the CONLL Shared Tasks[6], Automatic Labeling of Semantic Roles, identifying frame elements within a sentence and tag them with appropriate semantic roles given a sentence (Lluis et al., 2008), has become increasingly present among researchers worldwide. In recent years, a number of studies, such as (Chen and Rambow, 2003) and (Gildea and Jurafsky, 2002), has investigated this task on the FrameNet corpus. Role assignment has generally been modeled as a classification task. While using different statistical frameworks, most studies have largely converged on a common set of features to base their decisions on, namely syntactic information (path from predicate to constituent, phrasal type of constituent) and lexical

[2] FrameNet web page: http://framenet.icsi.berkeley.edu/
[3] VerbNet web page: http://verbs.colorado.edu/~mpalmer/projects/verbnet/downloads.html
[4] PropBank web page: http://verbs.colorado.edu/~mpalmer/projects/ace.html
[5] SemEval web address: http://www.senseval.org/
[6] ConLL web address: http://ifarm.nl/signll/conll/

information (head word of the constituent, predicate).

Semantic roles are classified in terms of how central they are to a particular verb. **Arguments** (or core semantic roles) instantiate required roles, which are in a close relation to the verb whose sense they complete, and **adjuncts** (or non-core semantic roles), which are more general roles that can apply to any verb.

Adjuncts represent circumstantial objects and can be of the following types: directions, locatives, temporal, manner, extent, reciprocals, secondary predication, purpose, cause, discourse, adverbials, modals, negation. For instance, temporal and locative adjuncts can be found in both sentences below:

John broke the window [at the school]$_{LOC}$ [yesterday]$_{TMP}$.

John visited his kids [at the school]$_{LOC}$ [yesterday]$_{TMP}$.

An important drawback in this domain is that most researches focus on text analysis, and text generation applications using semantic roles are not so well developed. In this context, using the semantic role labeling system presented in (Trandabat, 2010), we annotated the sentences containing entities from the input text with the semantic roles these entities play, and passed to the third step.

The semantic role system we used for Romanian was obtained by training 12 machine translation algorithms (see Trandabat, 2010) from the Weka framework (Hall et al., 2009) with different feature sets. After running all the classifiers for different modules (the module that separately identifies the semantic roles and classify them, or the module that jointly identifies semantic roles and classify them), their performance is compared, and the module that obtains the highest performance is considered the best configuration. The models for this best configuration are saved, and the best path is written to a configuration file. This configuration can then be used at a later time to annotate new texts with the developed SRL system.

The 10 fold cross-validation results of all classifiers are also saved since they provide a confusion matrix that can be used to see which classes were correctly predicted by different classifiers. The output of the system presented in (Trandabat, 2010) is a Semantic Role Labeling System, a sequence of trained models which can be used to annotate new texts..

2.3 Selecting relevant sentences

The third module of the summary generation system implies selecting, among the list of sentences from which summaries can be generated, the ones in which the entity has core semantic roles. The proposed method involves four main steps:

- Identifying the main character
- Extract sentences containing the main character
- Keep sentences with core roles for the specific character.
- Simplify sentences

There are two possible ways of *identifying the main character*: the easiest one is when the central character of the text is a-priori given as argument (in case a character-oriented summary is requested). Otherwise, the main character is considered to be the named entity having the higher number of occurrences in the text (including references, see Section 2.1). For the example below, the main character is considered to be Alcmene, with 9 occurrences.

Hercules was the son of Zeus and Alcmene. Alcmene's husband Amphiteryon was out avenging her brother's death at the hands of pirates. Zeus, disguised as Amphiteryon, came to her and told her stories of how he killed the pirates to avenge her brother's death. That night Zeus went to bed with Alcmene and impregnated her. The next day the real Amphiteryon returned with his stories of avenging the pirates, and he could not understand why his wife was irritated with him and seemed disinterested in the stories. It was then that Amphiteryon consulted a blind seer and became aware of what Zeus did.

For the *extraction of the sentences containing the main character*, both the entity as if, and its references, are considered. For the example above, the last sentence is kept out, as not containing the character or a reference to it.

The distinction between the situations when the *main character has core and non-core semantic roles* (or adjuncts vs. arguments) represents the backbone of our system. Thus, when the entity considered for the summary has a semantic role that is mandatory for a sentence meaning (it is a core semantic role, such as an *Agent*), the sentence containing it is kept. In contrast, if a sentence contains the entity in a non-core position (expressing temporal, spatial, modal, etc. circumstances), then its meaning is not essential for the summary, and the sentence containing the entity will be discarded from the summary. As an example, in the sentence below, Alcmene (refered as *his wife*) is only part of a non-core semantic role (Content for the verb *understand*), so this sentence will be discarded and not kept for the final summary:

`The next day the real Amphiteryon returned with his stories of avenging the pirates, and [he]Cognizer [could not understand]TARGET [why his wife was irritated with him and seemed disinterested in the stories]Content.`

The last step involved a *simplification of the sentences*. This simplification is based on a set of heuristics using semantic roles. Thus, in a sentence, not only one verb requiring semantic roles may appear. In order to simplify these complex sentences, we only keep the predicate[7] for which the entity is a semantic role. To give an example, consider the sentence below:

[Alcmene's]$_{Partner1}$ [husband]$_{TARGET}$ [Amphiteryon]$_{Partner2}$ was out avenging her brother's death at the hands of pirates.

In this case, two predicates are annotated with semantic roles: *husband* as a relationship predicate (according to FrameNet), and *avenging* as an activity predicate. Simplifying this sentence means keeping only the semantic roles for the first predicate (husband), for which the main character plays a semantic role, i.e. keeping only "Alcmene's husband, Amphiteryon was out".

3 Discussion and Further Work

In this paper, we presented a summary generation system based on semantic roles. The main components of the system are dedicated to identifying named entities, marking semantic roles, and selecting the sentences of the text to be kept in the summary.

[7] In general, predicates are associated with verbs. However, semantic roles theories have recently accepted the existence of predicate-like nouns and adjectives, which can gather around them semantic roles, just like verbs do.

We evaluated the method on 20 summaries extracted from the *Legend of the Olympus* novel. In a first batch, 5 volunteers received full version of the 20 texts, and were asked to generate short summaries (about 10% of the size if the full text). A second batch of 5 volunteers received the initial text marked with semantic roles, and were instructed to create short summaries (the same 10%) using the semantic role information. Although the evaluation was only intended to give a feedback on the method, and a proper evaluation is still to be developed, the volunteers reported that knowing the semantic roles of entities and guiding the summary on it makes the summary generation task easier.

Acknowledgments

The research presented in this paper was funded by the Sectoral Operational Programme for Human Resources Development through the project "Development of the innovation capacity and increasing of the research impact through post-doctoral programs" POSDRU/89/1.5/S/49944.

References

Baker G., Collin F., Fillmore, Charles J., and Lowe, John B. 1998. *The Berkeley FrameNet project*. In Proceedings of the COLING-ACL, Montreal, Canada. 1998

Chen J. and O. Rambow. 2003. Use of deep linguistic features for the recognition and labeling of semantic arguments. In Proceedings of the 2003 Conference on Empirical Methods in Natural Language Processing, 2003.

Christopherson, Steven L . 1981. *Effects of knowledge of semantic roles on summarizing written prose*. Contemporary Educational Psychology, Vol 6(1), Jan 1981, 59-65

Cristea and Iftene. 2011. If you want your talk be fluent, think lazy! Grounding coherence properties of discourse. Invited talk at SPED-2011, University of Brasov, May

Fillmore Charles J. 1968. The case for case. In Bach and Harms, editors, Universals in Linguistic Theory, pages 1-88. Holt, Rinehart, and Winston, New York, 1968.

Fillmore Charles J. 1982. *Frame semantics*, în Linguistics in the Morning Calm, Hanshin Publishing, Seoul , 1982, 111-137.

Gildea Daniel and Daniel Jurafsky. 2002. Automatic labeling of semantic roles. *Computational Linguistics*, 28(3):245-288, 2002

Hall, Mark, Eibe Frank, Geoffrey Holmes, Bernhard Pfahringer, Peter Reutemann, Ian H. Witten (2009); *The WEKA Data Mining Software: An Update*; SIGKDD Explorations, Volume 11, Issue 1

Levin B. and M. Rappaport Hovav. 2005. Argument Realization. Research Surveys in Linguistics Series. Cambridge University Press, Cambridge, UK, 2005.

Mani Inderjeet, automatic summarization, John Benjamins Pub Co; ISBN: 1588110591 (hardcover), 1588110605 (paperback), 2001.

Marquez Lluis, Xavier Carreras, Kenneth C. Litkowski, and Suzanne Stevenson. 2008. Semantic role labeling: An introduction to the Special Issue. *Computational Linguistics*, 34(2):145-159, 2008.

David Nadeau and Satoshi Sekine. 2007. *A survey of named entity recognition and classification*, Linguisticae Investigationes 30, no. 1, 3{26, Publisher: John Benjamin's Publishing Company

David Nadeau. 2007. *Semi-supervised named entity recognition: Learning to recognize 100 entity types with little supervision*, PhD Thesis.

Palmer Martha, Daniel Gildea, and Paul Kingsbury. 2005. The proposition bank: An annotated corpus of semantic roles. *Computational Linguistics*, 31(1):71-106, 2005.

Scurtu V., Stepanov E., Mehdad, Y. 2009. *Italian named entity recognizer participation in NER task@evalita 09*, 2009.

Suanmali, L., Salim, N. and Binwahlan, M. S.. 2010. SRL-GSM : *A Hybrid Approach based on Semantic Role Labeling and General Statistic Method for Text Summarization*. Journal of Applied Sciences 10(3) : 166-173

Trandabăţ D. 2010. *Natural Language Processing Using Semantic Frames*, PhD Thesis, University Al. I. Cuza Iasi, Romania

Trandabat Diana and Maria Husarciuc. 2008. *Romanian semantic role resource*. In Proceedings of the Sixth International Language Resources and Evaluation (LREC'08), Marrakech, Morocco, may 2008.

Building a Generator for Italian Sign Language

Alessandro Mazzei
Dipartimento di Informatica
Università degli Studi di Torino
Corso Svizzra 185, 10153
Torino, Italy
mazzei@di.unito.it

Abstract

This paper presents an ongoing work about the implementation of a CCG grammar for Italian Sign Language. This grammar is part of a generation system used for Italian-LIS translation.

1 Introduction

Italian Sign Language (Lingua Italiana dei Segni, henceforth LIS) is the sign language used by the Italian deaf (signing) community. LIS is a natural language that has a specific lexicon, morphology and syntax (Volterra, 2004). In the last years the computational linguistic community showed a growing interest toward sign languages (SLs), and a number of projects concerning the translation into a SL have recently started. Some of these projects adopt statistical techniques based on developing parallel corpora: English to Irish SL (Morrissey et al., 2007), Chinese to Chinese SL (Su and Wu, 2009). Some other projects adopt symbolic techniques: English to British SL (Bangham et al., 2000), English to American SL (Zhao et al., 2000; Huenerfauth, 2006). Recently a new project started for automatic translation from Italian to LIS: in this paper we present some features of the generation module adopted for the interlingua translation in this project.

The challenge of Italian-LIS translation depends on the complexity of the translation task as well as on the peculiar features of the LIS. Sign languages mix standard linguistics of vocal languages with a number of typical phenomena. Among others: there is a "spatial organization" of the sentence that interacts with the word order to determine syntactic/semantic dependencies and plays a role in the coordination; the presence of many articulators (two hands, eyebrow, eye gaze, torso etc.) allows for some form of parallelism; there are no prepositions, articles; finally, LIS is a poorly studied language and linguists often do not agree on basic linguistic properties (e.g. sentence word order). In order to reduce the difficulties of our ambitious project we concentrate on a specific application domain, i.e. weather forecasts. As starting point, the project is producing a parallel corpus of Italian-LIS sentence extracted from TV news and concerning weather forecasts.

Our interlingua[1] translation system has four distinct modules, that are: (1) a dependency parser for Italian; (2) an ontology based semantic interpreter; (3) a grammar based generator; (4) a virtual actor that performs the synthesis of the final LIS sentence. Here we give some details about the parser and the semantic interpreter, in the Section 2 we describe the generator.

In the first step, the syntactic structure of the source language is produced by the TUP parser (Lesmo, 2007). It uses a morphological dictionary of Italian (about $25,000$ lemmata) and a rule-based grammar. The final result is a *dependency tree*, that makes clear the structural syntactic relationships occurring between the words of the sentence (Hudson, 1984). Each word in the source sentence is associated with a node of the tree, and the nodes are linked via labeled arcs that specify the

[1] Our system can be defines as a knowledge based restricted interlingua, since it uses extra-linguistic information and deals with just two languages (Hutchins and Somer, 1992)

Proceedings of the 13th European Workshop on Natural Language Generation (ENLG), pages 170–175,
Nancy, France, September 2011.

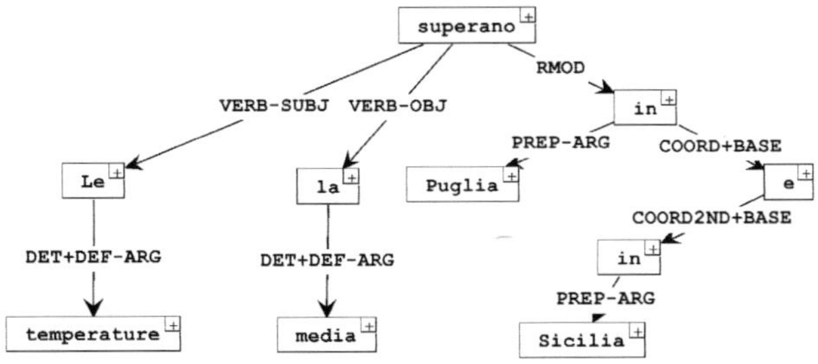

Figure 1: The syntactic structure of the sentence "Le temperature superano la media in Puglia e in Sicilia" (*The temperature exceeds the average in Puglia and Sicilia*).

onto(l_1:*meteo-status*,**exceed**)	event(e_0,l_1)
onto(l_2:*eva-entity*,**temperature**)	agent(l_1,l_2)
onto(l_3:*eva-entity*,**average**)	theme(l_1,l_3)
onto(l_4:*geo-area*,**Puglia**)	location(l_1,l_4)
onto(l_5:*geo-area*,**Sicilia**)	set(l_4,l_5)

Figure 2: The semantic interpretation of the sentence "Le temperature superano la media in Puglia e in Sicilia" given in terms of FoL predicates.

syntactic role of the dependents with respect to their head (the parent node). Consider the dependency tree n Fig. 1: *temperatura* (temperature) is the subject of the verb *superare* (exceed), while *media* (average) is the object; the coordinated words *Puglia* and *Sicilia* are modifiers of the verb.

The second step of the translation is the semantic interpretation: the syntax-semantics interface used in the interpretation is based on ontologies (Lesmo et al., 2011a; Nirenburg and Raskin, 2004). The knowledge in the ontology concerns the application domain, i.e. weather forecasts, as well as more general common knowledge about the world. Starting from the lexical semantics of the words in the sentence and on the basis of the dependency structure, a recursive function searches in the ontology providing a number of "connection paths" that represent the meaning of the sentence. Indeed, the final sentence meaning consists of a complex fragment of the ontology: semantic roles and other kind of semantic relations are contained in this fragment and could be extracted by translating it into First Order Logic (FoL) predicates. However, similar to other approaches (among others (Bunt et al., 2007)), our ontological meaning representation is unscoped. In Fig. 2 we report the semantic interpretation of the sentence "Le temperature superano la media in Puglia e in Sicilia" in terms of FoL predicates. The predicate onto expresses the lexical meaning of the words by using the ontology concepts: it assigns the concept instances exceed, temperature, average, Puglia, Sicilia to the FoL variables l1, l2, l3, l4, l5 respectively. Moreover, onto explicitly denotes the classes which these instances belong to: *meteo-status* is the ontological class of the events regarding the meteo; *geo-area* is the ontological class of the geographical areas; *eva-entity* is the ontological class of the evaluable entities. The predicates event, agent, theme, location express the semantics of the event in terms of predicate-arguments by using semantic roles (we adopt the set of semantic roles defined in the LIRICS project (Petukhova and Bunt, 2008)). Finally, the predicate set expresses a semantic relation that groups entities: this predicate allows to specify the cumulative reading, w.r.t. the distributive reading corresponding to have two not related locations.

2 A generator for LIS

Natural language generation can be described as a three steps process: text planning, sentence planning and realization (Reiterand and Dale, 2000). Text planning determines which messages to communicate and how to rhetorically structure these messages; sentence planning converts the text plan into a number of sentence plans; realization converts the sentence plans into the final sentences produced. Anyway, in the context of interlingua translation we simplify by assuming that generation needs only for the realization step. Our working hypothesis is that source and target sentences have as much as possible the same text and the same sentence plans. This hypothesis is reasonable in our projects since we are working on a very peculiar sub-language (weather forecasts) where the rhetorical structure is usually very simple.

In our architecture we use the OpenCCG realizer (White, 2006), an open source tool that has several appealing features with respect to our approach. OpenCCG is based on combinatory categorial grammars (CCG) (Steedman, 2000), a mildly context-sensitive formalism that is theoretically adequate to describe the complexity of natural language syntax (e.g. cross-serial dependencies, non-constituency coordination) and it has a very straight syntax-semantic interface. Moreover, OpenCCG adheres to the *bidirectional grammar* approach, i.e. there is one grammar for both realisation and parsing. It means that derivation and generation have the same structure and that we can develop a grammar by testing its correctness in realization in terms of parsing: as a result, we obtain a speed-up in the process of grammar development (White et al., 2010). Realization usually accounts for a standard number of morpho-syntactic phenomena, that are *inflection*, *agreement*, *word order*, *function words*. LIS has few function words but, similar to all SLs, it has a peculiar and rich system of inflection and agreement. OpenCCG allows to encode an inflectional system by using feature structures, which are part of the syntactic categories. The integration in one single elementary structure of the morphology-syntax-semantic information is appealing for sign languages where the absence of function words increases the importance of morpho-syntactic features to express the correct meaning of the sentence. Now we first give some specifications about the input/output of the generator (Section 2.1) and secondly we describe the treatment of some linguistic constructions by using a fragment of the CCG for LIS (Section 2.2).

2.1 Input and output

@l_1:*meteo-status* **exceed**	
@l_2:*eva-entity* **temperature**	@l_1 <agent> l_2
@l_3:*eva-entity* **average**	@l_1 <theme> l_3
@l_4:*geo-area* **Puglia**	@l_1 <location> l_4
@l_5:*geo-area* **Sicilia**	@l_4 <set> l_5

Figure 3: The semantic interpretation of the sentence "Le temperature superano la media in Puglia e in Sicilia" given in terms Hybrid logic predicates.

The input of the generator, that is the output of the semantic interpreter, are FoL predicates expressing a number of distinct semantic relations. Semantic situation type (e.g. event, state), semantic roles (e.g. agent, location), grouping relations (e.g. set, sequence), general semantic properties (as tense or plurality) can be produced by the semantic interpreter: we assume that at least semantic roles and grouping relations are explicitly expressed, as the interpretation in the Fig. 2. OpenCCG requires semantic interpretation in form of *hybrid logic* formulas, a kind of propositional modal logic that can be used to represent relational structures (Blackburn, 2000). Since hybrid logic is equivalent to a fragment of FOL, we could rewrite FoL predicates in terms of hybrid logic: (1) by identifying first order variables with *nominal* (a new sort of primitive logic elements which explicitly name the nodes of the relational structure); (2) by identifying first order predicate (of arity two) with *modality label* of hybrid logic (Brauner, 2008). Applying this algorithm to the FoL predicates in Fig. 2 we obtain the representation in Fig. 3.

Note that we assume a logical interpretation that does not adhere to the *linguistic meaning* notion that is usually adopted in OpenCCG, i.e. *Hybrid Logic Dependency Semantics* (HLDS) (Baldridge and Kruijff, 2002). HLDS defines semantic relations only between words, disallowing the definition of nominals that do not have a lexical predication (White, 2006). In contrast, our interpretation function produces a number of non-lexicalized structures for specific semantic constructions. One example is the interpretation of the ordinal numbers: the interpretation of "ultimo giorno del mese" (*last day of the month*) is $@X_0(\langle \mathsf{ODI}\rangle X_1 \wedge \langle \mathsf{ODRS}\rangle X_2 \wedge \langle \mathsf{ODS}\rangle X_3) \wedge @X_1\mathbf{day} \wedge @X_2\mathbf{month} \wedge @X_3\mathbf{last}$ (Lesmo et al., 2011b). In this hybrid formula, $\langle \mathsf{ODI}\rangle\langle \mathsf{ODRS}\rangle\langle \mathsf{ODS}\rangle$ are modalities which indicate specific semantic relations[2] and $X_0X_1X_2X_3$ are nominals: in this specific case X_0 does not have a lexical predicate.

A challenging requirement of our project is related to the target language: LIS, as all signed languages, does not have a *natural* written form. As a consequence we developed an *artificial* written form for LIS in order to "communicate" the output of the generator to the virtual interpreter. This written form encodes the main morphological features of the signs as well as a number of non-manual fea-

[2] $\langle$ODI$\rangle$ = Ordinal Description Iterator; $\langle$ODRS$\rangle$ = Ordinal Description Reference Sequence; $\langle$ODS$\rangle$ = Ordinal Description Selector.

Lexical Categories			
LEX	**PoS**	**SynCAT**	**SemCAT**
L_2_SUPERIORE_R_2	Verb	S [Y_0 ap=R_2] \ NP [Y_1 ap=R_2] \ NP [Y_2 ap=L_2]	@Y_0:*meteo-status* **(exceed** ^ <agent>Y_1:*eva-entity* ^ <theme>Y_2:*eva-entity*)
SICILIA_R_1	Noun	NP [X_0 ap=R_1]	@X_0:*geo-area* **Sicilia**
PUGLIA_R_3	Noun	NP [X_1 ap=R_3]	@X_1:*geo-area* **Puglia**
TEMPERATURA_R_2	Noun	NP [X_2 ap=R_2]	@X_2:*eva-entity* **temperature**
MEDIA_L_2	Noun	NP [X_3 ap=L_2]	@X_3:*eva-entity* **average**

Type Changing Rules				
SynCAT	**SemCAT**		**SynCAT**	**SemCAT**
NP [Y_0 ap]	@Y_0:*geo-area*	$\longrightarrow$	S [X_0] / S [X_0 ap]	@X_0:*meteo-status* <loc> Y_0:*geo-area*
NP [Y_0 ap=R_1]	@Y_0:*geo-area*	$\longrightarrow$	NP [X_0 ap=R_2] \ NP [X_0 ap=R_3]	@X_0:*geo-area* <set> Y_0:*geo-area*

Table 1: A fragment of the CCG for LIS: the articulatory position feature (**ap**) encodes the spatial location.

tures, as the gaze or the tilt of the head (Zhao et al., 2000). For sake of clarity we write a LIS sentence just as a sequence of *glosses*, that is the sequence of the names of the signs without representing any non-manual information. The only feature that we explicitly represent is the *spatial position* of the sign. In this paper we consider just the horizontal dimension in the signing space: we assume a discrete space of seven positions L_1 (the leftmost position), L_2, L_3, N (the neutral position), R_3, R_2, R_1 (the rightmost position).

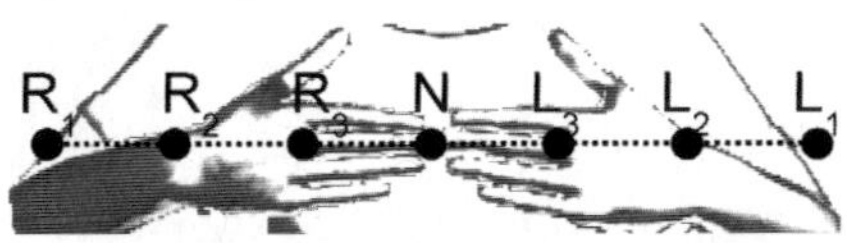

For signs that have just one articulatory position, we use the prefix L_i (R_j) in the gloss to indicate that a sign is performed on the left (and on the right) of the signer. For signs that have two articulatory positions (starting and ending position), we use the prefix L_i (R_j) in the gloss to indicate that a sign starts on the left (on the right) of the signer and the suffix L_l (R_m) in the gloss to indicate that a sign is performed on the left (and on the right) of the signer.[3]

2.2 A CCG for LIS

In Tab. 1 we present the fragment of the hand-written CCG: the grammar is organized in *Lexical Categories* and Type-changing rules. Each Lexical Category has four fields: **LEX**, that contains the lexical form of the item; **PoS**, that contains the part of speech category; **SynCAT**, that contains the syntactic category; **SemCAT**, that contains the semantic category. Note that SynCAT e SemCAT are related by using *semantic variables* (X_i and Y_j in Tab. 1): these variables appear in the syntactic categories, but are used as pointers to the semantic categories (Baldridge and Kruijff, 2002; White, 2006). Some Lexical Categories which have specific SynCAT-SemCAT values can change these values by using the type-changing rules.

The CCG accounts for two specific morpho-syntactic phenomena: (i) spatial agreement between verb and its arguments and (ii) NP-coordination. Similar to American SL in LIS we can tell a number of verb classes on the basis of spatial accord (Volterra, 2004; Wright, 2008). For instance the verb L_i_SUPERIORE_R_j (*exceed*) belongs to the class II-A, i.e. it is a transitive verb such that the

[3]As it is customary in the sign languages literature, we use names in uppercase for the signs that are related to their rough translation into another language, Italian in our work.

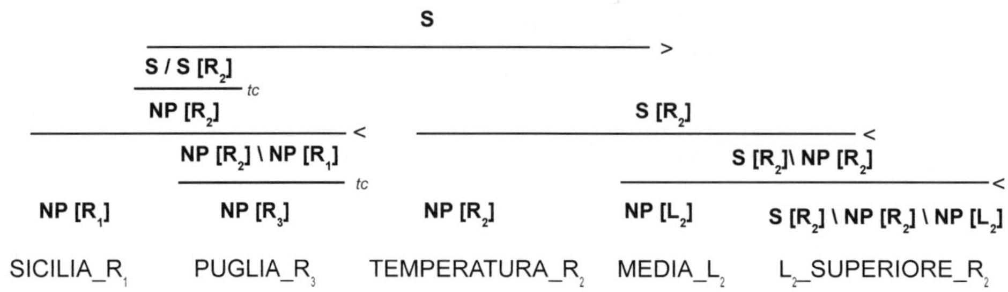

Figure 4: The realization/derivation of the LIS sentence "SICILIA_R$_1$ PUGLIA_R$_3$ TEMPERATURA_R$_2$ MEDIA_L$_2$ L$_2$_SUPERIORE_R$_2$" (for space reasons we do not show the semantics of the derivation).

starting position of the sign (L$_i$) coincides with the position of the agent, as well as the ending position of the sign (R$_j$) coincides with the position of the theme (or patient) (Volterra, 2004). Similar to (Wright, 2008), we model this feature in CCG by using a morphological feature called ap (articulatory position). The ap feature encodes the position of the noun in the atomic category NP, as well as the starting and ending position of a verb in the complex category $S\backslash NP\backslash NP$. NP coordination in LIS is realized in two distinct ways, i.e. (1.) by signing the NP in one single position but separating them by a *pause* and (2.) by signing the first NP into a particular position and signing the second NP in a distinct but related position: in our grammar we developed only the second option. Our CCG analysis of NP-coordination uses unary type-change operation and, in contrast to (Wright, 2008), does not assume a specific lexical unit that expresses coordination: Wright models the hand movement as a lexical unit (the "shift") that contains the category $NP\backslash NP/NP$. In contrast, we give a lexical value to the feature ap: similar to the CCG analysis of case-based language (e.g. Japanese, (Steedman, 2000)), we consider the position as a specific case. In particular, we suppose that the type-change operation is possible just with some specific ap values, obtaining a complex category for the second NP in the coordination.

In Fig. 4 we report the realization (coinciding with the derivation) of the LIS sentence "SICILIA_R$_1$ PUGLIA_R$_3$ TEMPERATURA_R$_2$ MEDIA_L$_2$ L$_2$_SUPERIORE_R$_2$" based on the lexicon in Tab. 1, that is the LIS translation of the Italian sentence "Le temperature superano la media in Puglia e in Sicilia". In accord to (Geraci, 2004) and in contrast with (Volterra, 2004) we assume that LIS respects the SOV order. In the generation, the unification mechanism on the feature *ap* constraints the NP arguments to accord with the starting and ending position of the verb: the agent TEMPERATURA is signed in the position R$_2$, that corresponds to the starting position of the verb SUPERIORE, while the theme MEDIA is signed in the position L$_2$, that correspond to the ending position of the verb. This mechanism avoids the generation of ungrammatical derivations as "TEMPERATURA_R$_1$ MEDIA_L$_2$ L$_2$_SUPERIORE_R$_2$", in which the positions of TEMPERATURA and SUPERIORE do not agree. Finally note that in the generation we have two type-change operations. The first one is used to account for NP coordination, as explained above. The second type-change is used to transform the NP into the complex sentence modification category S/S, since LIS does not have prepositions. Note that in order to limit over-generation we constrain both type-changes by using the semantics of the lexical category by requiring that the semantic ontological type of the lexical category is a *geo-area*, i.e. a geographic area.

3 Conclusion and ongoing work

In this paper we presented the main features of a generator for LIS. The generator is based on the OpenCCG tool and relies on a hand encoded CCG grammar to account for a number of peculiar linguistic phenomena of Sign Languages. Many improvements are necessary in order to encode further syntactic phenomena and to take account for a realistic large lexicon. In our opinion a crucial point is the encoding of topic-comment relations, that seem to have an important role in the word order of the LIS sentence.

Acknowledgments

This work has been partially supported by the ATLAS project, that is co-funded by Regione Piemonte within the "Converging Technologies - CIPE 2007" framework (Research Sector: Cognitive Science and ICT).

References

J. Baldridge and G.-J. Kruijff. 2002. Coupling ccg and hybrid logic dependency semantics. In *ACL '02*, pages 319–326, Morristown, NJ, USA. ACL.

J. Bangham, S. Cox, R. Elliott, J. Glauert, and I. Marshall. 2000. Virtual signing: Capture, animation, storage and transmission – an overview of the VisiCAST project. In. In *IEE Seminar on Speech and Language*.

P. Blackburn. 2000. Representation, reasoning, and relational structures: a hybrid logic manifesto. *Logic Journal of the IGPL*, 8(3):339–625.

T. Brauner. 2008. Hybrid logic. http://plato.stanford.edu/entries/logic-hybrid/.

H. Bunt, R. Muskensand M. Dzikovska, M. Swift, and J. Allen, 2007. *Customizing Meaning: Building Domain-Specific Semantic Representations From A Generic Lexicon*, volume 83, pages 213–231. Springer.

C. Geraci. 2004. L'ordine delle parole nella LIS (lingua dei segni italiana). In *Convegno nazionale della Società di Linguistica Italiana*.

R. Hudson. 1984. *Word Grammar*. Basil Blackwell, Oxford and New York.

M. Huenerfauth. 2006. *Generating American Sign Language classifier predicates for english-to-asl machine translation*. Ph.D. thesis, University of Pennsylvania.

W.John Hutchins and Harold L. Somer. 1992. *An Introduction to Machine Translation*. London: Academic Press.

L. Lesmo, A. Mazzei, and D. P. Radicioni. 2011a. An ontology based architecture for translation. In *Proceedings of the Ninth International Conference on Computational Semantics (IWCS 2011)*, The University of Oxford.

L. Lesmo, A. Mazzei, and D. P. Radicioni. 2011b. Ontology based interlingua translation. In *CICLing (2)'11*, pages 1–12.

L. Lesmo. 2007. The Rule-Based Parser of the NLP Group of the University of Torino. *Intelligenza Artificiale*, 2(4):46–47, June.

S. Morrissey, A. Way, D. Stein, J. Bungeroth, and H. Ney. 2007. Combining data-driven mt systems for improved sign language translation. In *Proc. Machine Translation Summit XI (MT'07)*.

Sergei Nirenburg and Victor Raskin. 2004. *Ontological Semantics (Language, Speech, and Communication)*. The MIT Press, September.

V. Petukhova and H. Bunt. 2008. Lirics semantic role annotation: Design and evaluation of a set of data categories. In *Proc. LREC'08*.

E. Reiterand and R. Dale. 2000. *Building natural language generation systems*. Cambridge University Press.

Mark Steedman. 2000. *The syntactic process*. MIT Press, Cambridge, MA, USA.

H . Su and C. Wu. 2009. Improving structural statistical machine translation for sign language with small corpus using thematic role templates as translation memory. In *IEEE Transactions on Audio, Speech and Language Processing, 17 (7), 1305-1315*.

Virginia Volterra, editor. 2004. *La lingua dei segni italiana*. Il Mulino.

M. White, R. A. J. Clark, and J. D. Moore. 2010. Generating Tailored, Comparative Descriptions with Contextually Appropriate Intonation. *Computational Linguistics*, 36(2):159–201.

M. White. 2006. Efficient realization of coordinate structures in combinatory categorial grammar. *Research on Language and Computation*, 2006(4(1)):39—75.

T. Wright. 2008. A combinatory categorial grammar of a fragment of american sign language. In *Proc. of the Texas Linguistics Society X Conference*. CSLI Publications.

L. Zhao, K. Kipper, W. Shuler, C. Vogler, N. Badler, and M. Palmer. 2000. A machine translation system from english to american sign language. *Association for Machine Translation in the Americas*.

Investigation into Human Preference between Common and Unambiguous Lexical Substitutions

Andrew Walker
University of Aberdeen
Department of
Computing Science
r05aw0@abdn.ac.uk

Advaith Siddharthan
University of Aberdeen
Department of
Computing Science
advaith@abdn.ac.uk

Andrew Starkey
University of Aberdeen
School of Engineering
and Physical Sciences
a.starkey@abdn.ac.uk

Abstract

We present a study that investigates that factors that determine what makes a good lexical substitution. We begin by observing that there is a correlation between the corpus frequency of words and the number of WordNet senses they have, and hypothesise that readers might prefer common, but more ambiguous words over less ambiguous but also less common ones. We identify four properties of a word that determine whether it is a suitable substitution in a given context, and ask volunteers to rank their preferences between two common but ambiguous lexical substitutions, and two uncommon but also unambiguous ones. Preliminary results suggest a slight preference towards the unambiguous.

1 Introduction

Paraphrasing is a sub-field of natural language processing (NLP) which aims to modify utterances from one form into another, without changing their meaning. One particular application of paraphrase is text modification to improve information access for low-level readers; e.g., syntactic simplification (Siddharthan, 2006; Siddharthan, 2003), paraphrase (Inui et al., 2003) and lexical simplification (Devlin and Tait, 1998).

Lexical simplification is typically defined as the task of replacing difficult words with simpler ones. However, there are many open question about when one word would be a good substitute for another in context. Our analysis of WordNet 3.0 entries (Miller, 1995) demonstrates an inverse correlation between word frequency rank in the BNC[1] and number of senses it has in WordNet (Pearson = -0.20; $p < 0.001$). In other words, more common (and perhaps simpler) words are also likely to be more ambiguous. This raises an interesting question about whether, given the choice between a common (and perhaps simpler) but ambiguous word and a less common but unambiguous word, readers would prefer one over the other.

2 Related work

Hayes (1988) found common patterns of word-usage in various textual genres, indicating that there may be some empirically derivable factors that predict lexical choice in speech and writing. His work focussed on word-frequency statistics, and in that work he highlighted that polysemy issues were important but difficult to analyse due to the limited technology of the time.

The PSET project (Devlin and Tait, 1998; Carroll et al., 1998) looked at simplifying news reports for aphasics and was perhaps the first computational work to focus on lexical simplification (replacing difficult words with easier ones). The PSET project used *WordNet* (Miller, 1995) to identify synonyms and the Oxford Psycholinguistic Database (Quinlan, 1992) to determine the relative difficulty of words (Devlin and Tait, 1998). Elsewhere, there has been interest in *paraphrasing*, including the replacement of difficult words (especially verbs) with their dictionary definitions (Kaji et al., 2002).

The tradeoff between brevity (and perhaps fluency) and clarity (or ambiguity) was studied by Khan et al. (2008) in the context of generating refer-

[1] The British National Corpus, version 3, 2007. Distributed by Oxford University Computing Services on behalf of the BNC Consortium. http://www.natcorp.ox.ac.uk

Proceedings of the 13th European Workshop on Natural Language Generation (ENLG), pages 176–180,
Nancy, France, September 2011.

ring expressions with the specific form "Adj Noun and Noun" (e.g., *old men and women*) where the scope of the adjective is ambiguous. They found that hearers prefer to read clear phrases over brief ones. Our study is similar in spirit, and we ask whether hearers prefer clarity to simplicity.

The 2007 SemEval lexical substitution task (McCarthy and Navigli, 2009) created a small corpus of manually selected lexical substitutions for 30 words in 10 contexts each. Participating systems had to submit lists of acceptable substitutions in these 300 contexts and were evaluated on recall and precision relative to the manually compiled gold standard. We reuse data from this corpus, focussing on the question of which of the valid substitutions would be preferred by readers.

3 Methodology

This paper has two parts. First, we briefly investigate factors that make a word substitution valid in context and present a machine learning approach to deciding the validity of word substitutions (§3.1). Then, in the second part (§4), we study whether readers prefer simpler but more ambiguous words. We use data from the 2007 SemEval lexical substitution task both parts.

3.1 Lexical substitution

In order to investigate the tradeoff between ambiguity and commonness, we need an algorithm to:

1. Discover possible lexical replacements, and
2. Rank the suitability of these replacements according to parameters such as ambiguity and commonness.

Our interest is really in the second step, but we need to identify valid replacements before we begin to rank them. For this purpose, we restricted ourselves to WordNet 3.0 (Miller, 1995) as a source of substitutions. The first step involved extraction of the "synsets" (synonym sets) that contain the word being replaced and then listing all of the elements in those synsets to find synonyms. For verbs and nouns, we also include any synsets bearing a "hypernym" relation to one of the originals; and similarly for adjective synsets via a "similar to" relation.

For this paper, we focus on the second step. This involved determining and weighting various properties of the words deemed as possible replacements. We identified the following properties:

1. **context**: a distributional measure of the likelyhood of each word in the context of the sentence;
2. **recognisability**: an estimation of how likely the word is to be recognised; i.e., whether the word is in the reader's vocabulary;
3. **suitability**: an estimate of whether the word is a suitable replacement, given the sense of the original word; and
4. **ambiguity**: how polysemous the word is.

In this way, words that are very common in the context should be more likely to be chosen, but might still be ranked lower than another less common word that is also less ambiguous. There should be a strong preference in the system output for any options that are both common and unambiguous.

3.1.1 Context

For the context, we produce a unit vector of the words surrounding the target item (maximum of 5 either side) weighted in proportion to their distance from it. To use an example from the task:

> "We cannot **stand** as helpless spectators while millions die for want in a world of plenty"

would be encoded as:

$$\begin{pmatrix} cannot, & 0.208\bar{3} \\ as, & 0.208\bar{3} \\ we, & 0.166\bar{6} \\ helpless, & 0.166\bar{6} \\ spectators, & 0.1250 \\ while, & 0.083\bar{3} \\ millions, & 0.041\bar{6} \end{pmatrix}$$

An entry in the corpus matching one of the substitutions (e.g., "remain") will have its surrounding vector similarly derived. The dot-product of the two is then calculated. The context score for that substitution option ("remain" here) is the sum of all such vector dot-products for entries in the corpus.

3.1.2 Recognisability

The recognisability score is an estimation of how likely a word is to be in a reader's lexicon. We observed that the form of a graph plotting word frequency against word rank does not appear to be plausible as a model of an individual's likely vocabulary. The Zipfian distribution of language would make such a simplistic model predict that the second most common word would only have a 50% chance of being recognised. We predict that a large number of the most common words are almost guaranteed to be recognised, and then a long-tail of the less frequently used words with diminishing recognisability. We model this with the logistic regression function $\frac{1}{1+e^{-z}}$ with $z = 6 - \frac{rank}{10000}$.

This model is so far unjustified though. It predicts a vocabulary of 60,000 words, as per Aitchinson (1994), following a logistic regression curve plateauing with the most common 30,500 words returning recognisabilities greater than 0.95 and then describing a long-tail of words with reducing recognisabilities.

3.1.3 Suitability

As there is no word-sense disambiguity process involved, all we can be sure of is that one of the original word's senses was the intended sense. The suitability score is calculated as the portion of the original word's senses that the substitution shares. Thus the suitability of a substitution ($subs$) given the original ($orig$) is

$$\frac{|senses(subs) \cap senses(orig)|}{|senses(orig)|}$$

3.1.4 Ambiguity

The ambiguity score is simply the inverse of the number of senses held by the substitution word:

$$\frac{1}{|senses(subs)|}$$

3.2 Lexical substitution task results

The 2007 SemEval lexical substitution task corpus consists of 30 selected words appearing in ten sentences each, giving 300 sentences in total. For each of these 300 sentences, there is a manually compiled list of valid lexical substitutions for the selected word. The challenge is to computationally derive suitable alternatives for the selected word in each of the 300 sentences. Results were scored for precision and recall relative to the manually compiled gold standard.

The SemEval 2007 task authors described a baseline for WordNet systems that achieved a precision of 0.30 and recall of 0.29. Our implementation (that multiplies the values of the four features defined above) scores a precision of 0.35 and a recall of 0.35. But, it should still be noted that solutions designed at the time used a much richer set of sources for replacements, including automatically constructed paraphrase corpora, and subsequently scored much better, with the best system achieving precision and recall of 0.72.

3.3 Learning a model to fit the data

The solution described above assumes (without justification) an equal weighting for each attribute. We also trained a machine learner to classify replacements as valid or invalid based on these four features. To create labelled data, we collated all of the possible replacements as found by our method described in §3.1. We then labelled the replacement word as "valid" if it was one of those found in the manually compiled gold standard for the task, and "invalid" otherwise.

A number of modifications were made to the attributes in order to make them more suitable for the machine-learning process. It was found that the context score had an extremely long tail, and taking the logs of each context score gave a much more reasonable distribution. The polysemy scores were, by their inverse-integer nature, skewed towards 0.0 with large gaps between each fractional value (e.g. no score could possibly be in the range $(0.5, 1.0)$). For this reason, we instead just used the number of senses the word could be used in, directly, rather than taking the inverse. The overlap scores were modified to be the raw number of senses shared (or the cardinality of the intersection of the two words' sets of senses), demonstrating that in the vast majority of cases only a single sense was shared, suggesting it might not be a very useful metric.

This data was then split into ten parts, each with the results and scores for three words. (Each section therefore did not have the same number of entries.) We tested each set on an IBk classifier (Aha et al.,

1991) trained on the other nine. After extracting the predicted "valid" results we scored them as we described in §3.2 with precision and recall of 0.291. The poor performance of machine learning is possibly due to the low number of words available for training.

4 Study on reader preference

We presented human volunteers with 21 sentences. Each sentence had a word singled out and four possible substitutions for it. These four substitutions are the most common and the least ambiguous words from the manually compiled list of valid substitutions in the 2007 SemEval lexical substitution corpus, and the most common and least ambiguous words from the list of words suggested by our algorithm (§3.1). The full matrix is presented in Table 1.

The 21 sentences used in this study were selected as follows:

1. The manually compiled gold standard contained at least two substitutions

2. The classifer predicted at least two different substitutions to the gold standard

Thus our data for the study comprises just the sentences for which there are four distinct lexical substitutions available, two each from the gold standard and the classifier. Our method for selecting data for this study filters out sentences for which the system recommendations overlap with the gold standard. Thus it is of interest to see whether these system recommendations are liked by readers.

Ten human volunteers, recruited by word-of-mouth, were presented with each original sentence in a random order, and offered the four possible replacements, again randomly ordered. They were asked to rank all four in order of preference as a substitution for the original word in context.

	Manual	System
Most Common	21	21
Least Ambiguous	21	21

Table 1: Matrix of word option types

Context: There are sound reasons for concluding that the long-run picture remains **bright**, and even recent signals about the current course of the economy have turned from unremittingly negative through the late fall of last year to a far more mixed set of signals recently.

Judge	Options			
ID	good	brilliant	gleaming	hopeful
1	2	4	3	1
2	3	4	1	2
...		...		
9	2	3	4	1
10	2	3	4	1
Totals:	21	34	34	11

Table 2: Example of result tabulation for lexical substitutions of the word "bright" in context.

	Pearson	p-value
frequency	0.087	0.216
log(frequency)	-0.164	0.073
polysemy	-0.196	0.037

Table 3: One-tailed correlations and p-values between average rankings and the listed word properties

4.1 Results

For each sentence we added up the ranks from all volunteers for each of the four replacements to get a final score. In Table 2, for example, "hopeful" was ranked as the most preferred replacement, with "good" following, and "brilliant" equalling "gleaming" as the least preferred.

These were analysed against each option's frequency (in the BNC) and its level of polysemy (in WordNet). The correlations are listed in Table 3. Table 3 shows a significant inverse correlation ($p < 0.05$) between the preferred words and their level of polysemy; i.e., readers prefer less ambiguous words. We did not find a significant correlation ($p > 0.05$) between word preference and corpus frequency.

Recalling the matrix in Table 1, we are intereste in the effect of two factors with two conditions each:

1. **source:** manual or system generated

2. **criterion:** most common or least ambiguous

The replacements from the manual gold standard were ranked significantly higher ($p < 0.05$) than the replacements from the system output. However, there were 7 out of 21 cases where a system suggestion was ranked the highest. This is interesting because we specifically selected sentences where the system recommended words that were not in the gold standard; these novel recommendations were preferred in a third of cases.

We did not find any effect of the criterion factor on preference. Indeed, there were 11 cases where an unambiguous word was preferred and 10 where a common word was. We suspect that this is because the words in the manual gold standard tended to be fairly common ones; the SemEval annotators did not have access to a thesaurus or lexical database when suggesting substitutions. Thus, our ranking of words by frequency was not very informative.

5 Conclusions

Our primary result was the significant inverse correlation between the word preference and level of polysemy; i.e., our participants showed a preference for less ambiguous words. We found no correlation between word frequency and preference. We might suppose that the critical matter is simply if a word is familiar or not, and so a more more common familiar word has little or no benefit to a reader over a slightly less common, but still familiar one.

The classifier performed well at predicting which words would be suitable, in line with expectations, and more investigation may be warranted to see if other attributes of words could factor into such a task. We suppose that there might be distinctions between the different parts-of-speech, or that more details about the word being replaced would also aid the classification process.

References

David W. Aha, Dennis Kibler, and Marc K. Albert. 1991. Instance-based learning algorithms. *Machine Learning*, 6(1):37–66.

Jean Aitchinson. 1994. *Words in the mind: An introduction to the mental lexicon.* Blackwell, Oxford, England.

John Carroll, Guido Minnen, Yvonne Canning, Siobhan Devlin, and John Tait. 1998. Practical simplification of English newspaper text to assist aphasic readers. In *Proceedings of AAAI98 Workshop on Integrating Artificial Intelligence and Assistive Technology*, pages 7–10, Madison, Wisconsin.

Siobhan Devlin and John Tait. 1998. The use of a psycholinguistic database in the simplification of text for aphasic readers. In J. Nerbonne, editor, *Linguistic Databases*, pages 161–173. CSLI Publications, Stanford, California.

Donald P. Hayes. 1988. Speaking and writing: Distinct patterns of word choice. *Journal of Memory and Language*, 27(5):572 – 585.

Kentaro Inui, Atsushi Fujita, Tetsuro Takahashi, Ryu Iida, and Tomoya Iwakura. 2003. Text simplification for reading assistance: a project note. In *Proceedings of the second international workshop on Paraphrasing - Volume 16*, pages 9–16, Stroudsburg, PA, USA. Association for Computational Linguistics.

Nobuhiro Kaji, Daisuke Kawahara, Sadao Kurohash, and Satoshi Sato. 2002. Verb paraphrase based on case frame alignment. In *Proceedings of the 40th Annual Meeting of the Association for Computational Linguistics (ACL'02)*, pages 215–222, Philadelphia, USA.

Imtiaz Hussain Khan, Kees van Deemter, and Graeme Ritchie. 2008. Generation of referring expressions: managing structural ambiguities. In *Proceedings of the 22nd International Conference on Computational Linguistics - Volume 1*, COLING '08, pages 433–440.

Diana McCarthy and Roberto Navigli. 2009. The english lexical substitution task. *Language Resources and Evaluation*, 43(2):139–159.

George A. Miller. 1995. Wordnet: a lexical database for english. *Commun. ACM*, 38(11):39–41, November.

Philip Quinlan. 1992. *The Oxford Psycholinguistic Database*. Oxford University Press, U.K.

Advaith Siddharthan. 2003. Preserving discourse structure when simplifying text. In *Proceedings of the European Natural Language Generation Workshop (ENLG), 11th Conference of the European Chapter of the Association for Computational Linguistics (EACL'03)*, pages 103–110, Budapest, Hungary.

Advaith Siddharthan. 2006. Syntactic simplification and text cohesion. *Research on Language and Computation*, 4(1):77–109.

Production of Demonstratives in Dutch, English and Portuguese Dialogues

Saturnino Luz
Department of Computer Science
Trinity College Dublin, Ireland
luzs@cs.tcd.ie

Ielka van der Sluis
Communication and Information Studies
University of Groningen, the Netherlands
I.F.van.der.Sluis@rug.nl

Abstract

A data elicitation study on the type of demonstratives and determiners selected to denote objects in English, Dutch and Portuguese dialogues is presented. Participants were given a scenario and a scripted dialogue in which a furniture seller identifies target objects to a buyer. They were then asked to choose a combination of a determiner or demonstrative and a referring expression to be uttered by the seller and told that the agent would point at the targets while uttering the chosen linguistic descriptions. The study was conducted with native speakers and rendered a total of 920 demonstratives and determiners. It focused on accessibility of the target referents and distance between agents and target referents. Results show that the three language groups largely agree in their preferences and, in contrast to previous work, align with a nearby/far away distinction.

1 Introduction

This paper investigates the use of indexical determiners (i.e. determiners employed for direct references to objects and that include a pointing gesture) by Dutch, Portuguese and English speakers. A comparison of the use of Dutch and English demonstratives in terms of the accessibility of the target by Piwek and Cremers (1996) suggested that English and Dutch speakers follow opposite strategies in their use of indexical demonstratives. Dutch speakers use proximal demonstratives for referents that are relatively difficult to access (*deze*), while English speakers use proximals (*this*, *these*) for referents that are relatively easy to access. Piwek et al.(2008) present an explanation for these differences in terms of the use of pointing gestures (Clark and Bangerter, 2004; Bangerter, 2004), suggesting that a pointing gesture functions as a "labelling" of the target object as being relatively accessible. Hence, where proximals require a pointing gesture, distal demonstratives (*dat/that* and *die/those*, which are more similar to definite determiners) can also be used non-indexically. This model corresponds to the 'folk-view' of demonstratives that considers distals to indicate objects far away from the speaker and proximals to indicate objects near the speaker (Bühler, 1934; Clark, 1996).

Byron and Stoia (2005) present a motivation for choosing either a proximal or a distal demonstrative based on three dimensions (i.e. spatial, temporal and task performance). Their analysis of a corpus of collaborative dialogues between participants solving a treasure hunt problem in a virtual space, shows that, in English: (1) distals are used both for objects located close to and far away from the speaker, whereas proximals are only used for objects located near the speaker; (2) proximals are used for objects that relate to the current time and to the future, while distals are used for past events; and (3) distals are less sensitive to the space and time dimension and more sensitive to the task than proximals.

While we acknowledge that these are important dimensions in the analysis of demonstratives, in the present paper we restrict ourselves to an elicitation study and analyse the use of indexical determiners in terms of accessibility and distance, in line with the model developed by Piwek et al. (1996; 2008).

Proceedings of the 13th European Workshop on Natural Language Generation (ENLG), pages 181–186,
Nancy, France, September 2011.

In addition to the languages compared by Piwek et al. (Dutch and English), we also analyse the use of demonstratives in Portuguese. The dialogue context designed for this study fits a discursive context in which the distal/proximal distinction is appropriate for Portuguese (Cavalcante, 2002), and thus enables us to compare the use of demonstratives across these three languages. Another difference between this study and those conducted by Piwek et al. is the data gathering method. While those authors relied on corpora collected from free task-based dialogues between participants, we employed scripted dialogues (André et al., 2000; Williams et al., 2007) presented to individual participants who were explicitly asked to choose among demonstratives.

2 Production Study

The study presented below originated from an investigation into the perception of multimodal referring expressions (REs) in a virtual world by Japanese an English speakers (Van der Sluis and Luz, 2011b; Van der Sluis et al., to appear). In this paper, the materials from a production study initially conducted for Japanese to validate our Japanese translation of a dialogue written in English, have been translated and further adapted to Dutch and Brazilian Portuguese. We draw on the results of this study to analyse the use of demonstratives in English, Dutch and Portuguese. The REs considered in this study are embedded in a scripted dialogue between two agents in a furniture sales setting. The study focuses on 'first-mention' REs which identify objects that have not been talked about earlier in the discourse.

A dialogue script was written for two agents in a furniture shop. The layout of the shop and the positions of the agents and furniture items is shown in Figure 1. The shop contains 26 objects, comprising distractors as well as target referents. The dialogue consists of 19 utterances and features a conversation between a female agent purchasing furniture for her office, and a male shop-owner describing some furniture items. The furniture seller agent refers to objects in the domain by uttering each scripted RE combined with a pointing gesture directed to the target object. Validation showed that the dialogue was acceptable to English speakers. Van der Sluis and Luz (2011a) describe the setting in greater detail.

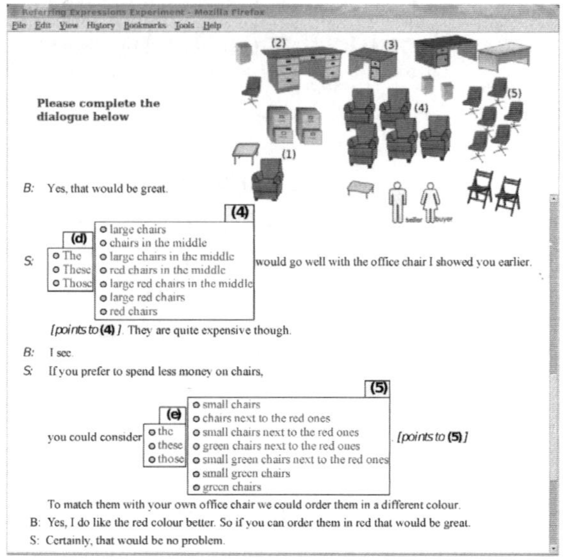

Figure 1: Screenshot of the application in which participants were asked to choose their preferred REs. Utterances by the Seller and Buyer are marked with "S:" and "B:", respectively. Options were presented as shown in the DE-boxes marked *(d)* and *(e)*, and RE-boxes marked *(4)* and *(5)*.

The dialogue was used as a template in which five first-mention referring expressions (REs) could be varied. The REs used to fill out these slots were chosen to cover various aspects of REs as are currently being studied in NLG: (1) cardinality, the REs targeted three singular objects and two larger sets of items; (2) locative expressions, the REs included three absolute locative expressions and two relative locative expressions; and (3) the position of the referent, the targets were distributed in the domain of conversation such that one referent was located near to the stationary agents, two referents were located far away from the agents, and two sets of referents were located somewhere in between those two extremes. Figure 1 shows 14 furniture items that are used for assessing multimodal GRE output: labelled (1) to (5), as well as a number of distractors. It was assumed that the agents would stay stationary and point in the direction of the targets.

The text was translated into Dutch and Brazilian Portuguese so as to adapt the dialogue to the normative, communicative and inferential rules of the respective cultures, but we attempted to keep the REs as close to the English originals as possible. The translations and localisations for Dutch and

Portuguese followed a similar pattern as the process for Japanese described in (Van der Sluis and Luz, 2011b). Validation of the translated dialogues was conducted by three native speakers in the respective languages and revisions were made accordingly.

Although the study was also conducted for Japanese, we will restrict our discussion in this paper to Dutch, English and Portuguese because the Japanese system for demonstratives differs from the ones discussed in this paper. It is a ternary, person-oriented system (Anderson and Keenan, 1985, p.282-286), in contrast to distance-oriented system such as the ones that seem to govern the use of demonstratives in Portuguese, English and Dutch. Although the Portuguese system also incorporates three classes of demonstratives, namely: *este(a)/s*, *isto*, (proximal), *esse(a)*, *isso (medial)* and *aquele(a)/s* (distal), these often operate as a binary system where the *este* and *esse* classes are used interchangeably as proximals whereas *aquele* is used as a distal (Cavalcante, 2002; Jungbluth, 2005).

Linguistic preferences were elicited through a web-based application. After being introduced to the scenario and task, participants were shown a screen similar to Figure 1. A picture of the domain was displayed at the top and kept visible throughout the dialogue. The bottom part of the screen contained the dialogue, through which the participants could scroll and select the REs and determiners or demonstratives from a set of options, all of which were simultaneously available to the participant while reading the sentence. The five REs were each presented with two boxes as illustrated in Figure 1: the DE-box, for determiner or demonstrative selection and the RE-box, for referring expressions. After each RE-box, it was stated that the agent's utterance would be combined with a pointing gesture in the direction of the target. The REs collected with the study are analysed elsewhere (Van der Sluis and Luz, 2011a) and will not be further considered in this paper. The DE-box included three options for Dutch, English and Portuguese: a definite determiner and a proximal and distal demonstrative.

3 Hypotheses

Two hypotheses, denoted H1 and H2 and summarised in Table 1, were tested for the five REs produced in the dialogue with respect to the use indexical demonstratives. H1 is related to the accessibility of the target (Gundel et al., 1993) and H2 concerns the physical distance between the speaker and the target object. Compared to the targets of RE2 and RE4, objects identified by RE1, RE3 and RE5 are relatively easier to access because they are located in the 'focus area' of the discourse (RE3 and RE5) or set visibly apart from the other objects in the domain (RE1). Hence, RE1, RE3 and RE5 call for demonstratives that indicate easy access. According to Piwek and Cremers (1996), Dutch speakers prefer proximal demonstratives for objects which are relatively hard to access, while English speakers apparently follow the opposite strategy. Portuguese speakers appear to follow a strategy which is similar to the latter (Cavalcante, 2002). In order to test these claims we set the accessibility hypothesis, H1, so that it predicts opposite strategies for Dutch, on the one hand, and Portuguese and English on the other.

Table 1: Expected *prox*imal and *dist*al demonstratives for *E*nglish and *D*utch for REs 1 to 5 with respect to ease of *a*ccess, (*H1*) and *d*istance, (*H2*).

RE	*a*	*H1-E/P*	*H1-D*	*d*	*H2-EDP*
RE1	easy	prox	dist	near	prox
RE2	difficult	dist	prox	far	dist
RE3	easy	prox	dist	far	dist
RE4	difficult	dist	prox	near	prox
RE5	easy	prox	dist	far	dist

Hypothesis H2 relates to the distance between target object and speaker. It predicts that participants will prefer distals over proximals to indicate objects further away (i.e. a proximal for RE1 and RE4 and distal demonstratives for the other REs). Since the dialogue script includes an explicit pointing gesture for all REs, we expected participants to choose either a proximal or an (indexical) distal demonstrative. We had no hypotheses about the use of definite determiners and exclude them from further analysis.

4 Results

Participants included 91 native English speakers (60% female, 40% male; age groups: 52% between 20 and 30, 33% between 31 and 40, and 25% over 41 years old; occupations: 44% students, 26% academics and 31% other), 42 native Brazilian Portuguese speakers (female: 60% female, 40% male;

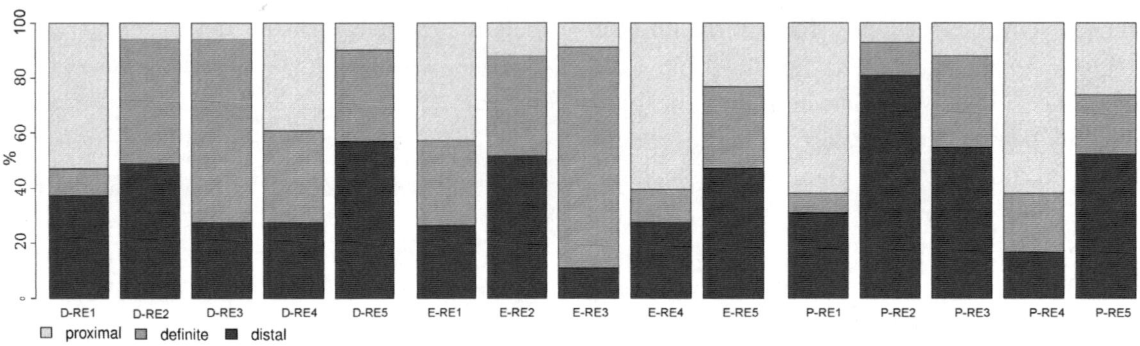

Figure 2: Percentages of definite determiners, distal and proximal demonstratives per referring expression (RE1 to RE5) for Dutch, English, and Brazilian Portuguese.

age groups: 71% between 20 and 30, 26% between 31 and 40, and 2% over 41 years old; occupations: 29% students, 57% academics and 14% other) and 51 native Dutch speakers (female: 55% female, 45% male; age groups: 21% between 20 and 30, 33% between 31 and 40, and 26% between 41 and 50 and 20% over 50 years old; occupations: 4% students, 14% academics and 82% other).

4.1 Demonstratives

Figure 2 presents the percentages of definite determiners, proximal and distal demonstratives selected per RE per language. Results show that native speakers of Portuguese, Dutch and English roughly agree in their choices. However, for RE3 we found some disagreement. The majorities of the English and Dutch participants, did not select a demonstrative, but selected a definite determiner for RE3 (i.e. 'the small desk next to it'). In contrast, the Portuguese speakers preferred a distal demonstrative.

Table 2 shows the frequencies of the demonstratives selected, determiners excluded. Again, Portuguese, Dutch and English speakers mostly agree in their choices. The majorities chose a proximal demonstrative for RE1 (i.e. 'this red chair'), a distal demonstrative for RE2 (i.e. 'that large desk'), a distal for RE3 (i.e. 'that small desk next to it'), a proximal demonstrative for RE4 (i.e. 'these red chairs') and a distal demonstrative for RE5 (i.e. 'those green chairs next to the red ones').

We computed χ^2 statistics to assess whether the data borne out the differences hypothesised (Table 1) and if those differences were statistically significant (i.e. whether the null hypotheses that no difference exists could be confidently rejected). The results of these tests are also summarised in Table 2.

Table 2: Frequencies of definite *De*terminers and *Distal* and *Proximal* demonstratives per *RE*ferring expressions for the *L*anguages *E*nglish, *D*utch and Brazilian *P*ortuguese, where differences are indicated with * = $p < .05$ and ** = $p < 0.01$. Where the null hypothesis is rejected, a + sign indicates a difference that agrees with the alternative hypothesis (H1, H2), and a − sign indicates a difference that disagrees with the alternative hypothesis.

RE	*Distal*	*Proximal*	*H1*	*H2*
E-RE1	38%(24)	62%(39)		
E-RE2	81%(47)	19%(11)	+**	+**
E-RE3	56%(10)	44%(8)		
E-RE4	31%(25)	69%(55)	−**	+**
E-RE5	67%(43)	33%(21)	−**	+**
D-RE1	41%(19)	59%(27)		
D-RE2	89%(25)	11%(3)	−**	+**
D-RE3	82%(14)	18%(3)	+**	+**
D-RE4	41%(14)	59%(20)		
D-RE5	85%(29)	15%(5)	+**	+**
P-RE1	33%(13)	67%(26)	+*	+*
P-RE2	92%(34)	8%(3)	+**	+**
P-RE3	82%(23)	18%(5)	−**	+**
P-RE4	21%(7)	79%(26)	−**	+**
P-RE5	67%(22)	33%(11)		

English participants agreed with our Access hypothesis and Distance hypothesis for RE2 ($\chi^2[1] = 22.35, p < .01$), which predict a distal demonstrative. English participants agreed with the Distance hypotheses for RE4 ($\chi^2[1] = 11.25, p < .01$) and RE5 ($\chi^2[1] = 7.56, p < .01$) and rejected the Access hypotheses for these REs (i.e. respectively a proximal and a distal demonstrative were preferred for RE4 and RE5). Dutch participants chose distal demonstratives for RE2, RE3 and RE5, respectively ($\chi^2[1] = 17.29, p < .01$), ($\chi^2[1] = 7.12, p < .00$) and ($\chi^2[1] = 16.94, p < .01$), thereby agreeing with the Distance and also with the Access hypothesis for RE3 and RE5. However, for RE2 the Dutch participants disagreed with the Access hypothesis. Portuguese speakers agreed with the Access hypothesis and the Distance hypothesis for RE1 ($\chi^2[1] = 4.333, p < .05$) and RE2 ($\chi^2[1] = 25.97, p < .01$) preferring respectively a proximal and a distal demonstrative. They also agreed with the Distance hypothesis for RE3 ($\chi^2[1] = 11.57, p < .01$) and RE4 ($\chi^2[1] = 10.94, p < .01$), preferring respectively a distal and proximal demonstrative, and thus rejected the Access hypothesis.

4.2 Access versus Distance

Table 3 summarises the participants' choices in terms of Access (H1) and Distance (H2) for the three language groups in the cases where the hypotheses differed. For English participants such differences were found for RE4 ($\chi^2[1] = 11.25, p < .01$) and RE5 ($\chi^2[1] = 7.56, p < .01$) indicating that their selections matched the Distance hypothesis better than the Access hypothesis. The Dutch participants also matched the Distance hypothesis better but only for RE2 ($\chi^2[1] = 17.29, p < .01$). Finally the demonstratives selected by the Portuguese participants matched the Distance hypothesis for RE3 ($\chi^2[1] = 11.57, p < .01$) and RE4 ($\chi^2[1] = 10.94, p < .01$) better than the Access hypothesis.

Table 3: Successful predictions of demonstratives for hypotheses *H1* (accessibility) and *H2* (distance) for *E*nglish, Brazilian *P*ortuguese and *D*utch. Significant differences between H1 and H2 are denoted with '**' ($p < .01$).

RE	*H1-Access*	*H2-Distance*	*H1 vs H2*
E-RE3	44%(8)	56%(10)	
E-RE4	31%(25)	69%(55)	**
E-RE5	33%(21)	67%(43)	**
D-RE1	41%(19)	59%(27)	
D-RE2	11%(3)	89%(25)	**
P-RE3	18%(5)	82%(23)	**
P-RE4	21%(7)	79%(26)	**
P-RE5	33%(11)	67%(22)	

5 Discussion and Conclusion

The Distance Hypothesis (H2) appears to be a better fit to the preferences of native speakers of the three languages than the Accessibility Hypothesis (H1). It agrees with the majority of choices for RE1, RE2, RE4 and RE5 in all language groups. Expression RE3, however, proved to be something of an exception, specially for Dutch and English, in that participants of those languages preferred to use a definite determiner in this RE rather than a distal or proximal demonstrative. It seems that in this case the increased accessibility of object (3), caused by the previous reference to 'the desk next to it', was transferred to the definite determiner rather than the distal demonstrative for Dutch and the proximal demonstrative for English, as predicted by H1.

In contrast to previous work, the data collected in our study show that the majorities of the three languages agree in their choices of demonstratives. This may be explained by the fact that pointing gestures were an explicit part of the REs that we tested, and therefore could be evidence for the post-hoc analysis presented by (Piwek et al., 2008), aligning with the folk view of a nearby/far away distinction.

Finally, this study introduced some methodological innovations. Unlike studies where data are collected from naturalistic conversations, we explicitly asked participants to make a judgement as to which demonstrative to use. This was done in a context which, although arguably still open to subjective interpretation, is much more tightly controlled and therefore better suited to cross-linguistic comparison. However, it could be argued that better control comes at the cost of naturalness. By asking the participants to respond from a third person's perspective and imagine the effects of communicative acts (including gestures) the study might have favoured reflective answers over spontaneous production. Such trade-offs seem to be characteristic of this sort of study, and getting them right is one of the many challenges in language generation research.

Acknowledgements

This research is supported by the Science Foundation Ireland (Grant 07/CE/I1142) as part of the Centre for Next Generation Localisation (www.cngl.ie) at Trinity College Dublin.

References

S. Anderson and E. Keenan. 1985. Deixis. In *Language Typology and Syntactic Fieldwork Vol. III*. Cambridge: Cambridge University Press.

E. André, T. Rist, S. Mulken, and M. Van Klesen. 2000. The automated design of believable dialogues for animated presentation teams. In *Embodied Conversational Agents*. MIT Press.

A. Bangerter. 2004. Using pointing and describing to achieve joint focus of attention in dialogue. *Psychological Science*, 15:415–419.

K. Bühler. 1934. *Sprachtheorie: Die Darstellungsfunktion der Sprache*. Fischer, Jena.

D. Byron and L. Stoia. 2005. An analysis of proximity markers in collaborative dialog. In *Proceedings of CLS-05*.

M. Cavalcante. 2002. O demonstrativo e seus usos. *Perspectiva*, 20(1).

H. Clark and A. Bangerter. 2004. Changing ideas about reference. In I. Noveck and D. Sperber, editors, *Experimental Pragmatics*, pages 25–49. Palgrave Macmillan, New York.

H. Clark. 1996. *Using Language*. Cambridge University Press.

J.K. Gundel, N. Hedberg, and R. Zacharski. 1993. Cognitive status and the form of referring expressions in discourse. *Language*, 69(2):274–307.

K. Jungbluth. 2005. Os pronomes demonstrativos do português brasileiro na fala e na escrita. *Cadernos de Linguagem e Sociedade*, 7:83–105.

P. Piwek and A. Cremers. 1996. Dutch and English demonstratives: A comparison. *Language Sciences*, 18(3-4):835–851.

P. Piwek, R. Beun, and A. Cremers. 2008. 'Proximal' and 'distal' in language and cognition: Evidence from deictic demonstratives in Dutch. *Journal of Pragmatics*, 40:694–718.

I. Van der Sluis and S. Luz. 2011a. A cross-linguistic study on the production of multimodal referring expressions in dialogue. In *Proceedings of the 13th European Workshop on Natural Language Generation*, Nancy, France.

I. Van der Sluis and S. Luz. 2011b. Issues in translating and producing Japanese referring expressions for dialogues. *Linguistic Issues in Language Technology*, 5(1):1–46.

I. Van der Sluis, S. Luz W. Breitfuß, M. Ishizuka, and H. Prendinger. to appear. Cross-cultural assessment of automatically generated multimodal referring expressions in a virtual world. *International Journal of Human-Computer Studies*.

S. Williams, P. Piwek, and R. Power. 2007. Generating monologue and dialogue to present personalised medical information to patients. In *Proc. of ENLG-07*.

Generation of Formal and Informal Sentences

Fadi Abu Sheikha and Diana Inkpen

School of Electrical Engineering and Computer Science
University of Ottawa
Ottawa, ON, K1N6N5, Canada

fabus102@uottawa.ca, diana@site.uottawa.ca

Abstract

This paper addresses the task of using natural language generation (NLG) techniques to generate sentences with formal and with informal style. We studied the main characteristics of each style, which helped us to choose parameters that can produce sentences in one of the two styles. We collected some ready-made parallel list of formal and informal words and phrases, from different sources. In addition, we added two more parallel lists: one that contains most of the contractions in English (short forms) and their full forms, and another one that consists in some common abbreviations and their full forms. These parallel lists might help to generate sentences in the preferred style, by changing words or expressions for that style. Our NLG system is built on top of the SimpleNLG package (Gatt and Reiter, 2009). We used templates from which we generated valid English texts with formal or informal style. In order to evaluate the quality of the generated sentences and their level of formality, we used human judges. The evaluation results show that our system can generate formal and informal style successfully, with high accuracy. The main contribution of our work consists in designing a set of parameters that led to good results for the task of generating texts with different formality levels.

1 Introduction

In this paper, we introduce an important technique that takes into account the differences between the formal text style and the informal text style. This technique is automatic text generation that can generate texts that are formal or informal, based on the user preferences.

There are linguistic studies that state that there are different levels of formality (Hayakawa, 1994). We focus on the coarse-grained level, formal and informal style, but finer-grained levels are possible (e.g., informal, less formal, formal, extremely formal).

The motivation for our work is the need for a software tool that helps people to generate formal or informal texts. One of the difficult issues of writing in English is the knowledge of how to adapt to formal or informal situations. Some situations (such as applying for a job) are likely to be formal, whereas others (such as emailing a friend or family member) are more likely to be informal. The real problem when writing is to know what words, phrases, or expressions to use. There are some words, phrases, and expressions that are either formal or informal; for instance, if the wrong word is chosen, then the reader may think we are being either too friendly or too formal.

The paper is organized as follows: in Section 2 we discuss related work; Section 3 addresses the main differences between the formal and the informal style; Section 4 presents the parameters that we used for generation; Section 5 describes our text generation system; results are shown in Section 6; Section 7 concludes the paper and suggests directions of future work.

2 Related Work

In this section, we briefly explain the natural language generation techniques (Reiter and Dale, 2000), the SimpleNLG package (Gatt and Reiter, 2009), and we discuss some of existing NLG

Proceedings of the 13th European Workshop on Natural Language Generation (ENLG), pages 187–193,
Nancy, France, September 2011.

systems that included stylistic variations.

2.1 Natural Language Generation (NLG)

Natural language generation is the process of constructing a natural language text from non-linguistic representation of information in order to meet specified communicative goals (McDonald, 1987). The aim is to build computer systems that automatically produce correct texts in English, and other human languages (Reiter et al., 1995). The main stages and the architecture of a typical NLG system were introduced by Reiter and Dale (2000).

2.2 SimpleNLG Package

The SimpleNLG[1] package (Gatt and Reiter, 2009) can be used to write a program which generates grammatically correct English sentences. It is a library, written in Java, which performs simple and useful tasks that are necessary for natural language generation. The main task that SimpleNLG performs is sentence realisation, which includes orthography, morphology, and simple grammar.

2.3 NLG and SimpleNLG

Following the architecture of Reiter and Dale (2000), the SimpleNLG performs Surface Realisation[2], which is one of the main components of an NLG System. The Surface Realiser does the following tasks:

- Linguistic realisation: this component uses the grammar rules to convert abstract representations of sentences into actual text.
- Structure realisation: converts sentences and paragraphs into mark-up symbols and displays the text.

2.4 Some NLG Systems that Include Style

There are many NLG systems implemented to generate texts for specific purposes. Many of them are commercial systems. For example, the Forecast Generator (FOG) system was designed in 1992 by CoGenTex[3] to generate weather reports in English and French; the inputs of the system were graphical and numerical weather depictions (Goldberg et al., 1994).

We discuss here related work in NLG systems that take into consideration generating text under pragmatic constraints, especially according to style. As far as we are aware, there are only a few researchers who investigated producing text with varied styles.

Hovy (1988, 1990) introduced an NLG system called PAULINE, which is considered as one of the earliest examples of Natural Language Generation systems. Hovy proposed to generate text under pragmatic constraints, including formality. Although small scale, his experiments generated the same text in different styles, to achieve different effects on the reader, and incorporated some pragmatics into language generation. He suggested using different words to generate different styles.

Stamatatos et al. (1997) proposed a system that can generate business letters based on different user requirements, such as style and tone.

Power et al. (2001) proposed the Iconoclast system that allows the users to choose a number of high-level parameters for the text style. These parameters could be sentence length, frequency of passive voice and pronouns, and the use of technical terms. This system allows the user to choose the parameters by manipulating slider bars in a graphical user interface.

Furthermore, Reiter et al. (2003) presented the STOP system that was developed in University of Aberdeen for the British Health Services; it generates tailored letters to help people stop smoking. The STOP system makes the text friendlier by adding more empathy; it also makes the text easier to read for people with poor reading skills.

3 Formal and Informal Language Style

In this section, we explain the main characteristics of informal versus formal style. We also present the parallel lists of words, phrases, and expressions for both styles, which we collected from different sources. The understanding of the main differences between the styles will help to build a system that generates sentences with formal and informal style, by implementing some of these characteristics in our NLG system.

[1] http://www.csd.abdn.ac.uk/~ereiter/simplenlg/

[2] http://www.ling.helsinki.fi/kit/2008s/clt310gen/docs/simplenlg-tutorial-v37.pdf

[3] http://www.cogentex.com/

3.1 Characteristics of Formal versus Informal Style

We briefly explain and summarize the main characteristics of informal style versus formal style, as we found them described in (Dumaine and Healey, 2003; Obrecht, and Ferris, 2005; Akmajian et al., 2001; Park, 2007; Zapata, 2008; Siddiqi, 2008; Redman, 2003; Rob S. et al., 2008; Pavlidis, 2009; Obrecht, 1999). These characteristics are used for building templates to generate sentences based on them. Here, we explain the characteristics of each style and provide examples:

A. Main Characteristics of Informal Style Text:

- It uses personal pronouns and the active voice.
- It uses short simple words and sentences.
- It uses Contractions (e.g., "won't").
- It uses many abbreviations (e.g., "TV").
- It uses many phrasal verbs.
- The words that express rapport and familiarity are often used in speech, such as "brother", "buddy", and "man".
- It uses a subjective style, expressing opinions and feelings.
- It uses vague expressions and colloquial (slang words are accepted in spoken not in written text (e.g., "wanna" = "want to")).

B. Main Characteristics of Formal Style Text:

- It uses impersonal pronouns and often the passive voice.
- It uses complex words and sentence.
- It does not use contractions.
- It does not use many abbreviations.
- It uses appropriate and clear expressions, business, and technical vocabulary.
- It uses politeness words and formulas such as "Please", "Sir".
- It uses an objective style, using facts and references to support an argument.
- It does not use vague expressions and slang words.

3.2 Formal versus Informal lists

We present our parallel lists of informal versus formal words, phrases, and expressions. These lists were collected manually from different sources: the first list is for formal versus informal words and phrases, the second list is for most of the contractions in English, and the third list is for some of the common abbreviations in English. These lists are important parameters for our system of sentence generation.

A. Informal/Formal list of words and phrases

This is a parallel list for informal versus formal words and phrases. We collected this list manually from different sources: (Gillett et al., 2009; Park, 2007; Redman, 2003; Rob et al., 2008). In addition, we obtained a new list that was extracted manually by Brooke et al. (2010) from the dictionary of synonyms *Choose The Right Word* (Hayakawa, 1994). Table 1 shows a sample of this parallel list.

Informal	Formal
about	approximately
anybody	anyone
ask for	request
buy	purchase

Table 1: Examples of formal and informal words from our parallel list

B. Contractions Lists

This is a parallel list for most of the contractions in English (short forms) that represent the informal style versus the full forms of the contractions that represent the formal style. We obtained this list manually from (Redman, 2003; Garner, 2001; Pearl Production, 2005; Woods, 2010). In Table 2, we show a sample of the parallel list of the contractions and their equivalent full forms.

Informal	Formal
aren't	are not
can't	cannot
I'm	I am

Table 2: Examples of contractions versus their equivalent full forms

C. Abbreviation Lists

This is a parallel list for some of the most common abbreviations in English that represent the informal style versus the full forms that corresponds to these abbreviations as used in formal style. However, there are some abbreviations that are acceptable in formal texts (Obrecht, 1999). We collected this list manually from (Redman, 2003; Gibaldi, 2003; Pearl Production, 2005). Table 3 shows a sample of pairs from the parallel list of the abbreviations and their equivalent full forms.

Informal	Formal
e.g.	for example
etc.	and so on
Feb.	February
Lab	Laboratory

Table 3: Examples of abbreviations and their equivalent full forms

4 Formality Parameters

In this section, we propose the following two main parameters that will be used in constructing formal/informal sentences. We hypothesize that both parameters might help to produce sentences in both styles.

a. Phrase, expression, and word choice (lexical choice): This parameter might help to generate sentences in both styles (Hovy, 1988). We implement this parameter in our system based on the parallel lists (formal/informal words, the contraction list, and the abbreviation list) that we have described in Section 3.
b. Passive/Active voice option: This parameter is based on the characteristics of both styles which we mentioned in Section 3. In addition, it was suggested by Hovy (1988). We added this parameter to our system and we let the system choose a sentence in the passive or the active voice, based on the preferred style.

5 Formal/Informal Sentence Generation

Our system can generate natural language sentences in a formal/informal style with different inputs of subject, verb, and complement (by complement, we mean one or more words including subordinate clauses, as expected in SimpleNLG). Therefore, the user might not worry about choosing any word that he/she is not very familiar with, whether the word is formal or informal, because the system will manage to replace some words with more appropriate words, based on the desired style. In addition, our system might interact with the user directly, or it can be integrated with any system that has the ability to send and receive commands from Java programs.

In the following, we explain the main steps for our system to generate sentences:

a. Ask the user which style is preferred to be generated in the sentence.
b. Ask the user to enter a template that represents the sentence in the form of a subject, a verb, and the rest of the sentence.
c. Ask the user about some syntactic features: the verb tense (present, past, future), progressive (yes, no), perfect (yes, no), and negation (yes, no).
d. The system then checks the verb in the formal/informal parallel list; if it is formal or informal, and the system will find a synonym of the verb in the list, it will replace it based on the preferred style. In addition, if the chosen style is Formal, then the system will choose to generate a sentence in passive voice.
e. After the sentence is constructed, the system will search for any word, phrase, or expression from the formal/informal list, the abbreviations list, and the contractions list, in order to replace it with a synonym, based on the preferred style.
f. Lastly, our system will generate a natural language sentence according to the preferred style, using SimpleNLG for surface realization.

6 Results and Evaluation

Natural language generation is most often evaluated using scores given by human judges (Reiter and Belz, 2009). Our evaluation target was to measure the degree of formality (Formal / Informal) of the generated sentences. We asked two human judges (graduate students in computational linguistics, native speakers of English) to annotate 100 generated sentences as having formal or informal style. Table 4 shows samples[4] of the generated sentences with the

[4] We will make the test set of annotated sentence available, on our website, in case other researchers need them for testing, as well as the three word lists used by our system.

judges' annotations. We estimate the correctness of our system by comparing the original class of the generated sentences (formal/informal) to the annotations of Judge1 and to the annotations of Judge2. We calculated several evaluation measures, to see if our proposed system achieves good quality in producing English sentences in formal and informal style. These measures are the accuracy (correctness) of our system according to each judge, and the precision for each class according to each judge.

Sentence	Actual Class	Judge1 annotate	Judge2 annotate
The plane is going to leave on Jan. 5th.	Informal	Formal	Informal
They were transmuting the raw materials to finished goods.	Formal	Formal	Formal

Table 4: Samples of the generated sentences with the annotations from both judges

		Predicted Class		Precision
		Informal	Formal	
Actual Class	Infor mal	TP = 45	FN = 0	0.90
	For mal	FP = 5	TN = 50	1.00

Table 5: The results compared to the annotations of Judge1, with the precision for each class

		Predicted Class		Precision
		Informal	Formal	
Actual Class	Infor mal	TP = 50	FN = 1	1.00
	For mal	FP = 0	TN = 49	0.98

Table 6: The results compared to the annotations of Judge2, with the precision for each class

The results of the annotations show high accuracy for the generated sentences. In Table 5 and Table 6, we show the results according to each of the two judges. The accuracy of our system is 95% according to Judge1 and 99% according to Judge2.

We also calculated the agreement between the two judges, and the kappa statistic that compensated for agreement by chance (Cohen, 1960) (Manning et al., 2008). The agreement between the two judges is 94% and the kappa value is 0.88. This shows a very good agreement for the task.

7 Conclusion and Future Work

In this paper, we have addressed the task of generation of formal and informal texts. The main characteristics of formal and informal style that we identified are success factors for our work, because they helped us to build the parameters that lead to good generation results. In addition, the parallel lists of formal versus informal words and phrases that we collected from different sources were very important in designing our system for the generation formal and informal sentences.

We developed an NLG system that can generate formal and informal sentences. We used template-based NLG techniques in the SimpleNLG package in order to implement our system. We proposed some important parameters that are used in generating formal and informal sentences. We think that these parameters were selected successfully because the evaluation with human judges showed a high accuracy in generating formal and informal sentences. Generating sentences with different formality levels is very useful for various applications (e.g., generating feedback for e-learning games, letters to clients, and other formal or informal documents).

Our future work will be on extracting more formal and informal lists; this should increase the possibility of generating more and more formal/informal sentences, with high accuracy. We will apply different techniques, such as bootstrapping, which can be used in order to extract more lists of words, based on some seed words. We also plan to extend the implementation of our NLG system to cover generating longer texts (e.g., generating several sentences, by adding aggregation, or replacing some nouns with pronouns to avoid repetitions).

References

Akmajian, Adrian, Demers, Richard A., Farmer, Ann K., and Harnish, Robert M. 2001. Linguistics: an introduction to language and communication. 5th Edition, MIT Press, Cambridge (MA), pp. 287-291.

Brooke, Julian, Wang, Tong, and Hirst, Graeme. 2010. Inducing Lexicons of Formality from Corpora. Proceedings. Workshop on Methods for the Automatic Acquisition of Language Resources and their Evaluation Methods, 7th Language Resources and Evaluation Conference, 17-22 May, Valetta, Malta, pp. 605—616.

Cohen, Jacob. 1960. Coefficient of agreement for nominal scales. Educational and Psychological Measurement. VOL. XX, No. 1, pp. 37-46.

Dumaine, Deborah, and Healey, Elisabeth C. 2003. Instant-Answer Guide to Business Writing: An A-Z Source for Today's Business Writer. 2003 Edition, Writers Club Press, Lincoln, pp. 153-156.

Garner, Bryan A. 2001. A Dictionary of Modern Legal Usage. 2nd Edition, pp. xxv, Oxford University Press, US.

Gatt, Albert, and Reiter, Ehud. 2009. SimpleNLG: A realisation engine for practical applications. In Proceedings of the 12th European Workshop on Natural Language Generation (ENLG 2009), 30-31 March, Athens, Greece, pp. 90-93.

Gibaldi, Joseph. 2003. MLA Handbook for Writers of Research Papers. 6th edition, Section 7.4, Modern Language Association of America, (ISBN: 0873529863 / 0-87352-986-3).

Gillett, Andy, Hammond, Angela, and Martala, Mary. 2009. Inside Track to Successful Academic Writing. Pearson Education, ISBN: 978-0273721710.

Goldberg, E., Driedger, N., and Kittredge, R. I. 1994. Using Natural Language Processing to Produce Weather Forecasts. IEEE Expert: Intelligent Systems and Their Applications, 9(2): 45-53.

Hayakawa, S. I., editor. 1994. Choose the Right Word: A Contemporary Guide to Selecting the Precise Word for Every Situation. 2nd Edition, revised by Eugene Ehrlich. HarperCollins Publishers, NY, USA.

Hovy, Eduard H. 1988. Generating Natural Language under Pragmatic Constraints. Lawrence Erlbaum Associates, Hillsdale, NJ, USA, pp. 82 – 87.

Hovy, Eduard H. 1990. Pragmatics and natural language generation. AI. vol. 43, pp. 153–197.

Manning, Christopher D., Raghavan, Prabhakar, and Schütze, Hinrich. 2008. Introduction to Information Retrieval. Cambridge University Press, Chapter 8, pp. 165- 166.

McDonald, David D. 1987. Natural language generation. In Stuart C. Shapiro, editor, Encyclopaedia of Artificial Intelligence, John Wiley and Sons, pp. 642-655.

Obrecht, Fred 1999. Minimum Essentials of English. 2nd Edition, Barron's Educational Series Inc., Los Angeles Pierce College, New York, page 13.

Obrecht, Fred, Ferris, Boak. 2005. How to Prepare for the California State University Writing Proficiency Exams. 3rd Edition, Barron's Educational Series Inc., New York, page 173.

Park, David. 2007. Identifying & using formal & informal vocabulary. IDP Education, the University of Cambridge and the British Council, the Post Publishing Public Co. Ltd.

Pavlidis, Mara. 2009. Target Your Study Skills: Optimise Your Learning. Faculty of Health Sciences. La Trobe University, Victoria, Australia, Chapter 5, page 3.

Pearl Production (Ed). 2005. English Language Arts Skills & Strategies Level 5. Saddleback Publishing, Inc. USA, ISBN 1-56254-839-5.

Power, Richard, Scott, Donia, and Bouayad-Agha, Nadjet. 2003. Generating texts with style. In: Proceedings of the 4th International Conference on Intelligent Text Processing and Computational Linguistics (CICLing'03), pp. 444-452.

Redman, Stuart. 2003. English vocabulary in use: Pre-intermediate & intermediate. 2nd Edition, Cambridge University press, UK.

Reiter, Ehud and Belz, Anja. 2009. An Investigation into the Validity of Some Metrics for Automatically Evaluating Natural Language Generation Systems. Computational Linguistics 25:529–558.

Reiter, Ehud and Dale, Robert. 2000. Building Natural Language Generation Systems (Studies in Natural Language Processing). Cambridge University Press 2000. ISBN 0-521-62036-8.

Reiter, Ehud, Mellish, Chris, and Levine, John. 1995. Automatic Generation of Technical Documentation. Applied Artificial Intelligence 9, pp. 259-287.

Reiter, Ehud, Robertson, Roma, and Osman, Liesl. 2003 Lessons from a Failure: Generating Tailored Smoking Cessation Letters. Artificial Intelligence, 144, pp. 41-58.

Rob, S. et al. 2008. How to Avoid Colloquial (Informal) Writing. WikiHow.

Siddiqi, Anis. 2008. The Difference Between Formal and Informal Writing. EzineArticles.

Stamatatos, E., Michos, S., Fakotakis, N., and Kokkinakis, G. 1997. A User-Assisted Business Letter Generator Dealing with Text's Stylistic Variations. The Ninth International Conference on Tools with Artificial Intelligence, (TAI-97).

Woods, Geraldine. 2010. English Grammar for Dummies. 2nd Edition, page 147, Wiley Publishing, Inc. NJ, USA.

Zapata, Argenis A. 2008. Inglés IV (B-2008). Universidad de Los Andes, Facultad de Humanidades y Educación, Escuela de Idiomas Modernos.

Glue Rules for Robust Chart Realization

Michael White
Department of Linguistics
The Ohio State University
Columbus, Ohio, USA
mwhite@ling.ohio-state.edu

Abstract

This paper shows how glue rules can be used to increase the robustness of statistical chart realization in a manner inspired by dependency realization. Unlike the use of glue rules in MT—but like previous work with XLE on improving robustness with hand-crafted grammars—they are invoked here as a fall-back option when no grammatically complete realization can be found. The method works with Combinatory Categorial Grammar (CCG) and has been implemented in OpenCCG. As the techniques are not overly tied to CCG, they are expected to be applicable to other grammar-based chart realizers where robustness is a common problem. Unlike an earlier robustness technique of greedily assembling fragments, glue rules enable n-best outputs and are compatible with disjunctive inputs. Experimental results indicate that glue rules yield improved realizations in comparison to greedy fragment assembly, though a sizeable gap remains between the quality of grammatically complete realizations and fragmentary ones.

1 Introduction

Robustness continues to be a problem for broad coverage chart realizers. Since Kay's (1996) pioneering work on chart realization with unification grammars, broad coverage chart realizers have been developed for LFG (Shemtov, 1997; Cahill and van Genabith, 2006; Hogan et al., 2007), HPSG (Velldal et al., 2004; Nakanishi et al., 2005; Velldal and Oepen, 2005; Carroll and Oepen, 2005) and CCG (White, 2006b; White, 2006a; Espinosa et al., 2008; White and Rajkumar, 2009), but none of these realizers come near 100% coverage. For example, both Cahill and van Genabith (2006) and White and Rajkumar (2009) report coverage below 90% for all Penn Treebank test section sentences (despite coverage near 100% for parsers with comparable grammars), and consequently both also report results with fragment concatenation for increased robustness. Earlier work with hand-crafted grammars for the XLE realizer has also made it possible to specify fragment concatentation rules.[1] Failure to generate a grammatically complete realization can be expected to become an even greater issue in surface realization shared tasks, where realizers must cope with non-native "common ground" inputs.

In contrast to grammar-based chart realization approaches, recent dependency-based approaches (Guo et al., 2008; Gali and Venkatapathy, 2009; Guo et al., 2010), which have eschewed explicit grammatical constraints, easily achieve 100% coverage by simply ensuring that each input word in a dependency structure ends up in the output. As the adage goes, if you can't beat 'em, join 'em, and thus in this paper we take a step in this direction by investigating the use of MT-inspired glue rules (Chiang, 2007) for enhanced robustness. The idea is that by using glue rules as a fall-back option, in the limit chart realization simply degenerates into dependency realization. The catch, of course—beyond computational concerns—is that in unmodified form, realization ranking models for grammar-based realiza-

[1] http://www2.parc.com/isl/groups/nltt/xle/doc/xle.html#SECG5

Proceedings of the 13th European Workshop on Natural Language Generation (ENLG), pages 194–199,
Nancy, France, September 2011.

tion are unlikely to work as well as ones designed explicitly for dependency-based realization.

Our approach to employing glue rules in chart realization is cached out in Combinatory Categorial Grammar (Steedman, 2000, CCG) and implemented in OpenCCG,[2] though as the techniques are not overly tied to CCG, we expect them to be applicable to other grammatical frameworks as well. To date, OpenCCG has made use of a greedy approach to assembling fragments when no grammatically realization is found within a time limit, which starts with the largest fragment and greedily adds non-overlapping fragments to one end or the other in a way that locally maximizes the realization ranking model score. In comparison to this earlier method, glue rules enable a much larger space of fragment concatenations to be explored, and since these rules are integrated into the general chart realization framework, they remain compatible with returning n-best outputs and allowing disjunctively specified inputs, in contrast to the earlier greedy concatenation method.[3]

2 Background

OpenCCG is a parsing/generation library for CCG which includes a hybrid symbolic-statistical chart realizer (White, 2006b). The chart realizer takes as input (quasi-) logical forms (LFs) represented using Hybrid Logic Dependency Semantics (HLDS), a dependency-based approach to representing linguistic meaning (Baldridge and Kruijff, 2002); see White (2006b) for discussion. Semantic dependency graphs are derived from the CCGbank (Hockenmaier and Steedman, 2007), modified to incorporate Propbank roles (Boxwell and White, 2008), where semantically empty function words such as complementizers, relativizers, infinitival-*to*, and expletive subjects are adjusted to reflect their purely syntactic status. Lexical category assignments are statistically filtered in a hypertagging step (Espinosa et al., 2008); Figure 1 illustrates the desired output of the hypertagger. As in Clark & Curran's (2007) approach to integrating supertagging and parsing, an adaptive strategy is employed, whereby a β-best list of supertags is returned for each lexical predication, and the hypertagger's β setting is progressively relaxed until a complete realization is found or the space/time limits are exceeded. Alternative realizations are ranked using an averaged perceptron model (White and Rajkumar, 2009) that makes use of three kinds of features: (1) the log probability of the candidate realization's word sequence according to a trigram word model and a factored language model over part-of-speech tags and supertags; (2) integer-valued syntactic features, representing counts of occurrences in a derivation, from Clark & Curran's normal form model; and (3) discriminative n-gram features (Roark et al., 2004), which count the occurrences of each n-gram in the word sequence. Section 4 of this paper also explores the use of a basic dependency model, with head-dependent and sibling dependent ordering features.

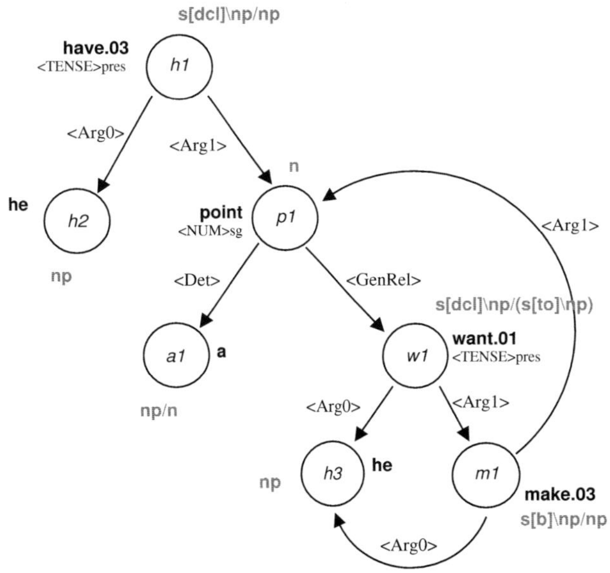

Figure 1: Semantic dependency graph from the CCGbank for *He has a point he wants to make [. . .]*, along with gold-standard supertags (category labels)

3 Glue Rules for Chart Realization

As in Chiang's (2007) approach to using glue rules in synchronous context-free grammars and the XLE approach to fragment rules in hand-crafted gram-

[2] http://openccg.sf.net

[3] While the greedy approach to fragment assembly could conceivably be generalized to a beam search that respected disjunctive constraints, doing so would introduce considerable redundancy with the core chart realization algorithm; indeed, generalizing the greedy approach by reusing the existing chart realization algorithm is essentially what the glue rules are designed to do.

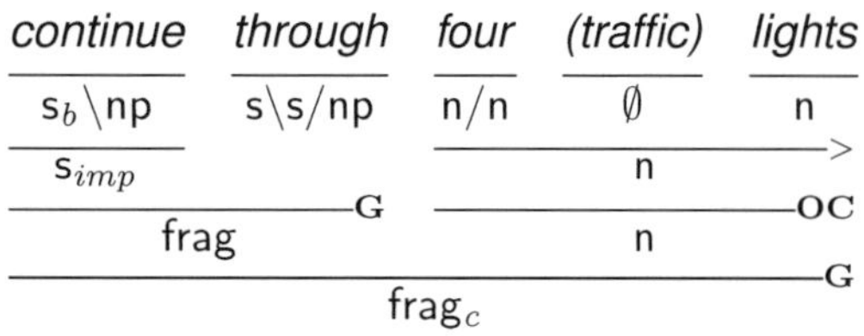

Figure 2: Syntactic derivation for *continue through four lights* using the glue rule (**G**) and opt-completion rule (**OC**), where *traffic* is left out for lack of a matching category, and *four lights* cannot be promoted to an NP because of a missing determiner semantic feature in the input.

mars, the basic idea is to concatenate top-level constituents that have been combined using other rules. As the example derivation (discussed further below) in Figure 2 shows, the glue rule (**G**) here is X Y[¬frag] ⇒ frag, where any two categories can be combined into a fragment category—except that only the left category may itself be a fragment, to avoid spurious ambiguities in how fragments are concatenated.

There are three twists to this basic story. First, on the assumption that derivations that follow the grammar are to be preferred to ones employing the glue rule, glue rules are only invoked after the chart has been completed with no grammatically complete derivation found to cover the input, and then only when the glue rule fills in an empty cell (i.e. set of covered elementary predications, or EPs). Additionally, to aid in the search for a fragment that covers the input completely, edges on the realizer's agenda are sorted first by the number of covered EPs, and secondarily by their model score.

The second twist concerns the LF chunking constraints in the realizer. In order to address the problem of proliferating semantically incomplete constituents (Kay, 1996), OpenCCG requires all the EPs in an LF chunk—by default, a non-trivial subtree in the input—to be covered by an edge before combination is allowed with another edge with EPs outside the chunk (White, 2006b). To effectively relax these constraints, if there are elementary predications within an LF chunk which are not covered by any lexical items or instantiated unary rules, those EPs are made optional; similarly, the EPs for instantiated unary rules are made optional, so that they can be checked off as covered by relevant fragments.[4]

```
Input LF:
@c(continue ^
   <Actor>(p ^ pro2) ^
   <Path>(t1 ^ through ^
          <Ref>(l ^ light ^ <num>pl ^
                <Card>(f ^ four) ^
                <Mod>(t2 ^ traffic))))

Preds:
ep[0]:  @p(pro2)
ep[1]:  @c(continue)
ep[2]:  @c(<Actor>p)
ep[3]:  @c(<Path>t1)
ep[4]:  @t1(through)
ep[5]:  @t1(<Ref>l)
ep[6]:  @f(four)
ep[7]:  @t2(traffic)
ep[8]:  @l(light)
ep[9]:  @l(<num>pl)
ep[10]:  @l(<Card>f)
ep[11]:  @l(<Mod>t2)

LF chunks:
chunk[0]:  {6-11}
chunk[1]:  {4-11}
chunk[2]:  {0-11}

LF optional parts:
opt[0]:  {0}
opt[1]:  {7,11}
```

Figure 3: Broken HLDS LF input for *continue through four traffic lights*, where *traffic* is given with the wrong relation and the determiner feature is missing. The elementary predications (EPs) for traffic are made optional, for lack of a matching category, and the EP for the implicit *you*, introduced by a unary rule, is also made optional. The sub-tree chunks for *four traffic lights*, *through four traffic lights* and all the entire input are also shown.

As a third and final twist, to allow glue rules to be applied recursively, fragments that complete an LF chunk or disjunction are marked as completed fragments (frag_c), so that they may be used with the glue rule as the right category (where fragments are normally disallowed). Note that it is the recursive use of glue rules, along with the connection to dependency realization discussed next, that perhaps most distinguishes the present approach from the use of fragment rules in hand-crafted grammars with XLE.

[4]Experiments with relaxed relation matching, which is similar to the use of relaxed unification constraints in grammar-based error detection (Schwind, 1988), have been inconclusive to date. In future work, it would be interesting to further explore the use of constraint relaxation and possibly other techniques from error detection, such as the use of mal-rules (Schneider and McCoy, 1998).

As glue rules are applied, LF chunking constraints are applied as usual, and thus the fragment gluing phase becomes tantamount to exploring different permutations of heads and phrases headed by their dependents, much as in dependency-based realization approaches. That is, since fragment edges are constructed by assembling existing edges in either order, all permutations of edges whose EPs fall within an LF chunk will eventually be tried (subject so search constraints), with preference given to the orderings with the best model scores. Note that with glue rules, tracking of disjunctive alternatives and optional EPs continues as usual too, so that n-best generation and realization from disjunctive logical forms can remain enabled.

To illustrate how glue rules enhance robustness, consider the input for the derivation in Figure 2 given in Figure 3, which shows a broken LF input for *continue through four traffic lights* using OpenCCG's `routes` sample grammar. Here, *traffic* is specified using the `Mod` relation instead of the `HasProp` relation required by the grammar, and the semantic feature for a zero determiner has been left out. Nevertheless, the realizer is able to generate *continue through four lights*, as follows. Initially, a nominal constituent (n) *four lights* is derived using the forward application rule, and the unary rule for promoting a bare verb phrase to an imperative sentence (s_{imp}) is applied to *continue*. As no further constituents can be formed, glue rules are enabled. At this point, *continue* and *through* combine via the glue rule (with X instantiated to s_{imp} and Y instantiated to $s\backslash s/np$), and the opt-completion rule (**OC**) is invoked so that *four lights* can be considered to cover the now optional EPs for *traffic* as well.[5] Finally, *continue through* and *four lights* combine via the glue rule to cover all the input EPs, making a completed fragment ($frag_c$).[6] If this clause were embedded in a larger sentence—e.g., *he said continue through four lights*—the completed fragment could again combine via the glue rule with *he said* to form a complete sentence.

[5]That is, since EPs 7 and 11 are optional, the edge for *four lights* can be promoted to one that covers all of the EPs 6–11 (White, 2006a).

[6]In n-best generation, other variants are generated as well, such as *you continue through four lights*, *continue through four lights you*, etc.

	perceptron −deps	perceptron +deps	oracle +deps
all: greedy	0.8133	0.8237	0.9409
all: glue rules	0.8198	**0.8308**	0.9570
gramm. complete	0.8686	0.8795	0.9747
greedy fragments	0.6039	0.6170	0.8158
glued fragments	0.6408	**0.6523**	0.8924

Table 2: Development set BLEU scores, CCGbank Section 00 (1575 grammatically complete sentences; 322 fragmentary ones)

	perceptron +deps
all incl. greedy fragments	0.8402
all incl. glue rule fragments	**0.8462**
grammatically complete	0.8879
greedy fragments	0.6116
glue rule fragments	**0.6477**

Table 3: Test set BLEU scores, CCGbank Section 23 (1932 grammatically complete sentences; 328 fragmentary ones)

4 Experimental Results

To further explore the connection to dependency realization, the dependency features illustrated in Table 1 were added to the baseline averaged perceptron realization ranking model.[7] These features, which depend on the input LF and candidate realization but not the CCG categories, count the occurrences of head-dependent and sibling dependent ordering configurations in a derivation. The features listed at the top record whether the head precedes the dependent or vice-versa, grouped by the broad part of speech (POS) of the head and the relation between the head and the dependent, with different combinations of words and POS tags. The features at the bottom record the order of sibling dependent words appearing on the same side of the head word, similarly grouped by the broad POS of the head and at different granularities of word or POS tag, and additionally with relation-relation orderings.

Table 2 shows the results of reverse realization with OpenCCG on the development section of the

[7]Features incorporating named entity classes (Rajkumar et al., 2009) and targeting agreement errors (Rajkumar and White, 2010) were not used in the experiments reported here.

Feature Type	Example
HeadBroadPos + Rel + Precedes + HeadWord + DepWord	⟨VB, Arg0, dep, wants, he⟩
... + HeadWord + DepPOS	⟨VB, Arg0, dep, wants, PRP⟩
... + HeadPOS + DepWord	⟨VB, Arg0, dep, VBZ, he⟩
... + HeadWord + DepPOS	⟨VB, Arg0, dep, VBZ, PRP⟩
HeadBroadPos + Side + DepWord1 + DepWord2	⟨NN, left, an, important⟩
... + DepWord1 + DepPOS2	⟨NN, left, an, JJ⟩
... + DepPOS1 + DepWord2	⟨NN, left, DT, important⟩
... + DepPOS1 + DepPOS2	⟨NN, left, DT, JJ⟩
... + Rel1 + Rel2	⟨NN, left, Det, Mod⟩

Table 1: Basic head-dependent and sibling dependent ordering features

CCGbank, Section 00, using a perceptron model with and without the dependency features as well as an oracle model using an n-gram precision score (approximating BLEU) against the reference sentence, which provides a topline result. Grammatically complete realizations were found for 83% of the development sentences within a 15-second time limit; in the remaining cases, outputs were constructed from the current chart either using the glue rules or the earlier greedy fragment assembly. With the glue rules, the realizer was run with packing enabled with a new 15-second limit, and complete edges were unpacked; with greedy fragment assembly, the realizer was run in best-first mode up to the new time limit, and then the available edges were greedily assembled. As the table shows, on the fragmentary cases the glue rules yield more than a three and a half point improvement in BLEU scores over greedy fragment assembly when using the perceptron scorer, both with the dependency features (from 0.6170 for 0.6523) and without them (from 0.6039 to 0.6408), showing that the modeling benefit of the dependency features carries over to the fragmentary cases. With the oracle scorer, the improvement is over 7.5 BLEU points, indicating that the glue rules may be capable of yielding even larger improvements with better ranking models.

Table 3 confirms the results of the averaged perceptron model with dependency features on the test section of the CCGbank, Section 23. As is evident in the table, the gap between the BLEU scores for the grammatically complete sentences and the fragmentary ones is quite large (more than 20 BLEU points). Thus, although the overall improvement in BLEU scores is modest (0.6-0.7 of a BLEU point) since the glue rules apply in only 15-17% of the cases, their effect is clearly noticeable with these sentences where the outputs remain generally mediocre.

5 Conclusions and Future Work

This paper has shown how glue rules can be used in OpenCCG as a fall-back option when no grammatically complete realization can be found, thereby increasing the robustness of chart realization. Unlike an earlier robustness technique of greedily assembling fragments, glue rules enable n-best outputs, are compatible with disjunctive inputs, and explore a larger space of possible fragment concatenations. They also differ from the fragment concatenation rules used in hand-crafted grammars for the XLE realizer in applying recursively, enabling the glue rules to emulate dependency realization. The experimental results indicate that by enabling this larger space of assembled fragments to be explored, glue rules can yield improved realizations in comparison to greedy fragment assembly, though a sizeable gap remains between the quality of grammatically complete realizations and fragmentary ones.

In future work, we plan to experiment with realization ranking models incorporating richer dependency-based features, with the aim of further reducing the quality gap between grammatically complete and fragmentary realizations. We also plan to examine the impact of such models and the glue rules on Generation Challenges shared task results.

Acknowledgments

This work was supported in part by NSF grant number IIS-0812297. Thanks go to the anonymous reviewers for helpful comments and discussion.

References

Jason Baldridge and Geert-Jan Kruijff. 2002. Coupling CCG and Hybrid Logic Dependency Semantics. In *Proc. ACL-02*.

Stephen Boxwell and Michael White. 2008. Projecting Propbank roles onto the CCGbank. In *Proc. LREC-08*.

Aoife Cahill and Josef van Genabith. 2006. Robust PCFG-based generation using automatically acquired LFG approximations. In *Proc. COLING-ACL '06*.

John Carroll and Stefan Oepen. 2005. High efficiency realization for a wide-coverage unification grammar. In *Proc. IJCNLP-05*.

David Chiang. 2007. Hierarchical phrase-based translation. *Computational Linguistics*, 33(2):201–228, June.

Stephen Clark and James R. Curran. 2007. Wide-Coverage Efficient Statistical Parsing with CCG and Log-Linear Models. *Computational Linguistics*, 33(4):493–552.

Dominic Espinosa, Michael White, and Dennis Mehay. 2008. Hypertagging: Supertagging for surface realization with CCG. In *Proceedings of ACL-08: HLT*, pages 183–191, Columbus, Ohio, June. Association for Computational Linguistics.

Karthik Gali and Sriram Venkatapathy. 2009. Sentence realisation from bag of words with dependency constraints. In *Proceedings of Human Language Technologies: The 2009 Annual Conference of the North American Chapter of the Association for Computational Linguistics, Companion Volume: Student Research Workshop and Doctoral Consortium*, NAACL '09, pages 19–24, Morristown, NJ, USA. Association for Computational Linguistics.

Yuqing Guo, Josef van Genabith, and Haifeng Wang. 2008. Dependency-based n-gram models for general purpose sentence realisation. In *Proc. COLING-08*.

Yuqing Guo, Haifeng Wang, and Josef van Genabith. 2010. A linguistically inspired statistical model for chinese punctuation generation. *ACM Transactions on Asian Language Information Processing*, 9:6:1–6:27, June.

Julia Hockenmaier and Mark Steedman. 2007. CCGbank: A Corpus of CCG Derivations and Dependency Structures Extracted from the Penn Treebank. *Computational Linguistics*, 33(3):355–396.

Deirdre Hogan, Conor Cafferkey, Aoife Cahill, and Josef van Genabith. 2007. Exploiting multi-word units in history-based probabilistic generation. In *Proc. EMNLP-CoNLL*.

Martin Kay. 1996. Chart generation. In *Proc. ACL-96*.

Hiroko Nakanishi, Yusuke Miyao, and Jun'ichi Tsujii. 2005. Probabilistic methods for disambiguation of an HPSG-based chart generator. In *Proc. IWPT-05*.

Rajakrishnan Rajkumar and Michael White. 2010. Designing agreement features for realization ranking. In *Coling 2010: Posters*, pages 1032–1040, Beijing, China, August. Coling 2010 Organizing Committee.

Rajakrishnan Rajkumar, Michael White, and Dominic Espinosa. 2009. Exploiting named entity classes in ccg surface realization. In *Proceedings of Human Language Technologies: The 2009 Annual Conference of the North American Chapter of the Association for Computational Linguistics, Companion Volume: Short Papers*, pages 161–164, Boulder, Colorado, June. Association for Computational Linguistics.

Brian Roark, Murat Saraclar, Michael Collins, and Mark Johnson. 2004. Discriminative language modeling with conditional random fields and the perceptron algorithm. In *Proc. ACL-04*.

David Schneider and Kathleen F. McCoy. 1998. Recognizing syntactic errors in the writing of second language learners. In *Proceedings of the 36th Annual Meeting of the Association for Computational Linguistics and 17th International Conference on Computational Linguistics, Volume 2*, pages 1198–1204, Montreal, Quebec, Canada, August. Association for Computational Linguistics.

Camilla Schwind. 1988. Sensitive parsing: error analysis and explanation in an intelligent language tutoring system. In *Proceedings of the 12th Conference on Computational Linguistics*, pages 608–613.

Hadar Shemtov. 1997. *Ambiguity Management in Natural Language Generation*. Ph.D. thesis, Stanford University.

Mark Steedman. 2000. *The Syntactic Process*. MIT Press.

Erik Velldal and Stefan Oepen. 2005. Maximum entropy models for realization ranking. In *Proc. MT-Summit X*.

Erik Velldal, Stephan Oepen, and Dan Flickinger. 2004. Paraphrasing treebanks for stochastic realization ranking. In *Proceedings of the 3rd Workshop on Treebanks and Linguistic Theories*.

Michael White and Rajakrishnan Rajkumar. 2009. Perceptron reranking for CCG realization. In *Proceedings of the 2009 Conference on Empirical Methods in Natural Language Processing*, pages 410–419, Singapore, August. Association for Computational Linguistics.

Michael White. 2006a. CCG chart realization from disjunctive logical forms. In *Proc. INLG-06*.

Michael White. 2006b. Efficient Realization of Coordinate Structures in Combinatory Categorial Grammar. *Research on Language & Computation*, 4(1):39–75.

Detecting Interesting Event Sequences for Sports Reporting

François Lareau **Mark Dras** **Robert Dale**

Centre for Language Technology
Macquarie University, Sydney, Australia
francois.lareau|mark.dras|robert.dale@mq.edu.au

Abstract

Hand-crafted approaches to content determination are expensive to port to new domains. Machine-learned approaches, on the other hand, tend to be limited to relatively simple selection of items from data sets. We observe that in time series domains, textual descriptions often aggregate a series of events into a compact description. We present a simple technique for automatically determining sequences of events that are worth reporting, and evaluate its effectiveness.

1 Introduction

We are developing a Natural Language Generation (NLG) system for generating commentary-style textual descriptions of Australian Football League (AFL) games, in both English and the Australian Aboriginal language Arrernte. There are a number of research questions to be tackled: one is how to handle a resource-poor, non-configurational language, the inherent complexities of which are outlined by Austin and Bresnan (1996); another, the focus of this paper, is the issue of content selection in the sports domain. More precisely, we are concerned with a kind of content aggregation that we call *aggregative inference*. Below is an extract from a typical human-authored commentary for a game:[1]

> Led by Brownlow medallist Adam Goodes and veteran Jude Bolton, the Swans kicked seven goals from 16 entries inside their forward 50 to open a 30-point advantage at the final change—to that point the largest lead of the match.

There is a corresponding database which contains quantitative and other data regarding the game: who scored when, from where, and so on. In the example given above, the phrase *the Swans kicked seven goals from 16 entries* goes beyond simply putting similar facts together; it involves an inference on the score progression to identify a strong moment of arbitrary duration in the game. In human-authored commentaries, we observed that this kind of aggregation is common; but existing content selection and aggregation techniques will not suffice here.

After surveying some related work on data-to-text generation and content selection (§2), we characterise our notion of aggregative inference, and present an analysis of our AFL data to demonstrate that it is a significant phenomenon (§3). We then propose a method for this task that can be used as a baseline for future work, and examine its adequacy for content selection (§4).

2 Related work

Time series Previous work has dealt with time series data and the particular problem of segmenting them meaningfully. Time series are typically continuous processes monitored at regular intervals; ours, in contrast, are irregular sequences of discrete events. The main difference is the number of data points: for example, a pressure sensor can produce thousands of readings in a day, but we only need to consider about 50 events in a game (see §3).

The SumTime project (Sripada et al., 2003b; Yu et al., 2004) aims to produce a generic time series summary generator. It has been applied to weather forecasts (Sripada et al., 2002; Sripada et al., 2003a), neo-natal intensive care (Sripada et al., 2003c; Portet et al., 2009), and gas turbine monitoring (Yu et al., 2006). For weather forecasts, Keogh et al. (2001) used a bottom-up segmentation technique that required thresholds to be set. In SumTime-Turbine, a search was made for patterns that had to be identified in a semi-automatic way using expert knowledge.

[1] All texts and data in this paper are from www.afl.com.au and stats.rleague.com/afl. For an explanation of the game, see en.wikipedia.org/wiki/Australian_rules_football.

Proceedings of the 13th European Workshop on Natural Language Generation (ENLG), pages 200–205,
Nancy, France, September 2011.

We want to do without thresholds and experts, using instead paired data and text (as in machine learning approaches, discussed below). In the domain of neonatal intensive care, Gao et al. (2009) focused on detecting unrecorded events in time-series; in contrast, we want to detect clusters of events rather than individual events. In the domain of air quality, Wanner et al. (2007) do not explain in detail how they segmented their curves, but they appear to have detected peaks and then considered the intervals between these peaks, assessing their slope. We need to be able to assess the slopes between any two data points, as human-authored texts refer to intervals other than those between peaks (cf. §3). Boyd (1998) used a signal processing technique called *wavelets* to detect trends in weather data. This is similar to a Fourier transform, except that it is not constrained to a specific time window, an important feature for detecting trends of arbitrary lengths. In her evaluation, 17 out of 26 trends (65.4%) mentioned by experts in human-authored texts were predicted by her system. Again, she did not have paired data and text.

Sports In general, content selection in the sports domain has so far amounted to selecting individual events in the game (Oh and Shrobe, 2008; Bouayad-Agha et al., 2011), with the exception of the work of Barzilay and Lapata (2005), discussed below. Some previous NLG systems for the sports domain were live speech generators (Herzog and Wazinski, 1994; André et al., 2000) that faced problems inherent to incremental NLG which are not relevant for us, in particular the fact that content selection must take place before the full course of the game is known. Robin (1994) focused mainly on *opportunistic generation*, i.e., the addition of background information, which is not the subject of our current work.

Machine learning Duboue and McKeown (2003) were the first to propose a machine learning approach to content selection; this and subsequent work has almost exclusively looked at selecting items from the raw tabular data. Taking aligned summaries and database entries in the domain of biographical texts, Duboue and McKeown (2003) construct a classification model for selecting both database rows that match the text exactly, and others that require some clustering across their graph-based representation. Barzilay and Lapata (2005) also take a classification approach, working on American football data. Formulating the problem as one of energy minimisation allows them to find a globally optimal set of database rows, in contrast to the independent row selection of Duboue and McKeown (2003). The goal of both approaches was to extract and present items that occur in the tabular data; Barzilay and Lapata (2005) explicitly restrict themselves to selecting from this raw data. Kelly et al. (2009), applying Barzilay and Lapata's approach to the domain of cricket, go beyond looking at raw data items to a limited 'grouping' of data, for example in pairing player data for batting partnerships.

In contrast, we are interested in presenting not just raw data, but data over which some inference has been carried out (as in the selection of time series data by Yu et al. (2004)), and the feasibility of using a machine learning approach to achieve this.

		Event		**Score**		
Time	**Player**	**H**	**A**	**H**	**A**	**M**
1′40″	Jesse White	G		6	0	6
4′42″	Jarrad McVeigh	B		7	0	7
10′05″	Patrick Ryder		B	7	1	6

Table 1: Sample scoring events data

Player	**K**	**M**	**H**	**G**	**B**	**T**
Jude Bolton	16	3	20	0	0	12
Adam Goodes	11	5	5	2	4	1
Heath Grundy	8	2	8	0	0	1

Table 2: Sample of in-game player statistics

3 Correlating data and texts

Our data comes in the form of tables that focus on different aspects of the game. The most important for our current purpose is the table of scoring events, which gives information about the score progression in the game: goals (worth 6 points) and behinds (1 point) scored by the home and away teams, their respective scores, and the margin[2] (see Table 1). There is also a table with statistics for each player during a given game, with his number of kicks, marks, handballs, goals, behinds and tackles for the match, as shown in Table 2. Other data is available that we do not have space to show here.

We collected human-authored summaries to see how they relate to the available data. The particular

[2]The home team's score minus the visitors'.

summaries we used are the published commentary of the sort found in newspapers: ours came from the Match Centre of the AFL website.[3] These are typically written by professional sports journalists as the game is taking place, and posted on the web shortly after the game has finished. The writers consequently have access to video of the game, and to the extensive set of statistics available from the Match Centre during the course of the game.

Each story is around 500 words long and consists of roughly 15–20 sentences organised in short paragraphs (a couple of sentences each). A typical text starts with a summary of the game's key facts: who won by how many points at which stadium, along with an overall characterisation of the match. It then continues with a more or less chronological presentation of the course of the game, an evaluation of each team's key players in the match, and a list of the injured; and it concludes with the consequences of the game's result on the season's rankings and a teaser about the upcoming games.

The stories essentially focus on in-game events (as opposed to background information), in particular scoring events. We also observed that more than half of the information conveyed required some sort of reasoning over the data. We identified three main types of propositions expressed in the text:

Raw data: propositions that refer to data readily available from the database, e.g., the margin in *The Swans led by 33 points at the final break.*

Homogeneous aggregative inferences: propositions that require reasoning over one type of data, e.g., *the Tigers kicked eight of the last 10 goals* (where there is no database entry that corresponds to this statistic, and it is necessary to carry out an aggregation over goals for an arbitrary time period) or *the result was never in doubt* (which is a more abstract assessment of the score over a period of time).

Heterogeneous aggregative inferences: propositions that require inferences on data of different types, e.g., *Melbourne physically dominated the Swans* (which refers to a combination of tackles, contested marks, players' physical attributes, and so on).

We distinguish *surface aggregation*, where information is packaged at the linguistic level, and *deep aggregation*, which takes place at the conceptual level; compare, e.g., *Johnson marked six goals and gathered 25 possessions* with *Johnson gave a stellar performance*. We are only concerned with the latter.

[3]See www.afl.com.au.

Type	#	%
Raw data	120	38.8
Score-based homo. aggreg. infer.	68	21.7
Other homogeneous aggreg. infer.	13	4.2
Heterogeneous aggregative infer.	112	35.8
Total	313	100.0

Table 3: Types of information conveyed in AFL stories

In a first step, we manually annotated ten of the collected texts using the above typology, leaving aside all propositions that did not refer to in-game information, and ignoring surface aggregations. Since scoring events are so important in this genre, we further divided the homogeneous aggregative inference type into two sub-categories—those based on score and those based on other data—and annotated the texts accordingly; Table 3 summarises the breakdown.[4]

Raw data accounts for just under 39% of the data expressed in these texts; the score at various points in time makes up the bulk of this category. In an AFL game, it is normal to see 30 goals and a similar number of behinds being scored. Consequently, not all are mentioned in the texts, so the problem with raw data in this context is to select the events that are mentionworthy; this problem has been explored already (cf. §2). More interesting, however, are score-based aggregative inferences, calculated from a sequence of goals and behinds. These account for almost 22% of our small corpus, and are not amenable to detection by existing approaches.

In a second step, we drew the curve for the score margin in every game, then took each expression marked as a score-based aggregative inference and identified the elements of the curve it referred to: (1) individual scoring events (points in time where the margin changes), (2) intervals between scoring events, or (3) the area under the curve (see Table 4). For the expressions that referred to intervals, we identified four subtypes: (1) those that refer to intervals where a team is on a roll (scoring points for a sustained period of time), or (2) when there is a

[4]We first annotated ten other stories with finer-grained categories, then two annotators went through three iterations of this mark-up until they agreed, before we annotated these ten stories.

Type	#	%
Intervals between events	40	58.8
Individual events	24	35.3
Area under the curve	4	5.9
Total	68	100.0

Table 4: Types of score inferences

Subtype	#	%
Team is on a roll	22	55.0
Tight struggle	7	17.5
Lead changes	5	12.5
Other	6	15.0
Total	40	100.0

Table 5: Subtypes of intervals referred to in texts

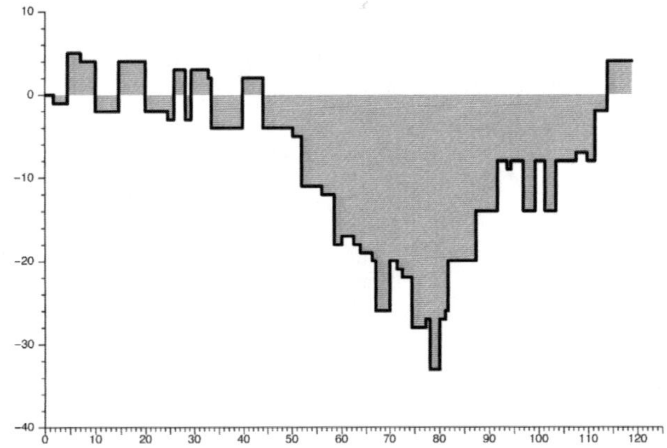

Figure 1: Sample score margin curve

tight struggle (a relatively extended period where no team is able to change the score margin significantly), (3) expressions that refer to the number of lead changes, and (4) other expressions (see Table 5).

It is clear from these observations that detecting when a team is on a roll is a very important kind of aggregative inference in this genre. We propose below a technique for doing this. Since detecting tight struggles is a closely related problem, we will also try to tackle it at the same time.

4 A curve segmentation technique

The goal is to identify clusters of events of arbitrary duration that form a unit of discourse. In contrast to the SUMTIME systems, where patterns in time series data are codified through discussions with experts or are subject to a user-defined threshold, we want to identify a measure such that content selection can be learned automatically, as an extension of techniques like those already used for homogeneous aggregative inferences (§2). We look for intervals in the score margin curve where the slope is either steep or rather flat (cf. Figure 1). What makes the problem non-trivial is that we do not know how steep or flat the curve needs to be in order to be interesting, how long the interval should be, and where it should start. There are 'natural time anchors' for intervals, namely the beginning and the end of the game or quarters, and peaks in the curve; however, human reporters also select intervals that are not bound to these anchors.

We calculate for each game the absolute value[5] of the slope between all pairs of scoring events (goals and behinds).[6] The slopes are then normalised relative to all other slopes that span the same number of events in the same game (by subtracting the mean and dividing by standard deviation); a steep slope over a short span (when a goal is scored right after another, say) is not as meaningful as an equally steep slope over a long span (which corresponds to a roll).

As an illustration, Figure 2 gives the matrix for the curve in Figure 1. Scoring events are numbered 1 to 49, and each cell corresponds to the interval between two events, with darkness indicating the normalised value. The shortest intervals appear along the diagonal edge, and as we move away from the edge and towards the upper-right corner of the matrix, we get longer intervals. The interval with the highest value in this matrix is the one between events 32 and 35 (at row 32, column 35). Indeed, it is the interval between the 78th and 82nd minutes of play, when the home team kicked back into the game. Notice that all the cells in row 32 and column 32 have a high value. This is because the 32nd event is the lowest point of the curve, so the slope between any point and this one is likely to be higher than normal. Hence, such dark bands identify important peaks in the curve. Notice also the contrast between the generally low values in the columns 1 to 17, and the generally higher ones in columns 18 and up. This contrast identifies another kind of inflection point in the curve: the event 17 is the one at the 50th minute of play, just before the curve plunges deep into negative values.

[5]The direction in which the margin changes is irrelevant.

[6]There are around 50 such events in a typical match, so there is a matrix of roughly 1200 pairs to consider (for n events in a game, there are $n \times \frac{n-1}{2}$ possible intervals).

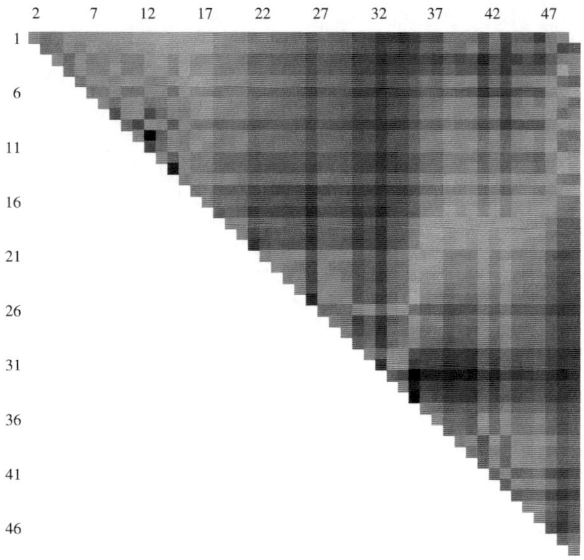

Figure 2: Sample matrix of normalised interval slopes

Rolls

Rank	#	%
≥ 0.9	15	68.2
≥ 0.8	17	77.3
≥ 0.7	20	90.9
Total	22	100.0
Median: 0.956		

Struggles

Rank	#	%
≤ 0.1	3	42.9
≤ 0.2	3	42.9
≤ 0.3	4	57.1
Total	7	100.0
Median: 0.204		

Table 6: Percentile ranks for normalised interval slopes

Finally, the normalised values are ranked in comparison with the other values for the game, and the ranks are expressed as percentiles. One would expect that when a team is on a roll, the slope for the corresponding interval will be comparatively high, and should rank towards the top, while in contrast, when the game is tight, the curve should look rather flat, and therefore the corresponding interval's normalised slope should have a low rank. The fact that the slopes are normalised relative to other slopes of equal intervals makes it possible to compare intervals of any duration and to rank them regardless of length.

We tested this technique on the data that corresponds to the texts we had annotated, and checked how many of the rolls and struggles mentioned in the texts received a rank that made sense (high ranks for rolls, low ones for struggles); see Table 6.

The technique works well for rolls, and could be used as a baseline and as a starting point for a stochastic reranking approach: taking the top 30%, say, and reranking based on other local score context.

For the rolls where the rank was lower than 0.9, most were cases where either it was not clear what interval was referred to in the text, or there was a reversal in the trend (and this was communicatively more important than the roll itself), or a roll was mentioned precisely because it was mild in contrast with another interval mentioned elsewhere.

The results are not as promising for struggles, probably because struggles tend to be in games with a generally flat curve, so that any segment of the game is likely not particularly more flat than the rest of the match, and therefore hard to detect. One possible alternative is to use a different score-related measure, e.g. a matrix of lead changes per time period. A second is to compare intervals with other intervals of the same duration in all games, rather than in the same game, as in the 'measures of interestingness based on unusualness' of Yu et al. (2004).

With respect to other work, our segmentation technique does not fit into any of the three types mentioned in Sripada et al. (2002): sliding window, top-down or bottom-up. It is not a pattern matching technique either, as in Yu et al. (2006). The normalisation of the segments aims to handle the variability of granularity that we need; this is the same goal as the wavelet technique of Boyd (1998), but our approach is technically much simpler. However, this method is only viable for curves with a limited number of data points, since it must take into account all possible sub-segments of the curve.

5 Conclusion

We have assessed the content of human summaries of football games in terms of the source of data for the facts they express, and have observed that a significant proportion of these facts were derived from inferences made on the score progression.

One frequent type of score inference is to detect exciting segments of the game, that is, either when a team is on a roll, or when there is a tight struggle. We have proposed a baseline technique to detect such intervals based on the slope between any two scoring events on a score margin curve. Our preliminary results show that this technique tends to do quite well at detecting when a team is on a roll, and somewhat less well at detecting tight struggles. We now plan to use it as a baseline for the evaluation of machine learning techniques.

Acknowledgements

The authors acknowledge the support of ARC Discovery DP1095443.

References

Elisabeth André, Kim Binsted, Kumiko Tanaka-Ishii, Sean Luke, Gerd Herzog, and Thomas Rist. 2000. Three RoboCup simulation league commentator systems. *AI Magazine*, 21(1):57–66.

Peter Austin and Joan Bresnan. 1996. Non-configurationality in Australian aboriginal languages. *Natural Language and Linguistic Theory*, 14(2):215–268.

Regina Barzilay and Mirella Lapata. 2005. Collective content selection for concept-to-text generation. In Chris Brew, Lee-Feng Chien, and Katrin Kirchhoff, editors, *Proceedings of Human Language Technology Conference and Conference on Empirical Methods in Natural Language Processing (HLT/EMNLP'05)*, pages 331–338, Vancouver.

Nadjet Bouayad-Agha, Gerard Casamayor, Leo Wanner, Fernando Díez, and Sergio López Hernández. 2011. FootbOWL: Using a generic ontology of football competition for planning match summaries. In *Proceedings of the Extended Semantic Web Conference (ESWC'11)*, Heraklion, Greece.

Sarah Boyd. 1998. TREND: a system for generating intelligent descriptions of time series data. In *Proceedings of the IEEE international conference on intelligent processing systems (ICIPS-1998)*.

Pablo Ariel Duboue and Kathleen R. McKeown. 2003. Statistical acquisition of content selection rules for natural language generation. In Michael Collins and Mark Steedman, editors, *Proceedings of the 2003 Conference on Empirical Methods in Natural Language Processing (EMNLP'03)*, pages 121–128, Sapporo.

Feng Gao, Yaji Sripada, Jim Hunter, and François Portet. 2009. Using temporal constraints to integrate signal analysis and domain knowledge in medical event detection. In *Proceedings of the 12th Conference on Artificial Intelligence in Medicine: Artificial Intelligence in Medicine (AIME'09)*, pages 46–55, Verona, Italy.

Gerd Herzog and Peter Wazinski. 1994. VIsual TRAnslator: Linking perceptions and natural language descriptions. *Artificial Intelligence Review*, 8(2–3):175–187.

Colin Kelly, Ann Copestake, and Nikiforos Karamanis. 2009. Investigating content selection for language generation using machine learning. In *Proceedings of the 12th European Workshop on Natural Language Generation (ENLG 2009)*, pages 130–137, Athens.

Eamonn Keogh, Selina Chu, David Hart, and Michael Pazzani. 2001. An online algorithm for segmenting time series. In *Proceedings of the IEEE International Conference on Data Mining (ICDM 2001)*, pages 289–296, San Jose, CA.

Alice Oh and Howard Shrobe. 2008. Generating baseball summaries from multiple perspectives by reordering content. In *Proceedings of the Fifth International Natural Language Generation Conference (INLG 2008)*, pages 173–176, Salt Fork.

François Portet, Ehud Reiter, Albert Gatt, Jim Hunter, Somayajulu Sripada, Yvonne Freer, and Cindy Sykes. 2009. Automatic generation of textual summaries from neonatal intensive care data. *Artificial Intelligence*, 173(7-8):789–816.

Jacques Robin. 1994. *Revision-Based Generation of Natural Language Summaries Providing Historical Background.* Ph.D. thesis, Columbia University, New York.

Somayajulu G. Sripada, Ehud Reiter, Jim Hunter, and Jin Yu. 2002. Segmenting time series for weather forecasting. In A. Macintosh, R. Ellis, and F. Coenen, editors, *Applications and Innovations in Intelligent Systems X*, pages 193–206. Springer.

Somayajulu G. Sripada, Ehud Reiter, and Ian Davy. 2003a. SumTime-Mousam: Configurable marine weather forecast generator. *Expert Update*, 6(3):4–10.

Somayajulu G. Sripada, Ehud Reiter, Jim Hunter, and Jin Yu. 2003b. Generating english summaries of time series data using the gricean maxims. In *Proceedings of the ninth ACM SIGKDD international conference on Knowledge discovery and data mining (KDD'03)*, pages 187–196, Washington.

Somayajulu G. Sripada, Ehud Reiter, Jim Hunter, and Jin Yu. 2003c. Summarizing neonatal time series data. In *Proceedings of the tenth conference on European chapter of the Association for Computational Linguistics (EACL'03)*, volume 2, pages 167–170, Budapest.

Leo Wanner, Bernd Bohnet, Nadjet Bouayad-Agha, François Lareau, Achim Lohmeyer, and Daniel Nicklaß. 2007. On the challenge of creating and communicating air quality information. In A. Swayne and J. Hrebicek, editors, *Proceedings of ISESS 2007*, Prague.

Jin Yu, Ehud Reiter, Jim Hunter, and Somayajulu Sripada. 2004. A new architecture for summarising time series data. In *Proceedings of INLG-04 Poster Session*, pages 47–50, Brockenhurst, UK.

Jin Yu, Ehud Reiter, Jim Hunter, and Chris Mellish. 2006. Choosing the content of textual summaries of large time-series data sets. *Natural Language Engineering*, 13(1):25–49.

Generation Challenges 2011 Preface

Generation Challenges 2011 (GenChal'11) was the fifth round of shared-task evaluation competitions (STECs) involving the generation of natural language. It followed four previous events: the Pilot Attribute Selection for Generating Referring Expressions (ASGRE) Challenge in 2007 which had its results meeting at UCNLG+MT in Copenhagen, Denmark; Referring Expression Generation (REG) Challenges in 2008, with a results meeting at INLG'08 in Ohio, US; Generation Challenges 2009 with a results meeting at ENLG'09 in Athens, Greece; and most recently Generation Challenges 2010 with a results meeting at INLG'10 in Trim, Ireland. More information about all these NLG STEC events can be found via the links on the Generation Challenges homepage (http://www.nltg.brighton.ac.uk/research/genchal11).

GenChal'11 brought together three STECs: the first Surface Realisation Challenge (SR'11) organised by Anja Belz, Deirdre Hogan, Michael White and Amanda Stent; the Challenge on Generating Instructions in Virtual Environments (GIVE) organised by Kristina Striegnitz, Alexandre Denis, Andrew Gargett, Konstantina Garoufi, Alexander Koller, and Mariët Theune; and the new Helping Our Own Challenge (HOO) organised by Robert Dale and Adam Kilgarriff.

In addition, GenChal'11 had a Future Task Proposals Track where researchers were invited to submit papers describing ideas for STECs to be run in the future. The proposals that were submitted to this track are the first two papers in this part of the proceedings: Janarthanam and Lemon's paper on the proposed GRUVE Challenge which can be seen as taking up where the GIVE Challenge is now leaving off; and Gervas and Ballesteros's paper on a Spanish version of the Surface Realisation Challenge.

For the first time this year, GenChal did not have an Open Track or Evaluation Methodologies Track, as these attracted very few submissions in the past.

The SR Task was based on Penn Treebank data and the organisers created two different input representations, one shallow, one deep, mainly from the annotations used in the CoNLL'08 Shared Task. The task for participating teams was to automatically generate surface realisations from the input representations. Five teams submitted six systems to the shallow and deep tracks. The submitted systems were evaluated using four automatic metrics and three human-assessed criteria. This volume includes the SR Task results report and the system reports by the participating teams.

In the GIVE Challenge, participating teams developed systems which generate natural-language instructions that help a human user solve a task in a 3D virtual world. The eight participating systems were evaluated by measuring how accurately and efficiently users were able to perform the task with a given system's instructions, and by collecting subjective ratings of the instruction quality from users. This year's GIVE Challenge maintained the same task as in GIVE-2 (with new evaluation worlds, of course), so that the participating teams could learn from the results of last year's edition and additional teams would be able to participate. The evaluation report for the GIVE Challenge as well as descriptions of the participating systems can be found in this volume. The software infrastructure (and at a later stage the collected data) is available on the GIVE website (http://www.give-challenge.org/research).

Proceedings of the 13th European Workshop on Natural Language Generation (ENLG), pages 206–207,
Nancy, France, September 2011.

The first HOO Challenge used a corpus of 1,000-word excerpts of text from papers in the ACL anthology that have been donated by their authors. Each excerpt was copy-edited by professional copy-editors and marked up with the resulting corrections. The task for participants was to produce such corrections automatically. Despite a relatively short turn-around time, six teams were able to participate in HOO. Their system reports and the results report by Dale and Kilgarriff are included in this volume.

The Question Generation Challenge did not run this year. However, the organisers have contributed a report outlining recent and future developments.

Once again, we successfully applied (with the help of support letters from many of last year's participants and other HLT colleagues) for funding from the Engineering and Physical Sciences Research Council (EPSRC), the main funding body for HLT in the UK. This support helped with all aspects of developing and running the SR Task and organising Generation Challenges 2011. It enabled us to create the SR Task data and to carry out human evaluations, as well as to pay for Deirdre Hogan and Eric Kow's time spent working on the SR Task.

Preparations are already underway for a sixth NLG shared-task evaluation event next year, Generation Challenges 2012, which is likely to include a first run of the GRUVE Challenge, a second run of the SR Task, hopefully as a multilingual task, including the Spanish version, and a second run of the HOO task. Results are likely to be presented at INLG'12.

Just like our previous STECs, Generation Challenges 2011 would not have been possible without the contributions of many different people. We would like to thank the students of Oxford University, KCL, UCL and Sussex Universities who participated in the SR Task evaluations; the ENLG'11 organisers, Claire Gardent and Kristina Striegnitz; the research support team at Brighton University and the EPSRC for help with obtaining funding; and last but not least, the participants in the shared tasks themselves.

Anja Belz, Albert Gatt, Alexander Koller and Kristina Striegnitz
September 2011

Generation Challenges Steering Committee:

Anja Belz, University of Brighton, UK
Robert Dale, Macquarie University, Australia
Albert Gatt, University of Malta and Unversity of Aberdeen, UK
Kevin Knight, ISI, University of Southern California, USA
Alexander Koller, Saarland University, Germany
Chris Mellish, Aberdeen University, UK
Johanna Moore, Edinburgh University, UK
Amanda Stent, Stony Brook University, USA
Kristina Striegnitz, Union College, USA

The GRUVE Challenge: Generating Routes under Uncertainty in Virtual Environments

Srini Janarthanam and Oliver Lemon
Interaction Lab, MACS
Heriot-Watt University
Edinburgh, United Kingdom
sc445,o.lemon@hw.ac.uk
www.macs.hw.ac.uk/InteractionLab

Abstract

We propose a shared task based around generation of instructions for pedestrian users navigating in open-world virtual environments. An important variant of this task involves handling uncertainty about the user's location (as would happen in the real world with a standard GPS system). We motivate and explain the task, propose metrics for evaluation of systems, describe the planned software setup, and propose a timeline for the challenge.

1 Introduction

Providing route instructions and descriptions for users is an interesting and a challenging task. Route-giving tasks have recently attracted active research in the NLG and dialogue systems communities (Dale et al., 2002; Cheng et al., 2004; Richter et al., 2008; Cuayhuitl et al., 2010; Dethlefs and Cuayáhuitl, 2011; Dethlefs et al., 2011). Route-giving (whether in virtual or real environments) involves many decisions, including when to instruct, what instructions and/or descriptions to give, and how to verbalize them. Research has shown that inclusion of landmarks in route instructions is highly effective (May et al., 2003; Schroder et al., 2011). In order to include landmarks in instructions, decisions such as which landmarks to include, how best to refer to them, and so on, must be taken. Another interesting issue for real-world route-giving is that it is not always possible to know where the user is, or where they are looking. Even when using tools like GPS trackers, there is an element of uncertainty in the pedestrian user's location, so generation under uncertainty becomes important (Lemon et al., 2010). Finally, instructions and referring expressions should also take into account the pedestrian's field of view or "viewshed", which is not directly observable but may be inferred from uncertain information about location and orientation.

Virtual environments provide an important development and test infrastructure for real-world systems. They avoid the need for costly and time-consuming real-world experiments and data-collections, while allowing manipulation of the spatial environment to investigate specific issues and contexts for NLG systems.

There is therefore an interesting and practical shared task in which research teams can collaborate using a shared infrastructure to investigate NLG issues in route giving tasks to pedestrians in outdoor virtual environments, where different types and degrees of uncertainty can be manipulated experimentally. The GRUVE challenge targets these tasks, with the expectation that its results will be informative for real-world pedestrian navigation systems.

2 Related work

The "Generating Instructions in Virtual Environments" (GIVE) challenge has been running successful shared tasks since 2009 (Koller et al., 2007; Byron et al., 2007). In this task, human users log into a virtual world over the Internet in which they are free to walk around inside building-like environments with several rooms and corridors. The objective (for users) of these tasks is to follow the instructions given to them (in text), navigate around, push buttons to disable or enable alarms, open or close doors, and finally recover a hidden trophy. Several teams participated in this shared task to build systems that will generate instructions online to the users. The generation systems were provided with the user's location and viewshed (i.e. what objects in the world are in the user's view). In the first version of the challenge, the users moved "block by block" in a grid-based virtual environment. Therefore it was possible to give instructions such as "move 3 steps forward".

Proceedings of the 13th European Workshop on Natural Language Generation (ENLG), pages 208–211,
Nancy, France, September 2011.

Figure 1: An outdoor virtual environment from SecondLife

However in the latest version of this challenge, the users move continuously and not discretely (Gargett et al., 2010). This challenge examined the issues concerning generating instructions and referring expressions in situated contexts. Our proposed challenge is similar to the GIVE challenge in the sense that it involves systems generating instructions for navigation, and generating referring expressions to refer to entities in the world. But in contrast, in this challenge, we propose to use an outdoor virtual environment where route instruction giving and referring to outdoor entities would be for pedestrian navigation in city-like environments, involving issues such as uncertainty in user's location and viewshed.

3 GRUVE Shared tasks

We propose a collection of shared tasks or challenges which will allow exploration of a number of issues in NLG:

- NLG under uncertainty
- the generation of instructions and route descriptions
- generation of referring expressions
- situated NLG
- optimisation of NLG
- adaptive NLG for different users
- NLG in interactive systems.

The proposed tasks will take place in an outdoor virtual environment and will be variants of route giving tasks. The basic task will be to get the user (who sees a first-person perspective, pedestrian view of the environment, see e.g. Figure 1) from location A to location B. The task can vary along the following dimensions of system knowledge:

- precision of user location information
- precision of user gaze direction / contents or user viewshed
- previous knowledge of user behaviour
- amount of feedback from user and its reliability/ noise.

We propose to evaluate NLG systems developed by the participating teams in route instruction giving tasks under various conditions discussed above. In the simplest case, the system has total information about the user location, heading/gaze direction, history of interaction/behaviour, and a clear and detailed set of feedback signals (e.g. "I am lost", "I am confused", "repeat", "rephrase", etc) as on-screen buttons. The challenge will be a case of constructing optimal messages for the user based on complete knowledge of their situation, which is akin to generating instructions for players of video games, as in an interactive version of the original GIVE task. (We discuss notions of optimality shortly). At the other end of the spectrum we may have to generate instructions for unknown users whose location we are very insure of, where feedback signals are very noisy, and where we don't have much idea what direction they are facing. This latter set of conditions is similar to real-world city navigation problems. There is a wide range of possibilities across this spectrum. For example, one task would be to generate instructions to users whose location is uncertain. In such situations, it becomes necessary to not only instruct the users but also question them in order to reduce uncertainty arising due to their location. Therefore, the NLG systems should be able to generate both instructions and questions in order to successfully complete the task. The NLG system should also be able to decide when to question the user and when to instruct him.

Instructions can also be generated in two formats: *a priori* or *in situ*. In the *a priori* format, the entire set of instructions to follow from source to destination are given to the user at the starting point. On the other hand, in the *in situ* format, a sequence of instructions are given to the user on the fly one by one as he walks along the route at appropriate times. We believe that all these generation tasks involve subtasks like content planning, referring expression generation, aggregation, realization, timing, and so on, and therefore this challenge would be of interest to many. We invite the community to discuss the range of tasks in detail.

4 Software infrastructure

As in the GIVE challenge, we will ask users to log in to a virtual environment, running on a server, and they will then encounter different NLG systems in a variety of tasks. We propose to reuse and modify the existing GIVE infrastructure for building a 3D interactive outdoor pedestrian environment. However, if it is not suitable, we propose to build the infrastructure using one of the following tools:

- OpenWonderLand[1]
- OpenSimulator[2]
- OpenSceneGraph[3]
- Unreal engine[4]
- Google Sketch Up[5]
- jMonkeyEngine[6]
- X3D[7]

One of these tools will be chosen and additional "feedback" buttons will be added to the user's GUI. These buttons will allow the user to "say" things like: 'Yes', 'No','OK', 'I'm lost', 'repeat', 'I'm confused', 'quit' and so on. Speech will be delivered to the user's browser via a TTS engine, or wizard voice, or prerecorded prompts can be used. A route planner will be a part of this infrastructure that will generate plans for navigation. This route plan will contain route directions from source to destination along with information on landmarks on the way. This route plan along with information specific to the user (i.e. location, viewshed, confidence scores, and button requests) will form the inputs to the NLG system. This infrastructure will then be made available to the teams for developing their own NLG system. Since this is the first time the challenge is organised, there will be no data available. All collected data will be released for future versions of the challenge.

5 Evaluation metrics

We propose to evaluate the participating systems based on objective metrics such as task completion, time taken, and so on. We also propose to obtain ratings from the users based on the quality of the interaction they had with the system. They will be asked to rate the features of the system based on how confusing or easy it was to follow the instructions, and so on.

6 Proposed Schedule

1. Software infrastructure in place: Oct 2011
2. Tasks and metrics defined: Nov 2011
3. Entrants collected: Dec 2011-Jan 2012
4. System development: Jan 2012- April 2012
5. Collect users/subjects via MTurk or other crowdsourcing method: April 2012
6. Run the challenge: April-May 2012

[1]http://openwonderland.org
[2]http://opensimulator.org/
[3]http://www.openscenegraph.org/
[4]http://www.unrealengine.com/
[5]http://sketchup.google.com/
[6]http://jmonkeyengine.org/
[7]http://www.web3d.org/

7. Report results: INLG 2012
8. Release data via web: post INLG 2012

7 Future work

In the future, we hope to extend this infrastructure so that users can interact with the system using text or speech input instead of propositional inputs using buttons. This will introduce an element of uncertainty in speech/text input as well in terms of ambient noise, underspecified referring expressions and so on.

8 Conclusion

In this paper, we presented a shared task for research teams to collaborate and investigate the issues and challenges in giving instructions for outdoor pedestrian navigation. We briefly presented a set of interesting new problems in this task. The GRUVE challenge targets route giving tasks to pedestrians in outdoor virtual environments, where different types and degrees of uncertainty can be manipulated experimentally, with the expectation that its results will be informative for real-world pedestrian navigation systems.

We hope to discuss with members of the NLG community how to modify the existing GIVE infrastructure for this task and how we can best collaborate with other researchers in developing and refining the challenge.

Acknowledgments

The research leading to these results has received funding from the European Community's Seventh Framework Programme (FP7/2007-2013) under grant agreement no. 216594 (SPACEBOOK project `www.spacebook-project.org`).

References

D. Byron, A. Koller, J. Oberlander, L. Stoia, and K. Striegnitz. 2007. Generating Instructions in Virtual Environments (GIVE): A challenge and evaluation testbed for NLG. In *Proceedings of the Workshop on Shared Tasks and Comparative Evaluation in Natural Language Generation*.

H. Cheng, L. Cavedon, and R. Dale. 2004. Generating Navigation Information Based on the Driver's Route Knowledge. In *Proceedings of the Coling 2004 Workshop on Robust and Adaptive Information Processing for Mobile Speech Interfaces*.

H. Cuayhuitl, N. Dethlefs, L. Frommberger, K.-F. Richter, and J Bateman. 2010. Generating Adaptive Route Instructions Using Hierarchical Reinforcement Learning. In *Proceedings of the International Conference on Spatial Cognition (Spatial Cognition VII), Portland, OR, USA*.

R. Dale, S. Geldof, and J. P. Prost. 2002. Generating more natural route descriptions. In *Proceedings of the 2002 Australasian Natural Language Processing Workshop*.

Nina Dethlefs and Heriberto Cuayáhuitl. 2011. Hierarchical reinforcement learning and hidden markov models for task-oriented natural language generation. In *Proc. of ACL*.

Nina Dethlefs, Heriberto Cuayáhuitl, and Jette Viethen. 2011. Optimising natural language generation decision making for situated dialogue. In *Proc. of SIGdial Workshop on Discourse and Dialogue*.

A. Gargett, K. Garoufi, A. Koller, and K. Striegnitz. 2010. The GIVE-2 Corpus of Giving Instructions in Virtual Environments. In *Proceedings of the 7th Conference on International Language Resources and Evaluation (LREC), Valletta, Malta*.

A. Koller, J. Moore, B. Eugenio, J. Lester, L. Stoia, D. Byron, J. Oberlander, and K. Striegnitz. 2007. Shared Task Proposal: Instruction Giving in Virtual Worlds. In *Workshop on Shared Tasks and Comparative Evaluation in Natural Language Generation*.

Oliver Lemon, Srini Janarthanam, and Verena Rieser. 2010. Generation under uncertainty. In *Proceedings of INLG / Generation Challenges*.

A. J. May, T. Ross, S. H. Bayer, and M. J. Tarkiainen. 2003. Pedestrian navigation aids: information requirements and design implications. *Personal and Ubiquitous Computing*, 7(6):331–338.

K.-F. Richter, M. Tomko, and S. Winter. 2008. A dialog-driven process of generating route directions. *Computers, Environment and Urban Systems*, 32(3):233245.

C. J. Schroder, W. A. Mackaness, and B. M. Gittings. 2011. Giving the 'Right' Route Directions: The Requirements for Pedestrian Navigation Systems. *Transactions in GIS*, 15(3):419–438.

A Proposal for a Spanish Surface Realization Shared Task

Pablo Gervás and Miguel Ballesteros
Departamento de Ingeniería
del Software e Inteligencia Artificial
Universidad Complutense de Madrid
Madrid, 28040 Spain
pgervas@sip.ucm.es, miballes@fdi.ucm.es

Abstract

We propose a competitive shared evaluation task for Surface Realization in Spanish. The task would be carried out in 2012. It would involve the generation of text in Spanish from a common ground input shared by all systems. Separate corpora for training/development (composed of pairs of common ground input and expected string result) and testing (only common ground input) will be provided. Automatic evaluation procedures will be provided. Submitted results will also be subject to human evaluation. The present proposal is tentative in two different ways. First, the authors intend to revise the proposal in view of the experience and feedback of the Surface Realization Pilot Task currently in process for English, once its results are made public (due in September, 2011). Second, the authors are willing to colaborate both with organizers of equivalent tasks for other languages or more researchers interested in surface realization for Spanish.

1 Background

Two main arguments motivate this proposal: the generally accepted need of establishing comparative forms of evaluation for NLG, and the overarching trend in NLP to extend tools and resources to languages other than English. In the context of the present call for proposals it should not be necessary to argue in favour of the first motivation. Interested readers can be referred to (Belz et al., 2010) and to the call for proposals itself for cogent argumentation on this point.

Regarding the second motivation, it can be defended by analogy with observed trends in Natural Language Analysis (NLA). The field of NLA has experienced a significant boom as a result of the success of statistical approaches. Crucial to this effort was the development of annotated corpora susceptible of being used for training. The existence of these corpora has made it possible to develop a large number of applications based on machine-learning. But this effort has been restricted to the languages for which corpora were available. This restriction has led to imbalances in the coverage that these tools provide across different languages, with a proliferation of tools for English and scarcity for many other languages. A large number of research efforts have been devoted in recent times to correct this imbalance, with researchers, universities, governments and international institutions focused on extending coverage to other languages. It would be a pity if a similar situation is allowed to arise in the field of NLG. The present call for proposals is designed to contribute to the development of a consensus in the use of comparative forms of evaluation in NLG. As such, it should include as soon as possible an effort to address the issue of extension of these methods to other languages.

Another argument in favour of extending these exploratory efforts to other languages can be found in the proliferation of statistical approaches to Surface Realization. Statistical approaches, in contrast to more knowledge-based approaches, should allow rapid development of solutions for alternative languages with little effort, provided the necessary training corpora are available.

Proceedings of the 13th European Workshop on Natural Language Generation (ENLG), pages 212–216,
Nancy, France, September 2011.

Finally, once comparative forms of evaluation start being available, generic observations concerning relative the merit of different approaches are likely to arise, such as for instance, empirical observations on whether statistical or rule-based approaches perform better. For the sake of completeness, it becomes important that any such observations be well founded on comparative studies across different languages. As an example, constituent-based parsing was prevalent for many years in computational approaches to languages while English was the primary object, and yet lost ground very quickly to dependency-based analyses once languages with more complex word order started to be considered. An effort should be made to avoid any similar oversight in Surface Realization.

Spanish is a good candidate as an alternative language for several reasons. First, it is widely used in the world, so any development efforts are likely to have potential application and a large market. Second, it differs from English sufficiently enough to provide a comparative view point. Issues that may introduce difficulties from the surface realization point of view include: long-range agreement in gender, more complex morphology of verbs, pronouns, nouns and adjectives. Gender agreement is particularly significant in languages were words have lexical gender as well as conceptual gender. In Spanish, different synomyms that refer to the same concept can be masculine or femenine, irrespective of the gender of the concept (which may even be neuter in gender). Spanish requires gender agreement between nouns and any accompanying adjectives, and between subjects and attributes in copulative sentences. Third, resources exist in Spanish that can be used as source for the development of a surface realization corpus. Finally, surface realizers have been developed for Spanish in the past, so it should be possible to compare modern approaches with earlier knowledge-based ones.

On the availability of surface realizers for Spanish, two classic surface realizers – FUF (Elhadad and Robin, 1992) and KPML (Bateman, 1995) – have a version for Spanish. These realizers have been deployed in applied contexts. A version of Surge adapted for Spanish was used for story narration (Callaway et al., 1999) although the coverage is inferior to the English original version. A Spanish version of KPML was applied in a chemistry querying system (Aguado et al., 1998). Melero (2006) combined rule–based approaches and machine–learning approaches for Spanish syntactic generation. This system was developed for a commercial machine–translation, the input was a deep syntactic representation and the output was grammatically aceptable text written in Spanish language.

Section 2 outline specifically our proposal considering the organization, data, evaluation and input/output representations. Finally, Section 3 presents some conclusions.

2 Our Shared Task Proposal

Surface realization normally requires an important quantity of knowledge about the structure of the target language, usually represented as a set of grammar rules or other linguistic constraints. Taking all of this into account and in order to continue providing a common forum for these activities, we propose the tools to include Spanish in a Surface Realization Task. In this Section we discuss specifically our proposal considering the organization, data, evaluation and input/output representations.

2.1 Data to be used

The data sets will be based on the Spanish AnCora corpus that was provided as training set for the CoNLL–2009 shared task. We will process this corpus to obtain a format suitable for the surface realization task.

2.1.1 AnCora Corpus: CoNLL 2009 Shared Task Data

AnCora (Palomar et al., 2004; Taulé et al., 2008) is a multilevel annotated corpus of Spanish texts. It has 528,440 lexical tokens. It is mainly based on newspaper texts with their dependency syntactic annotations, named–entity boundaries and semantic dependencies in Spanish. AnCora was developed by the Clic group at the University of Barcelona and it is annotated with morphological (PoS), syntactic (constituents and functions) and semantic (argument structure and thematic roles, semantic class, named entities and WordNet senses) information. The annotation was performed manually, semiautomatically, or fully automatically, depending on the encoded linguistic information, and it uses as a source the Cast3lb constituency treebank (Civit et al., 2006). It is the Spanish corpus provided for the CoNLL–2009 shared task[1] on "Syntactic and Semantic Dependencies in Multiple Languages" (Hajič et al., 2009).

We have contacted the Clic research group and we have their approval for carrying out the present proposal. They have suggested we may be able to use a forthcoming revised version of the AnCora corpus.

2.1.2 Our Future Data

Our future SR Task data will be derived from the CoNLL 09 AnCora corpus. We will process and adapt the treebank to make it useful for the generation task. It is expected that the actual format taken by this data wil depend largely on the insights obtained from the Surface Realization Pilot Task for English currently taking place during 2011.

It is worth to emphasize that AnCora contains a wide range of sentence lengths, though most of them are between 20 and 50 wordforms. This provides a good benchmark for a surface realization task, with realizations over a broad range of lengths. Moreover, as it is shown in (Gardent and Kow, 2006) surface realization is exponential in the length of the input. This makes the AnCora corpus very suitable for this proposal. Figure 1 shows the distribution of sentences in the AnCora corpus according to their length.

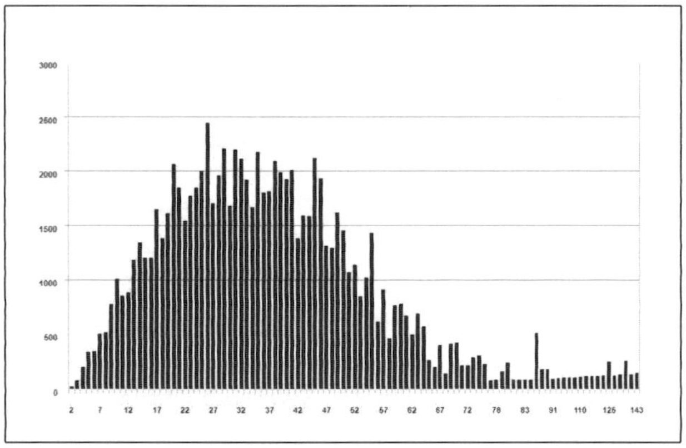

Figure 1: Distribution of sentences in the AnCora corpus according to their length. The x axis represents length and the y axis the approximate number of sentences.

We hope to produce two types of input representations, following the guidelines presented in (Belz et al., 2010), one shallow and one deep. For both shallow and deep representations relations will be randomly sorted and sentences will have single sentence roots.

- **Shallow Dependency Input**

  The shallow representation will include the dependency syntactic tree for every piece of text that is included in the CoNLL'09 data format. The information at each node will consist of a word's lemma, a number and a tense feature, and a coarse–grained POS-tag derived from the AnCora annotation. The edges between nodes will be labeled with the syntactic dependency annotations in the AnCora corpus.

  We have manually developed a transformation to the CoNLL'09 data format into the shallow representation, following the guidelines of the Surface Realisation Shared Task currently taking place in 2011. Figure 2 shows the output of our transformation for the sentence example: *Y, en la mesa, se acabó eso de usar los palillos una sola vez y tirarlos [And, at the table, no more using the toothpicks once and throw them out]*, the representation follows the same structure as the release of the current English Shared Task. It contains only lemmas and shallow dependency relations between nodes.

  If the forthcoming version of the AnCora corpus has a different data format and we decide to use it, we would have to modify the transformation or adapt the data to the expected output.

- **Deep Semantic Input** The deeper representation will be constructed by adding to the Shallow representation the semantic annotation included in the CoNLL'09 data format. Therefore, the information at each node will consist of a word's lemma, a number and a tense feature, and the sense tag (semantic tag). An, as done in (Belz et al., 2010), there will be no POS–tag information. The edges between nodes will be labeled with semantic labels derived from the AnCora annotation for the CoNLL'09 Shared Task.

  For the development of the deep representation, we have contacted Simon Mille and Leo Wanner who are trying to refine AnCora's tagset at

[1]http://ufal.mff.cuni.cz/conll2009-st/task-description.html

```
sentId=1
SROOT   1       0       acabar  CPOS=main       num=s|person=3|tense=past
        et      2       1       y       CPOS=coord
        cc      3       1       en      CPOS=prep
                f       4       3       ,       CPOS=comma
                sn      5       3       mesa    CPOS=common     gen=f|num=s
                        spec    6       5       el      CPOS=det        gen=f|num=s
                f       6       3       ,       CPOS=comma
        mprop   7       1       él      CPOS=pron_art   person=3
        suj     8       1       ese     CPOS=pron_dem   num=s
                sp      9       8       de      CPOS=prep
                        S       10      9       usar    CPOS=main       tense=infinitive
                                cd      11      10      palillo CPOS=common     gen=m|num=p
                                        spec    12      11      el      CPOS=det_art    gen=m|num=p
                                cc      13      10      vez     CPOS=common     gen=f|num=s
                                        spec    14      13      uno     CPOS=det_indef  gen=f|num=s
                                        s.a     15      13      solo    CPOS=qualif     gen=f|num=s
                                coord   16      10      y       CPOS=coord
                                S       17      10      tirar   CPOS=main       tense=infinitive
        f       18      1       .       CPOS=punct

Y, en la mesa, se acabó eso de usar los palillos una sola vez y tirarlos.
```

Figure 2: Shallow transformation of the following AnCora sentence: *Y, en la mesa, se acabó eso de usar los palillos una sola vez y tirarlos [And, at the table, no more using the toothpicks once and throw them out]*

the syntactic level (around 60 syntactic tags), and introduce temporary semantic tags in order to facilitate the mapping to the deeper levels (shallow and deep semantics) (Mille and Wanner, 2010). In this way, with their work and the forthcoming version of AnCora (Mariona's work) we should have a robust corpus that will be suitable for the generation task.

2.2 Evaluation

Evaluating surface realization is intrinsically difficult, due to the fact that there is usually no a single correct answer, but rather a range of possible correct answers, some of them better than others. To address this problem, based on the data resources described above we intend to develop evaluation techniques based on Fluency, Clarity and Appropriateness that take this difficulty into account. To this end, outputs will be evaluated by a variety of automatic metrics and human–assessed quality criteria.

We intend to revise this aspect of the proposal based on feedback from the SR pilot task for English. In principle, the evaluation techniques and methodology developed for English should be applicable to Spanish with little or no modification.

3 Conclusion

In this paper, we have proposed a Shared Task for Surface Realization of Spanish, as done in (Belz et al., 2010). The aim of the proposal is to extend the resources and techniques developed this year for the English Surface Realization Shared Task 2011 to a different language. This should test the techniques beyond the scope for which they were developed and provide resources for the development of surface realizers in a different language.

This proposal could be undertaken as a stand alone task, in tandem with the second iteration of the surface realization task for English, or as part of a multilingual shared task for surface realization. In general terms, the spirit of this proposal is that the use of languages, other than English, in NLG should be promoted. The authors are willing and qualified to provide or recruit the knowledge necessary to build the Spanish data and to evaluate the different participant systems.

We have developed a webpage[2], in which we explain our proposal and we invite people to collaborate in the task. In response to a recent call for expression of interest in this task we have received replies from research groups interested both in submitting and in colaborating in the development of the task.

Acknowledgments

This research is funded by the Spanish Ministry of Education and Science (TIN2009-14659-C03-01

[2] http://nil.fdi.ucm.es/srspa

Project), Universidad Complutense de Madrid and Banco Santander Central Hispano (GR58/08 Research Group Grant). We also want to thank Anja Belz, Bernd Bohnet, Simon Mille, Mariona Taulé, Leo Wanner and Michael White for their help, collaboration and availability.

References

G. Aguado, J. Bateman, S. Bernardos, M. Fernández, A. Gómez-Pérez, E. Nieto, A. Olalla, and A. Sánchez. 1998. Ontogeneration: Reusing domain and linguistic ontologies for spanish text generation. In *Proc. ECAI. Workshop on Applications of Ontologies and Problem Solving Methods*.

John A. Bateman. 1995. Basic technology for multilingual theory and practise: the kpml development viroment. In *Proc. IJCAI-95 Workshop on MULTILINGUAL TEXT GENERATION*, pages 1–12.

Anja Belz, Mike White, Josef van Genabith, Deirdre Hogan, and Amanda Stent. 2010. Finding common ground: towards a surface realisation shared task. In *Proceedings of the 6th International Natural Language Generation Conference*, INLG '10, pages 268–272, Stroudsburg, PA, USA. Association for Computational Linguistics.

Charles B. Callaway, Brent H. Daniel, and James C. Lester. 1999. Multilingual natural language generation for 3d learning environments. In *In Proceedings of the 1999 Argentine Symposium on Artificial Intelligence, pages 177190, Buenos Aires*, pages 177–190.

Montserrat Civit, Maria Antònia Martí, and Núria Bufí. 2006. Cat3lb and cast3lb: From constituents to dependencies. In *FinTAL*, pages 141–152.

Michael Elhadad and Jacques Robin. 1992. Controlling content realization with functional unification grammars. In *Proceedings of the 6th International Workshop on Natural Language Generation: Aspects of Automated Natural Language Generation*, pages 89–104, London, UK. Springer-Verlag.

Claire Gardent and Eric Kow. 2006. Three reasons to adopt tag-based surface realisation. In *Proceedings of the Eighth International Workshop on Tree Adjoining Grammar and Related Formalisms*, TAGRF '06, pages 97–102, Stroudsburg, PA, USA. Association for Computational Linguistics.

Jan Hajič, Massimiliano Ciaramita, Richard Johansson, Daisuke Kawahara, Maria Antònia Martí, Lluís Màrquez, Adam Meyers, Joakim Nivre, Sebastian Padó, Jan Štěpánek, Pavel Straňák, Mihai Surdeanu, Nianwen Xue, and Yi Zhang. 2009. The CoNLL-2009 shared task: Syntactic and semantic dependencies in multiple languages. In *Proceedings of the 13th Conference on Computational Natural Language Learning (CoNLL-2009), June 4-5*, Boulder, Colorado, USA.

Maria Teresa Melero Nogués. 2006. *Combining machine learning and rule-based approaches in Spanish syntactic generation*. Ph.D. thesis.

Simon Mille and Leo Wanner. 2010. Syntactic dependencies for multilingual and multilevel corpus annotation. Valletta (Malta), 05/2010.

M. Palomar, Montserrat Civit, A. Díaz, L. Moreno, E. Bisbal, M. Aranzabe, A. Ageno, M.Antonia Martí, and Borja Navarro. 2004. 3lb: Construcción de una base de datos de árboles sintáctico–semánticos para el catalán, euskera y español. In *Proceedings of the XX Conference of the Spanish Society for Natural Language Processing (SEPLN)*, pages 81–88. Sociedad Española para el Procesamiento del Lenguaje Natural.

Mariona Taulé, M.Antonia Martí, and Marta Recasens. 2008. AnCora: Multilevel Annotated Corpora for Catalan and Spanish. In *Proceedings of 6th International Conference on Language Resources and Evaluation*.

The First Surface Realisation Shared Task: Overview and Evaluation Results

Anja Belz[1] **Michael White**[2] **Dominic Espinosa**[2] **Eric Kow**[1]

[1]Computing, Engineering and Maths
University of Brighton
Brighton BN1 4GJ, UK
{asb,eykk10}@brighton.ac.uk

[2]Department of Linguistics
Ohio State University
Columbus, OH, 43210, US
{espinosa,mwhite}@ling.osu.edu

Deirdre Hogan
School of Computing
Dublin City University, Dublin 9, Ireland
dhogan@computing.dcu.ie

Amanda Stent
AT&T Labs Research
Florham Park, NJ 07932, US
stent@research.att.com

Abstract

The Surface Realisation (SR) Task was a new task at Generation Challenges 2011, and had two tracks: (1) Shallow: mapping from shallow input representations to realisations; and (2) Deep: mapping from deep input representations to realisations. Five teams submitted six systems in total, and we additionally evaluated human toplines. Systems were evaluated automatically using a range of intrinsic metrics. In addition, systems were assessed by human judges in terms of Clarity, Readability and Meaning Similarity. This report presents the evaluation results, along with descriptions of the SR Task Tracks and evaluation methods. For descriptions of the participating systems, see the separate system reports in this volume, immediately following this results report.

1 Introduction and Overview

Many different surface realisers have been developed over the past three decades or so. While symbolic realisers dominated for much of this period, the past decade has seen the development of many different types of statistical surface realisers. A significant subset of statistical realisation work (Langkilde, 2002; Callaway, 2003; Nakanishi et al., 2005; Zhong and Stent, 2005; Cahill and van Genabith, 2006; White and Rajkumar, 2009) has produced results for regenerating the Penn Treebank (PTB) (Marcus et al., 1995). The basic approach in all this work was to remove information from the Penn Treebank parses (the word strings themselves as well as some of the parse information), and then convert and use these underspecified representations as inputs to the surface realiser whose task it is to reproduce the original treebank sentence.

While publications reporting this type of work referred to each other and (tentatively) compared BLEU scores, the results were not in fact directly comparable, because of the differences in the input representations automatically derived from Penn Treebank annotations. In particular, the extent to which they were underspecified varied from one system to the next. Our aim in developing the Surface Realisation (SR) Task was to make it possible, for the first time, to directly compare different, independently developed surface realisers by developing a 'common-ground' input representation that could be used by all participating systems to generate realisations from. In fact, we created two different input representations, one shallow, one deep, in order to enable more teams to participate.

Five teams submitted systems to the SR Task (see Table 1), submitting six systems in total. We also used the corpus texts themselves as 'system' outputs, to provide a human topline. We evaluated participating systems using a range of intrinsic evaluation methods, both automatically computed and human-assessed (for an overview, see Table 2).

This report describes the data (Section 2), task definition, evaluation methods and results (Sections 3 and 4) for the SR Task, and then presents a discussion of some problematic issues in developing a shared surface realisation task for the first time (Section 5). The participating systems are described in the particpants' reports in this volume, immediately following this report.

Proceedings of the 13th European Workshop on Natural Language Generation (ENLG), pages 217–226,
Nancy, France, September 2011.

Team	Organisation(s)	Shallow systems	Deep systems
ATT	AT&T Labs Research	ATT-0 ^{y}	–
DCU	Dublin City University Toshiba (China) Research and Development Center	DCU	–
OSU	Ohio State University	–	OSU ^{y}
STUMABA	Universität Stuttgart Universitat Pompeu Fabra Université du Maine	STUMABA-S ^{x,y}	STUMABA-D ^{x,y}
UCM	Universidad Complutense de Madrid	UCM	–

Table 1: SR-Task teams and systems. The STUMABA systems are the version called 'System 2' in the team's report. ^{x} = resubmitted after fixing software bugs; ^{y} = late submission.

Quality criterion:	Type of evaluation:	Evaluation Method(s):
Humanlikeness	Intrinsic/automatic	BLEU, NIST, TER, METEOR
	Intrinsic/human	Human assessment of Meaning Similarity
Readability	Intrinsic/human	Human Readability judgements
Clarity	Intrinsic/human	Human Clarity judgements

Table 2: Overview of evaluation procedures used in the SR Shared Task.

2 Data

The SR Task data has two input representations—one for each track, shallow and deep. In both, sentences are represented as sets of unordered labeled dependencies (with the exception of named entities, see Section 2.4 below, which are ordered). The shallow input representation is intended to be a more 'surfacey', syntactic represention of the sentence. The deep(er) input type is intended to be closer to a semantic, more abstract, representation of the meaning of the sentence.

The input representations were created by post-processing the CoNLL 2008 Shared Task data (Surdeanu et al., 2008). For the preparation of the CoNLL-08 Shared task data, selected sections of the Penn WSJ Treebank were converted to syntactic dependencies via the LTH Constituent-to-Dependency Conversion Tool for Penn-style Treebanks (Pennconverter) (Johansson and Nugues, 2007). The resulting dependency bank was then merged with the Nombank (Meyers et al., 2004) and Propbank (Palmer et al., 2005) corpora. Named entity information from the BBN Entity Type corpus was also integrated into the CoNLL-08 data. Our shallow representation is based on the Pennconverter dependencies. The deep representation is derived from the merged Nombank, Propbank and syntactic dependencies in a process similar to the graph completion algorithm outlined in (Bohnet et al., 2010) (see Section 2.2 for differences).

2.1 Shallow representation

The shallow data consists of unordered syntactic dependency trees. Each word and punctuation marker from the original sentence is represented as a node in a syntactic dependency tree.

Nodes: The node information consists of a word's lemma, a coarse-grained POS-tag, and, where appropriate, number, tense and participle features and a sense tag id (as a suffix to the lemma). In addition, two punctuation features encode the quotation and bracketing information for the sentence.

The POS-tag set is slightly less fine-grained than the Penn POS-tag set. We removed the distinction between VBP and VBZ for example, so that determining agreement is a task left to the realiser.

Edges: Edges between nodes are labeled with the syntactic labels produced by the Penncoverter. See the SR Task Documentation[1] for a summary description of the label set. In addition to these *atomic* labels, edges can be labeled with *non-atomic* labels, which consist of multiple atomic labels (see Surdeanu et al. (2008) for details). See the SR Task

[1]Available here: `http://www.itri.brighton.ac.uk/home/Anja.Belz/pdf/SR-Task-2011-Doc.pdf`

Documentation for our current handling of long-distance dependencies and future plans for improvements.

2.2 Deep

The deep representation is in the form of dependency graphs and is not restricted to tree structures.

Nodes: Information at each node consists of a word's lemma, and where appropriate, number, tense and participle features and a sense tag id (as a suffix to the lemma). Two punctuation features encode the quotation and bracketing information for the sentence. Unlike in the shallow representation, there is no POS-tag information.

In a step towards removing punctuation, we removed commas from the deep representation.[2] In addition, some function words (specifically, that-complementizers and TO infinitives) were removed. For the future, we intend to remove further function words, such as relative pronouns and case-marking prepositions.

Edges: Semantic edges are labeled with semantic labels taken from the Propbank and Nombank semantic roles.

Where the PropBank/NomBank relations result in an unconnected structure, we connected the graph with edges from the corresponding syntactic tree, with the syntactic labels produced by the Penncoverter.

Some of these Pennconverter labels have been modified slightly in order to make them more general. See Table 3 for details. In the case of NMOD and AMOD, the syntactic head is typically a semantic argument of its modifier; accordingly, these syntactic relations were replaced with an AINV (Argument INVerse) semantic relation. The direction of Pennconverter edges remains unchanged.

2.3 Tokenisation

Tokenisation follows that of the CoNLL data, which differs from that of the Penn Treebank. Hyphenated words are split and dependencies between the split tokens are given. For example, *prime-time* is represented as three tokens with the dependencies: $[time]_{HMOD} \rightarrow [prime]_{HYPH} \rightarrow [-]$.

[2] There remain 55 occurrences where the comma had dependent nodes which we intend to remove in the future.

2.4 Named Entities

Named entity annotations from the BBN Entity Type corpus were used to derive NAME dependencies in the CoNLL corpus. For the SR Task data we have numbered all NAME dependencies with the order they appear in the original sentence because, arguably, the ordering of words in named entities is not a task that should be left to a surface realizer.

2.5 Coordination

Following the CoNLL format, the first conjunct is the head of coordinate structures in both shallow and deep representations. All other conjuncts, and the coordinating conjunction, are descendants of the leftmost conjunct. The order of the conjuncts is encoded in the dependency structure. The treatment of coordination will be revisited in future years.

2.6 Data Format

The data format for the shallow and deep tracks has the following components:

1. A line with the graph number (e.g. sentId=11055).
2. The graph represented as lines where each line represents a single node and consists of at least 4 and a maximum of 10 fields:

   RELATION ID PARENT_ID LEMMA[.sensetagID] [CPOS=POStag] [num=sg|pl] [tense=past|pres] [partic=past|pres] [quoted=d*s*] [bracket=r*c*]

   Each line contains at least the first 4 fields, except for nodes with multiple heads. In such cases, there is one line for each $head \rightarrow node$ relation. The first time this occurs the full information for the node is given. For subsequent occurrences only the relation label, the node ID, and the parent node ID are given. Note that, as the syntactic representations are strictly trees, multiple heads will only occur in the deep representation.

   The dependency structure of the graphs is reflected both through tabular indentation and the ID and PARENT ID fields.
3. A line containing the original sentence, followed by a blank line (the test set data did not include the sentence).

2.7 Training, Development and Test Sets

We followed the main data set divisions of the CoNLL'08 data. However, we removed 300 randomly selected sentences in chunks of 5 consecutive sentences for use in human evaluations. Of these,

Name	Description/Comments
RELATION (shallow)	Syntactic dependency relations. NAME dependencies are numbered with order information. The root of the tree has relation SROOT.
RELATION (deep)	Semantic relations when available. Otherwise, they are the shallow relations, some of which have been simplified as follows: $NMOD|AMOD \rightarrow AINV$, $HMOD \rightarrow MOD$, $PMOD \rightarrow A1$. Sentences have a single root, marked with relation SROOT.
ID	Token id of the node, starts at 1 for each new sentence
PARENTID	Token id of the parent of this node
LEMMA[.sensetagID]	Lemma with, when available, a sense tag id suffix. The lemma and sense tag id are the lemma and roleset id extracted from propbank/nombank. When this information is unavailable the lemma is the predicted lemma extracted from the CoNLL-08 data set.
CPOS (shallow)	Hand-annotated coarse grained POS tag (from PTB); $VBD|VBN|VBP|VBZ \rightarrow VB$, $NNS \rightarrow NN$, $NNPS \rightarrow NNP$, all other POS tags $\rightarrow$ original hand-annotated PTB POS tag.
NUM	Feature for nouns only. Values are singular or plural - derived from hand-annotated PTB POS tags. $NN|NNP \rightarrow singular$, $NNS|NNPS \rightarrow plural$.
TENSE	Feature for verbs only. Values are past or pres(ent) - derived from hand-annotated PTB POS tags. $VBD \rightarrow past$, $VBP|VBZ \rightarrow present$
PARTIC	Feature for participle tense derived from hand-annotated PTB POS tags (note: partic=pres could indicate a present participle or gerund). $VBN \rightarrow past$, $VBG \rightarrow pres$.
QUOTED	Feature for indicating whether the node is quoted in the original sentence. $d = doublequoted$, $s = singlequoted$. This feature value can consist of any number of d's followed by any number of s's. Multiple d's or s's occur when the node is embedded inside more than one quotation mark. Take for example the sentence: *He added : " Every paper company management has to be saying to itself , ' Before someone comes after me , I 'm going to go after somebody . ' "* The node corresponding to *paper* will have feature $quoted = d$ and the node for word *someone* will have $quoted = ds$.
BRACKET	Feature for indicating whether the node is inside brackets in the original sentence. $r = round\ brackets$, $c = curly\ brackets$. In a similar fashion to the QUOTED feature, this feature value can consist of any number of r's followed by any number of c's.

Table 3: Field descriptions for Shallow and Deep Representations.

we used 100 as the test set for human evaluation this year and will use the remainder in future editions of the SR Shared Task.

1. Training set: PTB Sections 02–21.
2. Development set: 1,034 sentences from PTB Section 24 (less 300 sentences for use in human evaluations).
3. Test set for automatic evaluations: PTB Sec. 23.
4. Test set for human evaluations: 100 sentences in chunks of 5 consecutive sentences, randomly selected (and removed) from PTB Section 24.

Note that a small number of sentences from the selected WSJ sections were not included in the CoNLL-08 data (and are thus not included in the SR Task data) due to difficulties in merging the various data sets (e.g. Section 23 has 17 fewer sentences).

3 Automatic Evaluations

We computed scores using the following well-known automatic evaluation metrics:

1. BLEU (Papineni et al., 2002):[3] geometric mean of 1- to 4-gram precision with a brevity penalty; recent implementations use smoothing to allow sentence-level scores to be computed.
2. NIST:[4,5] n-gram similarity weighted in favour of less frequent n-grams which are taken to be more informative.
3. METEOR (Banerjee and Lavie, 2005; Denkowski and Lavie, 2011):[6] lexical similarity based on exact, stem, synonym, and paraphrase matches between words and phrases.
4. TER (Snover et al., 2006):[7] a length-normalized edit distance metric where phrasal shifts are counted as one edit.

For each metric, we calculated system-level scores, the mean of the sentence-level scores and weighted n-best scores (described below).

Text normalisation: Output texts were normalised by lower-casing all tokens, removing any extraneous white space characters and ensuring consistent treatment of ampersands.

[3] http://www.itl.nist.gov/iad/mig/tests/mt/2009/

[4] http://www.itl.nist.gov/iad/mig/tests/mt/doc/ngram-study.pdf

[5] http://www.itl.nist.gov/iad/mig/tests/mt/2009/

[6] http://www.cs.cmu.edu/ alavie/METEOR/

[7] http://www.umiacs.umd.edu/ snover/terp/

N-best, ranked system outputs: Ranked 5-best outputs were scored using a weighted average of the sentence-level scores for each metric, with these sentence-level weighted sums averaged across all outputs. The weight w_i assigned to the ith system output was in inverse proportion to its rank r_i ($K = 5$): $w_i = \frac{K-r_i+1}{\sum_{j=1}^{K} K-r_j+1}$

Missing outputs: Missing outputs were scored as zero (one for TER); in the n-best evaluation, missing or duplicate outputs were scored as 0 (1 for TER). Since coverage was high for all systems (97% for OSU; 100% for all others), we only report results for all sentences (with the missing output penalty), rather than separately reporting scores for just the covered items.

3.1 Metric Scores

The automatic metric scores for all systems appear in Tables 4 and 5 for the Automatic Test Set and Human Test Set, respectively. Tables 6 and 7 give the means of sentence-level scores; the columns containing single capital letters show the homogeneous subsets of systems as determined by a post-hoc Tukey HSD analysis; systems whose scores are not significantly different (at the 0.05 level overall) share a letter.

In the tables, system scores are shown for all systems, both in the shallow and deep track; thus, it should be noted that the scores for STUMABA-D and OSU, which are deep-task systems, are not directly comparable to the scores for the remaining, shallow-task systems. Across the metrics and data sets, STUMABA-S is consistently the top-scoring system, with DCU between STUMABA-S and STUMABA-D. Since the automatic test set was much larger than the human test set, there were more significant differences between pairs of systems, as expected. TER and METEOR were less sensitive, with STUMABA-S and DCU falling into a top group for TER on the test section (i.e., there was no significant difference between STUMABA-S and DCU on the mean TER score at the 0.05 level overall), and STUMABA-S, DCU and STUMABA-D forming a top group for METEOR. On the human test set, the pattern was similar but with larger homogeneous subsets.

With the n-best results, it is difficult to make any firm conclusions with only two systems supplying n-best outputs. Nevertheless, it is evident that across the metrics, both the ATT and OSU systems have consistently higher 1-best scores than weighted n-best scores, indicating that they are generally successful in choosing a single-best output that is more similar to the reference sentence than the others in the top 5. In the absence of multiple reference sentences or human evaluation results for the n-best list though, it is unclear to what extent the outputs in the n-best list might represent valid paraphrases versus clearly less acceptable outputs.

4 Human Evaluations

4.1 Experimental Set-up

We assessed three criteria in the human evaluations: Clarity, Readability and Meaning Similarity. We used continuous sliders as rating tools (see Figures 1 and 2), because raters tend to prefer them (Belz and Kow, 2011). Slider positions were mapped to values from 0 to 100 (best).

The instructions relating to Clarity and Readability read as follows:[8]

> The first criterion you need to assess is **Clarity**. How clear (easy to understand) is the highlighted sentence within the context of the text extract?
>
> The second criterion to assess is **Readability**. This is sometimes called 'fluency', and your task is to decide how well the highlighted sentence reads; is it good fluent English, or does it have grammatical errors, awkward constructions, etc.
>
> Note that you should assess Clarity separately from Readability: it is possible for a text to be completely clear, yet not read well; conversely, it is possible for a text to read very well, and its meaning to be unclear.
>
> Please rate the highlighted sentence by moving each slider to the position that corresponds to your rating.

The part of the instructions relating to Meaning Similarity was as follows:

> This time you are being shown two extracts which are identical except for the highlighted sentences. You need to read both sentences within their context, and then decide how close in meaning the second sentence is to the first. [...] Once again use the slider to express your rating. The closer in meaning

[8]See `http://www.nltg.brighton.ac.uk/research/sr-task-evals/SR-1C/` for full instructions.

	BLEU			NIST			METEOR			TER		
System	sys	avg	nb	sys	avg	nb	sys	avg	nb	sys	avg	nb
STUMABA-S	0.8911	0.8827	—	14.87	14.74	—	0.9956	0.9851	—	0.0427	0.0476	—
DCU	0.8575	0.8532	—	14.63	14.52	—	0.9836	0.9747	—	0.0550	0.0535	—
STUMABA-D	0.7943	0.7853	—	14.40	14.21	—	0.9866	0.9744	—	0.0921	0.0946	—
ATT	0.6701	0.6711	0.4638	13.50	13.45	9.792	0.9780	0.9669	0.7106	0.1414	0.1322	0.3739
OSU	0.3566	0.3743	0.2882	10.92	10.66	7.918	0.8519	0.8483	0.6394	0.4674	0.4246	0.5547
UCM	0.2351	0.2527	—	2.782	4.611	—	0.6240	0.6079	—	0.5728	0.5570	—

Table 4: Automatic metric scores for automatic test data (PTB Section 23), including system-level scores (sys), mean of sentence-level scores (avg) and mean of weighted n-best scores (nb).

	BLEU			NIST			METEOR			TER		
System	sys	avg	nb	sys	avg	nb	sys	avg	nb	sys	avg	nb
STUMABA-S	0.8763	0.8621	—	10.81	10.70	—	0.9944	0.9842	—	0.0494	0.0537	—
DCU	0.8470	0.8319	—	10.73	10.65	—	0.9871	0.9791	—	0.0654	0.0650	—
STUMABA-D	0.7734	0.7510	—	10.59	10.43	—	0.9878	0.9754	—	0.1042	0.1096	—
ATT	0.6616	0.6262	0.4573	10.22	10.03	7.499	0.9788	0.9554	0.7135	0.1610	0.1664	0.3851
OSU	0.3975	0.4032	0.3164	9.056	8.850	6.736	0.8626	0.8546	0.6586	0.4226	0.3863	0.5189
UCM	0.2526	0.2652	—	2.466	3.620	—	0.6457	0.6268	—	0.5484	0.5416	—

Table 5: Automatic metric scores for human test data (PTB Section 24 100-sentence subset), including system-level scores (sys), mean of sentence-level scores (avg) and mean of weighted n-best scores (nb).

> the second sentence is to the first, the further to the right you need to place the slider.

For each test data item, raters were first shown the screen for the Readability and Clarity assessment (as shown in Figure 1), followed by the screen for Meaning Similarity assessment (see Figure 2). We displayed system outputs as they were. Raters were instructed to disregard spaces before punctuation and similar whitespace problems. Some systems produced lower-cased outputs, others (like the STUMABA-D one output of which is shown in Figures 1 and 2) produced outputs with capitalisations.

All experiments use a Repeated Latin Squares design which ensures that each subject sees the same number of outputs from each system and for each test set item. Following detailed instructions, raters first did three practice examples, followed by the texts to be rated, in an order randomised for each rater. Evaluations were carried out via a web interface. Raters were encouraged to take breaks, and in the case of the 2-hour long SR-Shallow evaluation they were required to take breaks.

In both experiments we used native-speaker raters from cohorts of 3rd-year undergraduate and postgraduate students (from Oxford, UCL, KCL and Sussex universities) currently doing, or having recently completed, a degree in linguistics. In the SR-Deep evaluation we used 6 raters evaluating half the test set each (roughly 1 hour). In the SR-Shallow evaluation we used 5 raters each evaluating the whole test set (2 hours). Their progress was logged at 10min intervals, and they received gift vouchers for their time.

In the following section, for each experiment we report the F-ratio as determined by a one-way ANOVA with the evaluation criterion in question as the dependent variable and System as the grouping factor. F is the ratio of between-groups variability over within-group (or residual) variability, i.e. the larger the value of F, the more of the variability observed in the data is accounted for by the grouping factor, here System, relative to what variability remains within the groups. We also report homogeneous subsets (sets of systems among which there are no significant differences) of systems as determined by a post-hoc Tukey's HSD analysis (with a significance threshold of 0.05).

4.2 Results

Table 8 shows three sets of means, for Clarity, Readability and Meaning Similarity,[9] for the systems in the Shallow Track. As mentioned above, we included the original PTB sentences as a topline ('Cor-

[9]Note that the Meaning Similarity results for the Corpus sentences should be 100 if the evaluators take care to place the slider pointer right at the end of the scale, but it's not easy to *see* whether the slider pointer is at 100 or 98.

	BLEU	Subset	NIST	Subset	METEOR	Subset	TER	Subset
STUMABA-S	0.8827	A	14.74	A	0.9851	A	0.0476	A
DCU	0.8532	B	14.52	B	0.9747	A B	0.0535	A
STUMABA-D	0.7853	C	14.21	C	0.9744	A B	0.0946	B
ATT	0.6711	D	13.45	D	0.9669	B	0.1322	C
OSU	0.3743	E	10.66	E	0.8483	C	0.4246	D
UCM	0.2527	F	4.611	F	0.6079	D	0.5570	E

Table 6: Tukey's HSD ($\alpha = 0.05$) homogeneous subsets for mean of sentence-level scores on automatic test data.

	BLEU	Subset	NIST	Subset	METEOR	Subset	TER	Subset
STUMABA-S	0.8621	A	10.71	A	0.9842	A	0.0537	A
DCU	0.8319	A	10.65	A B	0.9791	A	0.0650	A
STUMABA-D	0.7510	B	10.43	A B	0.9754	A	0.1096	A
ATT	0.6262	C	10.03	B	0.9554	A	0.1664	B
OSU	0.4032	D	8.850	C	0.8546	B	0.3863	C
UCM	0.2652	E	3.620	D	0.6268	C	0.5416	D

Table 7: Tukey's HSD ($\alpha = 0.05$) homogeneous subsets for mean of sentence-level scores on human test data.

pus' in the table). The results look similar across the three evaluation criteria: STUMABA-S has the highest mean, followed by DCU, but with no statistically significant difference between them; ATT is third and UCM fourth for Readability and Meaning Similarity, and the two systems are joint third for Clarity. Rankings are identical across the three criteria for the systems in the Deep Track, with STUMABA-D first in all three cases, and OSU second.

F-ratios were as follows. For the shallow systems and Clarity: $F_{(4,495)} = 49.402, p < .001$; Readability: $F_{(4,495)} = 52.839, p < .001$; and Meaning Similarity: $F_{(4,495)} = 82.565, p < .001$. For the deep systems and Clarity: $F_{(2,294)} = 120.020, p < .001$; Readability: $F_{(2,294)} = 162.22, p < .001$; and Meaning Similarity: $F_{(2,294)} = 197.27, p < .001$.

F-ratios are overall greater for the deep systems than for the shallow ones; and greater for Meaning Similarity than for Readability for which in turn is greater than for Clarity. The latter would indicate, perhaps surprisingly, that there was less variation (more agreement) among the evaluators about Meaning Similarity than about the other two evaluation criteria.

5 Discussion

Input Conversion Issues: The principal goal of the surface realisation shared task challenge is to make it possible to directly compare different approaches to surface realisation by encouraging the development of systems that start from a common ground input representation. In this year's SR shared task, the top-performing systems (StuMaBa-D, StuMaBa-S, DCU and ATT) were all statistical dependency realisers that do not make use of an explicit, pre-existing grammar. By design, statistical dependency realisers are robust and relatively easy to adapt to new kinds of dependency inputs; as such, they are well suited to the SR task in its current form. In contrast, there were only two systems that employed a traditional, hand-crafted generation grammar (UCM) or a reversible, Treebank-derived grammar (OSU), neither of which produced competitive results. In each case, difficulties in converting the common ground inputs into the "native" or expected inputs were cited as an unexpectedly large obstacle. Indeed, the UCM system report concluded that

> "[t]he reported results constitute a measure of the coverage achieved by the input conversion process more than a measure of the capabilities of the realizer employed."

Mapping inputs to other intermediate representations (such as logical forms or full LFG f-structures, for example) introduces additional complexity and noise into the pipeline, putting systems that require substantive input conversion at a disadvantage. Nevertheless, it could be that with more time, and greater use of machine learning in input conversion or grammars induced from the shared task data, it will be possible for participants to develop grammar-based systems that will produce more competitive realisers in future challenges.[10]

[10] Note that there are other conceivable shared tasks where the input conversion issue would not arise. For example, a text-to-text shared task on sentential paraphrasing could be agnostic as

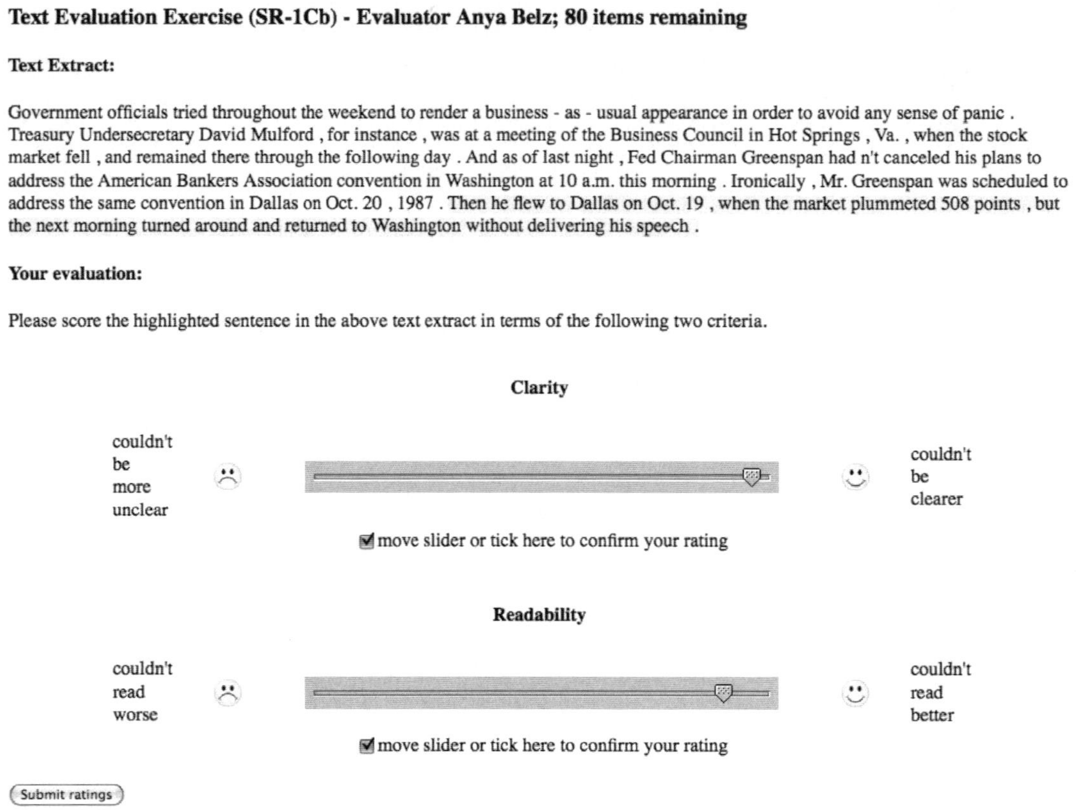

Figure 1: Screen shot of evaluation of a realisation in context, using sliders, for the criteria of *Clarity* and *Readability*.

To encourage the development of a greater variety of shared task systems, for next year we are actively considering ways of making it easier to participate, and welcome discussion of this topic.

Resources for the Community: A byproduct of running this shared task has been the development or refinement of various tools and data sets which can serve as resources for the generation community. These include:

- The training and test data sets, available from the Linguistic Data Consortium by request.
- The automated testing script, available from: http://www.ling.ohio-state.edu/ẽspinosa/genchal11/
- The test data from the six systems, with the human evaluation scores, available from: http://www.itri.brighton.ac.uk/research/sr-task/

As a result of the pilot SR Task, we have taken a first step forward in making results truly comparable in that researchers will be able to compare automatic results on this year's common ground inputs to the numbers reported in the tables, when submitting papers to conferences on the value of a given technique for surface realization. Furthermore, the human evaluation data can be used for system development, and in meta-evaluation of metrics.

6 Conclusion

The first Surface Realisation Shared Task was the result of a prolonged period of discussion and development which originally started as a heated debate about the comparability of the BLEU scores of different systems during the ACL-IJCNLP'09 reviewers' discussion period. We subsequently got together a working group of researchers interested in developing an SR input representation and presented an initial proposal at INLG'10 (Belz et al., 2010). Over the course of the past year we developed this into the fully specified SR Task we are reporting in this paper. The task in its present form should be regarded as a pilot, to be developed further over the coming years, with input from all interested parties.

to the kinds of internal representations systems employ. However, in such text-to-text tasks, it would be difficult to isolate text generation issues from text interpretation ones.

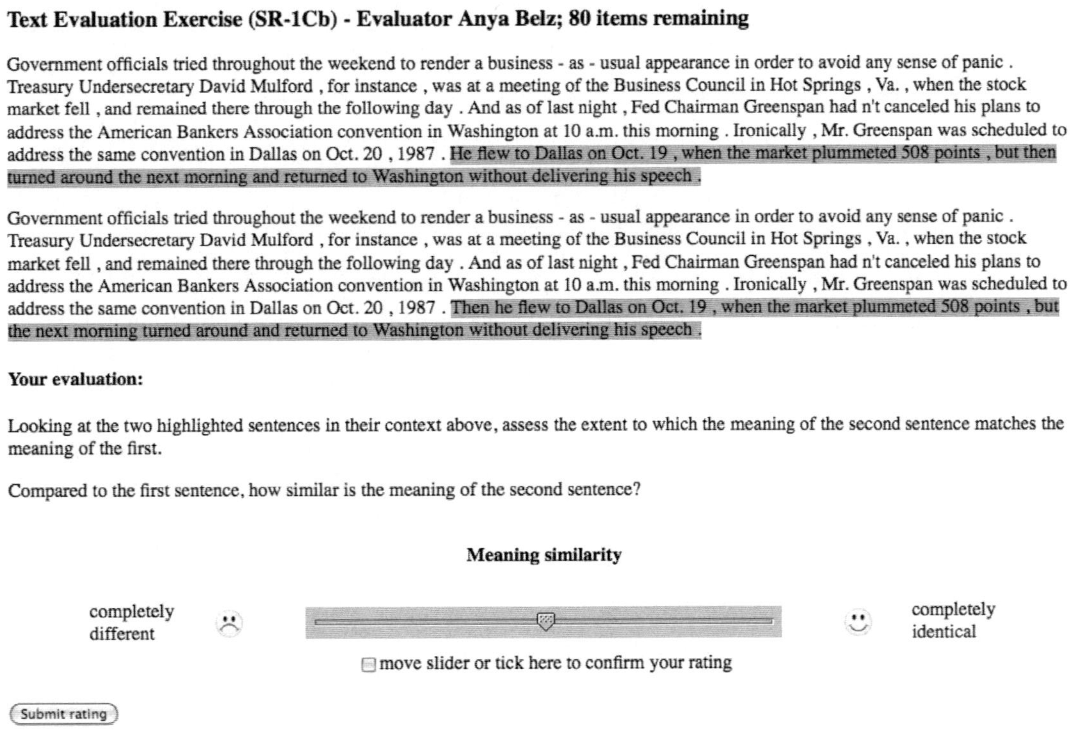

Figure 2: Screen shot of evaluation of the *Meaning Similarity* of a realisation compared to the original corpus sentence.

Clarity					*Readability*						*Meaning Similarity*					
System	Mean	Homogeneous subsets			System	Mean	Homogeneous subsets				System	Mean	Homogeneous subsets			
Corpus	88.55	A			Corpus	88.97	A				Corpus	96.68	A			
STUMABA-S	74.80		B		STUMABA-S	78.93	A	B			STUMABA-S	83.82		B		
DCU	64.26		B		DCU	77.32		B			DCU	81.14		B		
UCM	38.38			C	ATT	50.72			C		ATT	58.04			C	
ATT	38.06			C	UCM	38.43				D	UCM	30.27				D

Table 8: SR-Task, Shallow Track: Results for Clarity, Readability and Meaning Similarity evaluations, in terms of means and homogeneous subsets determined by post-hoc Tukey's HSD (sig. < 0.05).

We hope that ultimately, this initiative will evolve some degree of standardisation of realiser inputs, at two, or possibly more, levels, facilitating the development and re-use of off-the-shelf realiser tools.

Acknowledgments

The work reported here was supported by the Engineering and Physical Sciences Research Council (EPSRC), UK, under research grant EP/I032320/1. Work on the automatic evaluations and analysis was supported in part by NSF grant number IIS-0812297.

Many thanks to the other members of the working group for their valuable contributions: Bernd Bohnet, Johan Bos, Aoife Cahill, Charles Callaway, Josef van Genabith, Pablo Gervas, Stephan Oepen and Leo Wanner.

References

Satanjeev Banerjee and Alon Lavie. 2005. METEOR: An Automatic Metric for MT Evaluation with Improved Correlation with Human Judgments. In *Proc. of the ACL-05 Workshop on Intrinsic and Extrinsic Evaluation Measures for Machine Translation and/or Summarization*.

Anja Belz and Eric Kow. 2011. Discrete vs. continuous rating scales for language evaluation in nlp. In *Proceedings of the 49th Annual Meeting of the Association for Computational Linguistics (ACL-HLT'11)*.

A. Belz, M. White, J. van Genabith, D. Hogan, and A. Stent. 2010. Finding common ground: Towards a

Clarity					Readability					Meaning Similarity				
System	Mean	Homogeneous subsets			System	Mean	Homogeneous subsets			System	Mean	Homogeneous subsets		
Corpus	83.28	A			Corpus	88.06	A			Corpus	99.86	A		
STUMABA-D	60.30		B		STUMABA-D	64.91		B		STUMABA-D	72.54		B	
OSU	22.71			C	OSU	22.83			C	OSU	32.44			C

Table 9: SR-Task, Deep Track: Results for Clarity, Readability and Meaning Similarity evaluations, in terms of means and homogeneous subsets determined by post-hoc Tukey's HSD (sig. < 0.05).

Surface Realisation shared task. In *Proc. of INLG'10*, pages 267–271.

Bernd Bohnet, Leo Wanner, Simon Mille, and Alicia Burga. 2010. Broad coverage multilingual deep sentence generation with a stochastic multi-level realizer. In *Proceedings of the 23rd International Conference on Computational Linguistics*, Beijing, China.

A. Cahill and J. van Genabith. 2006. Robust PCFG-based generation using automatically acquired LFG approximations. In *Proc. ACL'06*, pages 1033–44.

Charles Callaway. 2003. Evaluating coverage for large symbolic NLG grammars. In *Proceedings of the 18th International Joint Conference on Artificial Intelligence (IJCAI 2003)*, pages 811–817.

Michael Denkowski and Alon Lavie. 2011. Meteor 1.3: Automatic Metric for Reliable Optimization and Evaluation of Machine Translation Systems. In *Proceedings of the EMNLP 2011 Workshop on Statistical Machine Translation.*

Richard Johansson and Pierre Nugues. 2007. Extended constituent-to-dependency conversion for english. In Joakim Nivre, Heiki-Jaan Kaalep, Kadri Muischnek, and Mare Koit, editors, *Proceedings of NODALIDA 2007*, pages 105–112, Tartu, Estonia.

I. Langkilde. 2002. An empirical verification of coverage and correctness for a general-purpose sentence generator. In *Proc. 2nd International Natural Language Generation Conference (INLG '02).*

Mitchell Marcus, Grace Kim, Mary Ann Marcinkiewicz, Robert MacIntyre, Ann Bies, Mark Ferguson, Karen Katz, and Britta Schasberger. 1995. The PENN treebank: Annotating predicate argument structure. Distributed on the PENN Treebank Release 2 CD-ROM, Linguistic Data Consortium.

Adam Meyers, Ruth Reeves, Catherine Macleod, Rachel Szekely, Veronika Zielinska, Brian Young, and Ralph Grishman. 2004. The nombank project: An interim report. In *NAACL/HLT Workshop Frontiers in Corpus Annotation.*

Hiroko Nakanishi, Yusuke Miyao, and Jun'ichi Tsujii. 2005. Probabilistic models for disambiguation of an hpsg-based chart generator. In *Proceedings of the 9th International Workshop on Parsing Technology (Parsing'05)*, pages 93–102. Association for Computational Linguistics.

Martha Palmer, Daniel Gildea, and Paul Kingsbury. 2005. The proposition bank: A corpus annotated with semantic roles. In *Computational Linguistics Journal*, pages 71–105.

Kishore Papineni, Salim Roukos, Todd Ward, and Wei-Jing Zhu. 2002. Bleu: a method for automatic evaluation of machine translation. In *Proceedings of 40th Annual Meeting of the Association for Computational Linguistics*, pages 311–318, Philadelphia, Pennsylvania, USA, July. Association for Computational Linguistics.

Matthew Snover, Bonnie Dorr, Richard Schwartz, Linnea Micciulla, and John Makhoul. 2006. A study of translation edit rate with targeted human annotation. In *Proc. of the Association for Machine Translation in the Americas (AMTA-06).*

Mihai Surdeanu, Richard Johansson, Adam Meyers, Lluís Màrquez, and Joakim Nivre. 2008. The conll-2008 shared task on joint parsing of syntactic and semantic dependencies. In *Proceedings of the Twelfth Conference on Computational Natural Language Learning*, Manchester, UK.

Michael White and Rajakrishnan Rajkumar. 2009. Perceptron reranking for CCG realisation. In *Proceedings of the 2009 Conference on Empririal Methods in Natural Language Processing (EMNLP'09)*, pages 410–419.

H. Zhong and A. Stent. 2005. Building surface realizers automatically from corpora. In A. Belz and S. Varges, editors, *Proceedings of UCNLG'05*, pages 49–54.

DCU*at Generation Challenges 2011 Surface Realisation Track

Yuqing Guo
Toshiba Research and Development Center
5/F., Tower W2, Oriental Plaza,
Dongcheng District, Beijing, China
guoyuqing@rdc.toshiba.com.cn

Deirdre Hogan and Josef van Genabith
NCLT/CNGL, School of Computing,
Dublin City University,
Glasnevin, Dublin 9, Ireland.
dhogan,josef@computing.dcu.ie

Abstract

In this paper we describe our system and experimental results on the development set of the Surface Realisation Shared Task. DCU submitted 1-best outputs for the Shallow subtask of the shared task, using a surface realisation technique based on dependency-based n-gram models. The surface realiser achieved BLEU and NIST scores of 0.8615 and 13.6841 respectively on the SR development set.

1 Introduction

DCU submitted outputs for SR-Shallow, the shallow sub-task of the surface realisation shared task, using a surface realisation technique based on dependency-based n-gram models, described in some detail in (Guo et al., 2010).

The generation method captures the mapping between the surface form sentences and the unordered syntactic representations of the shallow representation by linearising a set of dependencies *directly*, rather than via the application of grammar rules as in more traditional chart-style or unification-based generators (White, 2004; Nakanishi et al., 2005; Cahill and van Genabith, 2006; Hogan et al., 2007; White and Rajkumar, 2009). In contrast to conventional n-gram language models over surface word forms (Langkilde-Geary, 2002), we exploit structural information and various linguistic features inherent in the dependency representations to constrain the generation space and improve the generation quality.

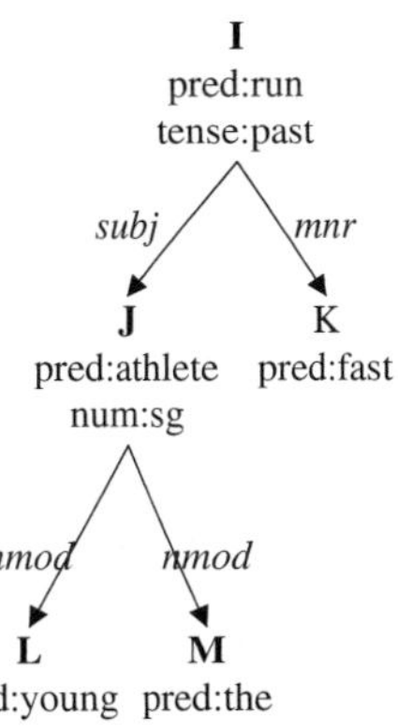

Figure 1: Unordered dependency tree for the input of the sentence: the young athlete ran fast

2 Dependency-based N-gram Models

The shallow input representation takes the form of an unordered dependency tree. The basic approach of the surface realisation method is to traverse the input tree ordering the nodes at each sub-tree based on local information. For each sub-tree the nodes are ordered according to a combination of n-gram models of increasing specificity. At the most general level, for a particular sub-tree, the n-gram model simply models the grammatical relations (including the predicate/head) of the sub-tree. Take for example the sub-tree rooted at node I from Figure 1. The realiser linearises the lemmas at nodes I, J and K by learning the correct order of the syntactic relations (in this case $subj \prec pred \prec mnr$).

Formally, in our most basic model, for a lo-

* Throughout this document DCU stands for the joint team of Dublin City University and Toshiba (China) Research and Development Center participating in the SR Task 2011.

Proceedings of the 13th European Workshop on Natural Language Generation (ENLG), pages 227–229,
Nancy, France, September 2011.

cal sub-tree t_i containing m grammatical relations (GRs) (including $pred$), generating a surface string $S_1^m = s_1...s_m$ expressed by t_i is equivalent to linearising all the GRs present at t_i. The dependency n-gram (DN-gram) model calculates probabilities for all permutations $GR_1^m = GR_1...GR_m$, and searches for the best surface sequence that maximises the probability $P(S_1^m)$ in terms of maximising $P(GR_1^m)$. Applying the chain rule and the Markov assumption, the probability of the surface realisation is computed according to Eq. (1).

$$P(S_1^m) = P(GR_1^m) = P(GR_1...GR_m) = \prod_{k=1}^{m} P(GR_k|GF_{k-n+1}^{k-1}) \quad (1)$$

The basic dependency n-gram model over bare GRs is not a good probability estimator as it only makes use of a few dozen grammatical function roles. For example there is no way to capture the difference between two nominal modifiers according to the labels of the two GRs. In order to facilitate better decisions, we extend the basic model to a number of more complex DN-gram models incorporating contextual information such as the syntactic relation of the parent of a node, as well as local node information (e.g. $tense$ and $number$ features). In the most specific model all grammatical relations are lexicalised (in the case of subtree rooted at node I from Figure 1 the model learns: *subj(athlete)* $\prec$ *pred(run)* $\prec$ *mnr(fast)*). Log-linear interpolations (LLI) are used to combine the estimates from the different DN-gram models:

$$P^{LLI}(S_1^m) = \prod_i P_i(S_1^m)^{\lambda_i} \quad (2)$$

3 The Realisation Algorithm

In order to generate the surface lexical form corresponding to an input lemma, morphological alternation has to be determined. From the training corpus, we use the grammatical properties like number, part-of-speech tag, tense, and participle feature which are encoded in the input nodes, to learn a mapping from lemma to the appropriate word form in the surface realisation.

The generation process proceeds as follows: Given an input tree T consisting of unordered projective[1] dependencies, the generation algorithm recursively traverses T in a bottom-up fashion and at each sub-tree t_i:

1. instantiates the local predicate $pred_i$ at t_i and performs morphological inflections if necessary
2. calculates DN-gram probabilities of possible GR permutations licensed by t_i
3. finds the most probable GR sequence among all possibilities by Viterbi search
4. generates the surface string s_i according to the best GR sequence as a realisation of t_i
5. propagates s_i up to the parent sub-tree.

4 Experimental Results

Results of the surface generator on the SR development set, trained exclusively on the SR training set, are displayed in Table 1.

BLEU-4	NIST	METEOR
0.8615	13.6841	0.8925

Table 1: Results on the development set

References

Aoife Cahill and Josef van Genabith. 2006. Robust PCFG-based generation using automatically acquired LFG approximations. In *Proceedings of the 44th Annual Meeting of the Association for Computational Linguistics (ACL).*

Yuqing Guo, Haifeng Wang, and Josef van Genabith. 2010. Dependency-based n-gram models for general purpose sentence realisation. *Natural Language Engineering*, 1(1):1–29.

Deirdre Hogan, Conor Cafferkey, Aoife Cahill, and Josef van Genabith. 2007. Exploiting multi-word units in history-based probabilistic generation. In *In Proceedings of the Joint Conference on Empirical Methods in Natural Language Processing and Conference on Computational Natural Language Learning*.

[1]The algorithm assumes all dependencies are projective and therefore has a somewhat inadequate handling of the non-projective dependencies that do exist in the SR data. For example, for the input dependency tree of sentence *Why , they wonder , should it belong to the EC ?* (training set sentId=32553) the algorithm can not generate the original word order. A further pre-processing step is needed to make all dependencies projective.

Irene Langkilde-Geary. 2002. An empirical verification of coverage and correctness for a general-purpose sentence generator. In *Proceedings of the 2nd International Natural Language Generation Conference (INLG)*.

Hiroko Nakanishi, Yusuke Miyao, and Jun'ichi Tsujii. 2005. Probabilistic models for disambiguation of an hpsg-based chart generator. In *Proceedings of the 9th International Workshop on Parsing Technologies (IWPT)*.

Michael White and Rajakrishnan Rajkumar. 2009. Perceptron reranking for ccg realization. In *Proceedings of the Conference on Empirical Methods in Natural Language Processing (EMNLP-09)*.

Michael White. 2004. Reining in ccg chart realization. In *Proceedings of the 3rd International Natural Language Generation Conference)*.

ATT-0: Submission to Generation Challenges 2011 Surface Realization Shared Task

Amanda Stent
AT&T Labs - Research
180 Park Avenue, Bldg. 103
Florham Park, NJ 07932
stent@research.att.com

1 Introduction

This abstract reports on our submission to the shallow track for the Generation Challenges 2011 Surface Realization Shared Task. This system is intended to be a *minimal* system in the sense that it uses (almost) no lexical, syntactic or semantic information other than that found in the training corpus itself. The system architecture was motivated by work done on FERGUS (Bangalore and Rambow, 2000). The system uses three information sources, each acquired from the training corpus: is a localized tree model capturing information from the dependency tree; a trigram language model capturing word order information for words in the same subtree; and a morphological dictionary. In the sections below we briefly present each of these models.

1.1 Tree Model

The tree model contains a set of counts for localized tree paths in the dependency trees in the training data. During training, for each lemma we extract several kinds of tree path:

- **three deep, lexicalized** – root, part-of-speech (POS) tag, and phrase type for the lemma; root and phrase type for the two ancestors nearest the lemma in the dependency tree
- **three deep, partly lexicalized** – root, POS tag, and phrase type for the lemma; phrase type for the two ancestors nearest the lemma
- **three deep, not lexicalized** – POS tag and phrase type for the lemma; phrase type for the two ancestors nearest the lemma
- **two deep, not lexicalized** – POS tag and phrase type for the lemma; phrase type for its parent

For each tree path, we record whether the lemma on this path was a *left child* or *right child* of its parent in the dependency tree. We use only localized tree paths to minimize data sparsity.

During realization, we work our way from the most to the least specific tree path for each input lemma, stopping when we find a tree path in the tree model. We assign to the lemma the most frequently occurring relative position of this tree path (to the right or to the left of the head). We do not currently take n-best tree path positions.

Use-lexicalized flag We can set a flag in the system to cause realization to use only the non-lexicalized tree paths, or to use the lexicalized tree paths (backing off to the non-lexicalized ones). We experimented with both settings (see Table 1).

1.2 Language Model

The language model is a capitalization-invariant trigram language model with Good-Turing discounting acquired from the training corpus using the SRI language modeling toolkit (Stolcke, 2002).

During realization, for each node in the dependency tree having more than one *left child*, we pass the possible orderings of the left children to the language model. We take the top two orderings, if they have similar likelihood; otherwise we take only the top one ordering. If the language model finds no likelihoods for the alternative orderings, they are all retained. The same process is applied to the *right children* of a node in the dependency tree.

Use-nbest flag We can set a flag in the system to cause realization to use only the most likely word ordering from the language model, or to consider n-

Proceedings of the 13th European Workshop on Natural Language Generation (ENLG), pages 230–231,
Nancy, France, September 2011.

System settings	Training data	Test data	Items	BLEU	NIST	Meteor	TER
Lexicalized, nbest	Train	Devel	1034	.670 (.344)	12.801	.975 (.435)	.146 (.418)
Non-lexicalized, nbest	Train	Devel	1034	.647 (.329)	12.685	.971 (.425)	.159 (.415)
Non-lexicalized, one-best	Train	Devel	1034	.623	12.587	.967	.174

Table 1: Automatic evaluation results. Single-best results are outside parentheses, 5-best are inside parentheses. *Lexicalized* = tree model has lexical information in tree paths.

best word orderings. Due to the vagaries of the testing software, we do not report results for different settings of this flag here. We used the same language model to rank order complete output sentences for the purposes of input to the testing software.

1.3 Morphological Dictionary

The morphological dictionary contains inflected forms found in the training data for each root form in the training data. It indexes root forms by part-of-speech and by verb tense, verb participle, number, and person (1/2/3) features. The person feature is approximated by assigning 1st person to first-person pronouns, 2nd person to second-person pronouns and leaving all other nouns alone.

We augment the morphological dictionary with 4 rules: add word-final *s* to plural nouns; add word-final *ed* to past tense verbs and past tense participles; add word-final *s* to present-tense singular verbs; add word-final *ing* to present tense participles. During post-processing of the entire sentence, we also add word-final *n* to the determiner *a* when it precedes a noun that starts with a vowel, remove multiple adjacent punctuation marks from the set {?!.;,} and ensure that the first letter of the sentence-initial word is upper case. This is the only information not found in the training data that we added to our system.

During realization, each input lemma is assigned inflection by looking up a tuple consisting of its root, POS tag and features in the morphological dictionary, or by using the rules mentioned above.

2 Results and Discussion

We evaluated the output of our surface realizer using the reference file and tool provided by Dominic Espinosa, which incorporates BLEU (Papenini and others, 2002), METEOR (Lavie and Denkowski, 2009) and TER (from TERp (Snover and others, 2009)). We used the subsets of the Penn Treebank (Marcus et al., 1993) provided by the Linguistic Data Consortium and converted into dependency trees by Deirdre Hogan. Table 1 shows the output of the automatic metrics for the development data. The absence of lexicalized information in the tree paths causes only a slight drop in accuracy because the language model duplicates some of that information; it also adds efficiency. Tracking only one-best possibilities for all phrases also adds efficiency at a cost of accuracy.

We have not done a formal error analysis, but we did notice during development that punctuation marks, especially those that need to be matched (brackets, quotes), and missing entries in the morphological dictionary, are the source of many errors in our system. It would be easy to use an external morphological dictionary with this system; for these experiments we wanted to be minimalist about the resources we used.

References

Srinivas Bangalore and Owen Rambow. 2000. Using TAGs, a tree model, and a language model for generation. In *Proceedings of the TAG+5 Workshop*.

Alon Lavie and Michael Denkowski. 2009. The METEOR metric for automatic evaluation of machine translation. *Machine Translation*, 23(2–3):105–115.

Mithcell Marcus, Mary Ann Marcinkiewicz, and Beatrice Santorini. 1993. Building a large annotated corpus of English: the Penn Treebank. *Computational Linguistics*, 19(2):313–330.

Kishore Papenini et al. 2002. BLEU: A method for automatic evaluation of machine translation. In *Proceedings of the ACL*.

Matthew Snover et al. 2009. Fluency, adequacy, or HTER? exploring different human judgments with a tunable MT metric. In *Proceedings of the Workshop on Statistical Machine Translation at the EACL*.

Andreas Stolcke. 2002. SRILM - an extensible language modeling toolkit. In *Proceedings of ICSLP*.

<StuMaBa>: From Deep Representation to Surface

Bernd Bohnet [1], **Simon Mille** [2], **Benoît Favre** [3], **Leo Wanner** [2,4]
[1]Institut für maschinelle Sprachverarbeitung (IMS)
Universität Stuttgart, {first-name.last-name}@ims.uni-stuttgart.de
[2]Departament de Tecnologies de la Informació i les Comunicacions
Universitat Pompeu Fabra, {first-name.last-name}@upf.edu
[3]Laboratoire d'Informatique de l'Universite du Maine
{first-name.last-name}@lium.univ-lemans.fr
[4]Institució Catalana de Recerca i Estudis Avançats (ICREA)

1 Setup of the System

We realize the full generation pipeline, from the deep (= semantic) representation (SemR), over the shallow (= surface-syntactic) representation (SSyntR) to the surface. To account systematically for the non-isomorphic projection between SemR and SSyntR, we introduce an intermediate representation: the so-called *deep-syntactic* representation (DSyntR), which does not contain yet (all) function words (as SemR), but which already contains grammatical function relation labels (as SSyntR).[1]

The system thus realizes the following steps:

1. *Semantic graph → Deep-syntactic tree*
2. *Deep-syntactic tree → Surface-syntactic tree*
3. *Surface-syntactic tree → Linearized structure*
4. *Linearized structure → Surface*

In addition, two auxiliary steps are carried out. The first one is part-of-speech tagging; it is carried out after step 3. The second one is introduction of commata; it is done after step 4.

Each step is implemented as a decoder that uses a classifier to select the appropriate operations. For the realization of the classifiers, we use Bohnet et al. (2010)'s implementation of MIRA (Margin Infused Relaxed Algorithm) (Crammer et al., 2006).

2 Sentence Realization

Sentence generation consists in the application of the previously trained decoders in sequence 1.–4., plus the two auxiliary steps.

[1]The DSyntR is inspired by the DSynt structures in (Mel'čuk, 1988), only that the latter are still "deeper".

Semantic Generation Our derivation of the DSynt-tree from an input Sem-graph is analogous to graph-based parsing algorithms (Eisner, 1996). It is defined as search for the highest scoring tree y from all possible trees given an input graph x:

$$F(x) = argmax\ Score(y), where\ y \in MAP(x)$$

(with $MAP(x)$ as the set of all trees spanning over the nodes of the Sem-graph x).

As in (Bohnet et al., 2011), the search is a beam search which creates a maximum spanning tree using "early update" as introduced for parsing by Collins and Roark (2004): when the correct beam element drops out of the beam, we stop and update the model using the best partial solution. The idea is that when all items in the current beam are incorrect, further processing is obsolete since the correct solution cannot be reached extending any elements of the beam. When we reach a final state, i.e. a tree spanning over all words and the correct solution is in the beam but not ranked first, we perform an update as well, since the correct element should have ranked first in the beam.

Algorithm 1 displays the algorithm for the generation of the DSyntR from the SemR. The algorithm performs a greedy search for the highest scoring tree. *extend-tree* is the central function of the algorithm. It expands a tree by one edge, selecting each time the highest scoring edge. The attachment point for an outgoing edge is any node; for an incoming edge, it can only be the top node of the built tree.

For score calculation, we use structured features composed of the following elements: (i) the **lemma**ta, (ii) the **dist**ance between the starting node

Proceedings of the 13th European Workshop on Natural Language Generation (ENLG), pages 232–235,
Nancy, France, September 2011.

Algorithm 1: Semantic generation

```
//(x_i, y_i) semantic graph and
// gold deep syntactic tree for training case only
// both trees contain an artifical root node
tree ← {} // empty tree
// search start edge
best ← −2^31
for all n_1 ∈ x_i do
    for all n_2 ∈ x_i & n_1 ≠ n_2 do
        for all l ∈ edge-labels do
            s ← score({(synt(n_1),synt(n_2),l)})
            if s > best then
                tree ← {(synt(n_1),synt(n_2),l)}
                best ← s ; root ← n_1
// computed remaining nodes to be added
rest ← nodes(x_i) − nodes(tree)
while rest ≠ ∅ do
  // extend tree: extend tree by one edge
  best ← −2^31
  for all n_r ∈ rest do
    for all n_t ∈ tree do
      for all l ∈ edge-labels do
        s ← score(tree, {(synt(n_t),synt(n_r),l)})
        if s > best then
          tree ← tree ∪ {(synt(n_t),synt(n_r),l)}
          best ← s ; rest ← rest - n_r
          continue with while
    // check for new root
    s ← score(tree, {(synt(n_r),synt(root),l)})
    if s > best then
      tree ← tree ∪ {(synt(n_r),synt(root),l)}
      root ← n_r ; best ← s ; rest ← rest - n_r
      continue with while
return tree
TRAINING: if predicted tree ≠ gold tree
then update weight vector in accordance with the trees
```

s and the target node t, (iii) the **dir**ection of the path (if the path has a direction), (iv) the sorted **bag** of in-going edges labels without repetition, (v) the **path** of edge labels between source and target node. The templates of the composed structured features are listed in Table 1. We obtain about 2.6 Million features in total. The features have binary values, meaning that a structure has/has not a specific feature.

Deep-Syntactic Generation: Since the DSyntR contains by definition only content words, function words must be introduced during the DSyntR–SSyntR generation passage in order to obtain a fully spelled out syntactic tree.

feature templates
label+dist(s, t)+dir
label+dist(s, t)+lemma$_s$+dir
label+dist(s, t)+lemma$_t$+dir
label+dist(s, t)+lemma$_s$+lemma$_t$+dir
label+dist(s, t)+lemma$_s$+lemma$_t$+dir
label+dist(s, t)+lemma$_s$+bag$_t$+dir
label+dist(s, t)+lemma$_t$+bag$_t$+dir
label+dist(s, t)+lemma$_s$+bag$_s$+dir
label+dist(s, t)+lemma$_t$+bag$_s$+dir
label+dist(s, t)+bag$_t$+dir
label+path(s, t)+dir

Table 1: Selected feature templates for the SemR → DSyntR mapping ('s' = "source node", 't' = "target node")

Algorithm 2: DSynt Generation

```
//(x_i, y_i^g) the deep syntactic tree
// and gold surface syntactic tree for training case only
// R set of rules
// traverse the tree depth-first
y_i ←clone(x_i)
node-queue ← root(x_i)
while node-queue ≠ ∅ do
  //depth first traversal
  node ← remove-first-element(node-queue)
  node-queue ← children(node, x_i)∪ node-queue
  // select the rules which insert a leaf node
  leaf-insert-rules ← select-leaf-rules(next-node,x_i,R)
  y_i ← apply (leaf-insert-rules,y_i)
  // during training, we update the weight vector
  // if the rules are not equal to the gold rules,
  // select the rules which insert a node into the tree
  // or a new node label
  node-insert-rules ← select-node-rules(node,x_i,R)
  // during training, we update here the weight vector
  y_i ← apply (edge-insert-rules,y_i)
```

For this passage, we use a tree transducer for which we automatically derive 27 rules by comparing a gold standard set of DSynt structures and SSynt dependency trees. The rules are of the following three types: 1) Introduction of an edge and a node: X ⇒ X *label$_s$* → Y; as 'X ⇒ X *P*→ ","' ; 2) Introduction of a new node and edges between two nodes: X *label$_d$*→ Y ⇒ X *label$_s^1$* → N *label$_s^2$* → Y, as 'X *OPRD*→ Y ⇒ X *OPRD*→ 'to' *IM*→ Y'; 3) Introduction of a new node label: X ⇒ N, as ' 'LOCATION' ⇒ 'on' ' .

Discriminative classifiers are trained for each of

the three rule types such that they either select a specific rule or NONE (with "NONE" meaning that no rule is to be applied). Algorithm 2 displays the algorithm for the generation of the SSyntR from the DSyntR.

Tree-based Part-of-Speech tagging: For linearization, i.e., word order determination, information on the part of speech (PoS) of the node labels of the SSynt tree is needed. For this purpose, we developed a tree-based PoS-tagger. The tagger works similarly to a standard PoS-tagger, except that we do not use (i) features derived from the context of the word (i.e., of the token to its left and of the token to its right) for which the PoS tag is being sought; and (ii) wordforms (since a semantic graph and thus also the trees derived from it in the course of generation are annotated only with lemmata and semantic grammemes). However, we use features derived from the SSynt structure that we obtained in the previous step and the grammemes provided in the semantic graph from which we start. As classifier, we use a linear support vector machine with averaging.

Linearization: For linearization and morphologization, we use a similar technique as Bohnet et al. (2010). Linearization is a beam search for optimal linearization according to a local and a global score functions.

In order to derive the word order, we use a bottom-up linearization method. We start by ordering the words of sub-trees in which the children do not have children themselves. We continue then with sub-trees in which all sub-trees are already ordered. This method allows us to use the order of the sub-trees to derive features. We order each sub-tree that includes a head and its children: (1) The algorithm creates sets of nodes for each sub-tree in the syntactic tree that contain the children of the node and the node itself. (2) The linearization algorithm orders the list of nodes in such that the node list of the children are ordered first. (3) Complete sentences are built by introducing the list of nodes in which only the head was included so far. The algorithm builds thus n-best lists of ordered sentences by adding ordered parts left-to-right.

Morphologization: Morphologization selects the edit script based on the minimal string edit distance (Levenshtein, 1966) in accordance with the highest score for each lemma of a sentence obtained during training and applies the scripts to obtain the wordforms.

System 1	
Mapping	Value
Semantics→Deep-Syntax (ULA/LAS)	99.0/95.1
Deep-Syntax→Surface-Syntax (correct)	98.6
Tree-based PoS tagging	97.8
Syntax→ Topology (% sent. eq. to reference)	54.2
Topology→Morphology (accuracy)	98.2
All stages from **deep representation**	
BLEU	76.4
NIST	13.45
All stages from **shallow representation**	
BLEU	88.7
NIST	13.89
System 2	
Semantics→Deep-Syntax (ULA/LAS)	99.0/95.1
Deep-Syntax→Surface-Syntax (correct)	98.9
Tree-based PoS tagging	98.2
Syntax→ Topology (% sent. eq. to reference)	57.7
Topology→Morphology (accuracy)	98.2
All stages from **deep representation**	
BLEU	79.6
NIST	13.55
All stages from **shallow representation**	
BLEU	89.6
NIST	13.93

Table 2: Performance of our realizer on the development set.

3 Evaluation

We submitted two systems ("System 1" and "System 2"). System 2 was a late submission. System 1 can be considered as a baseline system. System 2 introduces commata more accurately because of an improved feature set. In addition, System 2 uses the word order of the children of a node as context to derive features for the linearization. Furthermore, it uses a language model to rerank output sentences. For the language model, we use a 5-gram model with *Kneser-Ney* smoothing derived from 11 million sentences, cf. (Kneser and Ney, 1995). Table 2 displays the figures obtained for both the realization stages in isolation and the entire pipeline.[2]

[2]After the first submission of our system, we corrected a bug. As a consequence, the results improved. The bug occurred during the mapping of the data from HFG-format into CoNLL

References

B. Bohnet, L. Wanner, S. Mille, and A. Burga. 2010. Broad coverage multilingual deep sentence generation with a stochastic multi-level realizer. In *Proceedings of COLING '10*, pages 98–106, Beijing.

B. Bohnet, S. Mille, and L. Wanner. 2011. Statistical Language Generation from Semantic Structures. In *Proceedings of the International Conference on Dependency Linguistics*, Barcelona.

M. Collins and B. Roark. 2004. Incremental parsing with the perceptron algorithm. In *Proceedings of the 42nd Annual Meeting on Association for Computational Linguistics*, ACL '04, Stroudsburg, PA, USA.

K. Crammer, O. Dekel, S. Shalev-Shwartz, and Y. Singer. 2006. Online Passive-Aggressive Algorithms. *Journal of Machine Learning Research*, 7:551–585.

J. Eisner. 1996. Three New Probabilistic Models for Dependency Parsing: An Exploration. In *Proceedings of the 16th International Conference on Computational Linguistics (COLING-96)*, pages 340–345, Copenhagen.

R. Kneser and H. Ney. 1995. Improved backing-off for m-gram language modeling. In *Proceedings of the IEEE International Conference on Acoustics,Speech and Signal Processing.*

V.I. Levenshtein. 1966. Binary codes capable of correcting deletions, insertions, and reversals. *Soviet Physics*, 10:707–710.

I.A. Mel'čuk. 1988. *Dependency Syntax: Theory and Practice*. State University of New York Press, Albany.

2009 format, which was carried out to obtain training data in the format of our generator. It consisted in accessing a number of wrong columns and/or subcolumns of the annotation for a few features (which led to, e.g., the use of wordforms instead of lemmata).

The OSU System for Surface Realization at Generation Challenges 2011

Rajakrishnan Rajkumar and **Dominic Espinosa** and **Michael White**
Department of Linguistics, The Ohio State University
{raja,espinosa,mwhite}@ling.osu.edu

Abstract

This report documents our efforts to develop a Generation Challenges 2011 surface realization system by converting the shared task deep inputs to ones compatible with OpenCCG. Although difficulties in conversion led us to employ machine learning for relation mapping and to introduce several robustness measures into OpenCCG's grammar-based chart realizer, the percentage of grammatically complete realizations still remained well below results using native OpenCCG inputs on the development set, with a corresponding drop in output quality. We discuss known conversion issues and possible ways to improve performance on shared task inputs.

1 Introduction

Our Generation Challenges 2011 shared task system represents an initial attempt to develop a surface realizer for shared task inputs that takes advantage of prior work on broad coverage realization with OpenCCG (White, 2006; Espinosa et al., 2008; Rajkumar et al., 2009; White and Rajkumar, 2009; Rajkumar and White, 2010). OpenCCG is a parsing/generation library for Combinatory Categorial Grammar (Steedman, 2000). CCG is a unification-based categorial grammar formalism defined almost entirely in terms of lexical entries that encode sub-categorization as well as syntactic features. OpenCCG implements a grammar-based chart realization algorithm in the tradition of Kay's (1996) approach to bidirectional processing with unification grammars. The chart realizer takes as input logical forms represented internally using Hybrid Logic Dependency Semantics (HLDS), a dependency-based approach to representing linguistic meaning (Baldridge and Kruijff, 2002). To illustrate the input to OpenCCG, consider the semantic dependency graph in Figure 1. In the graph, each node has a lexical predication (e.g. **make.03**) and a set of semantic features (e.g. ⟨NUM⟩sg); nodes are connected via dependency relations (e.g. ⟨ARG0⟩). Such graphs are broadly similar to the "deep" shared task inputs. Note, however, that they are quite different from the shallow input trees, where many of the expected dependencies from coordination, control and relatization are missing. For example, in the figure, both dependents of **make.03** would be missing in the shallow tree, which involve control and relativization (with a null relativizer). As it would be difficult to hallucinate such dependencies, we have only attempted the deep task.

Grammar-based chart realization in the tradition of Kay is capable of attaining high precision, but achieving broad coverage is a challenge, as is robustness to any deviations in the expected input. Previous work on chart realization has primarily used inputs derived from gold standard parses, and indeed, native OpenCCG inputs have been obtained from gold standard derivations in the CCGbank (Hockenmaier and Steedman, 2007). Given the available time, our strategy was to make minor adjustments to OpenCCG's extracted grammars while devoting the bulk of our effort to converting the shared task inputs to be as similar as possible to the native inputs. Difficulties in conversion led us to employ machine learning for relation mapping and to introduce

Proceedings of the 13th European Workshop on Natural Language Generation (ENLG), pages 236–238,
Nancy, France, September 2011.

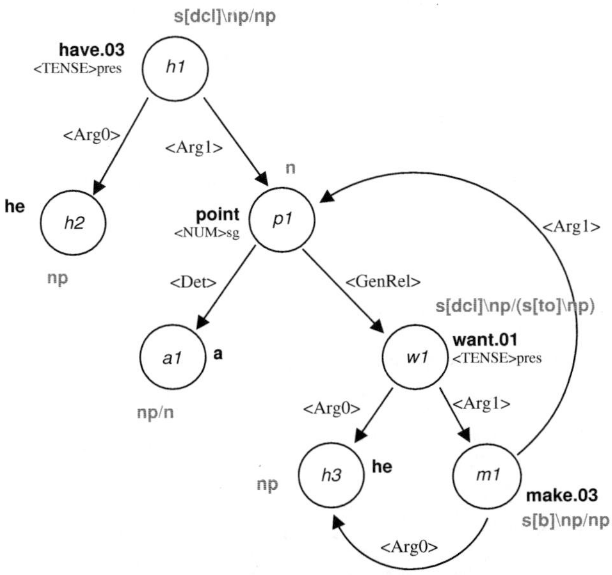

Figure 1: Semantic dependency graph from the CCGbank for *He has a point he wants to make [...]*, along with gold-standard supertags (category labels)

several robustness measures into OpenCCG's realization algorithm. Nevertheless, the percentage of grammatically complete realizations still remained well below results using native OpenCCG inputs on the development set, with a corresponding drop in output quality.

2 Conversion

In previous work, when extracting HLDS quasi–logical form graphs from the CCGbank, we removed semantically empty function words such as complementizers, infinitival-*to*, expletive subjects, and case-marking prepositions. For improved consistency with shared task inputs, we have instead left expletive subjects and all prepositions (but not complementizers and relativizers) in the native dependency graphs. Even so, the logical forms our system expects differed from the shared task inputs in many ways, the most notable being the structure of conjunctions, possessives and relative clauses, so manual conversion rules were written to handle these cases. In addition, named entities and hyphenated words were collapsed to form atomic logical form predicates, and for simplicity quotes were ignored. The conversion was effected by a Java converter augmented by XSL transforms. Table 1 provides frequencies of converted elements. Finally, to derive

Construction	Frequency
Collapsed NEs	703
Collapsed hyphenations	303
Conjunctions	691
Possessives	214
Relative clauses	90
Punct nodes excised	1672

Table 1: Conversion statistics for 1034 development section shared task graphs

possible word forms for unseen lemmas, `morphg` (Minnen et al., 2001) was used with heuristically derived POS tags.

3 Relation Tagger

Since the shared task graphs used relations between nodes which were often not easily mappable to native OpenCCG relations, we trained a maxent classifier to tag the most likely relation, as well as an auxiliary maxent classifier to POS tag the graph nodes, much like hypertagging (Espinosa et al., 2008). Training data for the classifier was extracted by comparing each relation between two nodes in the input shared task graph with the corresponding relation in the HLDS logical form. In case a labeled relation did not exist in the HLDS graph, a *NoRel* relation label was assigned. On the development data, we obtained accuracies of 90% for the POS tagger and 90.5% for the relation classifier. A substantial portion of the errors were related to the *NoRel* outcome. Of the 5154 *NoRel* cases in the dev sect, 444 were miscategorized as *Mod*, 344 as *Arg1*, 212 as *Arg0*, and 107 as *Det*. The other major error was that the *Mod* relation was often erroneously misclassified as *NoRel*.

4 Realization Results and Discussion

In spite of the graph structure and relation label changes described above, it still proved necessary to make several adjustments to both OpenCCG as well as the converted graphs. OpenCCG's strict relation checking had to be relaxed to permit divergences between the relations supplied by a lexical item and the ones in the input graph. In cases where no complete realization could be found, we also employed a novel approach to assembling fragments using MT-inspired glue rules (White, 2011), which enable a more exhaustive search of possible fragment com-

System	*Shared Task*			*Native*		
	BLEU	5-best	Coverage	BLEU	5-best	Coverage
OSU.1 (all)	0.4346	0.2483	95%	0.7838	0.5177	95%
OSU.2 (complete)	0.6564	0.3874	19%	0.8341	0.5413	76%

Table 2: Development set scores for all realizations (OSU.1) and grammatically complete realizations only (OSU.2) for the shared task inputs and using native inputs

binations and allow for n-best outputs. Additionally, we added optionality operators into the converted shared task graphs, in order to allow certain features or relations to be used as required by the grammar's constraints. The most notable cases were an optional $\langle$DET$\rangle$nil feature for nodes that could be expressed by bare nouns, and making certain relations optional, especially those derived from Nombank that yielded multiple parents for the child node.

For the experiments reported below, as in previous work, we used a lexico-grammar extracted from Sections 02–21 of our enhanced CCGbank with a similar model training procedure. Development set results appear in Table 2. Single-best and weighted 5-best BLEU scores, along with coverage percentages, are given for both the converted shared task inputs as well as native OpenCCG inputs, for comparison. The OSU.1 system includes outputs for all sentences, assembling fragments if no grammatically complete realizations are found; the OSU.2 system only includes outputs for complete realizations.[1] As the table shows, the percentage of grammatically complete realizations for the converted shared task inputs is well below the percentage using native inputs, with a corresponding drop in BLEU scores. Debugging efforts suggest that the remaining relation mismatches and other structural divergences are preventing complete realizations from being derived most of the time. The relative absence of punctuation-related features may also be an issue.

In future work, we plan to explore using machine learning more comprehensively to convert the inputs, beyond just relation tagging. We also plan to explore whether grammars can be induced that are more directly compatible with shared task inputs.

[1]Native coverage is less than 100% because of failures to derive a complete LF from the CCGbank; shared task coverage could have been 100% but the system was only run on the same inputs as in the native case.

Acknowledgements

This work was supported in part by NSF grant IIS-0812297 and by an allocation of computing time from the Ohio Supercomputer Center.

References

Jason Baldridge and Geert-Jan Kruijff. 2002. Coupling CCG and Hybrid Logic Dependency Semantics. In *Proc. ACL-02*.

Dominic Espinosa, Michael White, and Dennis Mehay. 2008. Hypertagging: Supertagging for surface realization with CCG. In *Proc. ACL-08: HLT*.

Julia Hockenmaier and Mark Steedman. 2007. CCGbank: A Corpus of CCG Derivations and Dependency Structures Extracted from the Penn Treebank. *Computational Linguistics*, 33(3):355–396.

Martin Kay. 1996. Chart generation. In *Proceedings of the 34th annual meeting on Association for Computational Linguistics*, pages 200–204, Morristown, NJ, USA. Association for Computational Linguistics.

G. Minnen, J. Carroll, and D. Pearce. 2001. Applied morphological processing of English. *Natural Language Engineering*, 7(3):207–223.

Rajakrishnan Rajkumar and Michael White. 2010. Designing agreement features for realization ranking. In *Proc. Coling 2010: Posters*.

Rajakrishnan Rajkumar, Michael White, and Dominic Espinosa. 2009. Exploiting named entity classes in CCG surface realization. In *Proc. NAACL HLT 2009 Short Papers*.

Mark Steedman. 2000. *The syntactic process*. MIT Press, Cambridge, MA, USA.

Michael White and Rajakrishnan Rajkumar. 2009. Perceptron reranking for CCG realization. In *Proc. of EMNLP-09*.

Michael White. 2006. Efficient Realization of Coordinate Structures in Combinatory Categorial Grammar. *Research on Language and Computation*, 4(1):39–75.

Michael White. 2011. Glue rules for robust chart realization. In *Proc. of ENLG-11*. To appear.

UCM Submission to the Surface Realization Challenge

Pablo Gervás
Universidad Complutense de Madrid / Ciudad Universitaria, 28040 Madrid, Spain
pgervas@sip.ucm.es

1 Introduction

This document describes the surface realization solution submitted by UCM to the Surface Realization Challenge. The UCM submission operates over the shallow representation of the challenge input. This submission to the surface realization challenge relies on an old-fashioned surface realizer based on unification with a grammar. Because this surface realizer requires fully specified inputs, a complex conversion process is required from the challenge input to the data that needs to be provided to the realizer. Where the challenge input is underspecified, the conversion process must provide any information that is missing from the input.

2 The TAP SurReal Surface Realizer

The UCM submission to the surface realization challenge relies on the TAP framework previously used for the Referring Expression Generation Challenge 2008 (Gervás et al., 2008) and 2009 (Hervás and Gervás, 2009). TAP (Text Arranging Pipeline) is a Java API for generating simple fluent text from a Java application. TAP is not itself a surface realizer. Instead it relies on existing surface realizers to carry out its task. The current TAP implementation is configured to rely on the SurReal surface realizer. The SurReal (SURface REALizer) implementation provides a lightweight partial Java implementation of the surface realization mechanisms of FUF described in Elhadad (Elhadad, 1993). SurReal relies on a grammar which is unified with the input. This grammar follows the conventions of the FUF grammar in Elhadad (Elhadad and Robin, 1996), but it is currently a much more simplified version than the original in its scope.

The TAP SurReal combination employed here was developed to provide a light weight surface realizer for Spanish, with particular features intended to facilitate the generation of literary texts (such as explicit control of construct placement within the sentence). For the submission described here an initial sketchy grammar for English has been expanded as required to match the demands presented by the challenge input. In spite of the effort invested, coverage may still be significantly improved.

3 Converting the Challenge Input

The challenge input data for the shallow representation consists of unordered syntactic dependency trees. Each word and punctuation marker from the original sentence is represented as a node.

An initial stage of preprocessing is applied to eliminate nodes that are not useful to the surface realizer. These include most of the punctuation signs (colons and interrogation and exclamation marks are retained as they may provide relevant information). The additional marks for indicating which nodes fall inside quotations or brackets are also eliminated, as no method has been found to make use of the information they provide (in the limited amount of time alloted to ponder this issue).

Proper nouns that include nodes of the form `NAME_*` (with the $\star$ a number indicating their relative ordering) are collapsed into single `NNP` node with a string for the full name (in the order indicated).

The differences in nature between these depen-

Proceedings of the 13th European Workshop on Natural Language Generation (ENLG), pages 239–241,
Nancy, France, September 2011. ©2011 Association for Computational Linguistics

dency trees and the input accepted by the surface realizer implies that the set of children nodes of any given node in a tree needs to be grouped into subsets that correspond to different subconstituents. Some of the information implicit in the surface form needs to be made explicit (such as agreement values for pronouns, or tense for clauses). Once this implicit information is explicit, the corresponding surface forms can be eliminated. These process is carried out by a set of hand-crafted tree rewriting rules. Rules rewrite, trim or relocate subtrees matching a given pattern, while respecting the rest of the tree (to ensure that a single abstract rule can cover a set of common cases in spite of ancillary local differences).

Due to the complexity of the task, at the time of writing only a limited set of such rules has been developed. Although an effort has been made to address the most generic constructions first, these rules fall short of covering the complete set of linguistic constructions available in the development data. The rules also fail to cover the full set of constructions that the realizer is capable of producing.

Although the shallow representation does have information on tense for specific nodes corresponding to verbs, the tense for each clause needs to be abstracted from the combination of tenses and the relative position of the various verb forms that make up the full verb phrase involved.

The explicit representation of pronouns in the shallow representation needs to be converted into the set of features that characterise them (person, number, gender).

Once the input trees have been rewritten to slimmer versions, a separate module converts them into suitable input for the realizer, using the TAP API.

Where the conversion process has failed to produce from the input successful data for the realizer, strings of the form "XXX*" has been introduced as place holders. Where the process resulted in no string, a place holder is required by the automation script, so the word "no" has been used.

4 Results over Development Data

The results obtained for the development data are reported on Table 1. These results are copied directly from the output of a version of the first automated script provided, adapted to run on a Windows machine.

BLEU	0.23791
BLEU (complete)	0.23791
Avg. BLEU	0.26100
Avg. BLEU (complete)	0.26100
NIST	2.59462
NIST (complete)	2.59462
Avg. NIST	4.48897
Avg. NIST (complete)	4.49331
METEOR	0.23061
Avg. METEOR	0.23061

Table 1: Single best results over development data

5 Discussion

The expected text provided with the development data is only used to provide feedback during the manual process of constructing the rewritting rules. This is a disadvantage with respect to alternative solutions capable of learning from the combination of input and expected text result.

The reported results constitute a measure of the coverage achieved by the input conversion process more than a measure of the capabilities of the realizer employed.

The TAP-SURREAL realizer provides rich features for controlling relative position of element within the sentence, however, as no information on relative position of elements in a sentence (other than for proper noun constructions) was available in the initial input data, the issue of relative position within the sentence has not been considered. The supplementary data with information on word position became available at too late a stage to be considered.

Acknowledgments

The research reported in this paper was research is partially supported by the Ministerio de Educación y Ciencia (TIN2006-14433-C02-01, TIN2009-14659-C03-01). Many thanks to Dominic Espinosa for his help in getting the automated evaluation scripts to run on a Windows machine.

References

M Elhadad and J Robin. 1996. An overview of SURGE: a reusable comprehensive syntactic realization component. Technical Report 96-03, Department of Computer Science, Ben Gurion University.

M Elhadad. 1993. FUF: The universal unifier. user manual, version 5.2. Technical Report CUCS-038-91, Columbia University.

P. Gervás, R. Hervás, and C. León. 2008. NIL-UCM: Most-Frequent-Value-First Attribute Selection and Best-Scoring-Choice Realization. In *Referring Expression Generation Challenge 2008, Proc. of the 5th International Natural Language Generation Conference (INLG'08)*.

Raquel Hervás and Pablo Gervás. 2009. Evolutionary and case-based approaches to REG: NIL-UCM-EvoTAP, NIL-UCM-ValuesCBR and NIL-UCM-EvoCBR. In *Proceedings of the 12th European Workshop on Natural Language Generation (ENLG 2009)*, pages 187–188, Athens, Greece, March. Association for Computational Linguistics.

Helping Our Own: The HOO 2011 Pilot Shared Task

Robert Dale
Centre for Language Technology
Macquarie University
Sydney, Australia
Robert.Dale@mq.edu.au

Adam Kilgarriff
Lexical Computing Ltd
Brighton
United Kingdom
adam@lexmasterclass.com

Abstract

The aim of the Helping Our Own (HOO) Shared Task is to promote the development of automated tools and techniques that can assist authors in the writing task, with a specific focus on writing within the natural language processing community. This paper reports on the results of a pilot run of the shared task, in which six teams participated. We describe the nature of the task and the data used, report on the results achieved, and discuss some of the things we learned that will guide future versions of the task.

1 Introduction

The Helping Our Own (HOO) Shared Task aims to promote the development of automated tools and techniques that can assist authors in the writing task. The task focusses specifically on writing within the natural language processing community, on the grounds that content matter familiar to Shared Task participants will be more engaging than content matter from another discipline. In addition, the ACL Anthology (Bird et al., 2008) provides us with a large and freely-available collection of material in the appropriate domain and genre that can be used, for example, for language modelling; obtaining similar material in other disciplines is more difficult and potentially costly. A broader discussion of the background to the HOO task can be found in (Dale and Kilgarriff, 2010).

In this first pilot round of the task, we focussed on errors and infelicities introduced into text by non-native speakers (NNSs) of English. While there are few native speakers who would not also have something to gain from the kinds of technologies we would like to see developed, the generally higher density of errors in texts authored by NNSs makes annotation of this material much more cost efficient than the annotation of native-speaker text. The focus on English texts is for purely pragmatic reasons; obviously one could in principle pursue the goals discussed here for other languages too.

This paper is structured as follows. In Section 2 we describe the development and test data that was provided to participants. Then, in Section 3 we describe the approach taken to evaluation. In Section 4, we summarise the results of the submissions from each of the six participating teams. Finally, in Section 5, we make some observations on lessons learned and comment on plans for the future.

2 The Data

2.1 Texts and Corrections

The data used in the pilot run of the task consisted of a set of *fragments* of text, averaging 940 words in length. These fragments were extracts from a collection of 19 *source documents*, each being a paper that had previously been published in the proceedings of a conference or a workshop of the Association for Computational Linguistics; the authors of these papers have kindly permitted their material to be used in the Shared Task. From each source document we extracted one fragment for development and one fragment for testing; each fragment is uniquely identifiable by a four-digit number used in all data associated with that fragment.

Each fragment was annotated with a number of *edits* to correct errors and infelicities, as discussed further below. Each fragment in the development set was annotated by two professional copy-editors, and each fragment in the test set was annotated by one copy-editor and checked by one of the organizers. Collectively, the development data contained a total of 1264 edits, or an average of 67 per file, with a minimum of 16 and a maximum of 100; and the test data contained a total of 1057 edits, an average of 56 per file with a minimum of 18 and a maximum of 107. In both data sets this works out at an average of one edit every 15 words.

Corresponding to each fragment, there is also a file containing, in stand-off markup format, the set of target edits for that file. Figure 1 shows some example *gold-standard edits*. The output of participating systems is compared against these files, whose contents we refer to as *edit structures*.

Proceedings of the 13th European Workshop on Natural Language Generation (ENLG), pages 242–249,
Nancy, France, September 2011.

```
<edit type="MY" index="0001-0004"
      start="631" end="631">
   <original><empty/></original>
   <corrections>
      <correction/>
      <correction>both </correction>
   </corrections>
</edit>
<edit type="RV" index="0001-0005"
      start="713" end="718">
   <original>carry</original>
   <corrections>
      <correction/>
      <correction>contain</correction>
   </corrections>
</edit>
<edit type="IJ" index="0001-0006"
      start="771" end="782">
   <original>electronics</original>
   <corrections>
      <correction>electronic</correction>
   </corrections>
</edit>
<edit type="RP" index="0001-0007"
      start="1387" end="1388">
   <original>;</original>
   <corrections>
      <correction>.</correction>
   </corrections>
</edit>
```

Figure 1: Some gold-standard edit structures.

Participating systems could choose to deliver their results in either one of two forms:

1. A set of plain text files that contain corrected text *in situ*; we provided a tool that extracts the changes made to produce a set of XML edit structures for evaluation.

2. A set of edit structures that encode the corrections their system makes.

There were advantages to providing the latter: in particular, edit structures provide a higher degree of fidelity in capturing the specific changes made, as discussed further below.

2.2 The Annotation of Corrections

By an *edit* we mean any change that is made to a text: from the outset, our intent has been to deal with textual modifications that go some way beyond the correction of, for example, grammatical errors. This decision presents us with a significant challenge. Whereas the presence of spelling and grammatical errors might seem to be something that competent speakers of a language would agree on, as soon as we go beyond such phenomena to encompass what we will sometimes refer to as 'stylistic infelicities', there is increasing scope for disagreement. Our initially-proposed diagnostic was that the annotators should edit anything they felt corresponded to 'incorrect usage'. A brief perusal of the data will reveal that, not surprisingly, this is a very difficult notion to pin down precisely.

2.3 Annotation Format

The general format of edits in the gold-standard edit files is as shown in Figure 1. Each `<edit>` element has an `index` attribute that uniquely identifies the edit; a `type` attribute that indicates the type of the error found or correction made;[1] a pair of offsets that specify the character positions in the source text file of the `start` and `end` of the character sequence that is affected by the edit; an embedded `<original>` element, which contains the text span that is subject to correction; and an embedded `<corrections>` element, which lists one or more possible corrections for the problematic text span that has been identified.

There are a number of complicating circumstances we have to deal with:

1. There may be multiple valid corrections. This is not just a consequence of our desire to include classes of infelicitious usage where there is no single best correction. The requirement is already present in any attempt to handle grammatical number agreement issues, for example, where an instance of number disagreement might be repaired by making the affected items either singular or plural. Also, it is usually not possible to consider the list of corrections we provide as being exhaustive.

2. A correction may be considered *optional*. In such cases we view the first listed correction as a null correction (in other words, one of the multiple possible corrections is to leave things as they are). When an edit contains an optional correction, we call the edit an *optional edit*. if the edit contains no optional corrections, then it is a *mandatory edit*. Note that deletions and insertions, as well as replacements, may be optional.

3. Sometimes edits may be interdependent: making one change requires that another also be made. Edits which are connected together in this way are indicated via indexed `cset` attributes (for *consistency set*). The most obvious case of this is where there is requirement for consistency in the use of some form (for example, the hyphenation of a term) across a

[1] The set of types is borrowed, with some very minor changes, from the Cambridge University Press Error Coding System described in (Nicholls, 2003), and used with permission of Cambridge University Press.

document; each such instance will then belong to the same `cset` (and consequently there can be many members in a `cset`). Another situation that can be handled using `csets` is that of grammatical number agreement. In such a case, there are two possible corrections, but the items affected may be separated in the text, requiring two separate edits to be made, connected in the annotations by a `cset`.

4. There are cases where our annotators have determined that something is wrong, but are not able to determine what the correction should be. There are two common circumstances where this occurs:

   (a) A word or fragment of text is missing, but it is not clear what the missing text should be.

   (b) A fragment of text contains a complex error, but it is not obvious how to repair the error.

   These two cases are represented by omitting the `corrections` element.

All of these phenomena complicate the process of evaluation, which we turn to next.

3 Evaluation

Each team was allowed to submit up to 10 distinct 'runs', so that they could provide alternative outputs. Evaluation then proceeds by comparing the set of gold-standard edit structures for a fragment with the set of edit structures corresponding to the participating team's output for a single run for that fragment.

3.1 Scoring

There are a number of aspects of system performance for which we can derive scores:

- Detection: does the system determine that an edit is required at some point in the text?
- Recognition: does the system correctly determine the extent of the source text that requires editing?
- Correction: does the system offer a correction that is amongst the corrections provided in the gold standard?

Detection is effectively 'lenient recognition', allowing for the possibility that the system and the gold standard may not agree on the precise extent of a correction. Systems can be scored on a fragment-by-fragment basis, on a data set as a whole, or on individual error types across the data set as a whole.

For each pairing of gold standard data and system output associated with a given fragment, we compute two *alignment sets*: these are structures that indicate the correspondences between the edits in the two edit sets. The *strict alignment set* contains those alignments whose extents match perfectly; the *lenient alignment set* contains those alignments that involve some overlap. We also have what we call *unaligned edits*: these are edits which do not appear in the lenient alignment set. An unaligned system edit corresponds to a *spurious* edit; an unaligned gold-standard edit corresponds to a *missing* edit. It is important to note that missing edits are of two types, depending on whether the gold-standard edit corresponds to an optional edit or a mandatory edit. A system should not be penalised for failing to provide a correction for a markable where the gold standard considers the edit to be optional. To manage the impact of this on scoring, we need to keep track of the number of *missing optional edits*.

3.1.1 Detection

For a given $\langle G, S \rangle$ pair of edit sets, a gold standard edit g_i is considered *detected* if there is at least one alignment in the lenient alignment set that contains g_i. Under conventional circumstances we would calculate Precision as the proportion of edits found by the system that were correct:[2]

$$(1) \qquad P = \frac{\textit{\# detected edits}}{\textit{\# spurious edits} + \textit{\# detected edits}}$$

Similarly, Recall would be conventionally calculated as:

$$(2) \qquad R = \frac{\textit{\# detected edits}}{\textit{\# gold edits}}$$

However, under this regime, if all the gold edits are optional and none are detected by the system, then the system's Precison and Recall will both be zero. This is arguably unfair, since doing nothing in the face of an optional edit is perfectly acceptable; so, to accommodate this, we also compute scores 'with bonus', where a system also receives reward for optional edits where it does nothing:

$$(3) \quad P = \frac{\textit{\# detected} + \textit{\# missing optional}}{\textit{\# spurious} + \textit{\# detected} + \textit{\# missing optional}}$$

$$(4) \qquad R = \frac{\textit{\# detected} + \textit{\# missing optional}}{\textit{\# gold edits}}$$

This has a more obvious impact when we score on a fragment-by-fragment basis, since the chances of a system proposing no edits for a single fragment are greater than the chances of the system proposing no edits for all fragments.

The detection score for a given $\langle G, S \rangle$ pair is then the harmonic mean (F-score):

$$(5) \qquad \textit{DetectionScore} = 2 \times \frac{\textit{Precision} \times \textit{Recall}}{\textit{Precision} + \textit{Recall}}$$

[2]Note that in all computations of Precision (P) and Recall (R) we take the result of dividing zero by zero to equal 1, but for the computation of F-scores we take the result of dividing zero by zero to be zero.

3.1.2 Recognition

The detection score described above can be considered a form of 'lenient' recognition. We also want to measure 'strict' recognition, i.e. the degree to which a participating system is able to determine the correct start and end locations of text to be corrected. We consider a gold-standard edit g_j to be *recognized* if it appears in the strict alignment set. *RecognitionScore* is defined to be 0 if there are no recognized edits for a given document; otherwise, we have:[3]

$$P = \frac{\#\ \textit{recognized edits}}{\#\ \textit{system edits}} \tag{6}$$

$$R = \frac{\#\ \textit{recognized edits}}{\#\ \textit{gold edits}} \tag{7}$$

The recognition score for a given $\langle G, S\rangle$ pair is again the harmonic mean.

Note that there is a deficiency in the scoring scheme here: it is quite possible that the system has decomposed what the gold-standard sees as a single edit into two constituent edits, or vice versa. Both analyses may be plausible; however, the scoring scheme gives no recognition credit in such cases.

3.1.3 Correction

Recall that for any given gold-standard edit g_j, there may be multiple possible corrections. A system edit s_i is considered a *valid correction* if it is strictly aligned, and the correction string that it contains is identical to one of the corrections provided in the gold standard edit. *CorrectionScore* is defined to be 0 if there are no recognized edits for a given document; otherwise, we have:[4]

$$P = \frac{\#\ \textit{valid corrections}}{\#\ \textit{system edits}} \tag{8}$$

$$R = \frac{\#\ \textit{valid corrections}}{\#\ \textit{gold edits}} \tag{9}$$

The correction score for a given $\langle G, S\rangle$ pair is, as before, the harmonic mean.

Just as in the case of recognition, correction scoring also suffers from the deficiency that if adjacent errors are composed or aggregated differently by the system than they are in the gold standard, no credit is assigned.

3.2 The Participating Teams

Submissions were received from six teams, as listed in Table 1. Some teams submitted only one run, while others submitted 10 (and in one case, nine); some teams submitted corrected texts, while others provided standoff XML edits.

[3] Again, we also compute a 'with bonus' variant of this that gives credit for missed optional edits.

[4] Once more, we also compute a 'with bonus' variant.

4 Results

In this section, we provide some comparative results across all six teams. Each team has also provided a separate report that provides more detail on their methods and results, also published in the present volume.

4.1 Total Scores

As a way of assessing the performance of a participating system overall, we compute each team's scores across the complete set of fragments for each run. Tables 2, 3 and 4 present the best scores achieved by each system under the 'no bonus' condition; and Tables 5, 6 and 7 present the best scores achieved by each system under the 'bonus' condition, where credit is given for missed optional edits. In each case, we show the results for the system run that produced the best F-score for that system; the overall best F-score is shown in bold.

4.2 Type-Based Scores

The numbers provided above, although they provide a means of characterising the overall performance of the participating systems, do not take account of the fact that some teams chose to attack specific types of error while ignoring other types of errors. Table 8 shows the number of edits of each type in the test data. Note that these are not the raw types from the CLC tagset that are used in the annotations, but are aggregations of these based on the part-of-speech of the affected words in the text; thus, for example, the Article type includes the CLC error tags FD (Form of determiner), RD (Replace determiner), MD (Missing determiner), UD (Unnecessary determiner), DD (Derivation of determiner), AGD (Determiner agreement error), CD (Countability of determiner), and DI (Inflection of determiner). 'Compound Change' corresponds to the tag CC, which is a new tag we added to the tagset to handle cases where there were multiple issues with a span of text that could not be easily separated; and 'Other' incorporates CL (collocation or tautology error), L (inappropriate register), X (incorrect negative formation), CE (complex error), ID (idiom wrong), AS (argument structure error), W (word order error), AG (agreement error), M (missing error), R (replace error), and U (unnecessary error).

The particular approaches each team took are discussed in the individual team reports; Tables 9 through 21 show the comparative performance by all teams for each of the error categories in Table 8. In each case, the we show each team's best results, indicating the run which provided them; and the best overall score for each error category is shown in bold. Note that the numbers shown here are the percentages of instances in each category that were detected, recognized and corrected; since we did not require teams to assign types to the edits they proposed, it is only possible to compute Recall, and not

Team	Country	ID	Submission Format	Number of Runs
Natural Language Processing Lab, Jadavpur University	India	JU	Text	1
LIMSI	France	LI	Text	10
National University of Singapore	Singapore	NU	Edits	1
Universität Darmstadt	Germany	UD	Edits	9
Cognitive Computation Group, University of Illinois	USA	UI	Text	10
Universität Tübingen	Germany	UT	Text	10

Table 1: Participating Teams

Team	Run	Precision	Recall	F-Score
JU	0	0.178	0.064	0.094
LI	8	0.409	0.063	0.110
NU	0	0.447	0.111	0.177
UD	5	0.050	0.137	0.073
UI	6	0.529	0.187	**0.277**
UT	2	0.134	0.119	0.126

Table 2: Best run scores for Detection, 'No Bonus' condition

Team	Run	Precision	Recall	F-Score
JU	0	0.125	0.045	0.067
LI	8	0.307	0.047	0.082
NU	0	0.399	0.101	0.162
UD	5	0.028	0.077	0.041
UI	1	0.583	0.153	**0.243**
UT	8	0.088	0.076	0.081

Table 3: Best run scores for Recognition, 'No Bonus' condition

Team	Run	Precision	Recall	F-Score
JU	0	0.104	0.038	0.055
LI	8	0.209	0.032	0.056
NU	0	0.291	0.074	0.118
UD	8	0.050	0.020	0.028
UI	1	0.507	0.133	**0.211**
UT	1	0.050	0.041	0.045

Table 4: Best run scores for Correction, 'No Bonus' condition

Team	Run	Precision	Recall	F-Score
JU	0	0.331	0.148	0.204
LI	8	0.606	0.141	0.229
NU	0	0.578	0.188	0.284
UD	3	0.388	0.113	0.174
UI	1	0.736	0.243	**0.366**
UT	2	0.200	0.193	0.197

Table 5: Best run scores for Detection, 'Bonus' condition

Team	Run	Precision	Recall	F-Score
JU	0	0.288	0.129	0.178
LI	8	0.539	0.125	0.203
NU	0	0.540	0.179	0.269
UD	6	0.913	0.090	0.164
UI	8	0.713	0.220	**0.337**
UT	5	0.334	0.104	0.159

Table 6: Best run scores for Recognition 'Bonus' condition

Team	Run	Precision	Recall	F-Score
JU	0	0.271	0.121	0.167
LI	8	0.473	0.110	0.178
NU	0	0.457	0.151	0.227
UD	6	0.894	0.088	0.160
UI	8	0.648	0.201	**0.306**
UT	7	0.898	0.083	0.152

Table 7: Best run scores for Correction, 'Bonus' condition

Type	Count
Article	260
Punctuation	206
Preposition	121
Noun	113
Verb	108
Compound Change	66
Adjective	34
Adverb	28
Conjunction	20
Anaphor	14
Spelling	9
Quantifier	7
Other	80

Table 8: Edits by Type

possible to calculate Precision or F-score. In the separate team reports, however, some teams have carried out these calculations based on the error types their systems were targettting.

5 Conclusions and Outstanding Issues

The task we set participating teams was an immensely challenging one. Much work in automated writing assistance targets only very specific error types such as article or preposition misuse; it is rare for systems to have to contend with the variety and complexity of errors found in the texts we used here.

We were very pleased at the level of participation achieved in this pilot run of the task, and we intend to run subsequent shared tasks based on the experience of the present exercise. We have learned a great deal that will hopefully lead to significant improvements in subsequent runs:

1. We are aware of minor tweaks that can be made to our annotation format to make it more useful and flexible.

2. There are various regards in which our evaluation tools can be improved to avoid artefacts that arise from the current scheme (where, for example, systems can be penalised because they decompose one gold-standard edit into a sequence of edits, or aggregate a sequence of gold-standard edits into a single edit).

3. We intend to provide better support to allow teams to target specific types of errors; we are also considering revisions to the tagset used.

Overall, the biggest challenge we face is the cost of data annotation. Identifying errors and proposing corrections across such a wide range of error types is a very labour intensive process that is not easily automated, and is not amenable to being carried out by unskilled labour.

6 Acknowledgements

Diane Nicholls and Kate Wild diligently annotated the data for the pilot phase. George Narroway spent many hours processing data and developing the evaluation tools. Guy Lapalme provided useful input on XML, XSLT and CSS; various members of our Google Groups mailing list provided immensely useful input at various stages of the project. We are especially grateful to all six participating teams for their patience in accommodating various delays that arose from unforeseen problems in creating and evaluating the data and results.

References

Steven Bird, Robert Dale, Bonnie Dorr, Bryan Gibson, Mark Joseph, Min-Yen Kan, Dongwon Lee, Brett Powley, Dragomir Radev, and Yee Fan Tan. 2008. The acl anthology reference corpus: A reference dataset for bibliographic research in computational linguistics. In *Proceedings of the Language Resources and Evaluation Conference (LREC 2008)*.

R. Dale and A. Kilgarriff. 2010. Helping Our Own: Text massaging for computational linguistics as a new shared task. In *Proceedings of the 6th International Natural Language Generation Conference*, pages 261–266, 7th-9th July 2010.

D. Nicholls. 2003. The Cambridge Learner Corpus—error coding and analysis for lexicography and ELT. In D. Archer, P. Rayson, A. Wilson, and T. McEnery, editors, *Proceedings of the Corpus Linguistics 2003 Conference*, pages 572–581, 29th March–2nd April 2001.

Team	Detection	Run	Recognition	Run	Correction	Run
JU	1.54	0	1.54	0	1.54	0
LI	3.46	1	3.46	1	2.31	1
NU	31.92	0	31.54	0	23.85	0
UD	1.92	5	0.77	1	0.00	0
UI	**41.54**	6	**39.62**	3	**35.38**	3
UT	8.46	0	3.85	0	3.08	1

Table 9: Best run scores for Article errors

Team	Detection	Run	Recognition	Run	Correction	Run
JU	14.08	0	11.65	0	9.71	0
LI	8.74	8	7.77	8	5.83	8
NU	0.00	0	0.00	0	0.00	0
UD	**16.99**	5	3.88	1	0.49	1
UI	15.53	4	**12.14**	4	**11.65**	0
UT	1.46	3	0.00	0	0.00	0

Table 10: Best run scores for Punctuation errors

Team	Detection	Run	Recognition	Run	Correction	Run
JU	4.13	0	2.48	0	2.48	0
LI	2.48	1	1.65	1	1.65	1
NU	15.70	0	15.70	0	9.92	0
UD	4.13	5	3.31	5	0.00	0
UI	32.23	1	32.23	3	23.97	3
UT	**60.33**	0	**52.89**	8	**28.10**	1

Table 11: Best run scores for Preposition errors

Team	Detection	Run	Recognition	Run	Correction	Run
JU	3.54	0	0.00	0	0.00	0
LI	6.19	7	5.31	7	2.65	7
NU	4.42	0	0.88	0	0.00	0
UD	**22.12**	1	**21.24**	1	**8.85**	1
UI	0.88	0	0.00	0	0.00	0
UT	0.00	0	0.00	0	0.00	0

Table 12: Best run scores for Noun errors

Team	Detection	Run	Recognition	Run	Correction	Run
JU	8.33	0	7.41	0	**7.41**	0
LI	1.85	1	0.93	0	0.00	0
NU	0.00	0	0.00	0	0.00	0
UD	**18.52**	5	**17.59**	5	2.78	8
UI	0.93	4	0.93	4	0.93	4
UT	3.70	2	0.00	0	0.00	0

Table 13: Best run scores for Verb errors

Team	Detection	Run	Recognition	Run	Correction	Run
JU	6.06	0	3.03	0	0.00	0
LI	15.15	7	1.52	6	0.00	0
NU	6.06	0	0.00	0	0.00	0
UD	**24.24**	5	**6.06**	1	**1.52**	1
UI	15.15	5	3.03	0	0.00	0
UT	18.18	3	0.00	0	0.00	0

Table 14: Best run scores for Compound Change errors

Team	Detection	Run	Recognition	Run	Correction	Run
JU	0.00	0	0.00	0	0.00	0
LI	14.71	6	14.71	6	5.88	6
NU	2.94	0	2.94	0	0.00	0
UD	**23.53**	5	**23.53**	5	**8.82**	3
UI	0.00	0	0.00	0	0.00	0
UT	5.88	0	5.88	0	0.00	0

Table 15: Best run scores for Adjective errors

Team	Detection	Run	Recognition	Run	Correction	Run
JU	7.14	0	0.00	0	0.00	0
LI	7.14	7	3.57	6	0.00	0
NU	3.57	0	0.00	0	0.00	0
UD	**28.57**	5	**14.29**	1	0.00	0
UI	0.00	0	0.00	0	0.00	0
UT	17.86	3	0.00	0	0.00	0

Table 16: Best run scores for Adverb errors

Team	Detection	Run	Recognition	Run	Correction	Run
JU	0.00	0	0.00	0	0.00	0
LI	5.00	0	5.00	0	5.00	0
NU	0.00	0	0.00	0	0.00	0
UD	0.00	0	0.00	0	0.00	0
UI	0.00	0	0.00	0	0.00	0
UT	**10.00**	0	**10.00**	0	**10.00**	0

Table 17: Best run scores for Conjunction errors

Team	Detection	Run	Recognition	Run	Correction	Run
JU	0.00	0	0.00	0	0.00	0
LI	0.00	0	0.00	0	0.00	0
NU	0.00	0	0.00	0	0.00	0
UD	**7.14**	2	**7.14**	2	0.00	0
UI	0.00	0	0.00	0	0.00	0
UT	0.00	0	0.00	0	0.00	0

Table 18: Best run scores for Anaphor errors

Team	Detection	Run	Recognition	Run	Correction	Run
JU	66.67	0	66.67	0	55.56	0
LI	**77.78**	6	**77.78**	6	**77.78**	6
NU	44.44	0	44.44	0	44.44	0
UD	55.56	2	55.56	2	44.44	3
UI	44.44	4	33.33	4	11.11	2
UT	0.00	0	0.00	0	0.00	0

Table 19: Best run scores for Spelling errors

Team	Detection	Run	Recognition	Run	Correction	Run
JU	0.00	0	0.00	0	0.00	0
LI	0.00	0	0.00	0	0.00	0
NU	0.00	0	0.00	0	0.00	0
UD	14.29	2	14.29	2	0.00	0
UI	0.00	0	0.00	0	0.00	0
UT	**57.14**	3	**57.14**	3	**14.29**	2

Table 20: Best run scores for Quantifier errors

Team	Detection	Run	Recognition	Run	Correction	Run
JU	7.04	0	1.41	0	0.00	0
LI	4.23	1	1.41	1	**1.41**	1
NU	0.00	0	0.00	0	0.00	0
UD	**22.54**	5	1.41	1	0.00	0
UI	4.23	3	0.00	0	0.00	0
UT	21.13	3	**4.23**	0	0.00	0

Table 21: Best run scores for Other errors

May I check the English of your paper!!!

Pinaki Bhaskar **Aniruddha Ghosh** **Santanu Pal** **Sivaji Bandyopadhyay**
Department of Computer Science and Engineering
Jadavpur University, Kolkata – 700032, India
pinaki.bhaskar@gmail.com arghyaonline@gmail.com santanu.pal@gmail.com sivaji_cse_ju@yahoo.com

Abstract

This paper reports about our work in the HOO shared task 2011. The task is to automatically correct the English of a given document. For that, we have developed a hybrid system of a statistical CRF based model along with a rule-based technique has been used. The system has been trained on the HOO shared task training datasets and run on the test set given by the organizer of HOO. We have submitted one run, which has been demonstrated F-score of 0.204, 0.178 and 0.167 for detection, recognition and correction respectively.

1 Introduction

Writing the research papers or thesis in English is a very challenging task for those researcher and scientist whose first language or mother tongue is not English. Express their research works properly in English is a hard job for them. Generally their paper, which is submitted to a conference and may be rejected not because of their research works but because of the English writing, which makes the paper harder for the reviewer to understand intention of author. This kind of problem will be faced in any field where someone has to provide material in a language other than his/her first language.

The mentoring [1] service of Association for Computational Linguistics (ACL) is one part of a response. This service can address a wider range of problems than those related purely to writing. The aim of this service is that a research paper should be judged only on its research content.

The organizer of "Help Our Own" (HOO) proposed and initiated a shared task, which attempts to tackle the problem by developing tools or techniques for the non-native speaker of English, which will automatically correct the English prose of the papers so that it can be accepted. All though the native English speakers are also be helped by this tools and techniques. This task is simply expressed as a text-to-text generation or Natural language Generation (NLG).

For this shared task, HOO, we have developed two models, one is rule-based model and another is statistical model. Then we have combined both these models and developed our system for HOO, 2011.

2 Related Works

English Language belongs to the Germanic languages branch of the Indo-European language family, widely spoken on six continents. HOO shared task is organized to help authors with the writing tasks. Identifying grammatical and linguistic errors in a text of a language is an open challenge to the researchers. In recent times, researchers (Heidorn, 2000) have acquired quite a benchmark for spell checker and grammar checkers, which is commonly available. In this task it is aimed to correct errors beyond the scope of these commonly available checkers i.e. detection and correction of jarring errors at part-of-speech (POS) level, syntax level and semantic level. Earlier Heidorn, 1975) developed augmented phrase structure grammar. Tetreault et.

[1] http://acl2010.org/mentoring.htm

Proceedings of the 13th European Workshop on Natural Language Generation (ENLG), pages 250–253,
Nancy, France, September 2011. ©2011 Association for Computational Linguistics

al., 2008, has dealt with error pattern with preposition by non-native speakers.

3 System Description

At the beginning of the work, we found that generation of list of rules to detect and correct the probable linguistic errors is a non-exhaustive set. So we have decided to list out the errors from the training corpus documents. We have listed the errors document wise. After a close inspection of the document wise error list, the author is prone to make similar type of errors, which depicts the attributes of the author. The errors types are classified in to some coarse groups like wrong form, something missing, needs replacing etc. We decided to resolve the errors at different levels like POS level, syntax level and semantic level. Our system contains two models – a rule based model and a statistical model as described in the next sections.

3.1 Rule based model

The total corpus is first checked using conventional grammar tool and spell checkers. The data set is parsed using Stanford dependency parser[2]. While detecting and correcting errors, we have considered the coarse groups one by one.

Wrong Form Preposition (FT) & Needs replacing Preposition (RT): To detect and to correct the wrong forms of preposition we have used a list of devised manually appropriate preposition list. Certain cases are solved based only syntax though in many cases we have to check the semantics. To identify the semantics we have used output of Stanford dependency parser and part-of-speech(POS).E.g. after verb "create", "by" preposition is used if an object follows the verb.

Wrong Form verb (FV): To detect the wrong forms of the verb we have used a verb paradigm table, which will help also in suggesting appropriate verbal inflection.

Wrong Form determiner (FD): To detect the wrong forms of determiner we have used the conventional spell checker system.

Wrong Form Adverb(FY)&& Wrong Form Adjective (FJ): To detect the wrong form of adverbs and adjectives, we have used positional aspect. Adverbs appear around the verbs, in most cases after the verbs whereas adjective appears around nouns, in most cases before the noun. A dictionary-based approach is implemented to correct the wrong forms of adverbs and adjectives.

Needs replacing conjunction (RC) & Needs replacing punctuation (RP): In case of serial comma, the last comma is replaced with "and".

Unnecessary punctuation (UP): In case of serial comma, if last comma is followed by "and" then that punctuation is treated as an error. Though it is an optional correction due to debate over serial comma issue, it is one of most frequent errors in the corpus.

Countability of noun errors(CN)and wrong quantifier because of noun countability(CQ): Countability errors are detected by the conventional grammar tools. For both these type of errors, we have considered agreement of quantifier, noun countability and verb of the sentence. Among these three, if two of them agree then the other one is corrected. As example,

"multiple error is found in the text".

In the above example, as "is" and "error" have same agreement over countability "multiple" will be corrected to "single".

Verb agreement error (AGV): To detect verb agreement error we have identified the subject using dependency parsing. We have detected the error using verb paradigm table.

The missing coarse group is the one of the bigger challenge of this task. Deriving rules for this missing coarse group needs a lot of in depth study. Few rules have been devised though in certain cases those corrections are optional. Few syntactic rules can be generated

Missing preposition (MT): For missing preposition we have used the appropriate preposition list but it wasn't enough to detect. We have devised some handcrafted rules based on linguistic features.

i. After the occurrence of "all", it might be followed by "of" and sometimes an article after "of".

ii. If there is a connecting word pair like "not only" and "but" then if either of them is followed and preposition then other one will also be followed by same preposition.

---

[2] http://nlp.stanford.edu/software/lex-parser.shtml

iii. A pronoun can't be used following number. There should be a preposition among them, mostly "of".

3.2 3.2 Statistical model

Devising rules for the appropriate determiner before nouns is quite difficult. Hence we decided to use a sequence labeling based statistical tool named Conditional Random Field (CRF++). For training, we have marked determiner along with the two words following the determiner in the training corpus. For better accuracy of the statistical model, a large data set is required for learning. Hence we have used our published papers for the training of the statistical model. If a preposition precedes the determiner then the determiner is also marked. As features to the statistical system, we have used word, root form, POS tag, number marker (singular/plural/null) and word position. The statistical tool is trained using the training corpus and it used tri-gram model.

3.3 Post Correction

After intense analysis, depending on the nature of errors in the output of statistical system we developed a set of rules.

i. In certain cases where the words are marked, we search for a gerund or noun after the marked word. If words are occurring for the first time in the paragraph then those cases are ignored.

ii. If there is gerund or noun after marked words and that gerund or noun has appeared before in the paragraph then "the" determiner is inserted before the marked word.

iii. If there is gerund or noun after marked words and that gerund or noun has appeared before in the paragraph and "a" determiner is present before the marked word then it will replaced with "the".

3.4 Merging output

The rule-based model identifies various errors based on linguistic syntactic and semantic features. The statistical model identified the missing determiner errors and wrong determiner errors. The post correction corrects the missing determiner error and wrong determiner errors detected by statistical parser. The output of the rule based model and the statistical model are merged to produce the final output. The block diagram is shown in the figure 1.

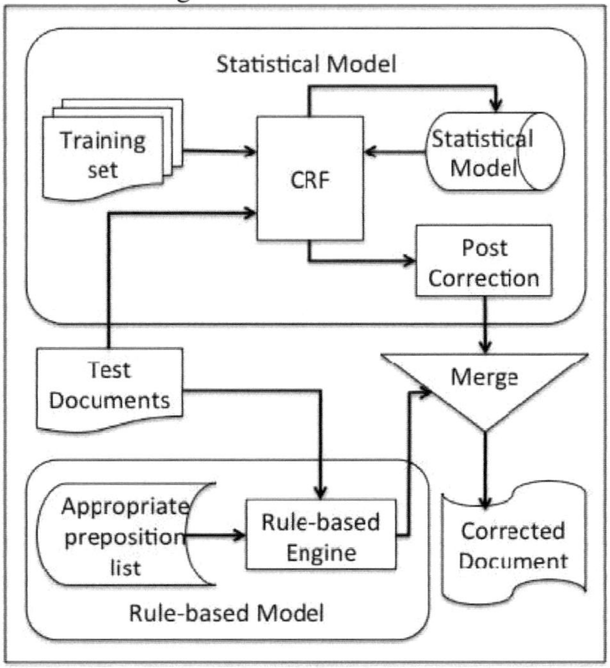

Figure 1:

4 Experimental Results

This paper reports about our research work as a part of HOO shared task. We have used a hybrid system consisting of a rule-based model and a statistical model followed by a post-processing. We have achieved F-score of 0.204, 0.178 and 0.167 in detection, recognition and correction respectively.

5 Conclusion

Our system has posed an accuracy of F-score 0.204, 0.178 and 0.167 in detection, recognition and correction respectively. Our system failed to detect and correct many syntactic and semantic errors like wrong "a" determiner. One error can be assigned with multiple tags. Hence deciding the appropriate tag is still an open debate.

Acknowledgments

The work has been carried out with support from Indo-French Centre for the Promotion of Advanced Research (IFCPAR) funded Project "An Advanced Platform for Question Answering System" (Project No. 4200-IT-1).

References

George Heidorn.2000.Intelligent writing assistance.In R Dale, H Moisl, and H Somers, editors, Handbook of Natural Language Processing, pages 181–207. Marcel Dekker Inc.

GE Heidorn. 1975. Augmented phrase structure grammars. In: BL Webber, RC Schank, eds. Theoretical Issues in Natural Language Processing. Assoc.for Computational Linguistics, pp.1-5.

Dale and Kilgarriff, 2010. Helping Our Own: Text Massaging for Computational Linguistics as a New Shared Task, International Natural Language Generation Conference 2010, Dublin, Ireland.

J R Tetreault and M S Chodorow. 2008. The ups and downs of preposition error detection in ESL writing. In Proceedings of the 22nd International Conference on Computational Linguistics.

http://en.wikipedia.org/wiki/Serial_comma

Strauss Jane, The Blue Book of Grammar and Punctuation, 10thEdition.

Handling Outlandish Occurrences: Using Rules and Lexicons for Correcting NLP Articles

Elitza Ivanova **Delphine Bernhard** **Cyril Grouin**
LIMSI–CNRS, BP133, F-91403 Orsay Cedex, France
elitza.ivanova@knights.ucf.edu
dbernhard@unistra.fr, cyril.grouin@limsi.fr

Abstract

This article describes the experiments we performed during our participation in the HOO Challenge. We present the adaption we made on two systems, mainly designing new grammatical rules and completing a lexicon. We focused our work on some of the most common errors in the corpus: missing punctuation and inaccurate prepositions. Our best experiment achieved a 0.1097 detection score, a 0.0820 recognition score, and a 0.0557 correction score on the test corpus.

1 Introduction

The number of articles written by non-native English speakers makes it necessary to provide the community with tools that can be helpful in checking and improving the linguistic quality of those articles (Dale and Kilgarriff, 2010).

The correction of errors made by English as a Second Language (ESL) writers has been addressed in several recent studies. Different kinds of errors are targeted, both concerning closed classes of words such as articles, prepositions, modals or auxiliaries and open classes of words, such as nouns and verbs (Lee and Seneff, 2006; Felice and Pulman, 2008; Gamon et al., 2009; Rozovskaya and Roth, 2011). In the case of closed classes and commonly confused words, it is possible to cast the problem as an automatic classification task. The goal of the classifier is to predict the most likely candidate from a confusion set in the given context. This requires large training corpora of mostly error-free texts.

Another approach to error correction consists in using manually developed rules to identify and correct erroneous occurrences. This approach has, for instance, been adopted in the open-source LanguageTool proofreading tool[1] (Naber, 2003; Miłkowski, 2010).

In this paper, we describe our participation to the HOO2011 challenge. We present our systems and the configurations we used while participating in the test stage of the challenge.

2 Material and methods

2.1 Corpus

Over a total amount of 1,264 annotated errors in the training corpus, we noticed that the most common errors are of three types: a missing punctuation (16.6%), a missing determiner (12.7%), and a preposition to be replaced (8.6%). Each other type of errors accounts for less than 5% of all errors in the corpus.

2.2 Systems

As the training corpus is only composed of 19 annotated files, we decided not to use machine-learning based approaches. Moreover, as we are non-native English speakers, finding and annotating English errors in scientific papers would have been a hard task.

2.2.1 Language Tool

Our first system consists of an extension of the LanguageTool system, as it has not been developed

[1] http://www.languagetool.org/

Proceedings of the 13th European Workshop on Natural Language Generation (ENLG), pages 254–256,
Nancy, France, September 2011.

```
<rule default="on" id="NEED_TO" name="need to">
    <pattern case_sensitive="no" mark_from="1">
        <token inflected="yes" postag="NN.*" postag_regexp="yes">need</token>
        <token postag="IN"><exception>to</exception></token>
        <token postag="VBG" postag_regexp="yes"/>
    </pattern>
    <message>Incorrect use of the preposition '\2' after '\1'. Normally, <suggestion>to <match no="3"
postag="VB"/></suggestion> is used.</message>
    <short>Wrong choice of preposition</short>
    <example correction="to seek" type="incorrect">I wish to stress the need <marker>of seeking</marker> a positive
outcome.</example>
    <example type="correct">I wish to stress the need to seek a positive outcome</example>
</rule>
```

Figure 1: Example LanguageTool XML rule.

specifically for text written by ESL writers. The system is based on linguistic resources and rules described in XML files that can be easily extended. We modified three resource files to deal with the HOO corpus: the grammar rules used to process the corrections, the compound words lexicon that lists the words that must be written with a dash, and the list of words that require "an" instead of "a" as a determiner, even though they do not begin with a vowel.

Figure 1 displays an example of an XML rule which deals with incorrect prepositions after the noun "need".

2.2.2 Commas module

In order to deal specifically with missing commas in figures larger than 1,000, we wrote an independent Python module.

2.2.3 CCAC

The second system[2] we used has been designed to perform both analyses of the quality, and spelling and grammatical correction of survey corpora and web content (Grouin, 2008). The final objective of this tool was to help indicate whether that noisy data could be used in an NLP chain of treatments to be applied further or not. This system is mainly based on unigrams of words and typographic rules. We adapted this system to English by producing a new lexicon of 19,000 unigrams of words from the *Financial Times* which we completed with 300 computational terms from the ACL corpus. This lexicon also includes the American version of British words.

[2]CCAC: Corpus Certification and Automatic Correction.

3 Experimental setup

We defined ten configurations based on several combinations of each system's parameters:

- Run 0: LanguageTool as it is from download;
- Run 1: LanguageTool with new rules;
- Run 2: As in run #1 plus commas module;
- Run 3: Run #0 plus new compounds lexicon;
- Run 4: Run #1 plus new compounds lexicon;
- Run 5: Run #4 plus commas module;
- Run 6: CCAC system;
- Run 7: CCAC system followed by run #5;
- Run 8: Run #5 followed by the CCAC system;
- Run 9: LanguageTool with punctuation correction only plus commas module.

4 Evaluation and discussion

The evaluation of our pipeline on the test corpus is given in Table 1. We achieved our best results using the combination of LanguageTool followed by CCAC (run #8); we obtained a 0.1097 detection score, a 0.0833 recognition score, and a 0.0589 correction score, without any bonus (Dale and Kilgarriff, 2011).

The CCAC system used independently did not obtain good results (#6). This system has been designed to process very noisy data using basic correction modules (to add or to remove diacritics, to process geminates, and at last to propose corrections based on the Levenshtein distance). Within the framework of the HOO challenge, the corrections to be made are finer than those of a web corpus.

While on the training data we achieved our best

Table 1: Official evaluation on the test corpus (no bonus scores)

Run	Det P	Det R	Det S	Rec P	Rec R	Rec S	Cor P	Cor R	Cor S
0	0.7143	0.0095	0.0187	0.7143	0.0095	0.0187	0.4286	0.0057	0.0112
1	0.4861	0.0331	0.0620	0.4085	0.0274	0.0514	0.2958	0.0199	0.0372
2	0.4868	0.0350	0.0653	0.4133	0.0293	0.0548	0.3067	0.0218	0.0406
3	0.5758	0.0180	0.0349	0.3333	0.0104	0.0202	0.2121	0.0066	0.0128
4	0.4835	0.0416	0.0767	0.3333	0.0284	0.0523	0.2444	0.0208	0.0384
5	0.4842	0.0435	0.0797	0.3404	0.0303	0.0556	0.2553	0.0227	0.0417
6	0.3056	0.0208	0.0390	0.2778	0.0189	0.0354	0.1528	0.0104	0.0195
7	0.4063	0.0615	0.1068	0.3019	0.0454	0.0789	0.2013	0.0303	0.0526
8	0.4085	0.0634	**0.1097**	0.3067	0.0473	**0.0820**	0.2086	0.0322	**0.0557**
9	0.4510	0.0218	0.0415	0.2745	0.0132	0.0253	0.2353	0.0114	0.0217

score using LanguageTool only,[3] on the test corpus, the combination of both LanguageTool and CCAC performed best. This demonstrates the complementarity of both tools when applied on a new corpus for which no specific rules had been designed.

For the time being, our systems only deal with some types of errors (especially punctuation and prepositions), due to time constraints for developing new resources and tools. Further work is thus needed to process all other kinds of errors. When improving the LanguageTool resources, we manually designed new rules and added new items in the lexicons. In order to improve this process, it would be interesting to automatically extract rules and missing words from the annotated corpus in order to reduce human intervention.

Acknowledgments

This work was partly realized as part of the Quaero Programme, funded by Oseo, French State agency for innovation. We thank the organizers for their work and reactivity during this challenge. We enjoyed being involved in this very fun task, even more so because such a correction tool would be useful for us non-native English speakers!

References

Robert Dale and Adam Kilgarriff. 2010. Helping Our Own: Text Massaging for Computational Linguistics as a New Shared Task. In *International Natural Language Generation Conference Proceedings*, pages 261–266, Dublin, Ireland.

Robert Dale and Adam Kilgarriff. 2011. Helping Our Own: The HOO 2011 Pilot Shared Task. In *Proc. of ENLG*, Nancy, France.

Rachele De Felice and Stephen G. Pulman. 2008. A Classifier-Based Approach to Preposition and Determiner Error Correction in L2 English. In *Proc. of Coling*, pages 169–176, Manchester, UK, August.

Michael Gamon, Claudia Leacock, Chris Brockett, William B. Dolan, Jianfeng Gao, Dmitriy Belenko, and Alexandre Klementiev. 2009. Using Statistical Techniques and Web Search to Correct ESL Errors. *Calico Journal*, 26(3).

Cyril Grouin. 2008. Certification and Cleaning-up of a Text Corpus: towards an Evaluation of the "grammatical" Quality of a Corpus. In *Proc. of LREC*, pages 1083–1090, Marrakech, Morocco.

John Lee and Stephanie Seneff. 2006. Automatic Grammar Correction for Second-Language Learners. In *Proc. of InterSpeech*, pages 1978–1981.

Marcin Miłkowski. 2010. Developing an open-source, rule-based proofreading tool. *Software – Practice and Experience*, 40:543–566.

Daniel Naber. 2003. A Rule-Based Style and Grammar Checker. Master's thesis, Technische Fakultät, Universität Bielefeld.

Alla Rozovskaya and Dan Roth. 2011. Algorithm Selection and Model Adaptation for ESL Correction Tasks. In *Proc. of the 49th Annual Meeting of ACL*, pages 924–933, Portland, Oregon.

[3]We obtained a 0.3487 detection, 0.2995 recognition and 0.2947 correction scores (with bonus) on run 5 and a 0.3485 detection, 0.2969 recognition and 0.2925 correction scores (with bonus) on run 8 on training corpus.

NUS at the HOO 2011 Pilot Shared Task

Daniel Dahlmeier[1], **Hwee Tou Ng**[1,2], and **Thanh Phu Tran**[2]
[1]NUS Graduate School for Integrative Sciences and Engineering
[2]Department of Computer Science, National University of Singapore
{danielhe,nght,thanhphu}@comp.nus.edu.sg

Abstract

This paper describes the submission of the National University of Singapore (NUS) to the Helping Our Own (HOO) Pilot Shared Task. Our system targets spelling, article, and preposition errors in a sequential processing pipeline.

1 Introduction

Helping Our Own (HOO) (Dale and Kilgarriff, 2010) is a new shared task for automatic grammatical error correction, a task which has attracted increasing attention recently. Instead of correcting errors in a general domain, e.g., essays written by second language learners of English, HOO focuses on papers written by non-native authors of English within the natural language processing community. In this paper, we describe the participating system from the National University of Singapore (NUS). The system targets spelling, article, and preposition errors. The core of our system is built on linear classification models and a large language model filter. We present experimental results on the HOO development and test data.

The next section describes the system in more detail. Section 3 describes the data sets used. Section 4 reports experimental results on the HOO development and test data.

2 System Architecture

The NUS system consists of a sequential pipeline of three processing steps:

1. Spelling correction
2. Article correction
3. Preposition correction

Sentence segmentation and tokenization are carried out on the HOO input files in a pre-processing step. Sentence segmentation uses the gold standard sentence boundaries. Each subsequent step takes a one-sentence-per-line plain text as input and outputs a one-sentence-per-line plain text in return. A post-processing step detokenizes the text and extracts the edit structures that encode the corrections.

2.1 Spelling Correction

We use the open-source spell checker Aspell[1] to correct spelling errors. Words are excluded from spelling correction if they are shorter than a threshold, or if they include hyphens or upper case characters inside the word. We use an in-domain Aspell dictionary constructed from all words that appear at least ten times in the ACL-ANTHOLOGY data set described in Section 3. Finally, we filter the corrections using a language model. The system only keeps corrections that strictly increase the normalized language model score of the sentence, defined as $\frac{1}{n}\log P$, where n is the length of the sentence, and P the language model probability.

2.2 Article Errors

Article error correction is treated as a multi-class classification problem. The possible classes are the articles *a*, *the*, and the empty article. The article *an* is normalized as *a* and restored later using a rule-based heuristic.

[1] http://aspell.net

Proceedings of the 13th European Workshop on Natural Language Generation (ENLG), pages 257–259,
Nancy, France, September 2011.

Each input sentence is tagged with part-of-speech (POS) tags and syntactic chunks. We use OpenNLP[2] for POS tagging and YamCha (Kudo and Matsumoto, 2003) for chunking. For each noun phrase (NP), the system extracts a feature vector representation. We use the features proposed in (Han et al., 2006) which include the words before, in, and after the NP, the head word, POS tags, etc. A multi-class classifier then predicts the most likely article for the NP. We employ a linear classifier trained with empirical risk minimization on NP instances from well-edited text (Dahlmeier and Ng, 2011). The features are only extracted from the surrounding context of the article and do not include the article itself, which would be fully predictive of the class.

During testing, a correction is proposed if the predicted article is not the same as the observed article used by the writer, and the difference between the confidence score for the predicted article and the confidence score for the observed article is larger than a threshold. Finally, we filter the corrections using a large language model and only keep corrections that strictly increase the normalized language model score of the sentence.

2.3 Preposition Errors

Preposition error correction follows the same strategy of multi-class classification and language model filtering. The system only corrects preposition substitution errors, not preposition insertion or deletion errors. The possible classes are the prepositions *about, among, at, by, for, in, into, of, on, to*, and *with*. For each prepositional phrase (PP) which is headed by one of these prepositions, a linear classifier predicts the most likely preposition from the above list. We use the features proposed by (Tetreault and Chodorow, 2008). Again, we apply a threshold to bias the classifier towards the observed preposition and filter corrections with a large language model.

3 Data Sets

We randomly split the files in the HOO development data into a tuning set HOO-TUNE (9 files) and a held-out test set HOO-HELDOUT (10 files). The official HOO test data HOO-TEST is completely unobserved during development. We create two training data sets from the ACL Anthology[3]: ACL-ANTHOLOGY includes all non-OCR documents from the anthology except the 2010 ACL conference and workshop proceedings as these overlap with the HOO data[4]. CL-JOURNAL contains all non-OCR documents from the *Computational Linguistics* journal. In both cases, we filter out section headings, references, tables, etc. The WEB 1T 5-GRAM CORPUS (Brants and Franz, 2006) is used for language modeling. Table 1 gives an overview of the data sets.

Data Set	Sentences	Tokens
HOO-TUNE	477	12,115
HOO-HELDOUT	462	10,691
HOO-TEST	722	18,789
ACL-ANTHOLOGY	708,129	18,020,431
CL-JOURNAL	22,934	611,334

Table 1: Overview of the data sets.

4 Experiments and Results

This section reports experimental results of our system on the HOO-HELDOUT and the HOO-TEST data set. The parameters of the system are as follows. The minimum length for spelling correction is four characters. The language model filter for article and preposition correction uses a 5-gram language model built from the complete WEB 1T 5-GRAM CORPUS using RandLM (Talbot and Osborne, 2007). For spelling correction, the language model filter is built from the ACL-ANTHOLOGY data set. The linear classifiers for article and preposition correction are trained on the CL-JOURNAL data set. Threshold parameters are tuned on HOO-TUNE when testing on HOO-HELDOUT, and on the complete HOO development data when testing on HOO-TEST.

4.1 Evaluation

We report micro-averaged detection, recognition, and correction F_1 scores as defined in the HOO overview paper. The scores are computed over the entire test collection.

For individual error categories, the HOO overview paper only reports the "percentage of

[2]http://opennlp.sourceforge.net

[3]http://www.aclweb.org/anthology-new

[4]Although the use of the HOO source documents was permitted, we believe that excluding them is more realistic.

Step	Detection		Recognition		Correction	
	wb	w/o b	wb	w/o b	wb	w/o b
PRE	.2152	.0000	.2152	.0000	.2152	.0000
+SPEL	.2219	.0095	.2190	.0063	.2162	.0031
+ART	.2681	.1093	.2520	.0917	.2455	.0846
+PREP	.2973	.1354	.2763	.1123	.2657	.1008

Table 2: Overall F_1 scores with (wb) and without bonus (w/o b) on the HOO-HELDOUT data after pre-processing (PRE), spelling (SPEL), article (ART), and preposition correction (PREP).

Step	Detection		Recognition		Correction	
	wb	w/o b	wb	w/o b	wb	w/o b
PRE	.1553	.0000	.1553	.0000	.1553	.0000
+SPEL	.1663	.0093	.1629	.0093	.1611	.0075
+ART	.2718	.1552	.2545	.1373	.2209	.1014
+PREP	.2840	.1774	.2686	.1615	.2274	.1177

Table 3: Overall F_1 scores with (wb) and without bonus (w/o b) on the HOO-TEST data.

instances in each category that were detected, recognized and corrected", but not precision or F_1 scores. Computing precision and F_1 is complicated by the fact that the HOO submission format does not require a system to "label" each proposed correction with the intended error category. As we know which correction was produced by which processing step for our own system, we know which error category a correction belongs to. Therefore, we can calculate micro-averaged precision, recall, and F_1 scores for spelling, article, and preposition errors individually by restricting the set of proposed edits and the set of gold corrections to a particular category.

4.2 Results

Tables 2 and 3 show the overall detection, recognition, and correction F_1 scores after each processing step on the HOO-HELDOUT and HOO-TEST set, respectively. Each processing step builds on the output of the previous step. The single biggest improvement in the score comes from the article correction step. The gap between the scores with and without bonus shows the large number of optional corrections in the HOO data. Tables 4 and 5 show the detection, recognition, and correction F_1 scores for individual error categories on the HOO-HELDOUT and HOO-TEST set, respectively.

Step	Detection		Recognition		Correction	
	wb	w/o b	wb	w/o b	wb	w/o b
SPEL	.2667	.2667	.2667	.2667	.2667	.2667
ART	.3455	.3011	.3455	.3011	.3246	.2796
PREP	.2692	.2353	.2308	.1961	.1731	.1373

Table 4: Individual F_1 scores for each error category with (wb) and without bonus (w/o b) on the HOO-HELDOUT data.

Step	Detection		Recognition		Correction	
	wb	w/o b	wb	w/o b	wb	w/o b
SPEL	.4706	.4706	.4706	.4706	.4706	.4706
ART	.3591	.3404	.3466	.3277	.2630	.2426
PREP	.3409	.2000	.3409	.2000	.2614	.1200

Table 5: Individual F_1 scores for each error category with (wb) and without bonus (w/o b) on the HOO-TEST data.

Acknowledgments

This research was done for CSIDM Project No. CSIDM-200804 partially funded by a grant from the National Research Foundation (NRF) administered by the Media Development Authority (MDA) of Singapore.

References

T. Brants and A. Franz. 2006. Web 1T 5-gram corpus version 1.1. Technical report, Google Research.

D. Dahlmeier and H.T. Ng. 2011. Grammatical error correction with alternating structure optimization. In *Proceedings of ACL*.

R. Dale and A. Kilgarriff. 2010. Helping Our Own: Text massaging for computational linguistics as a new shared task. In *Proceedings of INLG*.

N.-R. Han, M. Chodorow, and C. Leacock. 2006. Detecting errors in English article usage by non-native speakers. *Natural Language Engineering*, 12(2).

T. Kudo and Y. Matsumoto. 2003. Fast methods for kernel-based text analysis. In *Proceedings of ACL*.

D. Talbot and M. Osborne. 2007. Randomised language modelling for statistical machine translation. In *Proceedings of ACL*.

J. R. Tetreault and M. Chodorow. 2008. The ups and downs of preposition error detection in ESL writing. In *Proceedings of COLING*.

Helping Our Own 2011: UKP Lab System Description

Torsten Zesch
Ubiquitous Knowledge Processing (UKP) Lab
Technische Universitt Darmstadt, Germany
http://www.ukp.tu-darmstadt.de

Abstract

This paper describes the UKP Lab system participating in the Helping Our Own Challenge 2011. We focus on the correction of real-word spelling errors (RWSEs) that are especially hard to detect. Our highly flexible system architecture is based on UIMA (Ferrucci and Lally, 2004) and integrates state-of-the-art approaches for detecting RWSEs.

1 Introduction

Real-word spelling errors (RWSEs) occur when a word is replaced with another correctly spelled word which is not intended in that context. For example, file '0046' from the development data contains "... untagged *copra* are often used to do emotion classification research.", where the writer mistakenly replaced 'corpora' with 'copra'. As 'copra' (dried coconut meat) is a valid word, the error cannot be detected using a lexicon-based spell checker. In this case, the correction would rather be "... untagged copra *is* often used ..." because of the number agreement error. Real-word spelling errors like "copra/corpora" can only be detected using methods that analyze the context fitness of each term in a sentence.

The example above is tagged with the error class "S" together with other forms of spelling errors. The development data contains relatively few errors in this class, and only a the smaller part of them are RWSEs. However, RWSEs still pose a serious problem, as they give a sentence an unintended meaning which might heavily confuse the reader.

2 System Description

We implemented a general framework for error detection based on the open-source DKPro framework.[1] DKPro is a collection of software components for natural language processing based on the Apache UIMA framework (Ferrucci and Lally, 2004). It comes with a collection of ready-made modules which can be combined to form more complex applications.

Jazzy DKPro already provides a wrapper for the open-source spell checker Jazzy.[2]. Although it is not targeted towards RWSEs, we use it for reasons of comparison with other approaches.

Detecting RWSEs We re-implemented two state-of-the-art approaches: the knowledge-based approach by Hirst and Budanitsky (2005) (**BH2005**) and the statistical approach by Mays et al. (1991) (**MDM1991**). Both approaches test the lexical cohesion of a word with its context.

For that purpose, BH2005 computes the semantic relatedness of a target word with all other words in a certain context window to test whether the target word fits its context. Following Hirst and Budanitsky (2005), we use the semantic relatedness measure by Jiang and Conrath (1997) and WordNet (Fellbaum, 1998) as a knowledge source. If a target word does not fit its context, it is flagged as a possible error. Then, the set of valid words with low edit distance to the target word is computed. Each of the words in this set, that better fits into the given context than the target word, is selected as a possible correction.

[1] http://code.google.com/p/dkpro-core-asl/
[2] http://jazzy.sourceforge.net/

Proceedings of the 13th European Workshop on Natural Language Generation (ENLG), pages 260–262,
Nancy, France, September 2011. ©2011 Association for Computational Linguistics

Dataset	Detection P	Detection R	Detection S	Recognition P	Recognition R	Recognition S	Correction P	Correction R	Correction S
Jazzy	0.054	0.115	0.073	0.028	0.064	0.039	0.007	0.015	0.009
HB2005	0.093	0.028	0.043	0.048	0.013	0.020	0.009	0.002	0.003
MDM1991 (Google)	0.211	0.026	0.046	0.157	0.020	0.035	0.114	0.015	0.026
MDM1991 (ACL)	0.717	0.004	0.009	0.450	0.003	0.006	**0.450**	0.003	0.006
JoinRWSE	0.095	0.030	0.045	0.055	0.015	0.023	0.020	0.004	0.007
JoinAll	0.051	**0.136**	0.075	0.029	**0.073**	0.041	0.007	**0.016**	0.010
IntersectAll	**1.000**	0.006	0.013	**0.625**	0.004	0.009	0.313	0.003	0.005

Table 1: Overview of evaluation results. Best values are in bold.

The statistical approach (MDM1991) is based on the noisy-channel model assuming that the correct sentence s is transmitted through a noisy channel adding 'noise' which results in a word w being replaced by an error e leading the wrong sentence s' which we observe. Hence, the probability of the correct word w, given the error e is observed, can be computed using a n-gram language model and a model of how likely the typist is to make a certain error. We use two language models: (i) based on the Google Web1T n-gram data (Brants and Franz, 2006), and (ii) based on all the papers in the ACL Anthology Reference Corpus (Bird et al., 2008).

2.1 Combined Approaches

Our framework allows to easily combine spell checkers. In all the combination experiments, we used the MDM1991 with the Google n-gram model.

JoinRWSE Only the two approaches targeted towards RWSEs (i.e. BH2005 and MDM1991) are combined.

JoinAll All three spell checkers (Jazzy, BH2005, and MDM1991) are run in parallel and detections are joined as if only a single spell checker would have been used.

IntersectAll All three spell checkers (Jazzy, BH2005, and MDM1991) are run in parallel, but only errors that are detected by each of the spell checkers are retained.

3 Preliminary Results

As by the time of writing the final results are not yet available, we can only report preliminary results and analyses. Table 1 summarizes the results.

The knowledge-based approach (HB2005) does not perform well, as the documents contain a large amount of domain-specific vocabulary that is either not found in WordNet at all or not with the correct sense. The statistical approach (MDM1991) using the Google n-gram model yields a detection precision of .21 which translates into a still acceptable rate of false alarms, but the recall is very low. The detection precision of MDM1991 gets a significant boost using the ACL corpus n-gram model ($P = .72$), but at the price of an even lower recall. However, unlike the other models, MDM1991 with the ACL n-gram model is also able to provide quite good corrections ($P = .45$).

Regarding the combination experiments, we find that joining the two approaches for detecting RWSEs did not significantly increase recall indicating that both approaches more or the less detect the same errors. In contrast, recall significantly increases when joining all approaches which shows that the errors detected by Jazzy are largely complimentary to those detected by the two RWSE approaches.

The "join" combination strategy focuses on recall, but in the setting of this challenge high precision is more important than high recall, as writers might be tempted to take the detected errors and suggested corrections for granted. The result could be a document with more errors than before. Thus, we also used the "intersection" strategy which should yield better precision. When intersecting the results of all approaches, we obtain perfect precision, but very low detection recall (.06% translating into 8 overall detections).

When looking at the detected errors by type, we find that MDM1991 (with Google N-grams) detects

50% of all errors in the "S" class. However, to our surprise, it also detects 83% of errors in the "CN" class. Further analyses are necessary to investigate this behavior.

References

Steven Bird, Robert Dale, Bonnie Dorr, Bryan Gibson, Mark Joseph, Min-Yen Kan, Dongwon Lee, Brett Powley, Dragomir Radev, and Yee Fan Tan. 2008. The ACL Anthology Reference Corpus: A Reference Dataset for Bibliographic Research in Computational Linguistics. In *In Proceedings of Language Resources and Evaluation Conference (LREC 08). Marrakesh, Morocco.*

Thorsten Brants and Alex Franz. 2006. Web 1T 5-gram Version 1. Linguistic Data Consortium, Philadelphia.

Christiane Fellbaum. 1998. *WordNet: An Electronic Lexical Database*. MIT Press, Cambridge, MA.

David Ferrucci and Adam Lally. 2004. UIMA: An Architectural Approach to Unstructured Information Processing in the Corporate Research Environment. *Natural Language Engineering*, 10(3-4):327–348.

Graeme Hirst and Alexander Budanitsky. 2005. Correcting real-word spelling errors by restoring lexical cohesion. *Natural Language Engineering*, 11(1):87–111, March.

Jay J. Jiang and David W. Conrath. 1997. Semantic Similarity Based on Corpus Statistics and Lexical Taxonomy. In *Proceedings of the 10th International Conference on Research in Computational Linguistics*, Taipei, Taiwan.

Eric Mays, Fred. J. Damerau, and Robert L. Mercer. 1991. Context based spelling correction. *Information Processing & Management*, 27(5):517–522.

University of Illinois System in HOO Text Correction Shared Task

Alla Rozovskaya **Mark Sammons** **Joshua Gioja** **Dan Roth**
Cognitive Computation Group
University of Illinois at Urbana-Champaign
Urbana, IL 61801
{rozovska,mssammon,gioja,danr}@illinois.edu

Abstract

In this paper, we describe the University of Illinois system that participated in Helping Our Own (HOO), a shared task in text correction. We target several common errors, such as articles, prepositions, word choice, and punctuation errors, and we describe the approaches taken to address each error type. Our system is based on a combination of classifiers, combined with adaptation techniques for article and preposition detection. We ranked first in all three evaluation metrics (Detection, Recognition and Correction) among six participating teams. We also present type-based scores on preposition and article error correction and demonstrate that our approach achieves best performance in each task.

1 Introduction

The Text Correction task addresses the problem of detecting and correcting mistakes in text. This task is challenging, since many errors are not easy to detect, such as context-sensitive spelling mistakes that involve confusing valid words in a language (e.g. "there" and "their"). Recently, text correction has taken an interesting turn by focusing on context-sensitive errors made by English as a Second Language (ESL) writers. The HOO shared task (Dale and Kilgarriff, 2011) focuses on writing mistakes made by non-native writers of English in the context of Natural Language Processing community.

This paper presents our entry in the HOO shared task. We target several common types of errors using a combination of discriminative and probabilistic classifiers, together with adaptation techniques for article and preposition detection. Our system ranked first in all three evaluation metrics (Detection, Recognition, and Correction). The description of the evaluation schema and the results of the participating teams can be found in Dale and Kilgarriff (2011). We also evaluate the performance of two system components (Sec. 2), those that target article and preposition errors, and compare them to the performance of other teams (Sec. 3).

2 System Components

Our system comprises components that address article and preposition mistakes, word choice errors, and punctuation errors. Table 1 lists the error types that our system targets and shows sample errors from the pilot data[1].

2.1 Article and Preposition Classifiers

We submitted several versions of article and preposition classifiers that build on elements of the systems described in Rozovskaya and Roth (2010b) and Rozovskaya and Roth (2010c).

The systems are trained on the ACL Anthology corpus, which contains 10 million articles and 5 million prepositions[2]; some versions also use additional data from English Wikipedia and the New York Times section of the Gigaword corpus (Linguistic Data Consortium, 2003). Our experiments on the pilot data showed a significant performance gain when training on the ACL Anthology corpus,

[1] The shared task data are split into pilot and test. Each part consists of text fragments from 19 documents, with one fragment from each document included in pilot and one in test.

[2] We consider the top 17 English prepositions.

Proceedings of the 13th European Workshop on Natural Language Generation (ENLG), pages 263–266,
Nancy, France, September 2011.

Component	Relative Freq.	Targeted Errors	Examples
Article	18%	Missing/Unnecessary/ Replacement	Section 5.1 describes the details of ∅*/*the* evaluation metrics. The main advantage of *the*/∅* phonetic alignment is that it requires no training data.
Preposition	9%	Replacement	Pseudo-word searching problem is the same *to*/as* decomposition of a given sentence into pseudo-words.
Word choice	-	Various lexical and grammatical errors	
Punctuation	18%	Missing/Unnecessary	In the thesaurus we incorporate *LCSbased*/LCS-based* semantic description for each verb class.

Table 1: **System components.** The column "Relative frequency" shows the the proportion of a given error type in the pilot data. The category "Article" is based on the statistics for determiner errors, the majority of which involve articles.

compared to a system trained on other data, but we observed only a small improvement when other data were added to the ACL Anthology corpus.

The classifiers use features that are based on word n-grams, part-of-speech tags and phrase chunks. The systems use a discriminative learning framework and the regularized version of Averaged Perceptron in Learning Based Java[3] (LBJ, (Rizzolo and Roth, 2007)). This linear learning algorithm is known to be among the best linear learning approaches and has been shown to produce state-of-the-art results on many natural language applications (Punyakanok et al., 2008).

2.1.1 Adaptation to the Error Patterns of the ESL Writers

Mistakes made by non-native speakers are systematic and also depend on the first language of the writer (Lee and Seneff, 2008; Rozovskaya and Roth, 2010a). Injecting knowledge about typical errors into the system improves its performance significantly. While some approaches use this knowledge directly, by training a system on annotated learner data (Han et al., 2010; Gamon, 2010), there is often not enough annotated data for training. In our previous work, we proposed methods to adapt a model to the typical errors of the writers (Rozovskaya and Roth, 2010c; Rozovskaya and Roth, 2010b). The methods use error statistics based only on a small amount of annotation. The preposition and article systems use these methods with additional improvements.

An interesting distinction of the HOO data is that both the pilot and the test fragments are derived from the same set of papers. The size of the pilot data is not sufficient for training a competitive system, but applying the adaptation methods improves the quality of the system by a large margin (Table 2)[4].

System	No adaptation	Adapted
Articles	0.42	0.56
Prepositions	0.38	0.44

Table 2: **Adaptation to the typical errors**. F-score on detection on the pilot data. Error statistics are found in 10-fold cross-validation .

2.2 Word Choice Errors

This component of our system is the most flexible one and does not focus on one type of error but addresses various context-sensitive confusions: spelling errors, grammatical errors, and word choice errors. This component uses a Naïve Bayes classifier trained on the ACL Anthology corpus and the New York Times section of the North American News Text Corpus. The confusion sets include word confusions from the HOO pilot data. The Naïve Bayes formulation allows this component to be flexible with the types of confusions it addresses, unlike the discriminative framework.

2.3 Punctuation Errors

We address two types of punctuation errors, missing commas and misuse of hyphens. We define a set of rules to insert missing commas. Below we describe the hyphen checker.

2.3.1 Hyphen Checker

The hyphen corrector was developed to detect and propose corrections for: 1) inappropriate use of a hyphen to join two words that should be separate tokens; 2) inappropriate use of a hyphen to split

[3]`http://cogcomp.cs.illinois.edu.`

[4]The classifiers applied to the test data are adapted using error statistics based on the pilot data.

two words that should be conjoined to form a single word; and 3) omission of a hyphen, resulting in a pair of whitespace-separated words.

We extracted mappings between hyphenated and non-hyphenated sequences using n-gram counts computed from the ACL Anthology corpus by observing the frequency with which the same underlying token sequence occurs either as a single token, as two separate tokens joined by a hyphen, and as two separate tokens with no hyphen. Mappings were extracted for those sequences where one usage was at least 50% more frequent than the others. Discovered rules correct, for example, "para-linguistics" to "paralinguistics" and "pair wise" to "pairwise".

3 Evaluation

The task evaluation uses three metrics, Detection, Recognition, and Correction. In each metric, Recall, Precision and F-score are computed relative to the total number of edits in the corpus (see Dale and Kilgarriff (2011) for a description of the scoring metrics and for the overall ranking of the individual systems). We thought that it would also be interesting to see how the systems compare for two very common error types: articles and prepositions[5]. We have done a comprehensive and slightly different evaluation, computed relative to the edits that involve articles or prepositions, respectively, for each error type[6].

We also evaluate these two tasks by comparing the accuracy of the data before running the system (the "baseline") to the accuracy of the data after running the system. This evaluation shows whether the system reduces or increases the number of errors in the data. The accuracy and the baseline are computed as described in Rozovskaya and Roth (2010c) and the results are shown in Table 5.

Team	Run	Detection	Recognition	Correction
JU	0	0.029	0.029	0.029
LI	3	0.048	0.048	0.033
NU	0	0.372	0.368	0.276
UD	-	-	-	
UI	8	**0.505**	**0.505**	**0.449**
UT	1	0.040	0.025	0.025

Table 3: **Type-based performance: Articles**. For each team, the F-scores for the best run are shown. Results only shown for the teams that address these errors.

Team	Run	Detection	Recognition	Correction
JU	0	0.035	0.035	0.035
LI	8	0.039	0.039	0.039
NU	0	0.266	0.266	0.168
UD	5	0.079	0.079	0.000
UI	8	**0.488**	**0.488**	**0.363**
UT	4	0.202	0.202	0.117

Table 4: **Type-based performance: Prepositions.** For each team, the F-scores for the best run are shown.

Team	Run	Articles	Team	Run	Prepositions
JU	0	0.9280	JU	0	0.9488
LI	3	0.9372	LI	8	0.9546
NU	0	0.9149	NU	0	0.9436
UD	-	-	UD	8	0.9552
UI	5	**0.9424**	UI	9	**0.9562**
UT	7	0.9362	UT	6	0.9372
Baseline		0.9364	Baseline		0.9552

Table 5: **Accuracy results**. "Baseline" is the proportion of correct examples in the data.

4 Conclusion

The shared task is the first competition in text correction, and our team has learned a lot from participating in it – not least, the breadth of error types. We have described the system we entered in the shared task, outlining the approaches we took to address each error type. We also demonstrated the success of our technique for adapting classifiers to writer's errors.

Acknowledgments

The authors thank Jeff Pasternack for his help. This research is supported by a grant from the U.S. Department of Education and is partly supported by the Defense Advanced Research Projects Agency (DARPA) Machine Reading Program under Air Force Research Laboratory (AFRL) prime contract no. FA8750-09-C-018.

[5]Dale and Kilgarriff (2011) show evaluation by error type only for Recall because it is not possible to compute Precision for many other error types. Since it is easy to obtain high recall by proposing many edits (neglecting the precision performance) and, similarly, easy to obtain high precision by just proposing no edits, we present results sorted by F-score rather than by recall and/or precision, as in Dale and Kilgarriff (2011). For the same reason, we also choose the best run of each system based on this measure rather than choosing runs that are doing well just on one of the relevant measures (and, likely very poorly on the other).

[6]For articles, we consider all article edits (see Table 1). For prepositions, replacements involving the top 36 most frequent English prepositions are considered; they account for all preposition replacements made by the participating systems.

References

R. Dale and A. Kilgarriff. 2011. Helping Our Own: The HOO 2011 pilot shared task. In *Proceedings of the 13th European Workshop on Natural Language Generation.*

M. Gamon. 2010. Using mostly native data to correct errors in learners' writing. In *NAACL*, pages 163–171, Los Angeles, California, June.

N. Han, J. Tetreault, S. Lee, and J. Ha. 2010. Using an error-annotated learner corpus to develop and ESL/EFL error correction system. In *LREC*, Malta, May.

J. Lee and S. Seneff. 2008. An analysis of grammatical errors in non-native speech in English. In *Proceedings of the 2008 Spoken Language Technology Workshop.*

V. Punyakanok, D. Roth, and W. Yih. 2008. The importance of syntactic parsing and inference in semantic role labeling. *Computational Linguistics*, 34(2).

N. Rizzolo and D. Roth. 2007. Modeling Discriminative Global Inference. In *Proceedings of the First International Conference on Semantic Computing (ICSC)*, pages 597–604, Irvine, California, September. IEEE.

A. Rozovskaya and D. Roth. 2010a. Annotating ESL errors: Challenges and rewards. In *Proceedings of the NAACL Workshop on Innovative Use of NLP for Building Educational Applications.*

A. Rozovskaya and D. Roth. 2010b. Generating confusion sets for context-sensitive error correction. In *Proceedings of the Conference on Empirical Methods in Natural Language Processing (EMNLP).*

A. Rozovskaya and D. Roth. 2010c. Training paradigms for correcting errors in grammar and usage. In *Proceedings of the NAACL-HLT.*

A. Rozovskaya and D. Roth. 2011. Algorithm selection and model adaptation for esl correction tasks. In *Proc. of the Annual Meeting of the Association of Computational Linguistics (ACL)*, Portland, Oregon, 6. Association for Computational Linguistics.

Data-Driven Correction of Function Words in Non-Native English

Adriane Boyd **Detmar Meurers**
Seminar für Sprachwissenschaft
Universität Tübingen
{adriane,dm}@sfs.uni-tuebingen.de

Abstract

We extend the n-gram-based data-driven prediction approach (Elghafari, Meurers and Wunsch, 2010) to identify function word errors in non-native academic texts as part of the Helping Our Own (HOO) Shared Task. We focus on substitution errors for four categories: prepositions, determiners, conjunctions, and quantifiers. These error types make up 12% of the errors annotated in the HOO training data.

In our best submission in terms of the error detection score, we detected 67% of preposition and determiner substitution errors, 40% of conjunction substitution errors, and 33% of quantifier substitution errors. For approximately half of the errors detected, we were also able to provide an appropriate correction.

1 Introduction

We take as a starting point the preposition prediction approach of Elghafari, Meurers and Wunsch (2010). They explore a surface-based approach for predicting prepositions in English which uses frequency information from web searches to choose the most likely preposition given the context. For each preposition found in the text, the prediction algorithm considers three words of context on each side, building a 7-gram with a preposition slot in the middle:

`rather a question __ the scales falling`

For each prediction task, a *cohort* of queries is constructed with each of the candidate prepositions in the slot to be predicted:

1. `rather a question` **`of`** `the scales falling`
2. `rather a question` **`in`** `the scales falling`

...

9. `rather a question` **`on`** `the scales falling`

The queries are submitted to the Yahoo search engine and the query with the largest number of hits provides the predicted preposition. If no hits are found for any of the 7-gram queries, shorter overlapping n-grams are used to approximate the 7-gram query. If there are still no hits, the overlap backoff will continue reducing the n-gram length until it reaches 3-grams. If no hits are found at the 3-gram level, the most frequent preposition (*of*) is predicted.

Elghafari, Meurers and Wunsch (2010) showed that this surface-based approach is competitive with published state-of-the-art machine learning approaches using complex feature sets (Gamon et al., 2008; De Felice, 2008; Tetreault and Chodorow, 2008; Bergsma et al., 2009). For a set of nine frequent prepositions (*of, to, in, for, on, with, at, by, from*), they accurately predicted 77%. For these nine prepositions, De Felice (2008) identified a baseline of 27% for the task of choosing a preposition in a slot (choose *of*). Humans performing the same task agree 89% of the time.

2 Our Approach

We extend the preposition prediction approach to four function word categories: conjunctions, determiners, prepositions, and quantifiers. Table 1 shows the sets of function words for each category and the associated HOO error codes. The function word lists are compiled from all single-word substitution errors of these types in the HOO training data.[1] The counts show the number of occurrences of the error types in the test data, along with the total number of occurrences of the function word candidates.

[1] We also removed the correction *using* from the preposition list since it is not a preposition.

Proceedings of the 13th European Workshop on Natural Language Generation (ENLG), pages 267–269,
Nancy, France, September 2011.

Categ.	Codes	#	Candidates	#
Conj.	RC	2	but, if, whether, whereas, however, although	80
Det.	RD, FD, DD, AGD, CD, ID	17	a, whose, their, this, an, these, the, its, those	1572
Prep.	RT, DT	86	in, on, about, over, from, onto, for, among, of, into, within, to, as, at, under, between, with, by	2126
Quant.	RQ, FQ, CQ, DQ, IQ, AGQ	4	less, many, some, fewer, much, certain	78
Total		109		3856

Table 1: Function Words with Frequency in Test Data

To adapt the prediction approach for the HOO shared task, we replace the Yahoo search engine used by Elghafari et al. (2010) with the ACL Anthology Reference Corpus (ARC, Bird et al., 2008) and modify the prediction algorithm to keep the original token rather than predicting the most frequent candidate in cases where no hits for any n-grams are found. One drawback of ARC is that it contains native and non-native texts; we have not yet attempted to filter non-native texts.

Using ARC rather than web searches allows us to abstract away from the surface context by substituting POS tags and lemmas in the n-gram context. We use TreeTagger to tag and lemmatize ARC and create three different levels of context abstraction: a) surface context, b) POS context, and c) limited POS/lemma substitutions (POS for CD, SYM, LS; lemmas for comparative adjectives and most verbs). We use the same context throughout, though substitutions could be customized for each type, e.g., determiner selection depends on adjective and noun onsets (*a* vs. *an*), but preposition selection does not.

3 Results

We will discuss our results from two perspectives:

- **Global:** For each function word (correct or incorrect), was a correct prediction made?
- **Error detection:** For each function word substitution error, was the error detected/corrected?

For both perspectives, we can calculate precision and recall for the n-gram prediction approach:

$$\text{precision} = \frac{\text{correct predictions from n-gram approach}}{\text{\# predicted by n-gram approach}}$$

$$\text{recall} = \frac{\text{correct predictions from n-gram approach}}{\text{\# total prediction tasks}}$$

We here present the results for our run #2 in the HOO shared task, our best performing submission in terms of detection score. Run #2 uses the ARC reference corpus with limited POS/lemma substitutions, showing that an appropriate level of abstraction in the n-gram context can lead to improvement over purely surface-based contexts.

3.1 Baseline

The counts in Table 1 show that there is a high global baseline accuracy (= keep original word) for this subtask in the HOO challenge. The baseline for all four categories is 97.2% and the individual function category baselines vary from 94.9% to 98.9%. Thus, predicting the original word would give a high global accuracy for the function word prediction task in the HOO data; however, it would obviously not detect or correct any errors.

3.2 Global Results

Figure 1 shows the global accuracy, precision, and recall as the minimum n-gram length is increased from 3 to 7. The global precision, recall, and accuracy are ~70% for n-gram length 3. As the minimum n-gram length increases, the global accuracy and precision increase to 97% as recall drops to 1.5% since most 7-grams from the test data are not found in the reference corpus. Data sparsity issues are magnified by the fact that the n-gram context may contain additional errors.

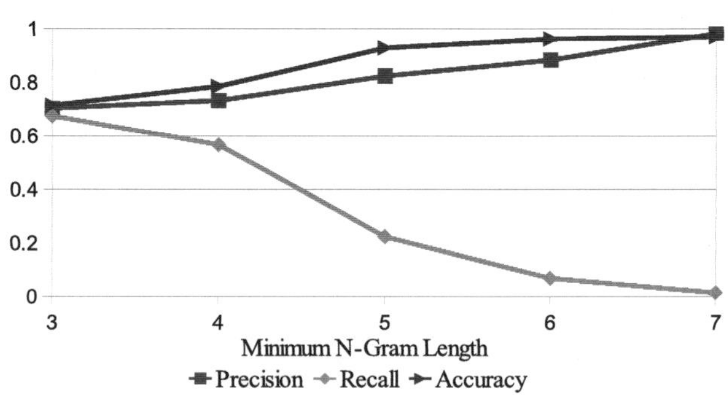

Figure 1: Global Accuracy, Precision, and Recall

3.3 Error Detection and Correction Results

Figure 2 shows the error detection/correction precision and recall as the minimum n-gram length increases from 3 to 6.

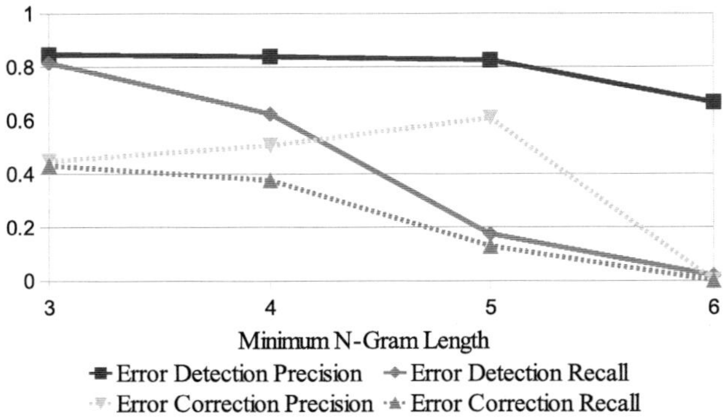

Figure 2: Error Detection and Correction F-Score

For 3-grams, the detection f-score is over 80% with a correction f-score of 44% (but keep in mind that the global accuracy is only 72% at this point). As the minimum n-gram length increases to 6, fewer errors are detected as longer n-grams are not found. From 3-grams to 5-grams, the detection precision stays relatively constant while the correction precision increases from 45% to 60%. Longer n-gram context thus leads to more accurate predictions.

4 Discussion and Conclusion

Extending the n-gram prediction approach (Elghafari, Meurers and Wunsch, 2010) with a genre-specific reference corpus and generalized contexts, we are able to detect 33%–67% of the targeted function word substitution errors in the HOO test corpus. We provide an appropriate correction for approximately half of the errors detected. However, our method currently miscorrects about ten function words for each one it detects as an error, which is reflected in the relatively low HOO detection precision score (14%) in the 'no bonus' condition.

As our approach was originally designed to predict rather than to correct function words, further customizations may improve the performance for correction tasks, which unlike prediction tasks have access to the word used in the original text. Instead of the raw counts we are currently using, one could weight the words in the candidate sets for each prediction task in order to account for global frequency (e.g., *the* is more frequent than *these* in contexts where both are correct) and in order to make it possible to add an explicit bias towards leaving the original word unmodified, since the HOO data shows that such a high percentage of function words in this genre are indeed correct.

The results we presented take into account only the four types of errors from the HOO error scheme of Table 1, however many errors involving function word substitutions in the HOO data are not actually annotated as such, but are part of other error types annotating multiple words. As a result, our system also detects some function word errors which were annotated as compound change, replace verb (e.g., phrasal verb error), wrong verb form, and replace adverb. The current HOO annotation scheme does not have the granularity to systematically identify all function word errors – a shortcoming worth addressing in order to support incremental, modular research on error detection. This is particularly relevant in light of the lack of inter-annotator agreement studies establishing which distinctions from the various error annotation schemes in the literature can reliably be annotated given the information present in the text (cf. Meurers, 2012, and references therein).

References

Shane Bergsma, Dekang Lin and Randy Goebel, 2009. Web-scale N-gram models for lexical disambiguation. In *IJCAI*.

Steven Bird, Robert Dale et al., 2008. The ACL Anthology Reference Corpus. In *LREC*.

Rachele De Felice, 2008. Automatic Error Detection in Non-native English. Ph.D. thesis, Oxford.

Anas Elghafari, Detmar Meurers and Holger Wunsch, 2010. Exploring the Data-Driven Prediction of Prepositions in English. In *COLING*.

Michael Gamon, Jianfeng Gao et al., 2008. Using Contextual Speller Techniques and Language Modeling for ESL Error Correction. In *IJCNLP*.

Detmar Meurers, 2012. Natural Language Processing and Language Learning. In *Encyclopedia of Applied Linguistics*, Wiley-Blackwell, Oxford. http://purl.org/dm/papers/meurers-12.html.

Joel Tetreault and Martin Chodorow, 2008. Native Judgments of Non-Native Usage: Experiments in Preposition Error Detection. In *COLING*.

Report on the *Second* Second Challenge on Generating Instructions in Virtual Environments (GIVE-2.5)

Kristina Striegnitz
Union College
striegnk@union.edu

Alexandre Denis
LORIA/CNRS
denis@loria.fr

Andrew Gargett
U.A.E. University
andrew.gargett@uaeu.ac.ae

Konstantina Garoufi
University of Potsdam
garoufi@uni-potsdam.de

Alexander Koller
University of Potsdam
akoller@uni-potsdam.de

Mariët Theune
University of Twente
m.theune@utwente.nl

Abstract

GIVE-2.5 evaluates eight natural language generation (NLG) systems that guide human users through solving a task in a virtual environment. The data is collected via the Internet, and to date, 536 interactions of subjects with one of the NLG systems have been recorded. The systems are compared using both task performance measures and subjective ratings by human users.

1 Introduction

This paper reports on the methodology and results of GIVE-2.5, the second edition of the Second Challenge on Generating Instructions in Virtual Environments (GIVE-2). GIVE is a shared task for the evaluation of natural language generation (NLG) systems, aimed at the real-time generation of instructions that guide a human user in solving a treasure-hunt task in a virtual 3D world. For the evaluation, we connect these NLG systems to users over the Internet, which makes it possible to collect large amounts of evaluation data at reasonable cost and effort.

While the shared task became more complex going from GIVE-1 to GIVE-2, we decided to maintain the same task in GIVE-2.5 (hence, the *second* second challenge). This allowed the participating research teams to learn from the results of GIVE-2 and it gave some teams (especially student teams), who were not able to participate in GIVE-2 because of timing issues, the opportunity to participate.

Eight systems are participating in GIVE-2.5. The data collection is currently underway. During July and August 2011, we collected 536 valid games, which are the basis for all results presented in this paper. This number is, so far, much lower than the number of experimental subjects in GIVE-1 and GIVE-2. Recruiting subjects has proved to be more difficult than in previous years. We discuss our hypotheses why this might be the case and hope to still increase the number of subjects during the remainder of the public evaluation period. When the evaluation period is finished, the collected data will be made available through the GIVE website.[1]

As in previous editions of GIVE, we evaluate each system both on objective measures (success rate, completion time, etc.) and subjective measures which were collected by asking the users to fill in a questionnaire. In addition to absolute objective measures, for GIVE-2.5 we also look at some new, normalized measures such as instruction rate and speed of movement. Compared to GIVE-2, we cut down the number of subjective measures and instead encouraged users to give more free-form feedback.

The paper is structured as follows. In Section 2, we give some brief background information on the GIVE Challenge. In Section 3, we present the evaluation method, including the timeline, the evaluation worlds, the participating NLG systems, and our strategy for recruiting subjects. Section 4 reports on the evaluation results based on the data that have been collected so far. Finally, we conclude and discuss future work in Section 5.

[1] http://www.give-challenge.org/research/

Proceedings of the 13th European Workshop on Natural Language Generation (ENLG), pages 270–279,
Nancy, France, September 2011.

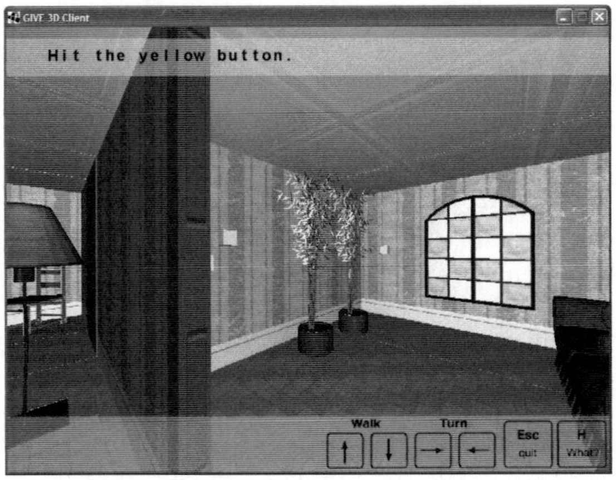

Figure 1: What the user sees in a GIVE world.

2 The GIVE Challenge

In GIVE, users carry out a treasure hunt in a virtual 3D world. The challenge for the NLG systems is to generate, in real time, natural language instructions that guide users to successfully complete this task.

Users participating in the GIVE evaluation start the 3D game from our website at `www.give-challenge.org`. They first download the *3D client*, the program that allows them to interact with the virtual world; they then get connected to one of the NLG systems by the *matchmaker*, which runs on the GIVE server and chooses a random NLG system and virtual world for each incoming connection. The game results are stored by the matchmaker in a database. After starting the game, the users get a brief tutorial and then enter one of three evaluation worlds, displayed in a 3D window as in Figure 1. The window shows instructions and allows the user to move around in the world and manipulate objects.

The task of the users in the GIVE world is to pick up a trophy from a safe that can be opened by pushing a sequence of buttons. Some floor tiles are alarmed, and players lose the game if they step on these tiles without deactivating the alarm first. Besides the buttons that need to be pushed, there are a number of distractor buttons that make the generation of references to target buttons more challenging. Finally, the 3D worlds contain a number of objects such as lamps and plants that do not bear on the task, but are available for use as landmarks in spatial descriptions generated by the NLG systems.

The GIVE Challenge took place for the first time in 2008–09 (Koller et al., 2010a), and for the second time in 2009–10 (Koller et al., 2010b). The GIVE-1 Challenge was a success in terms of the amount of data collected. However, while it allowed us to show that the evaluation data collected over the Internet are consistent with similar data collected in a laboratory, the instruction task was relatively simple. The users could only move through the worlds in discrete steps, and could only make 90 degree turns. This made it possible for the NLG systems to achieve a good task performance with simple instructions of the form "move three steps forward". The main novelty in GIVE-2 was that users could now move and turn freely, which made expressions like "three steps" meaningless, and made it hard to predict the precise effect of instructing a user to "turn left". Presumably due to the harder task, in combination with more complex evaluation worlds, the success rate was substantially worse in GIVE-2 than in GIVE-1. GIVE-2.5 is an opportunity to learn from the GIVE-2 experiences and improve on these results.

3 Evaluation Method

See (Koller et al., 2010a) for a detailed presentation of the GIVE data collection method. This section describes the aspects specific to GIVE-2.5, such as the timeline, the evaluation worlds, the participating NLG systems, and our strategy for recruiting subjects.

3.1 Software infrastructure

GIVE-2.5 reuses the software infrastructure from GIVE-2 described in (Koller et al., 2009) and (Koller et al., 2010b). Parts of the code were rewritten to improve how the visibility of objects is computed and how messages are sent between the components of the GIVE infrastructure: matchmaker, NLG system, and 3D client. The code is freely available at `http://code.google.com/p/give2`.

3.2 Timeline

GIVE-2.5 was first announced in July 2010. Interested research teams could start development right away, since the software interface would be the same as in GIVE-2. The participating teams had to make their systems available for an internal evaluation period by May 23, 2011. This allowed the organizing team to verify that the NLG systems satisfied at least a minimal level of quality, while the participating research teams could make sure that their server setup worked properly, accepting connections of the matchmaker and clients to their NLG system. Furthermore, the evaluation worlds were distributed to the research teams during this period so that they could test their systems with these worlds, adapt their lexicon, if necessary, and fix any bugs that coincidentally never surfaced with the development worlds. Of course, the teams were not allowed to manually tune their systems to the new evaluation worlds in ad-hoc ways. One team had built a system that learns how to give instructions from a corpus of human-human interactions. This team was given permission to use the evaluation worlds during the internal evaluation period to collect such a corpus.

The original plan was to launch the public evaluation on June 6th. Unfortunately, some problems with the newly reworked networking code delayed the start of the public evaluation period until June 21st. At the time of writing, the public evaluation is still ongoing so that all results presented below are based on a snapshot of the data collected by August 29, 2011.

3.3 Evaluation worlds

Figure 2 shows the three virtual worlds we used in the GIVE-2.5 evaluation. The worlds were designed to be similar in complexity to the GIVE-2 worlds, and as in previous rounds of GIVE, they pose different challenges to the NLG systems. World 1 has a simple layout and buttons are arranged in ways that make it easy to uniquely identify buttons. World 2 provides challenges for the systems' referring expression generation capabilities. It contains many clusters of buttons of the same color and provides the opportunity to refer to rooms using their color or furniture. World 3 focuses on navigation instructions. One part of the world features a maze-like layout, another room contains multiple alarm tiles that the player needs to navigate around, whereas a third room has several doors and many plants but only a few other objects, making it hard for the players to orient themselves.

3.4 NLG systems

Eight NLG systems were submitted (one more than in GIVE-2, three more than in GIVE-1).

A University of Aberdeen (Duncan and van Deemter, 2011)

B University of Bremen (Dethlefs, 2011)

C Universidad Nacional de Córdoba (Racca et al., 2011)

CL Universidad Nacional de Córdoba and LORIA/CNRS (Benotti and Denis, 2011)

L LORIA/CNRS (Denis, 2011)

P1 and **P2** University of Potsdam (Garoufi and Koller, 2011)

T University of Twente (Akkersdijk et al., 2011)

Compared to the previous GIVE editions, these systems employ more varied approaches and are better grounded in the existing CL and NLG literature. Systems A, C, L, and T are rule-based systems using hand-designed strategies. System A focuses on user engagement, T and C both focus on giving appropriate feedback to the user with C implementing the grounding model of Traum (1999), and L uses a strategy for generating referring expressions based on the Salmon-Alt and Romary (2000) approach to modeling the salience of objects.

System B uses decision trees learned from a corpus of human interactions in the GIVE domain (Gargett et al., 2010) augmented with additional annotations. System P1 uses the same corpus to learn to predict the understandability of referring expressions. The model acquired in this way is integrated into an NLG strategy based on planning. System P2 serves as a baseline for comparison against P1. Finally, system CL selects instructions from a corpus of human-human interactions in the evaluation worlds that the CL team collected during the internal evaluation phase.

See the individual system descriptions in this volume for more details about each system.

3.5 Recruiting subjects

We used a variety of avenues to recruit subjects. We posted to international and national mailing lists, gaming websites, and social networks. We had a

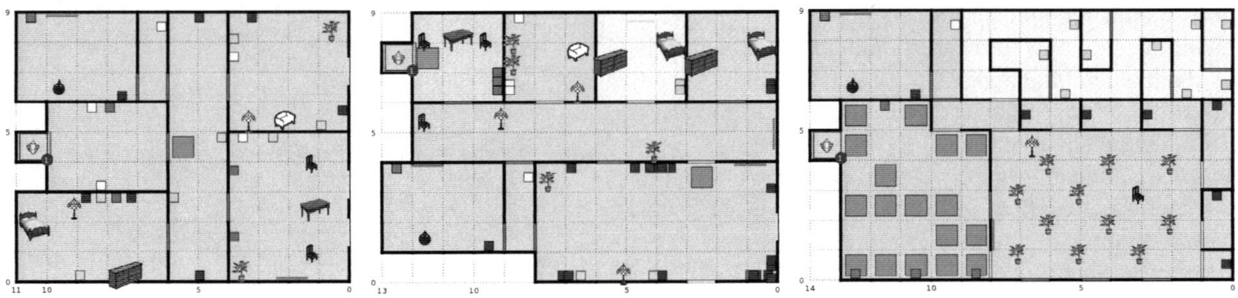

World 1 World 2 World 3

Figure 2: The 2011 evaluation worlds.

GIVE Facebook page and were mentioned on a relatively widely read blog. The University of Potsdam made a press release, we contributed an article to the IEEE Speech and Language Processing Technical Committee Newsletter, and submitted an entry to a list of psychological experiments online.

Unfortunately, even though we were more active in pursuing opportunities to advertise GIVE than in the last two years, we were less successful in recruiting subjects. In two months we only recorded slightly over 500 valid games, whereas in the previous years we were already well over the 1000 games mark at that point. What helped us recruit subjects in the past was that our press releases were picked up by blogs and other channels with a wide readership. Unfortunately, that did not happen this year. Maybe the summer break in the northern hemisphere, which coincided with our public evaluation phase, played a role. We are, therefore, extending the public evaluation phase into the fall, hoping to recruit enough subjects for more detailed and statistically powerful analyses than we can present in this paper.

4 Results

This section reports the results for GIVE-2.5, based on the data collected between June 21 and August 29, 2011. During this time period 536 valid games were played, that is, games in which players finished the tutorial and the game did not end prematurely due to a software or networking issue.

As in previous years, all interactions were logged. We use these logs to extract a set of objective measures. In addition, players were asked to fill in a demographic questionnaire before the game, and a questionnaire assessing their impression of the NLG system after the game. We first present some basic demographic information about our players; then we discuss the objective measures and the subjective questionnaire data. Finally, we present some further, more detailed analyses, looking at how the different evaluation worlds and demographic factors affect the results.

Again as in previous years, some of the measures are in tension with each other. For instance, a system that generates detailed and clear instructions will perhaps lead to longer games than one which tends to give instructions that are brief yet not as clear. This emphasizes that, as with previous GIVE challenges, we have aimed at a friendly challenge rather than a competition with clear winners.

4.1 Demographics

For this round of GIVE, 58% of all games were played by men and 27% by women; a further 15% did not specify their gender. While this means that we had twice as many male players as female players, we have a better gender balance than in the previous two editions of GIVE, where only about 10% of the players were female. Of all players whose IP address was geographically identifiable, about 32% were connected from Germany, 13% from the US, and 12% from the Netherlands. Argentina and France accounted for about 8% of the connections each, while 5% of them were from Sweden. The rest of the players came from 28 further countries. About half the participants (54%) were in the age range 20–29, 27% were aged 30–39, 4% were below 20, while the remaining 14% were between 40 and 69.

About 19% of the participants who answered the

task success: Did the player get the trophy?
duration: Time in seconds from the end of the tutorial until retrieval of the trophy.
distance: Distance traveled (measured in distance units of the virtual environment).
actions: Number of object manipulation actions.
instructions: Number of instructions produced by the NLG system.
words: Number of words used by the NLG system.

Figure 3: Summary of *raw objective* measures.

error rate: Number of incorrect button presses, over the total actions performed in a single game.
speed: Total distance over total time.
instruction speed: Total number of instructions over total time taken.
words per instruction: Length of instructions in number of words used.
word rate: Total number of words over total time taken.

Figure 4: Summary of *normalized objective* measures.

	A	B	C	CL	L	P1	P2	T
task success	42%	32%	70%	58%	68%	66%	65%	58%
			A	A	A	A	A	A
	B			B		B	B	B
	C	C		C			C	C
duration	687	701	538	539	341	407	415	480
					A	A	A	
						B	B	B
			C	C				C
	D	D						
distance	180	204	132	153	117	128	116	166
			A		A	A	A	
			B	B		B		
	C			C				C
	D	D						D
actions	17	35	14	15	14	14	16	16
	A		A	A	A	A	A	A
		B						
instructions	165	281	254	183	211	241	235	160
	A			A				A
	B			B	B			
					C	C	C	
		D	D			D	D	
words	1894	2693	1328	1269	962	1122	1139	1024
					A	A	A	A
				B		B	B	B
			C	C		C	C	
	D							
		E						

Figure 5: Results for the *raw objective* measures.

question were native English speakers, and an additional 73% of them self-rated their English language proficiency as at least good. The vast majority (84%) rated themselves as more experienced with computers than most people, while 47% self-rated their familiarity with 3D computer or video games as higher than that of most people. Finally, 16% indicated that they had played a GIVE game before in 2011.

4.2 Objective measures

Descriptions of the *raw* objective measures and of the *normalized* objective measures are given in Figures 3 and 4, respectively. Duration, distance travelled, and total number of actions, instructions, and words can only be compared meaningfully between games that were successful. The normalized measures, on the other hand, are independent of the result of the game. So, when comparing systems with the normalized objective measures, we have used all games in which the player managed to press at least the first button in the safe sequence.

Figures 5 and 6 show the results of raw and normalized objective measures, respectively. Task success is reported as the percentage of successfully completed games. For the other measures we give the mean value of that measure per game for each system. The figures also form groups of systems for each evaluation measure, as indicated by the letters. If two systems do not share the same letter, the difference between these two systems is significant with $p<0.05$. Significance was tested using χ^2 for task success, and ANOVA for the other objective measures, with all systems compared pairwise using post-hoc tests (pairwise χ^2 and Tukey).

4.3 Subjective measures

Subjective measures were collected using a post-task questionnaire, which asked users to rate the instructions delivered by the NLG systems with a series of ten questions. Figure 8 shows the questions that were asked, and the average responses received. The results are based on all games, independent of success. Ratings ranged from -100 to 100, non-responses were filtered out, and, following standard practice, negative items (e.g. Q2 on confusion caused by instructions) had their scores

	A	B	C	CL	L	P1	P2	T
error rate	21%	49%	10%	11%	12%	9%	15%	19%
			A	A	A	A	A	A
	B		B	B	B		B	B
		C						
distance per sec	0.22	0.24	0.26	0.28	0.36	0.29	0.27	0.35
					A			A
				B		B		B
		C	C	C		C	C	
	D	D	D	D			D	
instructions per sec	0.21	0.36	0.48	0.32	0.62	0.56	0.54	0.33
	A							
		B		B				B
			C				C	
						D	D	
					E			
words per instruction	11.9	9.6	5.2	7.1	4.6	4.7	4.8	6.5
					A	A	A	
			B				B	
								C
				D				
		E						
	F							
words per sec	2.4	3.4	2.5	2.3	2.9	2.6	2.6	2.1
	A		A	A				A
	B		B	B		B	B	
			C		C	C	C	
		D						

Figure 6: Results for the *normalized objective* measures.

A	B	C	CL	L	P1	P2	T
Q1: Overall, the system gave me good instructions.							
-18	-31	54	24	47	31	10	-3
		A	A	A	A		
			B		B	B	
			C			C	C
D						D	D
E	E						E
Q2–10: Remaining subjective measures (summed)							
98	47	414	245	347	323	231	146
		A		A	A		
			B	B	B	B	
			C			C	C
D	D						D

Figure 7: Results for the *subjective* measures.

reversed. Once again, systems were grouped by letters where there was no significant difference between them (significance level: $p<0.05$). We used ANOVAs and post-hoc Tukey tests to test for significance.

Figure 7 furthermore shows side by side the results for the first question, which asked users for their overall impression of the system, and the results for an aggregated score obtained by summing over the rest of the questions that tried to asses specific aspects of the system.

4.4 Effects of the evaluation world and demographic factors

Which NLG system subjects interacted with is not the only factor that affects their success rate. The evaluation worlds as well as some demographic factors also had statistically significant effects.

Not surprisingly, the evaluation world affects task success ($p<0.001$), with performance in worlds 1 and 2 around 67%, but much lower in world 3 (41%). Many systems reflect the same overall pattern in their task success rates, but individual systems behave very differently as shown in Figure 9. For example, systems A and P2 do much better in world 2 than world 1, while system B does much worse in world 2 than world 1. And while all other systems have their lowest success rate in world 3, system A is doing much better in worlds 2 and 3 than in world 1.

Male players have a somewhat higher task success rate than female players (65% vs. 54%). This difference is not statistically significant, but it is close ($p=0.052$). Unfortunately, we don't have enough data, yet, to do a by system analysis of the effects that demographic properties have on task success.

The results also indicate that proficiency in English affects task success ($p=0.047$). This overall significance is due to the task success rate of subjects who rate themselves as *near native* being, with 74%, much higher than the task success rate of subjects who think of themselves as merely *good* (58%), or *very good* (57%). *Native* English speakers have a task success rate of 65%, which in pairwise comparisons is not significantly different from any of the other groups. Subjects rated their English proficiency on a 5-point scale. However, we had to drop the lowest category (*basic*) due to data scarcity.

Finally, there were effects for both familiarity with video games ($p<0.005$), and computer expertise ($p<0.05$). The questionnaire asked sub-

A	B	C	CL	L	P1	P2	T
Q1: Overall, the system gave me good instructions.							
-18	-31	54	24	47	31	10	-3
		A	A	A	A		
			B		B	B	
			C			C	C
D						D	D
E	E						E
Q2: I was confused about which direction to go in.							
-22	-16	52	27	31	26	16	-17
		A	A	A	A		
			B	B	B	B	
C	C						C
Q3: I could easily identify the buttons the system described to me.							
37	3	60	46	42	39	16	23
A		A	A	A	A		
B			B	B	B	B	B
C	C					C	C
Q4: I had to re-read instructions to understand what I needed to do.							
14	-4	50	19	53	19	1	2
		A		A			
		B	B		B		
C	C		C		C	C	C
Q5: The system's instructions were visible long enough for me to read them.							
-10	-12	42	13	51	37	38	24
		A		A	A	A	A
		B	B		B	B	B
C	C		C				C
Q6: The system's instructions came too late or too early.							
-6	-10	36	-3	34	24	19	2
		A		A	A	A	
B			B		B	B	B
C	C		C			C	C
Q7: The system immediately offered help when I was in trouble.							
-13	1	52	17	38	48	35	1
		A		A	A	A	
			B	B		B	
	C		C				C
D	D						D
Q8: The system gave me useful feedback about my progress.							
-4	-16	62	37	23	57	33	27
		A	A		A	A	
			B		B	B	B
			C	C		C	C
D	D						
Q9: The system was very friendly.							
25	31	54	46	49	54	42	35
	A	A	A	A	A	A	A
B	B	B	B	B		B	B
Q10: I felt I could trust the system's instructions.							
0	-25	69	38	52	44	30	12
		A	A	A	A		
			B	B	B	B	
			C			C	C
D						D	D
E	E						

Figure 8: Results for individual questionnaire items.

jects to rate themselves as being much less familiar with video games/experienced with computers than most people, less familiar/experienced than most people, equally familiar/experienced, more familiar/experienced, or much more familiar/experienced. Again, due to data scarcity, we had to collapse the lowest two and highest two categories for familiarity with video games and the lowest three categories for computer expertise. On closer inspection, these overall significant effects are accounted for by a significant difference in task success ($p<0.001$) between players who rated themselves as *less familiar* with video games than most people (51% task success rate) and players who rated themselves as *more familiar* (69%). Similarly, the subjects who think of themselves as *much more* experienced with computers than most people (66%) are significantly more successful than subjects who think they are *less or equally* experienced than most people (49%).

4.5 Discussion

The objective and subjective measures largely agree in ranking systems C, CL, L, P1, P2, T before systems A and B. The first six systems do not differ significantly from each other in terms of task success or error rate. However, there are some significant differences between them when looking at the other objective measures. For example, games with

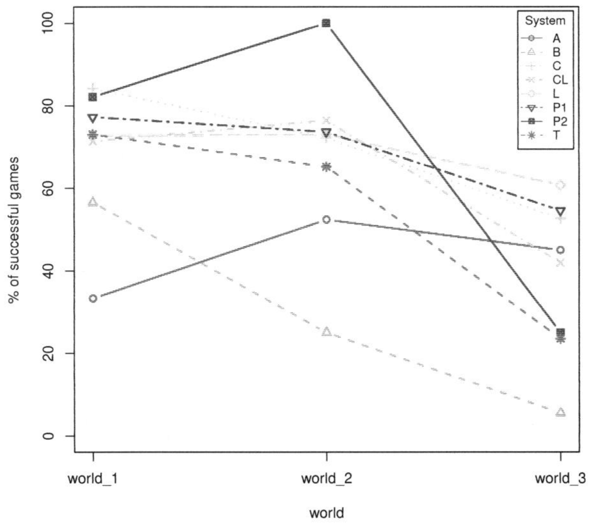

Figure 9: Effect of the different evaluation worlds on the task success rate of the NLG systems.

systems L, P1, and P2 are shorter than than those with systems C and CL, while system T is sitting in between the two groups.

Interestingly, shorter durations do not necessarily coincide with the players moving faster. For instance, players interacting with systems P1 and P2 move significantly slower than players who interact with system L. System L also delivers its instructions at a very fast pace, followed by systems P1 and P2. Those are the same systems that achieve the shortest game durations, and they also make the group of systems which produces the most concise instructions. However, it is not necessary for an NLG system to be as fast paced as the L and P systems to be successful. If we compare the two systems with the highest task success rates, systems C (70%) and L (68%), we see that L has very short games, fast moving players, and delivers its concise instructions at an extremely high rate. C, on the other hand, yields significantly longer games, has players that move at a significantly slower speed, and produces significantly longer instructions (though still concise compared to some other systems) at a much lower rate.

There is also some indication, though, that being too slow and wordy might be detrimental. Systems A and B, the least effective in terms of task success and error rate, have extremely long games, slow players, and long instructions that get sent at a slow pace.

As mentioned above, the subjective measures largely agree with the ranking suggested by the objective measures: systems C, CL, L, P1, P2, T are ranked before systems A and B. However, the top group is a little more split up. Systems C, L, and P1 are ranked highest both by Q1, the questionnaire item asking for an overall assessment, and by the summed scores for the remaining questionnaire items. Systems CL and P2, on the other hand, come in the next tier according to these subjective measures, while system T follows.

System C is doing well on questionnaire items that have to do with timing (such as Q6 and Q7), suggesting that even though it is slower than some of the other most successful systems, its instructions are well-timed. One interesting point to notice is that system A, which overall is not so successful, is doing relatively well on item Q3. In fact, referring expression generation is one of the aspects system A's team focused on.

Comparing this year's results to those of GIVE-2, we can report that task success has increased somewhat. The task success rate of systems in GIVE-2 ranged from 3% to 47% with a mean success rate of 29%. For GIVE-2.5, task success rates range from 32% to 70% with a mean of 57%. Though these results are measured in different worlds and are thus not directly comparable, they do provide some evidence of the overall increasing quality of systems entered in this round of GIVE.

Interestingly, the overall quality ratings (Q1) did not go up across the board in a similar way, although the systems that did best on this measure in GIVE-2.5 had somewhat higher scores than the best systems in the previous installment of GIVE. In GIVE-2, the systems had a mean score for that question that ranged from -33 to 36. In GIVE-2.5, the mean scores ranged from -31 to 54. Some of the other subjective measures improved more dramatically, though. For example, the systems' mean ratings for Q2 (*I was confused which direction to go in*) ranged from -32 to 21 in GIVE-2, but from -22 to 52 in GIVE-2.5.

Unfortunately, we don't have enough data, yet, to compare the effect that demographic factors have on

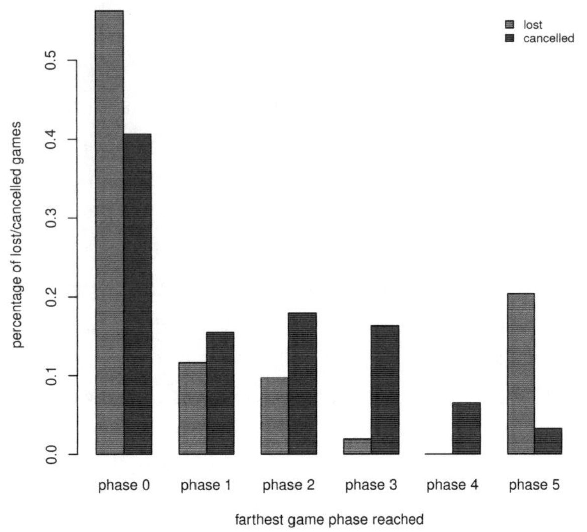

Figure 10: Player progress before they lose/cancel.

individual systems. By the end of our evaluation period, we will hopefully be able to make that analysis.

5 Conclusions and Outlook

This paper has described the methodology and results of GIVE-2.5, the second edition of the Second Challenge on Generating Instructions in Virtual Environments. In a number of ways, GIVE-2.5 expanded successfully on GIVE-2. Eight NLG systems participated in GIVE-2.5, one more than in GIVE-2. These systems represent a broader variety of approaches to NLG than seen before in a GIVE challenge, and the instructions they generate are of a higher quality.

Unexpectedly, our efforts to recruit subjects over the Internet were not as successful as in previous years. We think that this is mostly due to less luck with getting our advertising into channels that reach a broad audience, which was possibly exacerbated by the timing of the public evaluation period during the northern hemisphere summer break. It would be desirable to develop an advertising strategy for future editions of the challenge that can distribute our call to play GIVE more reliably.

One problem we already identified in GIVE-1 and GIVE-2 is that the task is not as engaging for players as modern 3D games are. As in GIVE-2, this is evidenced by the observation that many players cancel or lose the game before they ever press the first button in the safe sequence. (Figure 10 shows how close subjects got to finding the trophy before losing or canceling. Phase 0 means that not even the first button of the safe sequence was pressed successfully; phase 1 means that one button of the safe sequence was pressed successfully, etc.) The free text comments also contain complaints in that direction. We did not expect this problem to disappear, since the task is the same as in GIVE-2, but its persistence re-confirms that the next revision of GIVE needs to address this issue.

We are currently discussing the task and timeline for GIVE-3. The plan is to make a substantial change to the task. The specification of this new task and the implementation of the necessary software infrastructure needs some time, so that we will most likely not organize another edition of GIVE before 2013. However, Oliver Lemon and Srini Janarthanam will organize a challenge similar to GIVE in 2012, called *Generating Route Instructions under Uncertainty in Virtual Environments* (GRUVE). Its main features are that the game world will be an outdoor environment based on publicly available map data, and that it will be possible for NLG systems to interact with users in a more dialog-like fashion by generating questions plus a set of possible answers for the user to choose from. In addition, there will be an *uncertainty* track, where the player coordinates sent to the NLG system by the client will be artificially distorted in order to simulate a noisy GPS signal. (See Janarthanam and Lemon (2011) in this volume for more details.) We encourage everybody interested in GIVE to consider participating in GRUVE.

Acknowledgements

We would like to thank all participating research teams for their contributions, and the GIVE Steering Committee (Donna Byron, Justine Cassell, Robert Dale, Johanna Moore, Jon Oberlander) for their help and support in organizing the GIVE challenges.

References

S. Akkersdijk, M. Langenbach, F. Loch, and M. Theune. 2011. The Thumbs Up! Twente system for GIVE 2.5.

In *Proceedings of the Generation Challenges Session at the 13th European Workshop on Natural Language Generation*, Nancy, France.

L. Benotti and A. Denis. 2011. CL system: Giving instructions by corpus based selection. In *Proceedings of the Generation Challenges Session at the 13th European Workshop on Natural Language Generation*, Nancy, France.

A. Denis. 2011. The Loria instruction generation system L in GIVE 2.5. In *Proceedings of the Generation Challenges Session at the 13th European Workshop on Natural Language Generation*, Nancy, France.

N. Dethlefs. 2011. The Bremen system for the GIVE-2.5 Challenge. In *Proceedings of the Generation Challenges Session at the 13th European Workshop on Natural Language Generation*, Nancy, France.

B. Duncan and K. van Deemter. 2011. Direction giving: an attempt to increase user engagement. In *Proceedings of the Generation Challenges Session at the 13th European Workshop on Natural Language Generation*, Nancy, France.

A. Gargett, K. Garoufi, A. Koller, and K. Striegnitz. 2010. The GIVE-2 corpus of Giving Instructions in Virtual Environments. In *Proceedings of the 7th International Conference on Language Resources and Evaluation (LREC 2010)*, Malta.

K. Garoufi and A. Koller. 2011. The Potsdam NLG systems at the GIVE-2.5 Challenge. In *Proceedings of the Generation Challenges Session at the 13th European Workshop on Natural Language Generation*, Nancy, France.

S. Janarthanam and O. Lemon. 2011. The GRUVE Challenge: Generating Routes under Uncertainty in Virtual Environments. In *Proceedings of the Generation Challenges Session at the 13th European Workshop on Natural Language Generation*, Nancy, France.

A. Koller, D. Byron, J. Cassell, R. Dale, J. Moore, J. Oberlander, and K. Striegnitz. 2009. The software architecture for the First Challenge on Generating Instructions in Virtual Environments. In *Proceedings of the EACL-09 Demo Session.*

A. Koller, K. Striegnitz, D. Byron, J. Cassell, R. Dale, J. Moore, and J. Oberlander. 2010a. The First Challenge on Generating Instructions in Virtual Environments. In E. Krahmer and M. Theune, editors, *Empirical Methods in Natural Language Generation*, volume 5790 of *LNCS*, pages 337–361. Springer.

A. Koller, K. Striegnitz, A. Gargett, D. Byron, J. Cassell, R. Dale, J. Moore, and J. Oberlander. 2010b. Report on the Second NLG Challenge on Generating Instructions in Virtual Environments (GIVE-2). In *Proceedings of the Generation Challenges Session at the 6th International Natural Language Generation Conference*, Trim, Ireland.

D.N. Racca, L. Benotti, and P. Duboue. 2011. The GIVE-2.5 C generation system. In *Proceedings of the Generation Challenges Session at the 13th European Workshop on Natural Language Generation*, Nancy, France.

S. Salmon-Alt and L. Romary. 2000. Generating referring expressions in multimodal contexts. In *Proceedings of the Workshop on Coherence in Generated Multimedia (Co-located with INLG)*, Mitzpe Ramon, Israel.

D.R. Traum. 1999. Computational models of grounding in collaborative systems. In *Working Notes of the AAAI Fall Symposium on Psychological Models of Communication*, North Falmouth, MA, USA.

Direction giving: an attempt to increase user engagement

Bob Duncan and Kees van Deemter
Computing Science department, University of Aberdeen
(email: r.duncan.07@aberdeen.ac.uk, k.vdeemter@abdn.ac.uk)

Abstract

These notes describe a contribution to the 2011 GIVE Challenge from the University of Aberdeen. Our contribution focuses on an attempt to increase the extent to which participants felt engaged in the direction giving/following game on which the GIVE challenge focuses.

1 Introduction

These notes outline the first author's (undergraduate) final-year Computing Science project. Its main aim was to give the authors a hands-on understanding of the GIVE framework, and to see whether this framework should play a role in their future research on the generation of referring expressions (GRE). Our motivation was that previous assessments of GRE algorithms (Jordan and Walker 2005, Viethen and Dale 2007, Gatt and Belz 2010, Van Deemter et al. 2011) have typically focused on simplified experimental settings, where the domain is very small, and where the location of the hearer and speaker is not taken into account as a factor that influences the salience of the different domain objects. GIVE offers the possibility of doing away with these limitations in a rich, semi life-like environment, hence our interest.

The GIVE challenges place participants in a virtual world where they are going on a treasure hunt. To find the treasure, participants need to navigate through a building and push a series of buttons. GIVE asks for the submission of algorithms that help participants perform their treasure hunt. They should help them navigate through the building, and push the right buttons (while carefully avoiding others, which may set off alarms). An informal exploration of the systems submitted to the previous (2009) GIVE challenge suggested to us that there were three main areas in which there was substantial room for improvement of the algorithms submitted then: (1) user engagement, (2) special gadgets that might assist the user in his/her quest, and (3) the quality of the referring expressions generated. We elaborate briefly on each of these factors.

2 The Aberdeen system

2.1 User engagement

Subjective comments from participants to GIVE-2009 (see Koller et al. 2010) suggest that the algorithms submitted at the time were not well able to ``engage'' participants in the task, which may have felt more like a chore to them than like an enjoyable game. It seemed plausible that if user engagement could be improved, this would not only be a good thing in its own right, but that it might also lead to improved results on objective task performance metrics such as task completion rates (cf. Lester et al. 1997). In view of these observations, we attempted to increase users' engagement in the game by adding a "James Bond" theme to the utterances generated by the system. At the start of the game, for example, the system says: *"Hello, James Bond, Secret Agent 007, welcome to the GIVE World! Your mission is to get a trophy full of diamonds from a safe. To do this, you must turn off alarms, uncover the safe, and crack the safe combination. Now pay attention 007. I need to tell you three very important things: One, you need to get really close to a button before you press it! Two, if there is no message, go to the middle of the room to re-activate the scanner! Three, don't stand on the red tiles, 007. They are all alarmed!"*

Proceedings of the 13th European Workshop on Natural Language Generation (ENLG), pages 280–283,
Nancy, France, September 2011.

2.2 Gadgets

GIVE offers an electronic "world" that differs from real life. It seemed reasonable to us to make use of this fact by allowing the user to do things that might be impossible in real life. In particular, we decided to offer users the use of a gadget that we called ATAC (Automatic Target Acquisition Control). When activated, ATAC detects the correct target (for example, the button that needs to be pressed at a given moment in time) then checks whether it is "in view" (i.e., nearby). If it is, the system says "target acquired", otherwise it says that the target is not there. ATAC was expected to be particularly useful in preventing participants from pushing alarmed buttons.

2.3 Referring Expressions

A quick survey of the systems submitted to GIVE 2009 suggested to us that generation of referring expressions was generally a weak point. A good example is Denis (2009), which appears to rely on a strategy whereby the system indicates an underspecified referring expression (e.g., *"(push) a red button"*); if the user pushes the wrong button, the system proceeds to say that the wrong button was pushed, and another one needs to be attempted. While it is interesting to have a referential strategy that allows a degree of collaboration between speaker and hearer (cf. Heeman and Hirst 1995), this particular strategy seems error prone (particularly given the existence of alarmed buttons), and problematic in the presence of a large domain. (What if there are 10 red buttons, for example?)

Our initial plan was to use the algorithm of van Deemter (2006), originally designed to generate vague descriptions such as "The tall man". In a configuration of buttons on a wall, for example, this algorithm is able to identify any single button, by generating a sequence of gradable properties. Imagine a sequence of three buttons, for example, numbered 1,2,3 from left to right. Button 2 may be identified by the sequence *"Take the leftmost two buttons", "(From these) take the rightmost button"*. The problem, however, lies in Linguistic Realisation: a direct rendering of the sequence would give rise to a highly complex description, whereas an optimal rendering would simply say "The button in the middle". Programming this nontrivial Linguistic Realisation step proved too difficult a task within a final-year project that was full of other challenges. Moreover, the ATAC gadget (section 2.2) offers the user an additional technique, which might make complex referring expressions unnecessary in most situations. For these reasons, we decided to explore an alternative approach, which distinguishes a number of different referential situations, each of which is addressed by a largely separate procedure (though code was shared between these procedures as much as possible). Essentially, we used a large battery of small algorithms; an appropriate algorithm was chosen depending on the situation. This inelegant but flexible "engineering" approach made it easy for us to address a number of special situations which are often disregarded (e.g., the situation where the domain does not contain any distractors). It works by distinguishing a series of increasingly complex referential situations (programmed as CASE statements), starting with the simplest situations that a GIVE participant can encounter, and ending with the most complex ones. (In the list of cases, each case assumes that previous cases do not apply.)

CASE 1: There is only one button in the room, and this button is the target. System (example): *"There is a single blue button in this room. Push it, James!"*

CASE 2: The target button is the only one in its target region. System: *"There is a single button on the left wall. Push it."*

CASE 3: The target button has a colour that is unique in its target region. System: *"There is a row of four buttons on your right. Press the red button."*

CASE 4: There exists in the target region just one (horizontal or vertical) sequence of buttons, and the target button is one of these buttons. System: *"There is a horizontal sequence of buttons on your left. Push the rightmost button in this sequence."*

...

CASE n:
System: *"Use the ATAC scanner, James!"*

3 Evaluation of the Aberdeen system

The "objective" performance of our system, in terms of task completion percentages, times and words was largely unremarkable. In fact, our "James Bond" theme made our system more verbose than most, and the navigation aspect of our system drew a number of negative comments from participants, particularly regarding the timing of the system's messages (*"The system reacted very slowly on my progress. The commands were designed for really slow steps while I'm used to 'walk' quickly", "The message 'go through the doorway' was always too late", "The speed of the commands were a little bit too late."*) For details concerning objective performance, we refer to the organisers' figures. Here, we will attempt to assess to what extent the three innovations discussed in section 2 were successful. In each case, we start summarizing relevant parts of the questionnaire, followed by a summary of comments.

User engagement.
Questionnaire: The subjective questions did not address the extent to which a system managed to "engage" the user in the direction-giving game. Consequently, they did not shed light on our claim, neither confirming nor disconfirming it.
Comments: *"The fact that the system tells us that we are a secret agent, that's cool", "The salutation with 007 was very funny", "Altogether an acceptable game", "It was a fun game to play while it lasted."*

Gadgets.
Questionnaire: The subjective questions did not address this issue.
Comments: *"Saying 'target not here' or 'target in front of you' helped in letting me know if I'd reached the right place".*

Referring Expressions.
Questionnaire: The analysis of subjects' responses to the statement in the questionnaire that said "I could easily identify the buttons the system described to me" appears to confirm that the referring expressions produced by our system were clear. The results in this area were not statistically significant, however, so need to be treated with caution.
Comments: *"I'm impressed by the overall quality of the instructions I received. As an AI researcher I'm interested in such endeavors and will follow the progress in the near future", "The system worked better when I was near the correct buttons and it gave explicit instructions about which button to press", "It was quite good in describing which button was to be pressed", "The descriptions of which buttons to press were generally clear", "The descriptions of which buttons to push was quite clear", "The description of the buttons was most of the times unambiguous", "Good instructions", "Liked description of colors of buttons, numbers of buttons", "It's very good describing buttons positions, and has good relative references", "The button finding instructions were very easy to follow", "The identification of the buttons one must press is done almost impeccably."*

As it happens, these aspects of the system appeared to give rise to almost exclusively positive comments. Perhaps these positive comments need to be taken with a pinch of salt, given that they did not translate into better "objective" performance. (Compare Dehn and Van Mulken 2000 for a discussion of a similar asymmetry between subjective experience and objective task performance, in the area of Embodied Conversational Agents.)

4 Conclusion and general notes on the GIVE challenge

Mastering the GIVE software proved a major challenge for us, especially after the system was installed in the network, when a variety of new issues arose, relating to the use of ports, proxies and permissions. Taking part in GIVE became a very "technical" affair, with issues of Natural Language Generation and HCI taking a definite backseat.

We expect that researchers who want to use the GIVE framework itself (rather than participate in the GIVE challenge) are unlikely to experience these problems, however, because their programs will not need to be installed into the network. In regard of our plans to use the GIVE setting for our own future experiments, this is an encouraging conclusion.

In our initial exploration, we underestimated the

problems thrown up by navigation. Users can easily feel disoriented when they end up in an area where they should not be. Equally, if the user moves faster than the system can keep up with (in terms of producing the next instruction) then instructions can arrive too late to be of relevance, which can further disorient the user. Tackling these issues required more attention than we had anticipated. Having said this, it appears that those aspects of the system on which we decided to focus (user engagement, the ATAC gadget, and referring expressions) were fairly successful

Acknowledgments

We are grateful to Roman Kutlak and Margaret Mitchell for their assistance troubleshooting software issues, and to Chris Mellish for general advice.

References

Dehn and Van Mulken 2000. D.M. Dehn, S. van Mulken. The impact of Interface Agents: a Review of Empirical Research. *Journal of Human-Computer Studies* 52(1), p.1-22.

Denis, Alexandre. 2010. Generating referring expressions with reference domain theory. In Proceedings of the 6th International Natural Language Generation Conference
(INLG), Trim, Ireland.

Gatt, Albert and Anja Belz. 2010. Introducing shared task evaluation to NLG: The TUNA shared task evaluation challenges. In Emiel Krahmer and Mariët Theune (Eds.) Empirical Methods in Natural Language Generation. Springer Verlag, Berlin, pages 264–293.

Goudbeek, Martijn and Emiel Krahmer. 2010. Preferences versus adaptation during referring expression generation. In Proceedings of the 48th Annual Meeting of the Association for Computational Linguistics (ACL), pages 55–59, Uppsala, Sweden.

Gupta, Surabhi and Amanda Stent. 2005. Automatic evaluation of referring expression generation using corpora. In Proceedings of the 1st Workshop on Using
Copora in Natural Language Generation (UCNLG), pages 1–6, Brighton, UK.

Heeman, Peter A. and Graeme Hirst. 1995. Collaborating on referring expressions. *Computational Linguistics*, 21(3):351–382.

Jordan, PamelaW. and Marilyn Walker. 2005. Learning content selection rules for generating object descriptions in dialogue. *Journal of Artificial Intelligence Research,* 24:157–194.

Koller, Alexander, Kristina Striegnitz, Donna Byron, Justine Cassell, Robert Dale, Johanna Moore, and Jon Oberlander. 2010. The first challenge on generating instructions in virtual environments. In Emiel Krahmer and Mariët Theune, editors, Empirical Methods in Natural Language Generation. Springer Verlag, Berlin, pages 328–352.

Lester, J.C., S.A.Converse, S.E.Kahler, S.T. Barlow, B.A. Stone, R.S.Bhoga,. The Persona Effect.: Affective Impact of Animated Pedagogical Agents, in: Proc. CHI Conference, Atlanta, Georgia.

van Deemter, Kees. 2006. Generating Referring Expressions that involve gradable properties. *Computational Linguistics*, 32(2):195–222.

van Deemter, Kees, Albert Gatt, Ielka van der Sluis, and Richard Power (in press). Generation of Referring Expressions: Assessing the Incremental Algorithm. *Cognitive Science*. To appear Winter 2011-2012.

Viethen, Jette and Robert Dale. 2007. Evaluation in natural language generation: Lessons from referring expression
generation. *Traitement Automatique des Langues*, 48:141 –160.

The Bremen System for the GIVE-2.5 Challenge

Nina Dethlefs
University of Bremen
dethlefs@uni-bremen.de

Abstract

This paper presents the Bremen system for the GIVE-2.5 challenge. It is based on decision trees learnt from new annotations of the GIVE corpus augmented with manually specified rules. Surface realisation is based on context-free grammars. The paper will address advantages and shortcomings of the approach and discuss how the present system can serve as a baseline for a future evaluation with an improved version using hierarchical reinforcement learning with graphical models.

1 Introduction

Decision making in NLG systems for situated domains needs to be sensitive to a number of features concerning the spatial context, the user and the history of the interaction. Related work to situated NLG has explored different approaches to this problem. Stoia et al. (2006) use decision trees to learn a set of rules for referring expression generation (REG) in a virtual environment very similar to GIVE (Byron, 2005). Similarly, Dale and Viethen (2008) and Viethen (2010) use decision trees to inform REG in a spatial setting. Garoufi and Koller (2010) use AI planning for GIVE to principally guide the user to positions where unambiguous referring expressions (RE) can be generated. Denis (2010) uses an algorithm based on Reference Domain Theory to generate REs for GIVE based on context. Finally, Benotti and Denis (2011) use a corpus-based selection method to choose utterances from a human corpus to present to the user. In Dethlefs et al. (2011), we suggested to use Hierarchical Reinforcement Learning (HRL) for GIVE and compared it against decision trees. While results (based on simulation and human ratings) showed that the HRL system achieved significantly better performance, this paper presents a system that behaves based on decision trees learnt from human data. The system is developed as a reliable baseline for a comprehensive evaluation of an HRL-based system in the future (as part of the author's PhD thesis).

2 The GIVE Task

The GIVE task involves the generation of navigation instructions and REs in a virtual 3D world (Koller et al., 2010), where two participants go on a 'treasure hunt'. One participant instructs the other in navigating through the world, pressing a sequence of buttons and completing the task by obtaining a trophy.

2.1 GIVE-2 Corpus Annotation

While typically the task of instruction giver is taken by an NLG system, the GIVE-2 corpus (Gargett et al., 2010) provides 63 English and 45 German transcripts of human-human dialogues for the task. To design an NLG system for GIVE and automatically induce a set of rules to inform its design, the English dialogues were complemented with a set of semantic annotations. They include the string of words and time of an utterance as well as its type. Utterance types include *destination, direction, orientation, path* and *'straight'* for navigation and *manipulation, confirm* and *stop* otherwise. High-level navigation (e.g., 'go back to the previous room') and low-level navigation (e.g., 'go straight, then

Proceedings of the 13th European Workshop on Natural Language Generation (ENLG), pages 284–289,
Nancy, France, September 2011.

Utterance
string="turn left and press the blue button left of the yellow", *time*='20:54:55'

Utterance_type
content='orientation,manipulation' [straight, path, direction, destination, confirm, stop]
navigation_level='low' [high]

Referring_Expression
first_mention='true' [false], *within_field_of_vision*='true' [false]
discriminative_colour_distractor='true' [false], *mention_distractor_colour*='true' [false]
discriminative_colour_referent='false' [true], *mention_referent_colour*='true' [false]
mention_distractor='true' [false] , *mention_landmark*='false' [true]
spatial_relation='lateral_projection' [none, distance, middle, proximal, functional_control, functional_containment, non_projection_axial, frontal_projection, vertical_projection]

User
user_position='on_track' [off_track],
user_reaction='perform_desired_action' [perform_undesired_action, wait, request_help]

Figure 1: Sample annotation for a navigation instruction followed by a referring expression. Alternative annotation values are given in square brackets behind the actual values.

left and turn right') is distinguished. The former refers to contractions of the later. In terms of referring expressions (or *manipulation* utterances), annotations include whether a referent has been mentioned before, whether it has a discriminating colour, whether it has a distractor with a discriminating colour, whether a distractor or landmark was included in an utterance, whether the referent is visible and the type of spatial relation between a distractor or landmark and the referent. Spatial relations were annotated according to Bateman et al. (2010). Please see Figure 1 for an example annotation.

2.2 Generation Tasks

The NLG system was designed to perform four main tasks. **(1) High-level behaviour generation** is concerned with deciding what type of utterance to generate next among navigation instructions, referring expressions, confirmations or stop instructions. **(2) Navigation instruction generation** chooses a level of navigation (high or low), according to the degree of confusion of the user and their prior knowledge of the virtual world. **(3) REG** includes deciding to mention a referent's colour or not, mention a distractor (and its colour) or not, mention a landmark or not, and deciding what spatial relation to use (if any). **(4) Surface Realisation** produces a string of words for presentation to the user from the semantics determined by the previous components.

3 Algorithms for Content Selection

3.1 Learning Decision Trees

To learn a set of rules from the annotated GIVE corpus, Weka's (Witten and Frank, 2005) J48 classifier was used. We learnt one decision tree per annotated attribute. Rules for navigation instructions were learnt based on utterance type and user features, and RE rules were learnt based on the RE and user features. On average, the decision trees reached an accuracy of 91% in a 10-fold cross validation. The obtained rules were integrated into the algorithms designed for each behaviour.

3.2 High-level Behaviour

The high-level behaviour of the system was entirely hand-crafted. Whenever a game is started, the system greets the user and introduces them to the main task of the game. A first warning is then presented to the user to not step on any red tiles. After this first warning, additional warnings are generated whenever an alarm tile is visible and near to the user (so there is eminent danger of activating an alarm) or when a tile is visible and less than five warnings have been generated during the whole interaction. The objective of generating multiple warnings was to raise a strong awareness of their danger. Moreover, the system confirms successful manipulation actions of the user (to convey a notion of progress in the game), but not for successful navigation instruc-

Algorithm 1 Algorithm for generating navigation instructions.

```
1: function GENERATENAVIGATION(userConfusions c, nextGoal g, boolean leaving_room) return navigation
2:     instruction_type ← instruction type of destination, path, direction, orientation and straight
3:     navigation_level ← instruction level of high and low
4:     while navigation is not generated do
5:         if next room is known and userConfusions c = 0 then
6:             navigation_level = high
7:         else
8:             navigation_level = low
9:         end if
10:        if user is leaving_room is true and number of doors >1 then
11:            instruction_type = path + direction
12:        else if user is leaving_room is true and number of doors = 1 then
13:            instruction_type = path
14:        else if the user is leaving_room is true and the nextGoal g is in the same room then
15:            instruction_type = destination towards object
16:            if a salient landmark is present near the next goal then
17:                object = landmark
18:            else if a door is present then
19:                object = door
20:            else
21:                object = nextGoal g
22:            end if
23:        else if the user is leaving the room over a corridor then
24:            instruction_type = path
25:        else if the user is changing their orientation then
26:            instruction_type = orientation
27:        else if the user is going straight then
28:            instruction_type = straight
29:        else if the user is heading to another direction then
30:            instruction_type = direction
31:        end if
32:    end while
33: end function
```

tions (to not interrupt smooth interactions). Whenever the user requests help (by pressing the help button), the system either repeats the previous utterance or generates a paraphrase. The same behaviour is shown for user confusions (which we assume after five seconds that users do not do anything).

3.3 Navigation Instructions

Navigation instruction generation is partially learnt from decision trees and partially hand-crafted. It specifies that the agent should try to use high-level navigation behaviour whenever this is likely to be successful (i.e. when the user is not confused and the next room is already known). High-level instructions in this case could encourage shorter and more efficient interactions. Whenever the user leaves a room and a door needs to be mentioned, the direction of the door is included when there is more than one in the room. If a destination instruction to some object is given, the system prefers instructions to salient landmarks of the environment over buttons (since landmarks tend to be less ambiguous). Whenever no landmarks are present and a destination instruction to a button is generated, using the next referent as a destination is preferred over using a distractor. The resulting algorithm is shown in Algorithm 2. The behaviour specified in lines 5-9 (on high-level navigation) and in lines 16-22 (about choosing a salient object) were hand-crafted, the remaining behaviour was learnt.

Algorithm 2 Algorithm for generating referring expressions.

```
1: function GenerateRE(referent r, distractors d_{0...n}, landmarks l_{0...m}) return RE
2:     int reminders ← reminders to the user of getting close to r when pressing
3:     while RE is not generated do
4:         if r is visible and near then
5:             if utterance is of type repair and colour of r is discriminating then
6:                 include colour of r
7:             else if utterance is not of type repair then
8:                 include colour of r
9:             else
10:                don't include colour of r
11:            end if
12:            if colour of r is not discriminating and number of distractors d_{0...n} is not 0 then
13:                for d_i in d_{0...n} do
14:                    if colour of distractor d_i is discriminating and d_i is adjacent to r then
15:                        include d_i and colour of d_i
16:                    else if spatial_relation between d_i and r is vertical then
17:                        include d_i but not colour of d_i
18:                    else if spatial_relation between d_i and r is lateral or horizontal then
19:                        include d_i but not colour of d_i
20:                    end if
21:                end for
22:            else if colour of r is not discriminating and number of landmarks l_{0...m} is not 0 then
23:                include l_j that is closest to r
24:            end if
25:        else if d_i is visible and near but r is not then
26:            RE = 'Not this one, I mean the other button.'
27:        else
28:            RE = 'Try to find a button somewhere near.'
29:        end if
30:        if reminders <5 then
31:            RE = RE + 'Remember to get really close to press it.'
32:        end if
33:    end while
34: end function
```

3.4 Referring Expressions

The REG behaviour is again partially learnt and partially hand-crafted. The system mentions the colour of a referent whenever the current utterance type is not a repair or if the referent's colour is discriminating. If it is not, the system's next best choice is to use a distractor with a discriminating colour that is adjacent to the referent. Otherwise, it prefers to locate the referent using a vertical spatial relation over using a lateral or horizontal one. If no suitable distractor is present, a referent can be located with respect to a landmark. This set of rules was entirely learnt from decision trees (lines 6-25 in Algorithm 3). The remaining behaviour was designed manually. Whenever a distractor is near to the user and the only button visible, it was assumed that the user had the intention of pressing it. A warning is generated in this case that this was the wrong button. If no button is visible or near, the user is told to look for one in the vicinity. In addition, the system initially generates a set of reminders (up to five) to the user to get close enough to a button before pressing.

4 CFGs for Surface Realisation

The generation spaces of the system were represented as CFGs so that several alternative realisations of a semantic concept could be captured and alternated for more variable system output. In order to

CFG Generation Space for destination instructions

destination1 → desVerb1 desPrep1 desRel1
destination2 → desVerb1 desPrep2 desRel2
destination3 → desVerb2 desRel1|desRel2
desVerb1 → go | keep_going | walk | continue | empty
desVerb2 → you_need | you_want | get
desPrep1 → to | towards | until
desPrep2 → into | in
desRel1 → pointRelatum
desRel2 → roomRelatum

Figure 2: Example CFG for destination instruction. Non-terminal symbols represent semantic constituents, terminal symbols possible surface realisations.

obtain CFGs, we used the ABL algorithm (van Zaanen, 2000), which aligns strings based on Minimum Edit Distance and induces a CFG automatically from the aligned examples. The annotated GIVE corpus examples were used as input to the algorithm based on their instruction type, so that separate generation spaces were obtained for destination, direction, orientation, path and 'straight' instructions as well as REs. As an example, the CFG for destination instructions is shown in Figure 2. Here, a destination instruction can be phrased in three different ways. Type 1 generates instructions such as 'Go to the sofa' (referring to point-like destinations) and type 2 generates instructions such as 'Go into the next room' (referring to room-like destinations). Type 3 destination instructions use verb forms which are followed directly by either type of relatum. We use these CFGs to generate variation in surface forms.[1]

5 Results

The GIVE-2.5 evaluation revealed advantages as well as drawbacks of the presented approach. Some of the drawbacks that users commented on involved ambiguities with respect to doors or button referents, which were not identified uniquely, or the disambiguation occurred too late (e.g. when the system first generated an ambiguous phrase and then repaired it with an unambiguous paraphrase). This aspect would usually not affect task success measures, but can deteriorate user satisfaction scores. In terms of task success, the system reached roughly 56% which is a better number than any system achieved in the 2010 challenge, but is a bad number in comparison to the 2011 systems. This low number provides strong evidence that the generated tile warnings were insufficient, since a number of users lost the game here. Both points of criticism can be traced back to a lack in flexibility in system behaviour. A system with better (more adaptive) troubleshooting strategies to lead the user around tiles (instead of warning them) and avoiding ambiguous phrases at any time would likely have reached higher task success scores. This also affects positive feedback that users provided on the high-level navigation strategies. Several users stated that they wished the system had employed this strategy more globally.

6 Discussion and Conclusion

The reason for the system's lack of troubleshooting strategies and limited flexibility is likely found in the method itself: the human corpus data from which the decision trees were learned presented data sparsity problems with respect to learning troubleshooting strategies. This is because human users in the corpus react very flexibly to individual problematic situations which may stretch over several turns and therefore not be captured by the annotations.[2]

A powerful alternative to decision trees is reinforcement learning (or HRL for large systems) which has been applied to situated interaction (Cuayáhuitl and Dethlefs, 2011; Dethlefs et al., 2011) with promising results. Since RL agents are able to learn flexible behaviour strategies from a limited amount of data (using simulations), they often do not face the same data sparsity problems as supervised learning accounts. Rule-based systems may present a viable alternative for small and limited domains, but will not scale to complex real-world problems because of the large amount of manual work they require. Corpus-based selection methods that have been proposed recently (Benotti and Denis, 2011) appear to yield good results for clearly pre-specified tasks but will not present an alternative for tasks involving uncertainty or the need to gener-

[1]This variation is random in that it is not based on the likelihoods with which different forms appear in the human data.

[2]A more comprehensive annotation scheme could possibly improve performance in this case, but would probably not solve the data sparsity problems on the whole.

alise to new circumstances.

7 Future Directions

The presented system suffered from a number of drawbacks that future work will address. We observed a lack of flexibility in the system's behaviour especially when sophisticated troubleshooting strategies were needed. A hypothesis is that a system based on hierarchical RL could adapt more flexibly to different (unseen) conditions and provide better support to individual users. In addition, graphical models such as Bayesian Networks (Dethlefs and Cuayáhuitl, 2011a) or HMMs (Dethlefs and Cuayáhuitl, 2011b) can be used to formulate more sophisticated generation spaces based on corpus probabilities and support more coherent surface realisation. Both claims will be tested and evaluated against the baseline established in this paper.

Acknowledgments

Thanks to the German Research Foundation DFG and the Transregional Collaborative Research Centre SFB/TR8 'Spatial Cognition' for partial support.

References

John A. Bateman, Joana Hois, Robert Ross, and Thora Tenbrink. 2010. A linguistic ontology of space for natural language processing. *Artificial Intelligence*, 174(14):1027 – 1071.

Luciana Benotti and Alexandre Denis. 2011. Giving instructions in virtual environments by corpus based selection. In *Proceedings of the 12th Annual SIGdial Meeting on Discourse and Dialogue*.

Donna Byron. 2005. The osu quake 2004 corpus of two-party situated problem-solving dialogs. In *Technical Report OSU-CISRC-805-TR57, The Ohio State University Computer Science and Engineering Department*.

Heriberto Cuayáhuitl and Nina Dethlefs. 2011. Spatially-aware dialogue control using hierarchical reinforcement learning. *ACM Transactions on Speech and Language Processing (Special Issue on Machine Learning for Robust and Adaptive Spoken Dialogue Systems*, 7(3).

Robert Dale and Jette Viethen. 2009. Referring expression generation through attribute-based heuristics. In *Proceedings of the 12th European Workshop on Natural Language Generation*, ENLG '09, pages 58–65.

Alexandre Denis. 2010. Generating referring expressions with reference domain theory. In *Proceeding of the 6th International Conference on Natural Language Generation (INLG)*.

Nina Dethlefs and Heriberto Cuayáhuitl. 2011a. Combining hierarchical reinforcement learning and bayesian networks for situated dialogue. In *Proceedings of the 13th European Workshop on Natural Language Generation (ENLG), Nancy, France*.

Nina Dethlefs and Heriberto Cuayáhuitl. 2011b. Hierarchical Reinforcement Learning and Hidden Markov Models for Task-Oriented Natural Language Generation. In *Proceedings of ACL-HLT 2011, Portland, OR, USA*.

Nina Dethlefs, Heriberto Cuayáhuitl, and Jette Viethen. 2011. Optimising Natural Language Generation Decision Making for Situated Dialogue. In *Proceedings of the 12th Annual SIGdial Meeting on Discourse and Dialogue*.

Andrew Gargett, Konstantina Garoufi, Alexander Koller, and Kristina Striegnitz. 2010. The GIVE-2 corpus of giving instructions in virtual environments. In *Proceedings of the 7th International Conference on Language Resources and Evaluation (LREC)*.

Konstantina Garoufi and Alexander Koller. 2010. Automated planning for situated natural language generation. In *Proceedings of the 48th Annual Meeting of the Association for Computational Linguistics*, Uppsala, Sweden, July.

Alexander Koller, Kristina Striegnitz, Donna Byron, Justine Cassell, Robert Dale, Johanna Moore, and Jon Oberlander. 2010. The first challenge on generating instructions in virtual environments. In M. Theune and E. Krahmer, editors, *Empirical Methods on Natural Language Generation*, pages 337–361, Berlin/Heidelberg, Germany. Springer.

Laura Stoia, Darla Magdalene Shockley, Donna K. Byron, and Eric Fosler-Lussier. 2006. Noun phrase generation for situated dialogs. In *Proceedings of the Fourth International Natural Language Generation Conference*, INLG '06, pages 81–88, Morristown, NJ, USA.

Menno van Zaanen. 2000. Bootstrapping syntax and recursion using alginment-based learning. In *Proceedings of the Seventeenth International Conference on Machine Learning (ICML)*, pages 1063–1070, San Francisco, CA, USA.

Jette Viethen. 2010. *Generating Natural Descriptions: Corpus-Based Referring Expression Generation in Visual Domains*. Ph.D. thesis, Macquarie University, Sydney, Australia.

Ian H. Witten and Eibe Frank. 2005. *Data Mining: Practical Machine Learning Tools and Techniques*. Morgan Kaufmann, San Francisco, CA, 2. edition.

The GIVE-2.5 C Generation System

David Nicolás Racca, Luciana Benotti and **Pablo Duboue**
Universidad Nacional de Córdoba
Facultad de Matemática, Astronomía y Física
Córdoba, Argentina
{david.racca, luciana.benotti, pablo.duboue}@gmail.com

Abstract

In this paper we describe the C generation system from the Universidad Nacional de Córdoba (Argentina) as embodied during the 2011 GIVE 2.5 challenge. The C system has two distinguishing characteristics. First, its navigation and referring strategies are based on the area visible to the player, making the system independent of GIVE's internal representation of areas (such as rooms). As a result, the system portability to other virtual environments is enhanced. Second, the system adapts classical grounding models to the task of instruction giving in virtual worlds. The simple grounding processes implemented (for referents, game concepts and game progress) seem to have an impact on the evaluation results.

1 Introduction

GIVE-2.5 is the third instance of the challenge on Generating Instructions in Virtual Environments (Byron et al., 2007). The GIVE Challenge is an NLG evaluation contest in which natural language generation systems help human players complete a treasure hunt in virtual 3D worlds.

In GIVE, the C system and the human Instruction Follower (IF)—the player—establish a dialogue situated in a virtual world. The C system verbalizes, in real time, instructions that the IF must follow in order to complete the game. Generating instructions involves the generation of referring expressions and navigation instructions. The C system was designed independently of GIVE world's internal concepts by using the IF's visibility information. As a result, the main algorithms of the system can be ported to different virtual environments.

To make the communication more effective, the C system implements a grounding model for referents based on Traum's grounding acts model (Traum and Allen, 1992; Traum, 1999). The system also implements a grounding process for unknown objects, such as alarms, describing them to the player and specifying their effects.

The paper is structured as follows. Section 3 describes the system's strategy based on player's visibility. Section 2 introduces the architecture design of the system. Section 4 explains C system's grounding model. Section 5 briefly analyzes the evaluation results and Section 6 concludes.

2 System Architecture

In the virtual worlds, the player has to press several buttons to accomplish the target goal. These buttons, when pressed, modify the state of the virtual world. C system's architecture is an adaptation of Reiter and Dale (2000) NLG architecture to GIVE's dynamic context. Figure 1 presents the architecture diagram of the C System. The arrows between the different modules represent how data flows through modules. Note that data flows through a cycle that starts with the player's actions information and finishes with C system's text instructions. On each iteration, C system checks what the player did or is doing at the moment and uses this information as well as the plan's information to create one or more instructions in response to the player's activities.

The Monitor module is responsible for checking player progress and status. It collects targeted

Proceedings of the 13th European Workshop on Natural Language Generation (ENLG), pages 290–295,
Nancy, France, September 2011.

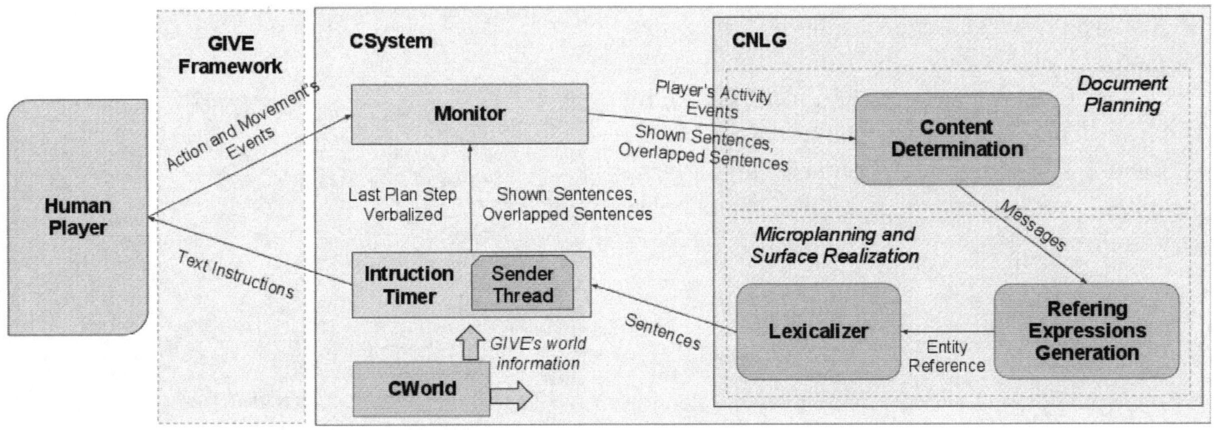

Figure 1: C system's architecture diagram.

player's actions which will be used later by the CNLG module to determine the content of the next instruction to be generated. Given a player's action, Monitor checks if the system's last verbalized plan step has now been accomplished by the player. That is, it verifies whether the player has performed the action previously indicated by the C system. This task is important for the grounding process implemented by the NLG as discussed in Section 4. The monitor also checks if the player is close to an alarm and whether an alarm is visible. In addition, it checks for player's inactivity using a set of timeouts which take into account the time the player is taking to perform the last issued instruction.

The CNLG module is the language generator of the system and is based on Reiter and Dale's architecture. The Content Determination unit uses the current plan and the monitor output to create a list of messages. Each message contains information corresponding to a CNLG's final utterance. Given a set of player's activity events such as a correct/incorrect object manipulation or player's inactivity, the Content Determination module selects from the plan the items that will form part of the next generated instructions. The Lexicalizer and Referring Expressions Generator (REG) modules convert the messages given by the Content Determinator module into a set of sentences objects (each representing a text utterance). The CWorld module provides information to all other modules about the current state of the GIVE World and player status.

Lastly, the Instruction Timer module sends the list of sentences to the human player ensuring that these are shown long enough to be considered completely read. It also determines which utterances will be shown using a priority hierarchy list of the sentence objects. Using this information, it classifies the sentences into shown and overlapped sentences.

3 Visibility-based Strategy

The main NLG task in GIVE is helping the human player by communicating a list of steps to reach the trophy. Thus, the NLG must communicate all the steps that compose the plan obtained using the GIVE framework planner. On this context there are three different types of plan steps (PS): movement plan steps (MoPS), object manipulation plan steps (MaPS) and object taking plan steps (TaPS). In GIVE, MaPS are related to pressing buttons where TaPS are actions that imply the possession of an object. MoPS are movement actions indicating the player must move from one region to another.

Since planners cannot handle continues environments, the virtual world has to be discretized. GIVE worlds are discretized into smaller rectangular regions such that, for all pairs of regions A and B, A is adjacent to B if and only if every point of A can be seen from B and every point of B can be seen from A. Two points in different regions can see each other if it is possible to draw a straight line between the two points without intersecting a wall. In GIVE, all rooms and hallways are rectangular and therefore so are all regions.

The strategy of the C system is based on player's

visibility. The C system chooses the next plan step to verbalize by checking whether the plan step's argument (e.g., button or target region) is visible by the player. The plan is a list composed of MaPS, MoPS and TaPS, sorted by the order in which these actions needs to be performed. A GIVE tipical plan has the following form:

$$\begin{pmatrix} MoPS_1^1, MoPS_2^1, ..., MaPS_1, \\ MoPS_1^2, MoPS_2^2, ..., MaPS_2, \\ ..., \\ MaPS_k, MoPS_1^{k+1}, MoPS_2^{k+1}, ..., TaPS \end{pmatrix}$$

Our algorithm selects one plan step at a time checking whether the argument of the first MaPS or TaPS is visible-360° by the player. An object is visible-360° by the player if she can visualize it directly by turning around 360°. If the first MaPS or TaPS do not satisfy this, then the C system takes the sublist $[MoPS_1^1, MoPS_2^1, ..., MaPS_1]$ and looks for the last MoPS that its "to" region is visible-360° by the player. A region is visible-360° when its center point is visible-360°. Therefore, the C system will first refer to the first object that the player has to manipulate if it is visible-360° and it will refer to the last visible region if that object is not visible. The principle of discretization given above ensures that such region exists if the plan is valid. The resulting behavior is to navigate the player referring to the furthest region until the first object to manipulate becomes visible. When giving MoPS instructions, the system replans only when the player has moved off the path enough to lose all MoPS region's visibility.

The C system replans if the player actions invalidate the current plan. This can happen if the player presses a button that was not the next button in the plan or when she goes so far away from the path established by plan that all the regions in the path are no longer visible-360°.

Object's visibility at 360° considers a circular visibility zone. This represents the points from which the player is able to visualize the object at 360°. The zone circle's radius determines the distance from which the system will consider that the player can see the object and it depends on the number of distractors that object has. This value is higher if there are few distractors and it is lower if there are many. By doing this, the C system forces the player to get closer to the target object if there are many distractors near, decreasing the number of visible distractors and thus, facilitating the generation of referring expressions. This also makes the C system capable of giving a button's reference from afar if the button is alone and then easily identifiable.

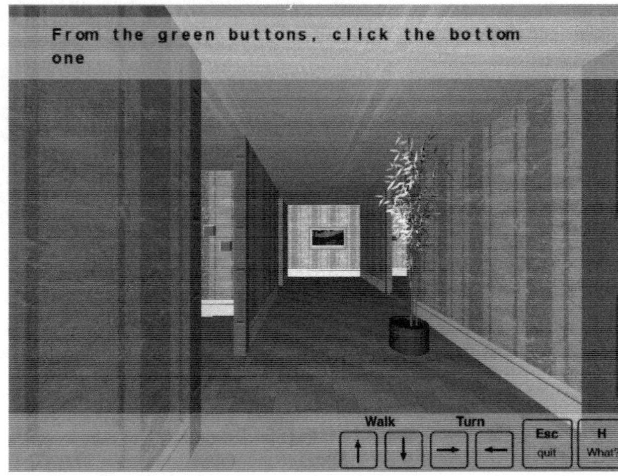

Figure 2: A referential expression from outside the button's room.

C system verbalizes MoPS referencing their region's center by using direction instructions such as —*Go straight*— or —*Move left*—. Also, while navigating, the system checks if there are alarms between the target region and player's location in a straight line and it warns the player about this. MaPS are verbalized using referential expressions for the target objects. To make this kind of references, the system uses object's type and color, its relative position with respect to others of the same type (e.g., first, second, in the middle) and its relative position with respect to player's location (e.g., on your left). It also implements visual focus and deduction by elimination types of references as —*That one*— or —*Not this one*—. Visual focus and deduction by elimination expressions are generated for trophy objects too, besides button's objects.

The C system visibility-based strategy is a general approach that allows to reference buttons as soon as they become visible (for example, the bottom green button in Figure 2). This strategy is, of course, not without its limitations. We can experience stability issues with respect to the generated descriptions for players that move abruptly (particularly if turning).

4 Grounding in Situated Dialogue

When people communicate, they constantly try to arrive to a state in which they believe to have understood, what has been said, well enough for current purposes. The process by which people arrive to this state is called *grounding*. The C system implements three different kinds of grounding.

First, the system grounds new virtual world objects such as alarms and safes. In this process what is grounded is the link between the graphical representation of alarms and safes inside GIVE with the role they play in the game. This grounding process is crucial for completing the GIVE task successfully since the player needs to identify the alarms in order not to lose the game, and she needs to identify the safe in order to win the game. The system implements this grounding process in two stages. The first time the player sees an alarm the system introduces the new object by first describing the object and prompting the player to pay attention to it—*Do you see that red region on the floor?*—then naming it—*That's an activated alarm* and finally describing its effects—*If you step over one of them, we'll lose the game*. In a second stage, every time the player gets too close to an alarm, the system will just present a warning—*There's an alarm, watch out*. The evidence that the alarms have been grounded is quite weak in the GIVE scenario since the player does not need to interact with them but to avoid them. However, we believe it had an impact in the number of lost games (see §5).

Secondly, the system grounds the state of completion of the task. In this process, what is grounded is the effect the player actions have on the state of the task. The C system implements this grounding process in order to minimize the amount of cancelled games following the hypothesis that the player will cancel less if she knows she is advancing in the task. This grounding process is implemented by indicating the effect of the player actions which advance the task—*We've opened one door. We need to open two more doors*—as well as those actions that were incorrect—*Wrong button! We've activated an alarm*. The evidence that the current state of the task has been grounded is non-existing in the GIVE scenario since the player does not react to it in any observable way. However, we believe it had an impact in the number of cancelled games and in the subjective metrics too (see §5).

Finally, the system needs to ground the buttons that the player has to manipulate in order to advance in the task. In this process, what is grounded is the identity of particular buttons that the player has to interact with. This is the grounding task which exhibits the strongest evidence, since the player interacting with the referred button is strong evidence that the intended referent was grounded. However, this is also the grounding task inside GIVE which is more complex since the GIVE worlds are designed such that the intended referents have many distractors (objects of similar characteristics). As a result, the best strategy to implement this grounding process is not to give a referring expression that uniquely identifies the referent but to implement it as a *collaborative* grounding process (as proven empirically by the GIVE-2 NA system (Denis et al., 2010)). The C system implements this grounding process adapting the model proposed by Traum (1992; 1999), which is a computational adaptation of the collaborative grounding model proposed by Clark and Schaefer (1989). In the rest of this section we explain how the C system adapts Traum's model to instruction giving in virtual environments.

Let's consider the following sample interaction with the system:

IG(1): Press the left blue button
IF(2): [Stares at the button on the right]
IG(3): Not that button
IF(4): [Stares at the left button]
IG(5): Yep, that button
IF(6): [Pushes the left blue button]

Traum models the grounding process as a finite state automata. Figure 3 illustrates the part of the automata of Traum's model that was implemented in the C system.

The arc (S,1) represents the contribution to be grounded— contribution (1) in our example. The remaining arcs represent contributions which do not need to be grounded because they are grounding acts—such as contributions (2) to (6)[1] in our example. Contributions (1) to (6) make the automata

[1]Notice that we consider that contributions are not only IG's utterances but also IF's actions.

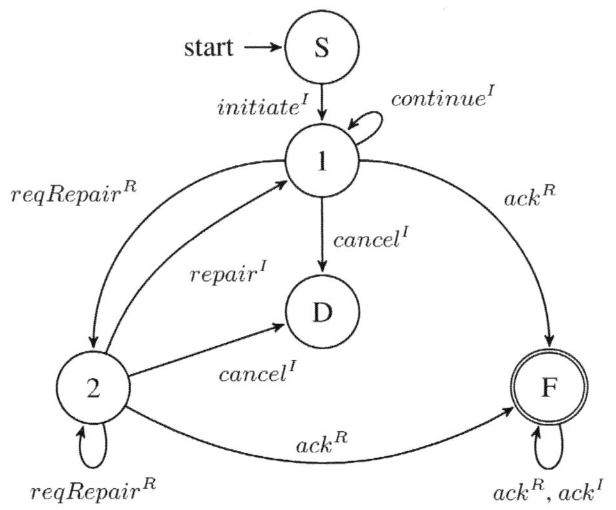

Figure 3: C system's grounding model.

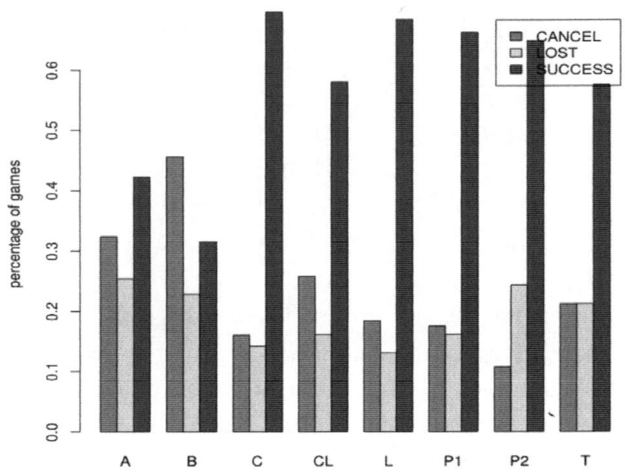

Figure 4: GIVE-2.5 results. Percentage of success, lost and cancelled games by system.

go through the states $\langle S, 1, 2, 1, 2, F \rangle$. That is, (2) and (4)—focusing a possible target and waiting—are treated as request repairs by the receiver R (the IG in this exchange). While (3) and (5) are treated as repairs by the initiator I (the IF in this exchange). Finally, (6) is modelled as an acknowledgement by the IF which grounds the instruction *Press the left blue button*; in the state F the contribution is considered grounded. If the IF would have pressed the correct button right after utterance (1) then the sequence followed would have been $\langle S, F \rangle$. While if the IF would have pressed the wrong button right after utterance (1) then the sequence followed would have been $\langle S, D \rangle$. The state D is a dead state, the contribution is considered ungroundable; after pressing a wrong button the system needs to find a new plan since the ongoing one may no longer be valid.

The C system implements only a part of Traum's grounding model because Traum's model includes the treatment of repairs contributed by the receiver. This is not possible in the GIVE scenario since the IF does not have enough information in order to correct the IG, the IG is the only one that is supposed to have knowledge of the task.

5 Evaluation Results

Figure 4 depicts the percentages for successful, lost and cancelled games of the results of the GIVE 2.5. C system's values for cancelled (16%) and lost(14%) games are lower than the observed on the other systems. We think this is a consequence of the grounding strategy for alarm objects and progress information used by C system.

The instructions about progress and effect's descriptions messages also enhanced the system's subjective metrics. For instance, most players thought that C system gave them useful feedback about their progress and most people considered they could trust on C's instructions.

6 Conclusions

In this work we have described the C natural language generation system for the GIVE-2.5 challenge. Our system classical grounding models (such as the ones from Traum (1992; 1999)) the process of giving instructions in virtual worlds. The simple grounding process for buttons, alarms, safes and game progress described in Section 4 had a positive impact on the evaluation metrics, as discussed in Section 5.

Moreover, the C system navigation and referring strategy (discussed in Section 3) is based on the area visible to the player. We believe this player-centric approach creates more natural-sounding instructions and reduces the chances for the player getting lost. The fact that these strategies make the C system also independent of the GIVE framework internal representations of concepts has portability implications we seek to explore in further work.

References

Donna Byron, Alexander Koller, Jon Oberlander, Laura Stoia, and Kristina Striegnitz. 2007. Generating Instructions in Virtual environments (GIVE): A challenge and evaluation testbed for NLG. In *Workshop on Shared Tasks and Comparative Evaluation in Natural Language Generation*.

Herbert H. Clark and Edward F. Schaefer. 1989. Contributing to discourse. *Cognitive Science*, 13:259–294.

Alexandre Denis, Marilisa Amoia, Luciana Benotti, Laura Perez-Beltrachini, Claire Gardent, and Tarik Osswald. 2010. The GIVE-2 Nancy Generation Systems NA and NM. Technical report, Loria/INRIA, France.

E Reiter and R Dale. 2000. *Building natural language generation systems*. Cambridge University Press.

David R. Traum and James F. Allen. 1992. A "speech acts" approach to grounding in conversation. In *ICSLP*. ISCA.

David R Traum. 1999. Computational Models of Grounding in Collaborative Systems. In *working notes of AAAI Fall Symposium on Psychological Models of Communication*, pages 124–131, November.

CL system: Giving instructions by corpus based selection

Luciana Benotti
PLN Group, FAMAF
National University of Córdoba
Córdoba, Argentina
luciana.benotti@gmail.com

Alexandre Denis
TALARIS team, LORIA/CNRS
Lorraine. Campus scientifique, BP 239
Vandoeuvre-lès-Nancy, France
alexandre.denis@loria.fr

Abstract

The CL system uses an algorithm that, given a task-based corpus situated in a virtual world, which contains human instructor's speech acts and the user's responses as physical actions, generates a virtual instructor that helps a user achieve a given task in the virtual world. In this report, we explain how this algorithm can be used for generating a virtual instructor for a game-like, task-oriented virtual world such as GIVE's.

1 Introduction

There are two main approaches toward automatically producing dialogue utterances. The most used one is the generation approach, in which the output is dynamically assembled using some composition procedure, e.g. grammar rules. The other is the selection approach, in which the task is to pick the appropriate output from a corpus of possible outputs. The selection approach has only been used in conversational systems that are not task-oriented such as negotiating agents (Gandhe and Traum, 2007a), question answering characters (Kenny et al., 2007), and virtual patients (Leuski et al., 2006). In this paper, we describe the algorithm used by the system CL for giving instructions by selecting utterances from automatically annotated human-human corpora. Our algorithm is the first one proposed for doing generation by selection for task-oriented systems, for details see (Benotti and Denis, 2011).

The advantages of corpus based generation are many. To start with, it affords the use of complex and human-like sentences without detailed analysis. Moreover, the system may easily use recorded audio clips rather than speech synthesis and recorded video for animating virtual humans. Finally, no rule writing by a dialogue expert or manual annotations is needed. Nowadays, most conversational systems require extensive human annotation efforts in order to be fit for their task (Rieser and Lemon, 2010). Semantic annotation and rule authoring have long been known as bottlenecks for developing conversational systems for new domains.

The disadvantage of corpus based generation is that the resulting dialogue may not be fully coherent. Shawar and Atwell (2003; 2005) present a method for learning pattern matching rules from corpora in order to obtain the dialogue manager for a chatbot. Gandhe and Traum (2007b) investigate several dialogue models for negotiating virtual agents that are trained on an unannotated human-human corpus. Both approaches report that the dialogues obtained by these methods are still to be improved because the lack of dialogue history management results in incoherences. Since in task-based systems, the dialogue history is restricted by the structure of the task, the absence of dialogue history management is alleviated by tracking the current state of the task.

In the next section we introduce the corpora used by the CL system. Section 2 presents the two phases of our algorithm, namely automatic annotation and generation through selection. In Section 3 we present a fragment of an interaction with a virtual instructor generated using the GIVE-2 Corpus (Gargett et al., 2010) and our algorithm. Finally, Section 5 discusses its advantages and drawbacks with respect to hand-coded systems.

Proceedings of the 13th European Workshop on Natural Language Generation (ENLG), pages 296–301,
Nancy, France, September 2011.

2 The algorithms

Our algorithm consists of two phases: an annotation phase and a selection phase. The *annotation phase* is performed only once and consists of automatically associating the DG instruction to the DF reaction. The *selection phase* is performed every time the virtual instructor generates an instruction and consists of picking out from the annotated corpus the most appropriate instruction at a given point.

2.1 The automatic annotation

The basic idea of the annotation is straightforward: associate each *utterance* with its corresponding *reaction*. We assume that a reaction captures the semantics of its associated instruction. Defining reaction involves two subtle issues, namely *boundary* determination and *discretization*. We discuss these issues in turn and then give a formal definition of reaction.

We define the *boundaries* of a reaction as follows. A reaction R_k to an instruction U_k begins right after the instruction U_k is uttered and ends right before the next instruction U_{k+1} is uttered. In the following example, instruction 1 corresponds to the reaction $\langle 2, 3, 4 \rangle$, instruction 5 corresponds to $\langle 6 \rangle$, and instruction 7 to $\langle 8 \rangle$.

DG(1): hit the red you see in the far room
DF(2): [enters the far room]
DF(3): [pushes the red button]
DF(4): [turns right]
DG(5): hit far side green
DF(6): [moves next to the wrong green]
DG(7): no
DF(8): [moves to the right green and pushes it]

As the example shows, our definition of boundaries is not always semantically correct. For instance, it can be argued that it includes too much because 4 is not strictly part of the semantics of 1. Furthermore, misinterpreted instructions (as 5) and corrections (e.g., 7) result in clearly inappropriate instruction-reaction associations. Since we want to avoid any manual annotation, we decided to use this naive definition of boundaries anyway.

The second issue that we address here is *discretization* of the reaction. It is well known that there is not a unique way to discretize an action into sub-actions. For example, we could decompose action 2 into 'enter the room' or into 'get close to the door and pass the door'. Our algorithm is not dependent on a particular discretization. However, the same discretization mechanism used for annotation has to be used during selection, for the dialogue manager to work properly. For selection (i.e., in order to decide what to say next) any virtual instructor needs to have a *planner* and a *planning problem*: i.e., a specification of how the virtual world works (i.e., the actions), a way to represent the states of the virtual world (i.e., the state representation) and a way to represent the objective of the task (i.e., the goal). Therefore, we decided to use them in order to discretize the reaction.

For the virtual instructor we present in Section 3 we used the planner LazyFF and the planning problem provided with the GIVE Framework. The planner LazyFF is a reimplementation (in Java) of the classical artificial intelligence planner FF (Hoffmann and Nebel, 2001). The GIVE framework (Gargett et al., 2010) provides a standard PDDL (Hsu et al., 2006) planning problem which formalizes how the GIVE virtual worlds work.

Now we are ready to define *reaction* formally. Let S_k be the state of the virtual world when uttering instruction U_k, S_{k+1} be the state of the world when uttering the next utterance U_{k+1} and $Acts$ be the representation of the virtual world actions. The *reaction* to U_k is defined as the sequence of actions returned by the planner with S_k as the initial state, S_{k+1} as the goal state and $Acts$ as the actions.

Given this reaction definition, the annotation of the corpus then consists of automatically associating each utterance to its (discretized) reaction. The simple algorithm that implements this annotation is shown in Figure 1.

$Acts \leftarrow$ *world possible actions*
for all utterance U_k in the corpus **do**
  $S_k \leftarrow$ *world state at* U_k
  $S_{k+1} \leftarrow$ *world state at* U_{k+1}
  $U_k.Reaction \leftarrow \text{plan}(S_k, S_{k+1}, Acts)$
end for

Figure 1: Annotation algorithm

2.2 Selecting what to say next

In this section we describe how the selection phase is performed every time the virtual instructor generates an instruction.

The instruction selection algorithm, displayed in Figure 2, consists in finding in the corpus the set of candidate utterances C for the current task plan P (P is the sequence of actions that needs to be executed in the current state of the virtual world in order to complete the task). We define $C = \{U \in \text{Corpus} \mid P \text{ starts with } U.\mathit{Reaction}\}$. In other words, an utterance U belongs to C if the first actions of the current plan P exactly match the reaction associated to the utterance U. All the utterances that pass this test are considered paraphrases and hence suitable in the current context.

$C \leftarrow \emptyset$
$Plan \leftarrow$ *current task plan*
for all utterance U in the corpus **do**
  if $Plan$ starts with $U.Reaction$ **then**
    $C \leftarrow C \cup \{U\}$
  end if
end for
return C

Figure 2: Selection algorithm

Whenever the plan P changes, as a result of the actions of the DF, we call the selection algorithm in order to regenerate the set of candidate utterances C.

While the plan P doesn't change, because the DF is staying still, the virtual instructor offers alternative paraphrases of the intended instruction. Each paraphrase is selected by picking an utterance from C and verbalizing it, at fixed time intervals (every 3 seconds). The order in which utterances are selected depends on the length of the utterance reaction (in terms of number of actions), starting from the longest ones. Hence, in general, instructions such as "go back again to the room with the lamp" are uttered before instructions such as "go straight", because the reaction of the former utterance is longer than the reaction of the later.

It is important to notice that the discretization used for annotation and selection directly impacts the behavior of the virtual instructor. It is crucial then to find an appropriate granularity of the discretization. If the granularity is too coarse, many instructions in the corpus will have an empty reaction. For instance, in the absence of the representation of the user orientation in the planning domain, instructions like "turn left" and "turn right" will have empty reactions making them indistinguishable during selection. However, if the granularity is too fine the user may get into situations that do not occur in the corpus, causing the selection algorithm to return an empty set of candidate utterances. It is the responsibility of the virtual instructor developer to find a granularity sufficient to capture the diversity of the instructions he wants to distinguish during selection.

3 A sample interaction

In this section we illustrate the interaction between the CL system and the user using the GIVE-2 Corpus (Gargett et al., 2010).

For the actual CL system we collected a corpus on each of the GIVE 2.5 evaluation worlds. The corpus was collected by using the GIVE Wizard (Gargett et al., 2010). 13 volunteers were recruited (4 female and 9 male) to play the DF role. The DG role was played always by the same person which was familiar with the virtual worlds.

On Figures 4 to 7 we show an excerpt of an interaction between the system and a user. The figures show a 2D map from top view and the 3D ingame view. In Figure 4, the user, represented by a blue character, has just entered the upper left room. He has to push the button close to the chair. The first candidate utterance selected is "red closest to the chair in front of you". Notice that the referring expression uniquely identifies the target object using the spatial proximity of the target to the chair. This referring expression is generated without any reasoning on the target distractors, just by considering the current state of the task plan and the user position.

After receiving the instruction the user gets closer to the button as shown in Figure 5. As a result of the new user position, a new task plan exists, the set of candidate utterances is recalculated and the system selects a new utterance, namely "the closet one".

The generation of the ellipsis of the button or the chair is a direct consequence of the utterances normally said in the corpus at this stage of the task plan

L	go
yes	left
straight	now go back
go back out	now go back out
closest the door	down the passage
go back to the hallway	nowin to the shade room
go back out of the room	out the way you came in
exit the way you entered	ok now go out the same door
back to the room with the lamp	go back to the door you came in
Go through the opening on the left	okay now go back to the original room
okay now go back to where you came from	ok go back again to the room with the lamp
now i ned u to go back to the original room	Go through the opening on the left with the yellow wall paper

Figure 3: All candidate selected utterances when exiting the room in Figure 7

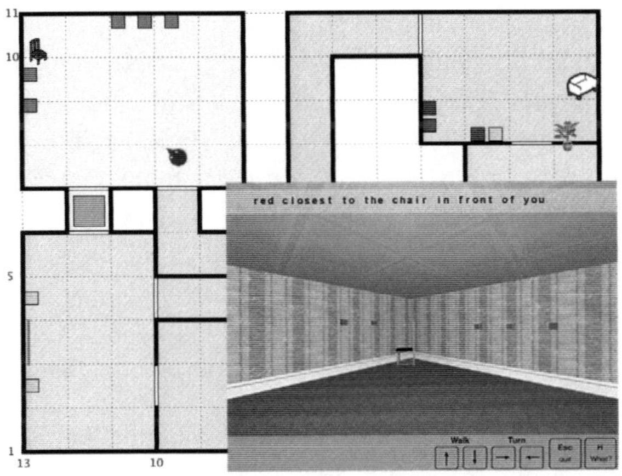

Figure 4: “red closest to the chair in front of you”

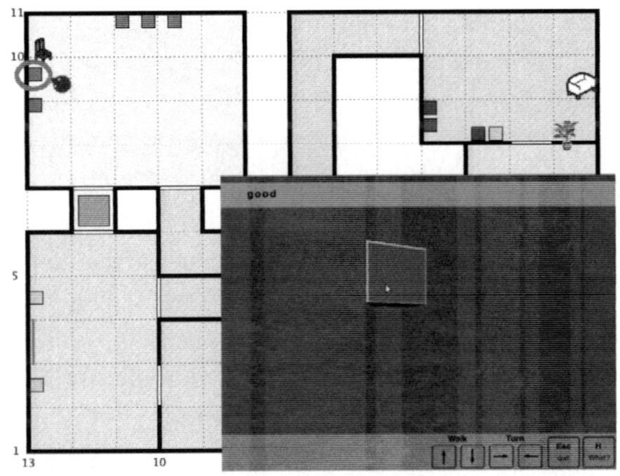

Figure 6: “good”

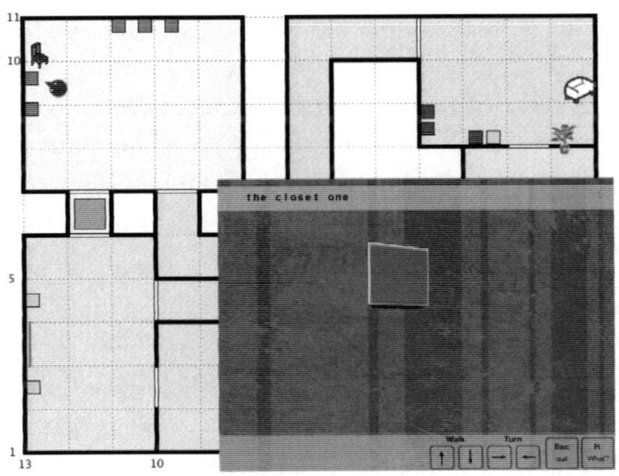

Figure 5: “the closet one”

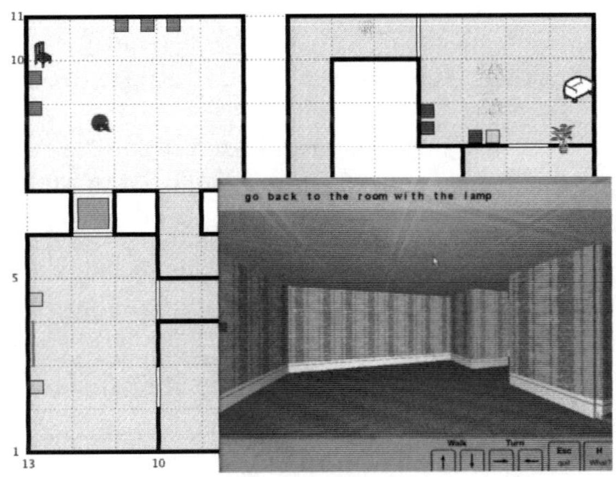

Figure 7: “go back to the room with the lamp”

(that is, when the user is about to manipulate this object). From the point of view of referring expression algorithms, the referring expression may not be optimal because it is over-specified (a pronoun would be preferred as in "click it"), Furthermore, the instruction contains a spelling error ('closet' instead of 'closest'). In spite of this non optimality, the instruction led our user to execute the intended reaction, namely pushing the button.

Right after the user clicks on the button (Figure 6), the system selects an utterance corresponding to the new task plan. The player position stayed the same so the only change in the plan is that the button no longer needs to be pushed. In this task state, DGs usually give acknowledgements and this is then what our selection algorithm selects: "good".

After receiving the acknowledgement, the user turns around and walks forward, and the next action in the plan is to leave the room (Figure 7). The system selects the utterance "go back to the room with the lamp" which refers to the previous interaction. Again, the system keeps no representation of the past actions of the user, but such utterances are the ones that are found at this stage of the task plan.

We show in Figure 3 all candidate utterances selected when exiting the room in Figure 7. That is, for our system purposes, all the utterances in the figure are paraphrases of the one that is actually uttered in Figure 7. As we explained in Section 2.2, the utterance with the longest reaction is selected first ("go back to the room with the lamp"), the second utterance with the longest reaction is selected second ("ok go back again to the room with the lamp"), and so on.

4 Portability to other virtual environments

The other systems that participated in the challenge do not need a corpus in a particular GIVE virtual world in order to generate instructions for any GIVE virtual world, while our system cannot do without such corpus. As a result these systems are more complex (e.g. they include domain independent algorithms for generation of referring expressions) and take a longer time to develop.

Our algorithm is independent of any particular virtual world. It can be ported to any other instruction giving task (where the DF has to perform a physical task) with the same effort than required to port it to a new GIVE world. This is not true for the other systems that participated in the GIVE-2.5 Challenge. The inputs of our algorithm are an off-the-shelf planner, a formal planning problem representation of the task and a human-human corpus collected on the very same task the system aims to instruct. It is important to notice that any virtual instructor, in order to give instructions that are both causally appropriate at the point of the task and relevant for the goal cannot do without such planning problem representation. Furthermore, it is quite a normal practice nowadays to collect a human-human corpus on the target task domain. It is reasonable, then, to assume that all the inputs of our algorithm are already available when developing the virtual instructor.

Another advantage of our approach is that virtual instructor can be generated by developers without any knowledge of generation of natural language techniques. Furthermore, the actual implementation of our algorithms is extremely simple as shown in Figures 1 and 2. This makes our approach promising for application areas such as games and simulation training.

5 Conclusions

In this paper we presented the system CL, which uses a novel algorithm for doing generation by corpus based selection from human-human corpora without manual annotation.

The algorithms we presented solely rely on the plan to define what constitutes the context of uttering. It may be interesting though to make use of other kinds of features. For instance, in order to integrate spatial orientation and differentiate "turn left" and "turn right", the orientation can be either added to the planning domain or treated as a context feature. While it may be possible to add orientation in the planning domain of GIVE, it is not straightforward to include the diversity of possible features in the same formalization, like modeling the global discourse history or corrections.

In sum, this paper presents the first existing algorithm for fully-automatically prototyping task-oriented virtual agents from corpora. The generated agents are able to effectively and naturally help a user complete a task in a virtual world by giving her/him instructions.

References

Luciana Benotti and Alexandre Denis. 2011. Giving instructions in virtual environments by corpus based selection. In *Proceedings of the SIGDIAL 2011 Conference*, pages 68–77, Portland, Oregon, June. Association for Computational Linguistics.

Sudeep Gandhe and David Traum. 2007a. Creating spoken dialogue characters from corpora without annotations. In *Proceedings of 8th Conference in the Annual Series of Interspeech Events*, pages 2201–2204, Belgium.

Sudeep Gandhe and David Traum. 2007b. First steps toward dialogue modelling from an un-annotated human-human corpus. In *IJCAI Workshop on Knowledge and Reasoning in Practical Dialogue Systems*, Hyderabad, India.

Andrew Gargett, Konstantina Garoufi, Alexander Koller, and Kristina Striegnitz. 2010. The GIVE-2 corpus of giving instructions in virtual environments. In *Proceedings of the 7th International Conference on Language Resources and Evaluation (LREC)*, Malta.

Jörg Hoffmann and Bernhard Nebel. 2001. The FF planning system: Fast plan generation through heuristic search. *JAIR*, 14:253–302.

Chih-Wei Hsu, Benjamin W. Wah, Ruoyun Huang, and Yixin Chen. 2006. New features in SGPlan for handling soft constraints and goal preferences in PDDL3.0. In *Proceedings of ICAPS*.

Patrick Kenny, Thomas D. Parsons, Jonathan Gratch, Anton Leuski, and Albert A. Rizzo. 2007. Virtual patients for clinical therapist skills training. In *Proceedings of the 7th international conference on Intelligent Virtual Agents*, IVA '07, pages 197–210, Berlin, Heidelberg. Springer-Verlag.

Anton Leuski, Ronakkumar Patel, David Traum, and Brandon Kennedy. 2006. Building effective question answering characters. In *Proceedings of the 7th SIGdial Workshop on Discourse and Dialogue*, SigDIAL '06, pages 18–27, Stroudsburg, PA, USA. Association for Computational Linguistics.

Verena Rieser and Oliver Lemon. 2010. Learning human multimodal dialogue strategies. *Natural Language Engineering*, 16:3–23.

Bayan Abu Shawar and Eric Atwell. 2003. Using dialogue corpora to retrain a chatbot system. In *Proceedings of the Corpus Linguistics Conference*, pages 681–690, United Kingdom.

Bayan Abu Shawar and Eric Atwell. 2005. Using corpora in machine-learning chatbot systems. volume 10, pages 489–516.

The Loria Instruction Generation System L in GIVE 2.5

Alexandre Denis
INRIA Grand-Est, LORIA-Nancy
54603 Villers les Nancy Cedex, France
denis@loria.fr

Abstract

This paper presents the instruction generation system L submitted by the LORIA and TALARIS team to the GIVE challenge 2011 (GIVE 2.5). The system L takes the same approach to instruction generation than its predecessor the system NA that participated to the GIVE challenge 2010 (GIVE 2), the two systems are almost the same except minor modifications. We present the strategy of these systems, namely a directive, low level, navigation strategy ("Go left") and a referring strategy based on focus and sub-contexts (Denis, 2010) ("Not this one! Look for the other one"). These strategies were successful, as shown by the GIVE 2 challenge, but also had some deficiences we tried to fix for GIVE 2.5. We explain these deficiencies and how we fixed them in GIVE 2.5. We eventually present the preliminary results that show that the system L, like the system NA, achieved a very good result both in objective and in subjective metrics.

1 Introduction

The GIVE challenge (Byron et al., 2009; Koller et al., 2010) is a framework that enables to evaluate instruction giving systems in a 3D setting. Players connect to the framework and are paired randomly with a system that will guide them through a 3D maze to retrieve a trophy. Each system must develop its own strategy to instruct the player to move (*navigation strategy*) and to push buttons to open doors or deactivate alarms (*referring strategy*). The systems must also make sure to monitor the player behaviour and provide him the necessary feedback to put him back on track if he performs wrong actions. From this framework we can draw two kinds of results, the objective results (task success rate, duration, number of words, etc.) and the subjective results (overall evaluation by the player, friendliness, etc.), see (Koller et al., 2010). These two metrics are both helpful to assess the quality of the systems.

We describe in this paper the system L, developed by the LORIA laboratory that participated to GIVE 2.5. The system is very close to the system NA that participated to the former challenge GIVE 2 (Denis et al., 2010). Thanks to GIVE 2 metrics, we were able to draw some interesting conclusions about the efficiency of the system and we tried to improve the existing flaws for GIVE 2.5. In section 2, we first present the previous system NA, and describe its navigation and referring strategies. We then show in section 3 what was wrong with the NA choices, in which situations it was not optimal, and how we circumvented the problems in the system L. We conclude in section 4 with the preliminary results and show that the performance of the system L is better than system NA.

2 NA System

In this section we describe the NA system that participated to the GIVE 2 challenge (Denis et al., 2010). We first present the whole instruction giving strategy and the main loop. Then we present the two kinds of instructions at hand, *move instructions* and *push instructions* and how these two instructions are both verbalized and monitored. We also describe three mandatory components, namely the replanning mechanism, the acknowledgement and warning system and the messaging manager.

2.1 Instruction giving

Like other systems, the NA system relies on the plan returned by the planner provided with the framework. However, it does not directly rely on this plan because of its too fine-grained granularity and builds an higher level plan. The general idea to build the high-level plan (or *instruction plan*) is to iterate through the plan returned by the planner (or *action plan*) and gather move actions. For instance,

Proceedings of the 13th European Workshop on Natural Language Generation (ENLG), pages 302–306,
Nancy, France, September 2011.

when a move action takes place in the same room than a push action, the move action and the push action are gathered into a single push instruction. Or when two move actions take place in the same room, they are gathered into a single move instruction. The plan is iterated and a rule-based matching algorithm rewrites the actions into instructions.

```
instr  (push(b3),
        actions:(move(r37,r42), push(b3)))
```

Figure 1: A push instruction gathering a move and a push action

Following the plan consists in providing the instructions at the right time, and monitoring the success or failure of actions. The main loop thus consists of two parts:

- pop a new expected instruction from the instruction plan when there is no current one
- evaluate the success or failure of the expected action and verbalize it

For each instruction, two functions have then to be specified:

- how to verbalize the instruction ?
- how to monitor the success or failure of the instruction ?

We now detail these two functions for both move and push instructions as they were implemented in NA.

2.2 Move instructions

2.2.1 Verbalizing move instructions

The verbalization of a move instruction consists basically in providing the direction to the goal region. If there is a door located at the goal region, the verbalization is *"Go through the doorway + direction"*, and if there is not, the verbalization is simply *"Go + direction"*. The direction is computed by taking the angle from the player position to the goal region, and we only consider four directions *"in front of you"*, *"to your right"*, *"to your left"* and *"behind you"*.

Nevertheless, there could be cases in which the goal region of the high level move instruction is not the most direct region. For instance, the room in figure 2 being shaped like an U, the player has to move to region $r3$, but because the moves to $r2$ and $r3$ are in the same room, they are aggregated in a single move instruction. But if we would directly utter the direction to the goal region $r3$, given the player orientation we would utter *"Go to your left"*. Instead, we need to consider not the goal region of the move instruction but the different regions composing the expected move. The trick is to take the region of the last low-level move action composing the move instruction which is theoretically visible (modulo any orientation) from his current position. The computation takes into account visibility by testing if an imaginary ray from the player position to the center of a tested region intersects a wall or not. Thus, in this case, because a ray from the player to $r3$ intersects a wall, it is not chosen for verbalizing while $r2$ is picked and the produced utterance is eventually *"Go behind you"* (this instruction has been changed in the system L to *"Turn around"*, see section 3).

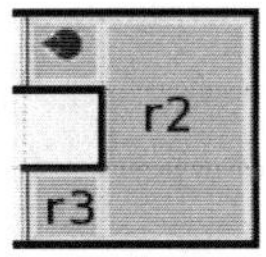

Figure 2: Example of U-turn

2.2.2 Monitoring move execution

The evaluation of the move instructions takes care of the lower action level. It simply tests if the player stands in a room for which there exists in the lower action level a region in the same room. In other words, a region is not on the way if it is located in a room where the player should not be. If this is the case, the failure of the move instruction is then raised (see replanning section 2.4). If the player reaches the goal region of the move instruction, then the success is raised and the current expectation is erased.

2.3 Push instructions

2.3.1 Verbalizing push instructions

Given the structure of the instruction plan, a push instruction can only take place in the room of the target button. The push instruction is actually provided in two steps: a *manipulate* instruction that makes explicit the push expectation *"Push a blue button"*, and a *designation* instruction that focuses on identifying the argument itself *"Not this one! Look for the other one!"*. The verbalization of the manipulate instruction does not make use of the focus, it only describes the object. On the other hand the verbalization of the designation instruction first updates the focus with the visible objects and then produces a referring expression.

This two steps referring process makes it easier to work with our reference setup. We tried applying Reference Domain Theory (RDT) for the reference to buttons (Salmon-Alt and Romary, 2000; Denis, 2010). The main idea of this theory is that the referring process can be defined incrementally, each referring expression relying on the previous referring expressions. Thus, after uttering a push expectation, a domain (or group) of objects is made salient, and shorter referring expressions can be uttered. For example, after uttering *"Push a blue button"*, the system can forget about other buttons and focus only the blue buttons. Expressions with one-anaphora are then possible, for instance *"Yeah! This one!"*. Spatial relations are only used when there is no property distinguishing the referent in the designation phase of the referring process. These spatial properties are computed, not from the player point of view, but to discriminate the referent in the domain, that is as opposed to other similar objects. For instance, we could produce expressions such as *"Yeah! The blue button on the right!"*. Vertical and horizontal orderings are produced, but only three positions for each of them are produced left/middle/right and top/middle/bottom. We also found it important to have negative designation instructions such as *"Not this one"* when there are focused buttons in the current domain that are not the expected buttons. Thanks to the referring model, we just have to generate *"Not"* followed by the RE designating the unwanted focus. More details about the use of Reference Domain Theory in the GIVE challenge can be found in (Denis, 2010).

2.3.2 Monitoring push execution

The evaluation of the success of a push expectation is straightforward: if the expected button is pushed it is successful, and the push expectation is erased such that the main loop can pick the next instruction, if a wrong button is pushed or if the region the player is standing in is not on the way (see section 2.2.2) then the designation process fails.

2.4 Replanning

It is often the case that the expected instructions are not executed. A simple way to handle wrong actions would be to relaunch the planning process, and restart the whole loop on a new instruction plan. However, we need to take into account that the player may move all the time and as such could trigger several times the planning process, for instance by moving in several wrong regions, making then the system quite clumsy. To avoid this behavior, we simply consider a *wait* expectation which is dynamically raised in the case of move or push expectation failure. As other expectations, the two functions, verbalize and evaluate have to be specified. A wait expectation is simply verbalized by *"no no wait"*, and its success is reached when the player position is not changing. Only when the wait expectation is met, the planning process is triggered again, thus avoiding multiple replanning triggers.

2.5 Acknowledging and warning

Acknowledging the behavior of the player is extremely important. Several kinds of acknowledgments are considered throughout the instruction giving process. Each time an action expectation is satisfied a *positive* acknowledgement is uttered such as *"great!"*, or *"perfect!"*, that is when the player reaches an expected region or pushes the expected button. We also generate acknowledgements in the case of referring even if the identification expectation is not represented explicitly as an action. When the player sees the expected button, we add *"yeah!"* to the generated referring expression. This acknowledgement does not correspond to the success itself of the action, but just warns the player that what he is doing is making him closer to the success. *Negative* acknowlegdments are also uttered, when there is an expectation failure ("no no wait") or when there is a visible button that could be the referent ("not this one").

However it is as necessary to warn the player when something went wrong as warning him that something *could* go wrong. Indeed, if the player steps on an alarm the game is lost. It is therefore quite important to warn the player about alarms. The NA system first provides a warning at the beginning of the game by explaining that there are red tiles on the floor and that stepping on them entails losing the game. But it also embeds an alarm monitor. If at any time, the player is close to an alarm, the system produces an utterance *"Warning! There is an alarm around!"*. In order to avoid looping these messages when the player passes by alarms, a timer forbids uttering several alarm warnings. But if the timer goes off, new alarm warnings could be potentially produced.

2.6 Messaging

Message management in a real-time system is a critical task that has to take into account two factors: the moment when an instruction is uttered and the time the instruction stays on screen. NA relies on a messaging system in which we distinguish two kinds of messages, the *mandatory* messages and the *cancellable* messages. Mandatory messages are so important for the interaction that if they are not received the interaction can break down. For instance, the manipulate instructions (e.g. *"Push a blue button"*) are crucial for the rest of the referring process. In the case they are not received, the player does not know which kind of button he has to press. Cancellable messages are messages which could be replaced in the continuous verbalization. For instance, the designation instructions (e.g. *"Yeah! This one!"*) or the direction instructions (e.g. *"Go straight"*) are continuously provided, each instruction overriding the previous one. We cannot force the cancellable messages to be displayed a given amount of time on the screen because of the fast update of the environment. Both types of messages are then necessary:

- if we would have only mandatory messages, we would risk to utter instructions at the wrong moment because of the delay they would stay on screen.
- and if we would have only cancellable messages, we would risk to miss critical information because they can be replaced too fast by next instructions.

The system then maintains a message queue in an independent thread called the message manager. Each message, either mandatory or cancellable, is associated to the duration it has or can stay on screen. The manager continuously takes the first message in the queue, displays it and waits for the given duration, then it displays the next message and so on. Before a new message is added to the queue, the message manager removes all pending cancellable messages while keeping mandatory messages. It then adds the message, and if the current displayed instruction is cancellable it stops the waiting.

3 Improvements in system L

We present in this section some of the problems of system NA and how we fixed them for GIVE 2.5 in system L.

3.1 Navigation strategy

While the NA navigation strategy was quite effective, and in general praised by the subjective assessment, it required some modifications. Some players were confused with the "doorway" verbalization either because they were not native speakers and did not know the word, or because they did not consider it as a natural wording. Indeed, because there was no visible door and only openings in walls, this verbalization was confusing. In system L, it simply has been removed and a shorter instruction "Go + direction" has been preferred. Moreover, thanks to the free-text feedback, we found out that the verbalization "Go behind you" of NA was clearly inappropriate, several players complaining about its non-naturalness and we replaced it by a simpler "Turn around" in system L.

3.1.1 Referring strategy

The changes in navigation strategy were purely cosmetic. On the contrary, despite its efficiency, the NA referring strategy had some serious flaws and thus required deeper modifications. In NA we separated the referring process into two steps that could make use of different discrimination features, the first step for instance did not make use of focus or spatial relationship, the second step used focus and spatial relationship but only to disambiguate between visible buttons. However this strategy was failing in at least two cases:

- the first descriptive step was not working well if the player was too close to a button. Because in most cases an indefinite referring expression was uttered e.g. "Push a blue button", it raised the presupposition that *any button was appropriate*, and if the player was too close to a matching button, he would directly press it, even if it was the wrong one.
- the second step mostly based on focus was not working well in rooms where *a lot of similar buttons were present.* The player would receive first "Push a blue button" and would continuously receive instructions like "Not this one! Look for another one!". He would then have to turn around, looking at each blue button until he would find the right one.

These two cases have been found out either by looking at the raw datas, situations where wrong buttons are pushed, or duration between the instruction and the actual push, or by looking at the subjective assessments of the players.

The common solution to these problems was to introduce player-relative spatial discrimination e.g. "to *your* left", as was done by another system that participated in GIVE 2, the NM system, see (Denis et al., 2010). For system L we also relaxed the difference between the two referring steps and both use a combination of focus, description and relative direction. In the first step, to address the indefinite presupposition problem, we forbid the simple utterance like "Push a blue button" but included either focus-based discrimination like "Push a blue button but not this one", or player-relative spatial discrimination like "Push a blue button, it is on your left".

Unfortunately time prevented us to model correctly the pronoun anaphora in the RDT framework (Denis, 2010) and it has been hardcoded. The player-relative discrimination also helped a lot to solve the second issue, instead of looking at each button, the player was directed immediately to the intended referent.

4 Results and conclusion

The preliminary results of the GIVE 2.5 challenge are consistent with the results of the GIVE 2 challenge (Koller et al., 2010). While the system NA achieved 47% average task success in GIVE 2, the preliminary results show that the system L achieves 67.2% in GIVE 2.5, and like last year it is in the top three systems. It is also the fastest system while using the smallest number of words to achieve task success. On the subjective level, the system has been positively evaluated and is in the first group for almost all metrics. The weakest point is shown by the *task progress feedback* metric. The system receives its lowest mark for the evaluation item "The system gave me useful feedback about my progress". This result is normal, and in line with the previous challenge, since the system does not provide any information about the task at hand but only gives move and push instructions. Other systems that participated to GIVE 2.5, for instance system C, are much more talkative (hence taking more time) and describe in details the task and the current progress like the remaining number of buttons. However, if giving task feedback is a necessary feature, we could question how much these approaches are task independent and if we could draw some general principles underlying the verbalization of task progress.

References

Donna Byron, Alexander Koller, Kristina Striegnitz, Justine Cassell, Robert Dale, Johanna Moore, and Jon Oberlander. 2009. Report on the First NLG Challenge on Generating Instructions in Virtual Environments (GIVE). In *Proceedings of the 12th European Workshop on Natural Language Generation (ENLG 2009)*, pages 165–173, Athens, Greece, March. Association for Computational Linguistics.

Alexandre Denis, Marilisa Amoia, Luciana Benotti, Laura Perez-Beltrachini, Claire Gardent, and Tarik Osswald. 2010. The GIVE-2 Nancy Generation Systems NA and NM. Technical report, INRIA Grand-Est/LORIA.

Alexandre Denis. 2010. Generating Referring Expressions with Reference Domain Theory. In *Proceedings of the 6th International Natural Language Generation Conference - INLG 2010*, Dublin Ireland.

Alexander Koller, Kristina Striegnitz, Andrew Gargett, Donna Byron, Justine Cassell, Robert Dale, Johanna Moore, and Jon Oberlander. 2010. Report on the second NLG challenge on generating instructions in virtual environments (GIVE-2). In *Proceedings of the International Natural Language Generation Conference (INLG)*, Dublin.

Susanne Salmon-Alt and Laurent Romary. 2000. Generating referring expressions in multimodal contexts. In *Workshop on Coherence in Generated Multimedia - INLG 2000*, Mitzpe Ramon, Israel.

The Potsdam NLG systems at the GIVE-2.5 Challenge

Konstantina Garoufi and **Alexander Koller**
Area of Excellence "Cognitive Sciences"
University of Potsdam, Germany
{garoufi, akoller}@uni-potsdam.de

Abstract

We present the Potsdam natural language generation systems P1 and P2 of the GIVE-2.5 Challenge. The systems implement two different referring expression generation models from Garoufi and Koller (2011) while behaving identically in all other respects. In particular, P1 combines symbolic and corpus-based methods for the generation of successful referring expressions, while P2 is based on a purely symbolic model which serves as a qualified baseline for comparison. We describe how the systems operated in the challenge and discuss the results, which indicate that P1 outperforms P2 in terms of several measures of referring expression success.

1 Introduction

The Challenge on Generating Instructions in Virtual Environments (GIVE; Koller et al. (2010)) is an evaluation effort for natural language generation (NLG) systems, which focuses on real-time generation of situated language. In this shared task, the role of the NLG system is to guide a human instruction follower (IF) through a 3D virtual world with the goal of completing a treasure-hunting task. As an internet-based evaluation, GIVE has been successful in attracting both a large number of volunteers for the IF role and a high level of interest from the research community.

In this paper, we report on our participation in the third installment of GIVE (GIVE-2.5; Striegnitz et al. (2011)). Although most of the work on the generation of referring expressions (REs) to date has focused either on logical properties of REs, such as uniqueness and minimality, or on their degree of similarity to human-produced expressions (see Krahmer and van Deemter (To appear) for a comprehensive survey), we believe that it would be desirable to optimize a system directly for usefulness. We therefore approach the RE generation task with a model that aims at computing the unique RE which is fastest for the hearer to resolve (Garoufi and Koller, 2011). The purpose of the Potsdam NLG systems P1 and P2 at the challenge was to assess with a task-based evaluation to what extent the model actually manages to do so.

While we cannot present the RE generation modules in detail here (see Garoufi and Koller (2011) for that), note that P1 implements the hybrid model mSCRISP of Garoufi and Koller, which extends the planning-based approach to sentence generation (Koller and Stone, 2007) with a statistical model of RE success. This model was learnt from a corpus of human instruction giving sessions in the GIVE domain (Gargett et al., 2010), in which every RE was annotated with a measure of how easy it has been for the hearer to resolve. System P1 is therefore designed to optimize the REs it generates for understandability. On the other hand, system P2 is an implementation of the baseline model EqualCosts of Garoufi and Koller. This is a purely symbolic model that always computes a correct and unique RE, but does so without any empirical guidance about expected understandability. System P2 behaves in the exact same way as P1 in all respects, with the exception of the RE generation module. It therefore serves as a qualified baseline against which we can

Proceedings of the 13th European Workshop on Natural Language Generation (ENLG), pages 307–311,
Nancy, France, September 2011.

compare the performance of the mSCRISP model.

Plan of the paper. We describe the two systems P1 and P2 in Section 2. As the RE generation modules have been presented in full detail in Garoufi and Koller (2011), we mostly focus on the other aspects of the systems' behavior here. We then comment on the evaluation results in Section 3 and conclude in Section 4.

2 The systems P1 and P2

The two systems operate on the same codebase, differing only in their RE generation modules. In particular, they follow identical strategies for determining their communicative goals, switching between navigation and reference, as well as issuing warnings and other feedback.

2.1 Determining the communicative goals

The GIVE framework provides an NLG system with a plan of what the IF must do in order to complete the task by picking up a trophy. This plan is a symbolic sequence of mixed moves and object manipulation actions such as move(reg_1, reg_2), manipulate(b_1, *off*, on, reg_2), take–t$_1$(reg_3). Our systems parse the plan in order to identify objects of interest and determine the nature of the communicative goals related to these: If a move action which involves going through a doorway from one room to another is encountered in the plan, then that doorway is registered as a target with the corresponding communicative goal that the IF should go through it. If, on the other hand, a manipulate or take action is encountered, then the patient of this action is registered as a target (be it a button to push or a trophy to take), while, accordingly, the manipulation of that target becomes a communicative goal for the systems to pursue.

2.2 Navigation and reference

Once the next target and the communicative goal have been determined, the systems go on to check whether a certain condition for reference is met; in particular, whether the target is currently in the IF's field of view. This precondition reflects empirical observations that human instruction givers typically manipulate the non-linguistic context of scenes in convenient ways (e.g. by making the referent visually salient) before referring to objects in these

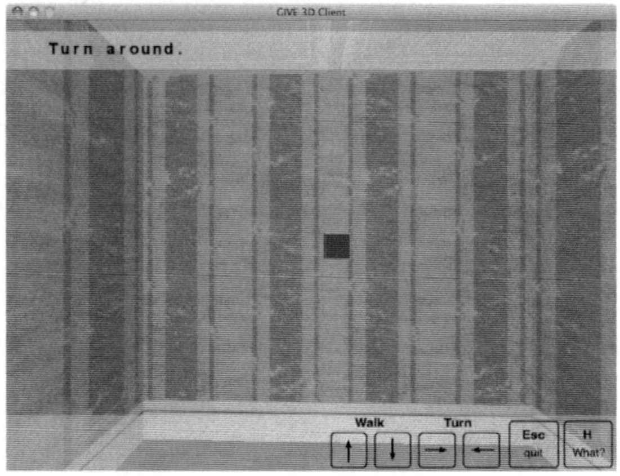

Figure 1: Example of a navigation instruction aiming at making the next target visible.

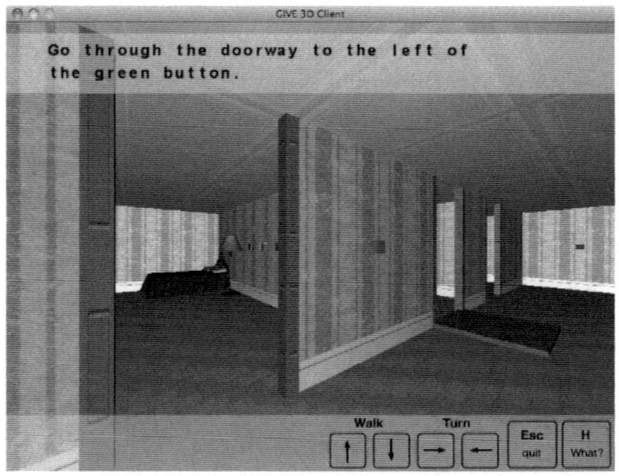

Figure 2: Example of a navigation instruction urging the IF to go through a doorway that they already see.

scenes (Stoia et al., 2006; Schütte et al., 2010). If the precondition is not fulfilled, then the systems resort to low-level navigation instructions such as "Turn left" or "Go straight" in order to change the IF's location to one that allows them to see the target (Figure 1). Because doorways are also perceived as targets, it is guaranteed that the next target is always located in the same room as the IF. As a result, this process usually involves no more than a few turns.

Once the target has become visible, the systems switch to referring expression generation mode so as to issue an instruction that describes the target and satisfies the communicative goal. Note that although the evaluation is concerned with REs to button targets only, we apply the same RE generation models to the description of all objects, including doorways and the trophy. Figure 2 shows an example of a navigation instruction that urges the IF to go through a visible doorway, while Figure 3 presents an example of an RE for a button target issued by system P1. In this scene, system P2 would generate the different RE "the right one to the right of the green button". The systems issue all these kinds of instructions at regular intervals repeatedly, until they detect that the IF has reacted. This is to make sure that the IF knows at all times what they are expected to do.

2.3 Execution monitoring

In real-time instruction giving it is crucial for a system to be able to monitor whether the IF actually executes the given instructions, assess how well they progress on the task, and finally react to such observations with appropriate feedback. Our systems issue three main types of such feedback:

- **Positive feedback.** The IF receives an affirmation (e.g. "Good job!", "Excellent!") as soon as they accommodate the given communicative goal by executing the associated action. These situations are important because apart from moving the task forward they establish that a system's RE has been resolved by the IF correctly.

- **Negative feedback.** Conversely, if the IF performs a different action than the one expected, e.g. by pushing the wrong button or going into the wrong room, they are immediately told so (Figure 4). This serves not only as feedback for the IF but also as an opportunity for the systems to reevaluate the situation and make the necessary computations for figuring out which communicative goal should come next.

- **Warnings.** Finally, certain regions in the GIVE worlds are equipped with alarms so that stepping on them would cause the IF to lose the game. If the systems detect that the IF has approached an activated alarm closely enough that this outcome becomes likely, they interrupt all their other functions and issue a brief warning about the danger (e.g., "Beware of the alarm on the floor!").

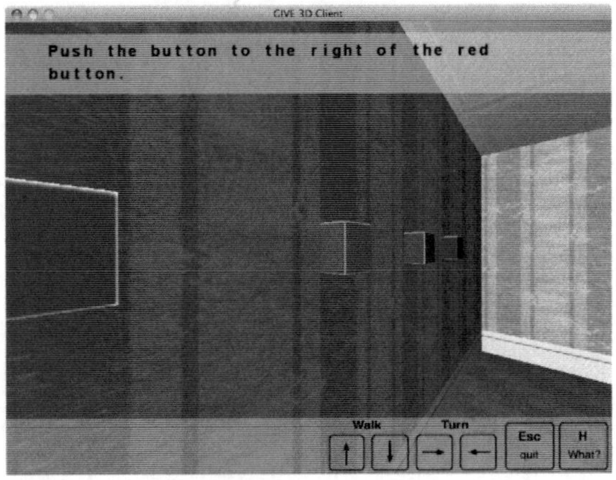

Figure 3: Example of an expression referring to a button target, as generated by P1.

2.4 Example instruction-giving session

Example (1) below presents a simplified excerpt from an interaction between system P1 and an IF, in which several of the instruction types listed above can be found.

(1) P1: *Turn left.*
IF: (turns left until the target becomes visible)
P1: *Push the yellow button.*
IF: (starts moving towards the button)
P1: *Push the button.*
IF: (pushes the button)
P1: *Good!*
P1: *Now turn right.*
IF: (turns right until the target becomes visible)
P1: *Go through the doorway.*
IF: (goes through the doorway)
P1: *Excellent!*
P1: *Turn right.*
IF: (starts turning right)
P1: *Go straight.*
IF: (starts moving straight ahead)
P1: *Don't step on the alarm!*
P1: *Go straight.*
IF: (continues moving ahead)
P1: *Push the green one in front of you.*

One meaningful detail is that, as lines 3–5 reveal, the REs that the system generates for a given target may change as the context of the scene changes. This particularly interesting aspect of the interaction follows from the fact that the system generates its REs newly for every new context, and thus decides newly which

Figure 4: Example of execution monitoring and negative feedback.

attributes to include in it and which not. Since the attribute selection process of P1 relies on the context features of the scene in a much more substantial way than that of P2, which simply uses the visual context in order to ensure that the RE is distinguishing in the domain, this phenomenon is observed in P1 more frequently than in P2. Indeed, P1 may change its decision of which attributes to include in an RE not because, say, a potential distractor has come into sight, but just because e.g. the IF has moved closer to the target, or even because the system has already attempted to refer to it in a particular way several times before without success.

3 Results

Although none of the objective and subjective evaluation measures of the challenge establish any significant differences between the two systems based on the current snapshot of the results, P1 does achieve better scores than P2 on most measures of RE success.

3.1 RE success

Areas in which P1 outperforms P2 include the objective measures of task success, number of actions executed by the IF (indicating incorrect resolution of REs), and game duration. But also in terms of subjective measures, as extracted by the IFs' responses to a post-task questionnaire, P1 scores higher than P2 for the most part: It is perceived as generating better instructions overall ("Overall, the system gave me good instructions"), better REs to buttons ("I could easily identify the buttons the system described to me"), and clearer, more trustworthy instructions ("I had to re-read instructions to understand what I had to do", "I felt I could trust the system's instructions"; see Striegnitz et al. (2011) for details).

More importantly, we compared the systems with respect to RE resolution success and successfulness, which is the exact measure of RE understandability that P1 was optimized for. This comparison does establish a significant difference between the two, indicating that P1 generates REs that are faster resolvable by the IFs after effects of RE rephrasing as described in Subsection 2.4 have been factored out (see Garoufi and Koller (2011) for details).

3.2 Error analysis

Finally, looking into possible causes of failure for the systems' REs, we find that the most apparent problem involves generating expressions which, though not semantically invalid, are of disputable linguistic acceptability. Typical instances of such REs are "the button to the left of the right button", "the button below the upper button" and variants of these. These cases arise due to the fact that we did not constraint the systems' grammar so as to disallow such constructions, while the systems often chose attributes for which this particular type of realization was possible.

It turns out that P2 was more prone to this type of REs than P1, which at first glance seems like a probable reason for the lower RE success rates of the system. However, examining the portion of REs of each system that did not fall into this category, we found that P1 still generated significantly more successful REs after factoring out the effects of rephrasing. It would be interesting for future work to compare the systems' REs in a more controlled way, so that their attribute selection and realization aspects can be evaluated in separation.

4 Conclusion

The systems P1 and P2 at the GIVE-2.5 Challenge implemented a novel model of RE generation and a qualified baseline from Garoufi and Koller (2011), respectively. Participating in the challenge allowed us to conduct a task-based evaluation of the model, collect data for both objective and subjective measures, and compare it against the baseline. The results indicate that the model outperforms the baseline with respect to the measure of RE understandability that it was optimized for.

Acknowledgments

Thanks to Kristina Striegnitz for clarifying important aspects of the evaluation methodology, and to all 148 internet users who went on a virtual treasure hunt to make this evaluation possible.

References

Andrew Gargett, Konstantina Garoufi, Alexander Koller, and Kristina Striegnitz. 2010. The GIVE-2 Corpus of Giving Instructions in Virtual Environments. In *Proceedings of the 7th Conference on International Language Resources and Evaluation*, Valletta, Malta.

Konstantina Garoufi and Alexander Koller. 2011. Combining symbolic and corpus-based approaches for the generation of successful referring expressions. In *Proceedings of the 13th European Workshop on Natural Language Generation*, Nancy, France.

Alexander Koller and Matthew Stone. 2007. Sentence generation as planning. In *Proceedings of the 45th Annual Meeting of the Association of Computational Linguistics*, Prague, Czech Republic.

Alexander Koller, Kristina Striegnitz, Donna Byron, Justine Cassell, Robert Dale, Johanna Moore, and Jon Oberlander. 2010. The First Challenge on Generating Instructions in Virtual Environments. In M. Theune and E. Krahmer, editors, *Empirical Methods in Natural Language Generation*, volume 5790 of *LNCS*, pages 337–361.

Emiel Krahmer and Kees van Deemter. To appear. Computational generation of referring expressions: A survey. *Computational Liguistics*.

Niels Schütte, John Kelleher, and Brian Mac Namee. 2010. Visual salience and reference resolution in situated dialogues: A corpus-based evaluation. In *Proceedings of the AAAI 2010 Fall Symposium on Dialog with Robots*, Arlington, VA.

Laura Stoia, Donna K. Byron, Darla M. Shockley, and Eric Fosler-Lussier. 2006. Sentence planning for realtime navigational instructions. In *Proceedings of the Human Language Technology Conference of the NAACL*, New York City, NY.

Kristina Striegnitz, Alexandre Denis, Andrew Gargett, Konstantina Garoufi, Alexander Koller, and Mariet Theune. 2011. Report on the Second Second NLG Challenge on Generating Instructions in Virtual Environments (GIVE-2.5). In *Proceedings of the 13th European Workshop on Natural Language Generation*, Nancy, France.

The Thumbs Up! Twente system for GIVE 2.5

Saskia Akkersdijk, Marin Langenbach, Frieder Loch, Mariët Theune
Human Media Interaction
University of Twente
P.O. Box 217, 7500 AE, Enschede, The Netherlands
{s.m.akkersdijk|m.langenbach|f.loch}@student.utwente.nl, m.theune@utwente.nl

Abstract

This paper describes the Thumbs Up! Twente system, a natural language generation system designed for the GIVE 2.5 Challenge. The purpose of the system is to guide a user through a virtual 3D environment by generating instructions in real-time. Our system focuses on motivating the user to keep him playing the game and trying to find the trophy.

1 Introduction

This report describes a natural language generation system called **Thumbs Up! Twente** (TU!T). It was developed for the Generating Instructions in Virtual Environments (GIVE) 2.5 Challenge,[1] which involves generating instructions that guide users to press coloured buttons and walk around the different rooms of a 3D-world. The goal is to find a trophy, which is located in a safe that can be opened by pressing a particular sequence of buttons.

Our system focuses on motivating the users through feedback to keep them playing. Before addressing this, we first describe other important aspects such as planning and the generation of instructions and referring expressions. We end with a presentation and discussion of evaluation results.

2 Planning

The basis for instruction generation in GIVE is a plan: a sequence of actions, created by a planner that was provided by the GIVE organisation. Each room in the 3D-world is divided into regions, and the initial plan consists of separate move actions for each region; see Figure 1 (left). TU!T aggregates these separate steps to enable the generation of high-level navigation instructions. This has several advantages (Braunias et al., 2010; McCoy et al., 2010):

- The users are free to choose their own way towards the instruction target, making the task more interesting.
- Fewer instructions are needed, leaving the user more time to read and understand the instructions, and (in the case of TU!T) leaving more room for motivational feedback.

Steps between regions in the same room are aggregated by TU!T as shown in Figure 1 (right). During aggregation it is checked whether the target region is still visible from the user's position. If this is not the case, plan steps are aggregated until the last visible region (see Figure 2).

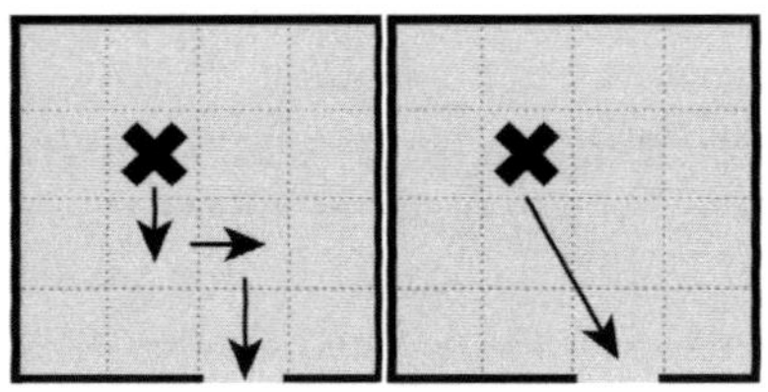

Figure 1: Aggregation of plan steps based on rooms.

3 Instruction Generation

When turning plan steps into verbal instructions, we tried to keep the instructions short and simply structured, because overly long instructions turned out

[1]http://www.give-challenge.org/research

Proceedings of the 13th European Workshop on Natural Language Generation (ENLG), pages 312–317,
Nancy, France, September 2011.

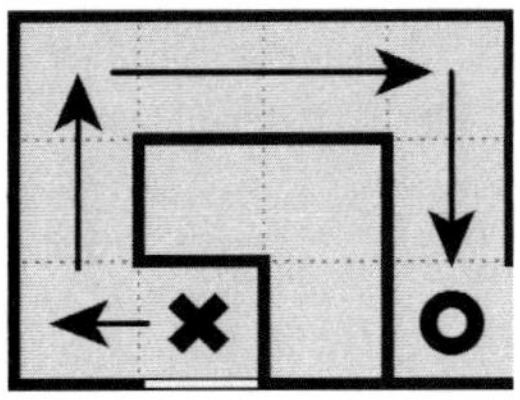

Figure 2: Aggregation of plan steps based on visibility of the target region.

to be a source of problems for systems from earlier challenges. According to the GIVE 2 report (Koller et al., 2010), the systems with the highest task success rate were those that produced the shortest instructions. We do not vary the wording of the instructions, because this might increase the difficulty in following and reading them quickly.

TU!T distinguishes three main instruction types (besides the final instruction to take the trophy):

- **Instructions to press a button** consist of the word *Press* followed by a reference to the target button, as described in Section 4.1.
- **Instructions to move to another room** refer to the door that the user needs to move through, as described in Section 4.2. This is the kind of situation shown in Figure 1.
- **Instructions to move to a location in the current room** are given in the kind of situation from Figure 2. They start with *Move around the corner,* since in most (but not all) cases the target region is, indeed, located around a corner. The direction in which the target region is located is added to form instructions such as *Move around the corner to your left.*

Note that TU!T also generates references to doors and buttons that are not currently visible to the user. If the target is behind the user, an instruction is added on how the user should turn to see it, e.g., *Press the blue button behind you. Turn around and go left.* If the instruction length does not exceed a certain threshold, explicit information about the visibility of the target is included in the instruction.

At fixed intervals, and after each button press, the system checks whether the user is still following the plan. If so, the generation of the next instruction is triggered. If the user has moved to the wrong room, TU!T informs the user of this. The user is given 6 seconds to move to the correct room without new instructions. If after this 'patience period' (Schütte and Dethlefs, 2010) the user has not corrected the mistake, a new plan is created starting from the user's current location. This is also done after the user has pressed a wrong button.

TU!T incorporates a mechanism to generate a new version of the current instruction when the user moves closer to the target. This may be helpful because at a shorter distance, referring expressions tend to become more specific. If the user is still at some distance the instruction may be fairly general, for instance *Press the blue button to your left* allowing the user to globally locate the button. When the instruction is repeated at a shorter distance it will generate a unique description, for instance *Press the left button in the middle row*, making it possible to successfully identify the target button. An updated version of the current instruction is also generated when the user presses "h" to call the *Help* function.

4 Referring Expression Generation

Referring expression generation (REG) in the GIVE worlds mainly involves referring to buttons and doors. We considered using the graph-based algorithm for this (Krahmer et al., 2003), but it turned out to be too slow for real-time, on-the-fly generation of expressions as required in GIVE. So we created our own referring expression generator, incorporating lessons learned from the GIVE 2 systems.

4.1 Referring to Buttons

TU!T uses two different methods for referring to buttons, *SimpleREG* and *GridREG*. Both methods always include the button's colour in the description, even when not strictly necessary for identification. This is done to prevent any possible confusion, and because humans tend to mention redundant properties as well (Dale and Reiter, 1995).

SimpleREG looks for landmarks around the button. We never include more than one landmark, otherwise the expressions might get too long and potentially confusing (Schütte and Dethlefs, 2010). Landmarks are selected by searching for the object closest to the target object, but some candidates are discarded. Open doors are never used, and buttons are only used as landmarks if there cannot be any confusion as to which button is meant. See Figure 3 for an example, where the lamp was chosen as the best landmark. We also include information about the button's location relative to the user, to form instructions such as *Press the green button on your right and to the right of the lamp.*

Figure 3: Referring to a button using a landmark.

GridREG creates a grid from all buttons, and counts them from left to right and from top to bottom. If there are, for example, nine buttons in a 3x3 grid the algorithm generates instructions such as *Press the blue button, it is the top left one.* If there is only one row of buttons, it generates references such as *Press the blue button, it is the second one from the left.* This approach is similar to that of Braunias et al. (2010) for GIVE 2.

The criterion for using SimpleREG or GridREG is the number of visible buttons with the same colour as the target button. As the name suggests, SimpleREG is used in relatively simple cases, when the target button is visible and maximally one other button of the same colour. SimpleREG is also used if the target button is not visible. In that case, TU!T generates instructions such as *Press the yellow button on your left. You cannot see it.* If there is a visible landmark, it is added to the description. GridREG is used when one or more buttons are visible with the same colour as the target button.

If there is only one other visible button with the same colour as the target button (as in Figure 3), one of the two methods is randomly selected, because they are equally suitable. TU!T records which method was used for the initial description, so that if the user presses "h", the other method can be used. This way the *Help* function can really clarify the situation if the user is confused, instead of only repeating the exact same instruction.

4.2 Referring to Doors

Referring to doors in the world is relatively simple, because their only distinguishing property is their location. TU!T never uses landmarks in connection to doors. If only the target door is visible, TU!T simply always says *Move through the door.* If the target door is not visible, its position relative to the user is mentioned, leading to instructions such as *Move through the door behind you.* If more than one door is visible, GridREG is used in a similar way as for buttons. But for door references an extra feature was added: TU!T searches for a hallway by looking at the coordinates of all visible doors in the user's current room, and checking if they are aligned in two rows. In this case the doors on each side are counted, to create instructions such as *Move through the second door on your right.*

We only include doors in the same room as the target door in the context set. If more doors are visible through an open door, these are not taken into account. This should be less confusing for the users, who probably assume they need to use a door inside the current room. We only consider open doors, because users never have to go through closed doors.

5 Motivation through Feedback

Keeping the user motivated is one of the main goals of our system. A motivated user is less likely to give up, which should reduce the number of canceled games and increase the number of successful games. Also, the overall experience of the user will be more positive. The way we make our system motivating is by giving two types of feedback.

Reflective feedback reports on the user's progress, triggered by a timer. The system randomly chooses a fitting feedback sentence, based on the number of remaining buttons to be pressed.[2] Examples are *You are in the second half of this game* and *Almost there!* The second type of reflective feedback is positive feedback after a correct action, which is known to enhance motivation (Harackiewicz, 1979; Vallerand and Reid, 1988). Examples are sentences such as *Well done!* and *Good job!* Finally, reflective feedback is given when a user enters the wrong room, for example *That's not the correct way*.

Anticipating feedback is feedback on what is visible for the user, based on what we think the user wants or needs to know. Confirmation that the user is looking at the correct object can be really useful and can make the user more confident. Telling the user that he/she is looking at the wrong object prevents wrong button presses, and makes navigation through the world more efficient.

When giving anticipating feedback on visible buttons we distinguish five situations:

- **Only the target button is visible:** in this case the system confirms that this is the correct button, for example by saying *Yes, that one.*
- **Only buttons of the wrong colour are visible:** in this case the system reminds the user that he/she needs a button with another colour, for example by saying *No, not this button. It should be blue* (Figure 4A).
- **Only wrong buttons, but of the correct colour are visible:** here, the system tells the user that another button is needed, for example by saying *This is the wrong button* (Figure 4B).
- **The target button is visible, as well as one or more other buttons, all of the wrong colour:** here, the system points out the target button, for example by saying *The blue one is the correct button* (Figure 4C).
- **The target button is visible, as well as one or more other buttons of the same colour:** in this case we give no feedback because it might be confusing (Figure 4D). Also, as the user comes closer, button visibility changes and one of the other situations will apply.

[2] Unlike instruction messages, feedback messages have variants with different wording.

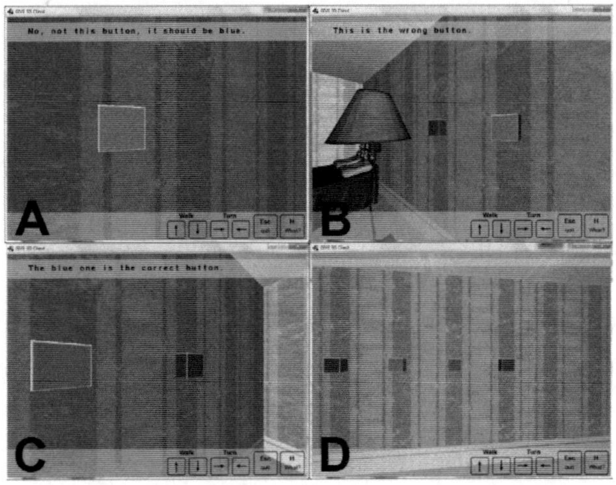

Figure 4: Four anticipating feedback situations.

For anticipating feedback on visible doors we distinguish three situations.

- **Only the target door is visible:** the system gives feedback that it is the correct door, for example by saying *Yes, that doorway*.
- **Another door than the target is visible:** the system tells the user that this is not the correct door, for example by saying *This is the wrong doorway*.
- **The target door and one or more other doors are visible:** in this case we give no feedback, for the same reasons as with buttons.

In addition to feedback on buttons and doors, TU!T also issues warnings when the user approaches an alarm tile. In GIVE 2, the lack of such warnings was identified as a major source of problems by McCoy et al. (2010) and Roth et al. (2010). To prevent irritation, TU!T keeps intervals of at least six seconds between warnings.

6 MessageQueue

The message queue sorts the messages to be displayed in order of importance. For example, navigational messages are always important, while progress feedback is less important. It also keeps track of how long a message should be displayed, which depends on the length of the message. As long as the queue is not empty, the first (most important) message is taken from the queue and displayed for the given duration.

It can be that while a message is displayed, a more important message is created. Then the current message is stopped and overwritten by the new message, to ensure that the displayed message accurately reflects the current situation. For example, if the user moves toward the target button while the system is giving feedback on a wrong button that was in view, the old feedback is replaced by a new message.

After each button press the message queue is emptied, to prevent it from becoming too full with old messages that may be no longer applicable.

7 Evaluation

GIVE 2.5 used three evaluation worlds, of which World 1 was the simplest. In World 2, the buttons were positioned in grids of different shapes, and World 3 had a large space with many doors, posing a challenge for direction giving. Table 1 shows the TU!T results for the three worlds, based on 22 games in World 1, 16 games in World 2 and 9 games in World 3, played between 1 July - 22 August 2011 in the online GIVE evaluation experiment. The subjective ratings indicate the level of agreement with statements such as "The system's instructions were visible long enough for me to read them" and "The system immediately offered help when I was in trouble." For readability, we reversed the polarity of ratings for negative statements.

TU!T performed relatively well in World 1, but it had problems with the button descriptions in World 2, and its performance in World 3 was bad overall. The evaluation participants did find the system friendly and appreciated its feedback, in particular in Worlds 1 and 2.

Measure	**World 1**	**World 2**	**World 3**
Successful games	68.2%	56.3%	22,2%
Lost games	13.6%	6.0%	44.4%
Cancelled games	18.2%	37.5%	33.3%
Q1: Overall quality	20.3	-6.0	-37.5
Q2: Directions	0.9	-31.9	-24.2
Q3: Button description	45.1	-17.9	19.9
Q4: Instruction clarity	9.4	-1.9	-3.4
Q5: Display duration	21.9	31.3	20.4
Q6: Instruction timing	10.4	3.4	-13.6
Q7: Help immediacy	18.6	-4.1	-27.8
Q8: Feedback	36.1	44.2	1.3
Q9: Friendliness	41.3	29.8	11.7
Q10: Trustworthiness	43.5	-2.4	-49.3

Table 1: Results for the GIVE 2.5 evaluation worlds. Subjective ratings are on a scale of -100 to 100.

8 Discussion

The evaluation results point to various flaws in the system. When referring to doors, TU!T naively assumes that they are aligned on one or two axes (walls). In a room with doors on three or more walls, as in World 3, this leads to confusing expressions. When the user approaches the doors the system's feedback will allow the user to find the correct one eventually, but this is far from efficient. Several evaluation participants commented that they reverted to 'trial and error' navigation when instructions were unclear, relying on the feedback to find out whether they were facing the right door or button.

Currently, TU!T generates non-unique descriptions such as *the blue button in front of you*, which are clarified automatically when the user approaches the target. This first description bears the danger of confusing the user (confirmed by participants' comments). Instead it would be better to first generate a move instruction that guides the user to a position from which a unique referring expression to the target button can be generated. A similar approach could be used for referring to doors.

As noted by Denis et al. (2010), instructions that are relative to the user's position (e.g., *behind you*) can be problematic because users can move through the world quite fast. We tried to make TU!T as fast as possible, but it still suffers from this problem. Sometimes the user moves around quickly and then receives an outdated instruction. The user can press *Help* for a new instruction, but this is an extra action that could be rendered unnecessary by improving the performance of our system.

The feedback mechanism incorporated in TU!T proved to be successful: almost all participants commented positively on this feature, in particular the anticipating feedback. It is hard to verify whether the feedback really had a motivational effect, but it was clearly perceived as helpful.

References

Johannes Braunias, Uwe Boltz, Markus Dräger, Boris Fersing, and Olga Nikitina. 2010. The GIVE-2 Challenge: Saarland NLG System. In *Online Proceedings of the GIVE-2 Challenge*.

Robert Dale and Ehud Reiter. 1995. Computational interpretations of the Gricean maxims in the generation of referring expressions. *Cognitive Science*, 19(2):233–263.

Alexandre Denis, Marilisa Amoia, Luciana Benotti, Laura Perez-Beltrachini, Claire Gardent, and Tarik Osswald. 2010. The GIVE-2 Nancy Generation Systems NA and NM. In *Online Proceedings of the GIVE-2 Challenge*.

Judith M. Harackiewicz. 1979. The effects of reward contingency and performance feedback on intrinsic motivation. *Journal of Personality and Social Psychology*, 37(8):1352–1363.

Alexander Koller, Kristina Striegnitz, Andrew Gargett, Donna Byron, Justine Cassell, Robert Dale, Johanna Moore, and Jon Oberlander. 2010. Report on the second NLG challenge on Generating Instructions in Virtual Environments (GIVE-2). In *Proceedings of the 6th International Natural Language Generation Conference (INLG 2010)*, pages 243–250.

Emiel Krahmer, Sebastiaan van Erk, and André Verleg. 2003. Graph-based generation of referring expressions. *Computational Linguistics*, 29(1):53–72.

Dermot Hayes McCoy, Ielka van der Sluis, and Saturnino Luz. 2010. The TCD system for GIVE-2. In *Online Proceedings of the GIVE-2 Challenge*.

Michael Roth, Michael Haas, Eric Hildebrand, and Eleftherios Matios. 2010. The Heidelberg GIVE-2 System. In *Online Proceedings of the GIVE-2 Challenge*.

Niels Schütte and Nina Dethlefs. 2010. The Dublin-Bremen System for the GIVE-2 Challenge. In *Online Proceedings of the GIVE-2 Challenge*.

Robert J. Vallerand and Greg Reid. 1988. On the relative effects of positive and negative verbal feedback on males' and females' intrinsic motivation. *Canadian Journal of Behavioural Science/Revue Canadienne des Sciences du Comportement*, 20(3):239–250.

Question Generation Shared Task and Evaluation Challenge – Status Report

Vasile Rus
Department of Computer Science
The University of Memphis
Memphis, TN 38152, USA
vrus@memphis.edu

Brendan Wyse
Centre for Research in Computing
The Open University
Walton Hall, Milton Keynes, UK
bjwyse@gmail.com

Paul Piwek
Centre for Research in Computing
The Open University
Walton Hall, Milton Keynes, UK
p.piwek@open.ac.uk

Mihai Lintean
Department of Computer Science
The University of Memphis
Memphis, TN 38152, USA
mclinten@memphis.edu

Svetlana Stoyanchev
Centre for Research in Computing
The Open University
Walton Hall, Milton Keynes, UK
s.stoyanchev@open.ac.uk

Cristian Moldovan
Department of Computer Science
The University of Memphis
Memphis, TN 38152, USA
cmldovan@memphis.edu

Abstract

The First Shared Task Evaluation Challenge on Question Generation took place in 2010 as part of the 3rd workshop on Question Generation. The campaign included two tasks: Question Generation from Sentences and Question Generation from Paragraphs. This status report briefly summarizes the motivation, tasks and results. Lessons learned relevant to future QG-STECs are also offered.

1 Introduction

Automatically generating questions is an important task in many different contexts including dialogue systems, intelligent tutoring systems, automated assessment and search interfaces. Questions are used to express informational needs: when we do not know something, the natural thing to do is to ask about it. As computer systems become more advanced and are expected to be more adaptive and autonomous, their informational needs grow, and being equipped with the ability to ask questions has clear advantages. State-of-the-art spoken dialogue systems are a good case in point: where would they be without the ability to ask questions, for example, about the user's goals ("Where would you like to travel to?") or about their understanding of the users' utterances ("Did you say 'London'?")?

Of course, the purpose of asking questions is not limited to satisfying straightforward informational needs. In a classroom, a teacher may ask a question, not because she doesn't know the answer, but because she wants to know whether the student knows the answer (or perhaps she wants to provide the student with a hint that will help him solve whichever problem he is dealing with). Generating such questions automatically is a central task for intelligent tutoring systems. Exam questions are

Proceedings of the 13th European Workshop on Natural Language Generation (ENLG), pages 318–320,
Nancy, France, September 2011.

another case in point. In the context of automated assessment, generating questions automatically from educational resources is a great challenge, with, potentially, tremendous impact.

2 QGSTEC Input and Output

Question Generation (QG) has recently been defined as the task of automatically generating questions (Piwek et al., 2008; Rus & Graesser, 2009). Whereas this definition more or less fixes the output of QG, it leaves open what the input is, and how the input relates to the output. For the First QGSTEC, the decision on input was aimed at attracting as many participants as possible and promoting a fair comparison environment. Thus, rather than adopting a specific semantic representation as input, the input for both tasks was raw text. Participants were free to (pre)process the text with their own and/or off-the-shelf NLP tools. As for the relation between input and output, the decision was made that the output question should be answered by (part of) the input text – thus the tasks were the inverse of Question Answering. Regarding the output evaluation, again to maximize participation in the tasks, only generic criteria (such as fluency and ambiguity), as opposed to application-specific criteria, were used.

Input data sources for both tasks were Wikipedia, OpenLearn, and Yahoo!Answers.

3 Question Generation from Sentences

Participants were given a set of inputs, with each input consisting of: (A) a single sentence and (B) a specific target question type (e.g., WHO?, WHY?, HOW?, WHEN?).

For each input, the task was to generate 2 questions of the specified target question type. For example, for input instance:

- The poet Rudyard Kipling lost his only son in the trenches in 1915.
- WHO

Two different questions of the specified type that are answered by input sentence were expected, e.g.: 1) "Who lost his only son in the trenches in 1915?" and 2) "Who did Rudyard Kipling lose in the trenches in 1915?"

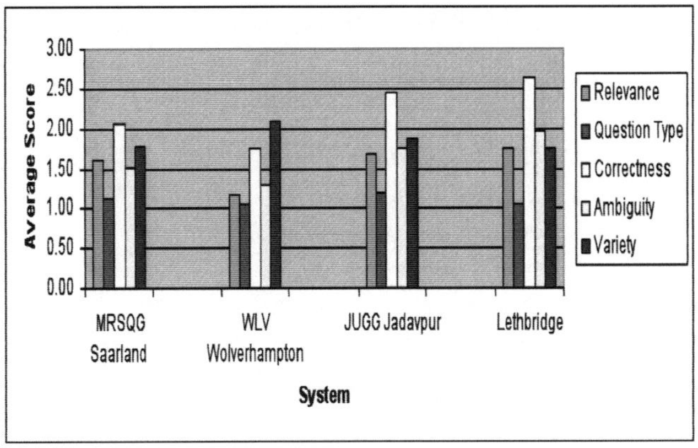

Figure 1: Results for QG from Sentences (without penalty for missing questions)

Five systems entered this task: MRSQG Saarland, WLV Wolverhampton, JUGG Jadavpur and Lethbridge; for descriptions of the systems we refer to Boyer and Piwek (2010). The system-generated questions were scored on five dimensions: Relevance, (Correct) Question Type, (Syntactic) Correctness, Ambiguity and Variety (of generated questions). The averaged results for the systems, based on both peer and independent reviewers, are depicted in Figure 1, with lower values indicating better scores. WLV scores best on all criteria except for "Variety". The picture changes when systems are penalized for missing questions (Figure 2). Now MRSQG outperforms the other systems on all criteria.

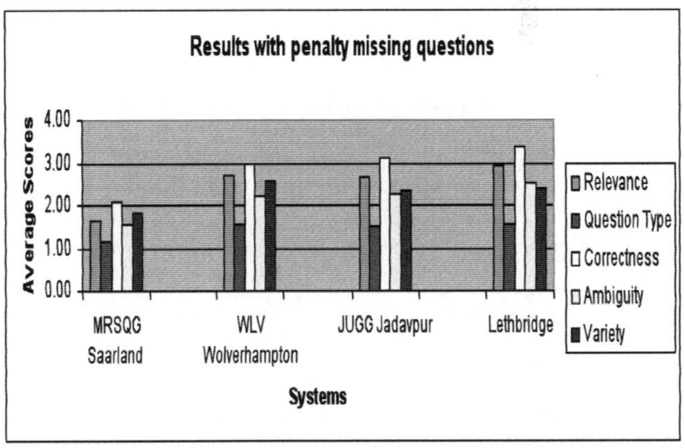

Figure 2: Results for QG from Sentence (with penalty for missing questions)

4 Question Generation from Paragraphs

The inputs for this task were paragraphs such as:

Two-handed backhands have some important advantages over one-handed backhands. Two-handed backhands are generally more accurate because by having two hands on the racquet, this makes it easier to inflict topspin on the ball allowing for more control of the shot. Two-handed backhands are easier to hit for most high balls. Two-handed backhands can be hit with an open stance, whereas one-handers usually have to have a closed stance, which adds further steps (which is a problem at higher levels of play).

For each paragraph, the task was to generate six questions at different levels of specificity: One question that is answered by the paragraph as a whole (e.g. "What are the advantages of two-handed backhands in tennis?"), two medium level questions (e.g., "Why is a two-hand backhand more accurate [when compared to a one-hander]?") asking about major ideas in the paragraphs, e.g. relations among larger chunks of text in the paragraphs such as cause-effect, and three specific question on specific facts (e.g., "What kind of spin does a two-handed backhand inflict on the ball?").

For this task, there was one submission out of five registered participants. The participating team was from University of Pennsylvania (for further details see Boyer & Piwek, 2010). We adopted an independent-judges approach in which two independents human raters judged the submitted questions using five criteria:

Score	Results/Inter-rater Reliability
Specificity	General=90%;Medium=121%; Specific=80%; Other = 1.39%/68.76%
Syntactic Correctness	1.82/87.64%
Semantic Correctness	1.97/78.73%
Question Diversity	1.85/100%
Question Type Correctness	83.62%/78.22%

Table 1: Summary of Results for University of Pennsylvania

5 Lessons Learned for Future QG-STECs

The first QG-STEC was a success by many measures including number of participants, results, and resources created. Here we highlight two recommendations for future QG-STECs. Firstly, it is worthwhile considering further fine-tuning of the instructions to judges to improve agreement and possibly replacing rating scales, which we used in evaluating the submissions, with preference judgments as the former seems to pose some challenges such as being unintuitive for raters and the inter-rater agreement tends to be low when using rating scales (Belz & Kow, 2010). Secondly, there is a case for extending the QGSTEC with a task that goes beyond raw text input, given the convergence of semantic representations that is driven by the semantic web.

Acknowledgments

We would like to thank the Engineering and Physical Sciences Research Council who partially supported this work through grant EP/G020981/1 (awarded to Paul Piwek) and the National Science Foundation who partially supported this work through grants RI-0836259 and RI-0938239 (awarded to Vasile Rus).

References

Belz, A. and Kow, E. (2010) Comparing Rating Scales and Preference Judgements in Language Evaluation. In Proceedings of the 6th International Natural Language Generation Conference (INLG'10), pp. 7-15.

Boyer, K.E. and P. Piwek (Eds) (2010). Proceedings of the 3rd Workshop on Question Generation. Carnegie Mellon University, Pittsburgh PA., June 18, 2010.

Piwek, P., H. Prendinger, H. Hernault, and M. Ishizuka (2008). Generating Questions: An Inclusive Characterization and a Dialogue-based Application. In: V. Rus and A. Graesser (eds.), online Proceedings of Workshop on the Question Generation Shared Task and Evaluation Challenge, September 25-26, 2008, NSF, Arlington, VA.

Rus, V. and Graesser, A.C. (2009). Workshop Report: The Question Generation Task and Evaluation Challenge, Institute for Intelligent Systems, Memphis, TN, ISBN: 978-0-615-27428-7.

Author Index

Association for Computational Linguistics
209 N. Eighth Street
Stroudsburg, Pennsylvania 18360